Understanding Allomorphy

Advances in Optimality Theory

Editors: Vieri Samek-Lodovici, University College London, and Armin Mester, University of California, Santa Cruz

Optimality Theory is an exciting new approach to linguistic analysis that originated in phonology but was soon taken up in syntax, morphology, and other fields of linguistics. Optimality Theory presents a clear vision of the universal properties underlying the vast surface typological variety in the world's languages. Cross-linguistic differences once relegated to idiosyncratic language-specific rules can now be understood as the result of different priority rankings among universal, but violable constraints on grammar.

Advances in Optimality Theory is designed to stimulate and promote research in this provocative new framework. It provides a central outlet for the best new work by both established and younger scholars in this rapidly moving field. The series includes studies with a broad typological focus, studies dedicated to the detailed analysis of individual languages, and studies on the nature of Optimality Theory itself. The series publishes theoretical work in the form of monographs and coherent edited collections as well as pedagogical texts and reference texts that promote the dissemination of Optimality Theory.

Published:

Optimality Theory, Phonological Acquisition and Disorders
Edited by Daniel A. Dinnsen and Judith A. Gierut

Modeling Ungrammaticality in Optimality Theory
Edited by Curt Rice and Sylvia Blaho

Phonological Argumentation: Essays in Evidence and Motivation
Edited by Steve Parker

Hidden Generalizations: Phonological Opacity in Optimality Theory
John J. McCarthy

Conflicts in Interpretation
Petra Hendriks, Helen de Hoop, Irene Krämer, Henriëtte de Swart and Joost Zwarts

The Phonology of Contrast
Anna Łubowicz

Prosody Matters: Essays in Honor of Elisabeth Selkirk
Edited by Toni Borowsky, Shigeto Kawahara, Takahito Shinya and Mariko Sugahara

Blocking and Complementarity in Phonological Theory
Eric Baković

Linguistic Derivations and Filtering: Minimalism and Optimality Theory
Edited by Hans Broekhuis and Ralf Vogel

Layering and Directionality: Metrical Stress in Optimality Theory
Brett Hyde

Understanding Allomorphy

Perspectives from Optimality Theory

Edited by Eulàlia Bonet, Maria-Rosa Lloret and Joan Mascaró

SHEFFIELD UK BRISTOL CT

Published by Equinox Publishing Ltd.

UK: Office 415, The Workstation, 15 Paternoster Row, Sheffield, South Yorkshire S1 2BX
USA: ISD, 70 Enterprise Drive, Bristol, CT 06010

www.equinoxpub.com

First published 2015

British Library Cataloguing-in-Publication Data

A catalogue record for this book is available from the British Library.

ISBN-13 978 1 84553 297 0 (hardback)

Library of Congress Cataloging-in-Publication Data
Understanding allomorphy : perspectives from optimality theory / Edited by Eulàlia Bonet, Maria-Rosa Lloret and Joan Mascaró.
pages cm. – (Advances in Optimality Theory)
Includes bibliographical references and index.
ISBN 978-1-84553-297-0 (hb)
1. Grammar, Comparative and general–Morphology–Psychological aspects. 2. Morphophonemics. 3. Psycholinguistics. 4. Optimality theory (Linguistics) I. Bonet i Alsina, M. Eulàlia, editor. II. Lloret-Romanyach, Maria-Rosa, editor. III. Mascaró, Joan.
P241.U86 2015
415'.9–dc23
2014039974

Typeset by S.J.I. Services, New Delhi
Printed and bound by Lightning Source Inc. (La Vergne, TN), Lightning Source UK Ltd. (Milton Keynes), Lightning Source AU Pty. (Scoresby, Victoria).

Contents

Introduction

Allomorphy is a particular case of deviance from the simplest way to implement morpheme exponence, namely a single morph for every morpheme, and a single morpheme for every morph. We get allomorphy under two conditions: first, there is more than one morph for a single morpheme, and second, the divergence among these morphs cannot be attributed to allophony, i.e. it cannot be predicted by the phonology of the language. Thus in a language in which the negative prefix *in-* appears in different shapes with the form [iN], where N is a nasal with different, predictable places of articulation, these forms are not allomorphs because their phonetic shape can be predicted by a process of nasal assimilation. But the phonology of languages with the privative prefix *a-/an-* (as in *a-symmetric*, *an-aerobic*), and no productive process of *n*-deletion or *n*-insertion, cannot derive their segmental differences from a single underlying form, and the prefix must be assigned two underlying forms, i.e. two allomorphs. Traditionally, allomorphs that have very dissimilar phonological shapes (e.g. the verbal forms *am, are, is* in English) have been called *suppletive.* However, sometimes the terms *suppletive*, *suppletion* have been extended to all cases of true allomorphy.

The contributors to this volume have tried to solve some of the many problems that the student of allomorphy faces, as we move towards a full understanding of it; of course, we have here by no means exhausted the variety of problems that allomorphy presents. One of the central questions that the chapters address more or less directly is how to express the different degrees of regularity that different instantiations of allomorphy display. In all cases of allomorphy the *form* of the allomorph is unpredictable (otherwise it would be allophonic), but the context that *controls* the allomorphic choice appears in many different forms and shows different degrees of regularity. Choice can be controlled lexically, it can be in free variation, or it can be both at once, as in the diminutive suffixes *-chen* and *-lein* in German; in fact, pure free variation, as in the Spanish imperfect subjunctive *-ra/-se* allomorphy (*cantara/cantase* 'sing-3sg.imp.subj') is not frequent. When the choice is grammatically controlled, the control can be phonological, or it can be non-phonological, usually morphological. In both cases it can be either regular or idiosyncratic. A case of idiosyncratic morphological control is the already mentioned allomorphy in the present of the verb *to be* in English: 1sg chooses /æm/, 3sg chooses /ɪz/, and the unnatural class {2sg, 1pl, 2pl, 3pl} chooses /ar/. A more regular morphological conditioning is found in the *bl* morpheme found in various languages: *bl(e)* appears in underived adjectives and *bil* in their derivatives (Catalan *varia-ble* 'variable', *varia-bil-íssim* 'variable-superlative', *varia-bil-itat* 'variability'). In this book we deal basically with phonologically conditioned allomorphy. Consider two prototypical examples of regular and idiosyncratic phonological control. In Moroccan Arabic the third person masculine singular enclitic (see Chapters 4 and 9) is /-u/ after a consonant, but /-h/ after a vowel ([ktab-u] 'his book', [xtˤa-h] 'his error'); the allomorphic choice avoids a complex coda in the first example and a hiatus in the second. The control is hence phonologically natural in that it yields a better, less marked ouput: [kta.bu] is more harmonic, on general markedness grounds, than [ktabh], and [xtˤah] more harmonic than [xtˤa.u]. The situation is however different in Jivaro where, according to the analysis in Paster (2006: 83-84), the genitive suffix has the allomorph /-na/ after consonants and the allomorph /-nu/ after vowels (*Yatzúm-na*, *Nucú-nu*). It is difficult to see why, on phonological grounds, *u* should be preferable after vowels and *a* after consonants; we would have in this case an arbitrary phonological choice. This situation raises two problems. On one hand it is difficult to determine, in many cases, to what extent we are in a situation like the regular one in Moroccan Arabic or in an idiosyncratic one like in Jivaro. In many chapters of this book there are extensive analyses that try precisely to determine how regular an allomorphic situation is. On the other hand we are faced with the problem of determining how to account for these cases. There are two opposing views. The one explicitly defended in the chapters by Bonet, Lloret, and Mascaró, Trommer, and Wolf accepts the view that allomorphic choice, in regular cases, can be determined by EVAL through TETU ('the emergence of the unmarked'). The opposing view, defended in the chapters by Paster and Bye, claims that allomorphic choice is not determined by phonological optimization, but rather, for both regular and idiosyncratic cases, by lexical selection. Some of the chapters focus on detailed case studies of one or few languages (Boyé and Plénat; Hargus, Rude, and Beavert; Booij and van der Veer; Steriade and Yanovich), while others cover a wide range of languages.

In their chapter, Bonet, Lloret, and Mascaró ('The prenominal allomorphy syndrome') examine several cases in which allomorph selection is governed by phonological, morphological, and syntactic factors; in particular prenominal versus postnominal position within the DP can determine selection. The authors base their analysis on an AGREE constraint and a constraint favouring lexically unmarked allomorphs. Booij and van der Veer ('Allomorphy in OT: The Italian mobile diphthongs') provide evidence for the selection of Italian 'mobile diphthongs' (as in *s*[jɛ́]*do* 'sit-1sg.pres.ind' – *s*[e]*diamo* 'sit-1pl.pres.ind') through language-specific ranking of universal phonological markedness constraints that control the structure of syllable nuclei. They extend their analysis to diachronic analogical levelling of the alternation. Boyé and Plénat ('L'allomorphie radicale dans les lexèmes adjectivaux en français. Le cas des adverbes en *–ment*') examine in great detail a case of 'inwards looking' allomorphy. The French adverbial suffix *-ment* attaches idiosyncratically to a specific base allomorph, usually coincidental with the feminine form of the adjective. But in some cases another allomorph is chosen because a nasal in the base activates a dissimilatory effect. Bye ('The nature of allomorphy and exceptionality: Evidence from Burushaski plurals') examines a complex case of allomorph selection in Burushaski. This language has several plural allomorphs whose selection is determined by semantic/pragmatic, phonological, and lexical factors. He argues for a non-optimizing theory of allomorph selection based on the constraint family SELECT, which takes two arguments, i.e. the context of selection and a specific allomorph. In the last sections he shows how patterned exceptionality can be derived through different kinds of 'attractors'. Paster ('Phonologically conditioned suppletive allomorphy: Cross-linguistic results and theoretical consequences') also contrasts the optimizing and non-optimizing models. She examines different languages located in different points in the optimizing–non-optimizing continuum and argues for an approach based on subcategorization frames that have to be met by specific allomorphs at the underlying level. The model predicts that allomorphy can be non-optimizing, must be determined at the underlying level, is always 'outward-looking', and takes place under adjacency. Hargus, Rude, and Beavert ('Obviative prefix allomorphy in Sahaptin and Nez Perce') study the distribution of the obviative prefix in Sahaptin and Nez Perce and consider the viability of an approach based on optimization. Furthermore, they reconstruct the Pre-Proto-Sahaptin situation and discuss the consequences for theories of language change. Steriade and Yanovich ('Accentual allomorphs in East Slavic: An argument for inflection dependence') show that in Ukrainian and Russian the stress pattern of derivatives is dependent on the stress pattern of the allomorphs found in the inflectional paradigm of their bases. This is accounted for in a modified version of base-derivative correspondence: inflective forms are generated independently, while the derivatives must be generated in a way that maintains similarity to them. Trommer ('Syllable-counting allomorphy by prosodic templates') discusses the set of cases of syllable-counting allomorphy that have been claimed to be non-optimizing by Paster (2005) and proposes that they can be successfully analysed as optimizing by using indexed constraints in a Stratal OT model. The indexed constraint favours a specific allomorph, while the competing allomorph is favoured by a conflicting markedness constraint that requires unmarked syllable count. Wolf ('Lexical insertion occurs in the phonological component') presents a theory in which morpheme realization takes place in the phonology and is controlled by constraints that are interleaved with phonological constraints ('Optimal Interleaving'). Using a serial approach, he applies this model to cases of allomorphy that have phonological control and at the same time show the influence of arbitrary and non-phonological preferences.

This book has a long history. Initially, the editor was Bernard Tranel, and the first versions of ten chapters were ready in 2006; after review, several revised versions were completed in 2007. After a period of inactivity, in 2011 the editors of the Equinox series *Advances in Optimality Theory* asked us to take over the editorship. Two of the intended authors could no longer contribute to the volume, but we managed to get an additional chapter (Chapter 7) by a new author. All authors have endeavoured to bring their respective chapters up to date, and after completion of the peer-review process, we believe we have compiled a volume which, in spite of the time elapsed since most of the first versions were written, represents a substantial contribution to our present understanding of allomorphy.

References

Paster, Mary (2005) Subcategorization vs. output optimization in syllable-counting allomorphy. In John Alderete, Chung-hye Han and Alexei Kochetov (eds) *Proceedings of the 24th West Coast Conference on Formal Linguistics*, 326–333. Somerville, MA: Cascadilla Proceedings Project.

Paster, Mary (2006) *Phonological Conditions on Affixation*. Doctoral dissertation, University of California, Berkeley. [Available on http://pages.pomona.edu/~mp034747/Paster_dissertation.pdf.]

1 The prenominal allomorphy syndrome*

Eulàlia Bonet (Universitat Autònoma de Barcelona)
Maria-Rosa Lloret (Universitat de Barcelona)
Joan Mascaró (Universitat Autònoma de Barcelona)

1.1 Introduction

The prenominal position X and the postnominal position Y within a DP $[_{DP}XNY]$, where N is the head noun, are asymmetric in various respects. Most typically, perhaps, a given category, definite article, demonstrative, numeral, qualifying adjective, etc. can appear in a given language in one position but not in the other. In some cases a category can appear in both positions, but one allomorph appears prenominally and the other allomorph appears postnominally. A simple case affecting a single lexical item is allomorph selection of the adjective for 'bad' in Catalan. The adjective *pèssim* 'awful' in (1a-b) is a normal adjective that presents the same form in both positions. But the adjective *mal/dolent* 'bad' (1c-d) presents its allomorphs in complementary distribution governed by position with respect to the N (M = masculine; F = feminine; Sg = singular; Pl = plural):

(1)	*Postnominal*		*Prenominal*	
a.	solució	pèssima	pèssima	solució
	solution-F	awful-F	awful-F	solution-F
	'awful solution'		'awful solution'	
b.	resultats	pèssims	pèssims	resultats
	result-MPl	awful-MPl	awful-MPl	result-MPl
	'awful results'		'awful results'	
c.	solució	dolenta	*dolenta	solució
	*solució	mala	mala	solució
	solution-F	bad-F	bad-F	solution-F
	'bad solution'		'bad solution'	

Affiliation: (Bonet) Associate Professor, Universitat Autònoma de Barcelona, Spain.

d.	resultats	dolents	*dolents	resultats
	*resultats	mals	mals	resultats
	result-MPl	bad-MPl	bad-MPl	result-MPl
	'bad results'		'bad results'	

More generalized left/right asymmetries of the same type can be found, for instance, in Ladin of Fassa (Romance, Italy), in Komi and Erzya (Finno-Ugric, Russia), and in Maasai (Nilo-Saharan, Kenya).[1] We illustrate these cases briefly. In Ladin (2) prenominal elements do not show agreement with the head, whereas postnominal elements can agree or not; Komi (3) shows postnominal agreement, (3b), and no agreement prenominally, (3a); Maasai presents a more complex situation, summarized in (4), with different kinds of prenominal agreement depending on category, but with full agreement postnominally.

(2) *Ladin of Fassa* (Rasom 2006)

a.	la	picola	cèses	de	Fascia
	the-Sg	little-Sg	houses-Pl	of	Fascia
	la	cèses	picoles	de	Fascia
	the-Sg	house-Pl	little-Pl	of	Fascia
	*les	picoles	cèses	de	Fascia
	the-Pl	little-Pl	house-Pl	of	Fascia
	'the little houses of Fascia'				

b.	duta	la	bezes	beles	ciaparà	na	resa
	all-Sg	the-Sg	girl-Pl	beautiful-Pl	will-get	a	rose
	'all beautiful girls will get a rose'						

(3) *Komi* (Croft and Deligianni 2001, Vilkuna 1998)

a.	ydɒyd	da	permyd	kerkajas
	big	and	dark	house-Pl
	'big and dark houses'			

b.	kerkajas	ydɒyd-ös	da	permyd-ös	tydalisny	matyn	n'in
	house-Pl	big-Pl	and	dark-Pl	be-visible-past1.3Pl	close	already
	'houses, big and dark, could already be seen close by'						

(4) *Maasai agreement in the DP* (Koopman 2003)

Categories (ordered)	Article-like	Other Triggering N	Quantifiers, numerals, As
Agreement in	Gender, Number	No agreement	Gender, Number, Case

In this chapter we focus on some specific cases of asymmetry which involve allomorphic choice that affects inflectional morphemes in Catalan and Spanish. In these languages, in normal circumstances, all prenominal and postnominal elements in the DP agree in gender and number with the N, as the Catalan phrase in (5) illustrates.

(5) tot**es** **les** mev**es** antigu**es** companyes italian**es** casad**es**
all-FPl the-FPl my-FPl old-FPl fellow-FPl Italian-FPl married-FPl
'all my old married Italian female colleagues'

In section 1.2 we present the analysis of DP agreement we assume throughout the chapter, which constitutes the origin of prenominal/postnominal asymmetries. We assume that postnominal agreement takes place in the syntax while prenominal agreement is established at PF and is controlled by constraint evaluation. The rest of the paper is organized as follows: section 1.3 is devoted to Northeastern Central Catalan, in which the plural morph *-s* does not appear in prenominal position under specific phonological conditions. We argue that the lack of agreement arises through the high ranking of a phonological markedness constraint interspersed with morphological constraints. In section 1.4 we examine a restricted set of lexical items in Spanish which require the bare stem, devoid of inflectional markers, to appear in prenominal position, while the same items in postnominal position appear fully inflected. We devote section 1.5 to a third case, from a variety of Spanish, in which the exceptional element that triggers asymmetric agreement in the DP is not the prenominal or postnominal element itself, but the N: it triggers regular agreement to the right and default masculine marking to the left. Finally, section 1.6 contains some concluding remarks.

1.2 Split concord

It is commonly held (see, e.g., Picallo 1991; Bernstein 1993; Cinque 1996, 2005) that the N is generated in the final, most embedded position within the DP. This assumption implies that when the noun surfaces in non-final position some movement has taken place. Different accounts can be found in the literature on the exact internal structure of the DP and as to whether N alone or the entire NP moves, for example. There is no clear consensus either as to whether concord within the DP and subject/verb agreement (clausal agreement) are the result of the same kind of operation.[2] Asymmetries in agreement can be found in both domains. More stable agreement appears in postnominal position within the DP and also with the order subject-verb, while prenominal elements within the DP and the verb in the verb-subject order often show weaker agreement. It is fairly common to assume that a Spec-Head relation, a local relation, is involved in the stable agreement of postnominal elements. For instance, Franck *et al.* (2006), following Guasti and Rizzi (2002), argue that agreement between a preverbal subject and the verb is achieved through the operations Agree and Move (which gives rise to a Spec-Head configuration), while with subject inversion only Agree takes place; Shlonsky (2004) relates clausal and DP-internal agreement and argues that full concord with postnominal elements within the DP is achieved by NP-movement to a position that ultimately enters a Spec-Head relation; Nevins (2011) also resorts to the Spec-Head relation to account for postnominal concord.

The idea we pursue in this chapter is that the syntax is responsible for postnominal concord, through Spec-Head agreement, and that at PF a family of constraints called CONCORD enforce general agreement in the DP, both prenominally and postnominally. This idea appears schematically in (6).

(6) $[_{DP}$ X N Y $t_N]$

SYNTAX (Agr. via Spec-Head)

PF (Agr. through CONCORD)

At PF the markedness constraints CONCORD compete, among others, with MAX constraints, which ensure that the inherent inflectional features on the N and those assigned by the syntax to postnominal elements are preserved; MAX will be irrelevant for prenominal elements. Candidates that violate CONCORD will be optimal when higher-ranked constraints rule out the agreeing candidate, causing the type of prenominal/postnominal asymmetries mentioned in the previous section. The duality of agreement (fixed agreement in the syntax, variable agreement at PF) is reminiscent of the proposal for sentential agreement in Guasti and Rizzi (2002) according to which if a morphosyntactic feature is checked in the overt syntax it must be expressed by the morphology, while if it is left unchecked its expression depends on morphological rules.

As pointed out by an anonymous reviewer, an alternative view would be to consider that all concord takes place in a single step, at PF, by two competing constraints, one that triggers local agreement and one that triggers general agreement. In section 1.5 we briefly describe this type of approach, following the lines of Samek-Lodovici (2002) for clausal agreement, and point out the difficulties it would face.

1.3 Northeastern Central Catalan s~Ø alternation

1.3.1 The data

As illustrated in section 1.1 (see (5)), number concord in Catalan is expressed by the plural morph *-s*. In general, the sibilant *s* deletes only in specific phonological contexts, namely before a rhotic (e.g., *les roques* [lə rɔ́kəs] 'the rocks') or before another sibilant (e.g., *les sopes* [lə sópəs] 'the soups') (for an OT analysis of these facts, see Bonet and Lloret 2002). In other contexts, *s* is retained and only assimilates in voicing to a following consonant or to a vowel across word boundaries (e.g., *les cases* [ləs kázəs] 'the houses', *les nenes* [ləz nɛ́nəs] 'the girls', *les àvies* [ləz áβjəs] 'the grandmothers'). In Northeastern Central (NEC) Catalan, however, the plural *-s* disappears in some additional cases, as illustrated in (7).[3] (In the examples, the low dash '_' is used for clarity to indicate the position of an inflectional element that should occur under general concord but does not show up.)

(7)		*NEC Catalan*			*Other Central Catalan varieties*
	a.	un_	meu_	companys	uns meus companys
		a	my	fellow-Pl	'some fellows of mine'
	b.	el_	bon_	vins	els bons vins
		the	good	wine-Pl	'the good wines'
	c.	aquell_	llibres		aquells llibres
		that	book-Pl		'those books'
	d.	quin_	nou_	problemes	quins nous problemes
		what	new	problem-Pl	'what new problems'

This apparent *s*-deletion occurs only when the three following conditions are met:

(8) a. *s* is preceded and followed by a consonant,
b. *s* occurs in prenominal position within the DP, and
c. *s* is the plural morph.

Thus, following (8a), *s* is retained if it can be syllabified as an onset, as in *els avis* [əl.**z**á.βis] 'the grandparents', or if it is the only consonant in a coda, as in *les nenes* [lə**z**.nɛ́.nəs] 'the girls'. Other examples in which the *-s* is retained because it is not preceded and followed by a consonant appear in (9). (We provide transcriptions only for cases of relevant discrepancies from orthography.)[4]

(9)					
	a.	aques**t-s**	**e**stra**ny-s**	**u**lls	[əkɛ̀dz əstràɲʒ úʎs]
		this-Pl	strange-Pl	eye-Pl	
		'these strange eyes'			
	b.	**el-s**	**a**nti**c-s**	**a**mics	
		the-Pl	old-Pl	friend-Pl	
		'the old friends'			
	c.	quin**e-s**	**m**al**e-s**	**c**arreteres	
		what-FPl	bad-FPl	road-FPl	
		'what bad roads'			

d. **tote-s dos-cente-s nove-s matriculades**
all-FPl two-hundred-FPl new-FPl registered-one-FPl
'all 200 new registered ones'

e. **quant-s últim-s instants** [kwànz ùltimz instáns]
how-many-Pl last-Pl instant-Pl
'how many last instants'

f. no **gaire-s bon-s aficionats**
not many-Pl good-Pl amateur-Pl
'not many good amateurs'

The plural *-s*, however, does not show up in the context C_C, i.e., if it would have to syllabify as the second element of a non-final coda, as, for instance, in (7a) *uns meus companys* [um_.mèw _.kum.páɲʃ], *[unz.mèws. kum.páɲʃ] 'some fellows of mine'. Further examples appear below:

(10) a. **aquell_ teu_ cabells**
that your hair-Pl
'those hairs of yours'

b. **el_ diferent_ grups**
the different group-Pl
'the different groups'

c. **quin_ mal_ camins**
what bad path-Pl
'what bad paths'

d. **tot_ dos-cent_ nou_ matriculats**
all two-hundred new registred-one-Pl
'all 200 newly registered ones'

e. **quant_ quart_ dies**
how-many fourth day-Pl
'how many fourth days'

f. **molt_ poc_ bon_ professionals**
very few good professional-Pl
'very few good professionals'

Following (8b), postnominal elements in the DP and the head of the NP itself do not lose the *-s* even in a C_C context, as shown in (11). Notice, in the illustrative examples in (10) and (11), that the same lexical items can show up prenominally without the *-s* and postnominally with the *-s* retained. This is the case for adjectives like *bons* 'good-Pl' and *nous* 'new-Pl', demonstratives like *aquells* 'that-Pl', and possessives like *teus* 'your-Pl'.

(11) a. aquest_ cabells llargs tenyits
this hair-Pl long-Pl dyed-Pl
'these long dyed hairs'

b. el_ vins blancs aquells tan cars
the wine-Pl white-Pl that-Pl so expensive-Pl
'those so expensive white wines'

c. quin_ camins bons desaprofitats
what path-Pl good-Pl wasted-Pl
'what wasted good paths'

d. dos-cent_ matriculats nous comprovats
two-hundred registered-one-Pl new-Pl checked-Pl
'200 checked newly registered ones'

e. quant_ parents teus francesos
how-many relative-Pl your-Pl French-Pl
'how many French relatives of yours'

f. molt_ poc_ professionals bons presents
much few professional-Pl good-Pl present-Pl
'very few good professionals present'

The plural element without *-s* must be strictly prenominal, since a gap causes the plural morph to reappear, as shown in the following pairs:

(12) a. el_ llums que tinc comprats
the lamp-Pl that I-have bought-Pl
'the lamps that I have bought'
els que tinc comprats
the(-one)-Pl that I-have bought-Pl
'the ones I have bought'

b. el_ llibres més venguts
the book-Pl most sold-Pl
'the most sold books'
Els més venguts
the(-one)-Pl most sold-Pl
'the most sold ones'

c. un_ cotxes grocs
a car-Pl yellow-Pl
'some yellow cars'
uns de grocs
a-Pl of yellow-Pl
'some yellow ones'

Finally, following (8c), a final *s* other than the plural morph does not delete even if it meets condition (8a), interconsonantal position, and condition (8b), prenominal position, as the following singular DPs illustrate (orthographic *ç* is [s]). The last example shows that the other suffix *-s*, i.e. the second-person singular morph, does not delete either, even though the phonological conditioning is met.[5] (2.Sg stands for second person singular.)

(13) a. un fals conseller
'a false counselor'
b. un dolç cant
'a sweet singing'
c. no ten-s pa?
not have-2.Sg bread
'don't you have bread?'

1.3.2 Untenable analyses

A simple morphological solution in terms of allomorphy would posit two allomorphs, *-s* and Ø, and their associated contexts (e.g., Ø in prenominal C_C contexts, *-s* elsewhere). Such an analysis is untenable because it would amount to reducing the natural prenominal/postnominal distinction and the equally natural C_C context to lexical listing.[6]

A purely phonological solution in terms of deletion is out of the question too, since the phenomenon is restricted to a single morph, i.e. plural *-s*. It is worth noting, though, that, historically, this phenomenon is probably the result of the morphologization of an earlier active, general process, which still operates in the neighboring Rossellonese dialect, where any word-final *s* deletes when it is preceded and followed by a consonant, as in *caps* vs. *cap_ grossos* ('heads' vs. 'big heads'), *dins* vs. *din_ tres dies* ('in' vs. 'in three days') (Fouché 1924: 254).

It is also impossible to resort to the prosodic hierarchy to explain why plural-*s* deletion (or, alternatively, Ø allomorph selection) applies within the 'prenominal+head' domain but never in the 'head+postnominal' domain. The size of a phonological phrase depends on the length of the constituents involved, but in this case we would need all prenominal elements plus the head to be grouped together into a single phonological phrase, regardless of prosodic weight, and all postnominal elements to each form a single phonological phrase of their own, again regardless of prosodic weight. The phonological phrasing in (14) would be plausible and would give the right results, with respect to the s~Ø alternation.

(14) (aquell_ plans)ϕ (desproporcionats)ϕ
that plan-Pl disproportionate-Pl
'those disproportionate plans'

However, a sequence of a monosyllabic noun followed by a monosyllabic adjective would give rise either to a forced phonological phrasing, as in (15a) (★ = prosodically ill-formed), or to a natural phrasing with illicit *s*-deletion, as in (15b).

(15) a. ★(xais)ϕ (blancs)ϕ
sheep-Pl white-Pl
b. *(xai_ blancs)ϕ
sheep white-Pl
'white sheep-Pl'

As just mentioned, all prenominal elements plus the N should form a single prosodic constituent, while each postnominal element should constitute a single prosodic constituent. This parsing is plausible for a sequence like (16a), but it would be extremely inadequate for a sequence like (16b). In (16b) several polysyllabic words must form a single prosodic constituent, while the postnominal word, which is monosyllabic, is forced to constitute an independent phonological phrase, giving rise to an extremely unnatural phrasing.

(16) a. (aquell_ pantalons) (vermells) (foradats) (llarguíssims)
that trouser-Pl red-Pl with-holes-Pl very-long-Pl
'those very long red trousers with holes'
b. ★(tots aquell_ complicadíssim_ càlculs) (nous)
all that very-complicated calculation-Pl new-Pl
'all those new very complicated calculations'

The fact is that the lack of *s* is at the same time (i) morphologically limited to the plural morph *-s*, (ii) syntactically conditioned (prenominal position), and (iii) phonologically conditioned (interconsonantal position), a sum of circumstances which in our view follows from concord for prenominal elements being established at PF.

1.3.3 Analysis under split concord

As said in section 1.2, our analysis is based on the assumption that there are two mechanisms for concord: Spec-Head agreement triggered by syntactic movement and PF-concord. For both cases, we assume that inflectional endings appear under the morphological constituent category FLEC(TION). Postnominal elements within the DP acquire concord through syntactic movement; they reach PF with the inflection assigned, and hence enter constraint evaluation with a specific ending in the input. In contrast, at the beginning of PF, prenominal DP elements do not show concord with the N and enter constraint evaluation without any specific inflection assigned. In this case, the input contains the stem of the word and all its possible inflectional endings. For example, in a DP such as *uns avis vells* 'some old grandparents' the N, *avis*, and its postnominal modifier, *vells*, reach PF with inflection assigned: the N has specified gender and number (masculine plural in our example) in the input to syntax; the postnominal modifier gets inflectional features in the syntax as a result of N movement and enters constraint evaluation (17a). We represent this structural relation between the stem and the specific inflectional morphs assigned before PF with a hyphen ('-').

The prenominal modifier, however, enters PF without inflection assigned. We assume that the input representation of inflectional categories is as follows: the input consists of two separate elements, the stem and the morphological constituent FLEC, which in this case hosts all possible gender and number morphs, i.e. Ø for masculine, *-a* for feminine, Ø for singular, and *-s* for plural (17b).[7] Here we represent the relation between the stem and the not yet incorporated morphological constitutent FLEC with a comma (',').

(17) a. Input to constraint evaluation for the N *avis* and the postnominal modifier *vells*
$[_{STEM}$ avi]-$[_{FLEC}$ $Ø_{M}$ $s_{PL}]$ $[_{STEM}$ vell]-$[_{FLEC}$ $Ø_{M}$ $s_{PL}]$
b. Input to constraint evaluation for the prenominal modifier *un-una-uns-unes*
$[_{STEM}$ un],$[_{FLEC}$ $Ø_{M}$, a_{F} ; $Ø_{SG}$, $s_{PL}]$

The inflectional information in (17) comes from different sources. One is idiosyncratic and, hence, is lexical. This is the case of the masculine gender for the N *avi* in (17a). The other one is regular and includes the fact that most nominal elements are inflected for gender and number; we leave aside the question as to what specific mechanisms derive (17b) from lexical entries.

Prenominal concord is ultimately governed by morphological constraints that require agreement within the DP. Two constraints require agreement of different strength: CONCORD demands agreement with the N (the nucleus of the NP, i.e. the agreement head) for all elements in the DP, prenominal or postnominal; MATCH bans only contradictory feature values, (18b). These two constraints interact with the morphological constraint *FEATURES, (18c), which militates against the presence of any agreement morphology.[8]

(18) a. CONC(ORD): If a N has an inflectional feature F, all other modifiers within the DP must have the inflectional feature F.
b. MATCH: No contradictory values of an inflectional feature F within a DP.
c. *FEAT(URES): "No agreement features." (Samek-Lodovici 2002: 59)[9]

The MAX constraint family prohibits deletion of input information. We distinguish between the well-established MAX(SEGMENT) constraint, which penalizes loss of input phonological segments, (19a), from MAX(MPH), penalizing loss of morphemes present in the input (19b).[10]

(19) a. MAX(SEGMENT): "Every segment of the input has a correspondent in the output. (No phonological deletion.)" (McCarthy and Prince 1995: 264)

b. MAX(MPH): Every morpheme of the input has a correspondent in the output. (No morphological deletion.)

As usual, MAX(SEGMENT) applies to input pre-established segments, including the inflectional endings of N and all postnominal elements because they are co-indexed for correspondence relations. As illustrated in (20a) for postnominal elements, an output with a deleted plural morph, like *vell*-[$_{\text{FLEC}}$ Ø$_{\text{M_PL}}$], and a phonetically identical output where all inflection has been erased, as in bare *vell*, both violate MAX(SEGMENT), because in both cases an input /s/ does not have a correspondent in the output. However, in prenominal position, (20b), inflectional endings are unspecified in the input; the only information FLEC contains is the actual realization if they turn out to be M, F, Sg, or Pl (in Distributed Morphology terms, Halle and Marantz 1993, FLEC contains all the potential Vocabulary items related to nominal inflection). In this position, then, MAX(SEGMENT) is violated only by candidates like *un*-[$_{\text{FLEC}}$ Ø$_{\text{M_PL}}$], because the plural morpheme has been chosen, but its exponent /s/ does not have a correspondent. Crucially, a candidate consisting of a bare stem like *un* does not violate MAX(SEGMENT), because no correspondence relation has been established between the candidate and input inflectional features. The constraint MAX(MPH), which is relativized here to gender and number morphemes, is violated by any candidate that consists of a bare stem, like *vell* or *un*, both in prenominal and postnominal position, because determiners and adjectives, among other elements, should be inflected. And since any nominal element should be inflected both for gender and for number (in Catalan), a bare stem violates MAX(MPH) twice. The N, having its inflectional endings determined already in the input to syntax, behaves like postnominal adjectives, (20a), with respect to MAX violations. The outputs *vell*-[$_{\text{FLEC}}$ Ø$_{\text{M_PL}}$] and *vell* in (20a), and the outputs *un*-[$_{\text{FLEC}}$ Ø$_{\text{M_PL}}$] and *un* in (20b) are phonetically identical. At the end of this section we provide empirical evidence for this distinction based on items in which the phonetic form of the bare stem and the phonetic form of the inflected form are different.

(20)

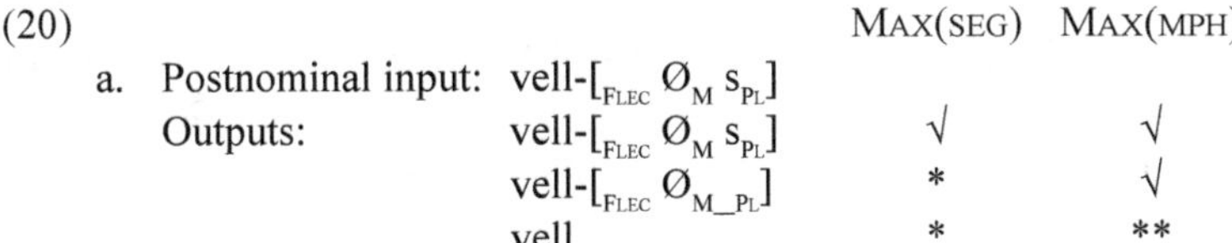

			MAX(SEG)	MAX(MPH)
a.	Postnominal input:	vell-[$_{\text{FLEC}}$ Ø$_{\text{M}}$ s$_{\text{PL}}$]		
	Outputs:	vell-[$_{\text{FLEC}}$ Ø$_{\text{M}}$ s$_{\text{PL}}$]	√	√
		vell-[$_{\text{FLEC}}$ Ø$_{\text{M_PL}}$]	*	√
		vell	*	**

b. Prenominal input:	un,[$_{FLEC}$ Ø$_M$, a$_F$; Ø$_{SG}$, s$_{PL}$]		
Outputs:	un-[$_{FLEC}$ Ø$_M$ s$_{PL}$]	√	√
	un-[$_{FLEC}$ Ø$_{M_PL}$]	*	√
	un	√	**

The interaction among the constraints discussed so far and the constraints responsible for banning CsC sequences (*CsC) is sufficient to account for the facts of NEC Catalan.[11] The ranking at work is the following:[12]

(21) MAX(SEG), MATCH >> *CsC >> CONCORD, MAX(MPH) >> *FEAT

We illustrate first the effect of (21) with an example that contains a head and postnominal material only. When inflection is already assigned in the input, MAX(SEG) >> *CsC forces input specifications to be retained, even when *CsC is violated. As shown in (22), in the sequence *taps vells* 'cork-MPl old-MPl' ('old corks'), the inflectional specifications of the head N *taps* are already present in the input to syntax. Syntactic movement provides the inflectional specifications of the postnominal element *vells*. Hence, at PF each of them consists of the stem and a FLEC constituent, which contains the number morph (*-s*, in the case of plural), as well as the gender morph (the masculine Ø in all the examples seen so far). For simplicity, in the examples below we omit the Ø gender morph from the representations: *tap*-[$_{FLEC}$ s$_{PL}$] *vell*-[$_{FLEC}$ s$_{PL}$]. The fully faithful candidate (22a) violates *CsC, but candidates satisfying *CsC must have lost the *-s*, either by segment deletion (22b), or by deletion of the FLEC constituent. In both cases there is a violation of MAX(SEGMENT). Other constraints are so far irrelevant.[13] From now on and for reasons of space, we also omit the label FLEC and the brackets delimiting affixes in the tableaux.

(22) *taps vells* 'old corks'

tap-s$_{PL}$ vell-s$_{PL}$	MAX (SEG)	MATCH	*CsC	CONC	MAX (MPH)	*FEAT
a. ☞ tap-s$_{PL}$ vell-s$_{PL}$			*			**
b. tap-_$_{PL}$ vell-s$_{PL}$	*!					**
c. tap vell-s$_{PL}$	*!				*	*

We now turn to the evaluation of prenominal elements, (23)–(25). A prenominal element, like *un* in *uns taps* 'some corks', for example, has an input without assigned inflectional features, i.e. [un],[$_{FLEC}$ [Ø]$_{SG}$, [s]$_{PL}$] (simplified to *un*,[$_{FLEC}$ Ø$_{SG}$, s$_{PL}$] in (23), and similarly in other tableaux). GEN generates, among others, the singular candidate *un*-[$_{FLEC}$ Ø$_{SG}$], the plural candidate *un*-[$_{FLEC}$ s$_{PL}$], and the bare stem *un* as well. Fully faithful candidates (23a-b) either violate *CsC because of the presence of the plural *-s,* or Match because of the contradiction between the singular Ø and the plural head *taps.* The offending *-s* can also be avoided through deletion, as in (23d), but high-ranked Max(segment) is violated in this case. Candidate (23c), the optimal candidate, is a bare stem and therefore violates Max(mph), since it has not retained the number morpheme from the input; it also violates Concord, because it does not have the plural feature of the head. But (23c) satisfies higher-ranked Match, because the bare stem and the plural *taps* contain no contradictory features, and it satisfies *CsC as well. Notice that candidates (23b-d) are phonetically identical.

(23) *uns taps* 'some corks'

un,Ø$_{SG}$, s$_{PL}$ tap-s$_{PL}$	Max (seg)	Match	*CsC	Conc	Max (mph)	*Feat
a. un-s$_{PL}$ tap-s$_{PL}$			*!			**
b. un-Ø$_{SG}$ tap-s$_{PL}$		*!		*		**
c. ☞ un tap- s$_{PL}$				*	*	*
d. un-_$_{PL}$ tap-s$_{PL}$	*!					**

When no conflict arises with *CsC, both prenominal elements and postnominal elements show explicit plural concord. In the sequence *uns avis* 'some grandparents', for example, concord applies within the whole DP and is fully expressed. In (24), deletion of the *-s* corresponding to the plural morpheme results in a Max(segment) violation, (24d). The prenominal elements of candidates (24a-c) do not violate Max(segment), because prenominal elements are not specified for any specific Flec morph in the input. Candidate (24b) is discarded by the constraint Match, because it contains contradictory values of the number feature; and the candidate containing the prenominal uninflected element, (24c), is ruled out by either Conc or Max(mph), which are ranked above *Feat.

(24) *uns avis* 'some grandparents'

un,Ø$_{SG}$, s$_{PL}$ avi-[s$_{PL}$]	Max (seg)	Match	*CsC	Conc	Max (mph)	*Feat
a. ☞ un- s$_{PL}$ avi-s$_{PL}$						**
b. un-Ø$_{SG}$ avi-s$_{PL}$		*!		*		**
c. un avi-s$_{PL}$				*!	*	*
d. un-_$_{PL}$ avi-s$_{PL}$	*!					**

The prenominal/postnominal asymmetry is illustrated in tableau (25) with the sequence *uns taps vells cars* 'some expensive old corks'; this example contains the N head and both prenominal and postnominal non-heads. Potential plural *-s* morphs in the interconsonantal context appear both in prenominal position (***uns** taps*) and in postnominal position (***taps** vells* and ***vells** cars*).

(25) *uns taps vells cars* 'some expensive old corks'

un,Ø$_{SG}$, s$_{PL}$ tap-s$_{PL}$ vell-s$_{PL}$ car-s$_{PL}$	MAX (SEG)	MATCH	*CsC	CONC	MAX (MPH)	*FEAT
a. un-s$_{PL}$ tap-s$_{PL}$ vell-s$_{PL}$ car-s$_{PL}$			***!			****
b. un-Ø$_{SG}$ tap-s$_{PL}$ vell-s$_{PL}$ car-s$_{PL}$		*!	**	*		****
c. ☞ un tap-s$_{PL}$ vell-s$_{PL}$ car-s$_{PL}$			**	*	*	***
d. un tap vell car-s$_{PL}$	*!*				***	*

As stated in (8c), the 'deleting' *s* must be the plural morph. Our next example in (26), *fals company* 'false colleague', illustrates the case of prenominal elements ending in an *s* that is not the plural morph, in which case the sibilant is maintained even if it appears in a C__C context. In this situation MAX(SEGMENT) penalizes the loss of the sibilant, because, as part of the stem, it is present in the input (26c-d).

Candidate (26e), with a regular *-os* plural form that avoids sibilant contact between the *s* of the stem and the *s* of plural concord, is discarded by MATCH, because the DP contains contradictory number features.[14] The two remaining candidates, (26a-b), fare evenly with respect to the following constraint, *CsC. Candidate (26a), being singular, wins because, unlike (26b), it satisfies CONC as well as MAX(MPH). Notice that in this case choosing the bare stem *fals* does not avoid the *CsC violation, because the *s* belongs to the stem.

(26) *fals company* 'false colleague'

fals,[Ø$_{SG}$, s$_{PL}$] company-[Ø$_{SG}$]	MAX (SEG)	MATCH	*CsC	CONC	MAX (MPH)	*FEAT
a. ☞ fals-[Ø$_{SG}$] company-[Ø$_{SG}$]			*			**
b. fals company-[Ø$_{SG}$]			*	*!	*!	*
c. fal_-[Ø$_{SG}$] company-[Ø$_{SG}$]	*!					**
d. fal_ company-[Ø$_{SG}$]	*!			*	*	*
e. fals-[os$_{PL}$] company-[Ø$_{SG}$]		*!		*		**

There is one piece of evidence that confirms that prenominal elements without the plural morph *-s* are elements showing lack of number concord, e,g., *un* in (25c), and not inflected singular forms, e.g., *un*-$[_{FLEC}Ø_{SG}]$ in (25b)). In Catalan in general, and in the NEC variety as well, there is a process of *n*-deletion: a large number of oxytone words that end in a vowel in the singular, show *n* elsewhere, as shown in (27a). Nevertheless, this process has a considerable number of exceptions, as shown in (27b). (For clarity, in the examples in (27) we separate the relevant stem from the rest of the word with a hyphen '-'; 'DIM' stands for 'diminutive'.)

(27)	a.	so	son-s	son-all
		'sound-MSg'	'sounds-MPl'	'rattle-MSg'
		funció	funcion-s	funcion-al
		'function-FSg'	'functions-FPl'	'functional-Sg'
		ple	plen-s	plen-itud
		'full-MSg'	'full-MPl'	'fullness-FSg'
		comú	comun-s	comun-itat
		'common-MSg'	'common-MPl'	'community-FSg'
	b.	son	son-s	son-eta
		'sleep-FSg'	'sleeps-FPl'	'sleep-DIM-FSg'
		Aran		aran-ès
		(place name)		'from Aran-MSg'
		segon	segon-s	segon-a
		'second-MSg'	'second-MPl'	'second-FSg'

The presence of a large number of exceptions has been a serious problem for a purely phonological analysis of *n*-deletion. (For a review of standard generative analyses, see Bonet and Lloret 1998: § 4.1; for attempts within OT, see Kikuchi 2002, 2005, and Bonet *et al.* 2004, 2005). An alternative account based on allomorphic terms is more plausible. Every morpheme that displays an n~Ø alternation has two allomorphs: one with final *n* and the other one with a final vowel. This is the view taken by Wheeler (2005: § 10.2), even though he retains the traditional assumption that the selection is done for (stipulated) phonological reasons. Contrary to Wheeler (2005), we assume that the selection is determined by morphological factors: the vowel-final allomorph is selected in singular forms in nouns and in masculine singular forms in adjectives; the unmarked *n*-allomorph is selected elsewhere. The cases relevant for NEC Catalan are illustrated in (28); (28a) illustrates, with one example from (27a), the case that presents allomorphy, and (28b) illustrates a case without allomorphy, with one of the examples from (27b).

(28)	a.	n~Ø alternation:	{*ple* MSg, *plen* elsewhere}	'full'
			ple poder	'full power'
			plen poders, *ple poders	'full powers'
	b.	Regular case:	*segon*	'second'
			segon classificat	'second classified'
			segon classificats	'second classified-Pl'

For normal prenominal adjectives like *vell* 'old', stem and masculine singular are phonetically identical, [vell], [vell]-[$Ø_{SG}$]. But they are not identical in the case of n-alternating nominals like *ple* 'full', whose stem is [plen] and whose masculine singular is [ple]-[$Ø_{SG}$]. If *s*-deleting prenominal elements were masculine singular forms, like candidate (23b) above, we would predict that in the case of *ple* we should get [ple]-[$Ø_{SG}$] in prenominal position, hence, **ple poders.* We get instead *plen poders,* as indicated in (29), where we show the variation of the adjective *ple* in prenominal position. The masculine and feminine singular (29a-b), and the masculine plural followed by a vowel (29c) do not create a CsC sequence. This sequence is created only when the masculine plural is followed by a C; then the stem *plen* is selected, (29d):[15]

(29)		*No CsC context*		*CsC context*
	a.	ple poder	'full power'	
	b.	plena vida	'full life'	
	c.	plens acords	'full agreements'	
	d.			plen poders 'full powers'
				*ple poders

Under the analysis we have proposed, (29d) is the predicted outcome: lack of number concord forces the *-n* alternant to appear in this position, since the final-vowel alternant occurs in singular (inflected) forms only. In the two following tableaux, for simplicity we do not consider candidates with the wrong n/Ø choice; we assume that *n*-deleting nominals like *ple* must be distinguished lexically from non-deleting ones like *segon,* a difference that we have indicated in the inputs through the informal notation /ple(n)/. (Candidates (30b) and (31a) do not violate MAX(SEG) because, as shown in (28a), items like 'full' have two allomorphs in the input, one with final /n/ and another one without it.) The form *ple* is selected in the masculine singular and *plen*, the bare stem, appears in other inflected forms and in derivatives.

(30) *plens poders* 'full powers (MPl)'

ple(n),$Ø_{SG}$, s_{PL} poder-s_{PL}	MAX (SEG)	MATCH	*CsC	CONC	MAX (MPH)	*FEAT
a. plen-s_{PL} poder-s_{PL}			*!			**
b. ple-$Ø_{SG}$ poder-s_{PL}		*!		*		**
c. ☞ plen poder-s_{PL}				*	*	*

The selection of the final-vowel alternant in (masculine) singular concord is illustrated in tableau (31).

(31) *ple acord* 'full agreement (MSg)'

ple(n),$Ø_{SG}$, s_{PL} acord-$Ø_{SG}$	MAX (SEG)	MATCH	*CsC	CONC	MAX (MPH)	*FEAT
a. ☞ ple-$Ø_{SG}$ acord-$Ø_{SG}$						**
b. plen acord-$Ø_{SG}$				*!	*!	*

In sum, by splitting concord we have been able to account for the facts of NEC Catalan concerning a very specific case of *s*-loss without resorting to (parochial) morph-specific constraints or unmotivated allomorphy (i.e. Ø for plural). Some of the empirical outcomes predicted by factorial typology are worth commenting on. NEC Catalan illustrates a pattern in which the phonological markedness constraint *CsC is interspersed between morphological constraints and different types of faithfulness constraints. Most varieties of Catalan are not sensitive to the markedness constraint *CsC. This constraint is ranked low in these varieties and that causes the plural morpheme to surface systematically. Rossellonese Catalan illustrates the opposite pattern: the very high ranking of *CsC prevents any interconsonantal *s* from surfacing. Finally, an unattested pattern is predicted by ordering MAX(MPH) above MATCH. Under such a situation, having a non-matching singular element will be preferred to having a bare root (with a missing morpheme). Thus, for an example like the one illustrated in (30), *plens poders*, the winning candidate would be the unattested form in (30b), 'ple-[$Ø_{SG}$] poder-[s_{PL}]'.

The data we have presented in this section provide evidence that agreement, at least partially, has to take place at PF, with interleaving of phonological and morphosyntactic constraints.

In the following sections we shall see other asymmetries between prenominal and postnominal elements involving true allomorphy that can also be better explained under the assumption of split concord.[16]

1.4 Spanish V~Ø alternation

1.4.1 The data

In Spanish, certain lexical elements show apparent vowel deletion when they occur prenominally, but not postnominally, within the DP.[17] The examples below include practically all the prenominal elements subject to the V~Ø alternation. We abstract away from the fact that prenominal and postnominal position of a specific element often entails some semantic difference. In (32a) and (33a) the relevant element appears in prenominal position and it surfaces without a final vowel. The final vowel is present when the relevant element is postnominal, (32b) and (33b).[18] In (32) the alternation is found only in the context of masculine nouns, while in (33) the alternation can be found with both masculine and feminine nouns, the modifier being invariable with respect to gender. Gender is indicated in cases where a contrast can be found between masculine and feminine forms.

(32)	a.	algún	compañero	b.	compañero	algun**o**
		some	fellow-M		fellow-M	some-M
		primer	día		Alfonso	primer**o**
		first	day-M		Alfonso-M	first-M
		tercer	cumpleaños		Carlos	tercer**o**
		third	birthday-M		Carlos-M	third-M
		mi	niño		niño	mí**o**
		my	child-M		child-M	mine-M
		tu	niño		niño	tuy**o**
		your	child-M		child-M	yours-M
		su	niño		niño	suy**o**
		his/her/their	child-M		child-M	his/her/their-M
		buen	caso		caso	buen**o**
		good	case-M		case-M	good-M
		mal	día		día	mal**o**
		bad	day-M		day-M	bad-M

(33)	a.	cualquier	libro	b.	libro	cualquier**a**
		any	book-M		book-M	any
		cualquier	libreta		libreta	cualquier**a**
		any	notebook-F		notebook-F	any
		gran	momento		momento	grand**e**
		great	moment-M		moment-M	great
		gran	persona		persona	grand**e**
		great	person-F		person-F	big

Comparing (34a) and (34b), it is clear that the Ø alternant is not possible when the noun is feminine singular or plural (either masculine or feminine).

(34)	a.	algún	compañero	
		some	fellow-MSg	
	b.	algun**a**	compañera	*algún compañera
		some-FSg	fellow-FSg	
		algun**os**	compañeros	*algún compañeros
		some-MPl	fellow-MPl	
		algunas	compañeras	*algún compañeras
		some-FPl	fellow-FPl	

In the case of gender invariable elements, like *gran~grande* and *cualquier~cualquiera*, the alternation is found when the noun is masculine or feminine singular (as in the examples in (35a), repeated from (33)), but not when the noun is plural, as illustrated in (35b).

(35)	a.	gran	momento	
		great	moment-M	
		gran	persona	
		great	person-F	
	b.	grand**es**	momentos	*gran momentos
		great-Pl	moment-MPl	
		grand**es**	personas	*gran personas
		great-Pl	people-FPl	

A second fact that will be crucial to our analysis concerns the elements that are affected by the V~Ø alternation. Even though all the elements affected by it either belong to functional categories or are adjectives like ‘good’ or ‘bad’, it is not the case that any masculine singular or invariable singular element with those properties will be subject to ‘deletion’ when it appears in prenominal position. For instance, even though numerals like *primer(o)* ‘first’ and *tercer(o)* ‘third’ are subject to the alternation, other numerals, like *noveno* ‘ninth’, are not (see (36a)); notice that a form like **novén* would not present any syllabification problem for Spanish (cf. *bien* ‘well’). A similar contrast can be found between the quantifiers *alguno* ‘some’ and *todo* ‘all’ (see (36b)): *todo* does not exist without the final vowel, **tod* (cf. *Madrid*).

(36)	a.	tercer	cumpleaños	*tercer**o** cumpleaños
		third	birthday-MSg	
		*novén	cumpleaños	noven**o** cumpleaños
		ninth	birthday-MSg	

b.	algún	compañero	*algun**o** compañero
	some	fellow-MSg	
	*tod	compañero	tod**o** compañero
	all	fellow(s)-MSg	

Similarly, even though adjectives like *buen(o)* 'good' and *mal(o)* 'bad' appear with the Ø alternant in prenominal position, *buen* and *mal*, (37a), other adjectives cannot be subject to 'deletion': *viej**o*** 'old' (**viej*, cf. *reloj* 'watch'), *plen**o*** 'full' (**plen*), *rar**o*** 'rare' (**rar*), *escas**o*** 'little' (**escás*), (37b).[19]

(37)	a.	buen	caso	*buen**o** caso
		good	case-MS	
		mal	día	*mal**o** día
		bad	day-MS	
	b.	*viej	reloj	viej**o** reloj
		old	watch	
		*plen	invierno	plen**o** invierno
		full	winter	
		*rar	ejemplar	rar**o** ejemplar
		rare	specimen	
		*escás	margen	escas**o** margen
		little	margin	

The facts illustrated in (36) and (37) bring us to the conclusion that the possibility of V~Ø alternation has to be specified somehow in the lexical entry of each item; it cannot be predicted from general properties of the grammar.

1.4.2 Previous approaches

Older approaches to the quite similar V~Ø alternation in Italian (Rizzi 1979, Vanelli 1979, Burzio 1989) claim or assume that the underlying form of items like *nessun* 'some' have a final vowel, *nessun**o***, and that a rule deletes it when the relevant item appears before a noun. Leaving aside the rule formulation, excluded in OT, deletion would have to be lexically restricted; it could not be triggered by some general mechanism. In addition, it would be hard to account for deletion when the relevant item is not adjacent to the noun, as in the sequence *nessun vecchio libro* 'no old book'.

Bernstein (1993a,b) proposes a syntactic approach to the V~Ø alternation in Italian and Spanish. Her analysis is mostly limited to pairs like *un libro* 'a/one book' vs. bare *uno* 'one' (as in *tengo uno* 'I have one') and does not deal with the prenominal/postnominal asymmetry found with other elements. She assumes the existence of a Word Marker Phrase (WM), generated between the category Number (Num) and the (lower) NP, which hosts the *-o* suffix. In sequences like *un libro* 'a/one book' the N (*libr-*) moves to Num as does the suffix *-o*. When the N is absent, as in *uno* 'one', the suffix *-o* moves to an empty Num and moves further to D so it can attach to some phonologically realized element, in this case *un-*. One of the problems with her approach is the very dubious nature of the WM syntactic category, which moreover is proposed only to account for the *-o* in nouns and in bare *uno* but not for other instances of *-o* (such as the one in adjectives like *rojo*; cf. *un libro rojo* 'a red book'). Another even more serious problem is that this type of approach does not enlighten us at all as to the causes of the asymmetries illustrated in (32) and (33). In her analysis she implicitly assumes that in *un libro* the determiner surfaces without a final *-o* because that is the form a determiner is supposed to have. But this type of approach does not say anything as to why an adjective like *buen(o)* 'good' surfaces without an *-o* in prenominal position (exactly like *un* does) and with *-o* in postnominal position (like many other elements do). For other arguments against the WM category see Alexiadou and Müller (2008).

Harris (1996) rejects Bernstein's Word Marker Phrase (WM) but follows her proposals about syntactic structure in other respects, and considers class (word) markers (CM) to be inserted by a morphological operation that applies to stems. In his analysis cases like *un_ libro* are derived from two mechanisms: a morphological 'rebracketing' operation that adjoins the items in a closed list to a following noun or adjective, and the failure of CM insertion in rebracketed elements; by stipulation, CM can only be inserted to the elements in the larger domains. Thus, sequences like *una tía* 'an aunt' end up with the structure [*un*]-CM [*tí*]-CM, while *un libro* is assigned the structure ${}_{N}[{}_{D}[un]\ {}_{N}[libr]]$-CM. The proposal is not explicit enough and raises many questions. For instance, it is not clear why postnominal elements do not have the same fate or why feminine (singular) items like *una* or *buena* show up with a CM in prenominal position. More generally, it is difficult to see how the proposals in Bernstein (1993a,b) and Harris (1996) could apply to related asymmetries/phenomena, like the non-realization of plural in NEC Catalan.

1.4.3 Analysis under split concord

Since the V~Ø alternation is not predictable (see section 1.4.1), it has to be specified somehow in the lexical entry of exceptional items (like *primer(o)* 'first'), while regular items (like *noveno* 'ninth') have the minimal lexical specifications. We assume that, since inflection is a regular property of nominal elements in languages like Catalan and Spanish, the fact that they are inflected is not part of their lexical entry. Being a regular property, this information is not supplied in the lexicon, but is expressed in the grammar. The fact that a particular category (D, A, N) is subject to inflection can be expressed in different places depending on the model of grammar assumed. (In Distributed Morphology, for instance, this information could be contained in the list of presyntactic morphosyntactic features.) Only in the case of idiosyncratic, exceptional elements that lack inflection will a lexical mark become necessary. This is the case of the so-called invariable adjectives which are not marked for gender (Spanish *amigo fiel* 'friend-MSg faithful-Sg', *amiga fiel* 'friend-FSg faithful-Sg', *amigos fieles* 'friend-MPl faithful-Pl', *amigas fieles* 'friend-FPl faithful-Pl'), or in cases of total lack of inflection. Thus for *noveno,* a regular adjective, the relevant morpho-syntactic operations will add inflectional features from the lexicon and will yield a structure with a FLEC constituent which includes both gender and number. However, adjectives like *primer(o)* are exceptional in that their lexical entries include two stem allomorphs, one that is regular, like the adjective *noveno*, and one that is idiosyncratic, like the adjective *fiel*. Thus the lexical entry of the adjective *primer(o)* will contain the regular stem allomorph *primer* and the irregular bare stem allomorph *primer¬*, where the symbol '¬' indicates that the stem is marked for not undergoing inflection.

As claimed in section 1.2, syntatic movement by the Noun triggers agreement on the postnominal elements within the DP. In the postnominal position, then, there is no difference between numerals like *primer(o)* and *noveno*. They will surface with the expected, unmarked, inflectional morphs for Spanish (*-o* for the masculine, *-a* for the feminine; Ø for the singular, *-s* for the plural): *primer**o*** (MSg), *primer**a*** (FSg), *primer**os*** (MPl), *primer**as*** (FPl); *noven**o*** (MSg), *noven**a*** (FSg), *noven**os*** (MPl), *noven**as*** (FPl). (38) illustrates the presence of postnominal inflection with respect to gender.

(38) a. piso primer**o**
floor-M first-M
planta primer**a**
floor-F first-F
b. piso noven**o**
floor-M ninth-M
planta noven**a**
floor-F ninth-F

As shown in section 1.4.1, since the V~Ø alternation is not predictable, it has to be specified somehow in the lexical entry of each item. On the one hand, regular items like *noveno* have the minimal lexical specifications (among others, the stem *noven*); since it is a regular adjective, the relevant morphosyntactic operations will pick up inflectional features from the lexicon and yield a structure with a FLEC constituent which includes both gender and number. On the other hand, the lexical entry of exceptional items like *primer(o)* will include, along with the regular stem *primer* (as for *noven*), the idiosyncratic, bare stem allomorph *primer*¬, where the symbol '¬' indicates that the stem is marked for not undergoing inflection.

At PF there is an asymmetry between prenominal elements and postnominal ones because the former, contrary to the latter, have not been assigned any inflection. In a parallel way to what we saw for NEC Catalan, nouns and postnominal elements, as in *piso noveno* or *piso primero*, enter constraint evaluation with an ending in the input: *pis*-[o_M $Ø_{SG}$] *noven*-[o_M $Ø_{SG}$], *pis*-[o_M $Ø_{SG}$] *primer*-[o_M $Ø_{SG}$]. Prenominal elements, however, yield a contrasting result. In the regular cases, like *noveno piso*, the input to PF contains the stem *noven* and all the possible inflectional endings, as shown in (39). Remember that we represent the relation between the stem and the not yet incorporated morphological constitutent FLEC with a comma (',').

(39) Regular cases (*noveno-novena-novenos-novenas*)
  a. Lexical entry: *noven*
  b. Input to PF (prenominal): noven,[$_{FLEC}$ o_M, a_F; $Ø_{SG}$, s_{PL}],
  Shorthand: noven,FLEC

In the exceptional cases, like *primer piso*, the input to PF contains the two allomorphs, which differ solely in the possibility of lacking inflection, as shown in (40).

(40) Exceptional cases (*primer-primero-primera-primeros-primeras*)
  a. Lexical entry: *primer*, *primer*¬
  b. Input to PF (prenominal): { primer¬ / primer,[$_{FLEC}$ o_M, a_F, $Ø_{SG}$, s_{PL}] }
  Shorthand: primer¬
  primer,FLEC

The constraints that are relevant in accounting for the V~Ø alternation include some of the ones that were already introduced for NEC Catalan, namely MAX(SEGMENT), MAX(MPH), CONCORD, and *FEAT. In a parallel way to what we saw for NEC Catalan, for inputs like *noveno*, MAX(MPH) is violated by candidates lacking inflectional morphemes present in the input. Crucially, however, for inputs like *primer(o)*, MAX(MPH) is not violated by candidates without inflection, because this item can exist as a bare stem (a word without inflection, *primer¬*). In the case of CONCORD, this general constraint has to be split into more specific constraints for marked choices in nominal inflection, feminine being more marked than masculine, and plural being more marked than singular. The more specific constraints do not have to be ranked with respect to each other and will appear as CONC(F,PL) in the tableaux. The ranking of the relevant constraints is given in (41). Justification for the splitting of CONC and some aspects of the constraint ranking can be found below. The constraint MATCH is not mentioned in the rest of this section because it is not crucial for any of the cases to be discussed here.

(41) Ranking: MAX(MPH), CONC(F,PL) >> *FEAT >> CONC, MAX(SEGMENT)

The tableau below illustrates, with the sequence *algún piso primero* 'some first floor', the prenominal/postnominal asymmetry with two masculine elements that are subject to the V~Ø alternation, *algun(o)* and *primer(o)*, and thus prenominally have input forms like those presented in (40b). The inflectional feature complex of the input elements *piso* and (postnominal) *primero*, [o$_{\text{M}}$ Ø$_{\text{SG}}$], is shortened to [o$_{\text{MSG}}$]. Similar abbreviations will be used in the rest of this section. For clarity, in (42) in the prenominal forms we indicate correspondence by indexation.

(42) *algún piso primero* 'some first floor'

	algun$_1$¬ pis-o$_{\text{MSG}}$ primer-o$_{\text{MSG}}$ algun$_2$,FLEC	MAX (MPH)	CONC (F,PL)	*FEAT	CONC	MAX (SEG)
a.	algun$_2$-o$_{\text{MSG}}$ pis-o$_{\text{MSG}}$ primer-o$_{\text{MSG}}$			6*!		
b.	algún$_1$ pis-o$_{\text{MSG}}$ primer	*!*		**	****	*
c. ☞	algún$_1$ pis-o$_{\text{MSG}}$ primer-o$_{\text{MSG}}$			****	**	

In (42) the constraint CONC(F,PL) is irrelevant because the N is masculine singular. The constraint *FEAT favours candidates with no inflection, but the ranking of MAX(MPH) above it rules out the candidate with fewer inflectional endings, (42b). In this candidate, MAX(MPH) is violated only by postnominal *primer* because the input contains specific inflectional morphemes that are not present in the output; prenominal *algún* satisfies MAX(MPH) because it is faithful to the bare stem *algun¬*, present in the input. *FEAT, ranked above CONC, still forces the candidate with *algún* to win over a candidate with *alguno*. In the tableaux that appear in the rest of this section, for clarity we do not show candidates with an N or postnominal elements without the desired inflection.

The lexical entry of a numeral like *noveno* 'ninth', unlike *algun(o)* or *primer(o)*, does not have an uninflected form, **novén*. The tableau in (43) shows how this ungrammatical form is ruled out in the sequence *noveno piso* 'ninth floor'. A crucial difference between items like *tercer(o)* and *noveno* is that *noveno* does not have an inflectionless bare allomorph *noven*¬; therefore, a candidate without inflection, like *novén* pis-o$_{MSG}$ in, (43b) violates MAX(MPH).

(43) *noveno piso* 'ninth floor'

noven,FLEC pis-o$_{MSG}$	MAX (MPH)	CONC (F,PL)	*FEAT	CONC	MAX (SEG)
a. ☞ noven-o$_{MSG}$ pis-o$_{MSG}$			****		
b. novén pis-o$_{MSG}$	*!*		**	**	

As mentioned above, feminine and plural are marked morphemes, compared to masculine and singular. As for the masculine, we know that when there are gender conflicts in coordinate elements, the masculine is chosen in concord, as illustrated below.

(44) a. El sol y la luna son bonitos
the-M sun-M and the-F moon-F are pretty-MPl
b. *El sol y la luna son bonitas
the-M sun-M and the-F moon-F are pretty-FPl

With respect to number, it is also well established that singular is less marked than plural. For instance, in Spanish, when agreement is not possible, as in impersonal sentences with weather verbs or *se* constructions, the verb appears in the singular (45a,c), while there is regular agreement when there is an explicit subject (45b,d).

(45) a. Llovió
rained.3Sg
'It rained'
b. Llovieron preguntas
rained.3Pl questions
'Questions poured'
c. Se sospecha lo peor
se fear.3Sg the worst
'The worst is feared'
d. Todos sospechan lo peor
all.3Pl fear.3Pl the worst
'All of them fear the worst'

In the V~Ø alternation the marked character of feminine and plural over masculine and singular also shows up: as we saw (see (34b)), the alternation never affects feminines or plurals; it only affects a form which is masculine singular (or invariable). The examples *alguna planta* 'some floor' and *algunos pisos* 'some floors' illustrate how candidates with *algún* or other not fully inflected forms are ruled out.

(46) *alguna planta* 'some floor'

algun¬ / algun,FLEC	plant-a_{FSG}	MAX (MPH)	CONC (F,PL)	*FEAT	CONC	MAX (SEG)
a. ☞ algun-a_{FSG}	plant-a_{FSG}			****		
b. algún	plant-a_{FSG}		*!	**	**	

In (46), candidate (46b) violates CONC(F,PL) (and is ruled out by it) because the N is feminine and *algún* is not. These types of examples justify the ranking CONC(F,PL) >> *FEAT.

(47) *algunos pisos* 'some floors'

algun¬ / algun (FLEC)	pis-o_M-s_{PL}	MAX (MPH)	CONC (F,PL)	*FEAT	CONC	MAX (SEG)
a. ☞ algun-o_M-s_{PL}	pis-o_M-s_{PL}			****		
b. algun-o_M	pis-o_M-s_{PL}	*!	*!	***	*	
c. algun-s_{PL}	pis-o_M-s_{PL}	*!		***	*	
d. algún	pis-o_M-s_{PL}		*!	**	**	

The non-plural modifiers in (47b,d) are ruled out by CONC(F,PL). Candidates (47b,c) have an inflected modifier, not a bare stem, but violate MAX(MPH) once each because they lack a number morpheme and a gender morpheme, respectively. Tableau (47) justifies the ranking MAX(MPH) >> *FEAT.

We saw in (33) that the invariable items *cualquier(a)* 'any' and *gran(de)* 'big, great' are also subject to the V~Ø alternation, and, in this case, the vowelless form (*gran* and *cualquier*) can co-occur in prenominal position with a feminine singular N, contrary to the cases with regular morphology we have seen so far (cf. *gran persona* 'great person-FSg' in (35a)). In what follows we concentrate only on the *gran-grande* alternation, which constitutes a clearer case than *cualquier(a)*, which can nevertheless be analysed along the same lines.[20] A first peculiar feature that *gran(de)* has is that it is invariable: it surfaces with the same form, with final *-e*, in postnominal position regardless of the gender of the N (cf. *pueblo grande* 'big town-M', *ciudad grande* 'big city-F'). Moreover, this final *-e* does not correspond to any of the expected vowel endings in nominals, *-o* for masculine and *-a* for feminine (a final *-e* can also be found in both masculine and feminine nouns, like *pase* 'pass-M' and *mole* 'bulk-F'). These two unpredictable characteristics, invariability and exceptional final vowel, must appear in the lexical entry of the adjective. Similarly to items like *algun(o)*, this lexical entry includes a bare, inflectionless form *grand¬*, which surfaces without the final /d/, *gran*, due to cluster simplification (common in current Spanish). For the *grande* allomorph, we assume that the input to constraint evaluation does not have full inflection like that which was illustrated in (39) for *noven(o)*, but rather has a nonspecified GEN(DER) feature with the (also lexically specified) ending *-e*. With respect to number, *grande*, having (unspecified) gender, is like any other adjective and thus can be either singular or plural.

(48) Input to constraint evaluation for prenominal *gran-grande-grandes*

a. { grand¬
 grand,[$_{\text{FLEC}}$GEN=e; $Ø_{\text{SG}}$, s_{PL}] }

b. Shorthand: grand¬
 grand,FLEC(GEN=e)

The syntax imposes inflection on the adjective when it appears in the postnominal position and it will thus surface as *grande(s)* (this is as much of an inflection as it can get). In the prenominal position inflection will not have been imposed and (48) will enter constraint evaluation. We illustrate the unusual appearance of the vowelless form with a feminine noun with the sequence *gran persona* 'great person-F', and the full form with the plural *grandes personas* 'great-Pl persons-FPl'.

(49) *gran persona* 'great person'

grand¬ / grand (GEN=e)	person-a$_{\text{FSG}}$	MAX (MPH)	CONC (F,PL)	*FEAT	CONC	MAX (SEG)
a. grand-e$_{\text{GSG}}$	person-a$_{\text{FSG}}$		*	***!*	*	
b. ☞ gran	person-a$_{\text{FSG}}$		*	**	**	*

Both (49a) and (49b) violate CONC(F,Pl) (and consequently also CONC) because the N requires all the other elements to be feminine, which is not the case here. The constraint *FEAT breaks the tie in favour of *gran persona*, with less inflection than its competitor **grande persona*.

Similarly to what we saw in (47), in (50), which contains a plural N, a fully inflected candidate (50a), is the optimal candidate. Even though this candidate fares worse than its immediate competitors with respect to *FEAT, it succeeds in expressing concord with a marked feature, Plural (partial satisfaction of CONC (F,PL)), and in having both a gender and a number morpheme (satisfaction of MAX(MPH)). In (49) and (50) we have ignored a candidate with the feminine morph *-a* (**granda persona* 'big-FSg person-FSg', **grandas personas* 'big-FPl person-FPl'). Following Bonet, Lloret and Mascaró (2007), we assume that unmarked endings of this type are ruled out by the constraint RESPECT, which demands lexical specifications (here, GEN=e) to be preserved in the output.

(50) *grandes personas* 'great persons'

grand¬ grand,FLEC(GEN=e)	person-a_F-s_{PL}	MAX (MPH)	CONC (F,PL)	*FEAT	CONC	MAX (SEG)
a. ☞ grand-e_G-s_{PL}	person-a_F- s_{PL}		*	****	*	
b. gran-s_{PL}	person-a_F- s_{PL}	*!	*!	***	*	*
c. gran	person-a_F- s_{PL}		**!	**	**	*

1.5 Spanish el~la alternation

1.5.1 The data

A well-known exception to the generalization that, in Spanish, nominals in the DP agree with the NP head in gender and number is, in Standard Spanish, the appearance of the masculine singular definite article *el* disagreeing with singular feminine nouns beginning with stressed /á/ (Harris 1987, 1989, 1991; Álvarez de Miranda 1993). (51a) illustrates cases of article disagreement, and includes a postnominal agreeing adjective which shows the feminine character of the noun. (51b-e) show that disagreement does not take place when one or more of the necessary conditions is not met: the initial /a/ must be stressed, must be adjacent to the definite article, must belong to the category noun, and must be singular. (51f) shows some exceptions. Nonorthographic stress is supplied.

(51) a. *Article disagreement*

el	árma	nueva	el	hámbre	aquella
the-M	weapon-F	new-F	the-M	hunger-F	that-F
el	águila	pequeña	el	área	fija
the-M	eagle-F	small-F	the-M	area-F	fixed-F

b. *Only stressed initial á*

la	alméndra	la	actríz
the-F	almond-F	the-F	actress-F
la	astúcia	la	hablánte
the-F	astuteness-F	the-F	speaker-F

c. *Only if adjacent*

la	nueva	árma
the-F	new-F	weapon-F
la	única	águila
the-F	only-F	eagle-F

d. *Only nouns*

la	hábil	maniobra	la_{Pr}	árma_{V}	
the-F	skillful-F	move-F	her-F	arms	's/he arms her'
la	$\text{ántes}_{\text{Adv}}$	mencionada			
the-F	before	mentioned-F			

e. *Only in the singular*

las	ármas
the-FPl	weapon- FPl
las	águilas
the-FPl	eagle-FPl

f. *Exceptions*

la	Ágata	la	árabe_{N}
the-F	'proper name-F'	the-F	arab-F (woman)
la	háche	la	ástro
the-F	letter h-F	the-F	(movie-)star-F

In colloquial usage that follows prescriptive norms (Real Academia Española 1931), disagreement affects the definite article and also *un* 'a', *algún* 'some', *ningún* 'no': *un*-M *arma*-F 'a weapon', *algún*-M *águila*-F 'some eagle', *ningún*-M *área*-F 'no area'. We will refer to this system in which some determiners ending in *-a* in the feminine singular take the masculine form when immediately preceding a noun beginning with /á/, as System I. But in colloquial speech, disagreement can extend to other lexical elements and to other contexts. In a common extension that we will call System II, all prenominal elements, no matter whether adjacent or not, appear in the masculine singular, instead of the expected feminine singular, before a feminine singular noun beginning with /á/. System II is illustrated in (52a). The example in (52b) shows that the same lexical element, *nuevo/a*, that disagrees in prenominal position (first example in (52a)) agrees regularly in postnominal position. (52c), which corresponds to the first example in (52a), presents agreement because the DP is plural. Other examples can be found in Eddington and Hualde (2008).

(52) a.

el	nuevo	arma	secreta		
the-M	new-M	weapon-F	secret-F		
todo	el	agua	perdida		
all-M	the-M	water-F	lost-F		
este	ave	migratoria			
this-M	bird-F	migratory-F			
un	amplio	área	abierta	al	público
a-M	wide-M	area-F	open-F	to-the	public
aquel	área	geográfica			
that-M	area-F	geographic-F			
el	mismo	agua	parecerá	fría	
the-M	same-M	water-F	will-seem	cold-F	
todo	su	área	delantera		
all-M	her-M/F	area-F	front-F		

b.

el	arma	nueva
the-M	weapon-F	new-F

c.

las	nuevas	armas	secretas
the-FPl	new-FPl	weapon-FPl	secret-FPl

1.5.2 Previous analyses

For System I, a variety of analyses have been proposed. Harris (1987) derives cases like *el água* from /ella á.../ via *a* deletion before á (ell) and depalatalization (el). Harris (1989) does not decide between two alternative options: lexical choice of the allomorphs *el/la* or a late *la* → *el* phonological rule. Halle *et al.* (1991) conclude that it should be a phonological rule, namely *la* → $l\ /\ _N[\_\_\_\ _N[$*á...*, the vowel *e* being supplied by epenthesis. Cutillas (2003: 175–184) proposes an OT analysis that avoids the ad hoc character of previous work. His solution is based on the fact that, in Spanish, sequences of identical vowels tend to be avoided (independently of the *el~la* alternation), and that identical vowels do not fuse when the second one is stressed. He proposes two allomorphs for the feminine singular definite article, {el, la}. Given allomorphic choice through Evaluation (see Mascaró 2007, and references), the most harmonic allomorph is selected. The candidate *la água* is disfavoured by a constraint $*V_iV_i$ banning identical vowel sequences, and fusion of both a's (l[á]gua) is ruled out by UNIFORMITY-σ, which prohibits fusion if the resulting vowel is stressed. The result is that the allomorph *el* is chosen in *el água*, but fusion is preferred in *la amiga* → *l[a]miga* because *el amiga* violates ONSET. In our view, all these accounts are problematic, but what is important for our present purposes is that they cannot be extended to the variety under examination here, System II, which is the one showing prenominal/postnominal asymmetries. For System II, it is impossible to sustain an analysis based either on a specific *la* → *el* or *la* → *l* rule, or on avoidance of *aá, given that adjacency of the disagreeing prenominal element and the noun is not necessary. In (53a) the ill-formedness of ***la*** in **toda* ***la*** *água* might be interpreted as phonological because of *aá, but this cannot be extended to *tod**a***, whose final *a* does not immediately precede *á*. In (53b-c), moreover, *todo* and *el* are separated from the á-initial potential trigger by an invariable prenominal element.

(53) a.	todo	el	água		*toda	la	água
	all-M	the-M	water-F		all-F	the-F	water-F
b.	todo	su	água		*toda	su	água
	all-M	its-M/F	water-F		all-F	its-M/F	water-F
c.	el	gran	árma		*la	gran	árma
	the-M	big-M/F	weapon-F		the-F	big-M/F	weapon-F

Spanish split concord (System II) is thus a case of regular postnominal agreement and prenominal non-agreement (with default masculine gender assignment) that is triggered by a small class of singular nouns. The fact that all these nouns begin with stressed á is a residue of an older stage (System I or, perhaps, an even older stage) in which the phenomenon had a true phonological conditioning.

1.5.3 Analysis under split concord

Since no regular phonological analysis is possible, we must assume that the class of around 25 nouns that trigger split agreement are lexically marked. The lexical mark will trigger deletion of the feminine feature [F] for this class of items in the singular only at the input to PF.[21] In Distributed Morphology terms, this would be an impoverishment operation that can be expressed as in (54).

(54) [F] → Ø / __ [Sg] for *agua, arma, ave …*

As illustrated in (55), where the FLEC constituent is shown below each stem, a noun like *agua* is lexically feminine, [F], (55a). Movement in syntax will determine any surface postnominal element to acquire the feature [F] as in (55b). At the input to PF the [F] feature will be deleted, (55c), and the unmarked, default gender, [M], will be chosen for prenominal elements, (55d).

(55) *Este agua fría* 'this cold water'

a. Input to Syntax	b. Syntax	c. Input to PF	d. Output
est- fri- agu-	*est- agua fría*	*est- agua fría*	*este agua fría*
[] [] [F Sg]	[] [f sg] **[F Sg]**	[] [_ Sg] [F Sg]	**[M Sg]** [_ Sg] [F Sg]

In the previous section we have seen cases in which a bare inflectionless form surfaces in prenominal position. Here this possibility is still available for items like *algún* (cf. *algún agua fría* 'some cold water'), but an additional constraint *FEM (feminine is prohibited) forces the unmarked masculine gender to surface for items that require inflection. In the tableaux of this section we omit the constraints MAX(SEGMENT) and CONC, because they are not relevant to the issues being discussed (their inclusion would not alter the results).

In a DP like *toda la sopa fría* 'all the cold soup', the non-exceptional feminine noun *sopa* 'soup' triggers syntactic postnominal agreement; at the output of syntax the representation of the DP is *tod*,FLEC *l*,FLEC *sopa*-FSg *fría*-FSg.[22] Postsyntactic feminine concord is enforced by CONC(F,PL) and affects nonvacuously all prenominal elements. The tableau in (56) also provides evidence for the ranking CONC(F,PL) >> *FEM.

(56) *toda la sopa fría* 'all the cold soup'

tod,FLEC l,FLEC sop-a$_{FSG}$ frí-a$_{FSG}$	MAX (MPH)	CONC (F,PL)	*FEM	*FEAT
a. ☞ tod-a$_{FSG}$ l-a$_{FSG}$ sop-a$_{FSG}$ frí-a$_{FSG}$			****	8*
b. tod-a$_{FSG}$ el$_{MSG}$ sop-a$_{FSG}$ frí-a$_{FSG}$		*!	***	8*
c. tod-o$_{MSG}$ el$_{MSG}$ sop-a$_{FSG}$ frí-a$_{FSG}$		*!*	**	8*

The DP *todo el agua fría* 'all the cold water', (57), contains the exceptional feminine noun *agua*. In the syntax, it is feminine and triggers feminine postnominal agreement, yielding *tod*,FLEC *l*,FLEC *agua*-FSg *fría*-FSg, but in the input to PF the singular noun *agua* loses its [F] feature (agu-a$_{_SG}$). Postsyntactic feminine concord (CONC(F,PL)) requires any feminine noun to trigger gender agreement with other nominals in the DP. Since *agua* has lost its F feature, CONC(F,PL) is not active. The masculine forms are favoured by the constraint *FEM that penalizes the more marked member of the M, F gender pair. A form without inflection (see (57d)) is ruled out by MAX(MPH). A form like **todo el agua frío* with general disagreement (not shown in the tableaux) would imply a change of the already inflected input ***fría*** to ***frío***, hence a faithfulness violation.

(57) *Todo el agua fría* 'all the cold water'

tod,FLEC l,FLEC agu-a$_{_SG}$ frí-a$_{FSG}$	MAX (MPH)	CONC (F,PL)	*FEM	*FEAT
a. tod-a$_{FSG}$ l-a$_{FSG}$ agu-a$_{_SG}$ frí-a$_{FSG}$			**!*	7*
b. tod-a$_{FSG}$ el$_{MSG}$ agu-a$_{_SG}$ frí-a$_{FSG}$			**!	7*
c. ☞ tod-o$_{MSG}$ el$_{MSG}$ agu-a$_{_SG}$ frí-a$_{FSG}$			*	7*
d. tod l agu-a$_{_SG}$ frí-a$_{FSG}$	*!***		*	***

Since deletion only affects the singular form, plurals will show regular prenominal agreement, as shown in (58):

(58) *Todas las aguas frías* 'all the cold waters'

tod,FLEC l,FLEC agu-a$_F$-s$_{PL}$ frí-a$_F$-s$_{PL}$	MAX (MPH)	CONC (F,PL)	*FEM	*FEAT
a. ☞ tod-a$_F$-s$_{PL}$ l-a$_F$-s$_{PL}$ agu-a$_F$-s$_{PL}$ frí-a$_F$-s$_{PL}$			****	8*
b. tod-a$_F$-s$_{PL}$ l-o$_M$-s$_{PL}$ agu-a$_F$-s$_{PL}$ frí-a$_F$-s$_{PL}$		*!	***	8*
c. tod-o$_M$-s$_{PL}$ l-o$_M$-s$_{PL}$ agu-a$_F$-s$_{PL}$ frí-a$_F$-s$_{PL}$		*!*	**	8*

So far, our basic assumption that the prenominal-postnominal asymmetry is derived from the interaction of two concord mechanisms has been implemented in a specific way. We have assumed that postnominal concord takes place in the syntax while general concord is contraint-driven at PF. However, this is not the only possible implementation; all concord could take place at PF. Adapting Samek-Lodovici (2002), one constraint AGR$_f$ would cover postnominal concord (a more local type of agreement), while another constraint, EXTAGR$_f$, would trigger more general agreement. The phenomenon just discussed would pose a potential problem for this type of approach, given that the lack of prenominal agreement is restricted to a closed class of nouns and only for the singular form of its inflectional paradigm. The impoverishment solution is not available for this alternative analysis. One must resort instead to one of the OT approaches to exceptionality, cophonologies (Orgun 1996; Inkelas and Zoll 2007), or indexed constraints (Itô and Mester 1999; Pater 2000). The fact that the lack of concord is restricted to the singular complicates a solution along these lines. See Bonet (2013) for more detailed discussion.

1.6 Concluding remarks

In this chapter we have examined three cases drawn from Catalan and Spanish in which an asymmetry between prenominal and postnominal elements within the DP arises with respect to inflectional features. We have argued that the prenominal/postnominal asymmetry, present also in many other languages, arises due to postnominal concord taking place in the syntax systematically and prenominal concord being established through constraint evaluation at PF. In one of the cases, from NEC Catalan, the failure to agree prenominally is controlled by a phonological markedness constraint *CsC interspersed with morphological constraints. We have shown that this context is avoided neither through the use of the singular form nor by simple deletion of the offending sibilant, but rather through the use of a bare stem, without inflection. The constraint that penalizes nominal items that have lost elements in the FLEC constituent, MAX(MPH), is ranked fairly low in NEC Catalan, but it becomes crucial in accounting for the two cases from Spanish examined in this chapter. The V~Ø alternation found in items like *algun(o)* 'some' and *primer(o)* 'first', but not in items like *noveno* 'ninth', is regulated both by MAX(MPH) and by a lexical difference: *algun(o)* and *primer(o)* have two allomorphs that differ solely in the possibility of existing as uninflected words, and thus can bypass the effects of MAX(MPH), while *noven(o)* does not have that possibility. In this case the irrelevance of the *CsC constraint and the presence of MAX(MPH) force the inflected form to surface in prenominal position. We have seen another case in which lexical specifications play a crucial role: in varieties of Spanish (System II) in which certain feminine singular lexical items trigger feminine agreement to their right and masculine agreement to their left, these feminine singular items lose their F feature in the input to PF. The combination of MAX(MPH) with the markedness constraint *FEM forces the masculine to surface prenominally with elements of the *noveno* type.

In this chapter we have further shown that it is possible to account for morphophonological alternations in a model of OT in which all constraints are universal; it is not necessary to resort to parochial constraints to deal with the peculiar cases we have examined here. All idiosyncratic properties that affect individual lexical items are part of the lexical entry of those items; they are not encoded in constraints.

Finally, an important result of our analysis is that we must allow for interleaving of at least some phonological and morphosyntactic constraints. This strengthens proposals along similar lines by Samek-Lodovici (2005) and Wolf (2008, this volume).

Notes

* We are specially indebted to Bernard Tranel for his very detailed comments on the first draft of the paper in 2006, and to an anonymous reviewer

for insightful suggestions. We would like to thank the audiences at the Seminari de Lingüística Teòrica (Universitat Autònoma de Barcelona, 2006), the Linguistic Symposium on Romance Languages 37 (University of Pittsburgh, 2007), the 6th Mediterranean Morphology Meeting (Ithaca, 2007), the University of Manchester (2012), and the Workshop on the Selection and Representation of Morphological Exponents (Tromsø 2012) for their suggestions, in particular Jonah Katz, Clàudia Pons, and Luigi Rizzi. Research for this paper was funded by grants FFI2013-46987-C3-2-P and FFI2013-46987-C3-1-P from the Spanish Ministerio de Economía y Competitividad, and 2014SGR1013 and 2014SGR918 from the Generalitat de Catalunya.

1 Croft and Deligianni (2001) examine other kinds of NP asymmetries in addition to agreement.

2 In this chapter we use the terms *concord* and *agreement* interchangeably when talking about DP-internal elements; only the term *agreement* is used for the subject/verb relation.

3 The varieties which present s~Ø alternation (referred to as NEC Catalan in this chapter) are spoken in the regions of Garrotxa, Pla de l'Estany, Gironès, and Alt Empordà. In some places in the area the phenomenon has slightly different properties.

4 *Aquests* 'these' is pronounced [əkɛ́ts] in isolation (cf. also singular *aquest* 'this', [əkɛ́t]). Final *-nts*, *-rts*, and *-lts* are pronounced without the 't'. In *estranys* 'strange-Pl' there is progressive place assimilation from the nasal.

5 In NEC Catalan, pronominal clitics ending in Cs, where *s* is the plural morph, followed by a verb beginning in a consonant always induce [ə] epenthesis for independent reasons; e.g., *els compro*: [əl.zə] *compro* 'I buy them', *ens compra*: [ən.zə] *compra* 's/he buys for us', and also *compra'ns* -[n.zə] 'buy for us' (cf. Bonet and Lloret 1998: 199).

6 In the morphology of Catalan, there is no clear evidence that a Ø plural allomorph can be posited since all plurals, except the NEC cases under discussion, end in *s*. The so-called 'invariable forms' always end in *s*; e.g., *tos* 'cough (singular and plural)', *temps* 'time (singular and plural)', *rentaplats* 'dishwasher (singular and plural)'. Hence, an alternative explanation based on fusion is plausible. For a review of different accounts for invariable forms regarding number inflection, see Lloret (1996).

7 For simplicity, we assume that the gender morphs are just Ø for masculine and *-a* for feminine. (Feminine *-a* is spelled *e* in the plural, but both spellings represent the same vowel, [ə].) There are, however, other less common allomorphs that occur in these morphological contexts (e.g., for masculine, *-o* and *-a*, as in *mic-o* 'monkey (M)', *map-a* 'map (M)'; for feminine, Ø, as in *sal* 'salt (F)'.) (For an analysis of gender allomorph selection in Catalan, see Bonet *et al.* 2007.) The situation is quite different with respect to number inflection. All plural forms, except the cases of NEC Catalan under discussion, end in *s* (see note 6).

8 The constraints (18a–c) are specific versions of more general constraints involving general agreement (AGREE; see Samek-Lodovici 2002 for sentence agreement) and *STRUC, which penalizes any and all structure (Prince and Smolensky 2004: 30, n. 13; 230). As is well known, languages differ in the set of features they express. For present purposes, we assume that the constraints are relativized to all inflectional nominal features, or to specific inflectional features when so indicated, as in Section 4.

9 Although we adopt the formulation of *FEAT from Samek-Lodovici (2002: 59), we understand the constraint in a slightly different fashion: for Samek-Lodovici only concord-dependent elements, but not the noun, can violate the constraint; for us the presence of any relevant phi-feature, either in the noun or in any modifier, constitutes a violation of the constraint.

10 MAX(MPH) is a pure morphological constraint, since it prevents deletion of a morphological constituent. Other related constraints posited in the literature are morphophonemic, since they prevent deleting segments from certain morphemes (e.g., MAX$_{\text{Lex}}$, informally defined as 'do not delete segments in lexical morphemes' in McCarthy 2002: 96). Given the data in this section, one could posit a markedness constraint (e.g., HAVEINFLECTION), instead of the faithfulness constraint MAX(MPH). However, for the facts from Spanish discussed in section 4 it is crucial that the relevant constraint be a faithfulness constraint.

11 We use *CsC as a shorthand for the interaction of the general markedness constraint *COMPLEXCODA with different faithfulness constraints of the MAX and IDENT families (cf. Wheeler 2005: § 7 and the references cited therein).

12 In section 4 we will see that the higher ranking of MAX(MPH) in Spanish is crucial for determining the possibility of V~Ø alternation for specific lexical items.

13 Faithfulness to specific values of features would be enforced by high-ranking the constraint IDENT(F), extended to inflectional features (IDENT(F): 'Correspondent segments have identical values for the feature F'; McCarthy and Prince 1999: 226). This constraint would prevent changes in the input feature values of specified segments (such as Sg for Pl in *tap*-[$_{\text{FLEC}}$ S$_{\text{PL}}$] *vell*-[$_{\text{FLEC}}$ S$_{\text{PL}}$]).

14 Regular masculine nominals ending in *s* in the singular add *-os* in the plural; cf. *falsos companys* 'false colleagues (Pl)'. (For an OT analysis of this plural formation, see Bonet *et al.* 2007.)

15 As expected, in postnominal position, only the fully inflected forms of the adjective can be found (e.g., *poder ple*, *vida plena*, *poders plens*).

16 In this chapter we do not analyse the situation illustrated in (12) in which a syntactic gap prevents '*s*-deletion' (*un_ cotxes grocs* vs. *uns de grocs*, **un_ de grocs*). These cases involve more intricate syntactic matters that force us to leave them for future research.

17 Italian has a similar phenomenon, though additional facts related to consonant clusters complicate matters slightly.

18 The final vowel also appears when there is no overt noun in the DP (cf. *Tengo un libro* 'I have a/one book' vs. *Tengo **uno*** 'I have one'; *Algún libro* 'some book' vs. *He leído **alguno*** 'I have read some'). We will not discuss these cases here because the presence of a phonologically empty N might involve movement operations that fall beyond the scope of this chapter. These cases are related to the Catalan examples mentioned in note 16.

19 Conversely, C-final adjectives like *seductor-a* 'captivating', *previsor-a* 'provident', *burlón-a* 'mocking', *parlanchín-a* 'talkative' that can appear in prenominal position do not add *-o* in the masculine in postnominal position (e.g., *seductor varón, varón seductor*, *varón *seductoro* 'captivating male', etc.).

20 *Cualquiera* was formed from two independent words, *cual* 'which' and the verbal form *quiera* (third person singular present subjunctive of the verb 'to want'). The final vowel *-a* was then a verbal ending. We can assume that the final *-a* was reanalysed as a gender-related vowel, a word marker in the sense of Harris (1991). Some evidence for this reanalysis is that, even though in the normative plural form of *cualquiera* the plural appears after the first element, *cual**es**quiera*, it is becoming more and more common to hear a plural *cualquiera**s***, with the plural morph at the end of the whole item.

21 The fact that deletion of the [F] feature has to be restricted to the singular must be a residue from a previous stage at which there was a clear phonological effect: only the singular *la*, and not the plural *las*, met the environment for the **aá* sequence that triggered the process.

22 Our analysis does not hinge on a particular lexical representation of the definite article, which has the paradigm *el*, *la*, *los*, *las*. A reasonable assumption, though, is that there is an allomorph *el* for the masculine singular, and that an allomorph *l* appears elsewhere, with the regular inflectional markers. As a convenient shorthand we use 'l,FLEC'.

References

Alexiadou, Artemis and Müller, Gereon (2008) Class features as probes. In Asaf Bachrach and Andrew Nevins (eds) *Inflectional Identity*, 101–155. Oxford: Oxford University Press.

Álvarez de Miranda, Pedro (1993) El alomorfo de *la* y sus consecuencias. *Lengua española actual* 15/1: 5–43.

Bernstein, Judy B. (1993a) *Topics in the Syntax of Nominal Structure across Romance*. Doctoral dissertation, The City University of New York.

Bernstein, Judy B. (1993b) The syntactic role of word markers in null nominal constructions. *Probus* 5: 5–38.

Bonet, Eulàlia (2013). Agreement in two steps (at least). In Alec Marantz and Ora Matushansky (eds) *Distributed Morphology Today: Morphemes for Morris Halle*, 167–184. Cambridge, MA: MIT Press.

Bonet, Eulàlia and Lloret, Maria-Rosa (1998) *Fonologia catalana*. Barcelona: Ariel.

Bonet, Eulàlia and Lloret, Maria-Rosa (2002) OCP effects in Catalan cliticization. *Catalan Journal of Linguistics* 1: 19–39.

Bonet, Eulàlia, Lloret, Maria-Rosa and Mascaró, Joan (2004) Crazy rules and markedness in Optimality Theory. Paper presented at the Workshop on Markedness in Phonology, 27th Generative Linguistics in the Old World (GLOW-27), Thessaloniki, April 18–21.

Bonet, Eulàlia, Lloret, Maria-Rosa and Mascaró, Joan (2005) How unnatural and exceptional can languages become? Paper presented at the Phonology Workshop: Crazy Rules and Lexical Exceptions, 3rd International Conference on Language Variation in Europe (ICLaVE-3). Amsterdam, June 23–25. [Handout available on http://www.uv.es/foncat/cat/Treballs/15.Bonet.et.al. pdf.]

Bonet, Eulàlia, Lloret, Maria-Rosa and Mascaró, Joan (2007) Allomorph selection and lexical preferences: Two case studies. *Lingua* 117 (6): 903–927.

Burzio, Luigi (1989) Prosodic reduction. In Carl Kirschner and Janet De Cesaris (eds) *Studies in Romance Linguistics. Selected Papers from the Seventeenth Linguistic Symposium on Romance Languages,* 51–68. Amsterdam and Philadelphia, PA: John Benjamins.

Cinque, Guglielmo (1996) The antisymmetric programme: Theoretical and typological implications. *Journal of Linguistics* 32 (2): 447–464.

Cinque, Guglielmo (2005) Deriving Greenberg's Universal 20 and Its Exceptions. *Linguistic Inquiry* 36 (3): 315–332.

Croft, William and Deligianni, Deligia (2001) Asymmetries in NP word order. Paper presented at the International Symposium on Deictic Systems and Quantification in Languages Spoken in Europe and Northern and Central Asia, Udmurt State University, Izhevsk, Russia, May 2001. [Available on http://lings.ln.man.ac.uk/ Info/staff/WAC/Papers/NPorder.pdf.]

Cutillas, Juan Antonio (2003) *Teoría lingüística de la optimidad. Fonología, morfología y aprendizaje*. Murcia: Servicio de Publicaciones de la Universidad de Murcia.

Eddington, David and Hualde, José Ignacio (2008) El abundante agua fría. Hermaphroditic Spanish nouns. *Studies in Hispanic and Lusophone Linguistics* 1: 5–31.

Fouché, Pierre (1924) *Phonétique historique du roussillonnais*. Toulouse: Privat. Reprint, Genève: Slatkine Reprints, 1980.

Franck, Julie, Lassi, Glenda, Frauenfelder, Ulrich H. and Rizzi, Luigi (2006) Agreement and movement: A syntactic analysis of attraction. *Cognition* 101 (1): 173–216.

Guasti, Maria Teresa and Rizzi, Luigi (2002) Agreement and Tense as distinct syntactic positions: evidence from acquisition. In Guglielmo Cinque (ed.) *Functional Stucture in DP and IP. The Cartography of Syntactic Structures, Volume 1,* 167–194. Oxford: Oxford University Press.

Halle, Morris, Harris, James W. and Vergnaud, Jean-Roger (1991) A reexamination of the Stress Erasure Convention and Spanish stress. *Linguistic Inquiry* 22 (1): 141–158.

Halle, Morris and Marantz, Alec (1993) Distributed Morphology and the pieces of inflection. In Kenneth Hale and Samuel J. Keyser (eds) *The View from Building 20. Essays in Linguistics in Honor of Sylvain Bromberger*, 111–176. Cambridge, MA: MIT Press.

Harris, James W. (1987) Disagreement rules, referral rules, and the Spanish feminine article *el*. *Journal of Linguistics* 23 (1): 177–183.

Harris, James W. (1989) The stress erasure convention and cliticization in Spanish. *Linguistic Inquiry* 20 (3): 339–364.

Harris, James W. (1991) The exponence of gender in Spanish. *Linguistic Inquiry* 22: 27–62.

Harris, James W. (1996) The syntax and morphology of Class Marker suppression in Spanish. In K. Zagona (ed.) *Grammatical Theory and Romance Languages*, 99–122. Amsterdam: John Benjamins.

Inkelas, Sharon and Zoll, Cheryl (2007) Is grammar dependence real? A comparison between cophonological and indexed constraint approaches. *Linguistics* 45 (1): 133–171.

Itô, Junko and Mester, Armin (1999) The phonological lexicon. In N. Tsujimura (ed.) *The Handbook of Japanese Linguistics*, 62–100. Malden, MA: Blackwell.

Kikuchi, Seiichiro (2002) Positional Markedness in Catalan Word-Final Deletion. Paper presented at the 125th Meeting of the Linguistics Society of Japan, Tohoku Gakuin University, November 3–4. [Available on http://www.sal.tohoku.ac.jp/~s_kiku/papers/catalan_deletion_LSJ125.pdf.]

Kikuchi, Seiichiro (2005) Relativised Contiguity and Word-Final Deletion in Catalan. *On'in Kenkyu [Phonological Studies]* 8: 25–32. [Available on http://www.sal.tohoku.ac.jp/~s_kiku/papers/kikuchi2005b_catalan_deletion.pdf.]

Koopman, Hilda (2003) Inside the 'Noun' in Maasai. In Anoop Mahajan (ed.) *Syntax at Sunset 3: Head Movement and Syntactic Theory (UCLA Working Papers in Linguistics, no. 10)*, 77–115. Los Angeles: UCLA.

Lloret, Maria-Rosa (1996) El tractament de les formes nominals 'invariables' quant a nombre. *Caplletra. Revista internacional de filologia* 19 (Tardor 1995): 215–227.

Mascaró, Joan (2007) External allomorphy and lexical representation. *Linguistic Inquiry* 38: 715–735.

McCarthy, John J. (2002) *A Thematic Guide to Optimality Theory*. Cambridge: Cambridge University Press.

McCarthy, John J. and Prince, Alan (1995) Faithfulness and Reduplicative Identity. In Jill Beckman, Laura Walsh Dickey and Suzanne Urbanczyk (eds) *University of Massachusetts Occasional Papers in Linguistics 18: Papers in Optimality Theory*, 249–384. Amherst, MA: Graduate Linguistic Student Association. [Available on Rutgers Optimality Archive #60, http://roa.rutgers.edu.]

McCarthy, John J. and Prince, Alan (1999) Faithfulness and identity in prosodic morphology. In René Kager, Harry van der Hulst and Wim Zonneveld (eds) *The Prosody-Morphology Interface*, 218–309. Cambridge: Cambridge University Press. [Available on Rutgers Optimality Archive #216, http://roa.rutgers.edu.]

Nevins, Andrew (2011) Convergent evidence for rolling up Catalan adjectives. *Linguistic Inquiry* 42 (2): 339–345.

Orgun, Cemil Orhan (1996) *Sign-based morphology and phonology: with special attention to Optimality Theory*. Doctoral dissertation, University of California at Berkeley.

Pater, Joe (2000) Non-uniformity in English secondary stress: the role of ranked and lexically specific constraints. *Phonology* 17: 237–274.

Picallo, M. Carme (1991) Nominals and nominalizations in Catalan. *Probus* 3 (3): 279–316.

Prince, Alan and Smolensky, Paul (2004 [1993]) *Optimality Theory: Constraint Interaction in Generative Grammar*. Malden, MA and Oxford: Blackwell. Technical report, Rutgers University Center for Cognitive Science and Computer Science Department, University of Colorado at Boulder.

Rasom, Sabrina (2006) Il plurale femminile nel ladino dolomitico tra morfologia e sintassi. In Nicoletta Penello and Diego Pescarini (eds) *Quaderni di Lavoro dell'ASIS 5: 20–35,* 1–16. *Atti dell'XI Giornata di Dialettologia 2005.* [Available on http://asis-cnr.unipd.it.]

Real Academia Española (1931) *Esbozo de una nueva gramática de la lengua española*. Madrid: Espasa-Calpe.

Rizzi, Luigi (1979) Teoria della traccia e processi fonosintattici. *Rivista di Grammatica Generativa* 4: 165–181.

Samek-Lodovici, Vieri (2002) Agreement impoverishment under subject inversion: a crosslinguistic analysis. In Gisbert Fanselow and Caroline Féry (eds) *Resolving Conflicts in Grammar: Optimality Theory in Syntax, Morphology, and Phonology,* 49–82. Linguistische Berichte Sonderheft 11. Hamburg: Helmut Buske.

Samek-Lodovici, Vieri (2005) Prosody-syntax interactions in the expression of focus. *Natural Language & Linguistic Theory* 23 (4): 687–755.

Shlonsky, Ur (2004) The form of Semitic Noun Phrases. *Lingua* 114 (2): 1465–1526.

Vanelli, Laura (1979) Una forma suppletiva dell'articolo e la sua fonosintassi. *Rivista di Grammatica Generativa* 4: 183–206.

Vilkuna, Maria (1998) Word Order in European Uralic. In Anna Siewierska (ed.) *Constituent Order in the Languages of Europe,* 105–149. Berlin and New York: Mouton de Gruyter.

Wheeler, Max W. (2005) *The Phonology of Catalan*. Oxford: Oxford University Press.

Wolf, Matthew (2008) *Optimal Interleaving: Serial Morphology-Phonology Interaction in a Constraint-Based Model*. Doctoral dissertation, University of Massachusetts at Amherst.

2 Allomorphy in OT: The Italian mobile diphthongs*

Geert Booij (Leiden University)
Bart van der Veer (Antwerpen)

2.1 Introduction

Allomorphy can be defined as the complementary distribution of morphemes with the same meaning. The traditional approach to allomorphy in generative phonology can be characterized as follows. Allomorphy is accounted for as much as possible in terms of a common underlying form for the relevant allomorphs, in combination with a set of phonological rules that derive these allomorphs as surface forms in different contexts.

This approach to allomorphy has been successful in cases of regular allomorphy where productive phonological rules can be invoked to derive the surface forms of a morpheme. However, there are many cases in which the allomorphs do not bear enough phonological similarity to even consider seriously the possibility that the allomorphs can be derived from a common underlying form. This kind of allomorphy is referred to as 'lexical allomorphy' or 'suppletive allomorphy', and it is usually assumed that such allomorphy must be accounted for by listing each of the allomorphs in the lexicon.

In some cases of lexical allomorphy, the selection of the right allomorph is a matter of morphology proper. This is, for instance, the case for competing suffixes from different strata of the Dutch lexicon: the native suffix *-heid* '-hood' can be attached to both native and non-native stems, whereas the synonymous suffix *-iteit* '-ity' can be attached to non-native stems only. In such cases, there is no phonology whatsoever involved in allomorph selection.

As pointed out in Carstairs (1988), the fact that allomorphs cannot be derived from a single underlying form and must be stored lexically does not necessarily imply that the choice between the allomorphs has nothing to do

Affiliation: (Booij) Emeritus Professor, Leiden University, Leiden, Netherlands.

with phonology. There are lots of cases in which the choice of a particular allomorph makes sense from a phonological point of view, and appears to have a phonological motivation. Carstairs qualifies such cases as 'phonologically conditioned suppletion'.

An example of suppletive allomorphy in Dutch, discussed in detail in Booij (1998), is the competition between two plural suffixes, *-s* and *-en*, which are – with some exceptions – in complementary distribution, but for which there is obviously no common underlying phonological form. What can be shown, however, is that the selection of the correct allomorph is governed by phonological constraints. The basic generalization is that the suffix *-en* [ən] occurs when the stem of the noun ends in stressed syllable, whereas *-s* appears after an unstressed syllable. The effect of this distribution is that plural nouns always end in a disyllabic trochee, the optimal prosodic foot of Dutch. This is illustrated by the following examples:

(1)	*Singular form*		*Plural form*
	kánon	'canon'	kánon-s
	kanón	'gun'	kanónn-en
	nátie	'nation'	nátie-s
	geníe	'genius'	geníe-en

This selection principle also predicts correctly – again, with some exceptions – that the plural forms of monosyllabic nouns require the plural suffix *-en*:

(2)	*Singular form*		*Plural form*
	non	'nun'	nonn-en
	knie	'knee'	knie-en
	bal	'ball'	ball-en

It is possible to account for this selection principle by assuming two morphological rules for the formation of plural nouns in Dutch, in which the phonological conditions for the selection of these plural suffixes are stated. Such an account, however, does not explain why this particular distribution of these allomorphs is found. The inverse situation, in which the suffix *-s* is added after a stressed syllable, and the suffix *-en* after an unstressed one, would be equally simple in terms of descriptive costs. What a rule-based analysis cannot express is the motivating force behind this distributional pattern, the tendency for an optimal prosodic shape of words. This can be expressed, however, in a theory that makes use of output constraints. Optimality Theory is such a theory.

In this article we will focus on a famous case of allomorphy in Italian, the phenomenon of the so called mobile diphthongs, a vowel alternation in the roots of inflectionally or derivationally related words. We will argue that this alternation is a case in which the two allomorphs have to be lexically listed, and hence is a case of lexical allomorphy. However, the selection of the right allomorph is performed by the language-specific ranking of a set of universal phonological constraints. This analysis follows the line of analysis as developed in Rubach and Booij (2001) for Polish, and in similar analyses listed in McCarthy (2002: 183). It is mainly based on work reported in the dissertation of the second author (Van der Veer 2006).

In Section 2.2, we will argue why we cannot account for this alternation by assuming a common underlying form. Instead, an OT- account will be presented, and the advantages of such an account will be highlighted. In Section 2.3 we will show that there is independent external evidence for this approach: the facts of analogical levelling require that inflected and derived words with a particular allomorph are stored in the lexicon. That is, this allomorphy must be lexical in nature. Section 2.4 will provide a summary of our findings.

2.2 Mobile diphthongs in Italian: An OT analysis

The 'mobile diphthong rule' refers to the alternation pattern of the stressed diphthongs [jɛ] and [wɔ] vs the unstressed corresponding monophthongs [e] and [o]. This alternation plays a role in the inflection of a number of verbs (see (3)) as well as some derivational processes (including diminutivization) (see (4)).

(3)	siedo	[ˈsjɛdo]	'I sit'	sederò	[sedeˈro]	'I shall sit'
	vieni	[ˈvjɛni]	'you come'	veniamo	[veˈnjamo]	'we come'
	muovo	[ˈmwɔvo]	'I move'	moviamo	[moˈvjamo]	'we move'
	suono	[ˈswɔno]	'I play'	soniamo	[soˈnjamo]	'we play'
(4)	dieci	[ˈdjɛtʃi]	'ten'	decina	[deˈtʃiːna]	'ten or so'
	muovo	[ˈmwɔvo]	'I move'	movimiento	[moviˈmento]	'movement'
	uomo	[ˈwɔmo]	'man'	omino	[oˈmiːno]	'little man'

In the phonological literature that has appeared on this topic, this alternation pattern has been analysed as a case of allomorphy in which the allomorphs are distributed according to phonological generalizations. Sluyters (1992) relates the alternation to stressed open syllable diphthongization. He argues that the mobile diphthongs are the result of a synchronic diphthongization rule, which is closely related to a rule that lengthens vowels: both phonological processes have the stressed open syllable as their domain of application and are aimed at creating well-formed binary feet. Conversely, Saltarelli (1970) invokes a monophthongization rule. He accounts for the monophthong-diphthong alternation by adopting the underlying diphthongs /iɛ:/ and /uɔ:/, from which simplex vowels are derived by means of a monophthongization rule. This rule applies after a rule which turns high vowels into glides when they are adjacent to a vowel.

Both Saltarelli and Sluyters analyse the monophthong-diphthong alternation as a synchronically productive phenomenon in Italian grammar. However, this synchronic approach is problematic, since it predicts the occurrence of diphthongization or monophthongization in cases where this is not correct. For instance, in a number of Italian verbs there is no monophthong-diphthong alternation at all: either the mid vowel or the diphthong is maintained throughout the paradigm. Examples of such verbs are given in (5).

(5)	spiegare	'to explain'	coprire	'to cover'
	chiedere	'to ask'	levare	'to lift'
	nuotare	'to swim'	notare	'to note'
	vuotare	'to empty'	votare	'to vote'
	abbuonare	'to forgive'	abbonare	'to subscribe'

Thus, the indicative present of the verbs *spiegare* and *coprire* is as follows:

(6)	SG	1	spiego	copro
		2	spieghi	copri
		3	spiega	copre
	PL	1	spieghiamo	copriamo
		2	spiegate	coprite
		3	spiegono	coprono

According to Sluyters' theory, we would expect the second person singular of the present indicative of the verb *coprire* 'to cover' to be **cuòpri*: the stressed mid-vowel diphthongizes in order to create a heavy stressed syllable. Likewise, Saltarelli's theory predicts that the second person plural of the present indicative of the verb *spiegare* 'to explain' is **spegàte*, in which the diphthong monophthongizes in unstressed position. The forms **cuopri* and **spegate* are not attested in modern Italian. Interestingly, in early Italian texts we do find forms such as *cuopro*, *cuopri*, *cuopre*, which suggests that stressed open syllable diphthongization may once have been a productive process in the language but no longer is. An analysis of the Italian monophthong-diphthong alternation in terms of phonological allomorphy, deriving the allomorphs from a single underlying representation, cannot differentiate between alternating and non-alternating vowels and diphthongs and would have to allow for many lexical exceptions.[1]

An alternative to positing a single underlying representation is to follow Rubach and Booij's (2001) analysis of Polish iotation and list the allomorphs in the lexicon. Rubach and Booij argue that this strategy does not imply that there is no task for phonology: the allomorphs may be arbitrary, but their distribution is regulated by the ranking of universal constraints. The listing requires that we posit multiple stems for each morpheme, so, for instance, the verb *sedere* would have two underlying allomorphs: /sɛd/ and /sjɛd/. Following the authors, the selection of either /sɛd/ or /sjɛd/ is predicted by the interaction of faithfulness and markedness constraints, as will be demonstrated in the remainder of this section.

As a preliminary, let us note that there is evidence that Italian onglides belong to the nucleus. Rising diphthongs have an autonomous phonological status since they occur after all kinds of consonants, as illustrated by the following examples:

(7)	[je]	piegare	'to fold'	[wi]	guida	'guide'
	[jɛ]	fieno	'hay'	[we]	quercia	'oak'
	[ja]	bianco	'white'	[wɛ]	guerra	'war'
	[jɔ]	pioggia	'rain'	[wa]	punt[wa]lità	'punctuality'
	[jo]	tempio	'temple'	[wɔ]	cuore	'heart'
	[ju]	fiume	'river'	[wo]	vuotare	'to empty'

Furthermore, acoustic experiments have shown that the duration of onglides interacts with the duration of the following vowel: the duration of the whole diphthong increases in stressed position (see van der Veer 2006). Therefore we assume that rising diphthongs are monomoraic in unstressed syllables and bimoraic in stressed (open) syllables, see (8).

(8)

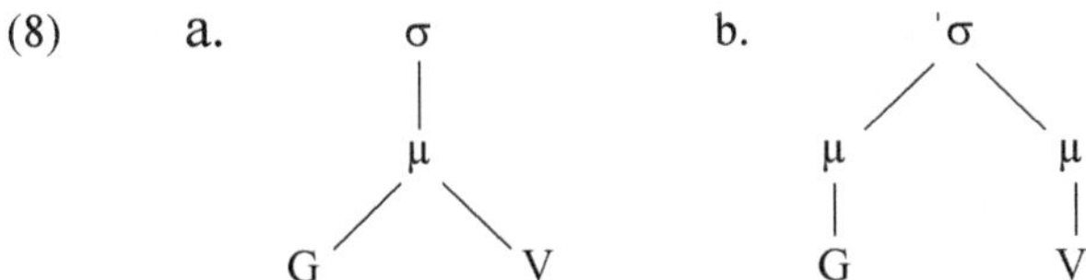

Now suppose we assume two underlying allomorphs for the root of the verb *sedere*: /sɛd/ and /sjɛd/. Subsequently, we would have to establish the constraint ranking responsible for the following alternation pattern:

(9) *sedere*, present indicative

SG	1	s[jɛ]do
	2	s[jɛ]di
	3	s[jɛ]de

PL	1	s[e]diamo
	2	s[e]dete
	3	s[jɛ]dono

In our OT analysis we use a metrical constraint 's$_{mm}$ ('bimoraic syllables are stressed; stressed syllables are bimoraic') and a faithfulness constraint DEP-M ('no epenthesis').[2] The interaction of these two constraints is responsible for the distribution of long and short vowels and diphthongs in Italian. as is illustrated in the following (simplified) tableaux for *casa* 'house' and *piano* 'flat', in which 's$_{mm}$ dominates DEP-M:

(10)

Input: /kasa/	'σ$_{\mu\mu}$	DEP-M
a. ☞ 'ka:.sa		*
b. 'ka.sa	*!	

(11)

Input: /pjano/	'σ$_{\mu\mu}$	DEP-M
a. ☞ 'pj$_{\mu}$a$_{\mu}$.no		*
b. 'pja$_{\mu}$.no	*!	

If we construct a tableau in the Rubach and Booij style, i.e. with two underlying allomorphs, we must conclude that the ranking 's$_{mm}$ >> DEP-M cannot determine which of the output candidates is optimal:[3]

(12) a.

/sɛd/ /sjɛd/ } + i	'σ$_{\mu\mu}$	DEP-M
i. ☞ 'sɛ:.di	*	
ii. ☞ 'sj$_{\mu}$ɛ$_{\mu}$.di	*	
iii. 'sɛ.di	*	

(12) b.

/sɛd/ /sjɛd/ } + ete	'σ$_{\mu\mu}$	DEP-M
i. ☞ se.'de:.te		
ii. ☞ sje$_{\mu}$.'de:.te		
iii. sj$_{\mu}$e$_{\mu}$.'de:.te		*

Candidates with light stressed syllables are ruled out immediately by $'s_{mm}$. Since both vowels and rising diphthongs can surface as either short or long, the constraint ranking in (12) does not suffice to select the correct output. In (12a) both candidates violate the faithfulness constraint, because both contain a mora which has no correspondent in the input. In (12b) no violation is incurred by either of the candidates. Therefore, the alternation pattern cannot be dealt with without additional constraints.

The key to the solution lies in the shape of the syllabic nuclei. The candidates in (12) exhibit the complete inventory of possible syllabic nuclei: (a) short vowels, (b) long vowels, (c) monomoraic diphthongs, and (d) bimoraic diphthongs. All languages have short vowels, but the occurrence of type b, c and d is dictated by markedness constraints on syllable structure. The following two constraints are crucial in the current analysis:

(13) a. $*N_{mm}$: No branching between a syllable nucleus and two moras.
b. $m \leftrightarrow \mu$: No branching between melody and mora.

Both anti-branching constraints militate complex nuclei, in the spirit of *COMPLEX-ONSET and *COMPLEX-CODA. Note that (13b) could be split up in a constraint against a more branching into two melodies (e.g. a glide-vowel combination) and one against a melody (e.g. a vowel) spreading over more than one mora. In general, one-to-one correspondences are preferred over branching within the syllable nucleus. The difference between the two constraints in (13) is where the branching and the one-two-one correspondence are located: either between syllable nucleus and mora, or between mora and melody. In the table below we summarize the violation types incurred by all four syllabic nuclei that occur in Italian:

(14)

	$*N_{\mu\mu}$	$m \leftrightarrow \mu$
$V_{\mu\mu}$	*	*
$G_{\mu}V_{\mu}$	*	
GV_{μ}		*
V		

From tableau (14) we can conclude that V_{mm} is doubly bad since it has a branching syllable node and a branching melody, and therefore it violates $*N_{mm}$ and $m \leftrightarrow \mu$.

We assume that within the syllable nucleus, branching violations at a higher level are more serious than branching violations at a lower level, and therefore propose that $*N_{mm}$ is ranked higher than m ↔ μ. The tableaux in (15) demonstrate how the proposed constraint ranking selects the optimal candidates in our case of allomorphy:

(15) a.

/sɛd/ /sjɛd/ } + i	$*N_{\mu\mu}$	m ↔ μ
i. ˈsɛː.di	*!	*
ii. ☞ ˈsj$_{\mu}$ɛ$_{\mu}$.di	*	

(15) b.

/sɛd/ /sjɛd/ } + ete	$*N_{\mu\mu}$	m ↔ μ
i. ☞ se.ˈdeː.te		
ii. sje$_{\mu}$.ˈdeː.te[4]		*!

Candidate (i) in (15a) loses as it violates both constraints. In (15b) the candidate with the short vowel, (i), wins because in unstressed syllables a short vowel is always the most optimal syllable nucleus. The point of interest is that stressed long vowels and unstressed monomoraic diphthongs are perfectly acceptable syllabic nuclei in Italian. In cases where these types of nuclei surface, the underlying representations do not parallel those of cases with different underlying allomorphs (as in (15)). For instance, the verb *coprire* 'to cover' only has /kɔpr/ as its underlying form and a high-ranked faithfulness constraint $\text{D}\textsc{ep}_{seg}$ ('no epenthesis') prevents the stressed nucleus from surfacing as a bimoraic diphthong by glide insertion, as shown in (16):

(16)

/kɔpr/ + i	$\text{D}\textsc{ep}_{seg}$	$*N_{\mu\mu}$
a. ☞ ˈkɔː.pri		*
b. ˈkw$_{\mu}$ɔ$_{\mu}$.pri	*!	*

Conversely, the bimoraic diphthong in candidate (ii) in (15a) is not an instance of glide insertion, because the glide is present in the /sjɛd/ allomorph and therefore $\text{D}\textsc{ep}_{seg}$ is not violated, as can be seen in the following tableau:

(17)

/sɛd/ } + i /sjɛd/	DEP$_{seg}$	*N$_{\mu\mu}$	m ↔ μ
a. ˈsɛː.di		*!	*
b. ☞ ˈsj$_{\mu}$ɛ$_{\mu}$.di			*

Similarly, monomoraic diphthongs surface because of high-ranked MAX$_{seg}$ ('no deletion'). The tableau in (18) evaluates the second person plural of the present indicative of *spiegare* 'to explain':

(18)

/spjɛg/ + ate	MAX$_{seg}$	m ↔ μ
a. spje.ˈgaː.te	*!	
b. ☞ spje$_{\mu}$.ˈgaː.te		

Candidate (18a) fatally violates MAX$_{seg}$, because the input glide is deleted. The verb *spiegare* has only one input /spjɛg/, as opposed to *sedere*. In (19) the tableau for the second person plural of *sedere* is presented once more, this time including the relevant faithfulness constraint. Since the input contains an allomorph without a glide, the winning candidate does not violate MAX$_{seg}$.

(19)

/sɛd/ } + ete /sjɛd/	MAX$_{seg}$	m ↔ μ
a. ☞ se.ˈdeː.te		
b. sje$_{\mu}$.ˈdeː.te		*!

The 'multi-input' analysis developed here has some major advantages with respect to the 'mono-input' analyses of Sluyters (1992) and Saltarelli (1970), who claimed that the monophthong-diphthong alternation was triggered by a diphthongization or monophthongization rule, respectively. Mono-input approaches to the monophthong-diphthong alternation suffer from overapplication effects – diphthongs or monophthongs occur where they should not. They rely on arbitrary and language-specific rules. In multi-input theories of allomorphy, the underlying allomorphs are arbitrary, but their distribution is governed by a language-specific ranking of universal constraints. The conclusion is that the monophthong-diphthong alternation is not a phenomenon triggered by active phonological processes but an instance of mixed phonological and morphological allomorphy: the allomorphs are posited in the input and the constraint ranking predicts where these allomorphs will appear.

Another advantage is that the newly proposed analysis also works for other alternation patterns in Modern Italian. For instance, velar palatalization, i.e. the palatalization of a velar sound in the context of a following high front vowel, has typically been considered as a readjustment phenomenon triggered by phonological factors (cf. Scalise 1984). It characterizes the flexion and derivation of a number of words, as in the following examples:

(20)	amì[k]o	'friend'	amì[tʃ]i	'friends'
	bèl[g]a	'Belgian'	bèl[dʒ]i	'Belgians'
	cattòli[k]o	'catholic'	cattoli[tʃ]ìssimo	'very catholic'
	stòri[k]o	'historian'	stòri[tʃ]i	'historians'

However, velar palatalization is not a generalized phenomenon in Italian, so it is not possible to interpret the [k]/[tʃ] and [g]/[dʒ] alternations as instances of exclusively phonological allomorphy (see Celata and Bertinetto 2005). Such an explanation would have to deal with too many lexical exceptions, as exemplified below:

(21)	grè[k]o	'Greek'	grè[tʃ]i	'Greeks'
	còmi[k]o	'comedian'	còmi[tʃ]i	'comedians'
	bèl[g]a	'Belgian'	bèl[dʒ]i	'Belgians'
			as opposed to:	
	tùr[k]o	'Turkish'	tùr[k]i	'Turks'
	càri[k]o	'freight'	càri[k]i	'freights'
	collè[g]a	'colleague'	collè[g]i	'colleagues'

Since it seems impossible to derive palatalization effects from a single underlying representation, an effective alternative is to list the allomorphs in the input. For instance, the underlying allomorphs of *greco* are /grɛk/ and /grɛtʃ/, whereas *turco* has only one input morpheme /turk/. Assuming a constraint PAL, which requires consonants to palatalize when they precede front vowels (cf. Łubowicz 2002), it is clear that PAL is dominated by IDENT(Place), a faithfulness constraint that calls for correspondents in input and output to have identical place features. Such a ranking blocks palatalization, as illustrated in the tableau for *turchi*, the plural of *turco*:

(22)

/turk/ + i	Id(Place)	Pal
a. ☞ ˈtur.ki		*
b. ˈtur.tʃi	*!	

The ranking in (22) will yield a different output when the input consists of multiple allomorphs, as in the following tableau for *greci*, the plural of *greco*. Here, the palatalized output will win, since it does not violate the faithfulness constraint.[5]

(23)

/grɛk/ /grɛtʃ/ } + i	Id(Place)	Pal
a. ˈgrɛː.ki		*!
b. ☞ ˈgrɛː.tʃi		

The current approach can be elegantly related to one of the key consequences of Optimality Theory, called 'the emergence of the unmarked' (McCarthy and Prince 1994). Consider the singular form *greco*: the constraint ranking in (23) does not prohibit the allomorph /grɛtʃ/ from surfacing before a back vowel and evaluates the candidates [ˈgrɛɔ.ko] and [ˈgrɛɔ.tʃo] as equally optimal. Rubach and Booij (2001) propose to solve this dilemma with the help of markedness constraints. In this case, it can be argued – in the spirit of Prince and Smolensky (1993) – that /tʃ/ is a more marked and cross-linguistically less frequent segment than /k/, resulting in the ranking *tʃ >> *k. The role that markedness constraints play in selecting the unmarked allomorph is demonstrated in the following tableau:

(24)

/grɛk/ /grɛtʃ/ } + o	Id(Place)	Pal	*tʃ	*k
a. ☞ ˈgrɛː.ko				*
b. ˈgrɛː.tʃo			*!	

A final advantage of the multi-input approach is that it makes an extremely interesting diachronic prediction. It was argued that irregular, non-productive alternations are lexicalized. As a consequence, the lexicon is more complex than in an approach that derives the allomorphs from one single input. This entails a substantially increased memorization burden on the speaker. When memory fails and analogical speech errors are produced, it is expected that errors of this kind – i.e. regularizations of non-productive alternations – are more easily accepted than forms that result from regularizations of productive alternations (cf. Wetzels 1981). This concept of analogical change is pursued in the next section.

2.3 Independent evidence for the lexical representation of allomorphy: Analogical change

The monophthong-diphthong alternation, 'just like all other alternations, represents a redundancy for the language' (Tekavčić 1972: 345, the translation is ours). In fact, written sources and experiments (Van der Veer 2001, 2006) provide evidence that this alternation is subject to a great degree of analogical levelling. In numerous cases the diphthongs are reported to have extended to unstressed syllables, as illustrated in (25).

(25) s[je]derò 'I shall sit'
p[je]dìno 'small foot'
m[wo]viàmo 'we move'
b[wo]nìno 'rather good'

The elimination of morphophonemic alternations, also referred to as analogical levelling, under the pressure of paradigm uniformity, is a fairly common phenomenon in the world's languages. Some salient observations about analogical change are made by Wetzels (1981). The central idea of this dissertation, couched in the SPE framework, is that opaque alternations are lexicalized by the speaker and, since they constitute an awkward allomorphy for the speaker, are subject to elimination (see also Kiparsky 1982).

There is good evidence that the 'mobile diphthong rule' had become opaque. Since the tenth/eleventh century, surface exceptions had been brought about by other changes in the language, such as the palatalization of post-consonantal /l/, the elimination of the onglides [j] and [w] after consonant clusters ending in /r/ or the introduction of loanwords, mostly latinisms (*voci dotte*):

(26) Sources of opacity of the 'mobile diphthong rule'
a. Palatalization of /l/ in the consonant clusters /pl/, /bl/, /kl/, /gl/ and /fl/ (10th/11th century, cf. Castellani 1976)
sp[jɛ]go ~ sp[je]ghiàmo 'I explain' ~ 'we explain' (cf. Latin *explico* 'I unfold')
p[jɛ]no ~ p[je]nézza 'full' ~ 'fullness' (cf. Latin *ple:nus* 'full')

b. Deletion of [j] and [w] after consonant clusters ending in /r/ (14th/15th century, cf. Castellani 1967)
   pr[jɛ]go > pr[ɛ]go ~ pr[e]ghiàmo 'I beg' ~ 'we beg'
   tr[wɔ]va > tr[ɔː]va ~ tr[o]viàmo 'he finds' ~ 'we find'
   pr[wɔ]va > pr[ɔː]va ~ pr[o]viàmo 'he tries' ~ 'we try'
c. Deletion of [w] after the palatal consonants /j/, /ʎ/, /ɲ/, /ʃ/, /tʃ/ and /dʒ/ (19th century, cf. Migliorini 1963)
   [dʒwɔ]ca > [dʒɔː]ca ~ [dʒo]chiàmo 'he plays' ~ 'we play'
   tova[ʎʎwɔ]lo > tova[ʎʎɔ]lo ~ tova[ʎʎo]lìno 'napkin' ~ 'small napkin'
d. Loanwords
   rip[ɛː]to ~ rip[e]tiàmo 'I repeat' ~ 'we repeat'

In (27) we summarize the history of the monophthong-diphthong alternation:

(27) History of the monophthong-diphthong alternation

	Output (stressed~unstressed)	*Input*
stage 1	mɔːv-~mov-	mɔv-
stage 2	mɔəv-~mov-	mɔv-
stage 3	muəv-~mov-	mɔv-
stage 4	mwɔv-~mov-	mɔv-
stage 5	mwɔv-~mov-	mɔv-/mwɔv-
stage 6	mwɔv-~mov-/mwov-	mɔv-/mwɔv-
(stage 7)	mwɔv-~mwov-	mwɔv-

Stage 1 reflects the pre-diphthongization stage in late spoken Latin; stressed open syllable diphthongization is assumed to have taken place in subsequent stages (stages 2-4) (cf. Sánchez Miret 1998). In stage 5, the diphthongization process became opaque and multiple inputs are posited. Stage 6 is a variation stage in which more and more speakers started to eliminate the alternation, extending the diphthong to the unstressed syllables; this levelling is almost complete, although back vowels/ diphthongs are slightly more resistant to the change. Complete levelling of the monophthong-diphthong alternation is reached in (hypothetical) stage 7. Conversely, the alternation between stressed mid-low vowels and unstressed mid-high vowels persists, because in Italian the mid vowels are neutralized in unstressed syllables. Therefore, the allophonic alternation between [jɛ], [wɔ] and [je], [wo] is predictable and persists.

It is clear that, as Van de Weijer (1999: 148) observes, 'analogical change touches on many different aspects of grammar: phonology, morphology and the (re-)representation of lexical items'. Recently, paradigm effects have received considerable attention in linguistics, for instance in Downing *et al.* (2005). These theories face the daunting challenge of covering the various aspects of paradigm effects and analogical change. In discussing the levelling effects concerning the mobile diphthongs, we will follow Albright and Hayes (2002) and Albright (2002, 2004, 2005a,b) and argue that access to allomorphy depends on access to lexically listed information in inflected and derived words. This point is also made in Celata and Bertinetto (2005) for Italian velar palatalization.

2.3.1 Paradigms and their bases

Albright and Hayes (2002) claim that language learners compare all the available paradigms and select the base form that allows one to construct the remaining members of the paradigm as reliably and efficiently as possible. They present a computational model of base discovery, which has been applied to a number of languages (e.g. Albright 2002, 2004, 2005a,b). Given paradigms of related words, the model learns the morphological and phonological rules needed to derive the entire paradigm from one single base form. In this section we use hypothetical language data to illustrate the premises of the model and construct a subgrammar of consonant alternation in nouns. Consider the following hypothetical language:

(28) Hypothetical language (stage 1)

SG	PL
pan	pani
tap	tapi
kam	kami
pak	paki
rak	ragi
mat	matʃi
pat	patʃi

In this language, phonology acts to neutralize the contrast between voiced /g/ and voiceless /k/: the contrast is present in plural nouns before the plural ending *-i*, but neutralized in word-final position in singular nouns, where we find only [k]. These data suggest that the language has a process of final velar devoicing. The language learner can discover this process (i) by comparing the singular (*rak*) with the plural (*ragi*) and (ii) by comparing *rak~ragi* with *pak~paki*. This second comparison is necessary to discover the direction of the process, which, in fact, is a process of final devoicing and not of prevocalic voicing, otherwise we would expect the plural of *pak* to be *pagi*. Since the neutralization affects the singular forms, the mapping from the singular to the plural is unpredictable. Therefore it is unlikely that the learner would memorize just the singular, since he would need two rules to project the plural ([k] → [ki] and [k] → [gi]) which would only have 50% accuracy in the form sets presented in (28). If, on the other hand, the learner were to derive the singular from the plural, he would still need two rules ([ki] → [k] and [gi] → [k]), but each of the rules would have 100% accuracy in the lexicon. Suppose the learner were confronted with a hypothetical new plural form *bagi*, the learner would, with 100% certainty, derive the correct form for the singular: *bak*.

The data further suggest that the language has a process of coronal palatalization, [t] becoming [tʃ] before the plural ending *-i*. To capture this process, the language learner will set up a morphological rule [tʃi] → [t], i.e. taking the plural form as the base, as he does for the cases of devoicing.

Albright and Hayes' base discovery model or algorithm assesses the reliability of these types of morphological rule and tries to find generalizations that have as few exceptions as possible. For more detailed analyses of real language data, the reader is referred to work by Albright, cited above. Not only does their model show that paradigms (including inflectional paradigms) are constructed around bases, it also claims to make correct predictions about the direction of analogical change. To illustrate this, let us assume that the hypothetical language considered so far reaches a new stage in which we encounter the following noun paradigms:

(29) Hypothetical language (stage 2)

SG	PL
mat	matʃi
kitʃ	kitʃi
pot	poti

Apparently, the process of coronal palatalization has been obscured by other generalizations and has become opaque. Now we find [t] in contexts where we would have expected [tʃ]. Besides, the morphological rule [tʃi] → [t], set up in a previous stage, has no longer 100% accuracy. As a result of the changes, contrasts are no longer more faithfully preserved in the plural. In such cases, Albright (2005b) proposes that the learner is forced to choose a single form that is generally most predictive: since the plural is most informative about other contrasts in the language (e.g. the contrast between [k] and [g]), it serves as the base for the words in (29) as well. If the non-alternating <kitʃ, kitʃi> type of paradigm becomes lexically more dominant in the language than the alternating <mat, matʃi> type of paradigm, the rule [tʃi] → [t] would have extremely low confidence.

Therefore, Albright suggests that the alternating forms are memorized as irregular exceptions, an idea which coincides with the multi-input approach presented in the previous sections.

The fact that opaque alternations tend to be eliminated (cf. Wetzels 1981; Kiparsky 1982), is also satisfactorily predicted by the current model. Albright (2005b: 17) assumes that ‘errors (by children or adults) are overwhelming overregularizations (that is, replacement of irregular forms by grammatically expected forms)’. On analogy with regular paradigms, the learner would expect the singular of *matʃi* to be *matʃ*. So, the model predicts that the <mat, matʃi> paradigm may change to <matʃ, matʃi>. Since the plural is adopted as the base form, converse changes are not predicted, i.e. the plural of *mat* becoming _*mati_, or the plural of *pot* becoming _*potʃi_ (on analogy with <mat, matʃi>). Thus, this model of paradigm acquisition predicts which forms will be affected and in which direction the change goes. It provides us with an explanatory generalization concerning analogical change, namely that analogical change is more than a phonological effect of paradigm uniformity; actually it can be interpreted as a morphological effect that results from the way that paradigms are learned. In the next section, we will see how the model makes the correct predictions for the monophthong-diphthong alternations in Italian and how this insight can be accommodated within an optimality-theoretic analysis.

2.3.2 Analogical levelling of the monophthong-diphthong alternation

In order to discover the generalizations behind the elimination of alternations caused by the ‘mobile diphthong rule’, we will construct a (simplified) subgrammar of vowel quality alternation in Italian verb paradigms. The implications of this subgrammar will – mutatis mutandis – also hold for other types of paradigms, including derivational ones.

Most verb paradigms in Italian do not show vowel quality alternations:

(30) Paradigms without alternations

PRES IND/3SG	INFINITIVE	Gloss
gr[iː]da	gr[i]dàre	‘to shout’
v[iː]ra	v[i]ràre	‘to bend’
c[uː]ra	c[u]ràre	‘to cure’
r[uː]ba	r[u]bàre	‘to steal’
[aː]ma	[a]màre	‘to love’
r[aː]sa	r[a]sàre	‘to shave’

However, in a large number of paradigms, surface contrasts are neutralized. Consider the following sets of forms, some of which do not show vowel alternations (31a), while others do (31b):

(31) Phonological neutralization

a. Non-alternating stems

PRES IND/3SG	INFINITIVE	Gloss
v[eː]de	v[e]dére	'to see'
m[eː]na	m[e]nàre	'to lead'
d[oː]na	d[o]nàre	'to donate'
v[oː]la	v[o]làre	'to fly'

b. Alternating stems

PRES IND/3SG	INFINITIVE	Gloss
ann[ɔː]ta	ann[o]tàre	'to note'
d[ɔ]rme	d[o]rmìre	'to sleep'
c[ɔː]pre	c[o]prìre	'to cover'
p[ɛ]nsa	p[e]nsàre	'to think'
pr[ɛː]da	pr[e]dàre	'to plunder'
r[ɛː]ca	r[e]càre	'to bring'

According to the paradigm acquisition model discussed in the previous section, the learner can discover that Italian has a vowel raising process which neutralizes the contrast between mid-low and mid-high vowels in unstressed syllables. The acquisition proceeds in two steps: (a) base discovery and (b) rule construction:

- Base discovery: by comparing the third person singular (*p*[ɛ]*nsa*) with the infinitive (*p*[e]*nsàre*) and by comparing *p*[ɛ]*nsa* ~ *p*[e]*nsàre* with *v*[eː]*de* ~ *v*[e]*dére*, the learner discovers that the language has a process of vowel raising and not lowering, since otherwise he would find 3SG **v*[ɛː]*de*; quality contrasts are preserved in the singular forms and therefore these forms constitute reliable bases to construct the remaining paradigm members.
- Rule construction: the learner sets up two rules: [ˈɛ, ˈɔ] → [e, o] and [ˈe, ˈo] → [e, o], each having 100% accuracy; from a hypothetical new form *pr*[ɔː]*pa* PRES IND/3SG, he would, with 100% certainty, derive the correct infinitive: *propare*.

This process of vowel raising is robust in modern Italian, whereas another process – stressed open syllable diphthongization – seems to have lost its robustness due to the emergence of other processes (see (26)). Thus, the learner may be confronted with the following forms:

(32) Opacity

PRES IND/3SG	INFINITIVE	Gloss
s[wɔ]na	s[o]nàre	'to ring'
n[wɔ]ta	n[wo]tàre	'to swim'
pr[ɔː]va	pr[o]vàre	'to try'

In a system in which the majority of the verbs have non-alternating nuclei and in which alternations due to vowel raising are robust, the <*s*[wɔ]*na*, *s*[o]*nàre*> type of paradigm is confusing and the only way to produce such alternating forms is, as argued above in our discussion of <mat, matʃi>, to memorize them as irregular inflectional (or derivational) forms. Albright's theory predicts that this double input may be regularized by error, on analogy with other paradigms. It also predicts the direction of the change. Since the third person singular of the indicative is more informative about contrasts in the nucleus of the verb stem than the infinitive, we expect the diphthong to be extended from the present indicative singular to the infinitive, i.e. <*s*[wɔ]*na*, *s*[wo]*nàre*>, on analogy with regular paradigms. And, as we know, this is the correct prediction.[6]

In a sense, then, Albright's theory of analogical change is determined by input regularization. In Optimality Theory this mechanism is referred to as Lexicon Optimization and it is precisely this strategy that we will focus on now. In (33) we repeat the forms listed in (32), this time with their respective input forms.

(33)

PRES IND/3SG	INFINITIVE	Input
s[wɔ]na	s[o]nàre	/sɔn/, /swɔn/
n[wɔ]ta	n[wo]tàre	/nwɔt/
pr[ɔː]va	pr[o]vàre	/prɔv/

It is unlikely that learners who – initially by error – eliminate the monophthong-diphthong alternation, still posit double input allomorphs. It is more plausible that the input forms of the levelled paradigms are reanalysed: if the output forms of a verb as *s(u)onare* are erroneously produced as <*s*[wɔ]*na*, *s*[wo]*nàre*>, the learner will choose /swɔn/ as the underlying form, because that form will do. In fact, the newly posited input is not merely stipulated, but it has the phonological shape of the form that, within the language under analysis, functions as a base within the paradigm, e.g. the third person singular of the present indicative in Italian verb paradigms. This strategy of selecting optimal inputs is called Lexicon Optimization in Prince and Smolensky (1993: 209).

In order to evaluate surface resemblances among morphologically related words, OT analysts have proposed to invoke either output-to-output correspondence constraints (Benua 1997) or uniformity constraints that evaluate the entire inflectional paradigm (Kenstowicz 1996) or a mix of both (McCarthy's 2005 Optimal Paradigm model). In these approaches, surface resemblance is schematized as the promotion of a constraint demanding this. With this background, we shall again take a look at the facts of Italian. The following tableau illustrates the early stage of the grammar, featuring the monophthong-diphthong alternation:

(34) Early grammar: alternation

/sɔn/ /swɔn/ } + a, are	DEP/MAX$_{seg}$	*N$_{\mu\mu}$	m ↔ μ
a. ˈsɔː.na, sɔˈnaː.re		*!	
b. ˈsw$_{\mu}$ɔ$_{\mu}$.na, swo$_{\mu}$.ˈnaː.re		*!	*
c. ☞ ˈsw$_{\mu}$ɔ$_{\mu}$.na, soˈnaː.re			*
d. ˈsɔː.na, swo$_{\mu}$.ˈnaː.re			**!

The next stage is one in which paradigm uniformity comes in when the effects of the mobile diphthong rule became less perceptible for language learners because of other changes in the languages (see (26)). Unlike Kenstowicz and McCarthy, we propose that the paradigm uniformity constraints do not interact directly with constraints such as MAX$_{seg}$ or N$_{mm}$. Following Van de Weijer (1999) we claim that constraints which inspect entire paradigms cannot be ranked alongside constraints which evaluate individual forms. Besides, paradigm uniformity constraints fail to explain analogy, since analogy is a diachronic phenomenon, occurring in the course of language acquisition, and as such it requires a diachronic solution (cf. Reiss 1997). A more appropriate account is Van de Weijers's idea of Paradigm Uniformity as a kind of (violable) meta-constraint that overlooks the whole grammar, in the spirit of the tableaux des tableaux technique suggested by Prince and Smolensky (1993) to formalize Lexicon Optimization.

In the following (meta-)tableau the non-levelled paradigm of the early grammar is compared to the levelled paradigm that occurs most frequently in the modern grammar:

(35) The meta-constraint Paradigm Uniformity

	Paradigm Uniformity
a. /sɔn/, /swɔn/ ˈsɔː.na, sɔˈnaː.re	*!*
b. /sɔn/, /swɔn/ ˈsw$_{\mu}$ɔ$_{\mu}$.na, swo$_{\mu}$.ˈnaː.re	*!*
c. /sɔn/, /swɔn/ ˈsw$_{\mu}$ɔ$_{\mu}$.na, swoˈnaː.re	*
d. /sɔn/, /swɔn/ ˈsɔː.na, so$_{\mu}$.ˈnaː.re	*

Note that all candidate paradigms incur violations of Paradigm Uniformity, because of the alternation between open and closed vowels (see (31b)). After a stage of variation, candidate (35c) won, for reasons that we explained in the first part of the section and which gave us the insight that analogical change, instead of being a merely phonological effect, is rather a morphological effect that results from the way that paradigms are learned.

If, in a subsequent language stage, language learners are constantly exposed to a candidate of the type (35c), there is no need to assume double inputs, hence the input form is restructured and Lexicon Optimization takes place, as shown in tableau (36).

(36) Modern grammar: no alternation and single input

/swɔn/ + a, are	Dep/Max$_{seg}$	*N$_{\mu\mu}$	m ↔ μ
a. ˈsɔː.na, soˈnaː.re	*!*	*	
b. ☞ ˈsw$_{\mu}$ɔ$_{\mu}$.na, swo$_{\mu}$.ˈnaː.re	*	*	
c. ˈsw$_{\mu}$ɔ$_{\mu}$.na, soˈna′.re	*!		*
d. ˈsɔː.na, swo$_{\mu}$.ˈnaː.re	*!		**

From written and spoken sources we know that both [e], [o] and [je], [wo] variants persisted for a very long time. In fact, variation – albeit little – is still found at present. It is also known that grammars and dictionaries included the *regola del dittongo mobile*, from the sixteenth century onwards until today. In the twentieth century the rule was still defended by a number of linguistic purists (Gabrielli 1956, 1976; Cappuccini and Migliorini 1962; Migliorini *et al.* 1969). This fact may certainly have slowed down the levelling process, especially in a community which only in the last century was unified linguistically.[7]

To conclude this section, we claim that analogical change shows that allomorphy must be listed lexically. As Wetzels (1981) puts it, analogical change is the effect of the competition between stored form and rule-based form; the rule-based form wins if the activation level of the stored form is low enough to be overruled by the rule-based form.

2.4 Storage versus computation

So far, we have argued that the allomorphs have to be listed lexically. This raises the question whether we should assume that the allomorphs are stored as such, or rather as parts of inflected or derived words? We think that the second answer is the correct one: allomorphs are memorized as parts of the words in which they appear, as was presupposed by the analysis of analogical change in section 2.3.

This assumption is in line with the general psycholinguistic and historical evidence that many inflected and derived words are stored in the lexicon. This is obviously the case for words with some unpredictable property, but this even applies to inflected and derived words that are completely regular, provided that they have a certain frequency of use. These frequency effects are found in lexical decision tasks (cf. Booij 1999 and the references cited there), and frequency effects presuppose lexical storage.

Historical phonological evidence for this assumption is that the outputs of a phonological rule may survive even though the relevant phonological rule got lost. Middle Dutch, for instance, had a rule of vowel lengthening in stressed open syllables. This rule is no longer active. Yet, we still find a number of plural forms with long vowels, whereas the singular form has a short vowel. That is, modern Dutch features pairs of nouns such as *pad* [pɑt] – *pad-en* [pa:dən] 'path' – 'paths'. Hence, the plural form *paden* must have been stored in order to survive after the loss of the rule of vowel lengthening (Booij 2002).

This assumption also explains why in particular derived words are often immune to analogical change, since derived words tend to be stored at a more extensive scale than inflected forms of words. For example, the word *pedone* 'pedestrian' will be listed besides the word *piede* 'foot'. Therefore, its phonetic form does not have to be computed, and the allomorph *pied-* will therefore not get the chance to be combined with *-one*.

In languages with rich inflectional paradigms such as Italian at least a subset of the inflectional forms will still be computed rather than stored, and hence analogical change can take place. Crucially, analogical change will only take place if computation is involved.

There are two ways of computing a new form. The first option is along the lines of the analysis of section 2.2. This applies in case the language user has both allomorphs as his disposition. If a word has to be used that is not available through direct lexical retrieval (or has a very low degree of activation which makes retrieval slow), the word will be computed. Both root allomorphs as listed in paradigmatically related words or word forms will occur in the candidate set. In this way the alternation will be maintained. The second option is that the language user takes only one root allomorph into account for the computation of the correct word (form), the allomorph that is lexically dominant (cf. section 2.3). This will lead to analogical change, with only one allomorph of the root being used in new word(form)s.

In conclusion, proper assumptions about the balance between storage and computation, in combination with a model of phonological computation in which allomorphs are listed and a set of ranked output conditions serves to select the optimal allomorph enabled us to give an insightful account of the Italian mobile diphthongs, both from a synchronic and a diachronic perspective.

Notes

* The names of the authors appear in alphabetical order. We are grateful to Bernard Tranel and the editors of this volume for their comments on earlier versions of this contribution that led to significant improvements, in particular as to the analysis of the distribution of the different types of syllabic nuclei in Italian, and the proper selection of the allomorphs. We also thank our colleague Marc van Oostendorp very much for his advice.

1 Cf. Vogel (1993:226), who also claims that 'a (morpho)phonological rule can be used to diphthongize the appropriate vowels', deriving the correct outputs from one single stem, although she admits that 'it is not predictable which verbs with *-e-* and *-o-* in their roots exhibit diphthongization'.

2 In OT literature the relationship between stress and bimoraicity is commonly captured by two different constraints: STRESS-TO-WEIGHT and WEIGHT-TO-STRESS. In some analyses, however, the distinction between these constraints becomes unclear. Following Van der Veer (2006), we argue that confusions of this type may raise the question whether these two separate constraints might not be better understood as the consequences of one single constraint which covers both directions in the stress/weight relationship.

3 In these tableaux constraint violations are only indicated if the relevant (i.e. first) syllable of each output candidate does not meet the requirements posited by a particular constraint.

4 As things stand in tableau (15), the not shown [ˈsj$_{\mu}$ε$_{\mu}$.de.te] candidate would win over the grammatical candidate [se.ˈde$_{\mu\mu}$.te]. However, high-ranked metrical constraints responsible for Italian stress (see D'Imperio and Rosenthall 1999) prevents stress from landing on the antepenultimate syllable here.

5 For a more detailed description of palatalization (or velar softening), the reader is referred to Halle (2005).

6 There is a very small number of exceptions. Alternations persist in the paradigms of highly irregular verbs such as *dolere* 'to hurt', *morire* 'to die', *tenere* 'to hold' and *venire* 'to come' and in a number of (etymological) derivations which are stored as indivisible items in the lexicon, such as *coraggio* 'courage' (cf. *cuore* 'heart') and *pedone* 'pedestrian' (cf. *piede* 'foot'). In three verb paradigms (*negare*, 'to deny', *levare* 'to raise' and *coprire* 'to cover') levelling has occurred in the opposite direction, i.e. the monophthong is found throughout the paradigm. The diphthongized forms of these verbs, e.g. *n*[jɛ]*go* and *c*[wɔ]*pro*, are archaic (cf. Sabatini and Coletti 1997) and we must assume that their paradigms were already levelled by the time the monophthong-diphthong alternation was levelled through extension of the diphthongs.

7 To get an idea of the linguistic diversity in Italy halfway through the twentieth century, we quote some numbers from De Mauro (1976): in 1951, 18.5% of the Italians used only the standard language, 13% only a dialect, 87% were capable of using standard Italian and 63.5% used a dialect in most situations.

References

Albright, Adam (2002) Islands of reliability for regular morphology: Evidence from Italian. *Language* 78: 684–709.

Albright, Adam (2004) Sub-optimal paradigms in Yiddish. In Vineeta Chand, Ann Kelleher, Angelo J. Rodríguez and Benjamin Schmeiser (eds) *WCCFL 23: Proceedings of the 23rd West Coast Conference on Formal Linguistics* 1–14. Somerville, MA: Cascadilla Press.

Albright, Adam (2005a) The morphological basis of paradigm levelling. In Laura J. Downing, Alan T. Hall and Renate Raffelsiefen (eds) (2005) *Paradigms in Phonological Theory,* 17–43. Oxford: Oxford University Press.

Albright, Adam (2005b) Explaining universal tendencies and language particulars in analogical change. Manuscript, Department of Linguistics, Massachusetts Institute of Technology.

Albright, Adam and Hayes, Bruce (2002) Modeling English past tense intuitions with minimal generalization. In Mike Maxwell (ed.) *Proceedings of the 6th Workshop of the ACL Special Interest Group in Computational Phonology (SIGPHON), Philadelphia, July 2002*, vol. 6 58–69. Stroudsburg, PA: Association for Computational Linguistics.

Benua, Laura (1997) *Transderivational Identity: Phonological Relations between Words*. Doctoral dissertation, University of Massachusetts at Amherst. [Available on http://roa.rutgers.edu/article/view/259.]

Booij, Geert (1998) Phonological output constraints in morphology. In Wolfgang Kehrein and Richard Wiese (eds) *Phonology and Morphology of the Germanic Languages,* 143–162. Tübingen: Max Niemeyer Verlag.

Booij, Geert (1999) Lexical storage and regular processes. *Behavourial and Brain Sciences* 22 (6): 1016.

Booij, Geert (2002) The balance between storage and computation in phonology. In Sieb Nooteboom, Frank Wijnen and Fred Weerman (eds) *Storage and Computation in the Language Faculty,* 133–156. Dordrecht: Kluwer.

Cappuccini, Giulio and Migliorini, Bruno (1962) *Vocabolario della lingua italiana.* Torino: Paravia.

Carstairs, Andrew (1988) Some implications of phonologically conditioned suppletion. In Geert Booij and Jaap van Marle (eds) *Yearbook of Morphology 1988,* 67–94. Dordrecht: Foris Publications.

Castellani, Arrigo (1967 [1980]) Italiano e fiorentino argenteo. In Arrigo Castellani (ed.) *Saggi di linguistica e filologia italiana e romanza (1946–1976)*, vol. 1, 17–35. Rome: Salerno. [Originally published in *Studi Linguistici Italiani* 7 (1967): 3–19.]

Castellani, Arrigo (1976 [1980]). Sulla formazione del tipo fonetico italiano. In Arrigo Castellani (ed.) *Saggi di linguistica e filologia italiana e romanza (1946–1976)*, vol. 1, 73–122. Rome: Salerno.

Celata, Chiara and Bertinetto, Pier Marco (2005) Lexical access in Italian: Words with and without palatalization. *Lingue e Linguaggio* 2: 293–318.

De Mauro, Tullio (1976) *Storia linguistica dell'Italia unita*. Bari: Laterza.

D'Imperio, Mariapaola and Rosenthall, Sam (1999) Phonetics and phonology of main stress in Italian. *Phonology* 16: 1–28.

Downing, Laura J., Hall, T. Alan and Raffelsiefen, Renate (eds) (2005) *Paradigms in Phonological Theory*. Oxford: Oxford University Press.

Gabrielli, Aldo (1956) *Dizionario linguistico moderno*. Milan: Mondadori.

Gabrielli, Aldo (1976) *Si dice o non si dice? Guida pratica allo scrivere e al parlare*. Milano: Mondadori.

Halle, Morris (2005) Palatalization/velar softening: What it is and what it tells us about the nature of language. *Linguistic Inquiry* 36 (1): 23–41.

Kenstowicz, Michael (1996) Base-identity and uniform exponence: alternatives to cyclicity. In Jacques Durand and Bernard Laks (eds) *Current Trends in Phonology: Models and Methods,* 36–395. Paris: CNRS and University of Salford Publications.

Kiparsky, Paul (1982) *Explanation in Phonology*. Dordrecht: Foris.

Łubowicz, Anna (2002) Derived environment effects in Optimality Theory. *Lingua* 112 (4): 243–280.

McCarthy, John J. (2002) *A Thematic Guide to Optimality Theory*. Cambridge: Cambridge University Press.

McCarthy, John J. (2005) Optimal paradigms. In Laura J. Downing, Alan T. Hall and Renate Raffelsiefen (eds) (2005) *Paradigms in Phonological Theory,* 170–210. Oxford: Oxford University Press.

McCarthy, John J. and Prince, Alan S. (1994).The emergence of the unmarked: Optimality in prosodic morphology. In Mercè Gonzàlez (ed.) *Proceedings of the North East Linguistics Society 24,* 333–379. Amherst, MA: Graduate Linguistic Student Association. [Available on http://roa.rutgers.edu/article/view/13.]

Migliorini, Bruno (1963) *Storia della lingua italiana.* Florence: Sansoni.

Migliorini, Bruno, Tagliavini, Carlo and Fiorelli, Piero (1969) *Dizionario della lingua italiana.* Firenze: Le Monnier.

Prince, Alan and Smolensky, Paul (1993 [2004]) *Optimality Theory: Constraint Interaction in Generative Grammar.* Technical Report, Rutgers University Center for Cognitive Science and Computer Science Department, University of Colorado at Boulder. Malden, MA and Oxford: Blackwell.

Reiss, Charles (1997) Explaining analogy. Manuscript, Concordia University Montreal. [Available on http://roa.rutgers.edu/article/view/199.]

Rubach, Jerzy and Booij, Geert (2001) Allomorphy in Optimality Theory: Polish iotation. *Language* 77 (1): 26–60.

Sabatini, Francesco and Coletti, Vittorio (1997) *Dizionario Italiano.* Florence: Giunto Gruppo Editoriale.

Saltarelli, Mario (1970) *A Phonology of Italian in a Generative Grammar.* The Hague: Mouton.

Sánchez Miret, Fernando (1998) *La diptongación en las lenguas románicas.* Munich: Lincom Europa.

Scalise, Sergio (1984) *Generative Morphology.* Dordrecht: Foris.

Sluyters, Willibrord (1992) *Representing diphthongs.* Doctoral dissertation, University of Nijmegen.

Tekavčić, Pavao (1972) *Grammatica storica dell'italiano 3: Morfosintassi.* Bologna: Il Mulino.

Van der Veer, Bart (2001) Eppur si muove: un'analisi critica dell'uso del dittongo mobile nel Novecento. *Studi di Grammatica Italiana* 20: 139–253.

Van der Veer, Bart (2006) *The Italian 'Mobile Diphthongs'. A Test Case for Experimental Phonetics and Phonological Theory.* [Doctoral dissertation, University of Leiden] Utrecht: LOT.

Van de Weijer, Jeroen M. (1999). Analogical Change in Optimality Theory. *On'in Kenkyu* [Phonological Studies] 2: 145–152.

Vogel, Irene (1993) Verbs in Italian morphology. In Geert Booij and Jaap van Marle (eds) *Yearbook of Morphology 1993,* 219–254. Dordrecht: Kluwer.

Wetzels, Leo (1981) *Analogie et lexique: le problème de l'opacité en phonologie générative.* Doctoral dissertation, University of Nijmegen.

3 L'allomorphie radicale dans les lexèmes adjectivaux en français

Le cas des adverbes en *-ment*

Gilles Boyé (ERSS: CNRS, UMR 5610 / Université Bordeaux 3)
Marc Plénat (Cercle Linguistique de Valence d'Albigeois)

3.1 Introduction

Les Formes de Liaison du Masculin Singulier (FLMS) de l'adjectif en français font figure de pont-aux-ânes dans les études sur l'allomorphie en Théorie de l'Optimalité (cf. en particulier Tranel 1996, 1998, 2000; Perlmutter 1998; Steriade 1999; Burzio 2005).[1] Mais, abstraction faite de cette question classique, très peu de travaux ont porté sur les variations des lexèmes adjectivaux dans cette langue. Ces variations, nombreuses et diverses,[2] restent en fait mal connues et peu étudiées. Faute de temps et de place pour aborder la question dans son ensemble, nous nous intéresserons ici aux seules allomorphies des radicaux des adverbes en *-ment*.[3]

Les grammaires enseignent que le radical de ces adverbes est le plus souvent identique au féminin de leur base adjectivale (cf. RIGOUREUX, fém. *rigoureuse* [rigurøz] → *rigoureusement* [rigurøz-mɑ̃]), mais que les adjectifs en [-ɑ̃]/[-ɑ̃t] donnent en règle générale des adverbes en [-amɑ̃] (ÉLÉGANT, fém. *élégante* [elegɑ̃t] → *élégamment* [elega-mɑ̃] et non *élégantement* [elegɑ̃t-mɑ̃]), qu'un petit nombre d'adjectifs donnent des adverbes en [-emɑ̃] (PROFOND, fém. *profonde* [prɔfɔ̃d] → *profondément* [prɔfɔ̃de-mɑ̃] et non *profondement* [prɔfɔ̃d-mɑ̃]), et qu'une poignée d'exceptions ont un radical tout à fait imprévisible (BREF, fém. *brève* [brɛv] → *brièvement* [brijɛv-mɑ̃] et non *brèvement* [brɛv-mɑ̃]). Comme c'est régulièrement le cas, une recherche systématique des formes sur la Toile permet de nuancer cette description traditionnelle et de dégager un certain nombre de généralisations inédites.[4] Nous observons en particulier que la finale [-amɑ̃] est

Affiliation: (Boyé) Université Bordeaux-Montaigne, France.

peu compatible avec une consonne labiale et/ou nasale dans l'attaque qui la précède. En présence d'une telle consonne, le radical de l'adverbe est souvent identique au féminin. De ce point de vue, VÉHÉMENT, qui fait *véhémentement* ([veemɑ̃t-mɑ̃]), et non **véhémemment* ([veema-mɑ̃]) est très loin d'être aussi isolé que ne le suggèrent les dictionnaires. On verra aussi que le nombre des formes en [-emɑ̃] s'accroît et que cette finale a tendance à s'adjoindre analogiquement à des adjectifs qui présentent des ressemblances avec ceux qui prennent déjà des finales en [-emɑ̃]. Par exemple FÉCOND ou IMMONDE donnent souvent *fécondément* ([fekɔ̃de-mɑ̃]) et *immondément* ([imɔ̃de-mɑ̃]), sur le modèle de *profondément*. Enfin, on verra qu'il existe une classe productive d'adverbes en [-mɑ̃] bâtis sur des bases nominales et que ces adverbes dénominaux ne se conforment pas aux régularités qui valent pour les déadjectivaux. Il se trouve en particulier que les substantifs en [-ɑ̃]/[-ɑ̃t] donnent des formes adverbiales en [-ɑ̃tmɑ̃] et non en [-amɑ̃]: alors, par exemple, que l'adjectif *collant* donne *collamment* ([kɔla-mɑ̃]), le substantif *collants* fait *collantement* ([kɔlɑ̃t-mɑ̃]). Cette description fait l'objet de la section 3.2.

La section 3.3 propose un traitement qui tient compte des généralisations décrites dans cette dernière. À notre sens, ni les radicaux en [-a], ni les radicaux en [-e] ne doivent en synchronie leur existence à l'influence de contraintes anti-marque. Comme les FLMS (Bonami et Boyé 2003, 2005), ces radicaux sont des manifestations d'un thème particulier de 'l'espace thématique' de l'adjectif (lequel est distinct de l'espace thématique du substantif). En règle générale, le choix de tel ou tel thème obéit à une préoccupation de conformité à des schèmes présents dans le lexique plutôt qu'à un conditionnement phonologique. En revanche, il saute aux yeux que le choix d'un thème d'apparence 'féminine' dans les cas du type *véhémentement* relève bien quant à lui d'un processus d'optimisation phonologique. On montre ainsi que les contraintes anti-marque interviennent dans la sélection des radicaux et que contraintes morphophonologiques et contraintes purement phonologiques sont entremêlées au sein d'une même hiérarchie.

3.2 Les adverbes en *-ment* du français

La tradition grammaticale distingue un cas général et trois cas particuliers.

Dans le cas général,

> Les adverbes en *ment* sont formés de l'adjectif féminin et du suffixe *ment* qui représente le latin **mente** (esprit et, par extension, manière): **bona mente**, *bonnement*, proprement 'd'un bon esprit, d'une bonne manière'. (Darmesteter 1920: 285)[5]

Les exemples de ce type abondent, point n'est besoin d'en citer beaucoup:

Tableau 3.1: Adverbes construits sur un thème de féminin

Lexème	Masculin	Féminin	Adverbe
LAID	lɛ	lɛd	lɛdmɑ̃
BEAU	bo	bɛl	bɛlmɑ̃
AVIDE	avid	avid	avidmɑ̃
JOLI	ʒɔli	ʒɔli	ʒɔlimɑ̃

Le fait que *-ment* s'adjoigne à un thème de féminin s'explique historiquement par l'origine périphrastique de l'adverbe et par l'accord en genre qui en découlait: *mens* était féminin. Dans la langue moderne, le choix de ce thème n'est assurément pas une question de syntaxe.

Premier cas particulier. Il existait en ancien français des adjectifs épicènes sans *e* sourd final (e.g. *fort*). Les adverbes en *-ment* correspondants étaient en conséquence bâtis sur la forme sans *e* commune aux deux genres (e.g. *fortment*). Ensuite, cette classe d'épicènes s'aligna peu à peu sur celle qui marquait le féminin par un *e* sourd, et les adverbes correspondants furent construits sur le nouveau féminin (e.g. *fortement*). Abstraction faite d'exceptions rarissimes comme *gentiment* ou *communément*, il ne subsiste plus dans la langue actuelle d'autre témoignage de l'état ancien que les adverbes bâtis sur les adjectifs en [-ɑ̃]/[-ɑ̃t]. Ces adjectifs donnent en effet des dérivés en [-amɑ̃], qui sont les héritiers directs des adverbes bâtis sur la forme unique en *-ant* ou *-ent* de l'ancienne langue. Les dictionnaires fournissent des dizaines d'exemples comme:

Tableau 3.2: Adverbes construits sur un thème en [-a]

Lexème	Masculin	Féminin	Adverbe
PESANT	pœzɑ̃	pœzɑ̃t	pœzamɑ̃
PRUDENT	prydɑ̃	prydɑ̃t	prydamɑ̃

Ces adverbes ont eu une histoire agitée. Malgré leur nombre, qui sans doute les protégeait, ils étaient soumis à l'attraction du cas général et l'on trouve dans les textes, notamment au XVe et au XVIe siècles, nombre d'adverbes en *-antement* et *-entement*. Les modernes *présentement* et *véhémentement* sont parfois présentés comme des restes de cette tentative de régularisation avortée. À l'inverse, du fait probablement de leur nombre, les adverbes formés sur d'anciens épicènes en *-ant* ou *-ent* ont servi de modèle pour des adverbes dérivés d'adjectifs en [-ɑ̃]/[-ɑ̃t] qui n'étaient pas épicènes à l'origine, comme *dolent* ou *violent*, qui ont donné *dolemment* et *violemment*.

Dans cette classe, seuls *lentement* et le très marginal *gentement* ont véritablement résisté à cette attraction.[6]

Second cas particulier. Les grammaires signalent à l'ordinaire qu'un petit nombre d'adverbes en *-ment* sont formés non pas sur le féminin ou le masculin de l'adjectif, mais sur un thème qui n'apparaît jamais comme forme libre. La liste de ces formes exceptionnelles est courte. Il s'agit la plupart du temps de dérivés anciens dont la base a évolué ou disparu. Exemple:

Tableau 3.3: Exemple d'adverbe construit sur un thème lié

Lexème	Masculin	Féminin	Adverbe
BREF	brɛf	brɛv	brijɛvmɑ̃

On trouve aussi dans la liste *grièvement, journellement, nuitamment, prodigalement, sciemment, traîtreusement.* Parmi les curiosités figure aussi *impunément*, un adverbe qui correspond à IMPUNI. C'est le seul cas relevé par les grammairiens où [e] se substitue non pas à un chva, mais à un [i].

Troisième cas particulier. Dans un petit nombre d'adverbes, en effet, le féminin de l'adjectif est augmenté d'un [e] 'sans règle prévisible', selon Bally (1965: 246). Exemple:

Tableau 3.4: Exemple d'adverbe construit sur un thème en [-e]

Lexème	Masculin	Féminin	Adverbe
OPPORTUN	ɔpɔrtɛ̃	ɔpɔrtyn	ɔpɔrtynemɑ̃

La liste des principales formes telle qu'elle est donnée par Grevisse (1975: 866–867) comprend: *commodément, communément, confusément, diffusément, énormément, expressément, exquisément, immensément, importunément, incommodément, indivisément, intensément, obscurément, opportunément, précisément, profondément, profusément, uniformément.* Cette liste est, dans l'ensemble, stable depuis cent ans et plus dans les grammaires. L'origine de ces adverbes a donné lieu à un assez grand nombre d'observations et de conjectures (cf., e.g., Brunot et Bruneau s.d.: 570; Darmesteter 1920: 286; Damourette et Pichon 1911–1930: 241 sqq.; Bally 1965: 246). Les auteurs s'accordent à penser qu'ils sont issus d'analogies et de confusions. De confusions entre des adverbes tirés d'adjectifs comme *précisement* et des adverbes tirés de participes passés comme *précisément*. D'analogies formelles avec des adverbes français (*immensément* aurait calqué sa finale sur *sensément*) ou même des adverbes latins (par exemple *impunément* aurait subi l'influence du latin *impune*). Et d'analogies fondées sur le sens: selon Bally (*ibid.*), *opiniâtrément* aurait emprunté sa finale à *obstinément.*

Il n'y a pas lieu d'épiloguer sur les formes exceptionnelles, dont le nombre demeure constant ou même régresse. Il n'y a pas lieu non plus de s'étendre sur le cas général: on trouve des dizaines d'adverbes nouveaux construits sur des thèmes de féminin. Signalons seulement en passant que ce mode de formation s'applique notamment dans le cas des adjectifs dont le thème de féminin résulte d'une allomorphie suffixale et non du simple réveil d'une consonne latente ou d'une allomorphie lexicale:

Tableau 3.5: Adverbes construits sur un féminin à allomorphie suffixale

Lexème	Masculin	Féminin	Adverbe
ACCROCHEUR	akrɔʃœr	akrɔʃøz	akrɔʃøzmɑ̃
MORALISATEUR	mɔralizatœr	mɔralizatris	mɔralizatrismɑ̃

Notre exposé portera sur les exceptions qui comportent au moins un certain caractère de systématicité.

3.2.1 Première exception: le type *opportunément*

Le compte-rendu que l'on vient de lire sur les adverbes en [-emɑ̃] est plus schématique que les discussions qu'il résume. Nombre d'auteurs signalent qu'il y a un certain flottement entre les thèmes de féminin et les thèmes en [-e] (cf., e.g., Bally 1965: 246; Grevisse 1975: 866–867; Chevalier, Blanche-Benveniste, Arrivé et Peytard 1964: 416). Nos propres observations confirment l'existence d'une telle variation, mais elles permettent aussi de commencer à en dessiner les contours: les cas où il y a hésitation se laissent pour la plupart regrouper en un petit nombre de types.

Les finales des adjectifs qui, selon les grammaires, donnent des adverbes en [-emɑ̃] ne forment pas une classe naturelle. Néanmoins, comme le remarque Huot (2001: 173–174), la majorité d'entre elles apparaissent à plusieurs reprises dans la liste habituelle, ce qui attire l'attention dans une énumération si courte. Pour évaluer la pertinence de cette remarque, nous avons quant à nous dénombré les occurrences des adverbes en *-ément* (avec un accent aigu marquant le timbre [e]) présents sur Google francophone à la fin du mois de mai 2006 et comparé pour chacun d'eux le nombre obtenu avec le nombre de leurs contreparties en *-ement* (sans accent). Nous ne nous faisons pas d'illusion sur la valeur des pourcentages obtenus, mais les résultats de cette enquête sont assez frappants pour être mentionnés. La proportion des formes en [-emɑ̃] est très variable; elle peut aller de 100% (*éprisément*, *multiformément*) à moins de 1/1.000.000. Nous ne nous intéressons ici qu'à la cinquantaine de formes pour lesquelles le pourcentage est supérieur à 5%. On y trouve, bien entendu, la vingtaine d'adverbes lexicalisés donnés par les grammaires, mais on y trouve aussi des formes construites sur des bases ayant les mêmes finales. Le tableau ci-dessous donne, pour chacune de ces finales, les adverbes que cite Huot (*ibid.*) et les adverbes que nous avons trouvés sur la Toile avec leur pourcentage.[7]

Tableau 3.6: Adverbes en -ément

Finale	Adverbes lexicalisés	Adverbes trouvés sur la Toile
-iz	*exquisément, indivisément, précisément*	*éprisément* (100%), *imprécisément* (93%), *divisément* (79%), *concisément* (64%)
-yz	*confusément, diffusément, profusément*	*obtusément* (92%), *infusément* (80%), *abstrusément* (25%), *inclusément* (22%)
-ɛ(C)s	*expressément*	*perplexément* (9%), *conversément* (9%)
-ɑ̃s	*immensément, intensément, densément*	*extensément* (100%)
-ɔd	*commodément, incommodément*	*malcommodément* (90%)
-ɔ̃d	*profondément*	*rotondément* (100%), *approfondément* (70%), *immondément* (53%), *fécondément* (53%), *nauséabondément* (11%), *furibondément* (8%)
-yn	*communément, importunément, opportunément, impunément*	*inopportunément* (98%)
-yr	*obscurément*	*immaturément* (18%)
-ɔrm	*énormément, uniformément*	*multiformément* (100%), *cruciformément* (100%), *informément* (90%), *difformément* (84%)

Certains des exemples nouveaux sont attendus, dans la mesure où leur base appartient à une famille d'adjectifs qui donne déjà des adverbes en [-emɑ̃] (cf., e.g., *imprécisément* ou *difformément*). Mais pour une majorité de formes l'analogie est purement phonique (cf., e.g., *obtusément*, *abstrusément* et *inclusément*). Certaines finales, qui étaient isolées dans la liste des grammaires, ne le sont plus: par exemple, *profondément* est rejoint par *rotondément*, *immondément*, etc. Le cas le plus notable, bien que très marginal, est celui de *approfondément*, où le [e] se substitue à un [i], comme dans *impunément*. En outre, dans notre collecte, les formes isolées ont pour ainsi dire toutes une finale qui, sans être identique à celles de la liste de Huot, s'en rapproche néanmoins. On y trouve ainsi *étanchément* et *absconsément* dont les finales sont très proches de [-ɑ̃semɑ̃]. Comme déjà, dans la liste des grammaires, certaines finales propices à [-emɑ̃] ne différaient l'une de l'autre que par un trait et se laissaient regrouper en familles (cf. [-iz] et [-yz],

[-ɔd] et [-õd], [-yn) et [-yr]), on se prend à penser que des analogies de forme avec des adverbes déjà présents dans le lexique ont bien joué un rôle prépondérant dans la naissance et l'extension de cette classe d'adverbes.

Les quelques sondages que nous avons pu faire dans les dictionnaires suggèrent que la diffusion des formes en [-emɑ̃] dépend du nombre des attracteurs potentiels et de leur ressemblance avec la forme nouvelle. Apparu vers la fin du XVIIIe siècle dans les dictionnaires, *immensément* est longtemps resté isolé; mais, modèle sans rival, il a attiré dans son orbite *densément* et *intensément* peu après leur création, et ces adverbes attirent à leur tour *extensément*. À l'inverse, *profondément*, qui se substitue à *profondement* dans les dictionnaires au milieu du XVIIIe siècle, n'a pas entraîné la mutation de *rondement* et de *secondement*, qui étaient bien ancrés dans le lexique; on comprend dès lors que les adverbes bâtis sur des adjectifs en [-õ]/[-õd] se conforment tantôt à un modèle (le dérivé de monosyllabe *blondement* se range du côté de son congénère *rondement*), tantôt à l'autre (*rotondément* ou *approfondément* sont attirés par le polysyllabe au vocalisme [ɔ … õ] *profondément*), et que certains hésitent entre les deux solutions (l'hésitation entre *fécondément* et *fécondement* ou *immondément* et *immondement* trouve peut-être une explication dans le fait que leur base dissyllabique ne comporte pas la voyelle [ɔ]).

Ce sommaire aperçu laisse bien des questions sans réponse. Le premier chaînon de la chaîne causale manque souvent: comment se fait-il par exemple qu'*immensement* ait fait place à *immensément* ou *profondement* à *profondément*? Et comment déterminer, dans le conditionnement des attractions, la part qui revient à l'existence d'un type dans le lexique de celle de sa fréquence d'utilisation dans le discours? L'histoire de ces formes reste à faire. Mais il semble assuré que le lexique existant pèse sur le lexique en création.

3.2.2 Deuxième exception: le type *élégamment*

On pourrait produire des dizaines d'exemples à l'appui de l'idée que la règle voulant que les adjectifs en [-ɑ̃]/[-ɑ̃t] donnent des adverbes en [-amɑ̃] est toujours productive.[8] La Toile abonde en néologismes de ce genre comme *accueillamment*, *affligeamment*, *affolamment*, *alléchamment*, *assourdissamment*, etc. Néanmoins, tous les adjectifs en [-ɑ̃]/[-ɑ̃t] ne sont pas également susceptibles de donner des adverbes en [-amɑ̃]. D'une façon générale, ces adjectifs sont assez peu productifs en formes adverbiales (cf. Molinier 1992), peut-être pour des raisons sémantiques. Mais il existe aussi de grandes disparités liées à la nature de la consonne qui précède immédiatement la finale [-ɑ̃]/[-ɑ̃t].

On trouvera ci-après les informations que l'on peut tirer à ce sujet de la banque de données lexicales *BDLEX* (cf. Calmès et Pérennou 1998). Pour chacune des consonnes du français, le tableau indique successivement le nombre d'adjectifs en [-ɑ̃]/[-ɑ̃t] construits sur un radical s'achevant par la consonne considérée, le nombre des adverbes en [-amɑ̃] pour la même consonne, la proportion des adverbes correspondant aux adjectifs, et, enfin, quelques exemples.

Tableau 3.7: Adverbes en -amment *et* -emment *dans BDLEX*

C	-Cɑ̃	-Camɑ̃	%	Exemples
d	37	13	35,14%	*abondamment, impudemment, indépendamment, prudemment*
g	10	3	30,00%	*arrogamment, élégamment, inélégamment*
ʒ	29	7	24,14%	*diligemment, indigemment, négligemment, obligeamment*
k	29	5	17,24%	*conséquemment, éloquemment, fréquemment, subséquemment*
l	75	10	13,33%	*équivalemment, excellemment, nonchalamment, violemment*
j	86	11	12,79%	*bienveillamment, brillamment, bruyamment, vaillamment*
v	16	2	**12,50%**	*savamment, fervemment*
z	46	5	10,87%	*complaisamment, pesamment, plaisamment, suffisamment*
ʃ	11	1	9,09%	*méchamment*
t	92	8	8,70%	*concomitamment, constamment, intermittemment, épatamment*
r	89	7	7,87%	*apparemment, concurremment, couramment, persévéramment*
n	70	4	**5,71%**	*éminemment, étonnamment, impertinemment, pertinemment*
s	146	7	4,79%	*décemment, incessamment, puissamment, récemment*
ɲ	7	0	**0,00%**	
f	6	0	**0,00%**	
p	11	0	**0,00%**	
b	6	0	**0,00%**	
m	19	0	**0,00%**	
Totaux:	785	83	10,57%	

Si la nature de la dernière consonne d'un adjectif en [-ɑ̃]/[-ɑ̃t] était sans influence sur la probabilité qu'existe ou non un adverbe en [-amɑ̃] correspondant, la proportion de ces adverbes serait sensiblement la même pour chaque consonne. Il n'en est rien et les disparités constatées ne doivent pas grand chose au hasard. Deux classes de consonnes sont incompatibles ou peu compatibles avec la finale adverbiale [-amɑ̃]: les labiales (en gris foncé) et les nasales (en gris clair). Il n'existe notamment pas dans la base d'adverbes dans lesquels [-amɑ̃] suive la nasale labiale [m] (en noir). Considérés isolément, les chiffres de chaque consonne sont trop faibles pour être vraiment probants. Mais les 96 adjectifs dans lesquels [-ɑ̃]/[-ɑ̃t] est précédé d'une nasale ne donnent un adverbe en [-amɑ̃] que dans 4,17% des cas, et ceux dans lesquels cette terminaison suit une labiale (58) dans 3,45% des cas seulement. Ces pourcentages sont très inférieurs à la moyenne, qui est de 10,5%.[9] Il apparaît manifestement qu'une contrainte relevant de l'*Obligatory Contour Principle* (OCP) est à l'œuvre et que, dans ce cas comme dans bien d'autres (cf. Plénat 2000, à paraître; Roché *et al.* 2011: chap. 4), le français évite la consécution de deux consonnes identiques ou similaires à faible distance l'une de l'autre.[10] Nous appellerons dans ce qui suit OCP le principe dissimilatif et les contraintes qui en découlent des contraintes dissimilatives, même si leur satisfaction ne passe pas toujours – loin de là – par une dissimilation proprement dite.

3.2.3 Une exception dans l'exception: le type *véhémentement*

Nous avons le sentiment que, lorsqu'une contrainte dissimilative s'oppose à la création d'une forme en [-amɑ̃], la langue recourt au mode de formation général consistant à concaténer [mɑ̃] au thème de féminin de l'adjectif (cf. Hathout *et al.* 2009). Faute de pouvoir dire *charmamment*, *probamment* ou *feignamment*, les locuteurs disent selon nous *charmantement*, *probantement* et *feignantement*, quand du moins ils oublient la règle apprise à l'école et prennent le droit de créer un néologisme qui s'en écarte.[11]

Les données ne laissent guère de doute sur ce point en ce qui concerne les adverbes en *-ment* dérivés d'adjectifs en [-mɑ̃]/[-mɑ̃t]. On trouvera dans le Tableau 3.8 ci-après les formes en [-mɑ̃tmɑ̃] et en [-mamɑ̃] *a priori* susceptibles d'être analysées comme des adverbes en *-ment* présentes sur Yahoo! français le 2 novembre 2006:

Tableau 3.8: Adverbes en [-mãtmã] et en [-mamã] sur Yahoo!

Base	[-mãtmã]	[-mamã]	Base	[-mãtmã]	[-mamã]
aimant	1	0	dément	4	1
alarmant	2	0	dormant	1	0
calmant	0	1	humant	0	1
charmant	26	4	inclément	0	1
clément	1	2	véhément	> 1000	16

Ce n'est pas un hasard que *véhémentement* figure parmi les deux ou trois adverbes lexicalisés issus d'adjectifs en [-ã]/[-ãt] originellement épicènes qui se sont alignés sur le cas général; son rival *véhémemment* est très minoritaire et ses attestations sont souvent suspectes. La même suspicion pèse sur nombre des formes en [-mamã] que nous avons relevées. *Calmamment* et *inclémemment* apparaissent dans un dictionnaire électronique qui applique aveuglément la règle des grammaires. *Clémemment, démemment* et *humamment* font partie de traductions maladroites dont les auteurs ne sont assurément pas des locuteurs français. L'un des quatre exemples de *charmamment* figure dans une discussion métalinguistique. Les deux ou trois exemples de cette forme qui paraissent légitimes font pâle figure à côté du nombre des attestations de *charmantement*, dont certaines sont anciennes et d'excellente qualité.[12] Il ne fait donc aucun doute que, pour une majorité de locuteurs, les adverbes correspondant à *aimant*, *alarmant*, *charmant*, *clément* ou *dément* sont *aimantement*, *alarmantement*, *charmantement*, *clémentement*, et *démentement*.

Les résultats de notre enquête concernant les autres consonnes labiales et les autres consonnes nasales sont moins nets. Il semble qu'il faille faire une différence entre d'une part [n] et [v], pour lesquels il existe dans le lexique des modèles en [-namã] et en [-vamã], et les autres. Pour ce qui est des nasales, le seul adjectif en [-ɲã]/[-ɲãt] qui, dans notre récolte, fournisse des adverbes apparemment légitimes est *répugnant*, qui fait *répugnamment* dans 4 cas et *répugnantement* dans 2 cas. En ce qui concerne les labiales, nous n'avons pas trouvé de tels adverbes formés sur des adjectifs en [-bã]/[-bãt] ou en [-fã]/[-fãt]. Mais, parmi les adjectifs en [-pã]/[-pãt], *frappant* donne tantôt *frappamment* (1 cas) et tantôt *frappantement* (2 cas) et l'on trouve aussi *anticipamment* d'un côté (1 cas) et *rampantement* de l'autre (1 cas aussi). Avec les consonnes [ɲ] et [p], la finale [-ãtmã] fait ainsi pratiquement jeu égal avec la finale [-amã], ce qui, compte tenu du fait que la première est bannie par la règle apprise à l'école, est assez remarquable. Lorsque, en revanche, l'adjectif se termine par [-vã]/[-vãt], les néologismes apparemment légitimes en [-ɑ̃tmɑ̃] (*émouvantement* [1 cas], *suivantement* [2 cas], *vivantement* [2 cas]) sont trois fois moins nombreux que les néologismes en [-amɑ̃] (*décevamment* [4 cas], *émouvamment* [5 cas], *suivamment* [4 cas], *vivamment* [3 cas]). Enfin, quand l'adjectif s'achève en [-nɑ̃]/[-nɑ̃t], les néologismes en [-ɑ̃tmɑ̃] font pâle figure à côté de leurs concurrents en [-amɑ̃]. Ces derniers sont les seuls qui comptent parmi eux des formes attestées à plusieurs dizaines d'exemplaires (*hallucinamment*, *impressionnament*, *lancinamment*, *prédominamment*, *prééminemment*, *suréminemment*, *surprenamment*) et ils sont très sensiblement plus nombreux que les formes en [-ɑ̃tmɑ̃] parmi les adverbes plus faiblement attestés. Il est possible que des adverbes bien ancrés dans le lexique comme *savamment* ou *éminemment* et *étonnamment* jouent dans ces deux cas un rôle d'attracteurs et contrebalancent les tendances dissimilatives. Comme dans le cas des formes en [-emɑ̃], le lexique existant semble peser sur le lexique naissant.

Vu la faible représentation de certains cas de figure et l'absence de points de comparaison bien établis du côté des consonnes non nasales et non labiales, nous renonçons à toute conclusion ferme sur le comportement des labiales et des nasales en général. Mais il est un point au moins qui ne fait aucun doute à nos yeux: la présence d'un [m] impose chez la très grande majorité des locuteurs le choix du thème en [-ɑ̃t] utilisé dans le cas général plutôt que celui du thème en [a] particulier aux adjectifs en [-ɑ̃]/[-ɑ̃t].

3.2.4 Les adverbes dénominaux

Au cours de notre enquête, nous avons trouvé d'assez nombreux exemples d'adverbes en *-ment* construits sur des substantifs. Ces dérivés, qui n'appartiennent pas au 'bon usage', sont peu ou mal décrits dans la littérature. Il ne nous appartient pas d'analyser leur syntaxe ni leur sémantique. Qu'il suffise sur ce point de signaler qu'ils sont particulièrement fréquents dans les formules de politesse en fin de lettre, immédiatement avant la signature, ou dans les expressions du type *X-ment parlant*. Mais leur morphologie est suffisamment différente de celle des adverbes déadjectivaux pour que nous la décrivions rapidement.

Voici un échantillon d'exemples trouvés sur la Toile:

Tableau 3.9: Adverbes en -ment *dénominaux*

Base nominale		Thème B	Adverbe	Exemple
(a)	bambou	bɑ̃buz-	*bambousement*	*Bambousement, Minidou.*
	Chirac	ʃirak-	*chiraquement*	*Chiraquement vôtre.*
	escargot	ɛskargɔt-	*escargotement*	*Mon fils alors s'avance escargotement.*
	kangourou	kɑ̃guru-	*kangouroument*	*Tes sauts sont kangouroument hauts.*
(b)	éléphant	elefɑ̃t-	*éléphantement*	*Tu te trompes, éléphantement.*
	collants	kɔlɑ̃t-	*collantement*	*Je suis pas riche collantement parlant.*
	résident	rezidɑ̃t-	*résidentement*	*Résidentement vôtre.*
(c)	acanthe	akɑ̃t-	*acanthement*	*Acanthement vôtre.*
	bande passante	bɑ̃dpasɑ̃t-	*bande passantement*	*Bande passantement parlant.*
	parapente	parapɑ̃t-	*parapentement*	*Parapentement vôtre.*

Convenons d'appeler thème A du substantif le thème employé au singulier dans les formes libres et thème B le thème utilisé devant les suffixes. On constate (cf. (a) et (b)) que les adverbes sont construits sur ce thème B: *chiraquement* est bâti sur le radical [ʃirak-], qui est à la fois la forme libre et la forme liée de CHIRAC (cf. *Chirac* et *chiraquien*), *bambousement* et *escargotement* sont construits sur les radicaux [bɑ̃buz-] et [ɛskargɔt-], comme *bambouseraie* et *escargotière*, et non sur les formes libres *bambou* ([bɑ̃bu]) et *escargot* ([ɛskargo]). Il faut noter que le thème B n'est pas spécifiquement un thème de féminin. Seuls les noms d'êtres sexués peuvent avoir à la fois un masculin et un féminin (il n'existe pas de *bambouses*). Pour ce qui est des noms du type *cousin* et *cousine*, on peut montrer que si leurs thèmes B sont identiques, ils donnent lieu au même adverbe, ici *cousinement.* En revanche, si les thèmes B des deux noms sont différents comme pour *animateur* et *animatrice*, ils donnent lieu à deux adverbes distincts: *animateurement* et *animatricement*. De la même façon, le substantif CRÉATEUR donne *créateurement,* un *créatricement* dénominal renverrait à une divinité féminine, alors que l'adjectif CRÉATEUR donne bien quant à lui *créatricement.*[13]

Ce qui est surprenant, c'est que cette règle voulant que les adverbes dénominaux en *-ment* prennent pour radical le thème B s'applique aussi lorsque le thème A de la base se termine par [-ɑ̃] et son thème B par [-ɑ̃t] (cf. (b): COLLANTS 'sous-vêtement féminin composé d'une culotte et de bas en une seule pièce', par exemple, fait *collantement* et non *collamment*[14] comme le fait l'adjectif COLLANT).[15] De même, les substantifs qui s'achèvent au thème A et au thème B par [-ɑ̃t] donnent des dérivés en [-ɑ̃tmɑ̃] (cf. (c): ACANTHE fait par exemple *acanthement* et non *acamment*). On voit que sur ce point, le substantif et l'adjectif ont un comportement très différent. On n'a pas d'exemple d'adverbes déadjectivaux bâtis sur des bases dont le thème libre soit en [-ɑ̃t], mais les adjectifs en [-ɑ̃]/[-ɑ̃t] donnent à l'ordinaire, on l'a vu, des adverbes en [-amɑ̃] et non en [-ɑ̃tmɑ̃].

Dernière curiosité, il semble bien que les noms en *-ment* donnent en général des dérivés qui ont la même forme que leur base, du moins quand celle-ci comporte au moins trois syllabes. Bernard Tranel nous fait justement remarquer que Jean-Pierre Chevènement pourrait faire précéder sa signature de *chevènement vôtre*, alors que Jacques Chirac devrait utiliser un suffixe: (cf. *Chiraquement vôtre* dans le Tableau 3.9). Nous avons trouvé quant à nous les exemples *amusement vôtre*, *environnement parlant* et *médicament parlant* (qui, plutôt mauvais quand ils sont considérés isolément, passent néanmoins assez bien dans leur contexte). Cette sorte d'haplologie ne semble possible ni avec les substantifs courts ni avec les adjectifs: le substantif *amant* fait *amantement* et l'adjectif *désarmant* fait *désarmantement*.

3.3 L'allomorphie radicale devant *-ment*

À la suite de Bonami et Boyé (2003, 2005), nous nous appuyons sur une conception dans laquelle les adjectifs sont représentés dans le lexique par plusieurs thèmes allomorphiques. Ces thèmes sont le plus souvent unis les uns aux autres par des relations systématiques dans un espace thématique. Chaque allomorphe remplit une ou plusieurs cases du paradigme flexionnel et dérivationnel de l'adjectif suivant un certain nombre de principes.[16] Dans ce qui suit, nous présentons ces notions en décrivant rapidement la flexion de l'adjectif au singulier, puis nous étendons leur utilisation au cas des adverbes en *-ment*. Nous montrons que, si, dans le cas général, les relations entre thèmes et les règles de sélection paraissent bien être morphologisées, il n'en va pas de même du processus de sélection qui aboutit à des formes en [-mɑ̃tmɑ̃] plutôt qu'en [-mamɑ̃] comme *charmantement*.

3.3.1 Le singulier de l'adjectif

3.3.1.1 Les relations entre le masculin et le féminin

Le français standard contemporain ne possède plus de marque de genre. Le masculin et le féminin peuvent être distincts l'un de l'autre, mais ce n'est pas toujours le cas, et, l'une des deux formes étant donnée, il n'est pas toujours possible de déduire l'autre avec certitude.

Tableau 3.10: le féminin des adjectifs

Lexème	Masc.	Fém.	Lexème	Masc.	Fém.
JOLI	ʒɔli	ʒɔli	SEC	sɛk	sɛʃ
PETIT	pəti	pətit	VIF	vif	viv
PRESBYTE	prɛsbit	prɛsbit	COURT	kur	kurt
VRAI	vrɛ	vrɛ	BLAFARD	blafar	blafard
LAID	lɛ	lɛd	NOUVEAU	nuvo	nuvɛl
SUSPECT	syspɛ	syspɛkt	VIEUX	vjø	vjɛj

Si le féminin se termine par une voyelle, le masculin est identique (cas de JOLI, VRAI),[17] mais l'inverse n'est pas vrai: le féminin correspondant à un masculin en voyelle peut prendre une consonne supplémentaire (cf. PETIT, LAID) ou même deux (cf. SUSPECT). Si le masculin se termine par une consonne, il y a de bonnes chances que le féminin soit identique (cas de PRESBYTE), mais il arrive aussi que la consonne du masculin soit différente de celle du féminin (cf. SEC, VIF) ou encore que le féminin comporte une consonne de plus que le masculin (cf. COURT, BLAFARD). Enfin le féminin peut se distinguer du masculin non seulement par une consonne supplémentaire, mais aussi par le timbre de sa dernière voyelle (cf. NOUVEAU, VIEUX).

La phonologie générative classique (cf., e.g., Schane 1968; Dell 1973) a proposé des solutions abstraites qui permettaient de dériver le plus souvent le masculin et le féminin d'une représentation sous-jacente unique. Dans ce cadre, les consonnes finales prononcées, notamment celles du féminin, étaient protégées de l'effacement par un chva destiné lui-même à disparaître dans la plupart des cas. Des solutions de ce genre sont transposables dans des cadres plus modernes (cf. Encrevé 1988: 222 sqq.). Mais le choix de ce type de solution repose sur des considérations d'élégance et d'économie, c'est-à-dire, en fin de compte, de goût. Pour savoir qu'à [pəti] correspond [pətit] et non [pəti] (cf. [ʒɔli]/[ʒɔli]) ou qu'à [pətit] correspond [pəti] et non [pətit] (cf. [prɛsbit]/[prɛsbit]), il faut avoir été exposé aux deux formes. Pourquoi supposer que le locuteur déduit de ces deux formes une représentation sous-jacente unique d'où il dérive ensuite l'une et l'autre plutôt que faire l'hypothèse qu'il les stocke dans son lexique?

Les différences que l'on observe entre le masculin et le féminin résultent pour la plupart de changements phonétiques motivés par des contraintes anti-marques. Mais ces contraintes ne semblent plus jouer aucun rôle. Prenez par exemple le cas de l'alternance [v]/[f] que l'on a dans VIF ([vif]~[viv]) ou dans BREF ([brɛf]~[brɛv]). Cette alternance est née du dévoisement d'un [v] qui se trouvait en position finale de mot au masculin (cf. Pope 1973: 98), conformément à une tendance universelle. Rien n'indique en synchronie, où les deux phonèmes se trouvent en position finale, qu'il en soit ainsi. Mieux même, certain locuteurs ayant à employer l'adjectif ROSBIF 'anglais' au féminin inventent [rɔzbiv]. Comme l'adjectif ROSBIF est issu d'une conversion du substantif ROSBIF ([rɔzbif]), le [v] de [rɔzbiv] trouve son origine dans le [f] et non l'inverse. On sait aussi que l'alternance C/Ø résulte de l'amuissement au masculin de consonnes finales de mot devant consonne (Pope 1973: 219 sqq.). Mais on constate en synchronie que des masculins en [-ar] de toutes provenances donnent à l'occasion des féminins en [-ard]: on rencontre par exemple [anard], [avard], [bizard] ou [vivipard] comme féminins de ANAR, AVARE, BIZARRE ET VIVIPARE, alors que ces adjectifs sont épicènes dans les dictionnaires. Il n'y a pas de [d] 'latent' dans ANAR, qui est une forme tronquée de ANARCHISTE, ni dans les autres cas. Ces formes trouvent leur origine dans une adjonction et non dans un effacement.

Le mécanisme qui régit les relations entre le masculin et le féminin ou le féminin et le masculin paraît bien être de nature analogique: c'est très certainement parce qu'il existe un très grand nombre de féminins en [-iv] et en [-ard] correspondant à des masculins en [-if] et [-ar], que ROSBIF peut donner [rɔzbiv] et BIZARRE: [bizard]. Et c'est parce qu'il existe de nombreux féminins en [-jɛr] correspondant à des masculins en [-je] (cf. *dernier* [dɛrnje] / *dernière* [dɛrnjɛr]) que *pécuniaire* ([pekyniɛr]) fait parfois *pécunier* ([pekynie]) au masculin. Nous ne chercherons pas ici à préciser la nature de ce mécanisme, mais son existence ne fait guère de doute.

Nous ne voyons donc pas quel avantage il y aurait à supposer que le masculin et le féminin ne pourraient pas être présents l'un et l'autre dans le lexique. Certes, tous les locuteurs n'ont pas les mêmes connaissances lexicales, et on vient de voir que l'on peut tirer un féminin d'un masculin ou un masculin d'un féminin. Mais les contraintes qui pèsent sur les formes nouvelles sont des contraintes morphophonologiques de fidélité à des schèmes lexicaux plutôt que des contraintes anti-marques (voir Tranel 1981: 51 sqq.).

3.3.1.2 Espace thématique et paradigme

On peut considérer des paires comme [pəti] et [pətit] ou [nuvo] et [nuvɛl] sous deux angles différents. Ce sont certes les éléments d'un paradigme (le masculin singulier et le féminin singulier de PETIT et de NOUVEAU). Mais on peut voir aussi en elles de pures formes, susceptibles de remplir aussi d'autres cases paradigmatiques. [nuvo], par exemple, sert de radical à NOUVEAUTÉ ([nuvote]) et [nuvɛl] à NOUVELLEMENT ([nuvɛlmɑ̃]). Aucun bon argument ne permet de dire que dans *nouveauté* le radical est masculin, ni qu'il est féminin dans *nouvellement*. Nous proposons donc (avec Bonami et Boyé 2003, 2005) de distinguer les thèmes, qui sont de pures formes (des morphomes au sens d'Aronoff 1994) de leurs instanciations dans les cases des paradigmes flexionnels ou dérivationnels.

Dans la section précédente, nous avons vu que les thèmes sont organisés: chaque adjectif a (au moins) deux thèmes qui peuvent être prédits l'un à partir de l'autre à des degrés divers. L'espace thématique est constitué de ces thèmes et de leurs relations. Les thèmes utilisés au masculin singulier et au féminin singulier seront appelés respectivement 'thème 1' et 'thème 2' et indexés conformément à ces appellations. Ainsi, par exemple, l'espace thématique de l'adjectif PETIT comprend-il les deux thèmes indexés $[\text{pəti}]_1$ et $[\text{pətit}]_2$. Pour remplir les cases masculines et féminines du paradigme flexionnel, les contraintes de sélection se réfèrent à l'index des différents thèmes:

(1) SÉLECTION (T1): Le masculin de l'adjectif sélectionne le thème 1.
(2) SÉLECTION (T2): Le féminin de l'adjectif sélectionne le thème 2.

De cette façon, c'est bien, par exemple, [pətit] qui sera sélectionné comme féminin singulier de PETIT:

Tableau 3.11: Sélection du féminin [pətit]

$\{\text{pəti}_1 \sim \text{pətit}_2\}_{\text{fém.sg}}$	DEP	MAX	SÉLECT (T1)	SÉLECT (T2)
$\text{pəti}_{1\ \text{fém.sg}}$				*!
☞ $\text{pətit}_{2\ \text{fém.sg}}$				

À notre sens, la sélection des thèmes n'obéit pas, en règle générale du moins, à des contraintes de marque, bien qu'il soit souvent tentant de faire intervenir de telles considérations. À titre d'illustration, nous reformulerons rapidement ici l'analyse des Formes de Liaison Masculin Singulier (FLMS) qui a été donnée dans Bonami et Boyé (2005).

Comme on sait, la FLMS peut être identique soit au masculin et au féminin à la fois (cas de JOLI et de SALE), soit au masculin seul (cas de VIF et de COURT), soit au seul féminin (cas de NOUVEAU et de VIEUX). Il arrive aussi qu'elle soit distincte à la fois du masculin et du féminin (cas de GRAND et de GROS), ou encore qu'elle n'existe tout simplement pas (cas de CHAUD et de FRAIS):

Tableau 3.12: Formes masculines, formes féminines et formes de liaison

Lexème	Masc. sing.	FLMS	Fém. sing.
JOLI	joli garçon [ʒɔligarsõ]	joli enfant [ʒɔliɑ̃fɑ̃]	jolie fille [ʒɔlifij]
SALE	sale coup [salku]	sale accident [salaksidɑ̃]	sale guerre [salgɛr]
VIF	vif succès [vifsyksɛ]	vif intérêt [vifɛ̃terɛ]	vive satisfaction [vivsatisfaksjõ]
COURT	court moment [kurmɔmɑ̃]	court instant [kurɛ̃stɑ̃]	courte durée [kurtədyre]
NOUVEAU	nouveau procédé [nuvoprɔsede]	nouvel outil [nuvɛluti]	nouvelle technique [nuvɛltɛknik]
VIEUX	vieux cousin [vjøkuzɛ̃]	vieil oncle [vjɛjõkl]	vieille tante [vjɛjtɑ̃t]
GRAND	grand copain [grɑ̃kɔpɛ̃]	grand ami [grɑ̃tami]	grande copine [grɑ̃dkɔpin]
GROS	gros salaire [grosalɛr]	gros héritage [grozeritaʒ]	grosse fortune [grosfɔrtyn]
CHAUD	chaud printemps [ʃoprɛ̃tɑ̃]		chaude saison [ʃodsɛzõ]
FRAIS	frais vallon [frɛvalõ]		fraîche vallée [frɛʃvale]

Notre proposition consiste d'abord à considérer la FLMS comme l'une des cases du paradigme flexionnel de l'adjectif, au même titre que le masculin singulier ordinaire ou le féminin singulier. Cette idée permet de rendre compte du fait que certaines FMLS comme [grɑ̃t] ou [groz] sont distinctes à la fois du masculin et du féminin et que certaines autres n'existent pas. Il est courant qu'un paradigme possède des formes qui ne sont pas déductibles des autres (cf., e.g., *je suis* en français, *I am* en anglais) ou que certaines cases ne soient pas remplies (cf. le pluriel du présent de FRIRE ou, parmi les adjectifs, le féminin de PREUX).

Dans le reste des cas, la bonne généralisation est que la FLMS est identique au masculin singulier si celui-ci se termine par une consonne et, sinon, au féminin. Pour rendre compte de cette généralisation, il suffit d'ajouter à la contrainte Sélection (T1), une contrainte voulant que la FLMS se termine par une consonne:

(3) $C]_{FLMS}$: Une FLMS se termine par une consonne.

Si cette contrainte domine SELECTION (T1) – contrainte à laquelle sont soumises les FLMS en tant que formes masculines –, elle donnera les résultats attendus (à condition, bien entendu, que le rang des contraintes de fidélité impose de choisir entre le thème 1 et le thème 2 à l'exclusion de tout remodelage de l'un ou de l'autre).[18] À titre d'exemple, voici les tableaux correspondant aux FLMS de JOLI, COURT et NOUVEAU:

Tableau 3.13: Formation régulière de la FLMS

		DEP	MAX	$C]_{FLMS}$	SÉLECT (T1)
JOLI:	$\{ʒɔli_1 \sim ʒɔli_2\}_{FLMS}$	DEP	MAX	$C]_{FLMS}$	SÉLECT (T1)
	$ʒɔlit_{1-FLMS}$	*!			
	$ʒɔl_{1-FLMS}$		*!		
	$ʒɔli_{2-FLMS}$			*	*!
	☞ $ʒɔli_{1-FLMS}$			*	
COURT:	$\{kur_1 \sim kurt_2\}_{FLMS}$	DEP	MAX	$C]_{FLMS}$	SÉLECT (T1)
	$kurt_{2-FLMS}$				*!
	☞ kur_{1-FLMS}				
NOUVEAU:	$\{nuvo_1 \sim nuvɛl_2\}_{FLMS}$	DEP	MAX	$C]_{FLMS}$	SÉLECT (T1)
	☞ $nuvɛl_{2-FLMS}$				*
	$nuvo_{1-FLMS}$			*!	

Comme ni le thème 1 ni le thème 2 de JOLI ne comportent de consonne finale, la FLMS n'en comporte pas non plus; c'est le thème 1 qui est retenu, parce que la forme est masculine – mais ce choix est sans conséquence. Les deux thèmes de COURT se terminant par une consonne, le thème 1 [kur] est choisi pour la même raison que le thème 1 [ʒɔli]. En revanche, le thème 1 [nuvo] de NOUVEAU, qui se termine par une voyelle, est concurrencé victorieusement par le thème 2 [nuvɛl] en dépit du fait qu'une forme masculine recourt normalement au thème 1.

Dans cette proposition, la contrainte qui impose la présence d'une consonne de liaison n'a rien d'une contrainte anti-marque universelle. C'est une contrainte qui porte exclusivement sur une catégorie de formes et n'est en rien destinée à conforter l'euphonie. De ce point de vue, cette proposition paraît bien moins attrayante que la solution voulant que, dans un cas comme *nouvel outil*, le féminin de l'adjectif soit retenu au mépris de l'accord en genre pour que ne soit pas transgressée la contrainte ONSET ou la contrainte NOHIATUS (cf. Perlmutter 1998; Tranel 1996). Quand on y regarde de plus près, cependant, on constate que cette approche morphologique de la forme des FLMS s'accorde avec une description cohérente de leur emploi, lequel se laisse résumer en une phrase: la FLMS est simplement la forme que prend l'adjectif antéposé à un nom recteur appartenant à une classe de noms déclencheurs de liaison.[19]

Le tableau ci-après illustre les notions dont nous nous servons:

Tableau 3.14: Espace thématique et paradigme des adjectifs

Lexème		Thème 1	↔	Thème 2	
	Masculin		FLMS		Féminin
BIZARRE	bizar	bizar	bizar	bizar/bizard	bizar/bizard
PETIT	pəti	pəti	pətit	pətit	pətit
GRAND	grɑ̃	grɑ̃	grɑ̃t	grɑ̃d	grɑ̃d
CHAUD	ʃo	ʃo	Ø	ʃod	ʃod

L'adjectif BIZARRE comporte dans sa représentation deux thèmes: le thème 1 [bizar] et le thème 2, qui est le plus souvent [bizar] aussi, mais qui peut être [bizard] pour certains locuteurs par analogie avec les adjectifs en [-ar]/[-ard]. Le thème 1 est employé au masculin singulier, et, se terminant par une consonne, également à la FLMS. Le thème 2 est utilisé au féminin singulier, mais aussi comme radical de dérivés comme *bizarresque~bizardesque*, *bizarrerie~bizarderie*, et *bizarrement~bizardement.* En ce qui concerne PETIT, l'absence de consonne finale au thème 1 et la présence d'une telle consonne au thème 2 ont pour conséquence que c'est ce dernier qui fournit la FLMS. Les adjectifs suivent généralement l'un ou l'autre patron. Mais, pour certains adjectifs comme GRAND ou CHAUD, la FLMS est une forme supplétive (éventuellement nulle). Elle figure directement dans le lexique comme une forme exceptionnelle au même titre que *je suis* ou *nous sommes* dans la conjugaison du verbe ÊTRE ou les 1ère et 2ème personnes du pluriel au présent de *frire* (cf. Bonami et Boyé 2003).

3.3.2 Les adverbes en *-ment*

Modéliser la morphologie des adverbes en *-ment* suppose que l'on détermine d'abord le statut de leurs radicaux: ceux-ci sont-ils modelés par la phonologie ou sont-ils choisis dans une liste d'allomorphes? À notre sens, c'est la seconde hypothèse qui est la bonne. Si tel est bien le cas, se pose alors une deuxième question? Comment s'opère le choix entre les divers allomorphes? Est-il le fait de la seule morphologie ou se plie-t-il à des contraintes phonologiques? Selon nous, le choix du radical obéit le plus souvent à une contrainte morphologique, mais cette contrainte morphologique est à la merci d'une contrainte phonologique occupant un rang plus élevé dans la hiérarchie des contraintes. C'est ainsi une contrainte dissimilative qui explique que CHARMANT donne *charmantement* plutôt que *charmamment.*

3.3.2.1 Les thèmes en [-a] et en [-e]

Un bon argument en faveur du caractère allomorphique des radicaux en [-a] et des radicaux en [-e] peut être tiré de la comparaison entre les adverbes en *-ment* et les déverbaux en *-ment.* Il existe en français des verbes déadjectivaux qui résultent d'une simple conversion: COURBE donne COURBER, CREUX: CREUSER, INNOCENT: INNOCENTER et PRÉCIS: PRÉCISER. Ces verbes donnent à leur tour des noms déverbaux en *-ment,* qui sont construits sur un thème identique au thème 2 de l'adjectif et prennent donc dans le cas général la même forme que l'adverbe en *-ment:*

Tableau 3.15: Déverbaux en -ment *et adverbes en* -ment *ordinaires*

Adjectif	Verbe	Thème 2	Nom	Adverbe
COURBE	COURBER	kurb-	kurbəmɑ̃	kurbəmɑ̃
CREUX	CREUSER	krøz-	krøzmɑ̃	krøzmɑ̃

Néanmoins, dans le cas des adjectifs qui donnent des adverbes en [-amɑ̃] ou en [-emɑ̃], le substantif déverbal se distingue de l'adverbe déadjectival:

Tableau 3.16: Déverbaux en -ment *et adverbes en* -ment *exceptionnels*

Adjectif	Verbe	Thème 2	Nom	Adverbe
INNOCENT	INNOCENTER	inɔsɑ̃t-	inɔsɑ̃tmɑ̃	inɔsamɑ̃
PRÉCIS	PRÉCISER	presiz-	presizmɑ̃	presizemɑ̃

Les paires minimales de ce genre sont peu nombreuses,[20] mais elles suffisent à montrer que le radical des adverbes en [-amɑ̃] ou en [-emɑ̃] ne saurait résulter du simple modelage d'un input identique à celui qui donne la forme libre de l'adjectif (si cet input est unique) ou, plus spécifiquement, le féminin de celui-ci (si le masculin et le féminin dérivent de deux allomorphes distincts): dans le même contexte phonologique, le même input donne un autre résultat.

En ce qui concerne plus particulièrement les adverbes en [-amɑ̃], un autre argument peut être tiré de la comparaison entre les adverbes déadjectivaux et les adverbes dénominaux. On se rappelle (cf. *supra* §3.2.4) que les noms en [-ɑ̃]/[-ɑ̃t] donnent des adverbes distincts de ceux qui proviennent d'adjectifs. Ainsi le nom *collant* donne-t-il l'adverbe *collantement*, alors que l'adjectif *collant* donne *collamment*. Cette différence est peu compatible avec l'idée que les adverbes en [-amɑ̃] résultent du simple jeu des contraintes anti-marque et des contraintes de fidélité appliquées à un input dans lequel *-ment* suivrait un thème non spécifique.

Dans l'hypothèse où les lexèmes seraient représentés dans le lexique par un thème unique, c'est clairement impossible. Le nom et l'adjectif *collant*, qui sont issus l'un de l'autre par conversion, sont nécessairement représentés par des thèmes identiques et l'adjonction de *-ment* à ces thèmes identiques ne pourrait donner que des formes identiques.

L'hypothèse dans laquelle l'adjectif possède un thème 1 et un thème 2 n'améliore guère la situation. Le nom et l'adjectif se manifestent sous la forme de deux radicaux analogues, l'un en [-ɑ̃], l'autre en [-ɑ̃t] (par exemple, l'adjectif COLLANT [kɔlɑ̃] donne COLLANTISSIME [kɔlɑ̃t-isim], et le nom COLLANT [kɔlɑ̃] donne COLLANTESQUE [kɔlɑ̃t-ɛsk] et COLLANTERIE [kɔlɑ̃t-ri]). La logique voudrait que le substantif possède un thème A et un thème B analogues au thème 1 et au thème 2 de l'adjectif (e.g. thème 1 et thème A: [kɔlɑ̃-], thème 2 et thème B: [kɔlɑ̃t-]). Il faudrait alors que, bizardement, *-ment* sélectionne des thèmes dissemblables (1 et B ou 2 et A) suivant que sa base est nominale ou adjectivale et que l'adjonction du suffixe à l'un des deux thèmes donne une finale en [-amɑ̃]. Comme un nom sans allomorphie comme *acanthe* donne *acanthement* et non **acamment*, il est clair que les thèmes en [-ɑ̃t] ne peuvent pas donner des dérivés en [-amɑ̃]. Reste la possibilité que ces dérivés résultent de l'adjonction de *-ment* à un thème 1 en [-ɑ̃]. Cette solution, qui reprend en synchronie l'explication diachronique, a certes de quoi séduire, mais elle se heurte à des difficultés graves.

Elle suppose que le thème 1 subit une dénasalisation de sa voyelle finale. C'est bien là ce qui s'est passé historiquement: les adverbes en [-amɑ̃] étaient encore prononcés avec une finale en [-ɑ̃mɑ̃] à la fin du XVIIe siècle,[21] avant que le premier [ɑ̃] ne subisse le sort de la plupart des voyelles nasales devant consonne nasale. Cependant, la dénasalisation des voyelles nasales dans ce contexte n'a jamais été complète et divers accidents ou évolutions ont introduit en abondance dans la langue de nouvelles séquences [ṼN] (cf. Tranel 1981: *passim*).[22] Il est par exemple significatif que la verlanisation d'un mot commençant par une consonne nasale et s'achevant par une voyelle nasale n'aboutissent pas à une dénasalisation de cette dernière (*maison* [mezõ] → [zõme] et non *[zome]). Il semble bien que la dénasalisation des voyelles nasales devant consonne nasale ne soit plus un processus phonologique actif en français, et que le processus ancien se soit morphologisé. Si les adjectifs en [-ɑ̃]/[-ɑ̃t], anciens ou nouveaux, donnent des adverbes en [-amɑ̃], c'est très probablement qu'ils reposent sur un allomorphe lexical en [-a], que l'on appellera le thème 3.

Comme la construction d'adverbes sur des substantifs est un phénomène récent ou qui, en tout cas, n'a pas fait l'objet d'une lexicalisation, la représentation lexicale des noms en [-ɑ̃]/[-ɑ̃t] ne comporte vraisemblablement pas d'allomorphe de ce genre et l'absence d'un tel allomorphe explique suffisamment que la morphologie des adverbes dénominaux diffère de celle des adverbes déadjectivaux.

3.3.2.2 La sélection du thème

La sélection du thème en [-a] des adjectifs en [-ɑ̃]/[-ɑ̃t] aboutit à une forme qui l'emporte sur ses rivales en termes de marque. Il serait de ce fait concevable que le choix entre les thèmes 1, 2 et 3 de ces adjectifs obéisse à un conditionnement phonologique. *Elégamment* ([elegamɑ̃]) satisfait deux contraintes que ses rivaux ne satisfont pas à la fois: dépourvu de [t] entre [ɑ̃] et [m], il respecte la contrainte NoCoda que transgresse *élégantement* ([elegɑ̃tmɑ̃]), et, présentant une voyelle orale et non une voyelle nasale devant le [m], il se conforme à la contrainte *ṼN responsable du processus historique qui dénasalisait les voyelles nasales devant consonne nasale. Peu importe que les contraintes *ṼN et NoCoda ne prévalent plus de nos jours contre les contraintes de fidélité. Si le thème en [-a] est dans l'input au même titre que le thème 1 et le thème 2, il satisfait par hypothèse les contraintes de fidélité autant que les deux autres thèmes. Et l'on comprend dès lors que ce soit la forme la moins marquée qui émerge:

Tableau 3.17: Sélection phonologique de élégamment

{$eleg\tilde{a}_1$ ~ $eleg\tilde{a}t_2$ ~ $elega_3$} + mɑ̃	Fidélité	NoCoda	*ṼN
(T1) elegɑ̃mɑ̃			*!
(T2) elegɑ̃tmɑ̃		*!	
☞ (T3) elegamɑ̃			

Cette façon de rendre compte des allomorphies par 'émergence du non marqué' est devenue classique en Théorie de l'Optimalité (cf. Mascaró 1996, 2007; McCarthy 2002: 152 sqq.). Elle permet d'expliquer avec élégance la généralisation en synchronie de configurations résultant historiquement de simplifications, même si ces simplifications ne sont plus actives de nos jours dans le cas général.

Cependant, toutes les allomorphies constatées ne résultent pas de la simplification de configurations marquées, et la généralisation de ce mode d'explication à l'ensemble des dérivés en *-ment* aboutirait à des échecs.

Appliquons par exemple cette façon de procéder au cas banal des adjectifs à deux thèmes, l'un consonantique l'autre vocalique comme PETIT (T1: pəti, T2: pətit):

Tableau 3.18: Sélection fautive de *petiment

{$pəti_1$ ~ $pətit_2$} + mɑ̃	FIDÉLITÉ	NOCODA
☛ (T1) pətimɑ̃		
(T2) pətitmɑ̃		*!

Le candidat *[pətimɑ̃], qui est dépourvu de la marque que constitue la coda [t], l'emporte haut la main sur son rival [pətitmɑ̃], qui pourtant seul est grammatical.

Prenons encore le cas d'un adjectif comme PRÉCIS qui, outre un thème 1 ([presi]) et un thème 2 ([presiz]), possède un troisième thème en [e] ([presize]):

Tableau 3.19: Sélection fautive de *préciment

{$presi_1$ ~ $presiz_2$ ~ $presize_3$} + mɑ̃	FIDÉLITÉ	NOCODA	TAILLE
☛ (T1) presimɑ̃			
(T2) presizmɑ̃		*!	
(T3) presizemɑ̃			*!

Dans ce cas, NOCODA éliminerait à juste titre le candidat bâti sur le thème 2 *[presizmɑ̃], mais les contraintes de taille, qui favorisent les dérivés dont le radical est dissyllabique (cf. Plénat et Roché 2003), imposent la sélection de *[presimɑ̃] au détriment de [presizemɑ̃], qui pourtant seul est grammatical.

La raison de ces échecs est simple. Le principe de l'émergence du non marqué fonctionne quand les allomorphes résultent du tranquille polissage des formes au cours du temps. Mais toutes les allomorphies n'ont pas cette origine. Le choix du thème 2 dans [pətitmɑ̃] découle de la morphologisation d'une vieille règle d'accord en genre, celui du troisième thème dans [presizemɑ̃] d'une analogie ou d'une confusion avec d'autres adverbes. Dans ces cas, la morphologie assure la 'rémanence du marqué' au détriment de l'émergence du non marqué.

3.3.2.3 Elargissement de l'espace thématique de l'adjectif

Pour rendre compte de l'ensemble des formes anomales, nous proposons d'élargir l'espace thématique de l'adjectif et de reconnaître, outre les thèmes

1 et 2, un thème 3. Par défaut, ce thème 3 est identique au thème 2, mais il accueille aussi les allomorphes sub-réguliers ou exceptionnels. Le tableau suivant illustre l'ensemble des cas de figure:

Tableau 3.20: Thèmes 1, 2 et 3 des adjectifs

Lexème	Thème 1	Thème 2	Thème 3	Adverbe
FRAIS	frɛ	frɛʃ	frɛʃ	frɛʃmɑ̃
RAGEUR	raʒœr	raʒøz	raʒøz	raʒøzmɑ̃
BREF	brɛf	brɛv	brijɛv	brijɛvmɑ̃
ÉLÉGANT	elegɑ̃	elegɑ̃t	elega	elegamɑ̃
OPPORTUN	ɔpɔrtɛ̃	ɔpɔrtyn	ɔpɔrtyne	ɔpɔrtynemɑ̃

Les cas illustrés par FRAIS, [frɛʃmɑ̃], et RAGEUR, [raʒøzmɑ̃], sont les cas par défaut, ceux dans lequel le thème 3 ne se distingue pas du thème 2. La seule différence, c'est que, dans le cas de RAGEUR, le thème 2 est lui-même obtenu par règle: la dérivation en -EUR engendre simultanément les thèmes 1 et 2 de l'adjectif déverbal (Bonami et Boyé 2005).

Il n'y a pas grand chose à dire du cas illustré par BREF, [brijɛvmɑ̃], sinon que les adverbes de ce genre sont nécessairement exposés à la concurrence. Leur existence dépend de connaissances lexicales dont tous les locuteurs ne disposent pas. Il s'ensuit que la règle par défaut trouve des occasions de s'appliquer à eux. C'est ce que confirme BRIÈVEMENT, dont la forme *brièvement* a eu du mal à s'imposer face à *brèvement* (que préféraient par exemple les grammairiens de Port-Royal) et subit de nos jours encore la concurrence de cette forme (*brèvement* est présent à des milliers d'exemplaires sur la Toile).

Le cas illustré par OPPORTUN, [ɔpɔrtynemɑ̃], mériterait une discussion approfondie. Ce cas recouvre en fait un ensemble de sous-cas assez différents les uns des autres. Certaines finales adjectivales (comme par exemple [-ɑ̃s]) entraînent quasi-systématiquement l'apparition d'un [e] (cf. *immensément, intensément, densément, extensément*); d'autres (comme par exemple [-ɔ̃d]) favorisent cette apparition sans toutefois l'imposer (cf. *profondément* vs. *rondement* vs. *immondément*/*immondement*). Cette situation n'est pas vraiment surprenante, puisque les règles de correspondance entre thèmes sont très loin d'être toutes systématiques (cf. *supra* §3.3.1.1). Enfin, dans ce cas précis, des indices existent qui suggèrent que le phénomène est bien *output-driven*, puisque [-ɔ̃demɑ̃] correspond à la fois à des inputs en [-ɔ̃d] et à des inputs en [-ɔ̃di] (cf. *profondément, immondément* vs. *approfondément*).

Le cas de ÉLÉGANT, [elegamɑ̃], a été longuement discuté dans la section précédente. Historiquement, les radicaux en [-a] sont issus d'une dénasalisation. Mais nous avons dit nos raisons de penser que la contrainte qui a imposé cette dénasalisation est inopérante en synchronie. Ces radicaux ont donc toutes chances d'être des allomorphes lexicaux. Comme ces allomorphes sont peu marqués, il serait concevable de confier à la phonologie le soin de les sélectionner. Nous choisissons ici de les aligner sur le cas général et de confier cette sélection à la morphologie.

Le dispositif que nous proposons comprend deux éléments: des règles de correspondances entre thèmes pour les cas réguliers et sub-réguliers et une contrainte de sélection:

(4) CORRESPONDANCES ENTRE LES THÈMES

- si le thème 2 a pour finale [-iz], [-yz], [-ɔd], [-õd], [-ɑ̃s], [-yn], [-yr], [-ɔrm], alors le thème 3 a la forme thème 2 + [e];
- si le thème 2 est du type [Xɑ̃t] ou (peut-être) [Xɑ̃d], alors le thème 3 est de forme [Xa];
- dans tous les autres cas, le thème 3 est identique au thème 2.

Cette formulation n'est pas tout à fait fidèle aux faits dans leur complexité, notamment en ce qu'elle oblige à considérer les idiosyncrasies comme *brièvement* ou *traitreusement* de la même façon que des 'exceptions' comme *rondement* ([rõdmɑ̃]), alors qu'il serait sans doute plus approprié de parler d'une pluralité de modèles en concurrence les uns avec les autres pour ces dernières. Et en ce qu'elle ignore le caractère *output-driven* du phénomène (*approfondément* n'est pas traité). Mais elle résume assez bien notre position: ce ne sont pas des considérations de marque qui sont responsables de la forme spécifique que prennent les radicaux des adverbes en *-ment*. Ce ne sont pas non plus des considérations de marque qui interviennent dans la sélection de ces allomorphes. Ce qui nous conduit à rendre compte de la morphologie des adverbes en *-ment* à l'aide de la contrainte de sélection suivante:

(5) SÉLECTION (T3): Les adverbes en *-ment* sélectionnent le thème 3 de l'adjectif.

Cette formulation est provisoire. L'essentiel pour nous était de disposer d'un mécanisme qui rende compte de la pression du lexique existant sur le lexique en création. Le lexique comporte pour chaque cas soit la forme elle-même (*brièvement*), soit des modèles nombreux (*fraîchement*, *élégamment*) ou saillants (*précisément*) et ce sont ces modèles qui s'appliquent. Il nous paraît assez plausible que l'on a affaire à des processus analogiques qui pourraient être modélisés comme le fait Burzio (2002) en supposant que les représentations lexicales constituent des faisceaux de contraintes et que les contraintes individuelles peuvent cumuler leurs effets. Les règles de correspondance entre thèmes pourraient être modifiées dans ce sens. Ici, elles sont formulées de façon à rendre compte du comportement majoritaire au niveau d'une finale donnée ([-iz], [-yz], etc.), elles pourraient être aménagées de façon à tenir compte d'un contexte phonologique plus large en utilisant par exemple un système de correspondances entre thèmes basées sur le Minimum Generalization Learner de Albright (2002).

3.3.2.4 Le type *charmantement*

Avec cette architecture, on obtient les résultats attendus sauf dans le cas des adjectifs en [-ɑ̃]/[-ɑ̃t] dans lesquels la rime finale est précédée d'une attaque en consonne nasale et/ou labiale (cf. *supra* §2.3). Dans ce qui suit, nous raisonnerons sur le cas des adjectifs en [-mɑ̃]/[-mɑ̃t], pour lesquels les données sont les moins contestables, mais la solution proposée peut être étendue au besoin au cas général. Si c'était le thème 3 qui était sélectionné, *charmant* donnerait l'agrammatical **charmamment*:

Tableau 3.21: Sélection fautive de *charmamment

{ʃarmɑ̃$_1$ ~ ʃarmɑ̃t$_2$ ~ ʃarma$_3$} + mɑ̃	FIDÉLITÉ	SÉLECT (T3)
(T1) ʃarmɑ̃mɑ̃		*!
(T2) ʃarmɑ̃tmɑ̃		*!
☛ (T3) ʃarmamɑ̃		

Dans ce cas particulier, il y a une exception dans l'exception, et, au lieu du thème 3, c'est le thème 2, celui que l'on trouve dans le cas général, qui est choisi.

Premier élément de solution: il y a manifestement lieu de penser que la phonologie intervient dans le choix du thème retenu et/ou dans son modelage. Les formes attendues et qui n'apparaissent pas ne sont pas phonologiquement quelconques. Si l'adverbe était construit sur le thème 3 [ʃarma-], *charmant* ferait *charmamment* [ʃarmamɑ̃], une forme dans laquelle deux [m] apparaîtraient de part et d'autre d'une voyelle. Dans la forme construite sur le thème 2 *charmantement* ([ʃarmɑ̃tmɑ̃]), cette consécution de deux [m] est interrompue par l'intrusion de l'occlusive orale coronale [t]. Avec les contraintes syllabiques et les contraintes de taille, les contraintes dissimilatives figurent parmi les contraintes anti-marque les plus actives dans la phonologie lexicale du français actuel (cf. Plénat à paraître). Il est donc tout à fait vraisemblable que l'apparition de radicaux inattendus soit à mettre sur le compte de contraintes de ce genre. Rien, effet n'indique que *véhémentement*, qui est isolé, littéraire et assez peu fréquent, serve de modèle. L'hypothèse que joue dans ce cas une contrainte dissimilative est la plus plausible.

Nous n'avons pas la place de détailler ici la variété des effets des contraintes dissimilatives en français. Mais on nous permettra au moins d'insister sur le fait que la consécution de deux [m] y est bien évitée autant que faire se peut. La construction des noms déverbaux recourt dans cette langue à trois procédés principaux: la suffixation en *-ment*, la suffixation en *-age* et la suffixation en *-ion*. (Ce dernier suffixe est adjoint à un thème spécial qui s'achève par [-ɑs] dans le cas par défaut, cf. Bonami, Boyé et Kerleroux 2009). Ainsi *passer* donne-t-il, suivant le sens considéré, tantôt *passage*, tantôt *passement*, et tantôt encore *passation*. Globalement, ces trois suffixations contribuent à peu près également au lexique attesté dans les dictionnaires. Mais elles ne sont pas également productives avec tous les types de bases. Leur productivité respective dépend en particulier de critères phonologiques. Plus précisément, l'adjonction des finales [-mɑ̃], [-aʒ] et [-ɑsjɔ̃] est gênée quand la consonne qui les précède est identique à celle qu'ils renferment eux-mêmes. *BDLEX* fournit les chiffres suivants:

Tableau 3.22: [-mɑ̃], [-aʒ] et [-ɑsjɔ̃] après [m], [ʒ] et [s] dans BDLEX

	-mɑ̃	-aʒ	-ɑsjɔ̃
Xm-	7	36	43
Xʒ-	53	11	0
Xs-	324	160	22
X-	1222	1301	1388

Il existe bien des dérivés comme *enfermement* ([ɑ̃fɛrməmɑ̃]), *limogeage* ([limɔʒaʒ]) ou *passation* ([pɑsɑsjɔ̃]) comportant deux consonnes identiques consécutives. Mais on voit que ces déverbaux sont bien moins nombreux qu'on ne s'y attendrait.[23] Dans le cas des dérivés en [-m(ə)mɑ̃], il faut en outre tenir compte du fait que *désarmement*, *réarmement* et *surarmement* subissent l'influence de *armement*. Cette faiblesse numérique ne peut guère être qu'un témoignage parmi tant d'autres de la vigueur des contraintes dissimilatives en français.

On sait aussi que les déverbaux en *-ment* sont à l'ordinaire construits sur le même thème que la 3ème personne du pluriel de l'indicatif présent (cf. *ils cheminent~cheminement*, *ils nettoient~nettoiement*, *ils franchissent~franchissement*, *ils abattent~abattement*, *ils braient~braiement*). Curieusement, toutefois, *endormir*, qui, en tant que verbe de la troisième conjugaison, devrait donner *endormement* (cf. *ils endorment*), fait exception et donne *endormissement* comme un verbe de la deuxième conjugaison alors que le thème *endormiss-* n'apparaît nulle part dans son paradigme. On ne peut s'empêcher de penser que cet emprunt à la deuxième conjugaison est une autre manifestation de la tendance à éviter la consécution de deux [m] sur la tire consonantique.

Dans le cas de ces déverbaux, l'existence de plusieurs suffixations équivalentes fournit l'exutoire le plus fréquent. Dans le cas des adverbes en [-mɑ̃], il n'existe pas de solution de rechange morphologique, et il est d'une certaine façon normal que la solution soit recherchée du côté du radical plutôt que de celui du suffixe.[24]

Pour modéliser ces phénomènes, on recourra ici à une contrainte phonologique générale contre la répétition de [m] sur le plan d'organisation des consonnes:

(6) *M (V) M: Pas de consonnes [m] consécutives sur la tire consonantique.

Dans le cas de *charmantement*, cette contrainte interagit avec la contrainte de sélection qui veut un thème 3 de la même façon que la contrainte qui requiert la présence d'une consonne finale interagissait avec la contrainte exigeant un thème 1 pour la FLMS. La contrainte dissimilative interdit que soit retenu le thème 3, dont la sélection aboutirait à une forme ([ʃarmamɑ̃]) qui l'enfreindrait.[25] Cette même contrainte s'oppose victorieusement aussi au choix du thème 1 ([ʃarmɑ̃mɑ̃]) qui la transgresserait également. Il n'y a que [ʃarmɑ̃tmɑ̃] qui respecte *M(V)M, et c'est cette forme qui est retenue:

Tableau 3.23: Sélection de charmantement

{ʃarmɑ̃$_1$ ~ ʃarmɑ̃t$_2$ ~ ʃarma$_3$} + mɑ̃	FIDÉLITÉ	*M(V)M	SÉLECT (T3)
(T1) ʃarmɑ̃mɑ̃		*!	*
☞ (T2) ʃarmɑ̃tmɑ̃			*
(T3) ʃarmamɑ̃		*!	

Contrairement néanmoins à ce qui se passe pour la FLMS, c'est une contrainte anti-marque à prétention universelle (de la famille de OCP) qui contrarie la règle morphologique de sélection du thème. Il s'agit donc là d'un cas peu contestable d'optimisation proprement phonologique.[26]

3.4 Conclusion

Dans la présente étude, nous avons essayé de renouveler la description de l'allomorphie radicale des adverbes en *-ment* du français en faisant intervenir des données nouvelles. Ces données, négatives, comme la faiblesse numérique des adverbes dans lesquels [-amɑ̃] est précédé d'une labiale ou d'une nasale, ou très rares, comme les formes en [-ɑ̃tmɑ̃] autres que les trois ou quatre adverbes signalés par les dictionnaires, échappaient nécessairement à nos prédécesseurs. Intéressamment, ces données font sens, en ce qu'elles plaident en faveur de l'idée qu'une contrainte dissimilative interdisant la consécution de deux consonnes nasales et/ou labiales joue un rôle non négligeable en français. Les contraintes de ce type sont omniprésentes en français et monnaie courante dans les langues. Elles peuvent prétendre au rang de contraintes universelles.

Nous n'avons en revanche pas à proposer de grandes nouveautés dans la description de la variété de radicaux propres aux adverbes en *-ment*. Ce qui frappe dans ce domaine, c'est le caractère étroitement paroissial des régularités établies. La comparaison avec ce qui se passe dans les déverbaux en *-ment* et dans les adverbes en *-ment* dénominaux montre que l'existence des radicaux en [-a] et en [-e] est exclusivement le fait de radicaux adjectivaux au sein d'adverbes en *-ment*. Le français actuel crée, abondamment pour les uns et sporadiquement pour les autres, de nouveaux radicaux de ce type, mais il ne fait là que reproduire des schèmes installés dans la langue. Les contraintes universelles n'ont probablement que très peu de part au choix de ces allomorphes, ou au choix d'un thème de féminin dans le cas par défaut.

Les deux types de contraintes, pourtant, interagissent: quand l'application de la contrainte de sélection des thèmes en [-a] aboutirait à une transgression de la contrainte dissimilative, c'est le thème par défaut qui est sélectionné (type *charmantement*). Il y a là, pensons-nous un exemple peu contestable du fait que les contraintes universelles peuvent intervenir dans le choix des allomorphes radicaux. Cet exemple n'est probablement pas isolé en français. Hathout, Namer, Plénat et Tanguy (2009) signalent en effet que le suffixe *-issime* sélectionne de préférence l'allomorphe 'populaire' des adjectifs en *-ique* dissyllabiques comme *logique* ou *lubrique*, d'où des superlatifs comme *logiquissime* ou *lubriquissime.* Comme le choix d'allomorphes 'savants' comme [lɔʒis-] ou [lybris-] aboutirait soit à des répétitions de [i] et de [s] (*[lɔʒisisim], *[lybrisisim]), soit, par troncation, à des formes dont le radical serait monosyllabique (*[lɔʒisim], *[lybrisim]),[27] il y a lieu de penser que l'allomorphie savant/populaire est, elle aussi, sensible aux contraintes dissimilatives et aux contraintes de taille. Mais il faudrait un autre article pour établir les faits.

Notes

1. Nous remercions Olivier Bonami, Michel Roché et Bernard Tranel, qui, par leurs remarques et leurs suggestions, nous ont permis d'améliorer très sensiblement une première version de ce travail. Il nous est cependant arrivé de persévérer dans l'erreur, et nous devons être tenus pour seuls responsables des faiblesses qui déparent encore ce chapitre.
2. Un même lexème adjectival peut se manifester sous des formes très différentes les unes des autres. Pour ne prendre qu'un exemple –plutôt exceptionnel, il est vrai–, RIGOUREUX est attesté comme [rigurø] dans *rigoureux*, comme [rigurøz] dans *rigoureux* (en position de liaison), *rigoureuse*, *rigoureusement*, *rigoureuseté*, *rigoureusité*, comme [rigurɔz] dans *rigourosité*, comme [rigɔrɔz] dans *rigorosité*, comme [rigur] dans *rigourissime* et comme [rigɔr] dans *rigorissime*. Certaines variantes sont phonologiquement tout à fait arbitraires en synchronie, soit qu'elles s'expliquent par l'emprunt ou l'imitation de la forme latine (*rigorōsus*), soit qu'elles résultent d'un conditionnement qui a disparu (par exemple une voyelle a longtemps protégé de la chute le [z] final au féminin). D'autres, en revanche, sont la conséquence directe de contraintes anti-marque actives en synchronie: c'est, par exemple, la coalition de contraintes de taille et de contraintes dissimilatives qui rend compte de la 'chute' de [ɔz] ou de [øz] dans *rigorissime* et *rigourissime* (cf. Plénat 2002). Cette prolifération d'allomorphes est masquée par le caractère très malthusien de la langue enseignée à l'école (qui ne connaît, par exemple, que *rigoureux*, *rigoureuse* et *rigoureusement*). Nous décrivons quant à nous un usage moins contraint, que reflètent une masse grandissante de textes sur la Toile.
3. Sur ces adverbes, voir en particulier Mørdrup (1976), Łozińska (1978), Nøjgaard (1992–1995), Molinier et Levrier (2000), Dal (2007).
4. Nous avons utilisé pour cette recherche systématique le script Webaffix (cf. Hathout et Tanguy 2005). L'utilisation de ce genre de données soulève parfois des problèmes difficiles; mais, pour peu que l'on soit un peu prudent, on affine sur bien des points les descriptions traditionnelles (cf. Hathout, Namer, Plénat et Tanguy 2009).
5. Cf. aussi, e.g., Bally (1965:162), Damourette et Pichon (1911–1930:241 sqq.), Grevisse (1975:865), Wagner et Pinchon (1962:375 sqq.).
6. Les dictionnaires signalent aussi que *dolentement* concurrence parfois *dolemment*.
7. Certaines formes sont extrêmement rares: nous n'avons, par exemple, trouvé qu'une attestation de *éprisément* et de *rotondément*. Mais d'autres sont bien attestées: plusieurs centaines de pages contiennent par exemple *concisément* ou *immondément*. Et le petit nombre des finales concernées est frappant.
8. On peut se demander si la règle ne doit pas être étendue aux autres adjectifs en [-ɑ̃]/[-ɑ̃C]. *Friamment*, de *friand*, est attesté chez Huysmans (*Les Sœurs Vatard* 161, Charpentier, Paris, 1879, citation dans le *TLF*). Tous les autres

adverbes dérivés d'adjectifs de ce type sont en [-ãCmã], mais ou bien leur base est en *-mand* (*allemandement, gourmandement, normandement, romandement*) ou bien elle est monosyllabique (*blanchement, franchement, grandement*). Il est possible et même probable que ces deux circonstances expliquent l'alignement sur le cas général (cf. *véhémentement* et *lentement*). Voir l'analyse proposée à la note 25 pour les dérivés de monosyllabes.

9. Parmi les nasales et les labiales, seul [v] donne une proportion d'adverbes supérieure (12,5%) à cette moyenne. Mais on notera que *fervemment*, qui est bien attesté dans les dictionnaires, est absent du lexique mental de nombreux locuteurs; pour notre part, nous dirions spontanément *ferventement*. *Savamment* est ainsi le seul cas universellement admis où une labiale précède [-amã].

10. Les données que nous avons recueillies automatiquement sur la Toile à l'aide de Webaffix ne contredisent pas cette conclusion: là aussi, les adjectifs dans lesquels [-ã]/[-ãt] suit une nasale (sauf [n]) ou une labiale donnent une proportion d'adverbes en [-amã] inférieure à la moyenne générale. Les écarts constatés, toutefois, sont trop faibles pour être très probants. Nous sommes tentés d'attribuer la faiblesse de cet écart au bruit considérable qui parasite les données. La Toile regorge d'archaïsmes, d'hypercorrectismes de locuteurs francophones, de généralisations abusives de locuteurs non francophones, de xénismes, de commentaires métalinguistiques et de confusions de toute sorte. Pour bien faire, il conviendrait de soumettre les données à une critique philologique serrée pour écarter les formes illégitimes et de dénombrer les formes légitimes en concurrence pour prendre la mesure de la variation. Ces vérifications auraient été trop lourdes à mener dans le cadre du présent travail. Nous n'avons pu examiner d'un peu près les données que sur des points particuliers, comme nous le verrons ci-après.

11. Ce sentiment qu'une contrainte dissimilative contrecarre l'apparition d'adverbes en *-mamment*/*-memment* est ancien. Ainsi, dans sa *Grammaire méthodique* de 1681, Vairasse d'Allais écrivait déjà:

    Il faut encore remarquer que des noms adjectifs qui sont terminez en, *ment*, comme, *vehement*, *clement*, on ne forme point d'adverbes en, *ment*, parce que la repetition de la lettre, *m*, dans les deux dernieres sillabes de ces mots serait tout à fait desagreable. Ainsi au lieu de dire, *Vehememment*, & *clememment*, on dit *avec vehemence*, *avec clemence*, &c.

    Il échappait à l'auteur que l'on pouvait éviter la cacophonie en utilisant le thème de féminin (*véhémentement* est employé depuis le XIVe siècle).

12. On trouve ainsi sur la Toile une citation attribuée à Gambetta ("Weiss, vous avez charmantement parlé.") figurant à l'origine dans un ouvrage du XIXe siècle, et une citation de l'abbé François Pascal, l'un des correspondants de Frédéric Mistral ("Le Préfet est charmantement & ardentement enfélibré").

Plus récemment, *charmantement* est employé par Albert Cohen dans *Mangeclous*.

13. Exemples trouvés sur la Toile: "Animateurement parlant, est-ce que les emplois d'anim spécialisé pour les classes sont des emplois ridicules et bouche-trous [...]"; "Ginette Migneault est l'animatrice pour l'Estran dans MRC Côte de Gaspé et Haute-Gaspésie. Pour me contacter, par courriel: migneaultg@yahoo.ca ou tel: 418 797-2457 Animatricement vôtre…"; "Un Créateur 'visage plus sévère que jamais et lourd de réflexions', [...], parlant 'très créateurement', [...]"; "On peut seulement réagir créatricement […]".
14. Il n'est pas aisé de trouver des données sur ce point: les exemples potentiels sont relativement peu nombreux, et il faut prendre soin d'écarter les formes susceptibles de recevoir une autre explication, comme les dérivés de féminins de noms en *-ant/-ent* ou les dérivés de noms masculins dans lesquelles cette finale est précédée d'un phonème nasal et/ou labial. Nous avons déniché sur la Toile une douzaine d'exemples qui nous paraissent satisfaisants: *collantement, commerçantement, étudiantement, Grand Intendantement, lance-ardentement, mécréantement, militantement, mutantement, néantement, occidentement, protestantement, résidentement.* Sur une base en *-d*, nous avons aussi trouvé *châteaubriandement.* Nous n'avons rencontré que trois exceptions: *engoulevemment, présidemment*, et une attestation isolée de *collamment. Confidemment*, qui doit être rapproché en synchronie du substantif *confident*, a conservé la forme qu'il avait dans l'ancienne langue.
15. Le dénominal *collantement* est abondamment attesté sur la Toile. Le déadjectival *collamment* est beaucoup plus rare, mais on trouve quelques attestations. Exemples: […] *une meuf dans mon entourage, amie d'un ami à moi, dont elle a longtemps été collament* (sic) *amoureuse sans retour*; […] *du nougat, avec une note de miel, bref, tout ce qui est collament* (sic) *sucré* […].
16. Ou, si l'on veut, de la 'déclinaison' de l'adjectif, cf. Morin (1992).
17. Si toutefois il existe: *bée, pie* n'ont pas de masculin, et, inversement, *preux* n'a pas de féminin.
18. Cette proposition est analogue dans son esprit à celle de Steriade (1999), qui, toutefois, s'intéresse à un dialecte où la contradiction entre contraintes peut aboutir à un remodelage des formes (adjonction de la consonne finale du féminin à la forme masculine, cf. des réalisations comme [prəmjeretaʒ] ou [plɛ̃nɑ̃plwa] au lieu de [prəmjɛretaʒ] ou [plɛnɑ̃plwa] pour *premier étage* et *plein emploi*).
19. Cette classe de déclencheurs de liaison ne se laisse pas définir en termes purement phonologiques. Si les mots à initiale consonantique en sont exclus, tous les mots à initiale vocalique n'en font pas partie: c'est le fameux problème des mots dits 'en *h* aspirée' (cf. *petit héros* [pti.e.ro], et non *[pti.te.ro]); et certains mots commençant par une semi-voyelle provoquent la liaison (cf. *petit oiseau* [pti.twa.zo], *petit hiatus* [pti.tja.tys], *petit huissier* [pti.tɥi.sje]). Sauf à compliquer les représentations phonologiques, il est donc difficile de supposer que la liaison a pour rôle de fournir au nom recteur une

attaque consonantique. On sait d'ailleurs (cf. Tranel 1990) que lorsqu'une rupture syntaxique sépare l'adjectif du nom, la consonne finale du premier ne s'enchaîne pas toujours sur la voyelle initiale du second: on dit *j'en ai un petit, éléphant* ([pti || t-e.le.fɑ̃]) en enchaînant la consonne, mais *j'en ai un bel, éléphant* ([bɛl || e.le.fɑ̃]) sans l'enchaîner. Les adjectifs dont la consonne finale s'enchaîne sont ceux dont l'enchaînement laisse devant la pausule une forme identique à la forme libre (cf. PETIT: FLMS [ptit], masc. [pti], vs. BEAU: FLMS [bɛl], masc. [bo]). Il y a donc lieu de croire que l'enchaînement permet dans ce cas de satisfaire simultanément la nécessité d'employer une FLMS devant un nom déclencheur de liaison et le besoin de recourir à la forme ordinaire devant une pause; quand les deux contraintes ne peuvent pas être satisfaites en même temps, la première prend le pas sur la seconde, et la FLMS n'est pas enchaînée. Autrement dit, l'enchaînement, dans ce cas, n'est qu'une conséquence secondaire du caractère contradictoire de deux règles syntaxiques présidant à l'emploi de deux formes du paradigme adjectival (Plénat 2008); il ne peut pas constituer la raison d'être de l'emploi de formes de liaison.

Le caractère syntaxique du choix des formes apparaît plus nettement encore dans le cas des coordinations adjectivales antéposées: dans cette configuration, les deux adjectifs prennent la forme d'une FLMS quand le nom recteur est un déclencheur de liaison, celle d'un masculin ordinaire quand c'est un inhibiteur de liaison: on dit *un bel et charmant enfant* et *un beau et charmant garçon, un grand* ([grɑ̃.t]) *et bel appartement* et *un grand* ([grɑ̃.]) *et beau salon.* Il arrive même que la FLMS soit employée devant *mais*: *un bel mais chétif enfant* (cf. Plénat 2013). Ce phénomène de liaison à distance montre clairement que la liaison de l'adjectif sur le nom n'est pas un phénomène de sandhi.

Comme la liaison non enchaînée, il suggère que l'on a affaire à la sélection d'une forme du paradigme adjectival en fonction de la classe du nom recteur: un nom singulier déclencheur de liaison impose une FLMS comme un nom au féminin singulier impose un adjectif au féminin singulier. Pour une vue d'ensemble des problèmes soulevés par la liaison de l'adjectif masc. sing. sur le nom, cf. Plénat et Plénat (2011).

20. On pourrait encore citer VIOLENT , [vjɔlɑ̃tmɑ̃]/[vjɔlamɑ̃], et COMMODE, [(a)kɔmɔdmɑ̃]/[kɔmɔdemɑ̃]. *Précisement* et *violentement* ne figurent pas dans les dictionnaires, mais on en trouve des attestations sur la Toile. Il en va de même de l'adverbe *courbement*.
21. Ou, du moins, telle était la prononciation recommandée par certains grammairiens, cf. Pope (1973:§444).
22. On trouve actuellement de telles séquences dans un grand nombre de configurations: à l'intérieur des morphèmes, du fait de la persistance –exceptionnelle– de certaines séquences (cf. *ennui* [ɑ̃nɥi]), du fait d'emprunts (cf. *samba* [sɑ̃mba], *Van Impe* [vɑ̃nimp]) ou encore du fait de la nasalisation d'occlusives

sonores après voyelle nasale dans la langue familière (cf. *chambre d'en haut* [ʃɑ̃mdɑ̃o]); à la jonction d'un préfixe et du radical qui le suit, par héritage en ce qui concerne *en-* (cf. *enivrer* [ɑ̃nivre], *emmancher* [ɑ̃mɑ̃ʃe]), dans les formes nouvelles pour ce qui est de *in-* négatif (cf. *immangeable* [ɛ̃mɑ̃ʒabl], *innavigable* [ɛ̃navigabl]); à la jonction du radical verbal et d'un suffixe personnel dans *(nous) tînmes* [tɛ̃m], *(nous) vînmes* [vɛ̃m]; dans les formes à redoublement: *maman* se prononce couramment [mɑ̃mɑ̃] et *Monmon* [mɔ̃mɔ̃] concurrence *Momon* comme diminutif de *Raymond*; à la jonction d'un clitique et de son hôte (cf. *en entrant* [ɑ̃nɑ̃trɑ̃], *en mangeant* [ɑ̃mɑ̃ʒɑ̃]).

23. Le fait qu'on ne trouve pas de déverbaux en [-ʒɑsjɔ̃] s'explique par le fait que le lexique 'savant' (emprunté directement au latin) ne comporte pas de fricatives prépalatales et que la suffixation en *-ion* supporte mal les radicaux 'non-savants'.
24. Pour les adverbes dénominaux, la répétition est généralement évitée en utilisant la forme du nom en tant qu'adverbe: *chevènement vôtre* (cf. *supra* §3.2.4).
25. Une explication du même ordre peut probablement être avancée pour expliquer que *lent* et *grand* donnent *lentement* et *grandement* au lieu de **lemment* et **gramment*. En français joue un rôle actif une contrainte voulant que le radical d'un dérivé suffixal comprenne au moins deux syllabes (cf. Plénat et Roché 2003). Placée au dessus de la contrainte SELECT (T3), cette contrainte est susceptible d'éliminer [lamɑ̃], [lɑ̃mɑ̃], [gramɑ̃] et [grɑ̃mɑ̃] au profit des formes attestées, à condition du moins que le [t] et le [d] de [lɑ̃tmɑ̃] et [grɑ̃dmɑ̃] comptent pour une syllabe ('dégénérée').
26. OCP interagit avec la morphologie d'une façon assez analogue dans la morphologie du pluriel catalan en déterminant l'apparition d'un allomorphe marqué de la marque de masculin dans des formes comme [pásus] (cf. Bonet, Lloret et Mascaró 2003).
27. La troncation est la solution retenue dans les polysyllabes: *britannique* fait *britannissime*, et *psychédélique*: *psychédélissime*.

Références

Aronoff, Mark (1994) *Morphology by Itself.* Cambridge, MA: MIT Press.

Albright, Adam (2002) *The Identification of Bases in Morphological Paradigms.* Thèse de doctorat, University of California at Los Angeles.

Bally, Charles (1965) *Linguistique générale et linguistique française.* Berne: Francke.

Bonami, Olivier et Boyé, Gilles (2003) La nature morphologique des allomorphies conditionnées: les formes de liaison des adjectifs en français. In Bernard Fradin, Georgette Dal, Nabil Hathout, Françoise Kerleroux, Marc Plénat et Michel Roché (eds) *Les unités morphologiques* [= *Silexicales* 3] 169–178. Villeneuve-d'Ascq: SILEX, Université de Lille 3.

Bonami, Olivier et Boyé, Gilles (2005) Construire le paradigme d'un adjectif. *Recherches linguistiques de Vincennes* 34: 77–98.

Bonami, Olivier, Boyé, Gilles et Kerleroux, Françoise (2009) L'allomorphie radicale et la relation flexion-construction. In Bernard Fradin, Françoise Kerleroux et Marc Plénat (eds) *Aperçus de morphologie du français* 103–125. Saint-Denis: Presses Universitaires de Vincennes.

Bonet, Eulàlia, Lloret, Maria-Rosa et Mascaró, Joan (2003) Phonology-morphology conflicts in gender allomorphy: a unified approach. Communication présentée au colloque Generative Linguistics in the Old World (GLOW), Colloque 26 (Lund, 9–11 Avril 2009).

Brunot, Ferdinand et Bruneau, Charles (s.d.) *Précis de grammaire historique de la langue française*. Paris: Masson.

Burzio, Luigi (2002) Surface-to-Surface Morphology: When your Representations turn into Constraints. In Paul Boucher (ed.) *Many Morphologies* 142–177. Somerville, MA: Cascadilla Press.

Burzio, Luigi (2005) Sources of Paradigm Uniformity. In Laura J. Downing, T. Alan Hall, Renate Raffelsiefen (eds) *Paradigms in Phonological Theory* 65–106. Oxford: Oxford University Press.

Calmès, Martine de et Pérennou, Guy (1998) *BDLEX:* a Lexicon for Spoken and Written French. In *1st International Conference on Langage Resources & Evaluation (LREC1998), Grenade, 28–30 mai 1998* 1129–1136. Paris: ELRA.

Chevalier, Jean-Claude, Blanche-Benveniste, Claire, Arrivé, Michel et Peytard, Jean (1964) *Grammaire Larousse du français contemporain*. Paris: Larousse.

Dal, Georgette (2007) Les adverbes en *-ment* du français: dérivation ou flexion? In Nabil Hathout et Fabio Montermini (eds) *Morphologie à Toulouse. Actes du Colloque International de Morphologie – 4èmes Décembrettes* 121–147. Munich: Lincom Europa.

Damourette, Jacques et Pichon, Edouard (1911–1930) *Des Mots à la pensée. Essai de grammaire de la langue française.* Paris: D'Artrey.

Darmesteter, Arsène (⁶1920) *Traité de la formation de la langue française*. In Adolphe Hatzfeld, Arsène Darmesteter et Antoine Thomas *Dictionnaire général de la langue française du commencement du XVIIe siècle jusqu'à nos jours* 1–300. Paris: Delagrave.

Dell, François (1973) *Les règles et les sons. Introduction à la phonologie générative*. Paris: Hermann.

Encrevé, Pierre (1988) *La liaison avec et sans enchaînement. Phonologie tridimensionnelle et usages du français.* Paris: Le Seuil.

Grevisse, Maurice (¹⁰1975) *Le Bon usage. Grammaire française avec des remarques sur la langue française d'aujourd'hui*. Gembloux: Duculot.

Hathout, Nabil, Namer, Fiammetta, Plénat, Marc et Tanguy, Ludovic (2009) La collecte et l'utilisation des données en morphologie. In Bernard Fradin, Françoise Kerleroux et Marc Plénat (eds) *Aperçus de morphologie du français* 267–287. Saint-Denis: Presses Universitaires de Vincennes.

Hathout, Nabil et Tanguy, Ludovic (2005) Webaffix: une boîte à outils d'acquisition lexicale à partir du Web. *Revue Québéquoise de Linguistique* 32.1: 61–84.

Huot, Hélène (2001) *Morphologie. Forme et sens des mots du français*. Paris: Armand Colin.

Łozińska, Maria (1978) *La formation des adverbes en* -ment *dans le français contemporain*. Varsovie: Państwowe Wydawnictwo Naukowe.

Mascaró, Joan (1996) External allomorphy as emergence of the unmarked. In Jacques Durand et Bernard Laks (eds) *Current Trends in Phonology: Models and Methods* 473–483. Salford: European Studies Research Institute.

Mascaró, Joan (2007) External allomorphy and lexical representation. *Linguistic Inquiry* 38: 715–735.

McCarthy, John J. (2002) *A Thematic Guide to Optimality Theory*. Cambridge: Cambridge University Press.

Molinier, Christian (1992) Sur la productivité adverbiale des adjectifs. *Langue française* 96: 65–73.

Molinier, Christian et Levrier, Françoise (2000) *Grammaire des adverbes. Description des formes en* -ment. Genève-Paris: Droz.

Mørdrup, Ole (1976) *Une analyse non-transformationnelle des adverbes en* -ment [= *Revue Romane. Numéro spécial* 11]. Copenhague: Akademisk Forlag.

Morin, Yves-Charles (1992) Un cas méconnu de la déclinaison de l'adjectif français: les formes de liaison de l'adjectif antéposé. In André Clas (ed.) *Le mot, les mots, les bons mots – Word, words, Witty Words. Hommage à Igor Mel'čuk par ses amis, collègues et élèves à l'occasion de son soixantième anniversaire* 233–250. Montréal: Presses de l'Université de Montréal.

Nøjgaard, Morten (1992–1995) *Les adverbes français. Essai de description fonctionnelle*, 3 vol. Copenhague: Munksgaard.

Perlmutter, David M. (1998) Interfaces: Explanation of allomorphy and the architecture of grammars. In Steven G. Lapointe, Diane K. Brentari et Patrick M. Farrell (eds) *Morphology and its Relation to Syntax and Phonology* 307 338. Standford, CA: CSLI Publications.

Plénat, Marc (2000) Quelques thèmes de recherche actuels en morphophonologie française. *Cahiers de lexicologie* 77: 27–62.

Plénat, Marc (2002) Jean-Louis Fossat: fossatissime. Note sur la morphophonologie des dérivés en - *issime*. In Lídia Rabassa (ed) *Mélanges offerts à Jean-Louis Fossat* [= *Cahiers d'Etudes Romanes* 11–12] 229–248. Toulouse: ERSS, Université de Toulouse-Le Mirail.

Plénat, Marc et Roché, Michel (2003) Prosodic constraints on suffixation in French. In Geert Booij, Janet DeCesaris, Angela Ralli et Sergio Scalise (eds) *Topics in Morphology. Selected Papers from the Third Mediterranean Morphology Meeting (Barcelona, September 20–22, 2001)* 285–299. Barcelona: Institut Universitari de Lingüística Aplicada, Universitat Pompeu Fabra.

Plénat, Marc (2008) La liaison 'obligatoire' avec et sans enchaînement. In Jacques Durand, Benoit Habert et Bernard Laks (eds) *Congrès Mondial de Linguistique Française – CMLF'08* 1657–1667. Paris: ILF.

Plénat, Marc (2013) La liaison à distance dans le groupe nominal. *Le français moderne* 81.1: 42–71.

Plénat, Marc (à paraître) Dissimilatory phenomena in French word-formation. In Peter O. Müller, Ingeborg Ohnheiser, Susan Olsen et Franz Rainer (eds) *Word-Formation. An International Handbook of the Languages of Europe*. Berlin/New York: Mouton De Gruyter.

Plénat, Marc et Plénat, Camille (2011) La liaison de l'adjectif sur le nom en français: morphologie, syntaxe, phonologie. In *Linguistica* LI 299–315. Ljubljana: Filozofska fakulteta univerze Edvarda Kardelja.

Pope, Mildred Katharine ([6]1973) *From Latin to Modern French with especial consideration of Anglo-Norman*. Manchester: Manchester University Press.

Roché, Michel, Boyé, Gilles, Hathout, Nabil, Lignon, Stéphanie et Plénat, Marc (2011) *Des unités morphologiques au lexique*. Paris/Londres: Hermès-Lavoisier.

Schane, Sandford A. (1968) *French Phonology and Morphology.* Cambridge, MA: MIT Press.

Steriade, Donca (1999) Lexical conservatism in French adjectival liaison. In Jean-Marc Authier, Barbara E. Bullock et Lisa A. Reed (eds) *Formal Perspectives on Romance Linguistics* 243–270. Amsterdam: John Benjamins.

Tranel, Bernard (1981) *Concreteness in Generative Phonology. Evidence from French.* Berkeley/Los Angeles/Londres: University of California Press.

Tranel, Bernard (1990) On suppletion and French liaison. *Probus* 2.2: 169–208.

Tranel, Bernard (1996) French Liaison and Elision Revisited: a unified account within Optimality Theory. In Claudia Parodi, Carlos Quicoli, Mario Saltarelli et María-Luisa Zubizarreta (eds) *Aspects of Romance Linguistics* 433–455. Washington, DC: Georgetown University Press.

Tranel, Bernard (1998) Questioning Generalized Suppletion. Communication présentée au Fourth South Western Optimality Theory Workshop, University of Arizona, Tucson, April 4.

Tranel, Bernard (2000) Aspects de la phonologie du français et la Théorie de l'optimalité. *Langue française* 126: 39–72.

Vairasse d'Allais, Denis (1681) *Grammaire méthodique, contenant en abrégé les principes de cet art et les règles les plus nécessaires de la langue française dans un ordre clair et naturel.* Paris: chez l'auteur.

Wagner, Robert-Léon et Pinchon, Jacqueline (1962) *Grammaire française classique et moderne*. Paris: Hachette.

4 The nature of allomorphy and exceptionality: Evidence from Burushaski plurals*

Patrik Bye (University of Tromsø, CASTL / University of Nordland)

4.1 Introduction

Linguistic theory is founded on two ancient dichotomies: the division between the predictable, or rule-governed ('the grammar'), and the unpredictable ('the listed', 'the lexicon') (cf. Joseph 2000), and the division between the functionally motivated, or natural, and the functionally arbitrary. What makes suppletive allomorphy so interesting is that it falls on the boundaries between these domains. Take the distinction between the rule-governed and the listed. On the one hand, the variation in suppletive allomorphs' *shape* cannot be derived by rule, and so distinct underlying forms must be posited for each suppletive allomorph. On the other hand, the *distribution* of suppletive allomorphs is largely rule-governed, ignoring of course lexically listed cases such as *oxen*. When we hold suppletive allomorphy up against the distinction between motivated and arbitrary, matters become more complicated still. The domain of rule-governed phenomena and the domain of natural phenomena very largely overlap in phonology – phonological rules by and large make good phonetic sense. This concurrence between the two domains has provided the impetus for most theoretical innovation in generative phonology, beginning with the SPE's flirtation with marked and unmarked feature values (Chomsky and Halle 1968), through the development of non-linear representations (e.g. Goldsmith 1979), right up to the advent of Optimality Theory (Prince and Smolensky 2004). As the theory has developed, the favoured locus for encoding substantive considerations of naturalness has changed. In the

Affiliation: Faculty of Professional Studies, University of Nordland, Bodø, Norway wake of SPE, it shifted from rules to representations and, most recently, from representations to output-oriented constraints.

Nevertheless, despite the fact that naturalness has remained a powerful criterion for evaluating competing theories of grammar in phonology, the concurrence of rule-governed and natural is far from perfect. In fact, natural language displays both possible types of mismatch: distributions that are predictable but not natural, and distributions that are natural but not predictable.

This chapter provides a detailed illustration of this drawing on the complex allomorphy of pluralization in Burushaski (pronounced [burúʃaski]), a language isolate spoken by approximately 90,000 people in the Hunza Valley in the Karakoram of northwestern Pakistan (Berger 1990).[2] Burushaski is spoken in three major dialects, the closely related Hunza and Nager dialects (Lorimer 1935–1938; Berger 1998), and the more divergent Yasin dialect (Lorimer 1962; Berger 1974, 1992; Tiffou and Pesot 1989; Morin and Tiffou 1989), which is the basis for the present study. The present paper relies on a sample of over 1,400 nouns and adjectives in Yasin Burushaski culled from the dictionaries by Berger (1974) and Morin and Tiffou (1989). The complete sample is supplied in the Appendix.

Burushaski's most significant linguistic neighbours are Shina and Khowar, both of which belong to the Dardic branch of the Indo-Aryan languages. At different times, both Shina and Khowar have exerted a great influence on the Burushaski lexicon. Most Yasin Burusho also speak Khowar as a second language (Berger 1974: 1), and according to Morin and Tiffou (1989: 5), Burushaski and Khowar have been in contact for two centuries. Most recently, Burushaski has borrowed from literary Urdu through military service and schooling. Loans from English are also found, most often having come via Urdu.

The remainder of the paper is structured as follows. Section 4.2 provides relevant empirical background about the phonological structure and gender system of Burushaski. Section 4.3 sets out the alternative theories of allomorphy. Section 4.4 describes the synchrony of allomorph selection in Burushaski and gives special attention to rule-governed but unmotivated distributions. Section 4.5 tackles the question of how exceptional patterns of allomorphy emerged diachronically and shows that much exceptionality is motivated. Section 4.6 concludes.

4.2 Empirical background

4.2.1 Inventory

The segment inventory of Yasin Burushaski is shown in (1). The most detailed description of the phonology of this variety to date is Tiffou and Pesot (1989: 7–14).[3] The system of transcription used in the inventory and throughout the article is the one used in Morin and Tiffou (1989), and Tiffou and Pesot (1989).[4] Where the conventions for transcription diverge from those of the IPA, the IPA counterparts are noted below in square brackets.

(1) *Yasin Burushaski segment inventory*[5]

p	t	c [ts]	č [tɕ]	ṭ [ʈ]	ç [ʈʂ]	k	q
ph	th		čh [tɕh]	ṭh [ʈʰ]	çh [ʈʂh]	kh	
		s	š [ɕ]		ṣ [ʂ]		x [χ]
b	d	z	j~ž [dʒ~ʒ]	ḍ[ɖ]	j̣~ẓ [ɖʐ~ʐ]	g [ɡ]	ɣ [ʁ]
m	n					ŋ	
	l			r			
w			y [j]				
							h
i		u		ī [iː]	ū [uː]		
e		o		ē [eː]	ō [oː]		
	a			ā [aː]			

Burushaski distinguishes three series of what we may broadly characterize as 'occlusives' (plosives and affricates): unaspirated fortis, unaspirated lenis, and aspirated.[6] The occlusive system distinguishes labial, coronal and dorsal places of articulation. The coronals are especially rich in contrasts. There are both alveolar and retroflex plosives, and alveolar, palatoalveolar and retroflex affricates. There is a distinction in dorsals between velar and uvular. Burushaski also has fricatives, nasals, liquids and glides. The sounds /c/ and /q/ stand out as exceptional both because they lack aspirated counterparts and their lenis counterparts are continuants [z, ʁ] rather than occlusives *[dz, ɢ]. The affricates /j/ and /j̣/ have continuant allophones [ž] and [ẓ] in coda position. I follow my sources in indicating this variation in the transcriptions.

Burushaski has a lexical accent distinction, as evidenced by minimal pairs like /baré/ 'behold!' vs. /báre/ 'of the valley', and /ḍuḍúr/ 'apricot species' vs. /ḍúḍur/ 'small hole'. Default accent falls on the second mora from the left edge of the word. The effect of this is seen most clearly in verbs when prefixes are added, e.g. *čaɣúrum* 'cold', *du-čáɣur-i* 'it (inanimate) gets cold', *du-mú-čaɣur-i* 'she gets cold', *a-tú-mu-čaɣur-i* 'she doesn't get cold'.

Monosyllabic nouns may be lexically accented on their stem or unaccented. With an unaccented CVC stem, the accent falls on the first mora of the suffix or the suffix train in line with the requirements of default accent, as shown in (2a). Accented CVC stems retain the accent on the root even when suffixed, as shown in (2b).

(2) a. Unaccented stems

/ṣaq+iŋ/	→	ṣaqíŋ	'mountain pasture'
/nal+iŋ/	→	nalíŋ	'yoke (in agriculture)'
/gir+iŋ/	→	giríŋ	'night'

b. Accented stems

/bál+iŋ/	→	báliŋ	'walnut'
/kél+iŋ/	→	kéliŋ	'wrinkle'
/ɣő́r+iŋ/	→	ɣő́riŋ	'fissure, cave'

Burushaski would also appear to have lexically accented suffixes. As far as I am able to tell, these suffixes invariably attach to CVC stems and they are always dominant, i.e. they suppress realization of whatever accent specification there is on the root (cf. Alderete 2001). The effect can be seen in monosyllabic nouns that vary in their choice of suffix in the plural, e.g. /čóṭ+a/→ *čóṭa* 'bud' (accented root + unaccented suffix), but /čóṭ+ánc/→ *čoṭánc* 'buds' (accented root + dominant accented suffix). In *čóṭa*, lexical accent on the stem is betrayed by the suppression of the default pattern, which would have given **čóṭa*. The suffix {-ánc}, however, is always accented, even where there is a lexical accent on the root, as in *čoṭánc*. In the absence of variation in choice of suffix, e.g. *mukánc* 'pearl', the default accent pattern and suffixal dominance converge on the same result and, in these cases, it makes no difference whether we posit a lexical accent on the root or not. Burushaski now has a large number of borrowed nouns, in which there seems to be no restriction on the location of the accent, e.g. *čatibói*, 'devastating flood' (< Khowar), *ešxuší*, 'great joy' (< Urdu), *boiexaná* 'kitchen' (< Urdu).

4.2.2 Syllable structure

In the Burushaski syllable, onsets are optional and codas are permitted. The language also allows complex onsets, but generally only where C_1 is a plosive and C_2 is /r/. Examples are: *prandélas* (type of insect), troq 'spicy', *crap* 'check a fever', *kraṣ* 'make a rubbing sound', *brik* 'resist', *drap* 'draughts (game)', *grinč* 'giant'. Berger mentions only two forms in which C_2 is /l/: *blok* 'bud', *phlak* 'upper part of cap', and one where C_1 is a fricative (*zran -mán-* 'to jerk').

In word-internal coda position, native words allow a liquid or a homorganic nasal, or one of the sibilants /s š ṣ/ followed by a voiceless oral stop, e.g. *pandár* 'wedding gift offered by guests', *xánjo* 'vegetable soup with ghee', *óṣṭana* 'half rupee', *dušmán* 'enemy', *γostá* 'leavened pastry'. These restrictions are apparently no longer synchronically meaningful, due to the inundation of the Burushaski lexicon with Urdu, Khowar and English loanwords, which abundantly violate the condition. Examples are *imdát* 'aide', *kiftén* 'captain', *takmá* 'medal, decoration', and *bažγalí* 'kind of wheat'. Word-finally a wider range of consonants is permitted, especially in loanwords from Urdu and Khowar. Examples: *baitáp* 'covetous', *baléṭ* 'experienced', *ajalúk* 'wave (< Kho.)', *abláq* 'piebald (< Urdu)', *čamáx* 'lighter', *ambróz* 'kind of pear', *buẓ* 'to get dishevelled', *ataléγ* (title of Yasin dignitary).

Word-finally complex codas of liquid/nasal + plosive, or sibilant + plosive are permitted, e.g. *balt* 'apple', *ronz* 'moufflon', *patráinč* 'hunting mask', *bakínç* 'razor', *xarč* 'expenditure', *išq* 'to love', just 'lined up', *margušt* 'climbing plant'.

4.2.3 Gender

Burushaski has four agreement classes or genders, assigned according to semantic criteria. The system has a great deal in common with those found in Dyirbal (Pama-Nyungan; Queensland), Ket (Palaeosiberian; Siberia), Lak (Caucasian; Dagestan) and the Dravidian languages (for references see Corbett 1991: 7–32). The traditional terms for the genders, due to Lorimer (1935–1938), are 'hm' (human male), 'hf' (human female), 'x' (non-human animate), and 'y' (inanimate). To illustrate the agreement classes, I give the paradigm for *-wár-* 'be tired' in (3). Agreement is signalled by means of a prefix on the predicate as well as variation in the form of the verb 'be'. In the first person, the suffix is {-am-} rather than {-um-}, which appears elsewhere.

(3) *Gender agreement in predicates* -wár- *'to be tired' present* (Tiffou and Pesot 1989:53)

	SG		PL	
1	ja a-wárčam ba	'I am tired'	mi mi-wárčam ban	'we are tired'
2	un gu-wárčum ba	'you are tired'	ma ma-wárčum ban	'you are tired'
3 hm	ne wárčum bái	'he is tired'	we u-wárčum ban	'they are tired'
hf	mo mu-wárčum bu	'she is tired'		
x	se wárčum bi	'it is tired'	ce (u-)wárčum bién	'they are tired'
y	te wárčum duá	'it is tired'	ke wárčum bicá	'they are tired'

With a few wrinkles, the semantic rules for gender assignment are straightforward. While all animals fall into the *x* gender without exception, not all inanimates are assigned to the *y* gender. Berger (1974: 13–14, §§ 43–47) explains that the *x* class, in addition to animals, takes substances in fragmentary and countable pieces, stone, wood, and objects made from these. Into *y* fall liquids, cohesive or finely grained substances, fire, collectives, abstracta and anything immaterial (language, dream, natural and supernatural forces, etc.). Smaller plants and body parts seem to be arbitrarily distributed between *x* and *y*. Fruits are *x* (individuable), while trees (conceived as fruit collectives) are *y*. Stone and wood are *x*. This is initially surprising, but natural if considered from the perspective of their use in manufacturing countable artefacts. Also, iron weapons are unexpectedly *y*. Tiffou and Pesot (1989: 16) explain this as follows: 'Pour les Bourouchos, le pouvoir de tuer constitue une force magique, qui l'emporte sur la réalité de l'objet.' As we shall see, aspects of the Burushaski worldview are also relevant to understanding semantically conditioned allomorphy.

For the purposes of plural formation, *h* nominals take a superset of the plural allomorphs associated with *x*. As we shall see in Section 4.4.1, nouns in the *h* gender evince some semantically conditioned allomorphy, but otherwise *x* and *h* have the same plural markers. There is no overlap in the sets of plural allomorphs used by the *x/h* and *y* classes.

4.2.4 Noun stem shape

The shape of the root plays an essential part in allomorph selection. The most important condition for choice of allomorph – important because it cuts across both the animate and inanimate classes – is whether the stem ends in a consonant or a vowel. For animates, if the stem ends in a consonant, the nature of the consonant also becomes relevant. Also for animates, there are allomorphs of the plural that attach exclusively to a special class of CVC stems, which always have a short vowel.[7] There are also monosyllabic stems with the shapes CV, CVV and CVVC, but these select from the same set of allomorphs as plurisyllabic stems. Examples of the three types of monosyllabic stem are shown in (4).

(4) *Monosyllables*

a. CV

nyá	'bear'
sú	'muzzle (of pot)'
pho	'scab, pustule'

b. CVC
   qaf 'claw, fork'
   blok 'bud'
   yoșț 'ambassador'
c. CVV
   șaú 'wild rose-bush'
d. CVVC
   jẫs 'small hoe'
   waíz 'preacher'
   taún 'wooden box for flower'

Finally, there are two subminimal stems, shown in (5), both of them inalienable.

(5) *Subminimal stems*
-s 'heart'
-ș 'throat'

4.3 Allomorph selection

4.3.1 Allomorphy as the emergence of the unmarked

Since the advent of Optimality Theory (Prince and Smolensky 2004; McCarthy and Prince 2001), there has been a great deal of work to show that phonologically conditioned suppletive allomorph distribution (SAD) is not only predictable but motivated, an effect of 'the emergence of the unmarked' (McCarthy and Prince 1994). Important references for this markedness-driven approach include Mester (1994), Tranel (1996a,b), Kager (1996), Mascaró (1996), Rubach and Booij (2001), McCarthy (2002: 153–156, 183–184), Green (2005), Wolf (2007), and many others.[8] In the markedness-driven view, allomorphs compete directly for insertion on the host. Because they compete, each allomorph has to be present in the input in the form of a disjunction and the task of choosing between them devolves to the constraint hierarchy. In the ideal case, given allomorphs X and Y which appear respectively in the environments A__B and C__D, there should be some markedness constraint M_1 that returns the harmonic ordering AXB over AYB and some (other) markedness constraint M_2 exerting the preference CYD over CXD. Exactly this situation is exemplified by Moroccan Arabic (Mascaró 1996), which has perhaps become the classic demonstration of markedness-driven allomorph selection. The third person masculine pronominal clitic in this variety varies in shape between {-u} after stems ending in a consonant and {-h} after stems ending in a vowel, e.g.

xtˤa-h 'his error' but *ktab-u* 'his book'. Inverting the distributions results in the violation of syllabic well-formedness constraints in each contrafactual stem-allomorph combination: ONSET in **xtˤa-u*, and NOCODA in **ktab-h*.

In other cases of SAD, it may be possible only to identify a single markedness constraint M_1, and there is no M_2 to enforce the preference CYD over CXD. A case of this type is found in Djabugay, a Pama-Nyungan language spoken in Queensland, Australia (Patz 1991:269; Kager 1996). In this language, there are two allomorphs of the genitive, {-n} after vowel-final stems, and {-ŋun} after consonant-final stems, e.g. *guludu-n* 'dove-GEN' vs. *gaɲal-ŋun* 'goanna-GEN'. Kager proposes that the distribution of {-n} derives from an independent fact about Djabugay prosody, that complex codas are disallowed. Given the choice between *gaɲalŋun* (6a) and *gaɲaln* (6b), (6a) is preferred by *COMPLEX CODA (*CXCODA), which in Djabugay is undominated.

(6)

/gaɲal+{-n, -ŋun}/	*CXCODA	MAX
a. ☞ gaɲalŋun		
b. gaɲaln	*!	

So far so good. For the vowel-final stems, however, an alternative explanation must be devised, since the contrafactual combination *guluduŋun is phonotactically unimpeachable. In (7), both (7a) and (7b) fare equally on the structural well-formedness constraint NOCODA. Kager observes, however, that since the expression we want to rule out contains more segments than the correct form guludun, *guluduŋun entails greater violation of *STRUC ('do not have structure').[9] In (7), *STRUC assesses a mark against each segment in the candidate representation.

(7)

/guludu+{-n, -ŋun}/	NOCODA	*STRUC
a. guluduŋun	*	********!*
b. ☞ guludun	*	*******

In this case, the expressions that we are comparing (in the abstract, CYD and CXD) are comparable and, in addition, CYD (*guludun*) has a proper subset of the violations of CXD (*guluduŋun*), making CYD optimal.

In still other cases, CYD and CXD will not be comparable in this way, and here the analyst must resort to other means to derive the preference. One way is to choose some low-ranked, perhaps otherwise inactive, markedness constraint to exert the preference CYD over CXD. There are many cases of this type. In Tahitian (Polynesian, French Polynesia; Tryon 1970; Lazard and Peltzer 2000; Paster 2006: 39f.), the causative/factitive is marked by attaching haʔa- to stems beginning with a labial /p f v m/ and {faʔa-} elsewhere. The observation that {faʔa-} does not attach to labial-initial stems looks suspiciously like an instance of the Obligatory Contour Principle (OCP) at work (Leben 1973, Goldsmith 1979, McCarthy 1986), and it is perfectly possible to get the pattern by, say, ranking $\text{OCP}_{\text{labial}}$ above *h. However, $\text{OCP}_{\text{labial}}$ is not demonstrably active in Tahitian phonology otherwise. This is borne out by the existence of a small number of labial-initial roots that idiosyncratically take {faʔa-} rather than the expected {haʔa-}, as well as the apparently happy coexistence of labials within roots (*faufaʔa* 'profit'). Beyond the limited and partially lexically governed variation between {faʔa-} and {haʔa-}, neither morpheme structure nor alternations provide support for the activity of $\text{OCP}_{\text{labial}}$ in Tahitian. Another point, which is usually missed in discussions of cases like this, is that we would also need some way of asserting the *default* preference {faʔa-} over {haʔa-} for stems that do not begin with a labial consonant, e.g. *h >> *f. In the classic case of the emergence of the unmarked, some low-ranked markedness constraint whose effect is generally invisible is allowed to emerge in certain circumstances. In Sanskrit, for example, complex onsets are generally permitted, providing an independent ranking argument for FAITH >> *COMPLEX ONSET. The effect of *COMPLEX ONSET emerges in reduplication, e.g. the intensive *kan-krand-* 'cry out', where the onset of the reduplicant *kan-* displays cluster simplification /kr/→ k. In the case of the default preference of {faʔa-} over {haʔa-}, on the other hand, an independent ranking argument is precisely what is lacking. The only evidence for ranking *h over *f is the distribution of the allomorphs itself, and so invoking the emergence of the unmarked in cases like these smacks of the *ad hoc* – the ranking serves the exclusive purpose of getting the default preference to work out right without having to appeal to notions like subcategorization. Hungarian furnishes a similar example. The second person present tense indefinite is marked by {-l} following a stem ending in a sibilant, and {-s} elsewhere. Again, the OCP seems to be the constraint favouring the {-l} allomorph (here $\text{OCP}_{\text{sibilant}}$), but the default preference {-s} over {-l} would have to be handled using an *ad hoc* ranking *LATERAL >> *SIBILANT.

In sum, the markedness-driven approach does not reduce to a single schema for dealing with cases where SAD appears phonologically motivated, or partially so. This fragmentation raises important questions about the attractiveness of the markedness-driven approach. In the next section I will introduce an alternative approach to allomorph selection.

4.3.2 Allomorphy as selection

In the last few years, work by Paster (2005, 2006, this volume) and Bye (2007) has challenged the markedness-based view, arguing instead that SAD should be encoded in terms of language-specific combinatorial requirements. This is prompted by the existence of a number of cases in which SAD is either neutral with respect to universal markedness, or the opposite of what markedness constraints would predict. Such cases may be said to be phonologically *conditioned* without being phonologically *motivated* – what Wolf (this volume) dubs 'arbitrary preference'. Wolf and a number of other researchers, such as Mascaró (2007), see arbitrary preference as tractable using mechanisms that complement rather than replace the markedness-driven type of account. We shall return to these approaches in more detail below.

According to the current proposal, SAD is governed by what Koenig (1999) calls 'medium-sized generalizations'. Medium-sized generalizations are language-specific and pick out classes of lexemes on the basis of some semantic, (morpho)syntactic or phonological property. Let us have a look at a few examples to get the flavour of the kind of thing intended.

In English, nouns for articles of clothing for the lower part of the body are systematically *pluralia tantum*, e.g. *trousers*, *pants*, *breeches*, *knickerbockers*, *tights*, *trunks*, *speedos*, *knickers*, *briefs*, *Y-fronts*, *boxers*. Although it hardly qualifies for inclusion in Universal Grammar, the pattern is clearly productive, as evidenced by the fact that novel slang words in the same semantic field receive the same treatment across the English-speaking world, e.g. *kecks* and *wabs* (Northern England), *tighty-whities* (US), *trolleys* (New Zealand).[10]

In Latin (Bennett 1999; Gildersleeve and Lodge 1999; Hale and Buck 1966), second declension nouns have a genitive in *-ōrum*, e.g. *hortus~hortōrum* 'garden', *bellum~bellōrum* 'war', *puer~puerōrum* 'boy'. Words denoting coins and measures in this declension, on the other hand, take *-um*, e.g. *talentum*, *sēstertium*, *modium* 'of measures', *iūgerum* 'of acres', *nummum* 'of moneys', *dēnārium*, *tetrachmum*, and so on.

Another good example is the kind of phonological and semantic criteria used in assigning gender in the Germanic languages. In German, nouns ending in an unstressed *-e* are generally feminine. Corbett (1991) is replete with examples of phonologically conditioned gender assignment. German also furnishes ample evidence of assignment rules based on inclusion within a semantic field, many of them quite specific and apparently unrelated to the gender's semantic core. Thus, nouns for musical instruments are generally neuter (Steinmetz 1986; Nelson 1998). The association, in a given semantic field, of nouns with a particular sound shape with a particular gender is functionally entirely arbitrary, and yet rule-governed.

Now let us turn to the question where such medium-sized generalizations fit into the overall scheme of things. The conception of the lexicon known from most generative linguistic theory is 'flat', a mere list of sound-meaning pairs. According to Koenig and Jurafsky (1995), and Koenig (1999), in addition to being a repository of lexical items, the lexicon also encodes generalizations over those lexical items. Koenig and Jurafsky's conception of the lexicon is as a hierarchical inheritance network, which Bye (2007) dubs the 'morpholexicon'.

The terminal nodes in the hierarchy are generally lexemes rather than fully inflected forms, which are underspecified and compiled on-line. Lexemes are organized into higher-order *classes*, each of which is represented in the hierarchy with a node and an associated feature structure. It is this property that allows us to deal with arbitrary language-specific properties (Koenig's 'medium-sized generalizations') as holding of *classes* of words rather than just individual items. For example, the English morpholexicon contains a feature structure for the lexical item 'play' specifying its semantic, morphosyntactic and phonological properties. The verb 'play' belongs to the superordinate class of intransitive verbs, which is represented in the hierarchy with its own feature structure, itself a proper subset of the feature structure for 'play'. The node for intransitive verbs is in its turn dominated by the node for verbs, and so on. Nodes are said to 'inherit' the information associated with the node that dominates them.

The hierarchical morpholexicon extends Saussure's notion of *l'arbitraire du signe* in a novel way. In the flat conception of mainstream generative grammar, entries form arbitrary pairings of sound and meaning. In the hierarchical conception of the lexicon, non-terminal nodes higher up in the hierarchy may also be paired with sound in a language-particular way. These pairings, which we may refer to as *constructions*, in essence constitute the *morphology* of the language: hence my proposed use of the term 'morpholexicon'. For example, in English the third person singular present of verbs is marked by affixing {-z}. The pairing of 'verb in third person singular present' and the form {-z} is a piece of language-specific (essentially lexical) knowledge, which may be encoded as the morpholexical constraint given in (8).

(8) SELECT($V_{3sg.pres}$, -z): Verbs in the third person singular present form select the suffix {-z}.

The constraint in (8) takes two arguments: a selector (a class of stems defined by some property, in this case the intensional property of being a verb in the third person singular), and a phonological realization, in this case an affix along with a specification of its attachment site (left/right edge of stem, here the right edge).[11] This has much in common with the idea that lexical entries are implemented by constraints, which has surfaced earlier in Optimality Theory (Hammond 1995; Russell 1995, 1999).

Some verbs have an irregular third person plural form, e.g. *is*, *has*, *does*. In such cases, the morpholexicon must supply a precompiled form, an exception to the general situation in which only lexemes are terminal nodes. The conditions for the precompiled form are more specific than the contrafactual regular forms (**bes*, **haves*, **does* [du:z]), and so the Elsewhere Principle gives the irregular forms priority. This may be translated into the strict domination of OT, such that the specific constraint SELECT($\text{BE}_{3sg.pres}$, [ɪz]) outranks general SELECT($V_{3sg.pres}$, -z).

In some cases, phonological properties of the lexeme or lexeme class influence exponence. It is natural to incorporate this information into the selector. However, if allomorph selection may be morpholexically determined, we predict that there should be cases of SAD that are phonologically arbitrary in that they are either neutral with respect to the demands of phonological markedness and faithfulness constraints, or go against them. French-lexified Haitian Creole (Hall 1953; Klein 2003; Bye 2007; Bonet *et al.* 2007) provides a striking example of this kind of case. Simplifying slightly, the suffixed definite article varies in shape between {-a} and {-la}, but the distribution is the exact opposite of what syllabic well-formedness constraints (ONSET and NOCODA) would predict: {-la} is selected by stems ending in a consonant, e.g. *malad-la* 'the sick (person)', and {-a} by stems ending in a vowel, e.g. *papa-a* 'the father'.[12] We would have the constraints (9) and (10). (Note that 'V]' stands here for a vowel-final stem.)

(9) SELECT($C]_{Ndef.sg}$, -la): Consonant-final nouns in the definite singular form select the suffix {-la}.

(10) SELECT($V]_{Ndef.sg}$, -a): Vowel-final nouns in the definite singular form select the suffix {-a}.

There would appear to be three ways in which morpholexical constraints may be integrated with the universal constraints supplied by CON. One possibility is that they interact directly in H-EVAL. Let us call this the 'Direct Interaction Hypothesis'.[13] In the case of Haitian Creole, the SELECT constraints given above in (9) and (10) must respectively dominate NOCODA and ONSET. The tableau in (11) illustrates how this approach works given an input with the stem /papa/ and the allomorphs of the definite in disjunction.

(11)

/papa+{-a, -la}/	Select(V]$_{\text{Ndef.sg}}$, -a)	Onset
a. ☞ pa.pa.|a		*
b. pa.pa.|la	*!	

Another possibility, issuing from Orgun and Sprouse's work on the theory of Control and further developed in Bye (2007), is that morpholexical constraints *filter* the output of Eval. This work explicitly attempts to relate the phenomenon of complementary distribution to the work on absolute ungrammaticality (cf. McCarthy and Wolf 2005; Rice 2007). Under the conception in Bye (2007), each allomorph is evaluated separately, and the Select constraints are relegated to the Morpholexical Control component, which is ordered after Eval. Once Eval has found the optimal candidate, the output must run the gauntlet of the language-specific constraints in Morpholexical Control, where it is either accepted or rejected (ruled absolutely ungrammatical). This is illustrated in (12) and (13) for /papa/. Both *papaa* and *papala* are phonotactically well-formed in Haitian Creole, but in Morpholexical Control the latter form is rejected by (10). Acceptance and rejection are indicated by '👍' and '👎' respectively.

(12)

	/papa+a/	Max	Dep	Onset
Eval	a. ☞ pa.pa.|a			*
	b. pa.pa.|la		*!	
	c. pa.pa	*!		
MControl		Select(V]$_{\text{Ndef.sg}}$, -a)		
	👍 pa.pa.|a	✓		

(13)

	/papa+la/	Max	Dep	Onset
Eval	a. pa.pa.|a	*!		*
	b. ☞ pa.pa.|la			
	c. pa.pa	*!		
MControl		Select(V]$_{\text{Ndef.sg}}$, -a)		
	👎 pa.pa.|la	*!		

The third possibility is that morpholexical constraints are operative *before* Eval. This possibility will not be pursued further here, but see Bye (2007) and the morpheme-based account of Bye and Svenonius (2012: 438f.) for detailed discussion. For expository purposes, I will in what follows be assuming the Direct Interaction Hypothesis.

It may be helpful to juxtapose the current proposal with others dealing with arbitrary preference. One such approach relies on an extended conception of faithfulness. Bonet (2004), Kikuchi (2006), Bonet *et al.* (2007), and Mascaró (2007) propose that allomorphs may be extrinsically ordered in the lexicon. Departures from the stipulated lexical priority are punished by the constraint PRIORITY (e.g. Bonet *et al.* 2007: 906), which requires that the output respect the lexically specified ordering. Given an ordering {X, Y, Z, …}, PRIORITY is only satisfied when allomorph X is used. Using allomorphs from lower down in the list gives progressively worse violations on PRIORITY (Y scores 1 mark, Z two). Picanço (2002) proposes to capture arbitrary preference through a language-specific ranking of PARSE-MORPH constraints. Our hypothetical arbitrary preference would be implemented with the ranking PARSE-MORPH(X) >> PARSE-MORPH(Y) >> PARSE-MORPH(Z). Neither of these implementations require any departure from the basic markedness-driven view. PRIORITY and PARSE-MORPH simply take care of those cases where allomorph preference cannot be attributed to markedness. Wolf (this volume), who argues that lexical insertion occurs in the phonological component, presents a proposal that is very similar in spirit to the one outlined here, although it differs in crucial respects. In his essentially morpheme-based approach, allomorphs are envisioned as spelling out morphosyntactic feature bundles emitted by the syntax. This conception leads Wolf to implement arbitrary phonological preference differently to the way proposed here. Adopting the mainstream assumption that the phonology plays no role in the selection of lexical items, Wolf ends up having to claim, given an arbitrary preference X over Y, that X spells out a featural superset of Y (i.e. X preempts Y because its morphosyntactic conditions are more specific). In the current approach, selection is governed by the morpholexicon, where the boundaries between autonomous syntactic, semantic and phonological modules break down. Allomorph selection under the current proposal calls not just on morphosyntactic features, such as gender, but calls directly on semantic and phonological information as well.

4.3.3 Duplication

All approaches that explicitly acknowledge the existence of arbitrary preferences, especially phonologically arbitrary preferences, raise the spectre of duplication. Given that some cases of SAD are phonologically conditioned without being phonologically motivated, learners must be capable of positing language-specific (morpholexical) constraints (or lexical priority orderings). The question is what, given this, learners do when faced with a case of SAD that is (or at least appears) phonologically motivated. There seem to be three possibilities. One possibility is that arbitrary and non-arbitrary preference are dealt with using *complementary* capacities. Learners only resort to language-specific strategies like morpholexical constraints or those discussed in the previous section when needed to capture distributions that cannot be laid at the door of markedness. A second possibility is that all allomorphy is dealt with one and the same type of capacity. Given that arbitrary preferences are established, the only conceptually necessary mechanisms for dealing with allomorphy in general would be the language-specific ones. In this case, the explanation for the overwhelming naturalness of SAD pointed out by researchers in OT must be sought in diachrony. This position, which is basically in agreement with Blevins' Evolutionary Phonology programme (2004, 2006), is the one explicitly adopted in Bye (2007) and in Paster (2006, this volume). (For another recent proposal in this direction, see also Embick 2010.) The third possibility is that the domains of arbitrary and non-arbitrary preference *overlap*, in which case universal 'true' phonological constraints and language-specific would partially duplicate each other. Considerations of theoretical parsimony would seem to disfavour the overlap model, and it is not obvious what the synchronic evidence for such duplication might be. It is, however, possible that both phonological and morpholexical generalizations are observable in speech processing errors. No such data exists for Burushaski, but in section 4.5, I will argue that it is reasonable to see certain kinds of exceptionality in SAD in Burushaski as deriving historically from speech processing errors that diagnose the covert activity of both morpholexical and markedness constraints.

4.4 Plural allomorph selection in Burushaski

Allomorph selection may be conditioned in one of three ways: (i) semantically/pragmatically, (ii) phonologically, or (iii) lexically. Section 4.4.1 addresses semantically and pragmatically conditioned allomorph selection, and Section 4.4.2 phonologically conditioned allomorph selection. In Section 4.4.3 we address the question of what happens when semantic/pragmatic and phonological criteria for allomorph selection conflict.

4.4.1 Semantically and pragmatically conditioned allomorph selection

The plural suffixes {-daru}, {-štaru}, {-tiŋ}, {-kón}, and {-bák} may only appear with nouns in the human class. Two of these, {-kón} and {-bák}, are only attested with one item each (*-cu -cukón* 'brother', *ṣádar ṣadarbák* 'servant'), and so are not considered further here. The remaining three are found with nouns referring to classes with quite well-defined semantic properties. The semantic basis of the class of nouns taking {-štaru} (or {-šteru}) is readily apparent – it contains all and only the nouns in the sample (12 in all) that refer to blood relatives (both lineal and collateral) in the parental generation or older, e.g. *bap* 'grandfather', *-nzu* 'aunt'.

There are 15 nouns in the sample that form their plural by suffixing {-daru}. Most of these refer to close family members in the same generation as or younger than ego, including consanguines, affines and 'fictive kin'. Thus, in addition to *-us* 'wife', we also find *raféq* 'beloved', and *-yál* 'friend'. It is interesting that this class also includes *aštán* 'ostler' (horses are very important in Burusho society) and *axón* 'mullah'.

The suffix {-tiŋ} is used with nouns referring to individuals that in one sense or another require 'handling with care', either because they are deemed especially worthy of consideration, or because they spell trouble, e.g. *sālé sālétiŋ* 'faithful woman' vs. *kančéni kančénitiŋ* 'fickle woman'. Classes based on a perceived need for circumspection are known from other languages, the most famous case being gender in Dyirbal (Dixon 1977; Lakoff 1990; Mylne 1995). In Burushaski, this 'handle-with-care' class includes royal personages (*badšá* 'king', *kaikaí* 'princess'), individuals with special spiritual gifts or in heightened spiritual states (*duagú* 'interpreter of the Qur'an', *hají* 'hajji, pilgrim to Mecca'), some supernatural beings (*parí* 'fairy', *phariště* 'angel'), people whose jobs entail working with sharp implements (*xansamá* 'cook', *lohár* 'knife-grinder'),[14] but also more socially disruptive character traits or the individuals that display them (*gadéru* 'crazy', *zenaxór* 'womanizer').[15]

For certain lexical items, there may be conflicting criteria for the choice of plural marker. Certain male relatives that otherwise might be expected to take {-daru} turn out in actual fact to select {-tiŋ}: *-yúhar yúhartiŋ* 'husband', and *-rar -rartiŋ*, *-rarišu* 'son-in-law', suggesting that, where both apply, the 'handle-with-care' tag has greater relative priority over that for kin.

Another issue has to do with variability. A number of {-tiŋ} nouns may also appear with the appropriate phonologically conditioned default suffix (see 4.2 below). Optionality in choice of suffix may reflect a lower perceived need for circumspection. Those nouns for which {-tiŋ} is obligatory in the plural refer to royalty and supernatural beings. Most other nouns that appear with {-tiŋ} permit variation.[16]

The basis for some assignments is not clear without deeper cultural knowledge, which has not been available to me. It is not obvious why *buzúrk* 'hermit, holy man' and *duagú* 'interpreter of the Qur'an, holy man' are listed as optionally taking {-tiŋ}, but *paiɣumbár* 'prophet', for example, is listed with {-išu}, the default suffix for consonant-final animate stems. Similarly, it is not clear why *hálkit* 'she-goat older than a year' should take the kin plural suffix {-daru} (*hálkitaru*) rather than {-išu}, or why *šarí* 'wife's brother' and *saróni* 'man's wife's sister/brother's wife' should take {-mu}, the default suffix for vowel-final animate stems, rather than {-daru}. Facts like these might raise questions about the productivity of the generalizations described here, but more insight into the cultural basis of these assignments is needed before reaching any such conclusion. The generalizations described so far are summed up as semantically conditioned SELECT constraints in (14).

(14) *Semantically conditioned plural allomorph selection in human stems*
   a. SELECT(HANDLE-WITH-CARE]$_{stem}$]$_{h.pl}$, -tiŋ): Human stems referring to persons that require circumspection select {-tiŋ} in the plural.
   b. SELECT(OLDER BLOOD RELATIVE]$_{stem}$]$_{h.pl}$, -štaru): Human stems referring to blood relatives in one's parents generation and older select {-štaru} in the plural.
   c. SELECT(KIN]$_{stem}$]$_{h.pl}$, -daru): Human stems referring to relatives select {-daru} in the plural.

Semantically conditioned allomorphy is not unknown in the world's languages. In Russian, the masculine plural is generally marked by {-i}, e.g. *blʲinɨ́* (блины) 'pancakes'. Nouns referring to jobs and professions ending in unstressed *-or* or *-er*, however, frequently take {-á}, and the pattern is gaining ground in colloquial Russian, e.g. *profʲésor profʲesorá* (профессора) 'professor', *dʲirʲéktor dʲirʲektorá* (директор) 'director', *inʒenʲér inʒenʲérɨ*, *inʒenʲerá* (инженеры, инженера) 'engineer' (Isačenko 1982: 97f.; cf. Janda 1999). The allomorphy of the ergative case in the Pama-Nyungan languages also turns up several examples. In Diyari (Austin 1981), for example, female personal names take {-ndu}, male personal names take {-li}, while other common nouns take {-yali}.

4.4.2 Phonologically conditioned allomorph selection

As mentioned earlier, the animate and inanimate classes are associated with distinct sets of plural allomorphs. Because each of these classes raise issues of their own, I have found it convenient to treat them in separate sections. Animates are dealt with immediately below in Section 4.4.2.1, inanimates in Section 4.4.2.2.

4.4.2.1 Animates

For the animate class, Berger (1974: 16f.) describes four phonologically delimitable types of stem associated with distinct plural suffixes. There are arguments for reducing this variation to three suffixes, {-yu} (*n*- and *s*-final stems), {-išu} (other C-final stems), and {-mu} (V-final stems).

The distributions of {-yu}, {-išu}, and {-mu} are formulated here on the basis of the 627 animate plurisyllables and non-CVC monosyllables (CV, CVV, CVVC) in the sample. Only a small fraction of these (21; 3%) are non-CVC monosyllables.

Consonant-final stems generally take the ending {-išu}. This rule has very high reliability. Out of a possible 244 stems, 226 (93%) take {-išu} in the expected manner. Examples of plurisyllables taking this suffix are shown in (15).

(15) aiždahár, aiždahárišu 'dragon'
humbák, humbákišu 'quiver'
soṭóp, soṭópišu 'stove'

CVVC stems behave in the same way, as shown in (16).

(16) sḗṭ, sḗṭišu 'merchant'
waíz, waízišu 'preacher'

Vowel-final plurisyllables take {-mu}, as shown in (17).[17] The generalization governing {-mu} is even more reliable. Of the 241 vowel-final plurisyllables and non-CVC monosyllables in the sample, 230 (95%) take {-mu}.

(17) cipíri, cipírimu 'person who blinks'
ɣormadí, ɣormadímu 'kind of bread'
ṭurpíču, ṭurpíčumu 'meadow lark'

There are only a few animate CV stems (7 in total), and these also take {-mu} as shown in (18).

(18) -mé, -mému 'tooth'
tá, támu 'leopard'
-ú, -úmu 'tear'

Given a markedness-driven approach, there is nothing unexpected about the distributions of {-išu} and {-mu}. Consider the vowel-final stem *ṭurpíču* 'meadow lark' shown in (19). The candidate that chooses {-išu} (19b) scores a violation of ONSET. Violation of ONSET can be repaired through deletion of the suffix-initial vowel (19c), or stem-final vowel (19d), but these repairs both entail violations of MAX. The least costly strategy, because it entails simultaneous satisfaction of both ONSET and MAX, is choosing the alternative allomorph {-mu} (19a).

(19)

/ṭurpíču+{-mu, -išu}/	ONSET	MAX
a. ☞ ṭur.pí.ču.|mu		
b. ṭur.pí.ču.|i.šu	*!	
c. ṭur.pí.ču.|šu		*!
d. ṭur.pí.|i.šu		*!

Now let us turn to the case where the input contains a consonant-final stem. This is shown in (20). Here, the selection of {-mu} results in a violation of NOCODA (20a). Again, repair by deletion is possible, as in candidates (20c) and (20d), but this results in violations of MAX. The actual winner (20b) achieves satisfaction of NOCODA and MAX in one fell swoop simply by selecting the other allomorph {-išu}.

(20)

/aiždahár+{-mu, -išu}/	NOCODA	MAX
a. aiž.da.hár.|mu	*!	
b. ☞ aiž.da.há.r|i.šu		
c. aiž.da.há.|mu		*!
d. aiž.da.há.r|u		*!

So far, the markedness-driven approach has fared well. Now let us consider stems ending in /n/ or /s/. Stems ending in a /n/ add the suffix {-yu}, as shown in (21). All 68 (100%) non-CVC stems in the sample use this suffix. The sequence [ny] is disallowed in Burushaski, at least word-medially (it occurs in initial position in the root *nya* 'bear'). In consequence, the stem-final /n/ is deleted.

(21) biṭán, biṭáyu (←/biṭán+yu/) 'soothsayer'
lanṭén, lanṭéyu (←/lanṭén+yu/) 'lantern'
taún, taúyu (←/taún+yu/) 'wooden box for flour'

Stems ending in /s/ generally add the ending {-u}. In addition, the stem-final /s/ always undergoes palatalization to [š]. Representative examples are shown in (22).

(22) éṣpaṭkus, éṣpaṭkušu (←/éṣpaṭkus+yu/) 'sheep between 6 and 12 months'
phópolanas, phópolanašu (←/phópolanas+yu/) 'blister'
úsas, úsašu (←/úsas+yu/) 'small stone for applying collyrium'

It is possible to see this as an instance of the same {-yu} suffix motivated for *n*-final stems in (21). In the case of *s*-final stems, the concatenation of /s/ and /y/ feeds coalescence to [š].[18]

The rule for suffixing {-yu} to *s*-final stems is less reliable than the rule for *n*-final stems. There are 67 *s*-final non-CVC stems in the sample. Of these, 52 (78%) are listed as exclusively occurring with {-yu}. As shown in (23), however, a smaller number of *s*-final stems form their plural with {-išu}, which, as we have seen, is the regular ending for stems ending in consonants other than /n/ or /s/. Eight *s*-final stems (13%) are listed only with {-išu}. The remaining two may occur with either {-yu} or {-išu}.

(23) ɣáqales, ɣáqalesišu 'scare-crow'
jāsús, jāsúsišu 'detective, informer, spy'
tapós, tapósišu 'eagle sp.'

Special mention must be made of items ending in a V+i diphthong /ei ai oi/. There are only six such items in the sample, but they all take {-išu}, not {-mu} as might be expected from the fact that they end in a vocalic segment. Examples are given in (24).

(24) čapléi, čapléišu 'sandal'
čatibói, čatibóišu 'devastating flood'
surunái, surunáišu 'oboe, bombard'

The pattern in (24) is partially explained if we assume that the second half of the diphthong is a coda glide. We shall return to this issue in below.

Assuming these generalizations are productive, one option is to account for the distributions directly using the following allomorph selection constraints in (25).

(25) *Phonologically conditioned plural allomorph selection in animate stems*

a. SELECT(n$]_{stem}$ $]_{anim.pl}$, -yu$_1$): Animate consonant-final stems ending in /n/ select {-yu} in the plural.

b. SELECT(s$]_{stem}$ $]_{anim.pl}$, -yu$_2$): Animate consonant-final stems ending in /s/ select {-yu} in the plural.

c. SELECT(C$]_{stem}$ $]_{anim.pl}$, -išu): Animate consonant-final stems select {-išu} in the plural.

d. SELECT(V$]_{stem}$$]_{anim.pl}$, -mu): Animate vowel-final stems select {-mu} in the plural.

The Elsewhere Principle allows us to rank the constraints in (25) as in (26). The constraints SELECT(n$]_{stem}$ $]_{anim.pl}$, -yu$_1$) and SELECT(s$]_{stem}$ $]_{anim.pl}$, -yu$_2$) do not conflict, and so they cannot be crucially ranked relative to one another. The same is true of SELECT(C$]_{stem}$ $]_{anim.pl}$, -išu) and SELECT(V$]_{stem}$$]_{anim.pl}$, -mu), whose conditions do not overlap.

(26) (25a), (25b) >> (25c), (25d)

Now let us compare this with the markedness-driven account of the same facts. In what follows I will develop such an account highlighting its strengths and weaknesses.

As shown earlier in (19) and (20), the selection of the correct allomorph in the markedness-driven approach is a trivial matter, as long as there is no more than a binary disjunction in the input. Adding a *third* allomorph into the equation, however, raises the problem of phonological underdetermination. In the case at hand, it is not obvious what decides between {-yu} and {-mu}. In terms of syllabic structure, both would seem to be equally good, and in tableau (27), the phonological grammar fails to return a unique optimal candidate. The undesired winner (27b) (marked with a frownie ☹) is as good as the desired winner (27a). Cf. (19).

(27)

/ṭurpíču+{-mu, -išu, -yu}/	ONSET
a. ☞ ṭur.pí.ču.|mu	
b. ☹ ṭur.pí.ču.|yu	
c. ṭur.pí.ču.|išu	*!

What seems to be missing from this picture is that there is an irreducible lexical element in SAD. The fact that vowel-final animate stems take {-mu} rather than {-yu} in the plural is an essentially arbitrary preference. Of course, it would be possible to pick some dimension on which {-yu} and {-mu} differ and where {-yu} comes off the worse, e.g. *GLIDE. But this would be an arbitrary move given that it is equally possible to identify dimensions on which [yu] is more harmonic than [mu], such as (to pick one) *NASAL. In order to generate the observed pattern we would have to rank *GLIDE above *NASAL, but there is no independent evidence for this – the only motivation for this ranking would be the distributional facts themselves, and so such an account would exploit the emergence of the unmarked in an *ad hoc* way. Inclusion of the constraint SELECT(V]$_{stem}$]$_{anim.pl}$, -mu) as in (28) makes the arbitariness of the preference explicit. Once we make this move, however, the markedness constraints no longer have any crucial role to play in the grammar, since SELECT(V]$_{stem}$]$_{anim.pl}$, -mu) is uniquely satisfied by the optimal candidate. This raises the question whether allomorphy should be seen as markedness-driven at all.

(28)

/ṭurpíču+{-mu, -išu, -yu}/	ONSET	SELECT(V]$_{stem}$]$_{anim.pl}$, -mu)
a. ☞ ṭur.pí.ču.|mu		
b. ṭur.pí.ču.|yu		*!
c. ṭur.pí.ču.|išu	*!	*

The distribution of {-yu} raises other serious problems for the markedness-driven approach, since it is at least partly non-optimizing. For *s*-final stems, a partial markedness-based account is possible. Adding {-išu} to a *s*-final stem would result in a violation of some form of the OCP, e.g. OCP$_{sibilant}$ in (29).

(29) OCP$_{sibilant}$: Adjacent sibilants are disallowed.

(30)

/éṣpaṭkus$_1$+{-mu, -išu, -y$_2$u}/	*sy	NOCODA	OCP$_{sib}$	UNIFORMITY
a. éṣ.paṭ.kus.|mu		*!		
b. éṣ.paṭ.ku.s|i.šu			*!	
c. ☞ éṣ.paṭ.ku.š$_{1,2}$u				*
d. éṣ.paṭ.kus$_1$.|y$_2$u	*!	*!		

In tableau (30), candidate (30a), although phonotactically possible, is eliminated by NOCODA. (30d) scores a violation mark on both NOCODA and the sequential constraint *sy, which is undominated in Burushaski. The choice comes down to choosing {-išu}, (30b), and coalescing /s+y/ to *š*, as in (30c), which violates the faithfulness constraint UNIFORMITY. The optimality of (30c) depends on being able to make the assumption that marks assessed on UNIFORMITY rank lower than those on OCP_{sib}. As was the case with {-yu} and {-mu} above, there is no independent evidence for this ranking.

Even if we allow for the possibility of constraint rankings whose only motivation is the distribution of allomorphs, there is no such story for *n*-final stems. Indeed, there is every reason why *n*-final stems *shouldn't* take {-yu}.

Apart from the one item *nya* 'bear', the sequence [ny] is disallowed, so the stem-final /n/ is deleted on addition of the suffix. Not only does the selection of the {-yu} allomorph force a gratuitous violation of MAX, but the condition for selecting {-yu} in the first place is, in the terminology of McCarthy (1999), also non-surface apparent. Consider the tableau in (31). The desired winner (31f), which is both unfaithful and opaque, is harmonically bounded over the constraints. Specifically, it is bested by (31c), which is unfaithful but transparent, and (31b), which is both faithful and transparent.

(31)

/girán+{-mu, -išu, -yu}/	NOCODA	*ny	MAX
a. gi.rán.|mu			*!
b. ☹ gi.rá.n|i.šu			
c. gi.rá.|mu			*!
d. gi.rá.n|u			*!
e. gi.rán.|yu	*!	*!	
f. ☞ gi.rá.|yu			¡*!

We can observe similar opacity in the stems with a final V+i diphthong in (24). If /i/ is actually parsed as a coda glide (e.g. *čatibóy* instead of *čatibói* 'devastating flood'), this would condition the selection of {-išu} (e.g. **čatibóyišu*), but this in turn results in a violation of the constraint against homorganic glide+vowel sequences: *yi and *wu do not occur in Burushaski. By way of repair one of the high vocoids is deleted, violating MAX. Again, this violation could be avoided more directly by simply selecting {-mu}, giving contrafactual **čatibóimu*.

Space restrictions prevent me from developing a full analysis of these opaque interactions here. There are a variety of ways that this may be dealt with, including Stratal OT (Kiparsky 2000), Sympathy Theory (McCarthy 1999), Paradigmatic Contrast (Łubowicz 2003, 2007), and Coloured Containment Theory (van Oostendorp 2007).[19] The essential point for present purposes is that the selection of the allomorph must make direct reference to the lexical form of the stem.

4.4.2.2 Inanimates

The Austronesian scholar Ken Rehg (2001: 218) remarks in a paper that 'one of the imperatives of generative phonology – that allomorphy must be minimized – is sometimes at odds with the data, typically in very subtle ways'. The fact of the matter is that suppletive allomorphy and phonologically conditioned alternations are not always easy to tell apart. Where two alternants are phonetically similar there will be an analytical temptation to derive the variation by phonological means. In some cases, further inspection reveals that the variation is actually lexically governed. An excellent example of this from Burushaski is the alternation of the inanimate plural marker between {-iŋ} and {-ŋ}. Naïvely, we'd expect the distribution of these variants to fall along phonologically sensible lines, as determined by, say, ONSET or *HIATUS. With consonant-final stems, naturally enough, we always find the {-iŋ} variant as in (32).

(32) áraz, áraziŋ 'complaint'
-hil, -híliŋ 'lip'
qaburstán, qaburstániŋ 'cemetery'

Equally unsurprisingly, the shape {-ŋ} is restricted to vowel-final inanimate stems. Representative examples are shown in (33).

(33) bulukáli, bulukáliŋ 'winter dish of meat, flour and onion'
óşţana, óşţanaŋ 'half-rupee'
barcé, barcéŋ 'fur worn over shoulders'
čakú, čakúŋ 'pen-knife'

However, three considerations warrant the belief that there is a significant (morpho)lexical element in the distribution of these allomorphs.

First, there is no evidence from the phonological processes of Burushaski of a general alternation between /i/ and Ø, be it epenthesis or deletion.

Second, for stems ending in a stressed vowel there is actually a lexical contrast between stems that take {-ŋ} and stems that take {-iŋ}. Although the default ending for such stems seems to be {-ŋ}, a sizeable minority of them nevertheless lexically select {-iŋ}, as in (34).[20]

(34) naɣé, naɣéiŋ 'excrement'
tasmá, tasmáiŋ 'ligature'

The forms in (34) would seem to be worse off phonologically than those in (33) in having a vowel sequence V+i. None of my sources provide information about the syllabification of sequences of non-identical vowels, but for the sake of discussion let us assume that such sequences entail a hiatus, which is penalized by the constraint in (35).

(35) *V.V: Hiatus is disallowed.

By phonological default, vowel-final stems take {-ŋ} by (35), as shown in (36).

(36)

/barcé+{-iŋ, -ŋ}/	*V.V
a. barcéiŋ	*!
b. ☞ barcéŋ	

For the plural forms in (34), (35) must be ranked below SELECT(V]$_{\text{stem\{nayé, tasmá ...\}}}$,]$_{\text{inan.pl}}$, -iŋ), as shown in (37) for *naɣé* 'excrement'.

(37)

/naɣé+{-iŋ, -ŋ}/	SELECT(V]$_{\text{stem\{nayé ...\}}}$,]$_{\text{inan.pl}}$, -iŋ)	*V.V
a. ☞ naɣéiŋ		*
b. naɣéŋ	*!	

Presence versus absence of hiatus appears to influence the relative frequencies of the plural allomorphs with stems ending in a stressed vowel. Of the 39 stems in the sample ending in stressed /í/, 34 (87%) take {-ŋ}, none takes {-iŋ}. Of the 75 stems ending in a final stressed /á/, 38 (51%) take {-ŋ} only. At 23 (31%), the number of á-final stems that take {-iŋ} only is much fewer. For stems ending in one of the other stressed vowels /ú é ó/, the preference picture is not clear because there are too few examples of each. Despite the phonological similarity of {-ŋ} and {-iŋ}, the existence of a contrast between words of the types shown in (33) and (34) would appear to diagnose suppletive allomorphy rather than lower level phonological variation.

Finally, {-ŋ} and {-iŋ} vary with a third allomorph, {-miŋ}, which appears to be the preferred suffix for stems ending in unstressed vowels other than /i/. Representative examples of unstressed V-final stems taking {-miŋ} are shown in (38).

(38) axránu, axránumiŋ 'stable'
xausóno, xausónomiŋ 'court case, legal dispute'
sénde, séndemiŋ 'sand'

Let us take a brief look at the numbers. The 33 stems ending in unstressed /i/ evince a modest preference for {-ŋ} (19 items) over {-miŋ} (7 items) or {-ŋ} and {-miŋ} in variation (7 items). The predominant pattern for stems ending in unstressed /i/ is illustrated in (39).

(39) ačaɣésti, ačaɣéstiŋ 'stitching'
kulupóŋgi, kulupóŋgiŋ 'weft'
ṣabulúki, ṣabulúkiŋ 'kind of clover'

The preference for the stems in (39) for {-ŋ} rather than {-miŋ} may be due to a constraint that militates against repeating unstressed /i/ in consecutive nuclei (*iC_0i). For stems ending in other unstressed vowels, however, the preference works in the opposite direction, and {-miŋ} is preferred. Only two stems ending in an unstressed vowel other than /i/ are listed as categorically taking {-ŋ}. The majority of such stems (17; 77%) take {-miŋ} only, and three (14%; all ending in the high vowel /u/) variably take {-ŋ} or {-miŋ}. Although the examples are few, we can tentatively conclude that the default ending for unstressed vowel-final stems is {-miŋ}. The consequence of assuming this is that the choice of {-ŋ} or {-miŋ} becomes a matter of arbitrary preference. Consider the factual-contrafactual pairs *barcéŋ* **barcémiŋ* 'furs worn over shoulders' and *xausónomiŋ* **xausónoŋ* 'court cases'. In both pairs, both forms fare equally well with respect to the avoidance of hiatus. Exchanging {-ŋ} and {-miŋ} doesn't make any difference to the phonotactics. In the case of the first pair, *barcéŋ* **barcémiŋ*, *Struc would be sufficient to enforce the optimization of *barcéŋ*, since the contrafactual form **barcémiŋ* has more segments. In the second pair however, *Struc actually prefers the contrafactual candidate **xausónoŋ* over the correct *xausónomiŋ*. Once again, we seem to have an irreducible lexical element. We can accordingly set up three allomorph selection constraints as in (40).

(40) *Plural allomorph selection in inanimate stems*

a. Select(V́$]_{stem}$ $]_{inan.pl}$, -ŋ): Inanimate stressed vowel-final stems select {-ŋ} in the plural.

b. Select(V$]_{stem}$ $]_{inan.pl}$, -miŋ): Inanimate unstressed vowel-final stems select {-miŋ} in the plural.

c. Select(C$]_{stem}$ $]_{inan.pl}$, -iŋ): Inanimate consonant-final stems select {-iŋ} in the plural.

Given (34), Select(V́$]_{stem}$ $]_{inan.pl}$, -ŋ) would also have to be dominated by a more specific constraint listing which vowel-final stems perversely take {-iŋ}, e.g. Select(V́$]_{stem\{nayé,\ tasmá\ ...\}}$, $]_{inan.pl}$, -iŋ).

In addition to the cases in (34), where the first vowel in the vowel cluster that is stressed, there are seven short unaccented CV stems with an unaccented vowel, all of which take {-iŋ} and receive default stress on the suffixal vowel. These are exemplified in (41).

(41) ba, baíŋ 'sorghum, millet'
ču, čuíŋ 'head (of grass); bunch (of grapes); knife-blade'
pho, phoíŋ 'scab, pustule'

There are two ways of dealing with the cases in (41). One solution is to say there is a more specific version of SELECT given in (42) that takes precedence to (40)a.

(42) SELECT($[CV]_{stem}\ ]_{inan.pl}$, -iŋ): Inanimate vowel-final stems select {-iŋ} in the plural.

Alternatively, the forms in (41) take {-iŋ} for some phonological reason. There is one respect in which the hypothetical form **baŋ* (for *baíŋ* 'sorghum') may be considered inferior to the actually occurring form. The right edge of the stem does not coincide with the right edge of the syllable. Compare the winning form *.ba.|íŋ.* with the contrafactual candidate **.ba|ŋ.* The latter violates (43).

(43) RALIGNSTEM: The right edge of the stem must be aligned with the right edge of some syllable.

However, violation of (43) cannot be sufficient, since, as we have seen, the plural forms of vowel-final stems will routinely violate this constraint. Consequently, (43) cannot be ranked highly enough to force the selection of {-iŋ}. Rather it must be ranked below *V.V (35), as in (44).

(44)

/barcé+{-iŋ, -ŋ}/	*V.V	RALIGNSTEM
a. .bar.cé.|iŋ.	*!	
b. ☞ .bar.cé|ŋ.		*

It is the misalignment combined with the shortness of the forms in (41) that seems to be the problem since, in stems of this type, the misalignment arises in the first syllable, which is especially important for lexical recognition. Building on Beckman (1998), there are positional faithfulness constraints sensitive to whether the violation occurs in the initial syllable of the word. One of these is a version of (43) relativized to the initial syllable. This constraint is formulated in (45)

(45) STEM_1-RALIGNSTEM: If it falls within the first syllable of the domain, the right edge of the stem must be aligned with the right edge of some syllable.

The facts are correctly accounted for on ranking (45) above *V.V (35), as shown in (46).

(46)

/ba+ŋ/	STEM_1-RALIGNSTEM	*V.V	RALIGNSTEM
a. ☞ .ba.|íŋ.		*	
b. .ba|ŋ.	*!		*

4.4.3 Competition between semantic and phonological selection

Other things being equal, nouns belonging to the human class take the same range of suffixes as the animate class unless, that is, they fall into one or more of the semantically defined classes described in section 4.4.1. Consider the examples in (47).

(47) a. narúci, narúcimu 'homosexual; hermaphrodite', kartópi, kartópimu 'person with protruding ears', aphiuní, aphiunímu 'opium smoker'
b. asaqál asaqálišu 'old man', ḍarawár, ḍarawárišu 'driver; conductor', ípholok, ípholokišu 'only child'
c. ambuxčán, ambuxčáyu 'secondary wife', insā́n, insā́yu 'human being' bedī́n, bedī́u 'atheist, glutton'
d. kamúnes, kamúnešu 'misanthrope, lone wolf', phópos, phópošu 'bastard, know-nothing', helés, helésu 'boy, servant'

Stems taking semantically conditioned plural markers in section 4.4.1 display a diverse set of terminals. If the semantic and phonological conditions conflict, the semantic condition takes precedence. For example, ordinarily, an *n*-final animate would take {-yu}, but this is overridden if the noun in question refers to kin, e.g. *salén, saléndaru* 'female relation (sister or daughter) of man' (not **saléyu*), *sáɣun, sáɣundaru* 'brother-in-law' (not **sáɣuyu*). The semantically-based SELECT constraints stated in (14) must therefore dominate the phonologically-based SELECT constraints stated in (25) *en bloc*. This is shown in (48) for sáɣundaru. For brevity, only the most relevant allomorphs are included in the input.

(48)

<table>
<tr><th>/sáɣun+{-yu, -daru}/</th><th>SELECT-daru</th><th>SELECT(n]$_{stem}$]$_{anim.pl}$, -yu)</th></tr>
<tr><td>a. sá.ɣun.|mu</td><td>*!</td><td>*</td></tr>
<tr><td>b. sá.ɣu.n|i.šu</td><td>*!</td><td>*</td></tr>
<tr><td>c. sá.ɣu.|yu</td><td>*!</td><td></td></tr>
<tr><td>d. ☞ sá.ɣun.|da.ru</td><td></td><td>*</td></tr>
</table>

The Burushaski facts seem to represent an instance of a principle that is well known from studies of grammatical gender assignment. This is the Core Semantic Override Principle (Nesset 2006). Nesset focuses on the fundamental importance of biological sex for assigning gender, but Dahl (2000) also shows that cross-linguistically a number of other semantic features may have override privilege. Examples include nouns denoting young or small animates, or nouns referring to certain kinds of animals.[21]

Since consonant-final stems with the right connotations may suffix {-tiŋ}, the relevant SELECT constraint must also interact with, and outrank, the phonological constraints, as shown in (49) for *gušpúr* 'prince'.

(49)

<table>
<tr><th>/gušpúr+{-mu, -išu, -tiŋ}/</th><th>SELECT-tiŋ</th><th>NOCODA</th></tr>
<tr><td>a. guš.púr.|mu</td><td>*!</td><td>*!</td></tr>
<tr><td>b. guš.pú.r|i.šu</td><td>*!</td><td></td></tr>
<tr><td>c. ☞ guš.púr.|tiŋ</td><td></td><td></td></tr>
</table>

4.5 Patterned exceptionality in allomorph selection and its evolution

One of the most striking features of plural formation in Burushaski is the great number of exceptions. Over a quarter (26%) of the nouns in the sample have an unpredictable choice of plural suffix. (See Vogt 1945 on similar facts from Hunza Burushaski.) It is helpful to distinguish between two kinds of exception. Some lexical items may take an allomorph that is particular to a closed class of items. For example, a unique item *hunc* 'arrow' takes the plural suffix {-é}. A small class of 20 animate nouns take the suffix {-a}. These plural markers are no doubt a legacy of an older stage of the language that have now ceased to be productive. Interestingly, many of the classes in question, though closed, have members that share some phonological property or resemble each other phonetically. Most strikingly, several plural suffixes attach exclusively to CVC-stems. In the animate class, this is true of suffixes like {-ánc}, {-áško} and {-ó}. In the inanimate class, the same is true of {-óŋ}. Let us dub these 'legacy' plurals.

Legacy plurals are to be distinguished from quirky lexical items that take a regular plural allomorph, but the 'wrong' one (cf. Fraser and Corbett 1997 on 'exceptional case default'). Synchronically, exceptionality may be dealt with using Select constraints that in addition to specifying any phonological or semantic condition also extensionally list the lexical items that take the suffix. For example, the unique item *hunc* 'arrow' that takes the marker {-é} in the plural might be captured by Select($C]_{\text{stem\{hunc\}}}\ ]_{\text{anim.pl}}$, -é). Since this constraint is more specific than Select($C]_{\text{stem}}\ ]_{\text{anim.pl}}$, -išu), it must dominate it.

4.5.1 The diachronic evolution of patterned exceptionality

As several studies have shown, exceptionality is 'patterned' (Zuraw 2000). This also turns out to be true of Burushaski plural allomorphy in a number of different ways. This section lays out the ways in which exceptions cohere and suggests directions for making sense of the patterns more fully. The data may be understood as providing a snapshot of a complex dynamic system in which there are 'attractors' of three kinds. First, general patterns may attract items away from specific patterns. In this case, the specific pattern ultimately ceases to be productive and the items that still behave according to the specific pattern have to be listed as doing so. Second, markedness constraints may inhibit the breakdown of existing exception classes or encourage the development of quirky plurals that match the stem to the 'wrong' suffix. Third, an exceptional item may serve as a nucleus around which other phonetically similar lexical items cluster, so that items that behave exceptionally in the same way tend to display a family resemblance. Of course, these attractors exert partly opposing forces on the behaviour of lexical items in actual performance.

4.5.2 The attraction of the unmarked

In addition to being constitutive of the grammar, markedness influences the frequencies of patterns in the lexicon. In this section, we will look at the ways in which markedness and exceptionality interact. Markedness considerations may either favour or disfavour an exceptional pairing of stem and allomorph. Let us first look at a case where markedness considerations statistically disfavour a particular combination. In section 4.4.2.2 we mentioned that inanimate stems ending in a stressed vowel may lexically select {-iŋ}, {-ŋ} or {-miŋ}. When we look at the relative frequencies of these suffixes with stems ending in a stressed /á/, we see a modest preference for {-ŋ} which may be attributed to the constraint *V.V in (35) acting in a gradient fashion.

The most famous case of gradient markedness comes from Standard Arabic. In Standard Arabic roots, cooccurrences of phonetically similar consonants are not categorically ruled out by the OCP but are statistically underrepresented in the lexicon. Frisch *et al.* (2004) argue that this is due to *gradient* OCP-Place, which is grounded in the difficulties repetition poses for processing in production, perception and working memory. Over time, the processing difficulties associated with adjacent similar consonants introduce asymmetries into the lexicon. In contrast to the view articulated by Blevins (2004, 2006) as part of the Evolutionary Phonology programme, these constraints cannot reside in language transmission, but must have a cognitive presence. The psychological reality of OCP-Place is revealed, amongst other things, by native speaker judgments of the 'wordlikeness' of nonsense test words that violate the gradient constraint to various degrees. In Burushaski, the OCP may be a factor in certain asymmetries in stem allomorph combinations. There is a set of common allomorphs that are exclusively used with animate CVC-stems.[22] These are the accented suffixes {-áško}, {-ánc} and {-ó}. Although these suffixes are exclusively used with CVC-stems, the reverse is not true. CVC-stems may also take one of the productive animate suffixes {-yu} or {-išu}. If we restrict our attention to the set of items that take {-áško} or {-ánc}, however, we find something close to complementarity in their distribution. Berger describes {-áško} as evincing a preference for attaching to nasal-final monosyllables. The number of items taking {-áško} obligatorily or optionally is only 20, but 17 of these end in a nasal, as in (50).

(50) ḍoŋ, ḍoŋánc, ḍoŋáško 'knoll'
khan, khanáško 'fort, fortified village'
sam, samánc, samáško 'hole in roof for smoke'

The suffix {-ánc}, on the other hand, preferentially attaches to non-nasal stems, as in (51). The number of items that (may) take {-ánc} is higher. Of 45 such items, only seven end in a nasal, and all but one of these optionally permit {-ánc}.

(51) barc, barcánc 'bridge'
čiq, čiqánc 'wooden tablet for separating wheat from chaff'
guk, gukánc 'chisel'
jip, jipánc 'shirt pocket'
sal, salanc 'mill stone'
uṭ, uṭánc 'camel'

There are examples that go against these tendencies, e.g. *ḍaṭ*, *ḍaṭánc* (also *ḍaṭášku*) 'supply trough for butter', *taɣ*, *taɣášku* 'twig, sapling', *mun munánc* (also *munášku*). On the face of it, these distributional facts appear to diagnose the gradient activity of $\text{OCP}_{\text{nasal}}$. In actual fact, {-ánc} is only strongly dispreferred when the stem ends in an alveolar nasal /n/. There are only two *n*-final stems that may take {-ánc}, and both of these are also recorded as allowing {-ášku}. For stems ending in a labial or dorsal nasal /m ŋ/, the preference for {-ášku} appears weaker. There is only one item that is reported as only taking {-ášku}, compared with three that only take {-ánc} and four that take either {-ášku} or {-ánc}. The constraint responsible then appears to militate against the repetition of /n/ that occurs when {-ánc} is suffixed to an *n*-final stem.

The previous example addressed the way in which markedness may structure preferences of closed classes. Markedness considerations may also favour exceptionality over regularity by impeding the breakdown of existing exceptional classes and encouraging the growth of new ones.

Where markedness is at stake, an exception class may display a more tenacious hold than might otherwise be expected. The following example involves OCP-Place. By default, consonant-final inanimate nouns suffix {-iŋ} in the plural. Inanimate stems ending in a velar obstruent /k x q/ or nasal /ŋ/ (abbreviated as K) are especially likely to evince exceptional behaviour in choice of plural allomorph.[23] The sample contains 407 C-final inanimates, 63 of which end in /K/. Of these 407 stems, 330 (81%) take {-iŋ} to form their plural. When we compare the set of K-final stems with those ending in other consonants, we find a marked asymmetry. Only 31 (49%) K-final inanimate stems take the productive inanimate plural suffix {-iŋ}. Examples of some of the ones that do are given in (52).

(52)	bardáq, bardáqiŋ	'bread in thin flour soup'
	čamáx, čamáxiŋ	'lighter'
	xoróŋ, xoróŋiŋ	'cloud'
	palaṣṭík, palaṣṭíkiŋ	'plastic'

Twenty-five (40%) K-final inanimate stems take the legacy suffix {-ičiŋ}, as illustrated in (53).

(53)	mundáq, mundáqičiŋ	'bread in thin flour soup'
	thux, thuxíčiŋ	'vapour'
	-phúiŋ, -phúiŋičiŋ	'nape of neck'
	hesk, heskíčiŋ	'comb; loom'

Compare this with the remaining 344 inanimate stems ending in consonants other than K. Of these, only two (0.58% of 344) take {-ičiŋ}, and both of these are monosyllables ending in /p/, which, like the velars and uvulars, is acoustically grave. In this case, OCP-Place seems to be slowing the breakdown of an unproductive class of legacy plurals.

Markedness may also encourage reassignment, giving quirky plural forms. As we have seen, inanimate stems ending in an unstressed vowel generally prefer the suffix {-miŋ} over {-ŋ}. However, when the stem final vowel is unstressed /i/, bare {-ŋ} is preferred over {-miŋ}. The constraint responsible for this apparent reversal may be a version of the OCP banning the repetition of /i/ in consecutive nuclei (*iC_0i). It is imaginable at an earlier stage of the language that {-miŋ} was the regular suffix for inanimate stems ending in any unstressed vowel. Subsequently, the operation of the OCP would have bled those stems ending in unstressed /i/ out of the {-miŋ} and into the {-ŋ} class.

In at least one case, markedness seems to be responsible for a unique case of quirky behaviour. A single item expected to take {-mu} optionally takes {-yu}, but the phonological form of the stem, *cúmu, cúmumu, cúmuyu* 'fish', suggests that this is no accident.[24] The form *cúmuyu* may be due to a constraint against repeating phonetically similar or identical material (here *mumu). In the variant *cúmumu*, the final /u/ of the stem is sandwiched between two identical labial consonants. Since /u/ also involves a lip gesture, this will increase the chances of undershooting the medial /u/ target. Substitution of the {-yu} suffix circumvents this. There is only one other animate noun root ending in /mu/, *ɣamú, ɣamúmu* 'ice', but the two do not form a perfect minimal pair because, in the latter case, the stem-final /u/ is stressed. The presence of stress here will likely diminish the tendency to coarticulate the last /m/ in the stem with the /m/ of the suffix. The very uniqueness of the *cúmu* example is significant. It cannot be a general pattern, so it indicates that markedness constraints are cognitively real presences (Fleischhacker 2002; Zuraw 2000, 2007).

Finally let us look at a case reminiscent of morphological haplology, which is normally accounted for in terms of markedness constraints, but where it turns out markedness cannot be at issue. The non-alternating forms *ɣašú* 'onion' and *khíšu* 'mosquito' are the only two forms in the language where the singular and plural forms are identical. Had they been formed regularly, the plural forms of these nouns would have been **ɣašúmu* and **khíšumu* (cf. *makú, makúmu* 'shuttle on loom', *bráɣu, bráɣumu* 'foal'). It can hardly be an accident that the final two segments correspond to the final two segments of a pluralized *s*-final animate noun, such as *kukúres kukúrešu* 'puppy'. What seems to have happened here is that the speaker takes advantage of the fact that the sequence *-šu-* word-finally activates a plural meaning. These two examples provide a clue as to what might really be going on in cases of morphological haplology (see e.g. de Lacy 1999 and references therein). Frequently haplology is grounded in the requirement to avoid repetition of identical or similar consecutive strings, but this would not work here. On the other hand, the explanation I have sketched here would generalize to other cases of morphological haplology.

4.5.3 The attraction of the general

A second way that exceptions arise is through the loss of items from specific allomorph classes to general allomorph classes. One possible result of this type of shift is a quirky kind of case where the noun takes a regular affix, but the 'wrong' one. For example there is a small group of *s*-final animate nouns that take {-išu} rather than the expected {-yu}, shown in (54).

(54) *Quirky s-final animates with* {-išu}

ɣáqales, ɣáqalesišu	'scarecrow'
jāsús, jāsúsišu	'detective, informer, spy'
kanjús, kanjúsišu	'miser, haggler'
panḍóles, panḍólesišu	'turf'

Shifts like these probably come about due to derailments of the Elsewhere Principle as allomorphs are selected on-line in actual language processing.[25] This happens because activation of the specific pattern entails the activation of the general pattern. Since the condition for selecting {-išu} (ending in a consonant) is properly included in the condition for selecting {-yu} (ending in a consonant that is an /s/ or /n/), {-išu} will be activated any time {-yu} is activated, though the reverse may not hold. Occasionally, the activation of the general pattern will reach the threshold faster than the specific pattern, and the wrong stem-allomorph combination will be produced and this, in turn, will increase the likelihood that the wrong stem-allomorph combination will be stored.[26]

There is evidence that this is also the source of the breakdown of the CVC condition in the animate stems. Judging from current distributions, it is imaginable that, until relatively recently, *n*-final animate CVC stems regularly took {-ášku}, and other C-final animate CVC stems took {-ánc}. At this hypothesized older stage, the selection of {-ášku} in *n*-final animate CVC stems would have taken precedence to the selection of {-yu} in other *n*-final animate stems via the Elsewhere Principle. Similarly, the selection of {-ánc} in C-final animate CVC stems would have had priority over selection of {-išu} in the rest of the C-final stems. For this hypothesized older stage, we would have had the constraints in (55) in addition to those in (25) above.

(55) *Plural allomorph selection in animate CVC-stems (hypothesized older stage)*
  a. SELECT($[CVn]_{stem}\,]_{anim.pl}$, -ášku): Animate CVC stems ending in /n/ select {-ášku} in the plural
  b. SELECT($[CVC]_{stem}\,]_{anim.pl}$, -ánc): Animate CVC stems ending in /s/ select {-ánc} in the plural

By the Elsewhere Principle, the hierarchy of defaults incorporating the constraints in (55) would have looked like (56).[27]

(56) SELECT($[CVn]_{stem}\,]_{anim.pl}$, -ášku) >> SELECT($(n]_{stem}\,]_{anim.pl}$, $-yu_1$), SELECT($(s]_{stem}\,]_{anim.pl}$, $-yu_2$), SELECT($[CVC]_{stem}\,]_{anim.pl}$, -ánc) >> SELECT($(C]_{stem}\,]_{anim.pl}$, -išu) >> SELECT($(V]_{stem}\,]_{anim.pl}$, -mu)

In modern Burushaski, the balance is shifting, or has already shifted, to the more general suffixes {-yu} and {-išu}. If we look at the *n*-final animate CVC stems that take either {-ášku} or {-yu}, the proportion taking one or the other is approximately half (13 take {-yu}, 12 take {-ášku}). For the animate monosyllables ending in consonants other than a nasal, the proportions of those taking the special suffix {-ánc} and those taking the general suffix {-išu} is the same (45 take {-išu}, 48 take {-ánc}). The direction of change may be established by examining the etymological make-up of each class. What we are taking to be the younger patterns with {-išu} and {-yu} should have a larger proportion of (relatively) recent loanwords, while the older pattern should have a higher proportion of native Burushaski words and older loans from Shina. In their dictionaries, Berger (1974) and Morin and Tiffou (1989) supply information about words shared between Burushaski and languages with which it has been or is in contact. Unfortunately, in the case of Shina and Khowar it is not possible to say anything about the direction of borrowing without further research. The figures that follow are therefore rather liberal estimates that assume that all the items Burushaski have in common with Shina and Khowar have been borrowed into Burushaski from these languages, which is unlikely. Loanwords from Khowar are nonetheless later and loanwords from Urdu and English are the most recent. Let us look at the composition of the {-išu} and {-ánc} classes more closely, restricting our attention to those words that are recorded uniquely with each suffix. In the {-ánc} class the proportion of native Burushaski and Shina loanwords is high (45% and 18% respectively), while that of Khowar and Urdu is relatively low (16% and 8% respectively). In the {-išu} class, on the other hand, these proportions are nearly reversed: the proportion of native Burushaski words drops to 30.5% and Shina to 3%, while Khowar and Urdu rise to 27.5% and 33% respectively. The etymological composition is thus consistent with the idea that the bleeding of lexical items from the {-ánc} to the {-išu} class is of relatively recent date and that {-ánc} formerly had a more regular distribution.

The corresponding picture for the smaller number of *n*-final animate stems is far less clear, although the weak asymmetry we see is of the same kind. What we expect to see is a greater proportion of recent loans with {-yu}. Of the 12 *n*-final nouns taking {-ášku}, six are loanwords (four Shina, one Khowar, one Urdu). Of the 13 *n*-final nouns taking {-yu}, six are loanwords (two Khowar, two Urdu, one Shina, one English). Although the proportion of native words in the two classes hardly varies, the proportion of Shina words in the {-ášku} class is greater, which is what we would expect assuming the Shina contribution is older. In the {-yu} class, the proportion of Shina words has fallen, and the languages with which Burushaski has had more recent contact (Khowar, Urdu and English) have taken over.

The picture that emerges, then, is that the generalization of the suffixes {-yu} and {-išu} to animate closed monosyllables has occurred (or at least accelerated) relatively recently hand in hand with recent borrowing. Extrapolating backwards, it is reasonable to suppose that, at an older stage, Burushaski had the more articulated default hierarchy as in (56), and where {-ášku} and {-ánc} were productive.

4.5.3 The attraction of the phonetically similar

Exceptional lexical items taking the same allomorph are often phonetically similar. For example, animate CVC stems ending in /m/ and /ŋ/ do not show the same profile as either *n*-final or CVC stems ending in some other oral consonant with respect to their relative affinities for {-ášku} and {-ánc}. They stand somewhere in between. If gradient OCP_n is responsible for the asymmetry between *n*-final and oral C-final CVC stems (rather than OCP-nasal, which would be to adopt Berger's account), then the profiles of m- and ŋ-final monosyllables result from attraction of a different kind. I propose that these items were drawn into the orbit of the {-ášku} by virtue of ending in a nasal.[28] The data furnish a number of cases that may be explained in a similar way.

There are 15 consonant-final forms with {-mu}, and these seem to fall into two unrelated classes. Two of these are idiosyncratic disyllables ending in /k/: *hánik, hánikmu* 'wooden key', and the variable *giṣṭék, giṣṭékmu, giṣṭékišu, giṣṭéka* 'brick or clay of salt'. Of the remaining 13 stems, two are prosodically defective inalienable stems consisting of a single sibilant (57a), the only two such stems in the Burushaski lexicon, and 11 are VC, CVC or CVVC monosyllables ending in a voiceless consonant (57b).

(57) *Consonant-final stems with* {-mu}
   a. -s, -smu 'heart', -ṣ, -ṣmu 'throat'
   b. es, esmu 'morsel', ɣáṣ, ɣáṣmu 'froth, cream', -ís, -ísmu 'child', nấš, nấšmu 'camel's nose-ring', muš, mušmu 'edge', -múš, -múšmu 'nose; snot', qáf, qáfmu, qáfišu 'claw, fork', ́-rič, ́-ričmu 'kidney', rū́h, rū́hmu 'soul', šā̃ṣ, šā̃ṣmu 'cover', tyoh, tyohmu 'kind of hawk'

I propose that the pattern in (57b) arose through analogy with the prosodically deficient items in (57a). Besides being monosyllabic, notice that seven of the 11 forms in (57b) end in a sibilant of some kind, like the two prosodically deficient stems. It is not possible to reconstruct the history of this state of affairs, but it is possible to offer a speculative model. The default suffix for C-final stems is {-išu}, but observe that the effect of affixing is subtly different for prosodically defective stems. For prosodically defective stems, affixing {-išu} results in a violation of RALIGNSTEM, given above in (43). The table (not a tableau) in (58) shows the violations.

(58)

	RALIGNSTEM	NOCODA
a. |.he.re.ṣ|i.šu.|	*	
b. |.he.reṣ.|mu.|		*

As we noted earlier, violations of RALIGNSTEM may be considered worse if they fall in the first syllable of the root-domain. When the root consists of a single consonant, violation of STEM_1-RALIGNSTEM results from suffixing the general post-consonantal ending {-išu}, but not {-mu}. This is shown in (59).

(59)

	STEM_1-RALIGNSTEM	RALIGNSTEM	NOCODA
a. ...|ṣ|i.šu.|	*	*	
b. ...|ṣ.|mu.|			*

Let us consider a few more examples of this kind. As we noted earlier, there are six items in the sample that end in a diphthong /ei ai oi/. All of them take {-išu} rather than {-mu} as might be expected. This choice is not altogether unexpected since /i/ may pattern as a glide rather than a prototypical consonant in these examples. Nevertheless, the final segment is vocalic, and this might be expected to serve as the magnet for the attraction of other stems ending in a vowel. There is indeed a small set of five vowel-final stems that (may) irregularly select {-išu} rather than the expected {-mu}, shown in (60) along with their variants. These end in a motley selection of vowels, including /i/ (2), /u/, /a/ and /o/ (1 each). Note that the initial /i/ of the suffix is deleted following an unstressed vowel.

(60) buyéki, buyékišu — 'goat with red hairs about the eyes'
daróɣo, daróɣošu, daróɣomu — 'staff'
guá, guáišu, guátiŋ — 'marriage witness before sufi'
išpaqéti, išpaqétišu, išpaqétimu — 'small white flightless bird'
kuráṭu, kuráṭišu — 'emaciated (animal)'

A significant number of ṣ-final stems form their plural by suffixing {-ha(ŋ)} or {-a(ŋ)}, with deletion or adjustment of the /ṣ/. Examples from the inanimate class are shown in (61).

(61) a. balkáṣ, balkáhaŋ, balkáṣiŋ 'cavity in wall', bayáṣ, bayáhaŋ, bayáṣiŋ 'ceiling, roof', -móqiṣ, -móqihaŋ 'face', noṣ nóhaŋ 'sapling', puṣ, púhaŋ 'shirt (of either sex)', teléṣ, teléhaŋ 'sinew on slingshot'

b. bálçikiṣ, bálçikiaŋ 'cow manure', biákuṣ, biákuaŋ 'cowstall', bisarṣ, bisáraŋ 'sickle', camáreṣ, camáraŋ 'part of wooden frame of smoke-hole in ceiling', cáreṣ, cáraŋ 'threshold', gíŋiṣ, gíŋiaŋ 'small leather pouch', gókoreṣ, gókoraŋ 'iron scraper', iṣqóreṣ, iṣqóraŋ 'thornbush', phutúneṣ phutúnaŋ 'charred log'

There are also a few consonant-final nouns that do not end in /ṣ/, but which form their plural in the same way. All of them end in /s/, which is the fricative most similar to /ṣ/.[29]

(62) burús, burúhaŋ — 'kind of milk product, lassi'
minás, mináhaŋ, minášiŋ — 'tale'
thánes, thánaŋ — 'cuff'

Osmosis in the opposite direction has apparently occurred in *barkáṣ, barkášu* 'balance, scales', which behaves like an *s*-stem in taking {-yu}.

A bit of prospecting in the appendix will turn up several other examples of this kind.

4.6 Conclusions

An implicit assumption in most work couched within the framework of OT is that motivated preferences are rule-governed preferences, while arbitrary preferences are lexically conditioned. As we have seen here, and in several other contributions to this volume, arbitrary preferences do not necessarily have to be listed but may be rule-governed. Conversely, certain kinds of lexically governed preferences turn out to be motivated. Although the rule-governed and the motivated largely overlap, the allomorphy of plural marking in Burushaski furnishes evidence for considering distributions under these two cross-classifying dimensions, as in (63).

(63) *Types of allomorphy*

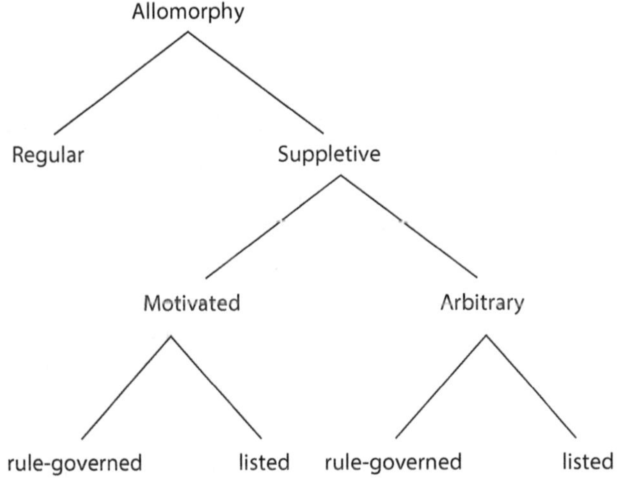

Rule-governed arbitrariness was developed in detail in Section 4, which compared the merits of markedness-driven and construction-based approaches to phonologically-conditioned suppletive allomorph distribution (SAD). The markedness-driven approach that has dominated theorizing about SAD within OT works only up to a point. When we examine the markedness-driven approach in detail, we find that it has to use more than one strategy to derive the correct distributions. Given allomorphs X and Y which appear respectively in the environments A__B and C__D, then ideally we should be able to identify two high-ranking markedness constraints M_1 and M_2 that exert the preferences AXB over AYB and CYD over CXD. In many cases, however, what we find is only partial phonological conditioning, that is, we can pin down M_1 and deal with AXB over AYB phonologically, but we can't identify any high-ranking M_2 to take care of the preference CYD over CXD. In some cases, the preference CYD turns out to have a proper subset of the violation marks of CXD, in which case appeal may be had to *STRUC. However, in other cases CYD and CXD are non-comparable, and it is here that the markedness-driven account appears least compelling. In such cases the analyst (and learner?) must arbitrarily select some constraint exerting the required preference and rank it accordingly. Since there will inevitably be some constraint exerting the opposite preference, this is not a particularly satisfactory solution in the absence of independent evidence for the ranking. Sooner or later, any complete theory of SAD must recognize the existence of arbitrary preferences between competing allomorphs. There is now increasing agreement that this view is correct.

Phonologically arbitrary, yet rule-governed, preferences between allomorphs manifest themselves in two ways in Burushaski. First, the selection of certain plural allomorphs is conditioned by the semantics or pragmatics rather than the phonology of the stem. Where semantic/pragmatic and phonological conditions conflict, the semantic/pragmatic conditions have priority by virtue of what we have called the Core Semantic Override Principle. Second, some preferences between phonologically conditioned allomorphs cannot be exerted by any known markedness constraint. In both of these cases we need to resort to some other mechanism to exert the observed preference. Here I have proposed that we deal with such arbitrary preferences by adopting a more highly articulated conception of the lexicon, what I call the 'morpholexicon'. This conception is independently motivated in the work on construction-based grammar and is explored at length in the computational work of Jean-Pierre Koenig and Dan Jurafsky. Other proposals for dealing with arbitrary rule-governed preferences exist (see for example Mascaró 2007, and Wolf, this volume), but I will leave it to future research to decide between the approaches on offer.

The main point of Section 4.5 was the existence of motivated exceptionality. Lexical preferences (exceptions) may be motivated by markedness and other considerations. I have argued that markedness as a cognitive presence is clearly implicated in the evolution of patterns of exceptionality in Burushaski. Markedness may favour the persistence of some types of exception, even encourage the development of new ones. Whatever markedness may do to favour exceptionality is opposed by the forces of regularization, which I have argued are represented by morpholexical constraints, some of which may duplicate the effects of phonological constraints. I have tentatively suggested that the breakdown of the CVC-stems as a distinct and productive inflectional class and the evolution of some quirky nominals (which lexically select the 'wrong' plural suffix) are due to the lexicalization of derailments of the Elsewhere Principle in on-line language processing. This account presupposes that all suppletive allomorphs have a distributional statement in the morpholexicon. Further exploration of this possibility, and its implications for the theory of the way the grammar and the lexicon interact I will leave to future investigation.

Appendix

Where the plural merely involves concatenation of the stem and suffix, only the base form is given. The plural form is given explicitly when it varies with some other form, or if concatenation triggers a non-trivial (morpho) phonological adjustment in the stem or suffix. Burushaski distinguishes between alienable and inalienable nouns. Nouns referring to body parts and relations only occur with a possessive prefix, e.g. *-rén, arén*, 'my hand', *-́çu*, *góçu* 'thy brother', *-́skil* 'his face'.

A Salient persons (65)

A.1 Kin {-daru} (15)
aštán, aštándaru 'ostler', *axón, axóndaru~axōya* 'mullah', *hálkit, hálkitaru* 'she-goat older than a year', *-húles, húlestaru* 'brother (of woman)', *-xákin, xákindaru* 'daughter-in-law', *raféq, raféqendaru* 'beloved', *-rék, -rékendaru* 'brother/sister-in-law', *salén, saléndaru* 'female relation (sister or daughter) of man', *sáγun, sáγundaru* 'brother-in-law', *-skir, -skirtaru* 'father-in-law', *-skus, -skušindaru* 'daughter-in-law', *šon, šondaru* 'blind, one-eyed', *-ús, -úšindaru* 'wife', *-yál, -yáldaru* 'friend', *-yást, yástaru* 'sister (of man)'

A.2 Blood relatives in parental generation or older {-štaru} (12)
bap, bápištaru 'grandfather', *dibáp, dibápišteru* 'great grandfather', *diwáw, diwáwišteru* 'great grandmother', *´-mi, ´-mištaru* 'mother', *nané, nanéštaru* 'uncle', *néne, néništaru* 'aunt', *´-ŋgu, ´-ŋguštaru* 'uncle', *´-nzu, ´-nzuštaru* 'aunt', *-pe, -pištaru* 'grandfather', *táti, tátištaru* 'father', *´-u, ´-uštaru* 'father', *wáu, wáuištaru* 'grandmother'

A.3 'handle-with-care' {-tiŋ} (35)
A.3.1 'handle-with-care' {-tiŋ} only (17)
badšá 'king', *bibí* 'wife of Pir', *čaŋgú* 'lame', *čarbú* 'night watchman', *çiloi* 'guardian', *guá* 'witness to marriage before sufi', *hají* 'hajji, pilgrim to Mecca', *kaikaí* 'princess', *kančéni* 'fickle woman', *lašá* 'lazy, unfit for work', *naí* 'barber', *mergí* 'epileptic', *parí* 'fairy', *pharištá* 'angel', *sālé* 'faithful woman', *šarmandá* 'shameful', *-yúhar* 'husband'

A.3.2 V-final {-tiŋ}~{-mu} (9)
baṭá, baṭátiŋ, baṭámu 'bald, lacking horns', *darzí, darzítiŋ, darzímu* 'tailor', *dobí, dobítiŋ, dobímu* 'launderer', *duagú, duagútiŋ, duagúmu* 'interpreter of the Qur'an, holy man', *gadéru, gadérutiŋ, gadérumu* 'crazy', *kamxordá, kamxordátiŋ, kamxordámu* 'someone who eats little', *kusá, kusátiŋ, kusámu* 'beardless man', *xansamá, xansamátiŋ, xansamámu* 'cook', *mučí, mučítiŋ, mučímu* 'blacksmith, cobbler'

A.3.3 C-final {-tiŋ}~{-išu} (9)
ajíz, ajíztiŋ, ajízišu 'submissive', *buzúrk, buzúrktiŋ, buzúrkišu* 'hermit, holy man', *gušpúr, gušpúrišu, gušpúrtiŋ* 'prince', *kusurwár, kusurwártiŋ, kusurwárišu* 'guilty', *lohár, lohártiŋ, lohárišu* 'knife-grinder', *-rar, -rartiŋ, -rarišu* 'son-in-law', *šeríf, šeríftiŋ, šerífišu* 'reliable/humble man', *zārgár, zārgártiŋ, zārgárišu* 'silversmith, goldsmith', *zenaxór, zenaxórtiŋ, zenaxórišu* 'womanizer'

A.4 Other (3)
-kón (1)
-cu, -cukón 'brother'
-bák (1)
ṣádar, ṣadarbák 'servant'
-iŋa (1)
-máŋgus, máŋgušiŋa 'secondary wife'

B Animate (784)

The frequency of each of the phonologically-defined classes of stem relevant to plural formation is summed up under the heading for each node. Note that the score for C-final excludes n- and s-final stems.
V-final 241, C-final 376, n-final 90, s-final 71, Vi-final 6

B.1 Plurisyllables and non-CVC monosyllables (627)
V-final 241, C-final 244, n-final 69, s-final 67, Vi-final 6

B.1.1 Plurisyllables (606)
V-final 232, C-final 234, n-final 68, s-final 65, Vi-final 6

B.1.1.1 Regular plural formation
B.1.1.1.1 Vowel-final stems {-mu} (223)
axtá 'castrated bull, horse or donkey', *alačí* 'cardamum', *alká* 'eyepiece', *ālú* 'potato', *aphiuní* 'opium smoker', *arabá* 'wheel of vehicle', *aramarí* 'cupboard', *badaγší* 'kind of horse', *baxtá* 'sheep with large tail', *bamphú* 'ball', *barxatúki* 'kind of night ghost or witch', *barmá* 'hand drill', *baṣá* 'turban', *baṭirí* 'electric battery', *beγéli* 'with big eyes', *behəští* 'one who fears God', *bijilí* 'electricty; electric lamp', *bráγu* 'foal', *búbu* 'flying black beetle', *buxári* 'stove', *bulá* 'grouse; strip of dough cooked in soup', *bulā́ni* 'dwarf; tripe prepared in little

parcels', *caq-legíni* 'uvula', *cípi* 'tiny worms (found in ditches filled with water)', *cipíri* 'person who blinks', *culá* 'uncastrated billy-goat', *čabí* 'key', *čaɣé* 'jackdaw', *čamaḍóri* 'iron frying pan', *čaní* 'burin, graver', *čantóro* 'person with extra digits', *čapáli* 'wine stain, branding mark', *čaré* 'desert plant', *čaréni* 'pouch to keep rags for cleaning rifle', *čarí* 'bedbug', *čarsí* 'hashish smoker', *čatánu* 'lintel', *češmá* 'glasses, spectacles', *čiríti* 'spark', *čorpóŋgi* 'one who crawls on all fours (baby, infirm)', *çéxi* 'goat/cow's horn; hook', *dairá* 'circle', *dáni, dánimu, dánimiŋ, dániŋ* 'kind of music', *daṣṭí* 'reserve of meat for winter', *dazbé* 'beads', *dildaŋgí* 'oven-baked bread', *diwá* 'lamp', *dučešmá* 'binoculars', *duldamá* 'kettle drum', *duṣṭá, duṣṭámu, duṣṭáiŋ* 'sapling', *ḍabí* 'packet (esp. of matches)', *ḍáku* 'walking stick', *ḍanḍá* 'rod, stalk, beam', *ḍanḍíni* 'kind of nappy', *ḍaŋgá* 'cairn, tower', *ḍóri* 'wooden ladle', *ḍuḍúru* 'nipple, teat', *ḍukúri* 'hunchbacked', *ḍulú* 'cord', *gabí* 'pipe; flute', *gadelá* 'mattress', *gaḍí* 'watch', *gajarí* 'horse blanket', *gáli* 'woollen blanket', *gambúri* 'flower', *gandá* 'good-for-nothing', *ganṭá* 'scales', *garaḍí* 'reel on fishing rod', *garpá* 'weed', *gawará* 'cradle', *gíli, gílimu, gíličiŋ* 'nail, peg', *girí* 'ibex', *góbi* 'cauliflower', *gunḍá* 'active pederast', *guŋgústi* 'lisper', *gúru* 'mirror', *gusgóyo* 'one who does a woman's work', *ɣalɣó* 'insect, worm, caterpillar', *ɣamú* 'ice', *ɣóni* 'air, bearing, comportment', *ɣonó* 'seed, sperm', *ɣorá* 'bump, swelling', *ɣormadí* 'kind of bread', *hamají* 'hammer used for cutting out recesses in upper millstone', *hatóḍa* 'hammer', *hunčá* 'pile', *hupúpu* 'hoopoe', *iškawá* 'wheel axle', *iṣqornó* 'small bird that makes home in thornbush', *jalá* 'raft', *jā́li* 'sieve', *jálu* 'dinghy, raft', *jamajī́ri* 'twin', *jaṭí* 'large wooden vat', *jandí* 'flag', *jawá* 'lazybones', *jermaní* 'heavy shell', *jilimčá* 'rug', *jiŋá* 'rockfall', *jolá* 'rucksack', *jorṓṭi* 'unripe apricot', *jundá* 'beggar's garment', *jurúni* 'curls, braids worn at sides', *ǰiŋá* 'boulder (rolling down)', *kačālú* 'Jerusalem artichoke', *kaḍí* 'beam, girder', *kajáti* 'match (for lighting fire)', *kakáči* 'stutterer', *kā́ku* 'cuckoo', *karmā́ci* 'alevin, young fish', *karmutá* 'parotid space', *kartópi* 'person with protruding ears', *kisá* 'rifle kit carried on belt', *kiṣí* 'line, verse of Qur'an', *karúṭu* 'deaf', *kíki* 'kind of falcon', *kikíu* 'dried powdered fruit', *kiṣí* 'line', *kunḍá* 'bolt', *kunú* 'butter vat', *kursí* 'chair', *kū́ru* 'system for fastening burden', *kurusmá* 'wild iris', *kuṭéni* 'rifle swab', *kháči* 'bucket', *kharéṭi* 'wicker basket', *khilaú* 'sweet made of walnuts/apricots in congealed grape concentrate', *khilí* 'sign', *khiṣṭí* 'small boat', *xālí* 'void', *xaltá* 'bag', *láɣu* 'laundry stick; bald', *láṣu* 'liar', *laqá* 'mountain plant sp.', *lóḍo* 'bastard, son of a bitch', *lṓṭi* 'food given to bull in form of ball; ball (for playing)', *loṭó* 'bare-headed', *makú* 'shuttle (on loom)', *mašá* 'trigger mechanism on shotgun with fuse', *mašarbá* 'watering can', *mašulá* 'mouthpiece of shalm', *mená* 'cake made with oil from apricot kernels', *muçá* 'horse-hair net for catching birds', *mulá* 'pack-saddle', *murdé* 'cord for regulating width of Dardic cap', *narí* 'wave, ripple', *náru* 'mill stone', *narúci* 'homosexual, hermaphrodite; man whose testicles have not dropped', *niginá* 'set precious stone', *-níni* 'pupil (of eye)', *´-ŋgitiki* 'white spot on horse's forehead', *paiséri* 'foot bridge, plank', *paltáṣu* 'wild bush sp.', *pálu* 'wedge', *panjí* 'stone wall', *páqu* 'bread', *patáxi* 'percussion cap', *pereṣú* 'side of cap', *pilíli* 'ant', *pinḍóro* 'spherical', *pultyá* 'wick, fuse', *phárce* 'cap', *phári* 'pond', *pháte* 'bowl', *-pháṭi* 'forehead', *pheraní* 'large basket for transport of straw', *phéru* 'maggot; spy', *phéṣu* 'pear', *phulúṭi* 'bud, willow catkin', *phurdónu*, *phurdónumu*, *phurdónumiŋ* 'woman's veil', *qašqá* 'white spot on horse's forehead', *qoqó* '(afflicted with) goitre', *quṭí* 'small leather pouch for gun-powder', *ráči* 'hunter's tutelary spirit', *sanḍá* '(male) buffalo', *sardóni* 'short truncheon', *sarká* 'part of field circumscribed by embankment', *saróni* 'man's WiSi/BroWi; woman's HuBro/SiHu', *suɣá* 'left hand, left-hander', *šamé* 'yoke (on neck of cattle)', *šarí* 'wife's brother', *-šáṭu* 'testicle', *šiŋálu* 'rosehip', *šišá* 'glass', *šónšimini* 'mouse', *šóṭo* 'mushroom', *šuɣurí* 'kind of hard pear', *šulú*, *šulúmu*, *šulúiŋ* 'driftwood', *šuqá* 'wide, long-armed woollen coat', *ṣaboqbánu* 'meal offered by father of suitor', *ṣáŋa* 'plant sp.', *ṣiéli* 'charming, lovely', *ṣóli* 'stopper', *tálu* 'inflammation of the tonsils', *tapóci* 'gobbledy-gook', *tarāzú* 'scales', *tauší* 'large bowl, basin', *tilíki* 'bread given to herdsman when animals throw', *tuxulí* 'castrated wether of 2–3 years', *tuléni* 'small stick for applying collyrium', *túli* 'wooden peg', *tumá* 'shell (of egg, nut); fruit stone', *túni* 'small basket', *thúči* 'hide from leg (used for leather bags)', *ṭéru* 'cross-eyed', *ṭíki* 'patch; thick loaf', *ṭóri* 'wooden bung', *ṭurpíču* 'meadow lark', *ṭhári* 'polo ball', *ṭhaṭhóri* 'poor man's bread (of corn or millet)', *učútu* 'nimble', *úhu* 'owl', *úju* 'otter', *uliná* 'protective roof', *úri* 'mountain summit', *-úru* 'nail, claw', *urusí* 'muzzle-loader; cup', *-wélji*, *-wéljimu*, *-wéljimiŋ* 'dream', *wezmá* 'measure of gun-powder for muzzle-loader', *yánji* 'mill', *zilimčá* 'hair blanket'

B.1.1.1.2 {-išu} (210)

B.1.1.1.2.1 Consonant-final {-išu} (204)

abláq 'dappled', *ainák* 'glasses', *aiždahár* 'dragon', *ajalúk* 'wave', *akhéṣ* 'dragon', *alám* 'flag, banner', *anáhar* 'sober, hungry', *anár* 'mango', *aqmáq* 'blockhead', *asaqál* 'old man', *ašéq* 'lover', *awarsír* 'overseer', *badā́m* 'almond', *badráŋ* 'cucumber', *bálaf* 'electric bulb', *baláŋ* 'pole for hanging clothes', *balbát* 'goose', *baléṭ* 'experienced', *behél* 'obedient', *behúš* 'beside oneself (with rage)', *beskáreṭ* 'two-year old wether', *biáṭar* 'cow of 1–2 years', *biḍír* 'large hammer for breaking stones', *buár* 'watermelon', *búmbal* 'wheel of spindle', *butál* 'bottle', *buṭár* 'castrated billy-goat 1–2 years old', *cadár* 'women's headscarf', *cigír* 'goat', *cimák* 'fine sieve', *cirík* 'small flightless bird with black head', *culdár* 'uncastrated (bull, ram, yak)', *čačír* 'thistle', *čainák* 'teapot', *čakást* 'tassle on back of bridegroom's cap', *čaqár* 'two-pronged fork, bifurcation', *čatír* 'tent', *čermék* 'supporting fork for spindle on spinning wheel', *čilpák* 'type of cake eaten after Ramadan', *čiráɣ* 'lamp', *čítaraŋ* 'swallow', *čópur* 'caper', *čumuṭkér* 'young woman', *ҫeҫér* 'small bird sp.', *damkutáh* 'asthmatic', *dinár* 'type of particularly valuable falcon', *dukandár* 'shopkeeper', *dumbalapúr* 'breech-loading rifle', *ḍáḍar* 'loose stones', *ḍakṭér* 'doctor, physician', *ḍambóz* 'stock or club carried by fakir', *ḍarawár* 'driver, conductor', *ḍonṭák* 'person with two teeth superposed', *gacér* 'vulture', *gádar* 'beam; wood for burning', *gáhal* 'kind of predator that eviscerates goats', *gaméš* 'buffalo', *gandál* 'ceiling beam', *gandár* 'garland of flowers', *gilám* 'rug', *giltír* 'straps for fastening yoke to shaft of plough', *girčáp* 'bedbug, louse', *ɣarbel* 'sieve', *ɣaṣép* 'magpie', *yaṣṭék* 'gusset of woollen coat', *yoçhár* 'waterfall', *yodút* 'ganglion', *yoriašút* 'someone who farts loudly', *yunḍíl* 'kind of dove', *yurér* 'butter vat', *haúlal* 'butterfly, moth', *henḍél* 'crank, starting-handle', *hómal* 'plant whose seeds are used for washing clothes', *hósar* 'pumpkin', *humbák* 'quiver', *hušiár* 'skilled, intelligent', *ísur* 'channel parallel to main irrigation channel', *íṣal* 'hinge', *ípholok* 'only child', *jabál* 'stone borer', *jādugár* 'magician, juggler', *janjabíl* 'ginger', *jaqár* 'fork', *jarnél* 'army general', *jerasím* 'microbe', *jiláu, jiláwišu* 'rein', *jiŋgóy* 'scorpion', *jiráŋ* 'chestnut brown (horse)', *jikáp* '(wild) rhubarb (edible part)', *kabút* 'white horse', *kākól* 'cultivated rhubarb', *kambál* 'blanket', *kamzór* 'weak', *kapál* 'head, skull', *kapčaléz* 'small wooden spoon', *karnél* 'colonel', *kawál* 'overhanging rock', *kinsár* 'ice axe', *kíusar* 'large walking stick', *kolóš* 'shoe of black plastic', *kuhméit* 'black horse', *kulúk* 'hoof', *kundáq* 'rifle support', *kundupičár* 'youngest child, Benjamin', *khámal* 'skull', *khamár* 'rifle kit carried on belt', *khánjul* 'kind of bird', *xačír* 'mule', *xambáx* 'container for flour made of flat stones or wood', *xarā́p* 'bad quality', *xarqár* 'donkey-driver', *xawáŋ* 'quilt', *xuṭúl* 'container on roof for grain', *laház* 'sick', *laxwár* 'kind of fast horse', *lapháṭ* 'stutterer', *likír* 'ligne de papier ligné', *lólum* 'eavesdropper, spy, guard', *luyár* 'animal sacrificed at funerary celebration', *macixór* 'kind of bird', *maxsúm* 'small child', *manḍáy* 'heron', *martól* 'sledgehammer', *mejár* 'major', *ménzer* 'marten', *meščikár* 'falconer', *murwát* 'screw', *muzī́r* 'jealous', *nabalét* 'friend', *nābehél* 'fatal', *natarā́š* 'disobedient', *naúhar* 'plant with edible white flowers', *niṭák* 'palate', *pāgál* 'idiot, half-wit', *paiyumbár* 'prophet', *pā́pal* 'solitary, misanthrope', *parašúṭ* 'parachute', *parčám* 'fringe', *pardúm* 'croupier', *parkál* 'dividers', *paṭík* 'hock (of animal)', *pelésk* 'cloth of goat's hair', *peléṭ* 'plate', *pisík* 'one of two front leather pieces of local boot', *pitík* 'sheep one year old', *punár* 'primrose with violet flowers', *púšuruk* 'grasshopper, cricket', *puṣṭúr* 'pockmarked', *phagál* 'bowl', *phaxúr* 'proud', *phal-phal* 'person with long ears', *phandár* 'wart', *phanús, phanúzišu* 'plateau', *phindár* 'eyesore, wen', *phoryóṭ* 'brown, russet', *phúrdum* 'cheetah', *qalám* 'feather pen', *qalíp* 'mould', *qandráq* 'ditch', *qerqér* 'juniper branch (whose fumes on burning inspire the shaman)', *qundáq* 'gun-stock', *rafḗq* 'loved one (man)', *rambóy* 'bean with red kernel', *raphál* '(European) shotgun', *samawár* 'samovar', *sandóq* 'box', *sapúk* 'type of game', *sayúrj* 'large, very expensive hunting falcon', *soṭóp* 'stove', *subadár* 'sergeant', *suyár* 'cooking pot', *suṭúl* 'small table', *šagárt* 'pupil, apprentice', *šanṭhér* 'cross-eyed', *šaxék* 'rifle swab', *šaŋkúr* 'nightblind individual', *šilák* 'bread without wheat', *šukúr* 'umbrella', *ṣáxur* 'branch; ray', *ṣíṣar* 'large winged beetle', *ṣiwíč* 'bird sp.', *tā́ām* 'food', *tābút* 'coffin, casket', *takabúr* 'proud', *taráq* 'naked; vagrant', *tauríč* 'plank fixed to joists of roof', *tuqúm* 'felt layer under saddle', *turčún* 'marmot', *turúy* 'dark brown horse', *thalóx* 'bag for toiletries', *thanáu* 'rope, cord; braid', *thóṣhalal* 'bride, bridegroom', *ṭákur* 'hair-dresser', *ṭaṭár* 'kind of large tailless forest rat', *ṭikadár* 'opponent', *ṭiṭírum* 'housing of door pivots', *uráy* 'part of horse where spurs driven', *usél* 'gift offered to father of bride', *ustát* 'master (term of respect for professional)', *úšam* 'adopted parent, dear friend (esp. in-law)', *waphadár* 'loyal, honest, faithful', *wāzgár* 'preacher', *yasaúl* 'servant of the mir', *yáṭhal* 'wild ewe'

B.1.1.1.2.2 Vi-final stems {-išu} (6)
anái, anáišu 'saddle button', *čapléi, čapleišu* 'sandal', *čatibói, čatibóišu* 'devastating flood', *goléi, goléišu* 'pill; ball of thread', *julái, juláišu* 'nut flour', *surunái, surunáišu* 'oboe, bombard'

B.1.1.1.3 {-yu} (123)

B.1.1.1.3.1 n-final {-yu} (68)
alɣán 'stirrup', *ambuxčán* 'secondary wife', *áŋan* 'chevaux de Frise of thornbush', *arɣón* 'cross-bred, hybrid, illegitimate child', *asúmun* 'star', *aúšin, aúšu* 'guest', *auzín, auzíu* 'abdomen', *báldan* 'whetstone', *balɣán* 'wound on horse', *bartún* 'pulley', *baṣqarikán* 'type of horse', *bedī́n, bedī́u* 'atheist; glutton', *bégamun* 'glutton', *beimā́n* 'infidel', *biṭán* 'bitan, soothsayer', *čidín* 'iron cooking-pot', *čilimčín, čilimčíu* 'basin', *damán* 'possession', *daṣmán* 'Sunna priest', *dióṣkun* 'friend who accompanies groom to seek bride', *dipcón* 'short-tailed tiger', *diucón* 'dog-like wild animal with short tail', *durbín, durbíu* 'longue vue', *dušmán* 'enemy', *gamún* 'foundation of house', *ganás* 'straw', *gármen* 'large bird of prey', *gikín* 'finger ring', *girán* 'large willow basket', *girwán* 'collar', *ɣā́mun* 'crow', *ɣaṣçún* (also *ɣaṣçúnc*) 'carrot', *ɣórkun* 'frog', *haján* 'harness for spade', *haldén, haldíu* 'ibex', *-hálmun* 'rib', *hírmen* 'yellow 'insect' with six legs on either side', *insā́n* 'human being', *jakún* 'donkey', *jamū́in* 'local functionary', *jikán* 'strap', *karmún* 'someone with cropped ears', *kiftén* 'captain', *lanṭén* 'lantern', *madyén* 'mare', *máɣun* 'pearl necklace', *maristán* 'slave', *milkón* 'kind of flower', *paṭigán* 'aubergine, brinjal', *pensén* 'pencil', *pharán* 'moth; soul', *qalín, qalíu* 'woven blanket', *rúmun* 'fringe', *sáhan* 'stone vat for fermenting wine', *sausán* 'iris', *-sésen* 'elbow', *siakhamán* 'rifle in which butt and bore form a single piece', *surxún* 'grey/white horse', šahín šahíu 'small hawk', *-šílan* '(yak's) tail', *šimán* 'sash', *-šípen, -šípiu* 'penis', *tasqán* 'earthquake', *tirdón* 'cartridge belt', *tuxmirán* 'parents-in-law', *turčún* 'marmot', *ṭiŋán* 'egg', *warɣán* 'animal cadaver', *zarxán* 'file'

B.1.1.1.3.2 s-final stems {-yu} (52)
ačás 'lamb older than two years, sheared for the first time', *barés* 'sinew, vein', *béles* 'sheep (older than 2 years)', *bónis* 'lumps of dough for making flatbread', *búndas* 'small wingless insect that bites sheep', *-čáɣanes* 'back of head', *čirkánas* 'stepping stones in ford', *čóqures* 'branches growing from a pruned tree', *čúkus* 'main beam', *daldénes* 'sieve', *dúlas* 'boy, youth', *éṣpaṭkus* 'sheep between 6 and 12 months up for second shearing', *ganás* 'straw', *gilás* 'drinking glass', *gírkis* 'rat, mouse', *gúṭas* 'corpse', *ɣárqas* 'lizard', *ɣólkos* 'cistern', *ɣónderes* 'water flowing over many rocks', *ɣóqares* 'raven', *haɣós* 'mountain pass', *harkunás* 'ice axe', *helés* 'boy, servant', *hundáres* 'floorbeam of a house', *húṭis* 'pedal', *huyés* 'sheep and goats', *imékus* 'small nail', *jikánderes* 'straps for attaching yoke', *júŋus* 'bracelet', *kamúnes* 'misanthrope, lone wolf', *kanjáres* 'wooded incline', *kukúres* 'puppy', *mátas* 'medium-sized beam in house', *mináis* 'doll', *moṭés* 'mill axis', *-núŋus* 'knee', *-phóɣonas* 'slave', *phópolanas* 'blister',

phópos 'bastard, know-nothing', *qaqā́s* 'kind of odorous plant', *qáqoles* 'bulb, blister', *ṣiṣíŋinas* 'small water conduit', *tanós* 'mortar', *tapús* 'kind of eagle', *turmúkuṭes* 'earwig (? believed fatal)', *thánes, thánešu, thánaŋ* 'point (of arrow, etc.)', *tharés* 'meadow', *úsas* 'small stone for applying collyrium', *-wáldes* 'back', *wélukus* 'one-year old sheep', *-yáṭes* 'head (of grass)', *-yúŋus* 'tongue'

B.1.1.1.3.2.2 c-final {-yu} (3)
biétarc, biétarču 'cowherder', *gamáic, gamáiču* 'neighbour', *huyéltarc, huyéltarču* 'shepherd'

B.1.1.2 Quirky plural formation (19)
B.1.1.2.1 C-final stems {-mu} (2)
hánik, hánikmu 'wooden key', *giṣṭék, giṣṭékmu, giṣṭékišu, giṣṭéka* 'brick of clay or salt'

B.1.1.2.2 Quirky stems with {-išu} (17)
B.1.1.2.2.1 Quirky V-final forms with {-išu} (5)
buyéki, buyékišu 'goat with red hairs about the eyes', *guá, guáišu, guátiŋ* 'marriage witness before sufi', *kuráṭu, kuráṭišu* 'emaciated (animal)'

B.1.1.2.2.1 Quirky V-final forms with {-išu}~{-mu} (2)
daróɣo, daróɣošu, daróɣomu 'staff', *išpaqéti, išpaqétišu, išpaqétimu* 'small white flightless bird'

B.1.1.2.2.2 Quirky s-final stems with {-išu} (10)

B.1.1.2.2.2.1 Quirky s-final stems with {-išu} only (8)
but-pharás(t), but-pharás(t)išu 'idolater', *ɣáqales, ɣáqalesišu* 'scarecrow', *ɣorqós, ɣorqósišu* 'water tank', *jāsús, jāsúsišu* 'detective, informer, spy', *kanjús, kanjúsišu* 'miser, haggler', *panḍóles, panḍólesišu* 'turf', *papóres, papóresišu* 'bump, boil', *tapós, tapósišu* 'species of eagle (considered lucky)'

B.1.1.2.2.2.2 Quirky s-final stems with {-išu}~{-yu} (2)
alɣás, alɣásišu, alɣášu 'bit', *čardaɣés, čardaɣésišu, čardaɣéšu* 'low wall delimiting inner entrance of dormitory',

B.1.1.2.2.3 Quirky C-final stems with {-yu} (5)
B.1.1.2.2.3.1 Quirky nC-final {-yu} (3)
gaṣíṣkin, gaṣíṣkuyu 'spider', *ɣaṣçúnç* (also *ɣaṣçún*) *ɣaṣçúyu* 'carrot', *phépenč, phépiu* 'rim of vessel'

B.1.1.2.2.3.2 Quirky ṣ-final {-yu} (1)
barkáṣ, barkášu 'balance, scales'

B.1.1.2.2.3.3 Quirky unstressed -mu final stem with {-yu}~{-mu} (1)
čúmu, čúmumu, čúmuyu 'fish'

B.1.1.3 Legacy plural formation (29)
B.1.1.3.1 Legacy V-final stem with {-kó} (1)
phínju, phinjukó 'polo stock'

B.1.1.3.1 Legacy C-final stem with {-u} (6)
B.1.1.3.1.1 Legacy C-final stem with {-u} only (3)
héreṣ, héreṣu, héreṣišu 'edge, bulge, seam; ridge; brink', *málhar, málharu, málharumu* 'rape, colza (eaten as vegetable)', *qarqámuš, qarqámušu* 'wing', *-yé, -yú* 'son'

B.1.1.3.1.2 Legacy C-final stem with {-u}~{-iau} (1)
héreṣ, héreṣu, héreṣišu 'edge, bulge, seam; ridge; brink'

B.1.1.3.1.3 Legacy C-final stem with {-u} and {-j-} stem augment (2)
tal, tálju 'dove', *búmbalten, búmbaltenju* 'knuckle'

B.1.1.3.2 Legacy ṣ-final {-ha} (3)
buláṣ, buláha 'childless, barren', *gaṣánç, gaṣáha* 'hunting falcon', *haménç, haméha* 'curd'

B.1.1.3.3 Legacy sibilant-final {-a} with subtraction (6)
B.1.1.3.3.1 Legacy ṣ-final {-a} with subtraction only (5)
asúkiṣ, asúkia 'rumen', *biškékiṣ, biškékia* 'hairy', *bupuṣ, búpua* 'pumpkin', *ɣaríŋkiṣ, ɣaríŋkia* 'singer', *híliŋkiṣ, híliŋkia* 'flame'

B.1.1.3.3.2 Legacy s-final {-a}+subtr. ~{-yu} (1)
phurúkus, phurúkua, phurúkušu 'container for unspun wool'

B.1.1.3.4 Legacy C-final {-a} (11)
B.1.1.3.4.1 Legacy C-final {-a} only (7)
giṣṭék 'clay or salt tablet', *haɣór* 'horse', *huráp* 'trough for kneading dough', *marúk* 'cream', šútum 'hearth', *tuéq* 'rifle', *ṭambúk, ṭambúka* 'slingshot'

B.1.1.3.4.2 Legacy C-final {-a}~{-iau} (3)
cigír, cigíra, cigíríšu 'goat', *čikít, čikíta, čikítišu* 'rifle with breech added', *meraxór, meraxórišu, meraxóra* 'stable boy'

B.1.1.3.4.3 Legacy C-final {-a}~{-aaku} (1)
surúŋ, surúŋa, suruŋášku 'path between two fields'

B.1.1.3.5 Haplological (singular = plural) (2)
ɣašú, ɣašú 'onion', *khíšu, khíšu* 'mosquito'

B.1.2 Non-CVC Monosyllables (21)
V-final 9, C-final 10, n-final 1, s-final 2

B.1.2.1 Regular plural formation
B.1.2.1.1 V-final {-mu} only (8)
xaú 'intestinal worm', ´-lči 'ice', *-mé* 'tooth; rung in ladder', *nyá* 'bear', *sa* 'month', *sú* 'muzzle (of pot)', *tá* 'leopard', *-ú* 'tear'

B.1.2.1.2 C-final stems with {-išu} (6)
dṓst 'friend', *rā́ṭ* 'fishing rod', *sḗṭ* 'merchant', *sī́x* 'spit, skewer', *tā́ž* 'hoopoe', *waíz* 'preacher'

B.1.2.1.3 *n*-final stems with {-yu} (1)
taún 'wooden box for flour'

B.1.2.1.4 *s*-final stems with {-yu} (1)
jā́s, jā́šu 'small hoe'

B.1.2.2 Quirky plural formation (3)
B.1.2.2.1 C-final stems with {-mu} (2)
rū́h, rū́hmu 'soul', *šā́ṣ, šā́ṣmu* 'cover'

B.1.2.2.2 *s*-final stems with with {-išu} (1)
saús 'carnation; green-blue colour'

B.1.2.3 Legacy plural formation
B.1.2.3.1 V-final stem with {-mu}~{-ha} (1)
kha, kháha, khámu 'hook, stirrup'

B.1.2.3.2 C-final stems with {-a} (2)
čaíṣk, čaíṣka, čéya 'wooden door-bolt', *máuṣk, máua, máuaha* 'rake'

B.2 CVC Monosyllables (157)
Where relevant, the existence of cognates languages in contact with Burushaski is indicated in parentheses to tie in with the discussion in § 5.2.2. Abbreviations used: B(urushaski), E(nglish), Kh(owar), P(ersian), Sh(ina), T(ibetan), U(rdu).
C-final 132, *n*-final 21, *s*-final 4

B.2.1 Regular plural formation
B.2.1.2 C-final {-išu} (37)
B.2.1.2.1 C-final {-išu} only (33)
B 10 (30.5%), Kh 9 (27.5%), Sh 1 (3%), Kh/Sh 2 (6%), U 11 (33%)
bált (B) 'apple', *bórj* (Kh) 'sparrowhawk', *čarx* (U) 'vulture, hawk', *čok* (B) 'bird sp.', *ḍúq* (B) 'hump, gibbosity', *guṭ* (Kh) 'pony', *hár* (Kh) 'garland', *jíp* (U < E) 'jeep', *jaç* (Kh) 'little bell', *jáẓ* (U < E) 'judge', *ker* (B) 'rival', *koš* (Kh)

'pod', *-khák* (Kh) 'skull', *khúš* (Sh/Kh) 'crippled in the hand or forearm', *xuk* (U) 'pig; churl', *léṣ* (Kh/Sh) 'kind of bird', *loq* (Kh) 'rag', *méz* (U) 'table', *pirč* (U) 'saucer', *phil* (U) 'elephant', *phúk* (B) 'morsel', *rónz* (B) 'mouflon', *rúl* (U < E) 'ruler (instrument)', *sír* (B) 'contraction of pain', *sur* (B) 'insidious, sinister', *ṣúṣk* (Kh) 'white ink for writing on slate', *táxt* (U) 'padded platform for taking meal', *tez* (U) 'swift', *-úl* (B) 'belly', *yoṣṭ* (Kh) 'ambassador'

Other N-final monosyllables {-išu} only (3)
bum, bumišu (Sh) 'ibex', *láŋ, láŋišu* (B) 'giant', *naŋ, naŋišu* (U) 'dragon'

B.1.1.3.4.1 C-final {-išu}~{-mu} (1)
qaf, qafišu, qafmu (Kh) 'claw, fork'

B.1.1.3.4.1 C-final {-išu}~{-a} (1)
tak, takišu, táka (Sh/Kh) 'tie on both sides of woollen coat',

B.2.1.3 {-yu} (13)
B.2.1.3.1 Nasal-final monosyllables {-yu} only (9)
B 5 (56%), Kh 2 (22%), Sh 0, Kh/Sh 0, U 2 (22%)
bran, bráyu (Kh) 'ram', *çen, çéyu, çíu* (B) 'bird', *-γán, -γáyu* (B) 'heel', *jin, jíu* (U) 'djinn', *phén, phíu* (B) 'fly', *-sán, -sáyu* (B) 'chin; spleen', *šen, šéyu* (Kh) 'vine-leaves', *-thán, -tháyu* (B) 'scalp', *ṭin, ṭíu* (U < E) 'can, tin'

B.2.1.3.2 s-final monosyllables {-yu} (4)
bes, bešú, bešó 'grease', *bus, búšu, bušó* 'bunch of grass', *gos, gošu* 'flat grinding stone', *-khús, -khúšu* 'posterior', *bóṣo, bóšu* 'calf'

B.2.2 Quirky plural formation (9)
Consonant-final monosyllables with {-mu} (9)
es, esmu 'morsel', *γáṣ, γáṣmu* 'froth, cream', *-ís, -ísmu* 'child', *náš, nášmu* 'camel's nose-ring', *muš, mušmu* 'edge', *-múš, -múšmu* 'nose; snot', *qáf, qáfmu, qáfišu* 'claw, fork', *´-rič, ´-ričmu* 'kidney', *tyoh, tyohmu* 'kind of hawk'

B.2.3 Legacy plural formation (99)
B.2.3.1 CVC {-ašku} (18)
B.2.3.1.1 *n*-final CVC {-ašku} (12)
B.2.3.1.1.1 *n*-final CVC {-ašku} only (7)
B 4 (57%), Kh 0, Sh 3 (43%), Kh/Sh 0, U 0
khan, khanášku (B) 'fort, fortified village', *khun, khunášku* (Sh) 'corner (in room)', *man, manášku* (B) 'walled platform for sitting or sleeping', *men, menášku* (B) 'earth-dwelling wasp', *pan, panášku* (Sh) 'place at either side of fireplace', *šon, šonášku* (Sh *śen*) 'bed frame', *yan, yanášku* (B) 'handle (on tool)'

B.2.3.1.1.2 *n*-final monosyllabic {-ašku} ~ {-yu} (3)
pen, péyu, penášku (U < E) 'pen', *phón, phóyu, phonášku* (B) 'dam in field', *thun, thúyu, thuŋášku* (B) 'irascible'

B.2.3.1.1.3 *n*-final monosyllabic {-ašku} ~ {-ánc} (1)
mun, munánc, munášku (Kh) 'treestump'

B.2.3.1.1.4 *n*-final monosyllabic {-ašku} ~ {-yu} ~ {-ánc} (1)
ɣón, ɣóyu, ɣonánc, ɣonášku (Sh) 'quail'

B.2.3.1.2 Other N-final CVC {-ašku} (5)
B.2.3.1.2.1 Other N-final CVC {-ašku} only (1)
ruŋ, ruŋášku (Sh) 'mountain pasture'

B.2.3.1.2.2 Other N-final CVC {-ašku} ~ {-ánc} (4)
duŋ, duŋánc, duŋášku (B) 'pole, post', *ḍoŋ, ḍoŋánc, ḍoŋášku* (B) 'knoll', *sam, samánc, samášku* (Sh *sugōm*) 'hole in roof for smoke', *ṣuŋ, ṣuŋánc, ṣuŋášku* (B) 'narrow gorge'

B.2.3.1.3 Other C-final CVC with {-ašku} (1)
B.2.3.1.3.1 Other C-final CVC with {-ašku} only (1)
taɣ, taɣášku (Kh) 'twig, sapling'

B.2.3.1.3.2 Other C-final CVC {-ašku}~{-ó}~{-iau} (1)
sanč, sančášku, sančó, sánčišu (Kh) 'floor beam'

B.2.3.2 CVC {-ánc} (42)
B.2.3.2.1 C-final CVC {-ánc} (43)
B.2.3.2.1.1 C-final CVC {-ánc} only (38)
B 17 (45%), Kh 6 (16%), Sh 7 (18%), Kh/Sh 3 (8%), U 3 (8%) Other 2 (5%)
barc (B) 'bridge', *buk* (Kh) 'throat, gullet; horn (musical instrument)', *buš* (Sh/Kh) 'cat', *buc* (B) 'wooden lever', *cal* (B) 'pile of corn', *čiq* (B) 'wooden tablet for separating wheat from chaff', *čiṣç* (Sh) 'guide', *çur* (B) 'wedge on catapult', *darč* (B) 'grain for threshing', *dau, dawánc* (Sh) 'tinplate', *deu, dewánc* (P) 'ghost, demon, nightmare', *dul* (Sh) 'collyrium', *ḍaf* (U) 'tambourine with shells', *ḍor* (Sh/Kh) 'hopper (in mill)', *ḍos* (B) 'breast (of hen)', *gap* (B) '(untreated) animal skin', *guk* (B) 'chisel', *ɣái, ɣayánc* (B) 'thread', *hurç* (B) 'pole', *jel* (Kh) 'blanket', *jip* (Kh/Sh < U) 'shirt pocket', *ju, juánc* (T) 'ball of wool', *khol* (Kh) 'overhanging rock that forms cave', *muk* (Sh) 'pearl', *mul* (Sh) 'wheatmeal gruel', *phlak* (Kh) 'rounded upper part of Dardic cap', *sal* (B) 'mill stone', *šar* (Kh) 'three-sided file for sharpening knives', *šol* (B) 'avalanche', *ṣar* (B) 'twig; roofless shelter for sheep', *ṣek* (B) 'funnnel', *tal* (Kh) 'castle', *tup* (U) 'canon', *uṭ* (U) 'camel', *yuk* (Sh) 'stretcher'

Other N-final CVC {-ánc} only (3)
ḍim, *ḍimánc* (B) 'piece of cloth forming back of coat', *sum sumánc* (B) 'female animal (esp. goat)', *ṣaŋ ṣaŋánc* (Sh) 'border'

B.2.3.2.1.2 C-final CVC {-ašku}~{-ánc} (1)
ḍaṭ, *ḍaṭánc*, *ḍaṭášku* (Kh) 'supply trough for butter'

B.2.3.2.1.3 C-final CVC with {-ánc} and {-i-} stem augment (2)
hur, *huriánc* 'water conduit', *tul*, *tuliánc* 'snake, eel'

B.2.3.2.1.4 C-final CVC with {-ánc} and {-kó} (1)
čar, *čaránc*, *čarkó* (Sh) 'rock'

B.2.3.2.1.5 C-final CVC {-išu}~{-ánc} (1)
phúl, *phúlišu*, *phulánc* (B) 'small wooden key'

B.2.3.2.1.6 C-final CVC with {-mu}~{-ánc} (1)
γaṣ, *γaṣánc*, *γáṣmu* (B) 'perilous mountain path'

(1)
B.2.3.3 {-ó} (21)
B.2.3.3.1 C-final CVC with {-ó} (8)
čaṭ, *čaṭó* 'small', *çirç*, *çirçó* 'bull, ox', *gaṣk*, *gaṣkó* 'long, thick rope', *gaṭ*, *gaṭó* 'knot', *γoṭ*, *γoṭó* 'silent', *jaṭ*, *jaṭó* 'old, hoary', *phut*, *phutó* 'species of hirsute spirit', *wec*, *wecó* 'cow, half a year after giving birth'

B.2.3.3.2 s-final CVC with {-ó} (4)
bes, *bešú*, *bešó* 'grease', *bus*, *búšu*, *bušó* 'bunch of grass', *has*, *hašó* 'ember', *gas*, *gašó* 'wool thread'

B.2.3.3.3 Liquid-final CVC with {-ó} with {-j-} stem augment (4)
bun, *bunjó*, *bundó* 'boulder', *dan*, *danjó* 'stone', *hal*, *haljó* 'fox', *ten*, *tenjó* 'bone'

B.2.3.3.4 C-final CVC with {-ó} and {-k-} stem augment (2)
čar, *čarkó*, *čaránc* 'rock', *čiṣ*, *čiṣkó* 'mountain, summit'

B.2.3.3.5 C-final CVC with {-ó}, {-k-} and {-V-} stem augments (1)
senç, *sençakó*, *sençukó* 'roof beam'

B.2.3.3.6 C-final CVC with {-ó} and {-i-} stem augment (2)
har, *harió*, *hariómu* 'bull, ox', *sar*, *sarió*, *sariómu* 'hare'

B.2.3.2.1.7 C-final CVC with {-mu} and stem augment (2)
kóč, *kóčimu* 'acne', *tah*, *tahamu* 'leopard'

B.2.3.4 Other (18)
B.2.3.4.1 C-final CVC Extended forms with {-nc} (2)
ɣask, ɣaskónc 'withies for basket-weaving', *wal, walénc* 'male animal'

B.2.3.4.2 C-final CVC {-a} (13)
blok, blóka 'bud', *bóṣo, bóṣa, bóṣu* 'calf', *čoṭ, čóṭa, čoṭánc, čoṭišu* 'bud, joint, knot', *ḍaḍáŋ* 'large drum', *du, duá* 'kid', *-ḍim, ḍíma* 'body, tree trunk', *huk, huká* 'dog', *sap, sápa* 'hoof', *ṣiŋ, ṣíŋa* 'spool, bobbin', *tak, táka* 'button', *tak, takišu, táka* 'tie on both sides of woollen coat', *ṭoq, ṭóqa* 'large block of wood', *urk, urká, urkás* 'wolf'

B.2.3.4.3 C-final CVC {-é} (1)
hunc, huncé, huncému 'arrow'

B.2.3.4.4 C-final CVC {-í} with ablaut (1)
hir, hurí, huríkia 'man'

B.2.3.4.5 C-final CVC {-u} (1)
tham, thámu 'prince'

B.3 V-final Disyllables (12)

B.3.1 V-final disyllables {-šku} (3)
kuná, kunášku stick', *kuṭu, kuṭušku* chalet', *ṭeṭé, ṭeṭéšku* rope'

B.3.2 V-final disyllables {-nc}
B.3.2.1 V-final disyllables {-nc} only (7)
bayú, bayúnc, bayónc 'salt', *behé, behénc* 'female animal', *biá, biánc* 'cow', *buá, buánc* 'sod of earth', *gaṭú, gaṭúnc* 'trousers',

B.3.2.2 V-final disyllables {-nc}~{-mu} (2)
bépa, bépanc, bépamu 'yak', *phurú, phurúnc, phurúmu* 'willow; reed'

B.4 Prosodically deficient C-stems {-mu} (2)
-s, -smu 'heart', *-ṣ, -ṣmu* 'throat'

C Inanimate (616)

C.1 Regular plural formation (429)
C.1.1 C-final {-iŋ} (301)
C.1.1.1 C-final {-iŋ} (269)
alɣaniwár 'dance tune', *ambúr* 'pincer', *axrán* 'stable', áraz 'complaint', *arzā́n* 'market', *asqór* 'flower', *aulán* 'leather patches for repairing boot', *baçár* 'peep-hole in entrenchment', *badā́m* 'almond tree', *bahúr* 'salty substance exuded from earth', *bakšawár* 'music marking end of polo game', *bal, balíŋ*

'wall; brains', *bal, báliŋ* 'walnut', *balbán* 'hole (in wall, ceiling)', *bálcir* 'mountain stream', *balt, báltiŋ* 'apple tree', *bandobár* 'fastener for shoulder strap', *banén* 'sweater, vest', *bar, baríŋ* 'mountain gorge; matter; size of piece of fabric', *baráncal* 'string made of intestine', *barénç* 'omen', *baríčum* 'threshing of grain', *barpéṭ* 'straps', *baspúr* 'grain fodder', *báṣqar* 'kind of tree with thorns', *baṭór* 'dried apricot', *bazár* 'market, bazaar', *bázum* 'enjoyment of dance with tambourine and hand-clapping', *beç, béçiŋ* 'badge', *bend, bendíŋ* 'place for sitting in house', *bérkat* 'summit', *besát* '(expensive) bed-clothes', *biabā́n* 'desert', *bóit* 'clear sky', *bṓṭ, bṓṭiŋ* 'blackboard', *budúl* 'rag', *bulásqor* 'square of purple flowers', *bupúr* 'fine hair, down', *búrj* 'corner', *burúš* 'brush', *buryán* 'scrambled eggs', *car, caríŋ* 'urine', *cart, cartíŋ* 'lateral slit in coat', *cel, celíŋ, celmíŋ* 'water', *-cér, -cériŋ* 'intestines', *colɣṓm* 'winter dish of meat and chapatis', *čakán* 'embroidery', *čáxur* 'stick with yarn wound around it', *čan, čaníŋ* 'gruel of wheat and meat', *čapár* 'scar', *-čar, -čáriŋ* 'voice, sound', *čémel* 'poison', *činár* 'plane-tree', *čočór* 'shavings', *čop, čopíŋ* 'beauty cream made from goat's horn and water', *čópur* 'caper (plant)', *čumúṣ* 'rhume', *čuturóɣ* 'water flow', *čuṭ, čuṭíŋ* 'fluid pattern', *daɣ, daɣíŋ* 'snow-free spot', *dā̄ɣ, dā̄ɣíŋ* 'leather button', *daɣóm* 'flour', *dam, damíŋ* 'lamé thread', *dap, dapíŋ* 'lump of clean wool', *darjét* 'pus', *dā̄s, dasíŋ* 'wasteland, wilderness', *dastúr* 'custom', *dawát* 'invitation', *dékharan* 'garden allotment', *del, delíŋ* 'oil, melted fat', *délčin* 'cinnamon', *den, deníŋ* 'year', *-dil, -diliŋ* 'breast', *díltar* 'butter-milk', *dī́n, dī́niŋ* 'believer', *diráxt* 'tree', *dráp, drápiŋ* 'draughts (game)', *dukán* 'shop, workshop', *ḍauḍáu, ḍauḍáwiŋ* 'dish made with chapatis in strips', *galt, galtíŋ* 'turn', *galtár* 'small twig', *gan, ganíŋ* 'road, path', *gar, garíŋ* 'wedding', *gasúndar* 'kind of hardwood tree', *gaṭbáṭ* 'confusion', *gert, gértiŋ* 'dust', *ginâhur* 'type of tree', *grinč, grínčiŋ* 'rice', *guc, gucíŋ* 'corner between wall and floor; river bank', *guláp* 'pink rose', *gumbát* 'cemetery', *gunc guncíŋ, gúnciŋ* 'day', *gunjaíš* 'solution', *gut gutíŋ* 'tent', *ɣar, ɣaríŋ* 'sound; pl. song', *ɣel, ɣeliŋ* 'dandruff', *ɣṓr, ɣṓriŋ* 'crevasse, cave', *ɣoṭúm* 'part of house', *ɣuṭúm* 'trough, mould', *haldénc* 'large sack of goat's hide', *harált* 'rain cloud; rain', *hayán* 'sign, token; gift', *hazíz* 'lead', *-híl, -híliŋ* 'lip (also of vessel)', *híŋbaltar* 'entrance to village (where people gather)', *hókum* 'spades (in cards)', *hukár* 'tamarind', *humáç* 'padding for socks', *hun, huníŋ* '(fire)wood', *hurt, hurtíŋ* 'wall dividing fields', *hurúp* 'letter of the alphabet', *il, íliŋ* 'eye (of needle)', *ílgaṭ* 'corner of the eye; notch; meeting of two valleys', *intihán* 'exam', *íŋgut* 'halter', *iskén* 'buttonhole', *išpén* 'leftovers', *išpít* 'lucerne', *iṣqór* 'narrow furrow for irrigation', *iṣṭám* 'paper bearing a stamp', *jal, jalíŋ* 'net', *janjér* 'chain, fetter', *jér, jériŋ* 'line, row', *jirā́p* 'sock', *juár* 'fight, war', *juláp* 'diarrhoea', *jut, jutíŋ* 'meadow', *jenjé*r 'chain, zip', *jiŋát* 'scree-slope', *jikáp* 'rhubarb plant', *kadán* 'kind of kitchen knife', *kaɣáz* 'paper', *kahkóɣ* 'chicken soup', *kaṭoɣár* 'fabric, material', *kauhán* 'shroud', *kél, kéliŋ* 'wrinkle, fold', *-ken, -keniŋ* 'liver', *ketép* 'book', *kiṭór* 'apricot dried with the stone', *kṓṭ, kṓṭiŋ* 'coat', *kuít* 'fig', *khačumár* 'iron hook', *khamarbánd* 'cummerbund', *khaṣ, khaṣíŋ* 'make-up', *xabár* 'piece of news', *xál, xáliŋ* 'taste', *xat, xatíŋ* 'letter', *-xát, -xátiŋ* 'mouth', *xerát* 'wooden tower', *xeréṭ* 'spittle', *-xóxaṭ* 'craw', *xorc, xorcíŋ* 'dust', *-xórpet* 'lung', *xōsiét* 'habit', *lam, lamíŋ* 'rheumatism', *-ltúmal* 'ear', *mac, macíŋ* 'ordeal in which red-hot axe-blade must be carried', *mahabát* 'law', *maxdúr* 'feeding trough for horses', *mal, malíŋ* 'field', *malhám* 'ointment', *manaḍér* 'money order', *máncel* 'whey', *mardán* 'perpetual meadow in otherwise cultivated land', *margúšt* 'kind of creeping plant', *mašín* 'machine (razor)', *mázur* 'lentil-like pulse', *-mélc, -mélciŋ* 'jaw-bone', *-mélmel* 'moustache', *menéṭ* 'minute', *mezpóš* 'table cloth', *mičíl* 'pomegranate tree', *-móqoṭ* 'cheek', *muxén* 'veranda', *multán* 'blood; blood money, wergeld', *múnḍal* 'willow tree', *muramát* 'repair', *-múṣpuṭ* 'trunk (of elephant)', *múṣt, múṣṭiŋ* 'handful; fist', *muṭhár* 'evergreen bush', *naɣár* 'fox-trap', *náqal* 'copy, reproduction', *nasyét* 'advice, counsel', *naúhar* 'plant with edible white flowers', *naukát* 'portion of food', *nawár* 'plaited ribbon', *niét* 'vow, wish', *niméž* 'prayer', *palíš* 'polish', *pánč* 'back of blade', *pandár* 'wedding gift', *paŋkaṭ* 'small change', *parawéz* 'border of herdsman's coat', *parkál* 'plan, sketch', *patráinč* 'hunting mask', *-pét, -pétiŋ* 'gall', *pétal* 'apricot blossom', *pubánd* 'fetter (on talon of hawk)', *phalál* 'peppermint', *phálpaṭ* 'rooster's comb', *phā́num* 'crack, fissure', *pharéṭ* 'scar', *phát, phátiŋ* 'residue', *phéč, phéčiŋ* 'hearth', *qaburstán* 'cemetery', *qalám* 'cabbage', *qamqám* 'mouse-trap', *qanún* 'law', *qóčawéz* 'bag for tinderwood', *qon, qoníŋ* 'embers for cooking', *qorbán* 'festival of Aid-el-Kebir; sacrificial victim at this festival', *rabáṭ* 'rubber', *rambóɣ* 'bean plant', *raxmát* 'benediction', *roɣán* 'paint', *sābút* 'proof, evidence', *san, saníŋ* 'white cotton', *saŋgesír* 'stew', *saphár* 'voyage', *sawál* 'question', *sarpúš* 'leather rifle protector', *séṭ, séṭiŋ* 'set', *sipiríṭ* 'spirit, ether', *siphér* 'period, full stop', *sitár* 'sitar', *siṭár* 'stock, reserve', *-skil, -skiliŋ* 'face, surfacc', *sukúl* 'school', *sópaṭ* 'ash of certain herb added to snuff', *sūrát* 'reflection', *-súsur* 'gums', *šaftál* 'clover', *šáhar* 'town', *šand šandíŋ* 'grain laid out in field to dry', *šarán* 'stone-walled enclosure', *šawáran* 'polo field', *šíl, šíliŋ* 'piece of wood used in joining by mortise and tenon', *šistuár* 'tune', *-šóɣon* 'hip', *šuáčal* 'kind of vegetable with round leaves', *ṣapáṭ* 'cermonial spoon', *ṣaú, ṣauíŋ, ṣaúŋ* 'wild rose-bush', *ṣolt, ṣoltíŋ* 'roof', *tal talíŋ* 'birch', *tam, tamíŋ* 'flash', *taréz* 'side part of shuqa', *-tátas* 'flat of hand', *tā́ž, tā́žiŋ* 'playing card', *tópon* 'piece of sheep-skin used in cleaning', *tumár* 'amulet', *túrum, túrumiŋ* 'horn (musical instrument)', *tušmáč* 'kind of tribunal', *thap, thapíŋ* 'night', *ther, theríŋ* 'dirt, filth', *ṭikéṭ* 'postage stamp', *waxt, waxtíŋ* 'time', *waskáṭ* 'waistcoat', *waṭ, waṭíŋ* 'bark', *-wáṭ, -wáṭiŋ* 'body, self', *yaqín* 'certitude, belief', *yárç, yárçiŋ* 'price, worth', *zabán* 'language', *záhar* 'poison', *zaŋgár* 'rust', *zā́r, zā́riŋ* 'gold', *zén* 'chainmail', *zián* 'injury', *zukám* 'rhume'

C.1.1.2 s-final {-iŋ} (8)

bakínās 'lancet for bloodletting', *bisás* 'yellow-flowering leguminous plant', *ɣoṭamús* 'disorder', *ɣupás, ɣupásiŋ, ɣupášiŋ* 'cotton', *hóras* 'sluice', *xuntís* 'sudden anger', *mirás* '(bad) habit', *pereṭís* 'training, exercise'

C.1.1.3 K-final {-iŋ} only (24)
balaṣṭíŋ 'explosion', *bardáq* 'bread in thin flour soup', *bobóq* 'muscle, esp. thigh', *čahalík* 'hearth', *čamáx* 'lighter', *dáštik* 'secondary hearth', *delk* 'manure, dung', *γaribík* 'gathering before transhumance', *héštik* 'office', *jirák* 'burn', *jéŋ* 'gap', *xork, xorkíŋ* 'chopped straw, chaff', *xoróŋ* 'cloud', *muçáṣk* 'milk strainer made of cow hair', *marmúk* 'handful', *muṣk* 'forest', *nawáq* 'iron ploughshare', *palaṣṭík* 'plastic', *paṭík* 'hock of dead animal', *-púnšak* 'shoulder blade', *šawálik* 'kind of trouser worn by women', *ṣaq, ṣaqíŋ* 'mountain pasture', *ṣúṣk, ṣúṣkiŋ* 'white efflorescence on mountain rocks', *waráq* 'sheet of paper'

C.1.2 V-final stems {-ŋ} (114)
C.1.2.1 Unstressed V-final stems {-ŋ} (21)
C.1.2.1.1 Unstressed i-final {-ŋ} (19)
ačaγésti 'stitching', *árdi* 'earth, area', *béšiki* 'puzzle', *bulukáli* 'winter dish of meat, flour and onion', *buxári* 'chimney', *dómaki* 'third visit before marriage', *γái, γáiŋ, γayánc* 'thread', *γašū́ši* 'nettle', *háški* 'harvest festival', *héqai* 'outer part of house (for keeping wood, etc.)', *kulupóŋgi* 'weft', *xarčíki* 'wedding night', *madíri* 'authority, power', *paṣóli* 'nostril', *suári* 'iron cross-piece in mill', *šíti* 'rupee', *ṣabulúki* 'kind of clover', *tā́li* 'strand (fibre)', *uγaríki* 'cereal mixture'

C.1.2.2 Unstressed V-final {-ŋ} (2)
boróndo 'ring', *óṣṭana* 'half-rupee'

C.1.2.2 Stressed V-final {-ŋ} (93)
C.1.2.2.1 Stressed i-final {-ŋ} (34)
abadí 'settlement', *arzí* 'request', *baltí* 'front room of house in which wood is kept', *barwazí* 'dance tune', *berbādí* 'ruin', *burí* 'silver', *čaní* 'walnut', *čilkí* 'half-rupee', *čuṭí* 'leave', *daṣṭí* 'reserve of meat for winter', *gaší* 'jaw', *γaibí* 'unexpected event', *γuskí* 'dough', *halí* 'birch-bark', *haulí* 'outside doorway', *istrí* 'clothes-iron', *išpirí* 'bread and butter (for special occasions)', *karanḍí* 'trowel', *khardačí* 'salad', *khirkí* 'window', *maçí* 'honey', *manḍaí* 'place where livestock accommodated on way to market in Gilgit', *mergí* 'epilepsy', *mōndarí* 'neighbour', *muzdurí* 'rent, wage', *nalí* 'seedling', *nanbaí* 'hotel, hostel', *nekí* 'good deed', *paxtí* 'lentil', *paṭí* 'bandage', *penṭirí* 'kitchen in bungalow', *qačí* 'shears', *suruŋgí* 'explosion', *šertí* 'bet, wager'

C.1.2.2.2 Stressed u-final {-ŋ} (4)
čakú 'pen-knife', *xaú* 'wild bush with sour fruit', *phuṭú* 'photo', *ṣaú, ṣaúŋ, ṣauíŋ* 'wild rose-bush'

C.1.2.2.3 Stressed e-final {-ŋ} (12)
C.1.2.2.3.1 Stressed e-final {-ŋ} only (7)
balčaŋgé 'board for kneading dough', *barcé* 'fur worn over shoulders', *dasé* 'patch', *gaçé* 'switch, rod', *garé* 'large sheep shears', *jamé* 'bow (for shooting)', *mesqé* 'saliva'

C.1.2.2.3.2 Stressed e-final {-ŋ}~{-iK} (5)
buyé, buyéŋ, buyéiŋ 'wooden shovel', *ɣamé, ɣaméiŋ, ɣaméčiŋ* 'spider's web', *ɣandé, ɣandéŋ, ɣandéiŋ* 'grass-plot', *musqé, musqéiŋ* 'saliva', *naɣé, naɣéŋ, naɣéiŋ* 'excrement'

C.1.2.2.4 Stressed o-final {-ŋ} (2)
C.1.2.2.4.1 Stressed o-final {-ŋ} only (1)
daɣó 'glue made from yak skin'

C.1.2.2.4.2 Stressed o-final {-ŋ}~{-iK} (1)
horgó, horgóŋ, horgóiŋ 'steep incline'

C.1.2.2.5 Stressed a-final {-ŋ} (41)
C.1.2.2.5.1 Stressed a-final {-ŋ} only (38)
baŋgalá 'bungalow', *bará* 'sitar-like string instrument', *bastá* 'strap for carrying across shoulder', *bayá* 'sole', *bistrá* 'bedding', *čaká* 'sour milk product', *dakxaná* 'post office', *dastá* 'handful', *jaɣá* 'place, location', *jaŋgyá* 'bermuda shorts', *janjá* 'torch, flare', *khiná* 'millet straw', *xadá* 'pole with snare on end for catching hawks', *xarčá* 'stock, provisions', *mahraká* 'row of people', *maliá* 'tax', *māmilá* 'affair, event', *maská* 'butter made the same day', *mewá* 'fruit', *moqá* 'occasion, chance', *moqabilá* 'match, competition, challenge', *naxšá* 'image, photo', *niphá* 'hem', *niwištá* 'conjugal bliss', *paisá* 'money', *paitawá* 'puttee', *qabzá* 'hinge', *qaphiá* 'pleasantry', *rozá* 'fast', *rupayá* 'rupee', *soḍá* 'baking powder', *surmá* 'collyrium', *širá* 'juice', *takmá* 'medal, decoration', *taxtá* 'tablet, slate', *tolyá* 'hand-towel', *tukazá* 'rifle stand', *ziadá* 'excess'

C.1.2.2.5.2 Stressed a-final {-ŋ}~{-iK} (3)
čamá, čamáŋ, čamáiŋ 'round brooch', *randá, randáŋ, randáiŋ* 'plane (tool)', *taɣá, taɣáŋ, taɣáiŋ* 'mortar made of earth and water'

C.1.2.3 Short CV-stem {-iŋ} (8)
ba, baíŋ 'millet; sorghum', *bo, boíŋ* 'seed grain', *ca, caíŋ, cáiŋ* 'kind of millet', *ču, čuíŋ* 'head (of grass); bunch (grapes); knife-blade; wedge (of melon)', *ge, geíŋ* 'snow', *pho, phoíŋ* 'scab, pustule', *ṣaú, ṣauíŋ, ṣaúŋ* 'wild rose-bush', *še, šeíŋ* 'wool'

C.2 Quirky plural formation (26)
C.2.1 V-final stems (28)
C.2.1.1 Unstressed V-final {-iŋ} (1)
kačā́lu, kačā́luiŋ 'Jerusalem artichoke (plant)'

C.2.1.2 Stressed V-final {-iŋ} (27)
C.2.1.2.1 Stressed u-final {-iŋ} (3)
čumuršú '(roasting) spit', *jumú* 'type of large coat', *šulú, šulúiŋ, šulúmu* 'driftwood'

C.2.1.2.2 Stressed o-final {-iŋ} (1)
doró 'work'

C.2.1.2.3 Stressed a-final {-iŋ} (22)
alaqá 'district', *bahá* 'hole, burrow', *baldá* 'burden', *barmá* 'borehole', *basá* 'day and night', *buçá* 'horse-hair net for catching birds', *burqá* 'veil for women', *doxná* 'flour ritually cast into fire', *duṣṭá* 'sapling', *humá* 'ford', *išqá* 'grass', *khamá* 'felt carpet', *pardá* 'veil; hymen', *šaldá* 'command', *tamašá* 'official festivity', *tasmá* 'ligature', *thaná* 'police district', *waɣdá* 'collateral'

C.3 Legacy plural formation (187)
C.3.1 C-final {-iŋ} with truncation (5)
-húṭis -húṭiŋ 'foot', *lamán lamániŋ, lamáiŋ* 'coat-tail', *mún múiŋ* 'artemisia', *-rén -réiŋ, -réiŋčiŋ* 'hand', *taxtabán taxtabániŋ, taxtabáiŋ* 'cupboard'

C.3.2 s/c-final with palatalization {-iŋ} (7)
ándus, ándušiŋ 'bog', *táuc, taučiŋ* 'puttee', *thas, thašiŋ* 'smoke', *phalc, phalčíŋ, phalčóŋ* 'kind of deciduous tree', *phópos, phópošiŋ* 'broom', *phúmbares, phúmbarešiŋ* 'fire signal'

C.3.3 {-haŋ} (11)
C.3.3.1 {-haŋ} only (10)
balkáṣ, balkáhaŋ, balkáṣiŋ 'cavity in wall', *bayáṣ, bayáhaŋ, bayáṣiŋ* 'ceiling, roof', *burús, burúhaŋ* 'kind of milk product, lassi', *ɣaṭénç, ɣaṭéhaŋ* 'sword', *-móqiṣ, -móqihaŋ* 'face', *milí, milíhaŋ* 'medicine', *muçúṣk, muçúhaŋ* 'implement for turning bread while roasting', *noṣ, nóhaŋ* 'sapling', *puṣ, púhaŋ* 'shirt (of either sex)', *teléṣ, teléhaŋ* 'sinew on slingshot'

C.3.3.2 {-haŋ}~{-iŋ} with palatalization (1)
minás, mináhaŋ, minášiŋ 'tale'

C.3.4 {-aŋ} (24)
C.3.4.1 {-aŋ} (10)
bálçikiṣ, bálçikiaŋ 'cow manure', *biákuṣ, biákuaŋ* 'cowstall', *bisarṣ, bisáraŋ* 'sickle', *camáreṣ, camáraŋ* 'part of wooden frame of smoke-hole in ceiling', *cáreṣ, cáraŋ* 'threshold', *gíŋiṣ, gíŋiaŋ* 'small leather pouch', *gókoreṣ, gókoraŋ* 'iron scraper', *iṣqóreṣ, iṣqóraŋ* 'thornbush', *phutúneṣ, phutúnaŋ* 'charred log', *thánes, thánaŋ* 'cuff'

C.3.4.2 {-aŋ} and {-i-} stem augment (2)
bur, buriáŋ 'single hair', *thur, thuriáŋ, thuriákiŋ, thuriákičiŋ* 'whip'

C.3.4.3 {-aŋ} with /ṣ/→/r/ C-final {-aK} (4)
barqáṣ, barqáraŋ 'removal', *barténç, bartéraŋ, barténçiŋ* 'edge', *ɣurpúṣ, ɣurpúraŋ* 'hayloft', *maltáṣ, maltáraŋ* 'butter'

C.3.4.4 C-final {-aŋ} (8)
bel, beláŋ, beléŋ 'shovel', *duk, dukáŋ* 'spindle', *gir, giráŋ, giríŋ* 'saw', *hesk, heskáŋ, heskíčiŋ* 'comb', *matél, matélaŋ* 'kind of crop disease', *sel, seláŋ* 'sewing needle', *teṣk, teṣkáŋ* 'dagger', *kač, kačáŋ* 'buttonhole'

C.3.5 {-miŋ} (63)
C.3.5.1 V-final (57)
C.3.5.1.1 V-final {-miŋ} only (38)
C.3.5.1.1.1 Unstressed V-final stems with {-miŋ} (24)
C.3.5.1.1.1.1 Unstressed i-final stems with {-miŋ} (7)
cáŋgi 'precipice', *čaqő̄ti* 'trouble', *éṣi* 'necklace', *ɣaréi* 'ornament', *phíṭi* 'papilla', *ṣuṣkáli* 'boiled makuti', *-wélji, -wéljimiŋ, -wéljimu* 'dream'

C.3.5.1.1.1.2 Other unstressed V-final stems with {-miŋ} (17)
axránu 'stable', *cáɣa* 'garden', *čódo* 'blame, accusation', *çáɣu* 'bush whose wood contains oil used in treating sunburn', *ɣardánu* 'whirlpool', *hálu, hal hálumiŋ, halmíŋ* 'goal (in polo)', *horóɣo* 'sweat', *járu* 'song for special occasion', *xausóno* 'court case, legal dispute', *nasálu* 'two-month old meat that has already begun to smell', *phurdónu* 'veil for women', *randíju* 'meat roasted on spit', *sáu* 'sand', *sénde* 'sand', *ṣaphéru* 'ash (used as vegetable fertilizer)', *-tóto* 'paw; palm of hand; ball of foot', *uŋgálu* 'old wound, cicatrice'

C.3.5.1.1.2 Stressed V-final stems with {-miŋ}
C.3.5.1.1.2.1 Stressed i-final stems with {-miŋ} (3)
darí 'window', *jí* 'life, soul, heart, spirits', *muṣkarí* 'good news'

C.3.5.1.1.2.2 Stressed o-final stems with {-miŋ} (1)
pašanó 'contention, noise'

C.3.5.1.1.2.3 Stressed a-final stems with {-miŋ} (10)
buqá 'ankle sock', *čardá* 'kind of small string instrument', *dabdawá* 'feast held in honour of guest', *ɣarbá* 'kind of small string instrument', *ɣustá* 'sourdough', *halwá* 'halva', *kačá* 'underpants', *pardá* 'intestine string', *patá* 'address', *talqá* 'gall-bladder',

C.3.5.1.2 V-final {-miŋ}~{-čiŋ} (1)
balá, balámiŋ, baláčiŋ 'misfortune', *bihái, biháimiŋ, biháimičiŋ* 'sickness'

C.3.5.1.3 V-final {-miŋ}~{-mičiŋ} (1)
bihái, biháimiŋ, biháimičiŋ 'sickness'

C.3.5.1.4 V-final {-miŋ}~{-(i)ŋ} (14)
C.3.5.1.4.1 Unstressed V-final stems with {-miŋ}~{-(i)ŋ} (10)
C.3.5.1.4.1.1 Unstressed i-final stems with {-miŋ}~{-(i)ŋ} (7)

cápi, cápimiŋ, cápiŋ 'tong, tweezers', *dáni, dánimiŋ, dániŋ* 'kind of music', *darséri, darsérimiŋ, darsériŋ* 'reserve of wood for winter', *dišáki, dišákimiŋ, dišákiŋ* 'winter reserve of flour', *jā́li, jā́limiŋ, jā́liŋ* 'fine wire mesh; mosquito screen; framework', *kurtáni, kurtánimiŋ, kurtániŋ* 'shirt', *useni, usénimiŋ, useniŋ* 'handkerchief'

C.3.5.1.4.1.2 Other unstressed V-final stems with {-miŋ}~{-(i)ŋ} (3)
bū́ru, bū́rumiŋ, bū́ruŋ 'kind of thorn bush', *ḍáuḍu, ḍáuḍumiŋ, ḍáuḍuiŋ* 'boiled crushed wheat', *páhlu, páhlumiŋ, páhluŋ* 'side'

C.3.5.1.4.2 Stressed V-final stems with {-miŋ}~{-(i)ŋ} (4)
C.3.5.1.4.2.1 Stressed i-final stems with {-miŋ}~{-(i)ŋ} (1)
šaní, šanímiŋ, šaníŋ 'garden patch'

C.3.5.1.4.2.2 Stressed e-final stems with {-miŋ}~{-(i)ŋ} (1)
-cé, -cémiŋ, -céiŋ 'foot print'

C.3.5.1.4.2.3 Stressed a-final stems with {-miŋ}~{-(i)ŋ} (2)
xestá, xestámiŋ, xestáiŋ 'leavened pastry', *laqá, laqámiŋ, laqáiŋ* 'kind of vegetable eaten in spring'

C.3.5.1.5 V-final {-miŋ}~{-čiŋ}~{-ŋ} (2)
buṣái, buṣáimiŋ, buṣáimičiŋ, buṣáiŋ 'settled land', *haúru, haúrumiŋ, haúriŋ, haúričiŋ* 'small dumplings cooled in water or milk'

C.3.5.2 C-final stems with {-miŋ} (6)
cel, celmíŋ, celíŋ 'water', *cer, cermíŋ* 'necklace', *sadáf, sadáumiŋ* 'precious pearl', *ter, termíŋ* 'summer pasture', *tiṣ, tiṣmíŋ* 'necklace', *uṣ, uṣmíŋ* 'debt'

C.3.6 {-čiŋ} (14)
C.3.6.1 V-final {-čiŋ} (9)
baryóndo 'sourdough', *gíli, gíličiŋ, gílimu* 'nail, peg', *yamé, yaméčiŋ, yaméiŋ* 'spider's web', *hói* 'vegetable', *xúi* 'fluid contents of animal intestines', *jeŋé, jeŋéčiŋ, jeŋéiŋ* 'sleeve', *mái* 'sour milk', *mamú* 'milk', *-mámu* 'breast; nipple, teat', *patári, patáričiŋ, patáriŋ* 'floorboard'

C.3.6.2 C-final {-čiŋ} (5)
giál, giálčiŋ 'pancake', *mel, melčíŋ* 'wine', *nal, nalčíŋ, nalíŋ* 'yoke (on plough)', *-phúiŋ, -phúiŋčiŋ, -phúiŋičiŋ* 'nape of neck', *-úl, -úlčiŋ* 'belly (of dead animal)'

C.3.7 K-final {-ičiŋ} (23)
C.3.7.1 K-final {-ičiŋ} only (14)
haŋ, haŋíčiŋ 'music', *hesk, heskíčiŋ* 'comb; loom', *jaŋ, jaŋíčiŋ* 'war', *kuṭéŋ* 'V-shaped eyepiece for aiming', *mundáq* 'large leather sack', *-qetaraŋ* 'armpit', *raŋ, raŋ(g)íčiŋ* 'colour', *sasáŋ* 'supporting wall', *-šák, -šákičiŋ* 'arm',

šask, šaskíčiŋ 'type of willow whose switches are used in wickerwork', *traŋ, traŋíčiŋ* 'saddle strap', *traq, traqíčiŋ* 'fissure (in rock, glacier)', *triŋ, triŋíčiŋ* 'curds from raw milk', *thux, thuxíčiŋ* 'vapour'

C.3.7.1 K-final {-ičiŋ}~{-iŋ} (7)
behék, behékičiŋ, behékiŋ 'willow', *peṭék, peṭékičiŋ, peṭékiŋ* 'head scarf of women', *ṣoq, ṣoqíčiŋ, ṣoqíŋ* 'gather (of a skirt)', *ṭambúk, ṭambúkičiŋ, ṭambúka, ṭambúkiŋ* 'slingshot', *taríŋ, taríŋičiŋ, taríŋiŋ* 'tube of goatskin (for making butter)', *tóq, tóqičiŋ, tóqiŋ* 'sludge, quagmire', *-yék, -yékičiŋ, -yékiŋ* 'name'

C.3.7.1 K-final {-ičiŋ}~{-čiŋ} (1)
-phúiŋ, -phúiŋičiŋ, -phúiŋčiŋ 'nape of neck'

C.3.7.4 K-final {-ičiŋ}~{-óŋ} (1)
phask, phaskíčiŋ, phaskóŋ 'edge'

C.3.8 K-final {-ičáŋ} (1)
hiŋ, hiŋíčaŋ 'door'

C.3.9 KV-final {-čiŋ} (10)
C.3.9.1 KV-final {-čiŋ} (7)
baŋgí 'Baumharz', *búiki* 'meal at funeral', *galgí* 'wing; arrow fletching; saddle wing', *gaŋgí* 'axe', *garíki, garíkičiŋ, garíkiŋ* 'torch', *hárki* 'ploughing', *thā̃ŋgi* 'bakery in royal kitchen'

C.3.9.2 P-final (3)
čhap, čhapíčiŋ, čhapíŋ 'meat', *harúm, harúmčiŋ* 'settled land', *kap, kapíčiŋ, kapíŋ* 'folded (of paper)'

C.3.10 {-óŋ} (23)
C.3.10.1 C-final CVC with {-óŋ} (21)
C.3.10.1.1 C-final CVC with {-óŋ} only (12)
baç, baçóŋ 'cabin for sheep and goats', *band, bandóŋ, bandúŋ* 'link, joint', *bat, batóŋ* 'flat stone', *baṭ, baṭóŋ* 'leather', *gark, garkóŋ* 'supply of peas', *harç, harçóŋ* 'plough', *manç, mançóŋ* 'broadaxe', *phaṭ, phaṭóŋ* 'hen's stomach', *salç, salçóŋ* 'beam of mill', *saṣç, saṣçóŋ* 'ploughwood', *tark, tarkóŋ* 'mill-wheel paddle', *yen, yenóŋ* 'thick pieces of bread'

C.3.10.1.2 C-final CVC {-óŋ}~{-iŋ} (6)
bac, bacóŋ, bacíŋ 'small irrigated mountain terrace', *balk, balkóŋ, balkóiŋ* 'plank', *can, canóŋ, caníŋ* 'straight, honest, true', *khaç, khaçóŋ, khaçíŋ* 'strand, desert', *mart, martóŋ, martíŋ* 'alluvial earth embankment', *phalc, phalčíŋ, phalčóŋ* 'kind of deciduous tree'

C.3.10.1.3 C-final CVC {-óŋ}~{-haŋ} (2)
branç, brançóŋ, bráhaŋ 'mulberry tree', *ganç, gançóŋ, gáhaŋ* 'spindle'

C.3.10.1.4 C-final CVC {-óŋ}~{-óiŋ} (1)
tap, tapóŋ, tapóčiŋ 'leaf'

C.3.10.2 C-final CVC with {-óŋ} with {-j-} stem augment (2)
gal, galjóŋ 'rope bridge, juniper', *phal, phaljóŋ* 'single grain'

C.3.11 {-éŋ} (2)
bel, beléŋ, beláŋ 'shovel', *bul, buléŋ* 'wellspring'

Acknowledgements

I would like to thank Sylvia Blaho, Laura Janda, Martin Krämer, Ove Lorentz, Bruce Morén-Duolljá, Tore Nesset, David Odden, Curt Rice, Bernard Tranel and Christian Uffmann for feedback on this work.

Notes

1. The corresponding ethnonym is 'Burusho'. Attempts have been made to establish a genetic connection between Burushaski and various other languages and language families, including Northwest Caucasian, Basque and Ket (a language isolate of Siberia). Most recently, Čašule (2003) has demonstrated systematic correspondences between Burushaski and Indo-European, arguing for a connection with the extinct Phrygian.
2. The phonology of Yasin Burushaski still awaits thorough elucidation. For a treatment of the Nager dialect, though, see Anderson (1997).
3. The Morin-Tiffou-Pesot system is itself little different from that of Berger, who uses /ċ ś ć ź/ for Tiffou, Pesot and Morin's /c č š ž/.
4. Tiffou and Pesot (1989:8) include two sounds in their inventory that Berger (1974:7) does not mention in his. These are the aspirated affricates / h/ and /c̣h/, although these are reported in Tiffou and Pesot's (1989) dictionary word-initially in only one word each. Their phonemic status is therefore somewhat in doubt.
5. For the phonetic properties of the fortis vs. lenis distinction, see Marchal, Tiffou and Warren (1977).
6. There is also a small class of allomorphs that attach exclusively to disyllabic vowel-final stems, but this class is so small it is ignored here.
7. An alternative to the Markedness-driven approach not discussed here is MPARSE Theory. See McCarthy and Prince (2001), and McCarthy and Wolf (2005). For a critique, see Orgun and Sprouse (1999) and Bye (2007).

8. Alternatively, more specific constraints might be invoked. The candidate we want to exclude (7a) also violates *u and *ŋ.
9. Systematic exceptions to this rule are garments consisting of a cache-sexe fastened to the body by means of thin ties, e.g. *gee-string*, *tanga*, *thong*. In other words, these items do not belong to the semantic field targeted by the *pluralia tantum* rule, and so do not constitute counterexamples.
10. Suffixation of {-z} in English is the phonological expression of being a verb in the third person singular. This is different to the morpheme-based view, according to which {-z} *means* 'third person singular'. Although this view rejects the idea that affixes are morphemes, it does not entail adopting a realization-based view of morphology (e.g. Aronoff 1994; Stump 2001). In common with the morpheme-based view, construction-based morphology recognizes the existence of phrase structure, whereas realizational morphology is flat. See Koenig (1999) for discussion.
11. Of course, it is always possible to argue about a particular case, and there may be some as yet undetected dimension of markedness given which the distribution of {-a} and {-la} in Haitian Creole works out as harmonic. See Klein (2003) for an attempt at deriving the pattern using the resources of OT. Unfortunately, there is no general strategy for dispensing with the cases of unnatural allomorph distribution in Paster (2006) or Bye (2007).
12. This is essentially the perspective adopted in Wolf (this volume) and (in a different way) Yu's work on infixation (Yu 2007). Building on a comprehensive survey of infixation patterns in the world's languages, Yu shows *contra* McCarthy and Prince (2001) that infixation site is generally not determined by considerations of phonological optimality. Instead, the positioning of infixes is determined by language-specific alignment constraints which reside in a stratum (M) dominating universal phonotactic and prosodic constraints (P).
13. Relevant to understanding the cultural basis of this last category, no doubt, is the fact that iron weapons are classified as 'magical forces' in the Burushaski gender system and are assigned to the inanimate *y* gender rather than *x*, which is generally used for countable nouns (cf. Tiffou and Pesot quoted above in section 4.2.4).
14. This class apparently does not extend to nouns denoting persons with negative qualities, e.g. *barxatukí* 'night ghost, witch', *láṣu* 'liar', *aqmáq* 'blockhead', *bégamun* 'glutton', *dušmán* 'enemy'. The basis for this difference in behaviour isn't clear.
15. On the basis of the available data it is not possible to conclude whether this variation is governed lexically or by the context of use. In a number of languages, variation in gender may be exploited to 'downgrade' or 'upgrade' nouns for rhetorical or pragmatic effect (Dahl 2000). It is possible that variation in plural allomorph serves a similar purpose in Burushaski, but this matter must be left to future research.
16. Tiffou and Pesot (1989:18) analyse the regular animate plural suffixes into a basic suffix {-u} and various stem augments ('élargissements'): {-m-}, {-iš-}

and {-y-}. For simplicity I adopt the view that the suffixes are not analysed further. Nothing crucial hangs on adopting either view, however.

17. There are also three *c*-final stems which, in fact, pattern with the s-final stems in taking {-yu}, causing palatalization of /c/ to: *biétarc bietárču* 'cowherd', *gamáic gamáiču* 'neighbour' and *huyéltarc huyéltarču* 'shepherd'.
18. The opaque selection of {-išu} by animate plurisyllables ending in V+i faces additional complications since, as in most languages, there is no underlying contrast between palatal vowel /i/ and palatal glide /y/ in Burushaski: the variation between the two is determined by the syllable structure. The opaque choice of allomorph can therefore not be understood as cuing an underlying constrast.
19. In vowel-final stems ending in an *unstressed* syllable, the bias against hiatus is virtually categorical. Of the 31 such stems in the sample, apparently only a single item (0.3%) takes {-iŋ}: *kačā́lu kačā́luiŋ* 'Jerusalem artichoke (plant)'. With the exception of this one form, if genuine, hiatus between unstressed vowels is disallowed.
20. These interactions are well studied in the Germanic languages. For German, see Zubin and Köpcke (1986), Steinmetz (1985, 1986, 1997), Nelson (1998), and Rice (2006). For Norwegian and Old Norse, see Trosterud (2001, 2006).
21. There are a few stems of this type ending in a diphthong whose second component is a high vowel. In these cases, the high vowel alternates with a glide, e.g. *dau dawánc* 'tinplate', *deu dewánc* 'ghost, demon, nightmare', *ɣái ɣayánc* 'thread'. There is only one open monosyllable animate in the sample, *ju̧ ju̧ánc* 'ball of wool' (a Tibetan loanword). It is possible that a more appropriate phonological interpretation might involve positing an underlying final glide (/ju̧w+ánc/ → ju̧wánc). See Berger (1974: § 37) and Tiffou and Pesot (1989:10) for relevant discussion.
22. Burushaski also has a number of inanimate stems ending in /ɣ/, but none of them take {-ičiŋ}. This may be because /ɣ/ is really a glide. For this reason, /ɣ/ is excluded from the class of true velar consonants here.
23. Berger (1974:17, § 66) also cites the adjective *-nyú* 'big', whose plural form is *-nóyu* as taking {-yu} in the plural, but given the change in the stem, it may be more appropriate to see this alternation as an instance of stem suppletion.
24. This is a variant of a well-known Hypernym Problem (Levelt 1989: 218). In language processing, semantic conditions may determine more than one lexical action (selection of a lemma). The semantic conditions for any given term will thus necessarily also access the hypernym, e.g. the semantic conditions for *ambassador* are a superset of those for *diplomat*.
25. An alternative account might take differences in the frequency of the patterns as its starting point. Since the highly specific suffixes in Burushaski are associated with fewer entries, the memory trace (activation potential) for the pattern may be weaker, and in on-line production we might get interference from patterns with stronger representation. A difficulty that the frequency-based account would have to overcome is that (at least on the evidence of the Burushaski lexicon) such production errors never cross genders, e.g. there

are no cases where {-iŋ} has ended up being substituted for {-yu}, despite the fact that {-iŋ} has considerably stronger representation. Assuming this could be overcome, we would need to find or devise a case where the general pattern has the lower frequency in order to compare the predictions of the two types of approach. One potential case is default *s*-plural in German (Marcus, Brinkmann, Clahsen, Wiese and Pinker 1991).

26. Interestingly, the grammar in (56) poses problems for conflict resolution between constraints for certain kinds of stem. The problem is s-final monosyllables. The presence of both SELECT([CVC]$_{stem}$, -ánc) and SELECT(s]$_{stem}$, -yu$_2$) in the grammar leaves the language-user without a unique way of determining the plural form of an *s*-final monosyllable because the two conditions do not stand in a proper inclusion relationship. Neither the Elsewhere not the Core Semantic Override Principle would resolve the conflict. What might have happened in the course of historical development is that speakers have resolved the issue in favour of the statistically best represented suffix, {-yu}. Five *s*-final monosyllables take {-yu}, and only one takes {-ánc}. Two take {-mu} and 4 take {-ó} with palatalization.
27. This is a special case of proportional analogy. See Hock (2005) for discussion and references.
28. Only one stem in the sample ends in /š/: *qarqámuš qarqámušu* 'fly'.

References

Alderete, John (2001) Dominance effects as tranderivational anti-faithfulness. *Phonology* 18: 201–253.

Anderson, Gregory D. S. (1997) Burushaski phonology. In Alan S. Kaye (ed.) *Phonologies of Asia and Africa (Including the Caucasus)*, vol. 2, 1021–1041. Winona Lake, IN: Eisenbrauns.

Aronoff, Mark (1994) *Morphology by Itself: Stems and Inflectional Classes*. Linguistic Inquiry Monograph 22. Cambridge, MA: The MIT Press.

Austin, Peter A. (1981) *A Grammar of Diyari, South Australia*. Cambridge: Cambridge University Press.

Beckman, Jill N. (1998) *Positional Faithfulness*. Doctoral dissertation, University of Massachusetts at Amherst.

Bennett, Charles E. (1999 [1895]) *New Latin Grammar*. Waucona, IL: Bolchazy-Carducci.

Berger, Hermann (1974) *Das Yasin-Burushaski (Werchikwar). Grammatik, Texte, Wörterbuch*. Neuindische Studien 3. Wiesbaden: Otto Harrasowitz.

Berger, Hermann (1990) Burushaski. In Ehsan Yarshater (ed.) *Encyclopaedia Iranica,* vol. IV, 567–568. London: Routledge and Kegan Paul.

Berger, Hermann (1992) *Das Burushaski – Schicksale einer zentralasiatischen Restprache*. Sitzungsberichte der Heidelberger Akademie der Wissenschaften (Philosophisch-historische Klasse). Heidelberg: Carl Winter.

Berger, Hermann (1998) *Die Burushaski-Sprache von Hunza und Nager. Teil I: Grammatik. Teil II: Texte. Teil III: Wörterbuch.* Neuindische Studien 13. Wiesbaden: Otto Harrasowitz.

Blevins, Juliette (2004) *Evolutionary Phonology. The Emergence of Sound Systems.* Cambridge: Cambridge University Press.

Blevins, Juliette (2006) A theoretical synopsis of Evolutionary Phonology. *Theoretical Linguistics* 32 (2): 117–166.

Bonet, Eulàlia (2004) Morph insertion and allomorphy in Optimality Theory. *International Journal of English Studies* 4 (2): 73–104. Special issue on 'Advances in Optimality Theory' ed. by Paul Boersma and Juan Antonio Cutillas. [Available on http://roa.rutgers.edu/article/view/734.]

Bonet, Eulàlia, Lloret, Maria-Rosa and Mascaró, Joan (2007) Allomorph selection and lexical preferences: Two case studies. *Lingua* 117 (6): 903–927.

Bye, Patrik (2007) Allomorphy – selection, not optimization. In Sylvia Blaho, Patrik Bye and Martin Krämer (eds) *Freedom of Analysis?*, 63–92. Berlin: Mouton de Gruyter.

Bye, Patrik and Svenonius, Peter (2012) Non-concatenative morphology as epiphenomenon. In Jochen Trommer (ed.) *The Morphology and Phonology of Exponence,* 427–495. Oxford: Oxford University Press.

Čašule, Ilija (2003) Evidence for the Indo-European laryngeals in Burushaski and its genetic affiliation with Indo-European. *The Journal of Indo-European Studies* 31 (1–2): 21–86.

Chomsky, Noam and Halle, Morris (1968) *The Sound Pattern of English.* Cambridge, MA: MIT Press.

Corbett, Greville G. (1991) *Gender*. Cambridge: Cambridge University Press.

Dahl, Östen (2000) Animacy and the notion of semantic gender. In Barbara Unterbeck and Matti Rissanen (eds) *Gender in Grammar and Cognition,* 99–115. Berlin: Mouton de Gruyter.

de Lacy, Paul (1999) Circumscriptive morphemes. In Catherine Kitto and Caroline Smallwood (eds) *Proceedings of the Sixth Meeting of the Austronesian Formal Linguistics Association,* 107–120. The Hague: Holland Academic Graphics.

Dixon, R. M. W. (1977) *A Grammar of Yidiɲ*. Cambridge: Cambridge University Press.

Embick, David (2010) Stem alternations and stem distributions. Unpublished manuscript, University of Pennsylvania.

Fleischhacker, Heidi (2002) Cluster-dependent epenthesis asymmetries. In Adam Albright and Taehong Cho (eds) *UCLA Working Papers in Linguistics* 7, 71–116. Los Angeles: UCLA Department of Linguistics.

Fraser, Norman M. and Corbett, Greville G. (1997) Defaults in Arapesh. *Lingua* 103 (1): 25–57.

Frisch, Stefan A., Pierrehumbert, Janet B. and Broe, Michael B. (2004) Similarity avoidance and the OCP. *Natural Language and Linguistic Theory* 22 (1): 179–228.

Gildersleeve, Basil and Gonzalez Lodge (1999) *Gildersleeve's Latin Grammar*. Wauconda, IL: Bolchazy-Carducci. Reprint of 1894 edition.

Goldsmith, John (1979 [1976]) *Autosegmental Phonology*. Doctoral dissertation, Massachusetts Institute of Technology. New York: Garland.

Green, Tonio (2005) Phonology Limited. [Available on http://roa.rutgers.edu/article/view/745.]

Hale, William Gardner and Buck, Carl Darling (1966) *A Latin Grammar*. Tuscaloosa, AL: University of Alabama Press.

Hall, Robert A. (1953) *Haitian Creole: Grammar, Texts, Vocabulary*. Memoirs of the American Anthropological Association 74. Menasha, WI: American Anthropological Association.

Hammond, Michael (1995) There is no lexicon! [Available on http://roa.rutgers.edu/article/view/43.]

Hock, Hans Heinrich (2005) Analogical change. In Brian D. Joseph and Richard D. Janda (eds) *The Handbook of Historical Linguistics*, 441–460. Oxford: Blackwell.

Isačenko, A. V. (1982) *Die russische Sprache der Gegenwart*. München: Max Hueber Verlag.

Janda, Laura A. (1999) From TORT to TŬRT/TRŬT: Prototype patterning in the spread of the Russian N(A)pl -á. In John Dingley and Leon Ferder (eds) *In the Realm of Slavic Philology: To Honor the Teaching and Scholarship of Dean S. Worth From his UCLA Students*, 145–161. Bloomington, IN: Slavica Publishers.

Joseph, John E. (2000) *Limiting the Arbitrary*. Studies in the History of the Language Sciences 96. Amsterdam: John Benjamins.

Kager, René (1996) On affix allomorphy and syllable counting. In Ursula Kleinhenz (ed.) *Interfaces in Phonology*, 155–171. Studia Grammatica 41. Berlin: Akademie Verlag.

Kikuchi, Seiichiro (2006) On Galician definite article allomorphy. *On'in Kenkyu [Phonological Studies]* 9: 41–48.

Kiparsky, Paul (2000) Opacity and Cyclicity. *The Linguistic Review* 17: 351–367.

Klein, Thomas (2003) Syllable structure and lexical markedness in Creole morphophonology: Determiner allomorphy in Haitian and elsewhere. In Ingo Plag (ed.) *The Phonology of Creole Languages*, 209–228. Tübingen: Max Niemeyer.

Koenig, Jean-Pierre (1999) *Lexical Relations*. Stanford, CA: CSLI.

Koenig, Jean-Pierre and Jurafsky, Daniel (1995) Type underspecification and on-line type construction in the lexicon. In Raul Aranovich, William Byrne, Susanne Preuss and Martha Senturia (eds) *WCCFL 13: The Proceedings of the Thirteenth West Coast Conference on Formal Linguistics*, 165–175.

Lakoff, George (1990) *Women, Fire, and Dangerous Things*. Chicago, IL: Chicago University Press.

Lazard, Gilbert and Peltzer, Louise (2000) *Structure de la langue tahitienne*. Paris: Peeters.

Leben, William (1973) *Suprasegmental phonology*. Doctoral dissertation, Massachusetts Institute of Technology.

Levelt, Willem J. M. (1989) *Speaking*. Cambridge, MA: MIT Press.

Lorimer, D. L. R. (1935–1938) *The Burushaski Language. Vol. 1: Introduction and Grammar. Vol. 2: Texts and Translations. Vol. 3: Vocabularies and Index*. Instituttet for sammenlignende kulturforskning. Serie B, Skrifter 29. Oslo: Aschehoug.

Lorimer, D. L. R. (1962) *Werchikwar-English Vocabulary*. Instituttet for sammenlignende kulturforskning. Serie B, Skrifter 51. Oslo: Norwegian Universities Press.

Łubowicz, Anna (2003) *Contrast Preservation in Phonological Mappings*. Doctoral dissertation, University of Massachusetts at Amherst. [Available on http://roa.rutgers.edu/article/view/554.]

Łubowicz, Anna (2007) Paradigmatic contrast in Polish. *Journal of Slavic Linguistics* 15 (2): 229–262.

Marchal, A., Tiffou, E. and Warren, R. (1977) A propos de «VOT»: le cas du bourouchaski. *Phonetica* 34 (1): 40–53.

Marcus, Gary F., Brinkmann, Ursula, Clahsen, Harald, Wiese, Richard and Pinker, Steven (1995) German inflection: The exception that proves the rule. *Cognitive Psychology* 29 (3): 189–256.

Mascaró, Joan (1996) External allomorphy as emergence of the unmarked. In Jacques Durand and Bernard Laks (eds) *Current Trends in Phonology: Models and Methods,* 473–483. Salford: European Studies Research Institute.

Mascaró, Joan (2007) External allomorphy and lexical representation. *Linguistic Inquiry* 38: 715–735.

McCarthy, John J. (1986) OCP effects: Gemination and antigemination. *Linguistic Inquiry* 17: 207–263.

McCarthy, John J. (1999) Sympathy and phonological opacity. *Phonology* 16: 331–399.

McCarthy, John J. (2002) *Thematic Guide to Optimality Theory*. Cambridge: Cambridge University Press.

McCarthy, John J. and Prince, Alan S. (1994) The emergence of the unmarked: Optimality in prosodic morphology. In Mercè Gonzàlez (ed.) *Proceedings of the North East Linguistic Society (NELS) 24*: 333–379. Amherst, MA: Graduate Linguistic Student Association. [Available on http://roa.rutgers.edu/article/view/13.]

McCarthy, John J. and Prince, Alan S. (2001) *Prosodic Morphology: Constraint Interaction and Satisfaction*. Revision of 1993 manuscript. [Available on http://roa.rutgers.edu/article/view/482.]

McCarthy, John J. and Wolf, Matthew (2005) Less than zero: Correspondence and the null output. [Available on http://roa.rutgers.edu/article/view/732; revised version published as Wolf and McCarthy (2009).]

Mester, Armin (1994) The quantitative trochee in Latin. *Natural Language and Linguistic Theory* 12 (1): 1–64.

Mylne, Tom (1995) Grammatical category and world view: Western colonisation of the Dyirbal language. *Cognitive Linguistics* 6 (4): 379–404.

Morin, Yves-Charles and Tiffou, Étienne (1989) *Dictionnaire complémentaire du bourouchaski du Yasin*. Asie et monde insulindien 17. Paris: Peeters.

Nelson, Donald (1998) A prolegomena to a German gender dictionary. *Word* 49 (2): 205–224.

Nesset, Tore (2006) Gender meets the Usage-Based Model: Four principles of rule interaction in gender assignment. *Lingua* 116 (9): 1369–1393.

Orgun, Cemil Orhan and Sprouse, Ronald L. (1999) From MParse to Control: Deriving ungrammaticality. *Phonology* 16 (2): 191–224.

Paster, Mary (2005) Subcategorization vs. output optimization in syllable-counting allomorphy. In John Alderete, Chung-hye Han and Alexei Kochetov (eds) *Proceedings of the 24th West Coast Conference on Formal Linguistics,* 326–333. Somerville, MA: Cascadilla Proceedings Project.

Paster, Mary (2006) *Phonological Conditions on Affixation.* Doctoral dissertation, University of California at Berkeley.

Paster, Mary (this volume) Phonologically conditioned suppletive allomorphy: Cross-linguistic results and theoretical consequences.

Patz, Elizabeth (1991) Djabugay. In R. M. W. Dixon and Barry J. Blake (eds) *The Handbook of Australian Languages IV,* 245–347. Melbourne: Oxford University Press.

Picanço, Gessiane (2002) Tonal polarity as phonologically conditioned allomorphy in Mundurukú. In Julie Larson and Mary Paster (eds) *Proceedings of the 28th Annual Meeting of the Berkeley Linguistics Society (BLS),* 237–248. Berkeley, CA: Berkeley Linguistics Society.

Prince, Alan and Smolensky, Paul (2004 [1993]) *Optimality Theory: Constraint Interaction in Generative Grammar.* Malden, MA and Oxford: Blackwell. Technical Report, Rutgers University Center for Cognitive Science and Computer Science Department, University of Colorado at Boulder.

Rehg, Kenneth L. (2001) Pohnpeian possessive paradigms: the smart solution, the dumb solution and the Pohnpeian solution. In Joel Bradshaw and Kenneth L. Rehg (eds) *Issues in Austronesian Morphology: A Focusschrift for Byron Bender.* Pacific Linguistics 519. Canberra: Research School of Pacific and Asian Studies, The Australian National University.

Rice, Curt (2006) Optimizing gender. *Lingua* 116 (9): 1394–1417.

Rice, Curt (2007) Gaps and repairs at the phonology morphology interface. *Journal of Linguistics* 43 (1): 197–221.

Rubach, Jerzy and Booij, Geert (2001) Allomorphy in Optimality Theory: Polish iotation. *Language* 77: 26–60.

Russell, Kevin (1995) Morphemes and candidates in Optimality Theory. Unpublished manuscript, University of Manitoba. [Available on http://roa.rutgers.edu/article/view/44.]

Russell, Kevin (1999) MOT: Sketch of an OT approach to morphology. Unpublished manuscript, University of Manitoba. [Available on http://roa.rutgers.edu/article/view/352.]

Steinmetz, Donald (1985) Gender in German and Icelandic: inanimate nouns. In J. T. Faarlund (ed.) *Germanic Linguistics. Papers from a Symposium at the University of Chicago,* 10–28. Bloomington, IN: IULC.

Steinmetz, Donald (1986) Two principles and some rules for gender in German: Inanimate nouns. *Word* 37: 189–217.

Steinmetz, Donald (1997) The Great Gender Shift and the attrition of neuter nouns in West Germanic: The example of German. In I. Rauch and G. Carr (eds) *New Insights in Germanic Linguistics II,* 201–224. New York: Peter Lang.

Stump, Gregory T. (2001) *Inflectional Morphology. A Theory of Paradigm Structure.* Cambridge: Cambridge University Press.

Tiffou, Étienne and Pesot, Jurgen (1989) *Contes du Yasin: Introduction au bourouchaski du Yasin avec grammaire et dictionnaire analytique*. Asie et monde insulindien 16. Paris: Peeters.

Tranel, Bernard (1996a [1994]) French Liaison and Elision revisited: A unified account within Optimality Theory. In Claudia Parodi, Carlos Quicoli, Mario Saltarelli and María-Luisa Zubizarreta (eds) *Aspects of Romance Linguistics,* 433–455. Washington, DC: Georgetown University Press. [Available on http://roa.rutgers.edu/article/view/15.]

Tranel, Bernard (1996b) Exceptionality in Optimality Theory and final consonants in French. In Karen Zagona (ed.) *Grammatical Theory and Romance Languages,* 275–291. Amsterdam: John Benjamins. [Available on http://roa.rutgers.edu/article/view/60.]

Trosterud, Trond (2001) Genustilordning i norsk er regelstyrt. *Norsk Lingvistisk Tidsskrift* 19: 29–58.

Trosterud, Trond (2006) Gender assignment in Old Norse. *Lingua* 116 (9): 1441–1463.

Tryon, Darrell T. (1970) *Conversational Tahitian: An Introduction to the Language of French Polynesia*. Berkeley, CA: University of California Press.

van Oostendorp, Marc (2007) Derived environment effects and consistency of exponence. In Sylvia Blaho, Patrik Bye and Martin Krämer (eds) *Freedom of Analysis?,* 123–148. Berlin: Mouton de Gruyter.

Vogt, Hans (1945) The plural of nouns and adjectives in Burushaski. *Norsk Tidsskrift for Sprogvidenskap,* 13: 96–129.

Wolf, Matthew (2007) For an autosegmental theory of mutation. In Leah Bateman, Michael O'Keefe, Ehren Reilly and Adam Werle (eds) *University of Massachusetts Occasional Papers in Linguistics* 32: *Papers in Optimality Theory III,* 315–404. Amherst, MA: Graduate Linguistic Student Association. [Available on http://roa.rutgers.edu/article/view/754.]

Wolf, Matthew (this volume) Lexical insertion occurs in the phonological component.

Wolf, Matthew, and McCarthy, John J. (2009) Less than zero: Correspondence and the null output. In Sylvia Blaho and Curt Rice (eds), *Modeling Ungrammaticality in Optimality Theory,* 17–66. London: Equinox.

Yu, Alan C. L. (2007) *A Natural History of Infixation*. Oxford: Oxford University Press.

Zubin, David and Köpcke, Klaus Michael (1986) Gender and folk taxonomy: The indexical relation between grammatical and lexical categorization. In C. Craig (ed.) *Noun Classes and Categorization,* 139–180. Amsterdam: John Benjamins.

Zuraw, Kie (2000) *Patterned Exceptions in Phonology*. Doctoral dissertation, University of California at Los Angeles.

Zuraw, Kie (2007) The role of phonetic knowledge in phonological patterning: Corpus and survey evidence from Tagalog infixation. *Language* 83 (2): 277–316.

5 Obviative prefix allomorphy in Sahaptin and Nez Perce*

Sharon Hargus (University of Washington)
Noel Rude (Confederated Tribes of the Umatilla Indian Reservation)
Virginia Beavert (University of Oregon)

5.1 Allomorphy and phonological constraints

The study of allomorphy brings Optimality Theory to a crossroads. Cases such as the one we will discuss in this article raise the question of whether the constraints required to describe linguistic systems with allomorphy can be expected to be universal.

The issue is the place of morphophonology in Optimality Theory, long controversial in rule-based approaches to phonology. As is well known, the major difference between structuralist and traditional generative approaches to phonology revolved around whether morphophonology was considered phonology or not (Halle 1957; Chomsky 1964, and much subsequent discussion). Dressler (1976) examined a number of characteristics which had been proposed to distinguish phonetic, phonological (PRs), morphophonological (MPhRs) and morphological rules (MRs), and noted that 'phonological or phonetic plausibility of synchronic processes' (p. 317) seemed to provide the best argument for a potential three-way distinction among PRs, MPhRs and MRs: 'PRs must be totally plausible, MRs implausible, and MPhRs should lie in between'. While he ultimately concluded that morphophonological rules as a distinct rule class do not exist,[1] others have argued for a distinction between phonology, morphophonology and morphology (e.g. Hooper 1976; Wurzel 1980; Haspelmath and Sims 2010).

We will not settle the question of the position of morphophonology in this article. Rather, we will suggest that the question is still with us in constraint-based models. Sometimes the constraints posited to describe allomorphy

Affiliation: (Hargus): Professor, University of Washington, Seattle, WA, USA seem undeniably phonological, as in the case of Latin *-i/-ī* 3rd/4th conjugation (Mester 1994). The long-vowelled allomorph is selected after a sequence of syllables which can be analysed as a well-formed foot ((re-si)(p-ī)-<mus> 'we taste of'), and the short-vowelled allomorph is selected in other cases ((dē)-(sip-i)-<mus> 'we are out of our minds'). In this case, the phonology which drives allomorph selection has much cross-linguistic justification.

However, in other cases of allomorphy the typological justification is questionable. For example, Hargus (2007) analysed verbal areal prefix alternations *w-* ~ *ho-* in the Athabaskan language Witsuwit'en in terms of an allomorph set {w, ho}. The *ho-* allomorph is selected before a full vowel (i.e. a vowel other than /ə/; e.g. hont'əy, /ho-in-t'i/ 'you (sg.) reside'), and the *w-* allomorph is used elsewhere (wəst'əy, /w-ə-s-t'i/ 'I reside'). The challenge presented by Athabaskan areal prefix allomorphy is to understand why *w-* + full vowel is phonologically ill-formed (hence *ho-* must be selected). In this case, a constraint against [w] followed by full vowel, inherited from Proto-Athabaskan, was responsible. (Leer (1979) posited that Proto-Athabaskan labio-uvulars lost their labialization before a full vowel – e.g. Proto-Athabaskan *-Gʷeʔt-ŋ 'dig' pf. > *-Gʷeʔt > *-Ge':t – but when the following vowel was reduced, as in super-heavy syllables, the labialization was transferred to the vowel – e.g. *-Gʷet-ɬ 'dig' prog. > *Gʷətɬ > *Gʊɬ.) Is this a markedness constraint for which we should seek and expect to find cross-linguistic justification? If phonological constraints are universal,[2] should *w+full vowel be considered part of the cross-linguistic arsenal even if it is not known to make an appearance outside of the Athabaskan language family (indeed, not even in all Athabaskan languages)?

The present case involves a cognate allomorph set in Nez Perce and Sahaptin, the only two languages in the Sahaptian family (Aoki 1962). The second author, who has a long history of research on both languages (e.g. Rude 1982, 2009), as well as their reconstructed ancestor, Proto-Sahaptian (Rude 2012), has estimated the degree of difference between Nez Perce and Sahaptin to be similar to that of a pair of Romance languages. Although languages probably do not change at a constant rate (Nettle 1999), the time-depth of Sahaptian might still be estimated at around 2,000 years. Rude (2012) has reconstructed the cognate allomorph set as follows:

> *ˀé. v. Obviative. [Nez Perce] /ˀe/; [Sahaptin] **á**. Allomorph [Nez Perce] /ˀew/ & [Sahaptin] /aw/ variously before a glottal or glottal plus sonorant. Codes 3rd person possessor subjects in intransitive clauses and 3rd person direct objects in transitive clauses in [Nez Perce], NE [Sahaptin] & [Columbia River Sahaptin]. The 2nd person pronoun *ˀé and obviative *ˀé are likely related.[3]

In both languages, one allomorph of the obviative prefix ends in a vowel and the other allomorph ends in a consonant, [w]. At first glance, the Sahaptian obviative prefix looks like a case of C/V allomorphy. We might expect the consonant-final allomorph to be used before a vowel and the vowel-final allomorph before a consonant, like the Korean nominative marker *-i/-ka* and other cases discussed by Hargus (2007). However, the present case turns out not to be so simple. Nez Perce *ew-* is only used before glottalized sonorants, and (simplifying somewhat) Sahaptin *áw-* is only used before vowel or glottal stop initial stems.

We will put forward the best case we can for phonological regulation of the Sahaptian allomorphs. An alternative to our phonological approach is to describe allomorphy via subcategorization frame matching. For example, in the case of the Witsuwit'en areal prefix mentioned above, in place of the negative constraint *w+full vowel, the *ho-* allomorph could positively subcategorize for a following full vowel and/or the *w-* allomorph could subcategorize for a following reduced vowel. In an analysis with subcategorization frames, there would be no need to posit a phonological constraint *w+full vowel nor the Sahaptian constraints that we posit in this article. The question then arises, if subcategorization frames are used in this case, why not in all cases of allomorphy, including Latin *-i/-ī*? And we are back to the very difficult question of where to draw the line between phonology and morphology.

5.2 Nez Perce obviative prefix allomorphy

5.2.1 Nez Perce phonological background

Nez Perce has the segment inventories given in (1)–(2) (Aoki 1970a; Crook 1999; Rude 1999):

(1) *Nez Perce consonant inventory*[4,5]

p p'	t t'		ts ts'	k k'	q q'	ʔ
		ɬ	s	x	χ	h
m m'	n n'	l l'				
w w'				j j'		

(2) *Nez Perce vowel inventory*

i ii		u uu
e ee		o oo
	a aa	

Nez Perce has vowel harmony, which has attracted some theoretical attention (e.g. Hall and Hall 1977): [e] (phonetically [æ]) alternates with [a], as do [o] and [u]. [i] is transparent, occurring with either the [a o] or [e u] harmonic sets. Nez Perce has both underlyingly accented and unaccented morphemes (Crook 1999, Rude 1999).[6] Underlying root-initial consonant clusters do not occur on the surface when word-initial; [i] is epenthesized within such clusters. [i] is also inserted to bear the stress of underlyingly accented words where the accent is not associated with an underlying vowel (Rude 1999). According to Crook (1999), underlying long vowels normally shorten unless they surface with primary stress. However, Rude (2006) notes that there are many examples of underlying long vowels (historically from the deletion of intervocalic consonants or Sahaptian ablaut) which do not shorten when unstressed.[7]

Nez Perce lacks vowel-initial words (Rude 1999). Crook (1999) lists only CVVC, CVV, CVC, CV as possible syllables.[8] The only dictionary entries for vowel-initial morphemes in the most comprehensive Nez Perce dictionary (Aoki 1994) are suffixes or bound roots, neither of which morpheme class would occur word initially.

5.2.2 Glottalized sonorants

As summarized in (1), the Nez Perce phonological inventory includes glottalized sonorant consonants (R'), which do not occur word-initially (Aoki 1970a, b). Glottalized sonorants occur post-vocalically before a vowel (*kál'a* 'just'), post-vocalically and word-finally (*hím'* 'mouth'), post-vocalically before a consonant (*sám'χ* 'shirt'), or pre-vocalically after a consonant (*ʔíisl'am* 'bull trout, Dolly Varden').

Rude (1999) notes that if glottalized sonorants are synchronically analysed as clusters of sonorant+/ʔ/ (also proposed by Aoki 1970b: 67), this explains their failure to occur word-initially, as clusters are not permitted in that position in Nez Perce, as mentioned above. Heteromorphemic glottalized sonorants clearly originate as sequences of sonorant+/ʔ/. Some examples are given in (3):

(3) *Some examples of [R'] (/R+ʔ/) from Aoki (1994)*

/m+ʔ/	[walíim'lapqat]	/walím-ʔlépqet/	'traditional moccasin' (p. 1016)
/n+ʔ/	[noon'aχ]	/núun-ʔaq/	'we wish' (p. 496)
/l+ʔ/	[ciq'áamqal'ajn]	/cq'ámqal-ʔajn/	'for the dog, dogsled' (p. 982)
/w+ʔ/	[hitéw'lesece]	/hi-téw-ʔlécen-se/	'he is making noise at night' (p. 1018)
/j+ʔ/	[hik'áaj'ajn]	/hik'aj-ʔajn/	'cupboard (i.e., 'for cups')' (p. 140)

Aoki (1970a) does not provide much information about the timing of the laryngeal and supralaryngeal events of the glottalized sonorants, only that glottalized sonorants and ejectives alike are 'distinguished [from non-glottalized sounds] by simultaneous coarticulation of glottal closure' (p. 16). Later, Aoki (1994: xii) describes [m'], etc. as 'like *m* with a catch before it'. Crook (1999: 28) similarly states that Nez Perce 'glottalized sonorants are preglottalized'. Aoki (1970b) provides a very limited number of spectrograms from two speakers. From his spectrograms and commentary on them, it appears that intervocalic glottalized sonorants are produced with glottalization timed at the midpoint of the sonorant. For the post-vocalic, word-final glottalized sonorants provided with that article, Aoki's description suggests post-glottalization. However, no spectrograms of minimal pairs for word-final glottalized vs. non-glottalized sonorants are provided, making it difficult to assess his remarks. In our own acoustic analysis of glottalized sonorant timing in Nez Perce with data from one native speaker, Eugene John, we have found overwhelming tendencies towards post-glottalization in our acoustic analysis of this speaker, but also some minor tendencies, such as timing of glottalization away from an adjacent vowel when the glottalized sonorant is adjacent to a fricative or nasal.

5.2.3 Distribution of obviative prefix allomorphs

The Nez Perce obviative prefix is presented in Aoki (1994:983) as *ʔe-* and glossed third-person object prefix. Rude (2006) refers to this morpheme instead as the obviative prefix, a categorization adopted in this article, as it 'codes a 3rd person possessor argument in an intransitive clause and a 3rd person direct object in a transitive clause'.

Rude (2006) further notes that the obviative prefix has two allomorphs, /ʔe/- and /ʔew/-. /ʔew/- is described as occurring before (underlying) clusters where the first element is /ʔ/ or /h/ and the second element is one of /m n l w j/, the class of sonorants. (Presuming epenthesis, Aoki (1994) states that 'ʔe has a [w] inserted before h or ʔ'.) Examples of the obviative prefix before /ʔ/[son] are provided in (4). In such cases, Rude transcribes the phonetic form as glottalized [w] followed by the supralaryngeal sonorant.[9] In (4)–(8), the first two segments of the underlying representation of the root are underlined.

(4) ʔew- before ʔ[son]
[ʔew'léesene] /ʔew-<u>ʔl</u>ésen-e/ Cf. [ʔiléesene] /ʔlésen-e/
'his made noise' 'I made noise'

[ʔew'níike] /ʔew-ʔnik-e/	Cf. [ʔiníike] /ʔnik-e/
'I placed it'	'I put mine away'
[ʔaw'jáaχna] /ʔew-ʔjáqn-e/	Cf. [ʔijáaχna] /ʔjáqn-e/
'I found him'	'I found mine'

An example of /h/[sonorant] is provided in (5). In this case, root-initial [h] is deleted.

(5) ʔew- before h[sonorant]

[ʔewíne] /ʔew-hn-e/ 'I told him'	Cf. [híne] /hn-e/ 'I said'

Continuing with Rude's description of obviative prefix allomorphy, 'if the second consonant in the cluster is not a [sonorant] (/m n l w j/) then /ʔe/ occurs'. Examples showing ʔe- before ʔC or hC, where C is an obstruent, are given in (6):

(6) ʔe- before ʔC or hC, where C = obstruent

[ʔeʔsíwene] /ʔe-ʔs´wen-e/ 'I skinned it'	Cf. [ʔisíwene] /ʔs´wen-e/ 'I skinned'
[ʔeʔpt'éeje] /ʔe-ʔpt'é-e/ 'I hit him'	Cf. [ʔipt'éeje] /ʔpt'é-e/ 'I hit mine'
[ʔehípe] /ʔ-hp-e/ 'I ate it'	Cf. [hípe] /hp-e/ 'I ate'

The allomorph ʔe- is also used before all other root-initial singleton consonants, including [ʔ] and [h]:

(7) ʔe- before ʔV or hV

[ʔaʔátsa] /ʔe-ʔáts-e/ 'his entered'	Cf. [ʔáatsa] /ʔáts-e/ 'I entered'
[ʔeʔwíje] /ʔe-ʔewi-e/ 'I shot it'	Cf. [ʔewíje] /ʔewi-e/ 'I shot'
[ʔehésne] /ʔe-hésn-e/ 'his breathed'	Cf. [héesne] /hésn-e/ 'I breathed'

Examples showing the allomorph ʔe- before a selection of other root-initial consonants are provided in (8):

(8) ʔe- before other C

[ʔóoptsij'awna] /ʔe-wáptsij'awn-e/	[wáaptsij'awna] /wáptsij'awn-e/
'I killed it'	'I killed mine'
[ʔamátna] /ʔe-m´tn-e/ 'his boiled'	[mátna] /m´tn-e/ 'mine boiled'
[ʔelíwne] /ʔe-l´wn-e/ 'his burnt'	[líwne] /l´wn-e/ 'mine burnt'
[ʔapáajna] /ʔe-pájn-e/ 'his arrived'	[páajna] /pájn-e/ 'I arrived'
[ʔekúje] /ʔe-ku-e/ 'his went'	[kúje] /ku-e/ 'I went'
[ʔak'óomajna] /ʔe-k'ómajn-e/	[k'óomajna] /k'ómajn-e/
'his got sick'	'I got sick'
[ʔetéemeke] /ʔe-témek-e/	[téemeke] /témek-e/
'I roasted it'	'I roasted mine'

To summarize, according to Rude (2006), the allomorph *ʔew-* is used before root-initial clusters of {h, ʔ}[sonorant], and *ʔe-* is used elsewhere.

5.2.4 /h/+sonorant

Taking a fresh look at the /h/[sonorant] verbs which require the *ʔew-* allomorph, it appears that there is only one such verb in Nez Perce. That verb is /hn/ 'say, tell', the lexical entry for which is given as '/hi/ (c-class)' in Aoki (1994), the c-class designation meaning that such verbs require certain inflectional suffix allomorphs which begin with [n] (see Aoki 1994: xv). The *ʔew-* allomorph of the obviative prefix which is used with 'say' is part of a suppletive inflectional paradigm for this verb, which is undoubtedly of high token frequency in Nez Perce.

We suggest that the use of the *ʔew-* allomorph with 'say' does not reflect productive synchronic phonology with /h/[sonorant] initial verbs in Nez Perce. Only one /h/[sonorant] initial verb, *hwíit* 'to whistle', is listed in Aoki (1994: 187).[10] While no obviative form of this verb is provided by Aoki, in (9) we show the obviative form of a phonologically similar /h/[sonorant] initial verb:[11]

(9) Obviative form of h[sonorant]-initial verb

Initial	*Obviative form*
hw /hwik/ 'slice up meat (for drying)'	[ʔeewikúʔ] 'I will cut it (meat) up'

Note that the form of the obviative prefix used with this verb is *ʔe-*, not *ʔew-*. Compensatory lengthening of [ʔe+hCV] to [ʔeeCV] is a regular phonological process in Nez Perce. Compare also [peepúʔ] /pe-hp-uʔ/ 'we will eat'; [ʔaapsáaqa] /ʔe-hp-sen-qa/ 'I was eating it'.[12]

A number of verbs which begin with [hi[sonorant]...] are listed in Aoki (1994). Following Rude (1999), these may be analyzed as underlyingly root-initial /h[sonorant].../ clusters with epenthetic [i]. Those verbs beginning with [hi[sonorant]] for which obviative forms are also provided by Aoki (1994) are listed in (10):

(10) Obviative forms of hi[sonorant]-initial verbs

Initial	*Lexical entry in Aoki (1994)*	*Obviative form*
hj	hijúum 'to be correct in guessing in a stick-game'	[ʔeejuumtse] 'I am right (in guessing) about it' (p. 172)
	hijíjiq 'to tickle (someone)'	[ʔeejíjiqce] 'I'm tickling her' (p. 170)
	hijémqe 'to cry after, hate to see someone go'	[ʔeejémqetse] 'I cry after him' (p. 170)

hm	himéj 'to suspect; to blame, accuse'	[ʔeeméjtse] 'I suspect him' (p. 144)
hl	hil'íiq 'to enjoy, have fun, be thrilled, revel'	[ʔeel'íiqetu] 'I used to enjoy it' (p. 142)

With the verbs in (10), the obviative prefix is again *ʔee-*, the result of compensatory lengthening before /hCV/ initial. Note that none of the verbs in (10) exhibits the *ʔew-* allomorph.

In this section, we have suggested that the *ʔew-* allomorph of the obviative prefix is in fact used with only one verb, 'say', and not before /h/[sonorant] initial roots more generally. The preference for the w-final obviative allomorph before /h/[sonorant]-initial roots appears to have historical significance only, a point which we return to in section 5.4.

5.2.5 One underlying representation or two?

Optimality Theory, like Natural Generative Phonology (e.g. Vennemann 1972) but unlike traditional generative phonology, has no requirement that morphemes contain single underlying representations, the problems with which have been pointed out by e.g. Hooper (1976) and Ohala (1992). However, given the phonetic similarity of the two allomorphs of the Nez Perce obviative prefix, the question arises as to whether two underlying representations must really be posited, or whether the obviative prefix might be either (1) /ʔew/-, with deletion before consonants other than ʔ[sonorant], or (2) /ʔe/-, with [w] insertion before ʔ[sonorant].

It is easy to show that neither analysis is tenable. Against (1), there is no general w-deletion before non-sonorants. When the verbal derivational prefix /sléw/- 'look, appear' (Aoki 1994: 641) precedes the consonant [ts] in (11), the prefix-final [w] is not deleted.

(11) [siléwtsukwetse] /sléw-tsúkwen-se/ 'I know by seeing'

Against (2), there is no general w-epenthesis before /ʔ/[sonorant]. When the verbal inflectional prefix /pe/- plural subject precedes root-initial /ʔ/ [sonorant], [w] is not inserted, as shown in (12):

(12) [peʔníike] /pe-ʔnik-e/ 'we put (it) away'

The obviative prefix thus contrasts with the non-alternating [w] in /sléw/- 'look, appear' and the non-alternating final vowel in /pe/- plural subject, indicating that multiple underlying representations are needed for the obviative prefix.

5.2.6 Glottalized sonorant phonology

In Nez Perce, the glottalized sonorant [w'] is preferred before a sonorant; otherwise, the allomorph with no supralaryngeal sonorant is used. We note first of all that this reflects a preference for monosegmental glottalized sonorants over bisegmental sequences of [sonorant][ʔ]. Overlapped, monosegmental articulations are presumably possible because the laryngeal and supralaryngeal articulations are independent events (Kingston 1990, 2005).

Second, as noted by Maddieson (1984) and Bird *et al.* (2008), glottalized sonorants are relatively rare in the world's languages, and those languages which have them often place restrictions on their distribution (Howe and Pulleyblank 2001). A small survey of distributional restrictions on glottalized sonorants is given in (13):

(13) *Distributional restrictions on glottalized sonorants*

<table>
<tr><td rowspan="2">Nez Perce (Sahaptian, Plateau Penutian)</td><td>post-vocalic</td><td>V_V, V_C, V_#</td></tr>
<tr><td>subset of pre-vocalic contexts</td><td>C_V</td></tr>
<tr><td rowspan="2">Klamath (Barker 1964; Blevins 1993) (Plateau Penutian)</td><td>pre-vocalic</td><td>#_V, C_V, V_V</td></tr>
<tr><td>subset of post-vocalic contexts</td><td>V_#, V_s, V_ sonorant (unless following sonorant is glottalized or voiceless)</td></tr>
<tr><td>Yowlumne Yokuts (Newman 1944; Plauché 1998) (Penutian)</td><td>post-vocalic only</td><td>V_C, V_V, V_#</td></tr>
<tr><td>Kashaya (Oswalt 1961; Buckley 1994) (Pomoan, Hokan)</td><td>subset of post-vocalic contexts</td><td>V_#, V_C</td></tr>
<tr><td>Nuu-chah-nulth (Kim 2003; Bird et al. 2008) (Wakashan)</td><td>pre-vocalic only</td><td>#_V, C_V, V_V</td></tr>
<tr><td>Witsuwit'en (Hargus 2006, 2007) (Athabaskan)</td><td>post-vocalic only</td><td>V_#, V_C</td></tr>
<tr><td>St'at'imcets (van Eijk 1997; Bird et al. 2008) (Salish)</td><td>adjacent to vowel</td><td>#_V, C_V, V_V, V_C, V_#</td></tr>
<tr><td rowspan="2">Nłeʔkepmxcin (Thompson et al. 1996; Bird et al. 2008) (Salish)</td><td>adjacent to vowel</td><td>#_V, C_V, V_V, V_C, V_#</td></tr>
<tr><td>syllabic</td><td>#_C, C_#</td></tr>
</table>

In all of the languages in (13) other than those from the Salish family,[13] the glottalized sonorants must be adjacent to at least one vowel, even when other sonorants have wider distributions. For example, in Nuu-chah-nulth, ordinary nasals can precede consonants (e.g. [ts'im̲t'u:] 'squirrel', [ʔin̲kʷ'ah̄s] 'lamp, ceiling light'; Howe and Pulleyblank 2001), whereas glottalized nasals (like all glottalized sonorants) must precede vowels.

Howe and Pulleyblank (2001) propose the constraint in (14) with reference to a similar restriction on the distribution of glottalized sonorants (R') in Yowlumne:

(14) IF R', THEN V__: If a sonorant is glottalized, then it must follow a vowel.

While some languages, such as Nłeʔkepmxcin, allow glottalized sonorants next to consonants with no adjacent vowel, there appear to be no languages that allow glottalized sonorants next to a consonant if a vowel is not also adjacent to the glottalized sonorant. This distribution suggests the pair of harmony scales in (15):

(15) *Harmony scales for glottalized sonorants*
a. R' / ___ V > R' / ___ C
b. R' / V___ > R' / C___

One can imagine finer distinctions of the scale in (15)a, such as R' / ___ sonorant > R' / ___ obstruent in place of the very general R' / ___ C. The intermediate stage R' / ___ sonorant is so far unattested, but Klamath comes close in allowing post-vocalic glottalized sonorants before ordinary sonorants but not obstruents (other than [s]). Phonetic motivation for R' / ___ sonorant might come from the need for an adjacent inherently voiced segment on which the glottalized sonorant might realize glottalization and/or place, in the manner suggested by Steriade (1999). The ranking of different steps on either harmony scale in (15) might well interact with the timing of glottalized sonorants, which is known to vary from language to language (Howe and Pulleyblank 2001; Hargus 2005; Bird *et al.* 2008) and within languages (Hargus 2007). For example, a language in which glottalized sonorants are predominantly post-glottalized might require that glottalized sonorants occur before vowels or sonorants, but not obstruents.

Recall that in Nez Perce, glottalized sonorants appear to be mainly post-glottalized, if our sample from Eugene John is representative of the language, and a following sonorant as opposed to obstruent may enhance the recoverability of post-glottalization. Accordingly, we posit the set of constraints in (16) on glottalized sonorant distribution, with predicted cross-linguistic ranking:

(16) *Constraints on distribution of glottalized sonorants (R') (O = obstruent, R = sonorant, V = vowel)*
   a. *R' / ___O >> *R' / ___R >> *R' / ___V
   b. *R' / O___ >> *R' / R___ >> *R' / V___

5.2.7 A formal model of Nez Perce obviative allomorphy

A model of Nez Perce obviative allomorphy was constructed for testing with OTSoft 2.1 (Hayes *et al.* 2003), using the Low Faithfulness Constraint Demotion algorithm proposed by Hayes (2004). Candidate sets were constructed for four types of root-initial consonants: /ʔ[sonorant].../, /ʔ[obstruent].../, /ʔV.../, and /CV.../ (for C other than glottal stop). The initial constraint set included both of the constraints on sequencing of glottal stop and sonorant (*ʔSON and *SONʔ), the proposed constraints on R' distribution in (16), UNIFORMITY, and NOCODA.

OTSoft results indicated that the pattern of winners and losers can be successfully modelled with the above seven constraints. In this model, the constraints are organized in two ranked strata. The top stratum consists of *R'/__O, *R'/__V, *ʔSON and *SONʔ, all unranked with respect to each other. The second stratum contains *R'/__R, UNIFORMITY, and NOCODA. Notice, somewhat surprisingly and contrary to the proposed ranking of constraints on glottalized sonorant distribution in (16), that *R'/ __ O and *R'/__ V have the same rank in Nez Perce, both outranking *R' / __ R. The crucial pairs of ranking relationships in this analysis are summarized in (17).

(17) *Constraint ranking for Nez Perce obviative allomorphy*

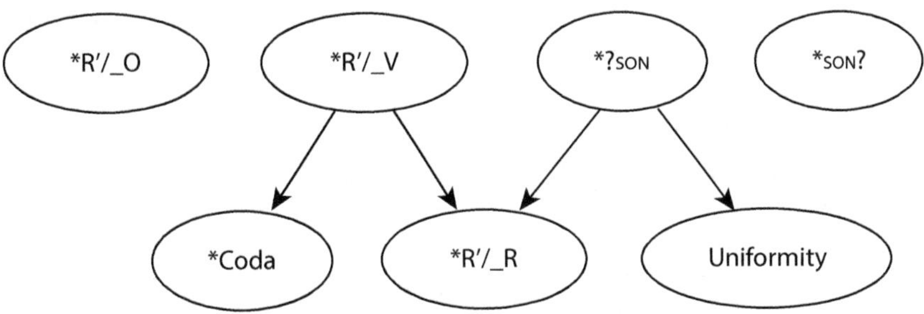

Next we illustrate this analysis with tableaux showing allomorph selection with the four root types. In the most interesting case, shown in (18), the winning candidate violates constraints against coalescence, codas and pre-sonorant glottalized sonorants, but alternatives violate the proposed constraints against sequences of sonorants and glottal stop or the distribution of glottalized sonorants, which are higher ranked. (In the tableaux in (18)–(21), constraints which are not applicable to a particular case have been omitted to simplify the presentation.)

(18) Why ʔew-, not ʔe-, is selected before ʔR

/{ʔew-, ʔe-}ʔnik-e/	*R'/__V	*ʔSON	*SONʔ	*R'/__R	UNIFORMITY	NO CODA
a. ʔewʔníike		*!	*			*
b. ☞ ʔew'níike				*	*	*
c. ʔeʔníike		*!				*
d. ʔen'íike	*!				*	

When the obviative prefix precedes root-initial glottal stop followed by an obstruent, the vowel-final allomorph is selected, as shown in (19). The losing candidates violate higher-ranked constraints against glottalized sonorants or sonorant-glottal stop sequencing:

(19) Why ʔe-, not ʔew-, is selected before ʔO

/{ʔew-, ʔe-}ʔs´wen-e/	*R'/__O	*SONʔ	UNIFORMITY	NOCODA
a. ʔewʔsíwene		*!		*
b. ʔew'síwene	*!		*	*
c. ☞ ʔeʔsíwene				*

When the obviative prefix precedes root-initial glottal stop followed by a vowel, the vowel-final allomorph is also selected, as shown in (21). The losing candidates violate constraints involving glottalized sonorant distribution or sonorant-glottal stop sequencing, whereas the winner, lacking a sonorant, incurs none of these violations.

(20) Why ʔe-, not ʔew-, is selected before ʔV

/{ʔew-, ʔe-}ʔáts-e/	*R'/__V	*SONʔ	UNIFORMITY	NOCODA
a. ʔawʔátsa		*!		*
b. ʔaw'átsa	*!		*	
c. ☞ ʔaʔátsa				

Finally, when the consonant following the obviative prefix is any other root-initial consonant, the preference for the *ʔe-* allomorph can be modelled on the basis of NOCODA:

(21) Why *ʔe-*, not *ʔew-*, is selected before other root-initial consonants

/{ʔew-, ʔe-}-ku-e/	NOCODA
a. ʔewkúye	*!
b. ☞ ʔekúye	

The reality of Nez Perce is that the sonorant-final obviative allomorph is preferred before glottalized sonorants. Hence it is not surprising that the computer model returns the result that *R'/__R must be low ranking in NP. But it is nonetheless troubling that the proposed cross-linguistic ranking in (16) immediately runs afoul of its first test case. Perhaps this is a testament to the difference between phonology and phonetically motivated constraints, and the fact that *morphologization*, as must be the case with the regulation of allomorph distribution, may cause a phonological constraint to become even further removed from its phonetic roots.

5.2.8 Nez Perce summary

In Nez Perce, the allomorph *ʔew-* is used before root-initial sequences of /ʔ/sonorant, and the allomorph *ʔe-* is used before other root-initials. We have suggested a phonological analysis for the preference for *ʔew-* before root-initial /ʔ/sonorant. At the heart of the analysis are newly proposed constraints on sequences of /ʔ/sonorant or sonorant/ʔ/.

5.3 Sahaptin obviative prefix allomorphy

Rigsby and Rude (1996) divide Sahaptin into three broad dialect areas: Northwest (NW), Northeast (NE), and Columbia River (CR). The Northwest (NW) Sahaptin dialects are Yakima, Klickitat, Kittitas, and Upper Cowlitz. The Northeast (NE) dialects are Walla Walla, Wánapam and Lower Snake R. The Columbia R. (CR) dialects are Umatilla, Warm Springs, John Day and Rock Creek.

The description of Sahaptin in this section is illustrated most thoroughly with data from the Yakima (a.k.a. Yakama) dialect, the only surviving representative of the NW dialect. The data in this section were provided by the third author, who is a native speaker of this dialect, and/or are taken from texts from this dialect by her late mother, Ellen Saluskin. Parallel data can often be found in Beavert and Hargus (2009), which has accompanying sound files. We also present a small amount of data from other dialect areas when the facts are different.

5.3.1 Sahaptin phonological background

Sahaptin has the phoneme inventories given in (22)–(23) (Jacobs 1931, Rigsby and Rude 1996, Hargus and Beavert 2014):

(22) *Sahaptin consonant inventory*[14]

p p’	t t’	tɬ tɬ’	ts ts’	ʧ ʧ’	k k’	k^w k^{w}’	q q’	q^w q^{w}’	ʔ
		ɬ	s	ʃ	x	x^w	χ	$χ^w$	h
m	n	l							
w				j					

(23) *Sahaptin vowel inventory*

i ii ɨ u uu
a aa

Sahaptin has a lexical accent system (Hargus and Beavert 2005, 2006). Accent is transcribed here with an acute accent over a vowel.

5.3.2 The obviative prefix

Amplifying somewhat the function of the obviative prefix as given by Rigsby and Rude (1996: 675), the Sahaptin obviative codes a third person possessor in intransitive clauses, as seen in (24), and a third person direct object with non-third person subjects in transitive clauses, as seen in (25):[15]

(24) ʔá-third person possessor
ʔá-pnu-ʃa pʧá
OBV-sleep-IMPF mother
‘his/her/their mother is sleeping’

(25) ʔá-third person direct object
ʔá-q’inu-ʃa=aʃ
OBV-sleep-IMPF=1SG
‘I see him/her/it/them’

The obviative prefix has two shapes, *(ʔ)á-* and *(ʔ)áw-*. The distribution of these allomorphs is described by Rigsby and Rude (1996:675) as follows: ‘*áw-* occurs before vowel-initial themes, *á-* elsewhere’. Rude (1997) refers to the allomorphs and their distribution as ‘…the pronominal *á-* (*áw-* before a glottal) …’. The discrepancy between the two descriptions is linked to another difficulty in the description of these prefixes, the parenthesized morpheme-initial glottal stops given above.

5.3.3 Glottal stop epenthesis

In Sahaptin, there is no contrast between words that begin with a glottal stop and words that begin with a vowel. Rigsby and Rude (1996: 670) state that 'many Sahaptin speakers pronounce [glottal stop] at the beginning of words that otherwise appear to have an initial vowel …', and in that article, as in the Yakima practical writing system, 'initial glottal stop before a vowel is not written' (Rigsby and Rude 1996: 666). In Yakima Sahaptin (and for other varieties of Sahaptin, we suspect), there is a contrast between vowel and glottal stop initial morphemes which emerges under prefixation. With a glottal stop initial morpheme like /ʔála/ 'grandchild (woman's son's child)', the first person singular possessive prefix is [ʔín]-. In (26), note the root-initial glottal stop after that prefix and also after the second person singular possessive prefix [ʔím]-:

(26) *Prefixed glottal stop initial noun*
ʔínʔala 'my grandchild'
ʔímʔala 'your grandchild'

With a vowel initial root like /ám/ 'husband', the first person singular possessive prefix is [ʔínm]-, and there is no root-initial glottal stop in prefixed forms of this noun:

(27) *Prefixed vowel initial noun*
ʔínmam 'my husband'
ʔímam 'your husband'

For Virginia Beavert (and other Sahaptin speakers, we suspect), the contrast between the vowel and glottal stop initial nouns is neutralized word-initially as glottal stop, as in the vocative forms of these nouns shown in (28)–(29). In the spectrograms shown in (28)–(29), note the sharp stop onset to both words, indicative of word initial glottal stop, apparently epenthesized in the case of the vowel initial morpheme /ám/ 'husband'.

(28) Word initial glottal stop (underlying): ʔála 'grandchild' (voc.)[16]

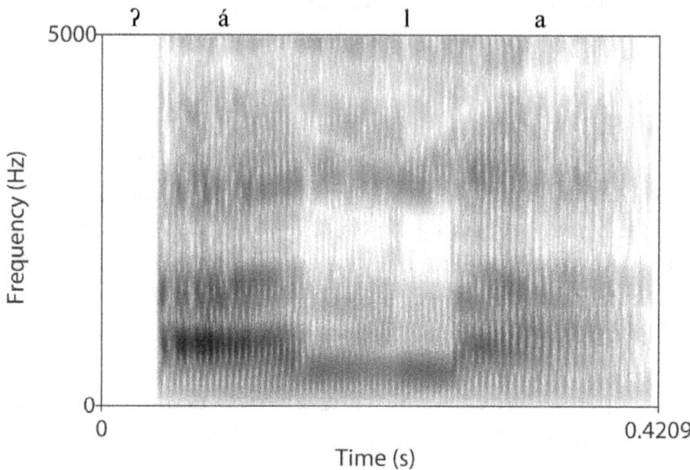

(29) Word initial glottal stop (epenthetic): ʔám 'husband' (voc.)

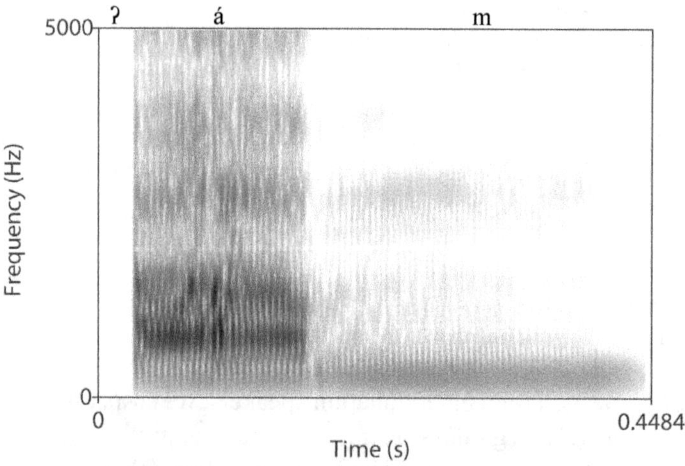

Vowel initial roots are less numerous than glottal stop initial roots in Yakima Sahaptin. For example, in the root index to Beavert and Hargus (2009), 14 are glottal stop-initial, four vary between glottal stop- and vowel-initial, and five are vowel-initial. Vowel initial verb roots can be recognized in the same way as vowel initial noun roots: by prefixation. When the vowel-final derivational prefix *wɨ́á-* is or was added to the verb root *ánakʷ-* 'abandon, divorce', the result is/was a long vowel:[17]

(30) *Vowel-final prefix + vowel-initial verb*
/wjá/- 'while walking'+ /ának^{w}/: wj<u>áan</u>ak^{w} 'leave behind'
/wilá/- 'wind' + /ának^{w}/: wil<u>áa</u>lak^{w} 'win' (*lit.* 'abandon in the wind')

However, when a vowel-final derivational prefix is added to a glottal stop initial verb root like /ʔajík/ 'sit', the result is a vowel sequence interrupted by the root-initial glottal stop:

(31) *Vowel-final prefix + glottal stop-initial verb*
/wjá/- 'while walking' + /ʔajík/: wj<u>áʔa</u>jk- 'sit down, take a break from walking'

5.3.4 Distribution of obviative prefix allomorphs

In the case of the obviative prefix, *(ʔ)á- ~ (ʔ)áw-*, the test of further prefixation, which was used with roots to determine whether a root is vowel- or glottal stop-initial, is not available, since there are no prefixes that can be added to the left of the obviative prefix. However, there is no question about the phonetic representation of words which contain the obviative prefix in word initial position: such words begin with glottal stop. Temporarily putting aside the analytical uncertainty about the underlying forms of the obviative prefix, we now illustrate the distribution of the contexts in which the two allomorphs occur.

As noted by Rigsby and Rude (1996), the allomorph *ʔáw-* occurs before vowel-initial roots like /ának^{w}/- 'abandon, divorce':

(32) ʔáw- before vowel-initial verb

ʧáw=PAT	*<u>ʔáw</u>*-anak^{w}-a	k'usík'usi-nan
neg=3PL	OBV-abandon-PAST	dog-OBJ

'they didn't abandon the dog'

The allomorph *ʔá-* is used before verb roots which begin with consonants other than glottal stop. A variety of different root-initial consonants are illustrated in (33). Singleton initial roots are shown in (33a-c)and cluster-initial roots in (33d-f).

(33) ʔá- before consonant-initial verbs (for C ≠ ʔ)

a.

ʃíin=nam	<u>ʔá</u>-k^{w}'ima-ʃa
who.OBJ=2SG	OBV-visit with-IMPF

'who are you visiting with?'

b.

<u>ʔá</u>-tamajnak-a=pat	ʔɨwínʃ-nan
OBV-incarcerate-PST=3PL	man-OBJ

'they incarcerated the man'

c. ʔíʧi ʔá-wa
this OBV-be.IMPF
'this is hers'

d. mɨ́l=nam ʔá-tq'iχ-ʃa?
how much=2SG OBV-want-IMPF
'how much do you want?'

e. ʔá-lst'a-m
OBV-join-CIS
'join me/us'

f. ʔá-mts'iχʷa=aʃ
OBV-listen to=1SG
'I'm listening to him'

/h/ initial verb roots are not as plentiful in Sahaptin as they are in Nez Perce, and root-initial clusters consisting of /hC/ are non-existent. An example of obviative allomorphy before an h-initial root is shown in (34). Here, the obviative allomorph used is *ʔá-*, the same as that used before a root-initial consonant other than glottal stop.

(34) ʔá- before /h/: /hananúj/- 'be busy'
ʔa-hananújwi-ʃa ʔámʧnik ʔájat
OBV-be busy-IMPF outside woman, wife
'his wife is busy outside'

Rude (1997) notes that the allomorph *ʔáw-* is also used before roots which begin with glottal stop. We will provide evidence below that this statement is too general for the Yakima dialect. But first note that in (35), the allomorph *ʔáw-* is used before roots beginning with /ʔV/. The initial glottal stop of the verb roots in the forms in (35) is best seen in the non-obviative forms provided for comparison, since the verb root initial glottal stop is actually missing in the obviative forms, a problem which we return to in section 5.3.6:

(35) ʔáw- before /ʔV/

a. /ʔajík/- 'sit'
ʃíin=nam ʔaw-ajk-twíi-ʃa
who.OBJ=2SG OBV-sit-COM-IMPF
'who are you sitting with?'
Cf. ʔi-wjá-ʔajk-ʃ
3.nom-while walking-sit-PF
'he's sat down, taking a break from walking'

b. /ʔátawi/- 'love' (< /ʔátaw/ 'valuable' -/i/ verb formative)
na-tílas-nan=naʃ ʔáw-atawi-ʃa
my-maternal grandfather-OBJ=1SG OBV-love-IMPF
'I love my grandfather'
Cf. pá-ʔatawi-ʃa
INV-love-IMPF
'he loves her'

In (36), the obviative allomorph *ʔáw-* is seen before verb roots beginning with glottal stop followed by one or more obstruents. Such verbs are diagnosable as having initial glottal stop by virtue of the fact that when word initial, [ɨ] is inserted following glottal stop and the second consonant of the cluster (Hargus and Beavert 2002). However, the obviative prefixed forms of these verb roots, like those in (35), also appear to lack morpheme-initial glottal stop:

(36) ʔáw- before /ʔ[obstruent]/
a. /ʔtámya/ 'buy'
ʃiin=nam ʔáw-tamj-iini-ʃa táatpas
who.OBJ=2SG OBV-buy-POSS-IMPF dress
'for whom are you buying the dress?' (*lit.* whose dress are you buying?)
Cf. ʔɨtámja-t
buy-GER
'buying'
b. /ʔʃnwáj(n)/ 'pity'
ʔáw-ʃnɨwajn-k
OBV-pity-IMPER.SG
'pity him'
Cf. ʔɨʃnɨwáj-t
pity-GER
'pity' (n.)
c. /ʔʃá/- 'lie, be in prone position'
Ku ʔɨwínʃ ʔáw-ʃa tɬ'jáwj-i.
and man/husband OBV-lie.IMPF die-PPL
'And her husband is lying dead.' (Saluskin no date-a)
Cf. lá-ʔɨʃa=aʃ
leisurely-lie.IMPF=1SG
'I'm relaxing.'
d. /ʔʃáp/- 'pack on back, shoulder'
Ku=yam ʔawkú tɬ'áaχʷ ʔáw-ʃap-ta.
then=actually.2SG then all OBV-pack-FUT
'And then you have to pack it all (gathered food).' (Saluskin no date-b)
Cf. ʔɨʃáp-i
pack-PPL
'packing'

When the verb root begins with /ʔ[sonorant]/, the allomorph *ʔá-* is used.

(37) ʔá- before /ʔ[sonorant]/

a. /ʔmasíχ/- 'joke around'
wáawk'a ʔɨlɨ́χ ʔá-ʔɨmasi χj-a ʔíʃt
too much lots OBV-joke around-PAST son/daughter
'her son joked around too much'

b. /ʔmújnak/- 'live with wife's family'
ʔá-ʔɨmujnak-ʃa ʔíʃt
OBV-live with wife's family-IMPF son/daughter
'her son is living with his wife's family'

c. /ʔwák/- 'dream, fantasize'
sts'át-pa=aʃ ʔá-ʔɨwak-ʃa-na palaláaj pjaχí
last night-LOC=1SG OBV-dream-IMPF-PAST lots bitterroot
'last night I dreamed about lots of bitterroot'

d. /ʔwájwi/- 'wear necklace'
ʔá-ʔɨwajwi-ʃa t'álpt ʔajat-mí ʔíʃt
OBV-wear necklace-IMPF bone bead woman-GEN son/daughter
'the woman's daughter is wearing a bone bead necklace'

In this context, root-initial /ʔ[sonorant]/, Yakima Sahaptin obviative allomorphy apparently differs from NE and CR dialects of Sahaptin. The example in (38) comes from Rude's fieldwork with NE dialect speakers. Note the use of the *ʔáw-* allomorph, where Yakima would use *ʔá-* in this context:

(38) /ʔník/ 'put away'[18] (NE Sahaptin)
ʔáw-nik-ʃa=aʃ
OBV-put away-IMPF=1sg
'I am putting it away'

Returning to Yakima Sahaptin, when the vowel separating the /ʔ[sonorant]/ sequence is stressed [ɨ́], an underlying vowel, two different patterns of obviative prefix allomorphy are seen. With 'say to, tell', the w-final obviative allomorph is preferred:

(39) /ʔɨ́n/- 'say to, tell'
Julie-nmí ʔáw-n-χa-na tíla "ʧʧúu tχána-tk".
-GEN OBV-say-HAB-PAST maternal grandfather quiet be-IMPER.PL
'Julie's maternal grandfather used to tell them, "be quiet".'
Cf. míʃ=nam pá-ʔɨn-χa-na?
what=2SG INV-say-HAB-PAST
'what did you tell me?'

However, with all other [ʔɨ́][sonorant] verbs we have checked,[19] a sample of which are shown in (40)–(42), the vowel-final obviative prefix is preferred:

(40) /ʔɨ́mʧak'ɨnk/- 'clamp mouth'
páp qɨ́s ʔá-ʔɨmʧak'ɨnk-a
man's daughter tight OBV-clamp mouth-PAST
'his daughter clamped her mouth shut'

(41) /ʔɨ́ntwana/- 'call after, talk to someone (while) walking away'
ʔá-ʔɨntwana-na=aʃ pʃwá-nan
OBV-call.after-PAST=1SG rock-ACC-OBJ
'I called after the rock'[20]

(42) /ʔɨ́mtɨmnajk/- 'kneel'
ʔá-ʔɨmtɨmnajk-ʃa pʧá
OBV-kneel-IMPF mother
'his mother is kneeling'

Strikingly, although /ʔɨ́ntwana/- is a historically *bipartite* verb (Beavert and Jansen 2011) formed from /ʔɨ́n/- 'say to, tell' and /twána/- 'accompany, follow', Beavert judges 'the Yakima pattern' of obviative allomorphy with this verb to be as shown in (41).

However, we note that other dialects of Sahaptin use the allomorph *ʔáw-* in this context, initial /ʔɨ́[sonorant]/. The example in (43) is from Umatilla:

(43) /ʔɨ́mttunwi/ 'be talkative'
ʔáw-ɨmttunwi-ʃa=nam paamijawáj
OBV-be talkative-IMPF=2SG 3PL.OBJ
'you're always talking to them'

We have searched earlier NW Sahaptin texts (Jacobs 1929, 1934, 1937) to determine whether the Yakima pattern is attested there, and have not found the crucial data, glottal stop initial verbs followed by [ɨ́][sonorant], except for 'say to, tell', which always takes the *áw-* allomorph. Interestingly, though, we have found the *ʔá-* allomorph of the obviative prefix before one glottal stop initial verb, *ʔɨ́χʷ-* 'magically wish' (*ʔúux-* in Yakima Sahaptin), attested in two texts, Yoke (1934) and Eyley Jr. (1934).

The distribution of Sahaptin obviative prefix allomorphy is summarized in (44):

(44) *Obviative prefix allomorphy summary*
a. Yakima Sahaptin
ʔáw- / ___ {V, ʔV, ʔ[obstruent]}
ʔá- / ___ {ʔ[sonorant], C (other than ʔ)}
ʔáw- ~ ʔá- / ___ ʔɨ́[sonorant] (lexically determined variation)

b. Other (NE, CR) Sahaptin
ʔáw- / ___ {V, ʔ}
ʔá- / ___ C (other than ʔ)

The distributional statements in (44) are complex, even in the NE and CR dialects, because the contexts which condition the allomorph sets do not fall into two neat classes. Part of the answer would seem to be connected with the fact that glottal stop initial verb roots are always followed by a vowel in surface form, and vowel initial verbs are always preceded by glottal stop word initially. Another piece of the answer might be the 'disappearing' morpheme-initial glottal stops in obviative prefixed verb roots noted above, to which we return in section 5.3.6.

5.3.5 One underlying representation or two?

The two allomorphs of the obviative prefix are phonetically close. The question therefore arises, just as for Nez Perce, as to why two underlying representations are needed, as opposed to a more traditional analysis with single underlying representation.

Suppose that the obviative prefix is /ʔá/-. Then [w] would need to be inserted before following vowel and glottal stop initial morphemes. However, there is no general phonological process of [w] insertion in this context in Sahaptin. Consider the inverse prefix *pá-* in (45). Before glottal stop initial roots, there is no [w] separating the inverse prefix from the root:

(45) pá- before a glottal stop initial root
/pá-ʔítuχ-ɨm/
INV-return[TR]-CIS[21]
'give it back to me'

The obviative prefix therefore cannot be (exclusively) vowel-final, like the inverse prefix.

Suppose that the obviative prefix is /ʔáw/-, with [w] deleted before a consonant other than [ʔ] and [ʔ] apparently deleting after [w]. This analysis predicts, first of all, that the sequence [wʔ] does not occur. However, [wʔ] is attested in Sahaptin. In the examples in (46), [wʔ] occurs within a verb root or across a prefix-verb root boundary:[22]

(46) [wʔ]
wawʔát- 'sprout, bud'
wawʔáwi- 'look for (with instruments)' (hands, eyes, etc.)

It is therefore not the case that [wʔ] is phonologically intolerable in Sahaptin. Moreover, sequences of [w] and other consonants are also well attested. A small sample is given in (47):

(47) [wC], C ≠ [ʔ]

ʔáwtkʷʃ	'ceiling, roof'
ʔáwtni	'sacred'
ʔáwqanin-	'roll around'
ʔáwʃnik-	'spread out on the floor, ground'

The examples in (46)–(47) indicate that there is no general [w]-deletion phenomenon in Sahaptin.

If neither w-epenthesis nor w-deletion can be motivated for Sahaptin, then we are left with positing two underlying representations for the Sahaptin obviative prefix.

5.3.6 Where did the glottal stop go?

Since the obviative morpheme is a prefix, the morphological structure of a word like *ʔáwʃnɨwajnk* 'pity him' might be expected to be /ʔáw-ʔʃnwájn-k/ (OBV-pity-IMPER.SG). We now turn to the question of why the root initial glottal stop is missing from the surface forms of such words.

Consider the fact that there are no surface vowel-initial words, at least in Yakima Sahaptin. Therefore the only relevant surface distinction is between words which begin with [ʔ] and words which begin with other types of consonants. Suppose that in words like *ʔáwʃnɨwajnk*, the obviative prefix *(ʔ)áw-* is infixed after the underlying glottal stop ([ʔ___ ʃnwájn]-). Then in words like *ʔ**á**wanakʷa*, the obviative prefix can also be described as infixed, except that in this form the glottal stop is epenthetic: /ánakʷ/ [ʔ___ánakʷ]. Then, if the w-final obviative prefix allomorph is vowel initial, there would be no need for glottal stop deletion when this allomorph is used with glottal stop initial verb roots: i.e. /ʔ-<u>áw</u>-ʃnwájn/- instead of /ʔ-<u>ʔáw</u>-ʃnwájn/-.

5.3.7 A formal model of Sahaptin obviative allomorphy

A Yakima Sahaptin obviative sample was constructed for testing with OTSoft. Six root types were selected: vowel-initial, singleton C initial (for C other than glottal stop), CC initial (for initial C other than glottal stop), and three types of glottal stop initial roots: ʔV, ʔ[obstruent], ʔ[sonorant].

The variable pattern seen with ʔɨ́[sonorant]-initial roots was not modelled. Initial candidate sets were limited to the following two inputs: prefixed *ʔá-* or infixed *áw-*. In section 3.7.3 we consider other possible prefixal inputs.

As we review the results of our formal modelling exercise, answers to the following questions will emerge.

(48) Is the vowel-final allomorph of the obviative prefix *ʔá-* or *á-*?

(49) Why is *áw-* infixed after glottal stop initial roots and *(ʔ)á-* prefixed to any other consonant?

(50) Why is the w-final allomorph used before clusters of ʔV or ʔ[obstruent] but not ʔ[sonorant]?

5.3.7.1 Constraints posited

Following Prince and Smolensky (2004) and McCarthy and Prince (1993), we assume that all infixes are really prefixes or suffixes. Affixes are positioned as close to an edge as possible. Infixation occurs only to mitigate some phonological problem and comes with a penalty: deviations from leftmost or rightmost position are penalized by the constraint EDGEMOST. Deviations from edge position are calculated categorically, in terms of one segment, one affix, one prosodic unit, etc., in the manner suggested by McCarthy (2003).

The asymmetry between ʔ[obstruent] and ʔ[sonorant] roots with respect to obviative allomorphy is captured in our analysis in terms of a minimal sonority distance requirement between a coda consonant and a following onset. Within the generative phonological literature, the need for such constraints has been argued for by Steriade (1982) and in such recent work as Baertsch and Davis (2001) and Gouskova (2004), although Henke, Kaisse and Wright (2012) argue against sonority as a primitive concept in phonology. For our purposes any [sonorant][sonorant] sequences in Sahaptin violate MINIMAL SONORITY DISTANCE (SONDIST), whereas [sonorant][obstruent] sequences do not.

The analysis of glottal stop initial roots requires the positing of a novel markedness constraint, *ʔVʔV, a constraint against contiguous glottal stop onsets. Cross-linguistically, this could be considered a type of haplology or OCP-like constraint. Independent evidence for *ʔVʔV in Sahaptin is provided by forms like those in (51). The third person singular nominative prefix *ʔi-* is variably present before verb roots which begin with [ʔ] followed by non-epenthetic vowel:

(51) Optional *ʔi-*

a. ʔi-ʔámtajk[23]-ʃa ʔájat ~ ʔámtajkʃa ʔájat
3S.NOM-live with husband's family-IMPF woman
'the woman is living with her husband's family'

b. ʔi-ʔílaʧχ-ʃa saplɨl ~ ʔílaʧχʃa saplɨl
3S.NOM-fry-IMPF bread
'she's frying bread'

Although we have not done a systematic sociolinguistic survey, our impression is that the variability is related to register. The forms with *ʔi-* above tend to occur in slow, careful speech, whereas those without *ʔi-* are more common in unguarded speech. Before glottal stop initial roots followed by epenthetic [ɨ], the facts are even messier. For the NE and CR speakers that Rude has worked with, either (52a) or b is possible, but not c. For Virginia Beavert, a is not possible. Either b or c is possible, and b is preferred over c.

(52) Realizations of ʔi- before a /ʔC/ root

a. ʔi-támja-ʃa
3S.NOM-buy-IMPF
'he is buying'

b. ʔɨtámja-ʃa
buy-IMPF
'he is buying'

c. ʔi-ʔɨtámja-ʃa
3S.NOM-buy-IMPF
'he is buying'

Crucially, the third person singular nominative prefix is not optional with verb roots which begin with any other consonant:

(53) Obligatory ʔi-

ʔi-pnú-ʃa *pnú-ʃa
3S.NOM-sleep-IMPF
'he's sleeping'

For this reason, despite the messiness of the data in (51)-(52), we feel justified in positing our constraint against contiguous glottal stops, *ʔVʔV.[24]

5.3.7.2 Results

OTSoft indicated that there is a ranking of the constraints which can generate the input data in our sample. The constraints are grouped into four strata. The highest ranked constraint in the analysis is SONDIST. The second and third constraint strata contain *ʔVʔV and EDGEMOST, respectively. The fourth constraint stratum contains DEP-ɨ and DEP-ʔ. The evidence for crucial rankings between these contraints is summarized in (54):

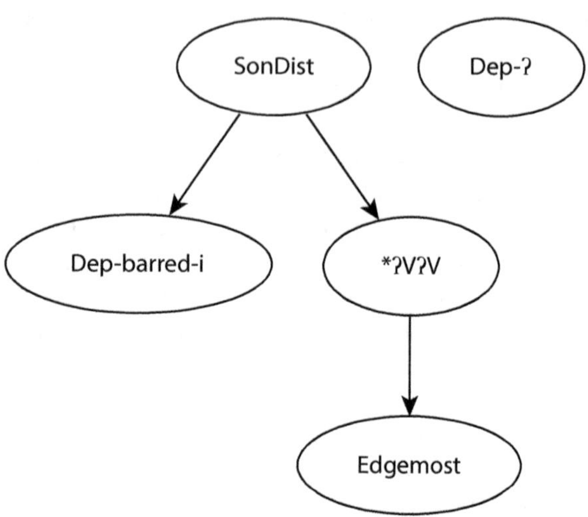

(54) *Constraint ranking for Yakima Sahaptin obviative prefix allomorphy*

In the remainder of this section, tableaux showing Yakima Sahaptin obviative prefix allomorphy for each of the six root types will be presented, omitting constraints which receive no penalties by any of the candidates. Again, for simplicity the only candidates shown in the tableaux in this section are infixed *áw-* and prefixed *ʔá-*. A larger set of candidates is considered in section 5.3.7.3.

C(C)V initial verb roots, where the initial C ≠ ʔ, are a relatively simple case to begin with. In this context, the preference for *ʔá-* over *áw-* (alternative output candidates are discussed in section 5.3.7.4) can be described with EDGEMOST. In (55), the verb root /kʷ'imá/ 'visit with' begins with a singleton consonant (cf. (33)a).

(55) Obviative allomorph selection before a CV-initial root

/{ʔá-, áw-}, kʷ'imá/	EDGEMOST
a. kʷ'-áw-ima	*!
b. ☞ ʔá-kʷ'ima	

In (56), the verb root /tq'íχ/ 'want' begins with a consonant cluster (cf. (33)e).

(56) Obviative allomorph selection before a CCV-initial root

/{ʔá-, áw-}, tq'íχ/	EDGEMOST
a. t-áw-q'iχ	*!
b. ☞ ʔá-tq'iχ	

Given the constraint set employed in the analysis, EDGEMOST dictates a preference for the prefixal allomorph. In these cases, nothing phonological is gained from infixation.

Now turning to glottal stop initial roots, a tableau showing the need for our novel markedness constraint *ʔVʔV is shown in (57) for a singleton glottal stop initial root, /ʔátawi/ 'love' (cf. (35)b.).

(57) Role of *ʔVʔV in obviative allomorph selection before ʔV roots

/{ʔá-, áw-}, ʔátawi/	*ʔVʔV	EDGEMOST
a. ☞ ʔ-áw-atawi		*
b. ʔá-ʔatawi	*!	

Without *ʔVʔV, there would otherwise be no phonological defect in the losing candidate in (57). The winning candidate avoids violating *ʔVʔV (via obligatory initial glottal stop epenthesis) via infixation, violating EDGEMOST instead. (See (64) for a tableau containing a larger set of candidates.)

The tableau in (61) illustrates obviative prefix allomorphy for a root beginning with a cluster of ʔ[obstruent], /ʔʃnwáy/ 'pity' (cf. (36)b.). Here, in addition to violating the markedness constraint *ʔVʔV, the winning candidate violates the faithfulness constraint DEP-ɨ.

(58) Obviative allomorph selection before ʔ[obstruent] initial roots

/{ʔá-, áw-}, ʔʃnwáj/	*ʔVʔV	EDGEMOST	DEP-ɨ
a. ☞ ʔ-áw-ʃn[ɨ]waj		*	*
b. ʔá-ʔ[ɨ]ʃn[ɨ]waj	*!		**

With root-initial clusters of ʔ[sonorant], the constraint SONDIST, which militates against coda-onset sequences which are too close in sonority, comes into play. The sonorant sequence in the losing candidate [wm] violates SonDist. Notice that the winning candidate contains a *ʔVʔV violation, unlike the losing candidate in the ʔ[obstruent] case, (58)b.

(59) Obviative allomorph selection before ʔ[sonorant] initial roots

/{ʔá-, áw-}, ʔmújnak/	SONDIST	*ʔVʔV	EDGEMOST	DEP-ɨ
a. ☞ ʔá-ʔ[ɨ]mujnak		*		*
b. ʔ-áw-mujnak	*!		*	

Finally, we turn to vowel-initial roots. With such roots, the allomorph *áw-* is used. Here, there is no root-initial consonant after which *áw-* may be infixed. In our tableau in (60) of obviative allomorphy with a vowel initial root, /ának^w/ 'abandon' (cf. (32)), we consider *ʔá-* and *áw*-prefixed candidates as usual. Both candidates contain epenthetic glottal stop, word-initial in the case of the candidate with *áw-* and word-internal in the case of the candidate with *ʔá-*. The ill-formedness of candidate b is due to the *ʔVʔV violation.

(60) Obviative allomorph selection before a V-initial root

/{ʔá-, áw-}, ának^w/	*ʔVʔV	EDGEMOST	DEP-ʔ
a. ☞ [ʔ]<u>áw</u>-anak^w		*	*
b. ʔ<u>á</u>-[ʔ]anak^w	*!		*

When other vowel final prefixes, like *wjá-* 'while walking' are added to this vowel-initial stem, a long vowel results: *wjáanak^w-* 'leave behind'. Recall that the obviative contrasts with prefixes like *wjá-* because the obviative, unlike other prefixes, has different surface allomorphs. In the formal analysis, the difference between these prefixes is attributed to a difference in inputs.

5.3.7.3 Vowel vs. glottal stop initial obviative prefix allomorphs

In this section, we justify our previous assumption that the vowel-final allomorph is glottal stop initial, rather than vowel-initial, by considering other inputs in a tableau des tableaux exercise.

Four analyses with the allomorph sets shown in (61) were constructed and submitted to OTSoft. Results for analysis 3 have already been presented above in section 5.3.7.2. Analyses 1, 2, and 4 are variants on this analysis. Each analysis contained the six verb roots illustrated in section 5.3.7. The same constraints as in section 5.3.7.2 were used, with one addition: MAX-ʔ. In the candidates considered in each analysis, the w-final allomorph was an infix, and the vowel-final allomorph was a prefix.

(61) *Possible allomorph sets for the obviative prefix*
Analysis 1: /ʔáw/-, /ʔá/-
Analysis 2: /ʔáw/-, /á/-
Analysis 3: /áw/-, /ʔá/-
Analysis 4: /áw/-, /á/-

Each analysis in (61) can be considered a possible analysis of the data, because each analysis predicted the right winning candidates via a consistent, analysis-internal ranking of the constraints (although each ranking was different in the four possible analyses). Each analysis can be compared in terms of the number of constraint violations presented by each of the winning candidates, as shown in (62):

(62) *Number of constraint violations of winning candidates in each analysis*

Analysis 1 (/ʔáw/-, /ʔá/-):	7
Analysis 2 (/ʔáw/-, /á/-):	10
Analysis 3 (/áw/-, /ʔá/-):	6
Analysis 4 (/áw/-, /á/-):	12

Analysis 3 is the simplest of the four in that it predicts the winning candidates with the fewest constraint violations. For this reason, we feel justified in analysing the Sahaptin obviative prefix allomorph set as /áw/-, /ʔá/-.

5.3.7.4 Prefixation vs. infixation

So far we have constructed an analysis of Sahaptin obviative allomorphy in which the allomorph set consists of a CV- prefix and a VC- 'infix'. In other languages with allomorph sets of this shape, prefix-infix variation is usually relatable to the gross difference in shape. For example, in Dakota, the agreement infixes have CV- and V- shapes which are infixed after the first CV of the root for consonant-initial roots, and VC- forms which are prefixed before V-initial roots (Moravcsik 1977; Shaw 1980; McCarthy and Prince 1993). The question therefore arises as to whether the difference in the placement of the Yakima Sahaptin CV- and VC- allomorphs is related to their shapes. We believe that it is.

To see why *áw-* is infixed, not prefixed, after glottal stop initial roots in Sahaptin, consider the tableau in (63), in which the obviative prefix is underlined in each candidate. Candidates (a) and (d) are phonetically identical, but if /áw/- were prefixed as in candidate (d) rather than infixed as in candidate (a), then both ʔ-epenthesis and ʔ-deletion would be needed to describe the winning candidate in the prefixation analysis, whereas neither is needed in the infixation analysis:

(63) Why /áw/- is infixed rather than prefixed

/{ʔá-, áw-}, ʔátawi/	*ʔVʔV	EDGEMOST	DEP-ʔ	MAX-ʔ
a. ☞ ʔ-<u>áw</u>-atawi		*		
b. <u>ʔá</u>-ʔatawi	*!			
c. ʔá-<u>ʔa</u>-tawi	*!	*		
d. [ʔ]<u>áw</u>-atawi			*	*!*

A comparison of candidates (a) and (c) in (63) also reveals why *áw-*, not *ʔá-*, is infixed after glottal stop initial roots. *ʔá-* here is phonologically and morphologically less well-formed: **ʔá-*<u>ʔa</u>*-tawi* violates *ʔVʔV in a way that candidate (a) does not.

Similar rationale for the prefixation rather than infixation of *ʔá-* to roots beginning with consonants other than glottal stop can be given. In (64), compare candidates (a) and (c). Candidate (c), with infixation, solves no phonological problems, and is morphologically less well-formed than candidate (a), the winner.

(64) Why /ʔá/- is prefixed rather than infixed

/{ʔá-, áw-}, kʷ'imá/	EDGEMOST	DEP-ʔ
a. ☞ <u>ʔá</u>-kʷ'ima		
b. kʷ'-<u>áw</u>-ima	*!	
c. kʷ'í-<u>ʔa</u>-ma	*!*	
d. [ʔ]<u>áw</u>-kʷ'ima		*!

Finally, we can see why *ʔá-*, not *áw-*, is prefixed to roots beginning with consonants other than glottal stop. Compare candidates (a) and (d) in (64). Candidate (d) violates DEP-ʔ, whereas candidate (a) does not.

5.3.8 Sahaptin summary

We have seen that the Yakima Sahaptin obviative prefix has VC- and CV-shapes. The VC- shape (*áw-*) is infixed after word-initial glottal stop or clusters of /ʔ[obstruent]/, whether underlying or epenthetic, and the CV-shape (*ʔá-*) is prefixed before consonants other than [ʔ] or before clusters of /ʔ[sonorant]/. In other Sahaptin dialects, the distribution is slightly different: *ʔáw-* is used before all vowel or /ʔ/-initial roots.

In either variety, the distribution of these allomorphs is complex. The formal analysis proposed here of the Yakima dialect requires the novel phonological constraint *ʔVʔV, which states a dispreference for contiguous glottal stop initial syllables. The obstruent vs. sonorant asymmetry in Yakima was accounted for via MINIMAL SONORITY DISTANCE. An output oriented approach to the Sahaptin obviative prefix allows us to make sense of the fact that the w-final allomorph occurs before underlyingly 'vowel or glottal stop' initial verb roots. In a surface-oriented approach, both classes can be referred to as glottal stop initial.

5.4 A possible scenario for historical change

In this section we outline a possible reconstruction and development of the obviative allomorph set. As summarized in (65), the obviative prefix distributions in Nez Perce and Sahaptin are rather different. In (65), 'C' represents any consonant other than [ʔ], and V represents any vowel other than [ɨ].

(65) *Distributions of obviative prefix allomorphs in Nez Perce and Sahaptin*

	___ʔ				'say'	___other C
	___ʔV		___ʔ[son]	___ʔ[obst]		
NEZ PERCE	ʔe-		ʔew-	ʔe-	ʔew-	ʔe-
SAHAPTIN	___ʔɨ́[son]	___ʔV				
Yakima	ʔá-	áw-	ʔá-	áw-	áw-	ʔá-
other Sahaptin	áw-	áw-	áw-	áw-	áw-	ʔá-

With only two languages in the Sahaptian family, it is difficult to determine which aspects of allomorphy in the daughter languages are innovative vs. conservative.[25]

First we tackle the reconstruction of 'say'. Rude (2012) reconstructs:

(66) *Proposed historical development of the obviative prefix*
*hɨn. vtt. Say, tell. NP /hn/; S ɨnn. Cf. Klamath hcm 'talk, speak'. (Barker 1963: 165)

Aoki (1962) had noted that Sahaptin [ʔ] can correspond to either Nez Perce [ʔ] (as with the obviative prefix) or [h], and posits the sound change root-initial PS *h > Sahaptin [ʔ]. This scenario still seems to be valid. (As a result of PS *h > Sahaptin [ʔ], root-initial /h/ is much less common in Sahaptin than it is in Nez Perce, as noted in section 5.3.4.) Initial *ʔ for 'say' can be ruled out on the grounds that there would not otherwise be any examples of PS *ʔ > NP /h/. Given that both languages use the w-final form of the obviative prefix with 'say', this suggests that at one point in the history of the family the w-final allomorph may have also been used more widely before root-initial /h/. We posit that this stage was Pre-Proto-Sahaptian, an internally reconstructed stage of Proto-Sahaptian. Proto-Sahaptian, however, differed from Pre-Proto-Sahaptian in that at the later stage the w-final allomorph was restricted to root-initial *ʔ. The w-final allomorph was lexicalized with 'say', which was still *h-initial at this stage. The w-final allomorph was not used with other *h-initial verbs in Proto-Sahaptian. We suggest that this lexicalization is due to the high frequency of the verb 'say to, tell'. A quick perusal of the texts in Jacob (1929, 1934) shows that this verb accounts for probably the majority of uses of the Sahaptin *ʔáw-* allomorph in this set of texts. As noted by Bybee (2001) and others, high token frequency can preserve an alternation.

In (66) we present our scenario for the reconstruction and historical divergence of this allomorph set. We suggest that originally the obviative allomorph occurred in a wider range of contexts than currently found in either Sahaptin or Nez Perce. We reconstruct the prefix as originally accented, as Sahaptin is more conservative with respect to accent than Nez Perce (Rude 2006).

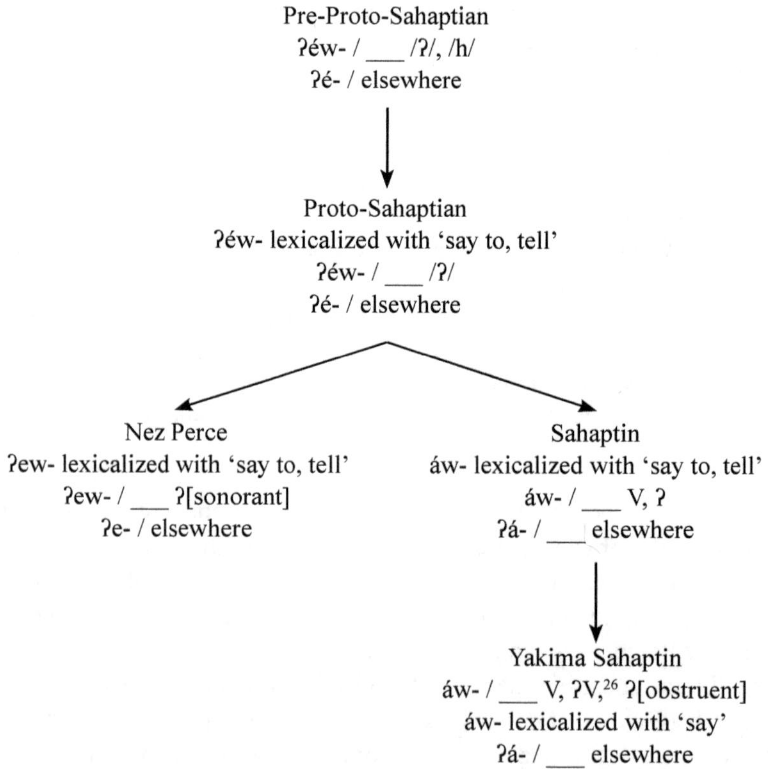

5.4.1 Nez Perce

Nez Perce has innovated by narrowing the context in which *ʔew-* is used. In Nez Perce, as we have seen, *ʔew-* only occurs before sequences of ʔ[sonorant]. The only other relevant innovation in Nez Perce is that the inherent accent of the obviative prefix was lost, so that this morpheme became unaccented.

According to our scenario, the use of the *ʔew-* allomorph before 'say' is a conservative retention of pre-PS allomorphy, despite the fact that the root-initial consonant of 'say' has changed from *ʔ to h in Nez Perce.

5.4.2 Sahaptin

*e > /a/ in the Sahaptin form of the obviative prefix, as is systematically the case for this vowel quality in Sahaptin (Aoki 1962; Rude 1999).

Unlike Nez Perce, the context for use of the [w]-allomorph of the obviative prefix has broadened slightly in Sahaptin, where it is now used before vowel-initial roots, according to our analysis.

The distribution of obviative prefix allomorphs in Nez Perce refers to glottalized sonorants. It can be noted in Sahaptin, there are no glottalized sonorants except sentence-finally (see Note 14). Nez Perce root-internal or root-final glottalized sonorants (including R' from /ʔ[sonorant]/) correspond to plain sonorants in Sahaptin in all known cases, and we posit that Proto-Sahaptian glottalized sonorants became plain sonorants in Sahaptin.

5.5 Conclusions

We have posited that in Pre-Proto-Sahaptian there was an allomorph set consisting of **ʔéw-*, used before laryngeal consonants, and **ʔé-* used elsewhere. We can speculate that previous to Pre-Proto-Sahaptian, obviative prefix allomorphy may have started out life as a simple epenthesis or deletion phenomenon, but even in Proto-Sahaptian there is evidence of morphologization (Hooper 1974; Wurzel 1980), in that the alternation is restricted to one morpheme in both daughter languages.

Two points of general interest arise from the present case. The first point is the theoretical issue raised in section 5.1: are phonological constraints always responsible for the distribution of allomorphs? We have suggested that the distribution of *ʔew-* in Nez Perce is related to typological tendencies in the distribution of glottalized sonorants. For Sahaptin, we have suggested that obviative allomorph distribution may be sensitive to constraints related to haplology and sonority. Recall that Dressler (1976, 1980) suggested that phonological rules should be 'totally plausible', morphological rules 'implausible', with morphophonological rules lying 'in between'. Perhaps what we really have here is an *in-between* case. Are the constraints we proposed plausible, implausible or in between? If implausible (or even in between), a description involving only subcategorization frames would be all that is needed.

The second general point is a historical one. We note that the form of the allomorphs has not changed (much). The main change has been in the context for use, and there only slightly. According to our historical scenario, the usage of **ʔéw-* with the verb 'say to, tell' must have been lexically conditioned even in Proto-Sahaptian. This usage of **ʔéw-* with 'say to, tell' has persisted in both languages to the present time, probably because of the apparently high token frequency of this verb. Moreover, the basic distribution of allomorphs **ʔéw-* and **ʔé-* in other contexts has also persisted. We therefore note that allomorphy can remain fairly stable over time. This finding is of interest because some linguists have predicted that change rather than stability might be the norm:

> Allomorphy tends to be minimized in a paradigm. (Kiparsky 1978: 41)
>
> We should first acknowledge that different pronunciations of the same morpheme, i.e., allomorphy, are largely nonfunctional and are rather to be viewed as an unfortunate but inevitable consequence of the ravages of sound change. It would serve the goal of communication better if there were a one-to-one mapping between pronunciation and meaning. (Ohala 1992: 229)

Both Ohala's and Kiparsky's comments indicate an expectation that languages might change in such a way that allomorphy is eliminated via analogical levelling. Hooper (1976:85); on the other hand, has predicted that alternations "that are strongly associated with meaning" tend to be extended rather than leveled, whereas suppletive alternations "tend to be leveled". In this case, neither levelling nor extension has occurred.

Notes

* We thank Nez Perce native speaker Eugene John for his help with data regarding glottalized sonorant timing. We thank Sonya Bird for helpful, on-going discussion of glottalized sonorants, and Bruce Rigsby for encouraging a comparative approach to the allomorphy sets in Sahaptin and Nez Perce. We also thank Bernard Tranel for his careful reading and comments on a previous draft of this article. Finally, we thank the editors for their helpful comments on our article, and for all their editorial service.

1. He concluded that there are 'simply PRs which have also some function in the morphological component; i.e. they are PRs and MRs at the same time' (Dressler 1976: 330). However, Ford and Singh (1996) argue that morphophonology is not 'phonology'. They would view the morphological characteristics of these rules as indicative of their morphological status.

2. However, see Rozelle (1998) for a thoughtful examination of this assumption on the basis of phonological differences between signed and spoken languages.
3. Aoki (1962) reconstructed the Proto-Sahaptian obviative prefix as **ʔá-, ʔé-* 'third person object prefix', giving Nez Perce *ʔa-*, *ʔe-* and Sahaptin *ʔá-* as reflexes. Aoki does not reconstruct the w-final allomorph.
4. According to Aoki (1970: 7), the Lower dialect of Nez Perce also has /kʷ/. Aoki (1994: xii) lists /kʷ k'ʷ qʷ q'ʷ/ as found (at least underlyingly) in the Lower dialect.
5. Transcriptional differences between sources have been eliminated in this article. All Nez Perce data are presented using the symbols in (1)–(2).
6. In words with no underlying accent, stress surfaces on the penultimate syllable if the word ends in a vowel or singleton consonant. Words that end in more than one consonant stress the ultima, as do also imperatives and a class of nondeclining adverbial/adjectival particles.
7. Likewise there are short vowels which do not lengthen when stressed (and which are missing in certain environments), which behave very differently than regular Nez Perce /a e i o u/. Many such vowels are historically epenthetic and correspond to Sahaptin [ɨ]. Vowels also fail to lengthen before [h] or [ʔ] (for an example see Note 12), or anywhere in the sequence [VʔV] or [VhV].
8. There are also phonetic word-final clusters of consonants, which have been analyzed as consonant clusters (Aoki 1970a; Crook 1999) or syllabic consonants (Rude 1985; Crook 1999).
9. Aoki (1970a) lists no prevocalic clusters of the shape [wʔC]. His one example of cluster type [ʔwC] (with C = sonorant, *ʔeʔwníise* 'I give it to him' (37), is transcribed *ʔew'niise* in (Aoki 1994), congruent with the transcription provided by Rude (2006) of the related form 'I gave it to him' as *ʔew'nije*. Aoki (1970a) gives one example of [w'C]: *hiléw'luutsix* 'they (fish) are resting in deep water'.
10. According to Eugene John (p.c.), Aoki's *hwíit* 'to whistle' is not Nez Perce but rather a borrowing from Sahaptin (*kwíikw*).
11. We are grateful to Eugene John for providing us with this example.
12. There must be a morpheme boundary between /V/ and /hC/, as shown by the preserved [VhC] in (e.g.) [wíhne] 'I have gone' (< /wíhnen-s/ 'go'). /h/ generally remains when the prefix is stressed; e.g., [ʔinéhl'iqtse] /ʔiné-hl'íqn-se/ 'I am amusing myself', in contrast to [ʔeel'íiqtetu] /ʔe-hl'íqn-tetu/ 'I used to enjoy it' (Aoki 1994: 142). However, with both /hn/ 'say, tell' and /hp/ 'eat', /h/ participates in compensatory lengthening even when the preceding vowel is stressed: [péene] /pé-hn-e/ 'he told him'; [ʔinéepse] /ʔiné-hp-se/ 'I am eating myself'; [péetsene] /pé-hn-sene/ 'he was telling him'; [péepe] /pé-hp-e/ 'he ate it'.
13. Even in Salish, only Nɬeʔkepmxcin in our sample allows glottalized sonorants which are not adjacent to vowels.

14. In Sahaptin, glottalized sonorants occur only sentence-finally. When the sentence-final yes/no question morpheme -ʔ follows a word ending in a sonorant, the result is a post-glottalized sonorant.
15. The obviative codes a third person direct object only in concert with a Speech Act Participant (first or second person) subject in the Columbia River and Northeast dialects of Sahaptin and in modern Yakima. However, in the Northwest Sahaptin dialects documented by Jacobs (1929), intransitive *ʔá-* does not always code a possessor and transitive *ʔá-* need not always occur with a first or second person subject.
16. In this article we use the morpheme glossing abbreviations of Rigsby and Rude (1996): CIS = cislocative, COM = comitative, GER = gerund, IMPER.SG = imperative singular, IMPF = imperfective, NOM = nominative, OBJ = objective case, OBV = obviative, POSS = possessive, VOC = vocative.
17. Some derivational prefixes have both productive and lexicalized functions. The productive instances of the prefix *wjá-* mean 'while walking' or 'keep Ving' (continuously). The verbs in (30) appear to be historical rather than synchronic formations.
18. In Yakima, this stem is *nítʃ*.
19. *ʔímani-* 'promise', *ʔímʔiyuuʃ-* 'promise to pay, pledge', *ʔímak'ink-* 'hold in mouth, close mouth, press lips together, tighten jaw', *ʔímtʃaʃiχ-* 'like taste of, develop taste for'.
20. Modelled after a traditional legend in which Coyote calls to a killer rock that he has defeated as he's walking away.
21. The final [ɨ] is epenthetic.
22. *wawʔáwi-* is synchronically morphologically complex, analyzable as *wá-* 'with instrument' + *w-* pl. (RED) + *ʔáwi-* 'look for'. However, the morphological structure of *wawʔát-* is less certain. If the sequence [waw] in *wawʔát-* 'sprout, bud' is etymologically prefixal, it is semantically opaque in modern Sahaptin. The final syllable is possibly an instance of ʔát- 'leave, go out, emerge'.
23. Careful readers will note the similarity of /ʔámtajk/ 'live with husband's family' and /ám/ husband', and may wonder why the former is glottal stop initial while the latter is vowel initial. The evidence for the distinction hinges on their different behaviours under affixation with different prefixes: /ʔi/- 3S.NOM in the case of the verb and /ʔin(m)/- 'my' in the case of the noun. It is possible that the nominative prefix differs from other vowel-final prefixes in terms of syntactic separability, but we have not fully explored this issue.
24. This constraint does not appear to be active in Nez Perce, e.g., [ʔaʔátsa] 'his entered'; [ʔeʔétise] 'hers is cooking'; [ʔeʔítey] 'put it in!'; etc.
25. A third, historically-related language might help. Sapir (1929) proposed that Sahaptian is a branch of Plateau Penutian, the other members of which are Klamath and the long-extinct Cayuse and Molala. Although Rigsby (1965) did a detailed assessment of the evidence and did not find support for Sapir's hypothesis, it is now generally accepted that Klamath and Sahaptian form a subgrouping within Plateau Penutian (Aoki 1963; Rude 1987, 1991;

DeLancey *et al.* 1988; DeLancey 1992). Unfortunately, Klamath lacks a prefix which is cognate with the Sahaptian obviative, as implicitly noted by Rude (1987).

26. For V other than [ɨ].

References

Aoki, Haruo (1962) Nez Perce and Northern Sahaptin: A binary comparison. *International Journal of American Linguistics* 28 (3): 172–182.

Aoki, Haruo (1963) On Sahaptian-Klamath linguistic affiliations. *International Journal of American Linguistics* 29 (2): 107–112.

Aoki, Haruo (1970a) *Nez Perce Grammar*. Berkeley, CA: University of California Press.

Aoki, Haruo (1970b) A note on glottalized consonants. *Phonetica* 21: 65–74.

Aoki, Haruo (1994) *Nez Perce Dictionary*. Berkeley, CA: University of California Press.

Baertsch, Karen and Davis, Stuart (2001) Turkic C+/l/(uster) phonology. In Mary Andronis, Christopher Ball, Heidi Elston and Sylvain Neuvel (eds.) *Chicago Linguistic Society*, vol. 37.1, 29–44. Chicago, IL: Chicago Linguistic Society.

Barker, M.A.R. (1963) *Klamath Dictionary*. Berkeley, CA: University of California Press.

Barker, M.A.R. (1964) *Klamath Grammar*. Berkeley, CA: University of California Press.

Beavert, Virginia and Hargus, Sharon (2009) *Ichishkíin Sínwit Yakama/Yakima Sahaptin Dictionary*. Toppenish and Seattle, WA: Heritage University and UW Press.

Beavert, Virginia and Jansen, Joana (2011) Yakima Sahaptin bipartite verb stems. *International Journal of American Linguistics* 77 (1): 121–149.

Bird, Sonya, Caldecott, Marion, Campbell, Fiona, Gick, Bryan and Shaw, Patricia A. (2008) Oral-laryngeal timing in glottalised resonants. *Journal of Phonetics* 36 (3): 492–507.

Blevins, Juliette (1993) Klamath Laryngeal Phonology. *International Journal of American Linguistics* 59 (3): 237–279.

Buckley, Eugene (1994) *Theoretical Aspects of Kashaya Phonology and Morphology*. Stanford, CA: CSLI Publications.

Bybee, Joan (2001) *Phonology and Language Use*. Cambridge: Cambridge University Press.

Chomsky, Noam (1964) *Current Issues in Linguistic Theory*. The Hague: Mouton.

Crook, Harold (1999) *The Phonology and Morphology of Nez Perce Stress*. Doctoral dissertation, University of California at Los Angeles.

DeLancey, Scott (1992) Klamath and Sahaptian Numerals. *International Journal of American Linguistics* 58 (2): 235–239.

DeLancey, Scott, Genetti, Carol and Rude, Noel (1988) Some Sahaptian-Klamath-Tsimshianic Lexical Sets. In William Shipley (ed.) *In Honor of Mary Haas: From the Haas Festival Conference on Native American Linguistics,* 195–224. Berlin: Mouton de Gruyter.

Dressler, Wolfgang (1976) Morphologization of Phonological Processes (Are there distinct morphonological processes?). In Alphonse Juilland (ed.) *Linguistic studies offered to Joseph Greenberg on the Occasion of his Sixtieth Birthday,* 313–337. Saratoga, CA: Anma libri.

Dressler, Wolfgang (1980) *Morphonology*. Ann Arbor, MI: Karoma.

Eyley Jr., Sam (1934) 2. Coyote tricks Eagle and takes his wives; he releases salmon. In Melville Jacobs (ed.) *Northwest Sahaptin texts. Part 1,* 90–94. New York: Columbia University Press.

Ford, Alan and Singh, Rajendra (1996) Quelques avantages d'une linguistique débarrassée de la morpho(pho)nologie. In Rajendra Singh (ed.) *Trubetzkoy's Orphan,* 119–139. Amsterdam: John Benjamins.

Gouskova, Maria (2004) Relational hierarchies in Optimality Theory: The case of syllable contact. *Phonology* 21 (2): 201–250.

Hall, Beatrice L. and Hall, R. H. R. (1977) Nez Perce vowel harmony: An Africanist explanation and some theoretical questions. In Robert M. Vago (ed.) *Issues in Vowel Harmony,* 201–236. Amsterdam: John Benjamins.

Halle, Morris (1957) *The Sound Pattern of Russian*. The Hague: Mouton.

Hargus, Sharon (2005) Distribution and timing of glottalized nasals in Athabaskan. Paper presented at Colloquium presentation, University of British Columbia, Department of Linguistics.

Hargus, Sharon (2006) Timing isn't everything: (Mostly) post-glottalized nasals in Witsuwit'en. Paper presented at the Linguistic Society of America, Albuquerque, NM, 5–8 January.

Hargus, Sharon (2007) *Witsuwit'en Grammar: Phonetics, Phonology and Morphology*. Vancouver: UBC Press.

Hargus, Sharon and Beavert, Virginia (2002) Yakima Sahaptin clusters and epenthetic [ɨ]. *Anthropological Linguistics* 44 (3): 1–47.

Hargus, Sharon and Beavert, Virginia (2005) A note on the phonetic correlates of stress in Yakima Sahaptin. In Daniel J. Jinguji and Steven Moran (eds.) *University of Washington Working Papers in Linguistics*, vol. 24, 64–95. Seattle, WA: Department of Linguistics, University of Washington.

Hargus, Sharon and Beavert, Virginia (2006) High-ranking Affix Faithfulness in Yakima Sahaptin. In Don Baumer, David Montero and Michael Scanlon (eds.) *Proceedings of the 25th West Coast Conference on Formal Linguistics,* 177–185. Somerville, MA: Cascadilla Proceedings Project.

Hargus, Sharon and Beavert, Virginia (2014) Northwest Sahaptin. *Journal of the International Phonetic Association* 44(3): 319–342.

Haspelmath, Martin and Sims, Andrea (2010) *Understanding Morphology* (2nd edn). London: Hodder Education.

Hayes, Bruce (2004) Phonological Acquisition in Optimality Theory: The Early Stages. In René Kager, Joe Pater and Wim Zonneveld (eds.) *Constraints in Phonological Acquisition*, 158–203. Cambridge: Cambridge University Press.

Hayes, Bruce, Tesar, Bruce and Zuraw, Kie (2003) OTSoft 2.1 (software package). [Available on http://www.linguistics.ucla.edu/people/hayes/otsoft/.]

Henke, Eric, Kaisse, Ellen M. and Wright, Richard (2012) Is the Sonority Sequencing Principle an epiphenomenon? In Steve Parker (ed.) *The Sonority Controversy,* 65–100. Berlin: De Gruyter.

Hooper, Joan (1974) Rule morphologization in natural generative phonology. In Anthony Bruck, Robert A. Fox and Michael W. La Galy (eds.) *Papers from the Parasession on Natural Phonology,* 160–170. Chicago, IL: Chicago Linguistic Society.

Hooper, Joan (1976) *An Introduction to Natural Generative Phonology*. New York: Academic Press.

Howe, Darin and Pulleyblank, Douglas (2001) Patterns and timing of glottalisation. *Phonology* 18 (1): 45–80.

Jacobs, Melville (ed.) (1929) Northwest Sahaptin Texts, 1. In *University of Washington Publications in Anthropology*, vol. 2, 175–244. Seattle, WA: University of Washington Press.

Jacobs, Melville (1931) A sketch of Northern Sahaptin grammar. *University of Washington Publications in Anthropology* 4: 85–291.

Jacobs, Melville (ed.) (1934) *Northwest Sahaptin Texts. Part 1*. Vol. 19. New York: Columbia University Press.

Jacobs, Melville (ed.) (1937) *Northwest Sahaptin Texts. Part 2*. Vol. 19. New York: Columbia University Press.

Kim, Eun-Sook (2003) *Theoretical Issues in Nuu-chah-nulth Phonology and Morphology*. Doctoral dissertation, University of British Columbia.

Kingston, John (1990) Articulatory binding. In John Kingston and Mary E. Beckman (eds.) *Papers in Laboratory Phonology I: Between the Grammar and Physics of Speech,* 406–434. Cambridge: Cambridge University Press.

Kingston, John (2005) The Phonetics of Athabaskan Tonogenesis. In Sharon Hargus and Keren Rice (eds.) *Athabaskan Prosody,* 137–184. Amsterdam: John Benjamins.

Kiparsky, Paul (1978) Historical Linguistics. In William Orr Dingwall (ed.) *A Survey of Linguistic Science,* 33–61. Stamford, CA: Greylock Publishers.

Leer, Jeff (1979) *Proto-Athabaskan Verb Stem Variation: I. Phonology*. Fairbanks, AK: Alaska Native Language Center, University of Alaska Fairbanks.

Maddieson, Ian (1984) *Patterns of Sounds*. Cambridge: Cambridge University Press.

McCarthy, John J. (2003) OT constraints are categorical. *Phonology* 20 (1): 75–138.

McCarthy, John J. and Prince, Alan S. (1993) *Prosodic Morphology I: Constraint Interaction and Satisfaction*. Amherst, MA and New Brunswick, NJ: Department, University of Massachusetts, Amherst and Rutgers University.

Mester, R. Armin (1994) The Quantitative Trochee in Latin. *Natural Language and Linguistic Theory* 12 (1): 1–61.

Moravcsik, Edith A. (1977) *On Rules of Infixing*. Bloomington, IN: Indiana University Linguistics Club.

Nettle, Daniel (1999) Is the rate of linguistic change constant? *Lingua* 108 (2–3): 119–136.

Newman, Stanley (1944) *The Yokuts Language of California*. New York: Viking Fund Publications in Anthropology 2.

Ohala, John J. (1992) The costs and benefits of phonological analysis. In Pamela Downing, Susan D. Lima and Michael Noonan (eds.) *The Linguistics of Literacy,* 211–237. Amsterdam: John Benjamins.

Oswalt, Robert L. (1961) *A Kashaya Grammar (Southwestern Pomo)*. Doctoral dissertation, University of California at Berkeley.

Plauché, Madelaine (1998) Glottalized sonorants in Yowlumne (Yawelmani). In Amanda R. Doran, Tivoli Majors, Claude E. Mauk and Nisha Merchant Goss (eds.) *Texas Linguistics Forum 41: Proceedings of the 1998 Texas Linguistics Society Conference,* 133–145. Austin, TX: Texas Linguistics Society.

Prince, Alan and Smolensky, Paul (2004) *Optimality Theory: Constraint Interaction in Generative Grammar*. Oxford: Blackwell Publishing.

Rigsby, Bruce (1965) *Linguistic Relations in the Southern Plateau*. Doctoral dissertation, University of Oregon.

Rigsby, Bruce and Rude, Noel (1996) Sketch of Sahaptin, a Sahaptian Language. In Ives Goddard (ed.) *Languages,* 666–692. Washington, DC: Smithsonian Institution.

Rozelle, Lorna (1998) Two Hands are Better than One: The Representation of the Non-Dominant Hand in American Sign Language and Finnish Sign Language. Manuscript, University of Washington.

Rude, Noel (1982) Promotion and topicality of Nez Perce objects. In Monica Macaulay, Orin D. Gensler, Claudia Brugman, Inese Čivkulis, Amy Dahlstrom, Katherine Krile and Rob Sturm (eds.) *Proceedings of the Eighth Annual Meeting of the Berkeley Linguistics Society,* 463–483. Berkeley, CA: Department of Linguistics, University of California at Berkeley.

Rude, Noel (1985) *Studies in Nez Perce Grammar and Discourse*. Doctoral dissertation, University of Oregon.

Rude, Noel (1987) Some Klamath-Sahaptian grammatical correspondences. *Kansas Working Papers in Linguistics*, vol. 12, 67–83. Kansas, KA: Department of Linguistics, University of Kansas.

Rude, Noel (1991) Verbs to Promotional Suffixes in Sahaptian and Klamath. In Elizabeth Closs Traugott and Bernd Heine (eds) *Approaches to Grammaticalization: Focus on Theoretical and Methodological Issues,* 185–199. Amsterdam: John Benjamins.

Rude, Noel (1997) Dative shifting and double objects in Sahaptin. In Talmy Givón (ed.) *Grammatical Relations: A Functionalist Perspective,* 323–349. Amsterdam: John Benjamins.

Rude, Noel (1999) Data for a Nez Perce Phonology. Manuscript.

Rude, Noel (2006) Proto-Sahaptian vocalism. In Masaru Kiyota, James J. Thompson and Noriko Yamane-Tanaka (eds.) *Papers for the Forty-first International Conference on Salish and Neighbouring Languages,* 264–277. Vancouver, BC: University of British Columbia.

Rude, Noel (2009) Transitivity in Sahaptin. *Northwest Journal of Linguistics* 3 (3): 1–37.

Rude, Noel (2012) Proto-Sahaptian Glossary. Manuscript.

Saluskin, Ellen (no date-a) Debt owed to Ellen Saluskin by Margaret Wahsise. Interlinear glossed text.

Saluskin, Ellen (no date-b) Root feasts. Interlinear glossed text.

Sapir, Edward (1929) Central and North American Languages. *Encyclopedia Britannica,* (14th edn), 138–141. London and New York: Encyclopaedia Britannica Co.

Shaw, Patricia A. (1980) *Dakota Phonology and Morphology*. New York: Garland.

Steriade, Donca (1982) *Greek Prosodies and the Nature of Syllabification*. Doctoral dissertation, Massachusetts Institute of Technology.

Steriade, Donca (1999) Phonetics in phonology: The case of laryngeal neutralization. In Matthew Gordon (ed.) *Papers in Phonology 3,* 25–146. Los Angeles: Department of Linguistics, University of California at Los Angeles.

Thompson, Laurence C., Thompson, M. Terry and Egesdal, Steven M. (1996) Sketch of Thompson, a Salishan Language. In Ives Goddard (ed.) *Languages,* 609–643. Washington, DC: Smithsonian Institution.

van Eijk, Jan (1997) *The Lillooet Language: Phonology, Morphology, Syntax*. Vancouver: UBC Press.

Vennemann, Theo (1972) Phonological uniqueness in natural generative grammar. *Glossa* 6: 105–116.

Wurzel, Wolfgang Ullrich (1980) Ways of morphologizing phonological rules. In Jacek Fisiak (ed.) *Historical Morphology,* 443–462. The Hague: Mouton.

Yoke, Jim (1934) 7. Coyote tricks Eagle and takes his wives, releases salmon, is duped by and dupes Wolves. In Melville Jacobs (ed.) *Northwest Sahaptin Texts. Part 1,* 167–176. New York: Columbia University Press.

6 Phonologically conditioned suppletive allomorphy:

Cross-linguistic results and theoretical consequences*

Mary Paster (Pomona College)

Introduction

Our understanding of phonology-morphology interface is still incomplete with respect to two important questions: What phonological effects are possible in morphology? And how should they be modelled? Some (actual and potential) types of phonological effects in morphology have already been subjected to studies involving large cross-linguistic surveys, e.g., reduplication (Inkelas and Zoll 2005), infixation (Yu 2003, 2007), affix ordering (Paster 2006c; see also Paster 2009), and ordering in coordinate compounds (Mortensen 2006). However, *phonologically conditioned suppletive allomorphy* (PCSA), although it has received some attention in the literature (see, e.g., Carstairs 1988, 1990; Mester 1994; Kager 1996; Mascaró 1996; Tranel 1996a,b; Carstairs-McCarthy 1998; Vaux 2003; Bonet 2004; Bye 2007), has not previously been the subject of a broad cross-linguistic study. This chapter summarizes an attempt to fill in this gap in our knowledge of phonologically conditioned morphology across languages. In this chapter I discuss the results of a cross-linguistic survey of PCSA, the full results of which are reported in Paster (2006a). This provides an understanding of the range of PCSA attested in the world's languages.

The larger aim of this chapter is a theoretical one. I contrast two competing models that have been proposed to account for phonological effects in morphology. The first is the 'P >> M' OT ranking schema proposed by McCarthy and Prince (1993a,b), in which P(honological) constraints are

Affiliation: Associate Professor, Pomona College in Claremont, California, Claremont, CA, USA ranked above M(orphological) constraints in OT. The second is a subcategorization-based approach where phonological elements of stems are incorporated into the subcategorization frames of affixes, and subcategorization frames specify the type of stem to which affixes attach, including syntactic, morphological, and (crucially) phonological features of stems. As I discuss, each model makes a number of important predictions regarding types and properties of PCSA that are expected to exist in the world's languages. As I will show, when one considers a large number of examples of PCSA (67 languages are represented in the survey), it is apparent that the predictions of the subcategorization approach match better with the empirical results than do the predictions of the P >> M approach. Thus, the results of the survey provide an important argument in favor of the subcategorization approach and against P >> M.[1]

6.1 Phonologically conditioned suppletive allomorphy (PCSA)

PCSA is a situation in which the distribution of two or more suppletive allomorphs is based on a phonological condition. One example is found in Dja:bugay (Patz 1991), a Pama-Nyungan language of Australia. As seen below, the genitive suffix in Dja:bugay has two different forms, *-n* and *-ŋun* (Patz 1991: 269).

(1)	a. With vowel-final stem		b. With consonant-final stem	
	guludu-n	'dove-GEN'	girrgirr-ŋun	'bush canary-GEN'
	gurra:-n	'dog-GEN'	gaɲal-ŋun	'goanna-GEN'
	djama-n	'snake-GEN'	bibuy-ŋun	'child-GEN'

When the stem ends in a vowel, as in (1a), the *-n* suffix is used. When the stem ends in a consonant, as in (1b), the *-ŋun* suffix is used. What distinguishes this as suppletive allomorphy for our purposes is that it is no plausible phonological process could relate the two allomorphs to a single underlying form, since this would involve the simultaneous deletion or insertion (depending on the analysis) of two segments, /ŋ/ and /u/. Under the traditional approach to allomorphy, we therefore conclude that there are two separate underlying forms that can be used to mark genitive. However, even though we are not able to write phonological rules or constraints to derive the allomorphs from a single underlying form, we nonetheless need to state the distribution of allomorphs in phonological terms, since the relevant property of the stem (consonant- vs. vowel-final) is phonological in nature.

Consonants vs. vowels at stem edges condition PCSA in many languages, but this is by no means the only type of condition that is found. In this chapter, I describe results of a survey aimed at discovering the precise range of possible phonological conditions on PCSA, and I show how these results bear on the question of how to model phonological conditions on affixation. The contributions of this chapter are twofold: to present a cross-linguistic overview of PCSA, and to show how the empirical findings point us towards a model of PCSA that is based on *morphological subcategorization* (Lieber 1980; Kiparsky 1982a,b; Selkirk 1982; Inkelas 1990; Orgun 1996; Yu 2003, 2007; Paster 2006a). In the approach that I advocate, phonology and morphology are maintained as distinct components of grammar, and phonological effects in morphology occur primarily because of morphological selection for phonological elements.

The structure of the chapter is as follows. In the remainder of section 6.1, I introduce the 'P >> M' and subcategorization models and discuss four predictions that each model makes for PCSA. I then contrast the predictions of the two models, setting the stage for the presentation of the survey data, and I give a brief introduction to the survey. In sections 6.2–6.5, I address each of the four pairs of contrasting predictions made by P >> M and subcategorization, presenting survey data that bear on the predictions. Finally, in section 6.6, I summarize the implications of the survey results for the two competing models. I evaluate the possibility of a hybrid approach that uses aspects of both models, and I conclude with some further remarks on strategies for modeling phonological conditions on affixation.

6.1.1 The P >> M model

As proposed by McCarthy and Prince (1993a,b), phonological effects in morphology are analyzed by ranking phonological (P) constraints over morphological (M) constraints in OT. This 'P >> M' ranking schema was assumed in the OT literature from the very beginning[2] and has featured in numerous OT analyses since that time. A prominent example is Kager (1996), which deals with 'syllable-counting allomorphy' (PCSA conditioned by the syllable count of the stem). Kager claims (1996: 170) that syllable-counting allomorphy is 'an output-oriented phenomenon' that is driven by P constraints and results from the Emergence of the Unmarked (TETU; McCarthy and Prince 1994).

In order to demonstrate how the P >> M schema works, I return to the Dja:bugay example presented above in (1). Recall that the pattern of allomorphy is that the genitive is marked by *-n* when the stem is vowel-final, and *-ŋun* when the stem is consonant-final. Kager (1996) characterizes the pattern as being driven by a constraint against clusters. Taking this approach, Kager proposes a P >> M analysis as follows. The relevant P constraint is shown in (2) (Kager 1996: 156, after Prince and Smolensky 1993).

(2) *COMPLEX: No complex syllable margins.

Kager (1996: 156) then proposes an M constraint as shown in (3).[3]

(3) GENITIVE = /-n/: Genitive is marked by /-n/.

Applying the P >> M ranking schema to this case yields the ranking in (4).

(4) *COMPLEX >> GENITIVE = /-n/

This constraint ranking correctly selects the candidate with the -ŋun suffix when the stem ends in a consonant, as shown in (5). Note that in a tableau where one of two suppletive allomorphs is to be selected, the input will include both possible allomorphs (shown in curly brackets), and it is the job of the constraints to select the correct allomorph.[4]

(5) *bibuy-ŋun* 'child-GEN'

/bibuy {-n, -ŋun}/	*COMPLEX	GENITIVE = /-n/
a. bi.buyn	*!	
b. ☞ bi.buy.ŋun		*

This ranking also correctly selects the candidate with the *-n* suffix when the stem ends in a vowel, as shown in (6).

(6) guludu-n 'dove-GEN'

/guludu {-n, -ŋun}/	*COMPLEX	GENITIVE = /-n/
a. ☞ gu.lu.dun		
b. gu.lu.du.ŋun		*!

Thus, the ranking of the P over the M constraint successfully accounts for Dja:bugay genitive allomorphy.

The P >> M approach as described above makes a number of predictions for PCSA. I will discuss four of them here. The first is that PCSA is 'optimizing'. This claim, made explicit by Kager (1996) with specific reference to syllable-counting allomorphy, is inherent in the P >> M approach more generally. If PCSA is driven by P constraints, and P constraints are universal as is widely assumed,[5] then all instances of PCSA should observably 'optimize' words with respect to some P constraint that is part of the universal inventory. In cases where PCSA is not obviously 'optimizing', the pattern of allomorphy should nonetheless be derivable from the interaction of M constraints with established P constraints.

A second prediction is that since P >> M does phonology and morphology in parallel, PCSA should be analyzable as being sensitive to phonological elements in surface forms, not in input forms. This means that we should never find any examples in which a pattern of allomorph selection is rendered opaque by a purely phonological process. Instead, we expect to find cases in which allomorphy is clearly surface-based such that the distribution of allomorphs cannot be captured with reference to inputs alone.

A third prediction is that there should be no limitation on directionality in PCSA. Specifically, the P >> M model, as it is commonly used, predicts there should be no asymmetry in terms of whether stems condition affix allomorphy or vice versa. It is common in P >> M analyses for input forms of complex words to consist of unordered sets of morphemes, and for the constraints to sort out the order of the morphemes (in fact, this is crucial to P >> M analyses of putative cases of phonologically driven affix order; see, e.g., Hargus and Tuttle 1997). For this reason, phonological properties of affixes can very easily trigger PCSA in stems under the P >> M approach, whereas in other models, words are built sequentially from the inside out so that affix-triggered stem allomorphy is not allowed.[6]

A fourth and final prediction is that conditions on allomorphy can come from anywhere in the word. There is no requirement that an affix be next to the part of the stem that conditions its distribution: PCSA in a prefix can be triggered by a segment at the right edge of the stem, and PCSA in a suffix can be triggered by a segment at the left edge of the stem. The reason this prediction is made is that there are P constraints that enforce relationships (identity, non-identity) between segments or features across long distances. For example, so-called 'long-distance OCP effects' can apply across long strings of intervening segments within a particular domain, within or across morpheme boundaries, as in, e.g., Suzuki's (1998: 27) GENERALIZED OCP. If a long-distance OCP constraint were involved in a P >> M ranking, we would expect that, for example, a stem-final labial could block the use of a prefix containing a labial segment.

The four predictions discussed above are summarized in (7).

(7) a. PCSA is 'optimizing' and analyzable using preexisting P constraints
b. PCSA is sensitive to phonological elements in surface forms, not underlying forms
c. Bidirectionality of phonological conditioning between stem and affix
d. Conditions on allomorph selection can be located anywhere in the word

Let us set aside these predictions for a moment and move on to discuss the subcategorization model.

6.1.2 The subcategorization model

In a subcategorization model, affixation is a process that satisfies missing elements specified in the lexical entries of morphemes. In this model, suppletive allomorphy is a phenomenon that results when two or more different affixes with the same meaning have different *subcategorizational requirements.* These requirements are schematized via subcategorization frames ('subcat frames'), which indicate the selectional requirements imposed by morphemes. By definition, a free morpheme has no subcategorizational requirements, meaning that stems usually do not have subcat frames, and therefore suppletive allomorphy is generally accounted for via the different subcat frames of competing affixes.

To demonstrate how the subcategorization model is used for PCSA, I return again to the Dja:bugay genitive allomorphy discussed earlier. In a subcategorization analysis, the distribution of allomorphs (*-n* with vowel-final stems, *-ŋun* with consonant-final stems) results from the different subcategorizational requirements of the two suffixes, as shown below.

(8) Dja:bugay genitive construction A — [[V#]$_{\text{noun}}$ *-n*]$_{\text{genitive noun}}$
Dja:bugay genitive construction B — [[ ]$_{\text{noun}}$ *-ŋun*]$_{\text{genitive noun}}$

'Construction A' creates genitive nouns using the -n suffix. As shown above, this suffix attaches to a morpheme of category 'noun' ending in a vowel. 'Construction B', on the other hand, creates genitive nouns using the *-ŋun* suffix. This suffix attaches to a noun with no specific phonological requirements. Because the phonological requirements of the *-n* form are more specific than those of the *-ŋun* form, *-n* is used when the stem is vowel-final; *-ŋun* is selected in the 'elsewhere case'.[7]

The particular version of the subcategorization model to be used here incorporates some mechanisms that are not inherent to the model itself but are compatible with the model and commonly assumed in analyses that make use of it. The first is an 'inside-out' word-building process as in, e.g., Lexical Morphology and Phonology (Kiparsky 1982a,b; Mohanan 1986). Starting with the root, complex words are built via successive 'layers' of affixes from the inside out,[8] and phonological processes apply to the output of the morphology at each level of affixation. This is significantly different from the standard account of affixation using P >> M, where the root and affixes are unordered in the input, and the surface order of morphemes is sorted out by M and/or P constraints.

A second mechanism incorporated into this version of the subcategorization model is the Generalized Determinant Focus Adjacency Condition (GDFAC; Inkelas 1990: 201), based on Poser's (1985) Determinant Focus Adjacency Condition. This is stated in (9).

(9) Generalized Determinant Focus Adjacency Condition: Each phonologically constrained element must be adjacent to each constraining element.

Although the GDFAC is not an inherent part of the subcategorization model, it is fully compatible with the subcategorization approach, and note that it is not easily incorporated into P >> M since that model does not refer to 'phonologically constrained/constraining elements'.

As I have characterized it here, the subcategorization model makes four important predictions for PCSA. I outline each of them here. The first is that PCSA is not always optimizing. In principle, an affix can subcategorize for any phonological unit, and there is no requirement that this unit have anything to do with the shape of the affix. The relationship is arbitrary, at least in terms of the synchronic grammar. This means that under the subcategorization model, we expect to find examples where the distribution of allomorphs does not appear to optimize the word. We predict that we should find some examples of PCSA in which no commonly accepted phonological OT constraint is sufficient to account for the pattern of allomorphy, and even examples in which the distribution of allomorphs makes words *less* optimal with respect to some well-formedness constraint.

A second prediction is that PCSA should be demonstrably sensitive to phonological elements in underlying forms rather than in surface forms. Though it is sometimes difficult to determine whether a given pattern is input- or surface-conditioned, there are some kinds of PCSA that could be used to distinguish between the two. One possible type of PCSA that would provide a strong argument in favour of input-conditioned allomorphy would be a case in which the operation of a purely phonological process renders the phonological motivation for allomorph selection opaque. Such a case would demonstrate that allomorph selection takes place in morphology *first*, and the output of this morphological process is the input to the phonological component, which *then* performs regular phonological operations on this input.

A third prediction made by the subcategorization model is that phonological conditions on suppletive allomorph selection can come only from the 'inside'. This is due to the assumed word-building model discussed above, in which words are built from the inside out. Since 'inner' material (roots and the affixes closest to it) does not have access to the 'outer' material (affixes farther away from the root) that will be attached later, roots and inner affixes cannot exhibit allomorphy conditioned by outer affixes in this model. The direction of conditioning will always be such that roots and inner affixes condition allomorphy in outer affixes. Any example of true 'outside-in' conditioning would counterexemplify the subcategorization model as I have defined it.

A final prediction of the subcategorization model (assuming the GDFAC, as discussed above) is that an allomorph must occur adjacent to the phonological element in the stem that conditions the allomorph distribution. An affix that subcategorizes for a general property of a stem (e.g., the syllable count of the stem) would not violate the adjacency requirement, but what would violate the requirement, and would therefore counterexemplify this version of the subcategorization model, would be a case in which a stem element that is not adjacent to the affix conditions PCSA in the affix. For example, a case of prefix allomorphy conditioned by the stem-final segment, or a case of suffix allomorphy conditioned by the stem-initial segment, would be problematic for the subcategorization model.

The predictions of the subcategorization model are summarized in (10).

(10) a. PCSA is not always phonologically optimizing
  b. PCSA is sensitive to phonological elements in underlying/input forms, not surface forms
  c. Phonological conditions on PCSA can come only from the 'inside' (stems can condition affix allomorphy but not vice-versa)
  d. Affix allomorphs occur adjacent to the phonological elements of stems that condition their distribution (assuming GDFAC)

We have now established some predictions that distinguish the two competing models being contrasted here. The predictions of the two models are summarized in the table in (11).

(11) Predictions of the two models

Prediction	P>> M	Subcategorization
a. PCSA is always optimizing	Yes	No
b. Input- or output-conditioned	Output	Input
c. Directionality of conditioning	Any	Inside-out only
d. Adjacency required	No	Yes

Given these predictions that differentiate the two models, we now have a way to determine which model is superior. What is needed to test the predictions is a large cross-linguistic survey of examples of PCSA. Below, I present a summary of the results of such a survey.

The survey described here involved consultation of over 600 grammars and descriptions. 137 examples of PCSA were uncovered in 67 languages representing 29 different language families (plus two isolates and one creole). The names, genetic affiliations, and references for each language are given in the Appendix.

The methodology of the survey construction is detailed in Paster (2006a); I summarize it briefly here. The survey cast a wide net, and a special effort was made to find examples in underrepresented language families in order to achieve broad coverage. No particular effort was made to balance the survey in any other sense; e.g., the survey was not deliberately statistically balanced to reflect the number of languages belonging to each language family. Instances of allomorphy were included in the survey if the source provided illustrative examples of each allomorph and if the allomorphy was determined to be both suppletive and phonologically conditioned. The question of suppletion is non-trivial; borderline cases were evaluated following Kiparsky's (1996) criteria with some modifications detailed in Paster (2006a). The result of using these criteria was such that if anything, the survey errs on side of inclusivity, meaning that some examples may have been included that really involve only one underlying form, and the allomorphy results from one or more phonological processes. Though I avoid making any important claims based solely on borderline cases, the inclusion of some cases of non-suppletive allomorphy may nonetheless slightly bias the results in favour of the P >> M approach with respect to prediction (11a). This is because regular phonological processes have long been observed to be (or to seem) phonologically 'optimizing', whereas the same is not necessarily true of suppletive allomorph selection. So including some cases of non-suppletive phonologically conditioned allomorphy will, on average, increase the proportion of 'optimizing' examples. As I show, even despite this potential for bias towards P >> M, that model falls short in comparison with the subcategorization model with respect to the survey data.

In the sections to follow, I present examples uncovered in the survey that bear on each of the predictions summarized above in (11). We begin with the question of optimization.

6.2 Phonological (non-)optimization in PCSA

Recall that the P >> M model predicts that every case of PCSA should be analysable in terms of phonological optimization, whereas the subcategorization model predicts that we should find cases of non-optimizing (i.e., arbitrary or 'neutral') PCSA. The argument as to whether a given pattern is optimizing or not can be somewhat subjective, but as we will see here, there are some cases of both the apparently optimizing and non-optimizing types that are clear representatives of their types.

A number of examples of apparently optimizing PCSA are found in the data. One such example is found in Modern Western Armenian (Vaux 1998; Andonian 1999). In this language, the definite article is *-n* when the noun ends in a vowel, as in (12a), or *-ə* when the noun ends in a consonant, as in (12b) (examples are from Vaux 1998: 252; Andonian 1999: 18).

(12)	a. With vowel-final stem		b. With consonant-final stem	
	lezu-n	'tongue'	atorr-ə	'the chair'
	kini-n	'wine'	kirk-ə	'the book'
	gadu-n	'the cat'	hat-ə	'the piece'

This pattern has an 'optimizing' quality for two reasons. First, with respect to the constraint against vowel hiatus, e.g., ONSET, it is preferable to use *-n* when the stem ends in a vowel, since the use of *-ə* would yield a VV sequence in this context. Second, with respect to *COMPLEX, it is preferable to use *-ə* when the stem ends in a consonant, since using *-n* would create coda clusters (or, when the stem already ends with a coda cluster, using *-n* would enlarge the cluster). Thus, this example appears to support the P >> M model, though it should be noted that the subcategorization model does not rule out the possibility of examples that seem optimizing, and therefore the existence of such examples does not counterexemplify the subcategorization model. What is needed to distinguish the two models is a case of non-optimizing PCSA, since these are not predicted by the P >> M model.

Several cases of apparently non-optimizing PCSA are indeed found in the survey data (Paster 2006a; see also Bye 2007, this volume). One such example is found in Tzeltal (Mayan, Mexico; Slocum 1948; Kaufman 1971; Walsh Dickey 1999). In Tzeltal, the perfective suffix has the form *-oh* when the stem is monosyllabic, as in (13a), and *-ɛh* when the stem has two or more syllables, as in (13b) (examples are from Walsh Dickey 1999: 328–329).

(13)	a. With monosyllabic stem		b. With polysyllabic stem	
	j-il-oh	'he has seen something'	s-maklij-ɛh	'he has listened to something'
	s-pas-oh	'he has made something'	s-hol-intaj-ɛh	'he has thought about it'
	s-kut͡ʃ-oh	'she has carried it'	h-pak'-antaj-ɛh	'I have patched it'
	s-jom-oh	'he has gathered it'	s-mak'lin-ɛh	'he has fed someone'
	s-nɛt'-oh	'he has squashed something'	s-tikun-ɛh	'he has sent something'

[o] and [ɛ] do not alternate elsewhere (Kaufman 1971: 28) in Tzeltal, so the allomorphy is not due to a general phonological property of the language. Stress in this language is word-final (Walsh Dickey 1999: 327), so the allomorphy is not stress-conditioned. A constraint banning [ɛ] in the second syllable has not to my knowledge been proposed as a universal constraint, making this unlikely to be a TETU effect, and any language-specific version of such a constraint in Tzeltal would have to refer to this particular morpheme and would be highly stipulative. This appears to be a case where the distribution of allomorphs is not phonologically optimizing in any meaningful way. Even though we can characterize the distribution in phonological terms, the distribution looks neutral with respect to phonological well-formedness constraints previously proposed in the literature. This is problematic for the P >> M model to the extent that this model characterizes PCSA as an optimizing phenomenon and attempts to account for PCSA using well-formedness constraints that have already been proposed to account for purely phonological phenomena.

Even more problematic for the P >> M model are cases of 'perverse' PCSA, where the distribution of allomorphs is the opposite of what it should be in order to be optimizing with respect to established well-formedness constraints. Several examples of this are discussed by Bye (2007), including one possible example from Dyirbal (Pama-Nyungan, Australia; Dixon 1972), where the ergative of vowel-final stems is formed with *-ŋgu* with disyllabic stems, and *-gu* with stems of three or more syllables (14).

(14)	a. With disyllabic stem	b. With larger stem
	yara-ŋgu 'man-ERG'	yamani-gu 'rainbow-ERG'

McCarthy and Prince (1990) characterize this as a 'compensatory relationship' in that the 'shorter' suffix goes with the 'longer' stem and vice versa. McCarthy and Prince acknowledge that coda consonants are not generally considered to be moraic in Dyirbal, but one would have to assume that codas are moraic, at least in this context, to give substance to the claim that the allomorphy is motivated by compensation. However, if the notion of a closed syllable does have some status in the language, then if anything, we would expect the exact opposite distribution of allomorphs from what actually occurs in Dyirbal. Here is why:

The stress pattern of Dyirbal is initial and alternating, and final syllables are unstressed (Dixon 1972: 274–276). This means that when we compare disyllabic stems with trisyllabic stems, the distribution of allomorphs causes words with *-ŋgu* to have closed unstressed syllables, while words with the *-gu* suffix have open stressed syllables. As seen in (15a) with a two-syllable stem, the *ŋ* of *-ŋgu* causes the penultimate syllable, which is unstressed, to be closed. And as seen in (15b), the use of *-gu* rather than *-ŋgu* with the three-syllable stem results in the stressed penultimate syllable being left open.

(15) a. ˈya.raŋ.gu ‘man-ERG’ *ˈya.ra.gu
b. ˈya.ma.ˌni.gu ‘rainbow-ERG’ *ˈya.ma.ˌniŋ.gu

If ‘syllable-counting allomorphy’ results from TETU as claimed by Kager (1996), then we would expect the distribution of allomorphs in Dyirbal to be reversed, since the Stress-to-Weight Principle should enforce a correspondence between heavy syllables (to the extent that closed syllables can be called ‘heavy’ in this language) and stress.

The observation that coda consonants are not moraic in Dyirbal may in fact render the Stress-to-Weight argument moot, and a further complication is that in at least some Pama-Nyungan languages, NC sequences can be syllabified as onsets and may even be single segments (i.e., prenasalized stops). However, if the Stress-to-Weight argument is rejected on these grounds, one must also reject McCarthy and Prince’s original comment on this example.[9] Without the notion of ‘compensation’, there is no clear way in which the distribution of ergative allomorphs is optimal in Dyirbal, and therefore this example is neutral at best. Even if the example is only neutral and not truly ‘perverse’, it is problematic for the P >> M approach because the relevant P constraint in such an analysis would have to be language-specific, arbitrary, and not externally motivated. If an advantage of P >> M is supposed to be the reduction of PCSA to phonological principles that are independently identified in the regular phonologies of the world’s languages, then proposing arbitrary, item-specific P constraints for individual languages completely undermines the spirit of the model.

Another example of a perverse pattern of PCSA is found in Haitian creole (Hall 1953; see also Bye 2007; Bonet *et al.* 2007). In this language, there is a determiner whose form alternates between *-a* and *-la* in a pattern that is the exact opposite of what would be expected if the pattern optimized CV syllable structure: *-a* occurs after vowel-final stems while *-la* occurs after consonant-final stems. Some examples are shown below (Hall 1953: 32).

(16)	panié-a	‘the basket’	pitit-la	‘the child’
	trou-a	‘the hole’	ãj-la	‘the angel’
	figi-a	‘the face’	kay-la	‘the house’
	chẽ-ã	‘the dog’	madãm-lã	‘the lady’

In this example, if regular phonological well-formedness constraints were responsible for the allomorphy, we would have expected the opposite distribution, since this would avoid coda consonants and vowel hiatus.[10] Note that the existence of such cases of non-optimizing PCSA is problematic not only for the P >> M model but for any optimality-based approach, including Stratal OT, Optimal Interleaving (Wolf 2008), and others.

6.3 Input- vs. output-based conditions in PCSA

As discussed above, the P >> M model predicts that conditions on PCSA should be statable in output-based terms, since P and M apply in parallel and therefore there is no opportunity for, e.g., P to apply to the output of M. The subcategorization model, on the other hand, predicts that we should be able to capture all instances of PCSA with reference to inputs. This is because morphological allomorph selection applies *before* the regular phonological processes, and then the output of the morphology is the input to phonology (at each level, as in Lexical Morphology and Phonology). This pair of predictions is significant because it shows how each of the models being contrasted here might be falsified: an example of PCSA that can only be stated in input terms and not in output terms would counter-exemplify the P >> M model, while an example of PCSA that can only be stated in output terms and not in input terms would counterexemplify the subcategorization model. In the vast majority of cases, the distribution of allomorphs is statable both in input- and output-based terms. For example, as was demonstrated in section 6.1, the Dja:bugay example discussed at the beginning of the chapter is easily statable both in output-based terms (in the P >> M analysis using *COMPLEX) and in input-based terms (in the subcategorization analysis with *-n* subcategorizing for vowel-final stems, and *-ŋun* as the 'elsewhere' allomorph). This is true of most of the examples of PCSA found in the survey. However, it is not true of every example.

There are a few examples in the survey that are clearly input-based. One such example is found in Turkish (Lewis 1967), where the third person possessive suffix has /-i/ and /-si/ allomorphs. As seen in (17), the /-i/ form occurs when the stem ends in a consonant, while /-si/ occurs when the stem ends in a vowel (examples are from Aranovich *et al.* (2005) and from Gizem Karaali, p.c.; note that vowel alternations are due to regular Turkish vowel harmony).

(17) a. With consonant-final stem

bedel-i	'its price'
ikiz-i	'its twin'
alet-i	'its tool'

b. With vowel-final stem

deri-si	'its skin'
elma-sɪ	'its apple'
arɪ-sɪ	'its bee'

A proponent of the P >> M approach might cite this as an example of syllable structure optimization since the distribution of allomorphs serves to avoid both vowel hiatus and syllable codas. However, as pointed out by Aranovich *et al.* (2005), there are examples in which the distribution of allomorphs is rendered opaque by a regular phonological process. Turkish exhibits a regular process of Velar Deletion (see, e.g., Sezer 1981), which deletes /k/ in intervocalic position. This interacts with the third person possessive suffix allomorphy in an interesting way: underlyingly /k/-final stems take the /-i/ suffix allomorph since the stems are underlyingly consonant-final, but then because of the addition of the vowel suffix, the /k/ is in intervocalic position and is therefore deleted. Thus, as seen in (18), the interaction of PCSA and Velar Deletion produces the very vowel hiatus that the distribution of /-i/ vs. /-si/ was supposed to avoid.

(18)			
	açlı-ɪ	'its hunger'	(cf. açlık 'hunger')
	bebe-i	'its baby'	(cf. bebek 'baby')
	gerdanlı-ɪ	'its necklace'	(cf. gerdanlık 'necklace')
	ekme-i	'its bread'	(cf. ekmek 'bread')

The explanation for this situation seems to be that suppletive allomorph selection takes place first in the morphology, and then the regular phonology of the language (including Velar Deletion) applies to the *output* of morphology, in some cases rendering the conditions on PCSA opaque. This is easy to capture in the subcategorization model, since we can say that /-i/ subcategorizes for stems that are consonant-final in the *input*, and then the output of morphology is the input to phonology. It is much more difficult to capture using P >> M because the constraints on allomorph distribution are not surface-true. The distribution cannot be stated using only output-based constraints in P >> M because that model does phonology and morphology together in parallel; it is crucial that morphology apply before phonology in this case.

While the survey revealed a small number of examples of crucially input-conditioned PCSA, it did not reveal any cases of crucially output-based PCSA. Every pattern of PCSA found in the survey is statable via conditions on inputs.

6.4 Directionality of conditioning in PCSA

A third set of predictions differentiating P >> M from the subcategorization approach involves the directionality of conditioning in PCSA. In P >> M, since roots and affixes are unordered in inputs, either type of morpheme can affect the selection of the other: roots can condition PCSA in affixes, and affixes can condition PCSA in other affixes and in roots. The subcategorization model is more restrictive in this regard. Because words are built from the inside out, starting with roots and applying 'layers' of affixes in succession, PCSA is only allowed to be conditioned from the 'inside'. This means that a root can condition PCSA in an affix, but an affix cannot condition PCSA in a root. Similarly, an 'inner' affix (one close to the root) can condition allomorphy in an 'outer' affix (one farther away from the root), but not vice versa. The subcategorization model therefore makes a specific, falsifiable claim that distinguishes it from P >> M. While 'inside-out' conditioning of PCSA is allowed under both models, a clear example of 'outside-in' conditioning will counterexemplify the subcategorization model.

There are many examples of 'inside-out' conditioning; in fact, the vast majority of PCSA cases found in the survey are clear examples of this type. A representative example is found in Kwamera (Central-Eastern Oceanic, Vanuatu; Lindstrom and Lynch 1994). The perfective prefix in this language has two allomorphs that are distributed based on the initial vowel/segment of the stem as follows (Lindstrom and Lynch 1994: 12): /ɨn-/ occurs before verbs beginning with non-high vowels, while the /uv-/ allomorph occurs before verbs beginning with consonants and high vowels. Some examples are shown in (19) (Lindstrom and Lynch 1994: 10, 21, 23).

(19) a. ia-p-ɨn-ata
1exc-COND-PERF-see
'if I had seen'

ia-p-ɨn-osi
1exc-COND-PERF-hit
'I would have hit it'

ik-ɨn-ata
2-PERF-see
'you saw'

b. r-uv-kusi
3sg-PERF-weave
'she wove'

iak-uv-regi
1exc-PERF-hear
'I heard'

Thus, the /ɨn-/ allomorph is used when the following vowel is [−high], and the /uv-/ allomorph is used elsewhere, including before [+high] vowels (though the /uv-/ prefix is only shown before consonant-initial roots among Lindstrom and Lynch's examples). The point of the example is that, like many other examples in the survey, this is a case where stems condition PCSA in affixes.

In contrast with the large number of 'inside-out' examples, very few cases were found in the survey that look like possible examples of 'outside-in' conditioning. The most promising example comes from Italian (Hall 1948). In Italian, some stems have allomorphs ending in /isk/ that occur only in morphological contexts where the word stress falls on the stem-final syllable, namely, in the present and subjunctive 1sg, 2sg, 3sg, and 3pl and in the 2sg imperative (Hall 1948: 25, 27).[11] One such stem is *fin-* 'finish'; some examples are shown below (Hall 1948: 214).

(20) Present

finísk-o	'I finish'	fin-iámo	'we finish'
iníšš-i	'you (sg.) finish'	fin-íte	'you (pl.) finish'
finíšš-e	's/he finishes'	finísk-ono	'they finish'[12]

Subjunctive

finísk-a	'that I finish'	fin-iámo	'that we finish'
finísk-a	'that you (sg.) finish'	fin-iáte	'that you (pl.) finish'
finísk-a	'that s/he finish'	finísk-ano	'that they finish'

Imperative

		fin-iámo	'let's finish'
finíšš-i	'(you (sg.)) finish!'	fin-íte	'(you (pl.)) finish!'

Other stems of this type include ağ- 'act' (Hall 1948: 43), argu- 'argue' (1948: 44), dilu- 'add water' (1948: 45), mɛ́nt- 'lie' (1948: 45), diminu- 'diminish' (1948: 52), and ammon- 'admonish' (1948: 61). There appears not to be any semantic or phonological generalization regarding which stems pattern with this class.

This example is important because it is the most convincing out of a very small number of stem PCSA examples found in the survey.[13] The subcategorization approach does not allow affixes to condition PCSA in roots; this does allow us to explain the extreme rarity of putative examples, but it also requires us to analyse these examples in such a way so that they do not contradict the 'inside-out' generalization. One important fact to note about this example is that, segmentally, the shorter stem allomorph is a subset of the longer allomorph. This allows us to analyse *-isc* as a separate affix. In fact, in modern analyses of Italian stem allomorphy (e.g., DiFabio 1990; Schwarze 1999), *-isc* is considered to be an affix or 'stem extension' (Schwarze 1999). Therefore, it is already assumed that stems containing *-isc* do not exhibit *root* allomorphy; instead, the root always remains the same, and it is the presence or absence of a separate affix *-isc* that is determined by the stress pattern of the word. Analysing *-isc* as an affix is helpful, but still problematic since this looks like an example of PCSA in an 'inner' suffix being conditioned by an 'outer' suffix. A further move that we need to make in order to maintain the 'inside-out' generalization is to assume that *-isc-* is actually an infix rather than a suffix. This allows us to assume that the word is built as follows: first, the subject agreement suffix is added to the root, and *then* the *-isc-* infix (which I assume to have inherent stress) will be inserted between the root and the suffix whenever the suffix is not inherently stressed.

The infixing analysis may provoke some scepticism, but in fact, this has been proposed independently (and in the pre-OT literature having nothing to do with the present debate): DiFabio (1990) analyses *-isc-* as an infix.[14] While the infixing analysis may seem like a clever trick to uphold the 'inside-out' generalization, one must concede that the lack of cases of phonologically conditioned stem allomorphy is striking given the number of cases involving affix allomorphy. Furthermore, it is not the case that any possible putative case of stem allomorphy could be explained away. The infixation account is possible for Italian because *isc* is present in all of the extended stems, but imagine a language Italian', which is like Italian but with etymologically unrelated stem pairs, e.g. *fin-* ~ *complet-* instead of the Italian *fin-* ~ *finisc-*. This would make it impossible to claim that the allomorphy resulted from the addition of a stem extension, and we would have to conclude that this was a counterexample to our model. But, in fact, no such cases were revealed by the present survey. Of the small number of stem allomorphy examples found in this survey, none are compelling examples of true 'outside-in' conditioning (see Paster 2006a for details). Thus, the survey provides no solid evidence for the existence of this type of PCSA that is predicted by P >> M.

6.5 Adjacency requirements in PCSA

A final prediction that differentiates P >> M from subcategorization involves adjacency. As discussed in sections 6.1.1 and 6.1.2, the P >> M model allows conditions on PCSA to come from anywhere in the word, whereas the subcategorization model predicts that the affix exhibiting allomorphy should be adjacent to the element in the stem that conditions the allomorphy. This means that the subcategorization model predicts that prefix allomorphy should be conditioned by elements at the left edge of the stem (or by general properties of the stem), and suffix allomorphy should be conditioned by elements at the left edge of the stem (or, again, by general properties of the stem). What is not predicted by the subcategorization model is suffix allomorphy conditioned by an element at the left edge of the stem, or prefix allomorphy conditioned by an element at the right edge of the stem. Examples of either of these types would counterexemplify the subcategorization model.

Examples of the first two types are quite common. For instance, there are numerous examples in the survey in which prefix allomorphy is conditioned by a stem-initial element. One such case is found in Tahitian (Polynesian, French Polynesia; Lazard and Peltzer 2000). In Tahitian, the causative/ factitive is marked by *ha'a-* when the root begins with a labial, as in (21a), and *fa'a-* elsewhere, as in (21b) (Lazard and Peltzer 2000: 224–225).[15]

(21)	a. With labial-initial stem		b. Elsewhere	
	ha'a-fiu	*'ennuyer, s'ennuyer'*	*fa'a-'amu*	*'faire manger, nourrir'*
	ha'a-mana'o	*'se rappeler'*	*fa'a-rave*	*'faire faire'*
	ha'a-veve	*'appauvrir'*	*fa'a-tai'o*	*'faire lire'*

Note that the segment conditioning the prefix allomorphy is at the left edge of the stem and therefore ends up being adjacent to the affix.

There are also numerous examples in the survey where suffix allomorphy is conditioned by a stem-final element. An example of this is found in Hungarian (Kenesei *et al.* 1997; Rounds 2001). In present tense indefinite verbs, when the stem ends in a sibilant, as in (22a), the 2sg is marked by *-El* (where *E* is a mid-vowel that undergoes backness and rounding harmony). Elsewhere, the 2sg subject is marked by [-s], as in (22b). Examples are from Abondolo 1988: 102, Kenesei *et al.* (1997: 289–290), and Rounds (2001: 27); note that Hungarian orthographic <sz> represents [s].

(22)	a. With sibilant-final stem		b. Elsewhere	
	vonz-ol	'you attract'	rak-sz	'you place'
	edz-el	'you train'	vág-sz	'you cut'
	hajhász-ol	'you seek'	vár-sz	'you wait'
	foz-öl	'you cook'	nyom-sz	'you press'

Thus, it is a stem-final segment that conditions suffix allomorphy, so that the affix exhibiting the allomorphy is adjacent to what conditions it.

A related type of PCSA is examplified in Nakanai (Austronesian, New Britain; Johnston 1980). In Nakanai, as seen below, the *-il-* form of the nominalizing affix occurs when it can be in the first syllable and adjacent to main stress (23a); *-la* occurs elsewhere (23b) (examples are from Johnston 1980: 177–178; note that stress is on the penult, Johnston 1980: 256).

(23)	a. Affix in first syll. and next to main stress		b. Elsewhere	
	au	'steer'	vi-gile-muli	'tell a story'
	il-au	'steering'	vigilemulimuli-la	'story'

peho	'die'	vi-kue	'fight (v.)'
p-il-eho	'death'	vikue-la	'fight (n.)'
loso	'dive'	go-ilo	'go in'
il-oso	'diving'	goilo-la	'entrance'

Thus, the affix that is alternately a prefix and an infix always occurs next to the phonological element that conditions its occurrence.[16]

There are also numerous examples in the survey where an overall property of the stem conditions affix allomorphy. In Kaititj (Pama-Nyungan, Australia; Koch 1980), for example, the ergative/instrumental/locative is marked by *-ŋ* when the stem is disyllabic, and by *-l* when the stem is trisyllabic or larger. Examples are given below (Koch 1980: 264–266; [N] is a prestopped apical nasal).

(24) a. With disyllabic stem

aˈki-ŋ	'head-ERG'
ilˈtʸi-ŋ	'hand-ERG'
aNˈmi-ŋ	'red ochre-ERG'
aynˈpi-ŋ	'pouch-ERG'

b. With larger stem

aˈliki-l	'dog-ERG'
aˈʈuyi-l	'man-ERG'
aˈɣirki-l	'sun-ERG'
ˈɭuNpiri-ɭ	'forehead-ERG'

Examples where a general property of the stem conditions affix allomorphy are quite common; like the previous three types of examples, they do not bear on the comparison between the two models being considered here since both allow for all of these types of allomorphy. As an aside, however, it should be pointed out that the Kaititj example is another instance of the apparently non-optimizing type of PCSA discussed in section 6.2.[17] There is no obvious way in which this pattern of allomorphy optimizes words, and any P constraint written to account for it will be language-specific, *item*-specific, and not motivated by any well-known phonological or phonetic principle.

One type of allomorphy predicted by the P >> M model and *not* by the subcategorization model is one in which an element at the left edge of the stem conditions suffix allomorphy. In fact, *no* examples of this type were found in the survey. While one must be cautious when considering negative evidence, it is nonetheless striking that no examples of this type are found, given the large sample set.

Similarly predicted by P >> M, but unattested in the surveyed languages is the symmetric type of allomorphy in which an element at the right edge of the stem conditions prefix allomorphy. This type of PCSA is ruled out by the subcategorization approach, and is also not found in the survey. In combination with the other apparently nonexistent type of PCSA predicted by P >> M, this is an important finding. It suggests that the lack of such examples is not a coincidence or an accidental gap, but is a principled gap that reveals an important fact about PCSA. The subcategorization model is the only one of the two that predicts and accounts for this gap.

6.6 Conclusion

Now that we have discussed examples relating to the predictions made by P >> and subcategorization, we are in a position to evaluate how well each of the models fares when tested against a large number of examples. The results of this test are summarized below in (25).

(25) Testing predictions of the two models

Prediction	P >> M	Subcategorization	Result favors
a. PCSA is optimizing	Yes	(✓) **No**	(Subcategorization)
b. Input- or output-conditioned	Output	✓ **Input**	Subcategorization
c. Directionality of conditioning	Any	✓ **Inside-out only**	Subcategorization
d. Adjacency required	No	✓ **Yes**	Subcategorization

As indicated by the check marks, the subcategorization model clearly fares better than P >> M with respect to predictions (b-d). Although the results for prediction (a) lean towards the subcategorization model, there is more to be said about this prediction.

The issue with regard to optimization is that many examples in the survey do appear to be optimizing, while others do not. The reason that the results 'lean' towards the subcategorization model is that this model is equally capable of handling both the optimizing and non-optimizing types of PCSA, while the P >> M model has difficulty in capturing the non-optimizing cases since this requires unusual, stipulative P constraints. However, one could argue that the subcategorization model is not fully adequate to account for the optimizing examples because it assumes that they are arbitrary, and that the apparent optimization is coincidental. Therefore, even though it can capture the distribution of allomorphs, the subcategorization-based analysis fails to capture the motivation for PCSA in the optimizing cases.

6.6.1 Two types of PCSA?

One possible way around the problem mentioned above is to model the cases that seem to be optimizing using P >> M, and to use subcategorization frames for the other, non-optimizing cases. Proposals similar to this have been made by Booij (1998) and Lapointe (1999); this also corresponds with Mascaró's (1996) distinction between 'internal' and 'external' allomorphy.

There are a number of problems with this strategy. First, even the 'optimizing' examples still appear to fulfil predictions (b-d) of the subcategorization approach more closely than those of the P >> M approach: they are never demonstrably output-based, they are conditioned from the 'inside' and not the 'outside', and they never violate the adjacency requirements of the GDFAC. Thus, even those examples for which we would give a P >> M analysis under the dual approach still fail to fulfil three other predictions of the P >> M approach that distinguish it from the subcategorization model.

A second problem has to do with how we might establish the split between optimizing and non-optimizing cases to determine which model to use for a given example. Optimization vs. non-optimization is not a black-and-white distinction, but rather a continuum, as schematized in (26). On the left-hand side of the continuum are cases that appear to be optimizing and may be considered TETU effects as claimed by Kager (1996). To the right of these are examples where the distribution of allomorphs is non-arbitrary, is optimizing for some types of examples but not others, and cannot be claimed to result from TETU. Farther along the continuum are examples of the arbitrary or 'neutral' cases of PCSA that are not optimizing in any obvious way, and on the far right are examples of the 'perverse' type that seem to have an anti-optimizing effect.

(26) A continuum of optimization in PCSA

Optimizing; possible TETU effects	*Non-arbitrary distribution; not necessarily optimizing*	*Arbitrary distribution; non-optimizing*	*'Perverse'*
◄———	———	———	———►
e.g. Armenian	Nakanai	Tzeltal, Kaititj, Dyirbal	Haitian creole

The continuum is problematic because it is not clear where optimization ends and non-optimization begins. In order to analyse the optimizing examples in one way and the non-optimizing examples in a different way, we need a clear dividing line between the two types.

A related problem is that there is no independent basis for two different types of PCSA. The split would therefore have to be made based on which examples lend themselves to analysis in P >> M and which do not. This is circular because the claim that there are two types of allomorphy that should be analysed differently would rest upon the fact that we analysed the two types differently. A useful comparison can be made between this situation and the situation faced by Alderete *et al.* (1999) in their study of fixed segment reduplication (FSR). Alderete *et al.* proposed that there are two types of FSR, a phonological type and a morphological type; the former follows phonological principles and is analysed phonologically, while the latter does not follow phonological principles (e.g., the identity of the fixed segment in morphological FSR is an arbitrary segment, not a phonologically unmarked 'default' segment) and is analysed morphologically. Unlike in our present study of PCSA, Alderete *et al.* (1999: 355–356) identified several independent differences between their proposed phonological and morphological types of FSR. We have no such independent criteria to distinguish two types of PCSA.

A final problem with the dual approach has to do with how to formalize it. Even if we decide that there are two types of PCSA that should be analysed differently, how can we ensure that the grammar will 'do' the optimizing type using P >> M and the non-optimizing type using subcategorization? A possible way to encode the distinction in the grammar would be to put limits on subcategorization frames so that affixes *can't* subcategorize for the elements that commonly condition the optimizing type of PCSA. As discussed in Paster (2006a), PCSA conditioned by prosodic units such as feet, syllables, and moras, as well as the C/V distinction, account for most of the optimizing examples, while PCSA conditioned by specific segments and/or features are more commonly non-optimizing. Suppose, then, that subcategorization frames were limited so that an affix could only subcategorize for small units like segments and features, and not for larger prosodic units or C/V. Then suppose that the grammar were set up so that it would 'try' a subcategorization-based generalization first, and failing this, would then default to the P >> M generalization. This would achieve the effect of having the grammar (rather than the analyst) distinguish the two types of PCSA, but there is a major problem with this move. The problem is that it directly contradicts the set of things that have previously been established as elements that affixes can subcategorize for. In his study of infixation, Yu (2003, 2007) found that the set of phonological elements that *can* be morphologically subcategorized for is exactly: {foot, syllable, mora, C, V}. Thus, preventing affixes from subcategorizing for these elements would have unintended negative consequences for other types of phonologically conditioned morphology.

The bottom line is that while the subcategorization model can handle both the examples that seem to optimize and those that do not, the P >> M model can handle only the optimizing examples well. And with no independent evidence to distinguish two separate types of PCSA, the subcategorization model is the one that should be used.

Assuming that one accepts these arguments for the subcategorization model, one may reasonably ask whether this means that the apparent optimization found in so many examples in the survey is merely a coincidence. The answer is no, not necessarily. One possible way that PCSA can develop is from a phonological process that is lost and gets morphologized, as discussed in Paster (2006a). If the original phonological process was optimizing (and it is widely held that phonological processes often do have this characteristic), then the resulting PCSA can retain the appearance of optimization without this having to be encoded in the synchronic grammar (Paster 2006a,b). Paster (to appear) describes some other historical pathways through which apparently optimizing PCSA may arise in languages without the involvement of optimization at any stage of the pattern's development.

6.6.2 M >> P vs. separate components

If P >> M is rejected as a way of modelling phonological conditions on affixation, how might we rule out this ranking schema? There are at least two possibilities. One, proposed by Yu (2003: 108) is a universal ranking M >> P.[18] Alternatively, P and M may be distinguished as separate components of grammar that are not evaluated in parallel and therefore have no ranking relationship. Both of these options are sufficient to rule out P >> M, but they make different predictions.

The M >> P proposal makes at least two important claims. The first is that PCSA is surface-based, since if M and P have a ranking relationship, they will be evaluated in parallel just as in P >> M. The second is that P constraints will drive morphology whenever M constraints underdetermine outputs.

The 'separate components' proposal, on the other hand, makes opposing claims. In this approach, assuming that the output of morphology is the input to phonology, PCSA should be an input-based phenomenon. A second claim is that P constraints cannot drive morphological processes; instead their effects should be seen on the outputs of morphology only.

There is some evidence suggesting that the 'separate components' approach is the correct one. First, as we have seen above, PCSA is crucially an input-based phenomenon, not output-based. This is demonstrated in the Turkish example discussed in section 6.3. Thus, a prediction of the M >> P proposal is contradicted by PCSA. The second type of evidence against M >> P comes from affix ordering. Assuming that affix order is handled by M constraints (an assumption that is explicitly made in some treatments of putative phonologically conditioned affix order, e.g. Hargus and Tuttle 1997), then under M >> P, we expect that anytime the M constraints do not fully determine affix order, P constraints should be able to step in and select a winner. However, as I discuss in Paster (2006c), no good cases of phonologically driven affix order are attested. Furthermore, there are at least two attested examples of free affix order, in Chintang (Bickel *et al.* 2007) and in Filomeno Mata Totonac (McFarland 2007)). Under M >> P, we would expect that if the morphology left the affix order free, then the lower-ranked P constraints should come into play, as in TETU, and select a winner. Free affix order should not exist because the P constraints should always pick a consistent winner. Thus, the existence of free affix order, in combination with the other observations discussed here, favours the 'separate components' approach.

6.6.3 Summary

Based on the survey results and the arguments presented here, I conclude that the superior account of PCSA assumes that phonology and morphology are separate components of grammar, not evaluated in parallel as in P >> M (or M >> P). PCSA occurs because the subcategorization frames of affixes can make reference to phonological properties of stems, and sometimes there are two affixes that express the same feature but have different phonological shapes and different subcategorizational requirements. The selection of suppletive allomorphs takes place specifically in morphology, and the output of morphology is the input to phonology at each level. This account seems to make the most accurate predictions with respect to cross-linguistic generalizations about PCSA and other types of phonological effects in morphology.

Notes

* I am grateful to Sharon Inkelas, Andrew Garrett, and Kristin Hanson for input into the development of this research. I also thank Bernard Tranel for comments on an earlier draft of this chapter. All errors are, of course, my own.

1. It is important to note that the argument against the P >> M ranking schema is not necessarily an argument against OT approaches to phonology or morphology in general, since there is nothing inherent in OT that requires P >> M to be a possible ranking. More recent approaches to PCSA in OT address some of the deficits of the original model in various ways, but to the extent that these approaches retain aspects of the P >> M approach, they also retain the problems associated with those aspects of the model, which will be discussed.

2. In fact, it was originally claimed that prosodically conditioned morphology is *always* driven by P >> M. McCarthy and Prince assert (1993a: 24) that '[f]or morphology to be prosodic at all within OT, the ranking schema **P** >> **M** must be obeyed, in that at least **some** phonological constraint must dominate some constraint of the morphology'. A similar assertion is made in McCarthy and Prince (1993b).
3. As Kager points out in a footnote, one could try to use a more general M constraint than the one in (3). Kager (1996: 156) suggests '... a universal constraint requiring that morphological categories are marked by minimal means (e.g. the "phonologically shortest" morpheme)'. However, this is untenable because there are numerous examples of PCSA in which the 'preferred' allomorph is just as long as, or even longer than, the allomorph that occurs in the more specific environment. Wolf and McCarthy (2009) discuss examples from Dyirbal and Axininca Campa to make this point: in their analysis of Dyirbal, the ergative suffix allomorph *-ŋgu* has preference over the shorter allomorph *-gu*, and in Axininca Campa, the genitive suffix allomorph *-ni* has preference over the equally short (and no more marked) allomorph *-ti*.
4. This seems to be the most common implementation of P >> M; Wolf and McCarthy (2009) refer to this as a 'standard approach in OT,' though they argue against including both allomorphs in inputs.
5. OT constraints were assumed from the beginning (Prince and Smolensky 1993) to be universal, and many phonologists continue to adhere to this view (see, e.g., McCarthy 2002 for discussion).
6. The P >> M schema could be recast in terms of Stratal OT (Kiparsky 2000), which is an OT model that incorporates the level ordering concept of Lexical Morphology and Phonology (Kiparsky 1982a,b; Mohanan 1986), and therefore shares the 'inside-out' word-building property that I have associated here with the subcategorization model. However, since we are evaluating models of PCSA as they are commonly implemented (and not how they *could* be implemented), the P >> M model that I will refer to throughout the paper is one that is not couched within Stratal OT and therefore does not have the 'inside-out' word-building property. As will be discussed, the lack of sensitivity to morphological constituency in classic OT is not its only problem with respect to PCSA; therefore, a Stratal OT implementation of P >> M does not necessarily avoid all the problems of classic OT in this domain.
7. There are a variety of ways to incorporate the 'elsewhere' concept into an analysis. One way is via serial ordering: 'try' allomorph A first, then use allomorph B in cases where allomorph A fails. This is roughly the approach taken by Wolf and McCarthy (2009). Another way to handle this is in OT morphology: a constraint requiring category X to be marked by allomorph A outranks a constraint requiring category X to be marked by allomorph B; an undominated constraint requiring adherence to subcategorizational requirements outranks both. The effect of this ranking will be that allomorph A is

used to mark category X except when this would violate the subcategorizational requirements of allomorph A; then (and only then), allomorph B is used. Note that the OT morphology approach is perfectly compatible with the argument against P >> M, since the OT analysis described here is purely morphological and does not involve any P constraints.

8. This description implies a step-wise, serial process of affixation, though it can also be thought of in a parallel model in terms of morphological constituency (bracketing).

9. It should be noted that in later work, McCarthy and Prince (1993b:117-120) abandon reference to a 'compensatory relationship' between the root and affix in Dyirbal ergative allomorphy. Instead, they propose a P >> M account of this pattern in which the relevant P constraint is AFX-TO-FT, which requires the *-ŋgu* suffix to attach to a base that consists of a foot. The AFX-TO-FT constraint in this account is in some respects similar to a subcat frame, except that McCarthy and Prince explicitly define it as phonological rather than morphological in nature: '... Afx-to-Ft is a **P**-constraint, because it crucially refers to a prosodic notion, the foot, as well as to a morphological one ...' (1993b: 114). In this analysis, failure to satisfy AFX-TO-FT results in a null parse, in which case the *-gu* allomorph is used by 'default'. Wolf and McCarthy (2009: §6.1) discuss this aspect of the analysis further, proposing that there is a 'stipulated priority relationship' between the two suffix allomorphs such that the *-ŋgu* allomorph is 'tried first', and if this yields a null parse, then *-gu* is used since *-gu* is 'not indexed to AFX-TO-FT'.

10. cf. Bonet *et al.*'s (2007) analysis of the Haitian example, which does involve a phonological well-formedness constraint (one based on the Syllable Contact Law that prohibits vowel-initial syllables after a consonant), but not directly: the analysis also requires a constraint aligning syllable edges to morpheme boundaries as well as a stipulated ordering relation between the two allomorphs using a PRIORITY constraint. See Wolf (2008: 97–99) for criticisms of the PRIORITY approach.

11. Indeed, the editors point out that this could be the motivation for the pattern from an optimization perspective, since it serves to avoid root stress such that roots are uniformly atonic throughout the paradigm, and that an OT approach might have an advantage in that, unlike the present analysis, it would not crucially depend on underlying stress.

12. Thanks to Anna Thornton for correcting the transcription of this form, which was incorrectly reported in Paster (2006a).

13. Only one other was uncovered, from Zahao (Chin, Burma; Osburne 1975; Yip 2004), and it is not at all clear that the stem allomorphy in that example is phonologically conditioned (Paster 2006a: 122–124).

14. The fact that separate stems *fin-* and *finisc-* co-existed at an earlier stage in the history of Italian does not preclude an infixation analysis, since speakers could have created the infix *-isc-* on the basis of the existence of other such pairs of verbs in the language. However, if each of the two separate stems previously was able to occur in all of the morphological/phonological environments in

(20), then we are faced with the question of how the stem allomorphs came to be distributed in the modern language (after the stems collapsed into a single suppletive paradigm) in just such a way so as to avoid stress clash. One possibility is that forms of each stem with every possible inflectional suffix co-existed at some stage, and as the separate stems merged, perhaps via the creation of the *-isc-* infix, the forms without *-isc-* preferentially survived in the stressed suffix environment because they had a more harmonic rhythmic pattern than those with *-isc-* (this would be true whether *-isc-* had inherent stress or not; for example, the modern form *fin-íte* 'you (pl.) finish' has an alternating stress pattern, whereas its hypothetical competitors *finísk-íte* and *finisk-íte* do not). Note, however, that this historical scenario does not require that speakers ever utilized a phonological constraint in determining when *fin-* vs. *fin-isc-* would be used. In the P >> M model, P constraints are used to determine which affixes will be allowed to combine with which stems, not to choose between multiple pre-existing semantically equivalent words. Perhaps the choice between words already existing in a language is more a conscious stylistic decision than one that is driven by constraints or rules of grammar.

15. One might suspect that the allomorphy here is not suppletive, since only one segment differs between the two allomorphs. However, as discussed by Paster (2006a: 39–41), *ha'a-* and *fa'a-* are best analysed as suppletive allomorphs because there is no general labial dissimilation process in the language.

16. McCarthy (2003: 101–102) discusses this example, claiming that in Nakanai, *-il-* is attracted to the main stress of the word but is also a 'formal prefix', and the pattern is driven by dispreference for a stress shift with respect to the base. In McCarthy's analysis, OO-PK-MAX penalizes the stress shift caused by *-la*, while the constraints AFX-TO-HD(-il-) and PREFIX/σ(-il-) limit *-il-* to occurring with disyllabic and smaller stems. Each of these constraints presumably outranks UNIFORMEXPONENCE, which requires each morphological category to be marked by a single affix across all forms (though McCarthy does not explicitly propose such a constraint), making this a case of P >> M. A subcategorization account for the Nakanai allomorphy is characterized as follows: the *-il-* affix subcategorizes for the first vowel and main stress (under a cyclic account of stress). *-il-* can then attach only to disyllabic and smaller stems (see Yu 2003 on using subcategorization for infixation), and *-la* will attach to all other stems by virtue of its less restrictive subcategorization frame. The Nakanai example is thus exactly the type of case predicted and accounted for by subcategorization.

17. Although Kaititj is in the same language family (Pama-Nyungan) as Dyirbal, a language cited earlier as having non-optimizing PCSA, this is by no means a property of all of the languages in this family, so these constitute distinct examples. As detailed in Paster (2006a,b), there is a wide range of patterns of allomorphy (including languages with no suppletive allomorphy at all) in the ergative suffix in Pama-Nyungan languages, even within branches of

Pama-Nyungan (and note that Kaititj and Dyirbal are not classed within the same branch according to the Ethnologue (Gordon 2005)).

18. Note, however, that Yu (2007), which is based on Yu (2003), does not pursue this option.

References

Abondolo, Daniel M. (1988) *Hungarian Inflectional Morphology*. Budapest: Akadémiai Kiadó.

Alderete, John, Beckman, Jill, Benua, Laura, Gnanadesikan, Amalia, McCarthy, John and Urbanczyk, Suzanne (1999) Reduplication with fixed segmentism. *Linguistic Inquiry* 30 (3): 327–364.

Andonian, Hagop (1999) *Beginner's Armenian*. New York: Hippocrene Books.

Aranovich, Raúl, Inkelas, Sharon, Orgun, Orhan and Sprouse, Ronald (2005) Opacity in phonologically conditioned suppletion. Paper presented at the Thirteenth Manchester Phonology Meeting, University of Manchester, 26–28 May.

Austin, Peter (1981) *A Grammar of Diyari, South Australia*. Cambridge: Cambridge University Press.

Bickel, Balthasar, Banjade, Goma, Gaenszle, Martin, Lieven, Elena, Paudyal, Netra Prasad, Rai, Ichchha Purna, Rai, Manoj, Rai, Novel Kishore and Stoll, Sabine (2007) Free prefix ordering in Chintang. *Language* 83 (1): 43–73.

Biggs, Bruce (1961) The structure of New Zealand Maaori. *Anthropological Linguistics* 3: 1–54.

Blevins, Juliette (2001) *Nhanda: An Aboriginal Language of Western Australia*. Honolulu, HI: University of Hawai'i Press.

Bonet, Eulàlia (2004) Morph insertion and allomorphy in Optimality Theory. *International Journal of English Studies* 4 (2): 73–104.

Bonet, Eulàlia, Lloret, Maria-Rosa and Mascaró, Joan (2007) Allomorph selection and lexical preferences: Two case studies. *Lingua* 117 (6): 903–927.

Booij, Geert (1997) Non-derivational phonology meets Lexical Phonology. In Iggy Roca (ed.) *Derivations and Constraints in Phonology*, 261–288. Oxford: Clarendon Press.

Booij, Geert (1998) Phonological output constraints in morphology. In Wolfgang Kehrein and Richard Wiese (eds) *Phonology and Morphology of the Germanic Languages*, 143–163. Tübingen: Niemeyer.

Booij, Geert (2005) *The Grammar of Words*. Oxford: Oxford University Press.

Breen, J. G. (1976a) Bidjara. In R. M. W. Dixon (ed.) *Grammatical Categories in Australian Languages*, 339. Canberra: Australian Institute of Aboriginal Studies.

Breen, J. G. (1976b) Wangkumara. In R. M. W. Dixon (ed.) *Grammatical Categories in Australian Languages*, 336–339. Canberra: Australian Institute of Aboriginal Studies.

Breen, J. G. (1976c) Warluwara and Bularnu. In R. M. W. Dixon (ed.) *Grammatical Categories in Australian Languages*, 331–335. Canberra: Australian Institute of Aboriginal Studies.

Bye, Patrik (2007) Allomorphy – Selection, not optimization. In Sylvia Blaho, Patrik Bye and Martin Krämer (eds) *Freedom of Analysis?* (*Studies in Generative Grammar* 95), 63–91. Berlin: Mouton de Gruyter.

Bye, Patrik (this volume). The nature of allomorphy and exceptionality: Evidence from Burushaski plurals.

Carstairs, Andrew (1988) Some implications of phonologically conditioned suppletion. *Yearbook of Morphology* 1988: 67–94.

Carstairs, Andrew (1990) Phonologically conditioned suppletion. In Wolfgang U. Dressler, Hans C. Luschützky, Oskar E. Pfeiffer and John R. Rennison (eds) *Contemporary Morphology,* 17–23. New York: Mouton de Gruyter.

Carstairs-McCarthy, Andrew (1998) Phonological constraints on morphological rules. In Andrew Spencer and Arnold Zwicky (eds) *The Handbook of Morphology,* 144–148. Oxford: Blackwell.

Conathan, Lisa J. (2002) Split intransitivity and possession in Chimariko. In Lisa Conathan and Teresa McFarland (eds) *Survey Report #12: Proceedings of the 50th Anniversary Conference of the Survey of California and Other Indian Languages,* 18–31. Berkeley, CA: Survey of California and Other Indian Languages.

de Maria, Jose (1918) *Gramatica y vocabulario jibaros*. Quito: Imprenta de la Universidad Central.

Dench, Alan (1995) *Martuthunira: A Language of the Pilbara Region of Western Australia*. Canberra: Pacific Linguistics.

Dench, Alan (1998) *Yingkarta*. München: LINCOM Europa.

DiFabio, Elvira G. (1990) *The Morphology of the Verbal Infix isc in Italian and Romance.* Doctoral dissertation, Harvard University.

Dimmendaal, Gerrit J. (1983) *The Turkana Language*. Dordrecht: Foris.

Dixon, R. M. W. (1972) *The Dyirbal Language of North Queensland.* Cambridge: Cambridge University Press.

Dixon, R. M. W. (1977) *A Grammar of Yidiɲ.* Cambridge: Cambridge University Press.

Dixon, R. M. W. (1980) *The Languages of Australia.* Cambridge: Cambridge University Press.

Dolbey, Andrew (1997) Output optimization and cyclic allomorph selection. In Brian Agbayani and Sze-Wing Tang (eds) *Proceedings of the Fifteenth West Coast Conference on Formal Linguistics,* 97–112. Stanford, CA: CSLI.

Donaldson, Tamsin (1980) *Ngiyambaa: The Language of the Wangaaybuwan*. Cambridge: Cambridge University Press.

Elías-Ulloa, José (2004) Variable syllable weight and quantity-insensitive allomorphy in Shipibo. Paper presented at the 35th meeting of the North Eastern Linguistic Society, University of Connecticut, 22–24 October.

Gordon, Raymond G., Jr. (ed.) (2005) *Ethnologue: Languages of the World.* Fifteenth edition. Dallas: SIL International. [Available on http://www.ethnologue.com.]

Hall, Robert A. (1948) *Descriptive Italian Grammar*. Ithaca, NY: Cornell University Press and Linguistic Society of America.

Hall, Robert A. (1953) *Haitian Creole: Grammar, Texts, Vocabulary. Memoirs of the American Anthropological Association* 74. Menasha: American Anthropological Association.

Hargus, Sharon and Tuttle, Siri G. (1997) Augmentation as affixation in Athabaskan languages. *Phonology* 14 (2): 177–220.

Harrell, Richard S. (1962) *A Short Reference Grammar of Moroccan Arabic.* Washington, DC: Georgetown University Press.

Inkelas, Sharon (1990) *Prosodic Constituency in the Lexicon.* New York: Garland.

Inkelas, Sharon and Zoll, Cheryl (2005) *Reduplication: Doubling in Morphology.* Cambridge: Cambridge University Press.

Johnston, Raymond Leslie (1980) *Nakanai of New Britain: The Grammar of an Oceanic Language*. Canberra: Australian National University.

Kager, René (1996) On affix allomorphy and syllable counting. In Ursula Kleinhenz (ed.) *Interfaces in Phonology,* 155–171. Berlin: Akademie Verlag.

Karlsson, Fred (1999) *Finnish: An Essential Grammar*. London and New York: Routledge.

Kaufman, Terrence (1971) *Tzeltal Phonology and Morphology. University of California Publications in Linguistics* 61. Berkeley and Los Angeles, CA: University of California Press.

Kenesei, István, Vago, Robert and Fenyvesi, Anna (1997) *Hungarian.* New York: Routledge.

Kikuchi, Seiichiro (2001) Spanish definite article allomorphy: A correspondence approach. *Phonological Studies* 4: 49–56. Tokyo: Kaitakusha.

Kiparsky, Paul (1982a) Lexical morphology and phonology. In I.-S. Yange (ed.) *Linguistics in the Morning Calm,* 3–91. Seoul: Hanshin.

Kiparsky, Paul (1982b) Word-formation and the lexicon. In Frances Ingemann (ed.) *1982 Mid-America Linguistics Conference Papers* 1–29. Lawrence, KS: Department of Linguistics, University of Kansas.

Kiparsky, Paul (1996) Allomorphy or morphophonology? In Rajendra Singh (ed.) *Trubetzkoy's Orphan: Proceedings of the Montreal Roundtable 'Morphophonology: Contemporary Responses',* 13–31. Amsterdam and Philadelphia, PA: John Benjamins.

Kiparsky, Paul (2000) Opacity and cyclicity. *The Linguistic Review* 17: 351–366.

Kite, Suzanne and Wurm, Stephen (2004) *The Duuŋidjawu Language of Southeast Queensland.* Canberra: Pacific Linguistics.

Koch, Harold J. (1980) Kaititj nominal inflection: Some comparative notes. In B. Rigsby and P. Sutton (eds) *Papers in Australian Linguistics 13: Contributions to Australian Linguistics,* 259–274. Canberra: Pacific Linguistics.

Kosch, Ingeborg M. (1998) Thoughts on suppletion in Northern Sotho. *South African Journal of African Languages* 18 (2): 33–40.

Kramer, Ruth (2005) Root and pattern morphology in Coptic. Ms, University of California, Santa Cruz.

Lapointe, Steven G. (1999) Stem selection and OT. *Yearbook of Morphology* 1999: 263–297.

Lazard, Gilbert and Peltzer, Louise (2000) *Structure de la langue tahitienne*. Paris: Peeters.

le Bleis, Yves and Barreteau, Daniel (1987) Les extensions verbales en Mafa. In Herrmann Jungraithmayr and Henry Tourneux (eds) *Etudes tchadiques: Classes et extensions verbales,* 99–114. Paris: Geuthner.

Lee, Hansol H.B. (1989) *Korean Grammar*. Oxford: Oxford University Press.

Lewis, Geoffrey L. (1967) *Turkish Grammar*. Oxford: Clarendon Press.

Li, Bing (1996) *Tungusic Vowel Harmony*. The Hague: Holland Academic Graphics.

Lieber, Rochelle (1980) *On the Organization of the Lexicon.* Doctoral dissertation, Massachusetts Institute of Technology.

Lindstrom, Lamont and Lynch, John (1994) *Kwamera*. München: LINCOM Europa.

Lipkind, William (1945) *Winnebago Grammar*. New York: King's Crown Press.

Mascaró, Joan (1996) External allomorphy as emergence of the unmarked. In Jacques Durand and Bernard Laks (eds) *Current Trends in Phonology: Models and Methods,* 473–483. Manchester: European Studies Research Institute, University of Salford.

McCarthy, John J. (2002) *A Thematic Guide to Optimality Theory*. Cambridge: Cambridge University Press.

McCarthy, John J. (2003) OT constraints are categorical. *Phonology* 20: 75–138.

McCarthy, John J. and Prince, Alan (1990) Foot and Word in Prosodic Morphology: The Arabic broken plural. *Natural Language and Linguistic Theory* 8 (2): 209–282.

McCarthy, John J. and Prince, Alan (1993a) Generalized Alignment. *Yearbook of Morphology* 1993: 79–153.

McCarthy, John J. and Prince, Alan (1993b) Prosodic Morphology I: Constraint interaction and satisfaction. Ms, University of Massachusetts, Amherst and Rutgers University.

McCarthy, John J. and Prince, Alan (1994) The Emergence of the Unmarked. Ms., University of Massachusetts, Amherst, and Rutgers University.

McFarland, Teresa (2007) Free affix order in Filomeno Mata Totonac. Paper presented at the 2007 Linguistic Society of America Annual Meeting, Anaheim, California, 4–7 January.

McGregor, William (1990) *A Functional Grammar of Gooniyandi*. Amsterdam and Philadelphia, PA: John Benjamins.

Melnar, Lynette R. (2004) *Caddo Verb Morphology*. Lincoln, NE: University of Nebraska Press.

Mester, R. Armin (1994) The quantitative trochee in Latin. *Natural Language and Linguistic Theory* 12 (1): 1–61.

Mohanan, K. P. (1986) *The Theory of Lexical Phonology*. Dordrecht: Reidel.

Mortensen, David (2006) *Logical and Substantive Scales in Phonology*. Doctoral dissertation, University of California, Berkeley.

Mürk, Harri William (1997) *A Handbook of Estonian: Nouns, Adjectives, and Verbs*. Bloomington, IN: Indiana University Research Institute for Inner Asian Studies.

Nash, David (1986) *Topics in Warlpiri Grammar.* New York: Garland.

Newman, Stanley S. (1965) *Zuni Grammar*. *University of New Mexico Publications in Anthropology* 14. Albuquerque, NM: University of New Mexico Press.

Oates, Lynette F. (1988) *The Muruwari Language.* Canberra: Pacific Linguistics.

Odden, David (1996) *The Phonology and Morphology of Kimatuumbi*. Oxford: Clarendon Press.

Orgun, Cemil Orhan (1996) *Sign-Based Morphology and Phonology with Special Attention to Optimality Theory*. Doctoral dissertation, University of California, Berkeley.

Osburne, A. (1975) *A Transformational Analysis of Tone in the Verb System of Zahao (Laizo) Chin.* Doctoral dissertation, Cornell University.

Oswalt, Robert L. (1960) *A Kashaya Grammar (Southern Pomo)*. Doctoral dissertation, University of California, Berkeley.

Parker, E. M. and Hayward, R. J. (1985) *An Afar-English-French Dictionary (with Grammatical Notes in English)*. London: School of Oriental and African Studies, University of London.

Paster, Mary (2006a) *Phonological Conditions on Affixation*. Doctoral dissertation, University of California, Berkeley. [Available on http://pages.pomona.edu/~mp034747/Paster_dissertation.pdf.]

Paster, Mary (2006b) Pama-Nyungan ergative allomorphy: Historical reconstruction and theoretical consequences. Paper presented at the 2006 Linguistic Society of America Annual Meeting, Albuquerque, New Mexico, January 5-8.

Paster, Mary (2006c) A survey of phonological affix order with special attention to Pulaar. In Leah Bateman and Cherlon Ussery (eds) *Proceedings of the 35th Annual Meeting of the North Eastern Linguistic Society: Volume 2,* 491–506. Amherst, MA: University of Massachusetts Graduate Linguistics Student Association.

Paster, Mary (2009) Explaining phonological conditions on affixation: Evidence from suppletive allomorphy and affix ordering. *Word Structure* 2 (1): 18–47.

Paster, Mary (To appear) Diachronic sources of allomorphy. In Stephanie Shih and Vera Gribanova (eds) *The Morphosyntax-Phonology Connection: Locality and Directionality at the Interface*. Oxford: Oxford University Press.

Paster, Mary and Beam de Azcona, Rosemary (2005) A phonological sketch of the Yucunany dialect of Mixtepec Mixtec. In Lea Harper and Carmen Jany (eds) *Proceedings of the Seventh Annual Workshop on American Indigenous Languages,* 61–76. University of California, Santa Barbara.

Patz, Elizabeth (1991) Djabugay. In Robert M.W. Dixon and Barry J. Blake (eds) *The Handbook of Australian Languages* 4: 245–347. Oxford: Oxford University Press.

Patz, Elizabeth (2002) *A Grammar of the Kuku Yalanji Language of North Queensland.* Canberra: Pacific Linguistics.

Payne, David L. (1981) *The Phonology and Morphology of Axininca Campa.* Dallas and Arlington, TX: Summer Institute of Linguistics and University of Texas at Arlington.

Poser, William (1985) There is no domain size parameter. *GLOW Newsletter* 14: 6–67.

Prince, Alan and Smolensky, Paul (1993) *Optimality Theory: Constraint Interaction in Generative Grammar. Technical Report* 2. New Brunswick: Rutgers Center for Cognitive Science, Rutgers University.

Radhakrishnan, R. (1981) *The Nancowry Word: Phonology, Affixal Morphology, and Roots of a Nicobarese Language*. Edmonton: Linguistic Research, Inc.

Rounds, Carol (2001) *Hungarian: An Essential Grammar*. New York: Routledge.

Schuh, Russell G. (1998) *A Grammar of Miya. University of California Publications in Linguistics* 130. Berkeley and Los Angeles, CA: University of California Press.

Schwarze, Christoph (1999) Inflectional classes in Lexical Functional Morphology: Latin -sk- and its evolution. In Miriam Butt and Tracy Holloway King (eds) *The Proceedings of the LFG '99 Conference.* [Available on http://cslipublications.stanford.edu/LFG/4/schwarze/lfg99-schwarze.html.] Stanford, CA: CSLI.

Selkirk, Elisabeth (1982) *The Syntax of Words*. Cambridge, MA: MIT Press.

Sezer, Engin (1981) The k/Ø alternation in Turkish. In G. N. Clements (ed.) *Harvard Studies in Phonology* 354–382. Bloomington, IN: Indiana University Linguistics Club.

Sharp, Janet Catherine (2004) *Nyangumarta: A Language of the Pilbara Region of Western Australia*. Canberra: Pacific Linguistics.

Shaw, Patricia A. (1980) *Theoretical Issues in Dakota Phonology and Morphology*. New York: Garland.

Slocum, Marianna C. (1948) Tzeltal (Mayan) noun and verb morphology. *International Journal of American Linguistics* 14 (2): 77–86.

Sohn, H.M. (1975) *Woleaian Reference Grammar*. Honolulu, HI: University Press of Hawai'i.

Spagnolo, L. M. (1933) *Bari Grammar*. Verona: The Nigrizia Printing Press School.

Suzuki, Keiichiro (1998) *A Typological Investigation of Dissimilation*. Doctoral dissertation, University of Arizona.

Terrill, Angela (1998) *Biri*. München: LINCOM Europa.

Thompson, D.A. (1976) Kuuku Yaʔu. In R. M. W. Dixon (ed.) *Grammatical Categories in Australian Languages* 329–331. Canberra: Australian Institute of Aboriginal Studies.

Timberlake, Alan (2004) *A Reference Grammar of Russian*. Cambridge: Cambridge University Press.

Tranel, Bernard (1996a) French liaison and elision revisited: A unified account within Optimality Theory. In Claudia Parodi, Carlos Quicoli, Mario Saltarelli and María-Luisa Zubizarreta (eds) *Aspects of Romance Linguistics,* 433--455. Washington, DC: Georgetown University Press.

Tranel, Bernard (1996b) Exceptionality in Optimality Theory and final consonants in French. In Karen Zagona (ed.) *Grammatical Theory and Romance Languages,* 275–291. Amsterdam and Philadelphia, PA: John Benjamins.

Tryon, Darrell T. (1970) *Conversational Tahitian: An Introduction to the Language of French Polynesia*. Berkeley and Los Angeles, CA: University of California Press.

Valentine, J. Randolph (2001) *Nishnaabemwin Reference Grammar*. Toronto: University of Toronto Press.

Vaux, Bert (1998) *The Phonology of Armenian*. Oxford: Oxford University Press.

Vaux, Bert (2003) Syllabification in Armenian, Universal Grammar, and the Lexicon. *Linguistic Inquiry* 34 (1): 91–125.

Walsh Dickey, Laura (1999) Syllable count and Tzeltal segmental allomorphy. In John R. Rennison and Klaus Kühnhammer (eds) *Phonologica 1996: Syllables!?* 323–334. The Hague: Thesus.

Watson, Janet C.E. (2002) *The Phonology and Morphology of Arabic*. Oxford: Oxford University Press.

Werner, Roland (1993) *Tidn-Aal: A Study of Midob*. Berlin: Dietrich Reimer Verlag.

Wolf, Matthew (2008) *Optimal Interleaving: Serial Phonology-Morphology Interaction in a Constraint-Based Model.* Doctoral dissertation, University of Massachusetts, Amherst.

Wolf, Matthew and McCarthy, John J. (2009) Less than zero: Correspondence and the null output. In Sylvia Blaho and Curt Rice (eds) *Modeling Ungrammaticality in Optimality Theory,* 17–66. London: Equinox.

Wordick, F. J. F. (1982) *The Yindjibarndi Language.* Canberra: Pacific Linguistics.

Yip, Moira (2004) Phonological markedness and allomorph selection in Zahao. *Language and Linguistics* 5 (4): 969–1001.

Yu, Alan C. L. (2003) *The Morphology and Phonology of Infixation.* Doctoral dissertation, University of California, Berkeley.

Yu, Alan (2007) *A Natural History of Infixation.* Oxford: Oxford University Press.

Zwicky, Arnold M. (1986) The general case: Basic form versus default form. In Vassiliki Nikifordou, Mary VanClay, Mary Niepokuj and Deborah Feder (eds) *Proceedings of the Twelfth Annual Meeting of the Berkeley Linguistics Society,* 305–314. Berkeley, CA: Berkeley Linguistics Society.

Appendix: Surveyed languages

Note: references to languages in the text included what was deemed the most useful or relevant level of specificity in classification. Here, I list the phylum to which each language belongs, in order to facilitate assessment of the range of languages surveyed. Affiliations are from Ethnologue (Gordon 2005).

Abbreviations: AA = Afro-Asiatic; IE = Indo-European; MP = Malayo-Polynesian; NC = Niger-Congo; NS = Nilo-Saharan; PN = Pama-Nyungan; ST = Sino-Tibetan

Language name	*Phylum*	*Location*	*Reference*
Armenian	IE: Armenian	Armenia	Andonian (1999)
Axininca Campa	Arawakan: Maipuran	Peru	Payne (1981)
Bari	NS: Eastern Sudanic	Sudan	Spagnolo (1933)
Biak	Austronesian: MP	New Guinea	Booij (2005)
Bidjara	Australian: PN	Australia	Breen (1976a)
Biri	Australian: PN	Australia	Terrill (1998)
Caddo	Caddoan: Southern	Oklahoma	Melnar (2004)
Chimariko	Hokan: Northern	NW California	Conathan (2002)
Coptic	AA: Egyptian	Egypt	Kramer (2005)
Dakota	Siouan: Siouan Proper	Northern US	Shaw (1980)
Diyari	Australian: PN	Australia	Austin (1981)
Dja:bugay	Australian: PN	Australia	Patz (1991)
Dutch	IE: Germanic	Netherlands	Booij (1997)
Duuŋidjawu	Australian: PN	Australia	Kite and Wurm (2004)
Dyirbal	Australian: PN	Australia	Dixon (1972)
English	IE: Germanic	United Kingdom	Zwicky (1986)
Estonian	Uralic: Finnic	Estonia	Mürk (1997)
Finnish	Uralic: Finnic	Finland	Karlsson (1999)
Gooniyandi	Australian: Bunaban	Australia	McGregor (1990)
Haitian Creole	creole	Haiti	Hall (1953)
Hungarian	Uralic: Finno-Ugric	Hungary	Rounds (2001)
Italian	IE: Italic	Italy	Hall (1948)
Jivaro	Jivaroan	Ecuador	de Maria (1918)
Kaititj	Australian: PN	Australia	Koch (1980)
Kashaya	Hokan: Northern	Northern California	Oswalt (1960)
Kimatuumbi	NC: Atlantic-Congo	Tanzania	Odden (1996)
Korean	isolate	Korea	Lee (1989)
Kuku Yalanji	Australian: PN	Australia	Patz (2002)
Kuuku Yaʔu	Australian: PN	Australia	Thompson (1976)
Kwamera	Austronesian: MP	Vanuatu	Lindstrom and Lynch (1994)

Latin	IE: Italic	Vatican State	Mester (1994)
Mafa	AA: Chadic	Cameroon	Le Bleis and Barreteau (1987)
Manchu	Altaic: Tungus	China	Li (1996)
Maori	Austronesian: MP	New Zealand	Biggs (1961)
Martuthunira	Australian: PN	Australia	Dench (1995)
Midob	NS: Eastern Sudanic	Sudan	Werner (1993)
Mixtepec Mixtec	Oto-Manguean: Mixtecan	Mexico	Paster and Beam de Azcona (2005)
Miya	AA: Chadic	Nigeria	Schuh (1998)
Moroccan Arabic	AA: Semitic	Morocco	Harrell (1962)
Muruwari	Australian: PN	Australia	Oates (1988)
Nancowry	Austro-Asiatic: Mon-Khmer	Nicobar Islands	Radhakrishnan (1981)
Ngiyambaa	Australian: PN	Australia	Donaldson (1980)
Nhanda	Australian: PN	Australia	Blevins (2001)
Nishnaabemwin	Algic: Algonquian	Ontario	Valentine (2001)
Northern Sotho	NC: Atlantic-Congo	South Africa	Kosch (1998)
Nyangumarta	Australian: PN	Australia	Sharp (2004)
Qafar	AA: Cushitic	Ethiopia	Parker and Hayward (1985)
Russian	IE: Slavic	Russia	Timberlake (2004)
Saami	Uralic: Sami	Norway	Dolbey (1997)
Sa'ani Arabic	AA: Semitic	Egypt	Watson (2002)
Shipibo	Panoan: North-Central	Peru	Elías-Ulloa (2004)
Spanish	IE: Italic	Spain	Kikuchi (2001)
Tahitian	Austronesian: MP	French Polynesia	Tryon (1970)
Turkana	NS: Eastern Sudanic	Kenya	Dimmendaal (1983)
Turkish	Altaic: Turkic	Turkey	Lewis (1967)
Tzeltal	Mayan: Cholan-Tzeltalan	Mexico	Slocum (1948)
Wangkumara	Australian: PN	Australia	Breen (1976b)
Warlpiri	Australian: PN	Australia	Nash (1986)
Warluwara	Australian: PN	Australia	Breen (1976c)
Warrgamay	Australian: PN	Australia	Dixon (1980)
Winnebago	Siouan: Siouan Proper	Wisconsin	Lipkind (1945)
Woleaian	Austronesian: MP	Micronesia	Sohn (1975)
Yidiɲ	Australian: PN	Australia	Dixon (1977)
Yindjibarndi	Australian: PN	Australia	Wordick (1982)
Yingkarta	Australian: PN	Australia	Dench (1998)
Zahao	ST: Tibeto-Burman	Burma	Osburne (1975)
Zuni	isolate	New Mexico	Newman (1965)

7 Accentual allomorphs in East Slavic: An argument for inflection dependence*

Donca Steriade (Massachusetts Institute of Technology)
Igor Yanovich (Universität Tübingen)

For Morris Halle, on his birthday

1 Introduction

The stress of Ukrainian and Russian derivatives depends on the range of accentual allomorphs found in the inflectional paradigm of their base. The stem of a derivative can adopt a certain accentual profile – unstressed, or stressed on a particular syllable – only if some inflected form of its base contains a stem allomorph with the same accent. This creates a distinction between variable and invariant nouns, illustrated below with Ukrainian data.

(1) Derived adjectives of accentually variable vs. invariant base nouns, in Ukrainian

	Nominative Sing.	Nominative Pl.	Adjective in *ov-yj*
(a) Variable bases: stressed and stressless stems	garbúz 'melon' jármarok 'fair' paljt-ó 'overcoat'	garbuz-ý jarmark-ý páljt-a	garbuz-óv-yj jarmark-óv-yj paljt-óv-yj
(b) Invariable bases: only stem-stressed	abrykós 'apricot' káktus 'cactus'	abrykós-y káktus-y	abrykós-ov-yj káktus-ovyj

The nouns in (1a) have a stressless stem allomorph, in the singular or in the plural, and use that stem to generate penultimate stressed *-óv-yj* forms. The nouns in (1b) have invariant stem stress in inflection and keep that stress in derivation, yielding *-ov-yj* forms with pre-penultimate stress.

The two languages analysed here have different accentual systems, but the phenomenon of interest to us, the freedom to use in derivation any stem allomorphs of the inflected base, is found in both. Our chapter provides a description of this pattern, connects it to related data outside of Slavic, and analyses it based on a modified conception of the phonological cycle.

The remainder of section 7.1 outlines the better known mechanisms of Proto-Slavic accentuation and the difference between Proto-Slavic accent and the two East Slavic systems analysed here. The basic accentual generalization we defend for modern East Slavic is introduced in section 7.1.2. Section 7.2 presents the Ukrainian evidence for it and its analysis. Section 7.3 is a sketch of some of the Russian evidence for the same idea. Section 7.4 is an extension of this idea beyond accent and beyond Slavic languages.

7.1.1 Proto-Slavic accentual classes and their modern East Slavic counterparts

The accent of derivatives in Proto-Slavic and East Slavic is predictably related to the mobility of accent in their bases (Bulaxovsjkyj 1927; Hartmann 1936; Halle 1973; Garde 1976; Dybo 1981; Zaliznjak 1985; Halle and Kiparsky 1981; Melvold 1989, among others; cf. also review in Lehfeldt 2001). In this section we briefly outline the Proto-Slavic accent system, seeking to establish a common point of departure for the two East Slavic systems of interest to us.

Accent in Proto-Slavic inflected nouns can be derived from the underlying accentual properties of stems and suffixes (Dybo 1981). The same underlying properties that predict stress in inflectional paradigms determine stress in derivatives.[1] This pattern is illustrated below:

(2) Proto-Slavic accent as a function of the underlying accent of the stem and the suffix.[2]

a.	Underlyingly accented stem:	**báb*- 'old woman'
	with unaccented infl. suffix:	**báb-ǫ* (Acc Sg)
	with accented infl. suffix:	**báb-a* (Nom Sg)
	with unaccented deriv. suffix:	**báb-ьsk-ъ*, **báb-ьsk-a* (Adj, 'related to women')
	with accented deriv. suffix:	**báb-ьj-ь*, **báb-ьj-a* (Adj, 'related to women')
b.	Underlyingly post-accented stem:	**os*- 'wasp', **žen*- 'woman'
	with unaccented infl. suffix:	**os-ǫ́*, **žen-ǫ́* (Acc Sg)
	with accented infl. suffix:	**os-á*, **žen-á* (Nom Sg)
	with unaccented deriv. suffix:	**žen-ь́sk-ъ*, **žen-ь́sk-a* (Adj, 'related to women')
	with accented deriv. suffix:	**os-ь́j-ь*, **os-ь́j-a* (Adj, 'related to wasps')

c. Underlyingly unaccented stem: **mǫž-* 'male human', **vorg-* 'enemy'
with unaccented infl. suffix: **mǫ́ž-ъ*, **vórg-ъ* (Nom Sg)
with accented infl. suffix: **mǫž-ý*, **vorg-ý* (Inst Pl)
with unaccented deriv. suffix: **mǫ́ž-ьsk-ъ*, **mǫž-ьsk-á* (Adj, 'related to men')
with accented deriv. suffix: **vorž-ьj-ь́*, **vorž-ьj-á* (Adj, 'related to enemies')

The class of nouns illustrated in (2a) – known as class (a) or type (a) nouns (Stang 1957) – have fixed accent on the stem. Accent remains on the stem in all inflected forms, and in all derivatives. This pattern can be generated if the stem is underlyingly accented and if faithfulness to the stem accent outranks faithfulness to any suffix, inflectional or derivational.

The nouns in (2b) illustrate *post-accenting*, or class (b) nouns. Proto-Slavic post-accentuation occurs when a stem-final vowel is short and underlyingly accented (Illich-Svitych 1963; Dybo 1981). Assume that Proto-Slavic accent was a tonal accent and had to be realized on two moras. When the stress-bearing unit was a long vowel, the tonal accent could be realized within the stressed nucleus. When stress fell on a short vowel, the tonal accent had to extend to the next syllable. This produced the post-accentuation reflexes of modern languages, perhaps because the stressed syllable was identified as containing the end-point of the tonal accent's domain.[3] Stress in words containing a post-accenting stem always lands on the syllable immediately following the stem, regardless of the underlying accent of the suffix. In inflection, the ending is stressed after a type (b) stem, whether underlyingly stressed, as in **os-á,* or not, as in **os-*ǫ́. In derivation, it is always the derivational suffix immediately following the root-final syllable that gets the stress: **os-ь́j-ь*.

The nouns in (2c) illustrate the Proto-Slavic mobile nouns, class (c). Their stems were underlyingly stressless. When combined with an accented derivational or inflectional suffix, that affixal accent surfaced: **mǫž-ý, *mǫž-ьsk-á*, **vorž-ьj-ь́*.[4] When combined with unaccented suffixes, an initial stress was assigned to the prosodic word: **mǫ́ž-ъ*, **mǫ́ž-ьsk-ъ*.

Summing up, the reconstructed Proto-Slavic accentual alternations can be derived from the underlying accent of stems and affixes, the mechanism of postaccentuation, and two additional assumptions: only one stress can surface in each word; and faithfulness to stems outranks faithfulness to affixes (McCarthy and Prince 1994).

The systems of modern East Slavic languages are nowhere near as transparent. Consider inflection first. While the Proto-Slavic accentual types are derivable from the underlying accent of the stem and the ending, no such analysis is possible for modern East Slavic accent. There are fixed-stress types which continue the Proto-Slavic types (a) and (b) and are still referred to by those terms. In addition, there is a variety of different accentual types, with the same endings surfacing as stressed in some and stressless in others, in multiple combinations. The abbreviated Russian paradigms in (3) illustrate this. Ukrainian, seen in section 7.2, is similar.

(3) Accentual variety in Russian: some accentual types of the *-o* nouns.[5]

Class (a), fixed stem stress: *udod* 'hoopoe'			Class (b), fixed ending stress: *dožď* 'rain'		
Sg		Pl	Sg		Pl
N	udód □■	udód-y □■-○	N, A	dóždj ■	doždj-í □-●
G, A	udód-a □■-○	udód-ov □■-○	G	doždj-á □-●	doždj-éj □-●
L	udód-e □■-○	udód-ax □■-○	L	doždj-é □-●	doždj-áx □-●

Class (c), stem stress in sg., ending stress in pl.: *dub* 'oak'			Class (d), ending stress in sg., stem stress in pl.: *kazak* 'cossack'		
Sg		Pl	Sg		Pl
N, A	dúb ■	dub-ý □-●	N, A	kazák □■	kazák-i □■-○
G	dúb-a ■-○	dub-óv □-●	G	kazak-á □□-●	kazák-ov □■-○
L	dúb-e ■-○	dub-áx □-●	L	kazak-é □□-●	kazák-ax □■-○

Class (e): same as class (c), but stem stress in Nom.pl.: *volk* 'wolf'			Class (f): same as class (b), but stem stress in Nom.pl.: *gvozď* 'nail'		
Sg		Pl	Sg		Pl
N	vólk ■	vólk-i ■-○	N, A	gvózdj ■	gvózdj-i ■-○
G, A	vólk-a ■-○	volk-óv □-●	G	gvozdj-á □-●	gvozdj-éj □-●
L	vólk-e ■-○	volk-áx □-●	L	gvozdj-é □-●	gvozdj-áx □-●

These accentual paradigms lend themselves to multiple analyses. Some assign stress to each individual case/number form (Zaliznjak 1967, § 6: 15–22; Halle 1973); others use some paradigmatic cells as bases for deriving still others (Butska 2002; Feldstein 2006; Ivlieva 2009; Yanovich and Steriade 2010). All analyses must appeal to lexically indexed rules or constraints (Pater 2010) to differentiate the attested types of accentual paradigms. This contrasts sharply with the Proto-Slavic system, where each ending is reconstructed as having been invariably stressed in all mobile words, or invariably stressless in all.

Despite the variety of accentual types in inflection, fewer distinctions affect accent placement in derivatives. Thus Halle's (1973) analysis of Russian derivatives distinguishes underlyingly stressed bases, type (a), and underlyingly stressless post-accented bases of type (b) from all others. Zaliznjak's (1985) analysis of Russian derivatives distinguishes fixed stem-stress bases from all others. So, surprisingly, while inflection displays a wide range of accentual alternations, most differences between accent patterns are irrelevant in derivatives (cf. Feldstein 1984: 506). This is different from Proto-Slavic, where the same properties of morphemes – underlying accent and post-accentuation – determined stress in both inflection and in derivation.

7.1.2 Match Stem Stress and lexical conservatism

To explain this collapse of accentual distinctions in the derivational morphology of modern East Slavic we will propose the following: the faithfulness of candidate derivatives to their base is assessed by letting the derivative's stem correspond to *any stem allomorph* found in the inflectional paradigm of the base. Words belonging to different mobile paradigms – recall from (1) *garbúz, garbuz-ý*; *jármarok, jarmark-ý*; *paljt-ó, páljt-a* – behave similarly *qua* bases insofar as these paradigms contain among their allomorphs a stressless stem. This stem is used to optimize the derivatives' stress. That's all that matters in derivation: the existence of some stem allomorph possessing a desirable accentual profile, anywhere in the inflectional paradigm of the base. The accentually immobile class (a) nouns differ from the mobile bases in lacking *any* unaccented stem allomorph in its inflectional paradigm. The generalization we anticipate is that, for a large class of derivatives, the only relevant base-faithfulness constraint is the one in (4).

(4) Match Stem Stress: A syllable in the stem of the derivative is [α stress] only if a correspondent of that syllable *in some inflected form of its surface base* is also [α stress].

Derivative: $[\ldots s_{[\alpha\ \text{stress}]} \ldots]_{\text{stem}} - [\ldots]_{\text{derivational}} - [\ldots]_{\text{ending}}$

An inflected form of its base: $[\ldots s_{[\alpha\ \text{stress}]} \ldots]_{\text{stem}} - [\ldots]_{\text{ending}}$

To make (4) concrete, imagine a disyllabic, accentually mobile base noun like Ukrainian *jármarok* (class (c) in (2), common to Russian and Ukrainian). Some of its inflected forms have stem stress, e.g. *jármarok.* Others, like *jarmark-ý,* have a stressless stem. The totality of these forms make up a pool of accentual allomorphs from which derivatives choose their own stem. (5) depicts the two choices that Match Stem Stress sanctions, plus a third option which the constraint penalizes. The forbidden option consists of stressing in derivation a stem syllable that is never stressed in inflection:

(5) Satisfying MATCH STEM STRESS

Pool of stress profiles in surface inflected forms of a disyllabic base		Options for stressing derivatives of this base are limited to profiles in the pool
$[\acute{\sigma}\sigma]_{stem} - [\sigma\ldots]_{ending}$	⟵	$[\acute{\sigma}\sigma]_{stem} - [\sigma\ldots]_{derivational\ suffix} - ([\sigma\ldots]_{ending})$
$[\sigma\sigma]_{stem} - [\acute{\sigma}\ldots]_{ending}$	⟵	$[\sigma\sigma]_{stem} - [\acute{\sigma}\ldots]_{derivational\ suffix} - ([\sigma\ldots]_{ending})$
		$*[\sigma\acute{\sigma}]_{stem} - [\sigma\ldots]_{derivational\ suffix} - ([\sigma\ldots]_{ending})$

The Ukrainian forms in (6) provide a preview of the material explained by MATCH STEM STRESS, expanding on (1). As seen before, base nouns with fixed stem stress have one allomorph and must use that form in derivatives, (6a). Most bases with ending stress, (6b), and with mobile stress, (6c), also provide a stressless allomorph. This can be used in *-ov-yj* derivatives to produce the penult stress favoured by Ukrainian (*obruč-év-yj*, *pojizd-óv-yj*).[6] The *-n-yj* and *sjk-yj* derivatives prefer allomorphs stressed on the stem-final syllable, to promote penult stress in the suffixed form, and use these wherever available: cf. (6b.ii; 6c.ii-iii) compared to (6a.ii).

(6) Effects of MATCH STEM STRESS (in Ukrainian)

a. Fixed stem stress (type a) w. non-final stress => pre-penultimate stress in the derivative
   i. *osýk-a* 'asp', GenSg *osýk y*, NomPl *osýk-y* => *osýk-ov-yj* 'of an asp'
   ii. *Úžgorod* (toponym), GenSg *Úžgorod-u* => *Užgorod-sjk-yj* 'from U.'

b. Post-accentuation (type b) => penultimate stress in the derivative
   i. *obrúč* 'hoop', GenSg *obruč-á*, NomPl *obruč-í* => *obruč-év-yj* 'of a hoop'
   ii. *obrúč* 'hoop' => *obrúč-n-yj* 'of a hoop'

c. Mobile stress (types c, d) => penultimate stress in the derivative
   i. type (c): *pójizd* 'train', GenSg *pójizd-a*, NomPl *pojizd-ý* => *pojizd-óv-yj* 'of train'
   ii. type (c): *nébo* 'heavens', NomPl. *nebes-á*, Genpl. *nebés* => *nebés-n-yj* 'heavenly'
   iii. type (d): *častot-á* 'frequency', NomPl *častót-y* => *častót-n-yj* 'related to frequency'

None of the derivatives in (6) violates MATCH STEM STRESS. All are *lexically conservative*, in the sense that they use only stem variants independently guaranteed to occur elsewhere (Steriade 1999a,b 2007).

The data in (6) also provides a summary of the differences between the modern Ukrainian system and Proto-Slavic. First, the derivatives of Ukrainian post-accenting nouns, type (b), are not invariably post-accenting themselves: attested *obrúč-n-yj* (6b.ii) is not post-accenting **obruč-n-ýj*. Second, the Ukrainian derivatives of *stressed* stems, types (a) and (c),[7] are not invariably stem-stressed: *pojizd-óv-yj* (6c.i) is not. In general, only the derivatives of class (a) nouns are stem-stressed with any consistency in East Slavic. These are first indications that the analysis sketched above for Proto-Slavic doesn't fit the modern East Slavic data considered here.

While the data in (6) suggests certain regularities, defended in detail below, the empirical picture in modern East Slavic is much more complex. First, there exist *dominant* derivational suffixes that create forms whose stress is unaffected by any form of faithfulness to the stem. In their presence, all base properties are overridden.[8] For example, all Ukrainian *-yčn-yj* derivatives are stressed on the penult no matter what forms they are based on. Naturally, we concentrate here on the non-dominant, or *recessive* derivatives.

Second, we will see that a minority of Ukrainian recessive derivatives have penult or final stress even when no appropriate stem allomorph of the base exists. Historical studies show that reassignment of stress types and restructuring of accentual paradigms took place in East Slavic dialects throughout their documented history (cf. Zaliznjak (1985) for eastern East Slavic, Vynnycjkyj (2002) for south-western East Slavic, among others). The contemporary lexicons of Ukrainian and Russian contain both remnants of these historical developments and innovations still productive today. This is as expected for ongoing changes that spread, sometimes incompletely, through a lexicon. Because of this mix of forms reflecting old and new systems, we find strong tendencies but no categorical restrictions in our East Slavic data. Nonetheless, we can show that MATCH STEM STRESS is a factor in the Ukrainian and Russian derivational morphology. That constraint alone does not determine the form of the derivative, but it is a central part of the interplay that does.

We focus on three noun-to-adjective derivational suffixes of Ukrainian (*-n-yj, -sjk-yj* and *-ov-yj*), and three suffixes of Russian (*-ostj, -išš-e*, and possessive *-ov*). The evidence for MATCH STEM STRESS in East Slavic is not limited to those. Ivlieva (2009) provides additional evidence from Russian for the same idea; see also Melvold (1989: 48ff).

7.1.3 Predictably derived stem allomorphs; inflection dependence

The principles that distribute listed allomorphs of roots and affixes have been investigated by Bonet *et al.* (2007); Kager (1996); Drachman *et al.* (1996); Paster (2005); Tranel (1996), among others. The conclusion reached in most of those studies is that when a morpheme offers multiple listed variants, markedness constraints are at least in part responsible for their surface distribution.

Our study follows in this line of thought, with a difference: the markedness-driven distribution documented in this chapter involves not underlying allomorphs of the base noun but predictably derived ones. Thus the difference between the stem allomorphs in Nom. Sg. *obrúč* vs. Gen.sg. *obruč-á* is predictable for a post-accenting noun: the noun must be listed as post-accenting, in a way we outline below, but its two stems, the result of its being post-accenting, need not be listed in the permanent lexicon. The scenario we defend is one in which the inflected forms of the base words have their phonology, including their accent, regularly derived by the grammar in a first derivational step. The results are stored in a derived lexicon of inflected forms. In a later step, the grammar computes the accent of the derivatives of these words. At this later stage, all inflected surface forms of the base, and their stress profiles, are available for look-up. Those forms function as a collective base in the evaluation of candidates for the derivative: MATCH STEM STRESS checks the stem stress of the derivative against this set.

We call this phenomenon *inflection dependence* (Steriade 2007). We do not deny the relevance of additional correspondence constraints seeking a match with a specific form in the inflectional paradigm of the base. When such constraints dominate the output, it may appear that a single form serves as the base. We suggest that such constraints do have an effect in Ukrainian. But the focus here is on the evidence for the less well documented constraint type that characterizes the inflection dependence effect: MATCH STEM STRESS.

7.1.4 The alternatives to MATCH STEM STRESS

Our main finding will be that the accentual profile of *any inflected form of the base* can be adopted by its derivatives for the purpose of optimizing their stress, regardless of the morphosyntactic features expressed in that inflected base form. There is no unique base form in the computation of the derivative (Burzio 1998, 2005; Steriade 1999a,b).

We compare this anticipated finding to baseline analytical expectations derived from current views on how bases influence the shape of their derivatives. We spell these out starting from the theory of cyclic rule application (Chomsky *et al.* 1956; Chomsky and Halle 1968), its Optimality Theoretic offshoots (Kenstowicz 1996; Benua 1997; Kiparsky 2000; Bermúdez-Otero 2011), and other recent work.

The essence of the baseline alternative to our analysis is that only two forms can influence the derivative. One of them is the underlying representation of the root (for a mono-morphemic base stem), or the root with derivational affixes (in the case of a complex stem). What is the other form? That would correspond to the output of a derivative's first cycle in a rule-based theory of the cycle, or in Kenstowicz's (1996) OT reconstruction of the cyclic idea, and in Stratal OT (Kiparsky 2000; Bermúdez-Otero 2011).

What is the *domain* of this earlier cycle whose output might be inherited by the derivative? Here the theories cited abide, mostly tacitly, by the assumption that any cyclic domain contained in the derivative corresponds to a subconstituent of the derivative's syntactic structure. Chomsky *et al.* (1956) were the first to spell out this assumption. Benua (1997: 30) too upholds something akin to it, as does Kager (1999). This rules out the possibility that any inner cycle to in a derived word might be a case- or number-inflected form of the base. Nominal case is licensed by syntactic structures inaccessible inside a derivative. As a result, overtly case-inflected forms are rarely if ever found as stems of derived words. This is true in East Slavic as well: the derivatives we consider do not contain in their stems any case suffix. As for number, most derivatives are interpreted as having bases insensitive to number information. The forms discussed here are no different in this respect.

A further class of possibilities is reviewed in Albright's (2002, 2005, 2010) studies of bases in inflectional paradigms. The in-principle options reviewed there can be considered for derivational morphology as well. They include: the base as the most informative surface form of the inner lexeme (the form preserving most phonological contrasts between bases), the base as the on-average most frequent form of the lexeme, the base as citation form or as a syntactically unmarked form – whatever *unmarked* may mean. All these possible theories of what a base may be are based on the assumption (empirically supported in Albright's work) that there is a *unique* base in every inflectional paradigm. In an extension to derivational morphology, this means a unique base for each derivative.

The East Slavic evidence documented here should be evaluated against these two expectations: each derivative has a unique base, and this base is an uninflected form.

7.2 Ukrainian evidence for Match Stem Stress

This section documents the effects of inflection dependence in the recessive Ukrainian denominal adjectives. We show that these derivatives obey a revised version of the constraint Match Stem Stress (4), and do so frequently to the exclusion of other forms of faithfulness. In sections 7.2.1–7.2.6 we introduce the necessary background on Ukrainian, and show the effects of faithfulness for fixed-stress bases. Then, in sections 7.2.7–7.2.12, we examine derivatives of post-accenting and mobile-stress nouns, and show that they are faithful to their bases under the Match Stem Stress interpretation of faithfulness, but not on alternative interpretations that require a unique base.

Our sources are: the Ukrainian dictionaries of Pogribnyj (1984) and Andrusyshen and Krett (1957); the inverse dictionary of Ukrainian by the Potebnja Linguistics Institute of the Ukrainian Academy of Sciences, to which we refer as ISUM (1985); the Ukrainian grammar of Pugh and Press (1999); the on-line declension help for individual nouns, provided by the Ukrajinsjkyj Lingvistyčnyj Portal at http://lcorp.ulif.org.ua/dictua/; Butska's (2002) analysis of Ukrainian nominal accentuation, continued in Truckenbrodt and Butska (2003); and finally Vynnycjkyj (2002), an extensive description of Ukrainian stress in all parts of speech, for historical and dialectal data on accentual changes. Our assumptions about underlying accent in different noun classes and the mechanisms that derive accentual mobility come from Yanovich and Steriade (2010).

7.2.1 Preference for penult stress in modern Ukrainian

The East Slavic accentual systems have a shared characteristic: the position of the stress is in principle unconstrained. In Ukrainian, however, penultimate stress is preferred. In some Western Ukrainian dialects, this preference is reported as an invariant fact (Zilynskyj 1979: 184, 194; Reiter 1969; Baerman 1999). The data we analyse – from standard Ukrainian, based on Eastern dialect – show that aspects of the penult preference are present in general. Having relied on secondary literature and dictionary data for the evidence of penult-stress preference, we do not know its exact extent across Ukrainian vernaculars. As we consistently use standard-Ukrainian stress facts as explananda, this is not problematic for our purposes here.

We infer the penult preference in Eastern Ukrainian from two kinds of data. The first are Zilynskyj's (1979) observations about his own productions (in standard Ukrainian) accompanied by transcriptions that assign stress numbers – 1 'main' to 6 'very weak or no stress' – to every syllable. These data indicate that at least a secondary stress is present on the penult whenever clash avoidance allows it. The examples below illustrate two points: under clash with final or antepenult main stress, Zylinskyj reports the penult as weakly stressed or unstressed, a 4, 5, or 6 stress (7a). Everywhere else, the penult is recorded as a 1 or a 2 (7b). We indicate the position of main and secondary stresses using acute and grave accents.

(7) Degrees of stress in E. Ukrainian (1 the strongest, 6 the weakest): Zilynskyj's transcriptions (1979: 187–190; accents added by us)

a. weak or no stress on the penult under clash with main stress

dòbrotá	*pèrenočuválysjmo*
2 4 1	2 4 3 4 1 4 3

b. strong (secondary or main) stress on the penult everywhere else
ròzgovórjuvàly *pèrenočuvály*
2 4 1 4 2 4 2 6 4 3 1 5

Lehr-Splawinsky (*apud* Zylinskyj 1979: 189) makes a supporting point: 'When more than two syllables follow the primary accent, there is a tendency for the end of the word to be trochaic, i.e. for secondary accent to fall on the second syllable from the end, i.e. ˊ- -.'

These descriptions suggest an analysis in which lapse avoidance (*LAPSER) and final stress avoidance (NONFINALITY) are active. Their joint effect is to promote some stress on the penult. In the unmarked case, MAINSTRESSRIGHT (MSR) will make this the main stress of the word. Competing with *LAPSE and NONFINALITY are clash avoidance (*CLASH) and faithfulness to lexically specified stress (IDENTSTRESS IO) – or, as we shall see, correspondence to a surface base. In *dòbrotá* 'goodness', lexical stress on the final is preserved in violation of NONFINALITY. In *pèrenočuválysjmo* (from *pèrenočuváty* 'to pass the night') the base stress on *vá* is preserved: here IDENTSTRESS BD, *CLASH and NONFINALITY make it impossible to satisfy *LAPSER. Aside from such circumstances, a penult stress will always surface. Penult stress becomes the main stress in e.g. *pèrenočuvály* in (7b). Deviations from MSR in nominal forms and their derivatives are analyzed below. Constraint definitions are found in the Appendix.

A second class of observations, on the distribution of stress in derived forms compared to their bases, shows a preference to maintain the penult stress *as main stress*. The table in (8) provides data on the stress patterns of the citation forms of polysyllabic nouns and derived adjectives from a Ukrainian database described in section 7.2.5. Based on the information reported above, we interpret the dictionary stress data as reporting only the position of *main* stress.

(8) Lexical frequencies of main stress positions in a database of nouns and derived adjectives

	Pre-antepenult	Antepenult	Penult	Final
bases	1	55	450	370
derivatives	48	376	413	184

This data shows that the prevalent position of main stress, for both bases and derivatives, is on the penult. Pre-penultimate stress is found, with rare exceptions, only among derivatives. We interpret this restriction as the result of the interaction between the MSR and faithfulness to the main stress position of the base, MATCHSTEMSTRESS(MAIN). The vast majority of pre-penult main stresses arise when a derivational suffix is added to a stem that keeps the main stress of its base: e.g. *káktus, káktus-ov-yj* 'of a cactus', or, as we learn from Zilynskyj and Lehr-Splawinsky, [káktusòvyj], with a secondary stress on the penult and a violation of MSR. Main stress on a pre-antepenult is essentially impossible *in bases* because the sole competitor to MSR is irrelevant to base accentuation: it's the Base Derivative (BD) faithfulness constraint MATCH STEM STRESS(MAIN).

Pre-penultimate stress is, to an extent, also under-represented in *derivatives*: that's because MSR isn't always outranked by base faithfulness. This argument emerges from the table in (9), which provides rates of stress by position in *-ov-yj* adjectives. These data come from ISUM (1985).

(9) Lexical frequency of main stress positions in Ukrainian *-ov-yj* adjectives: *N* = 3385

	Pre-antepenult	Antepenult	Penult	Final
Main stress	6%	40%	37%	17%

Two facts about this distribution indicate a preference for the penult as the locus of main stress. First, the majority of the base nouns belong to class (a), by far the best populated accentual class in East Slavic. Most derivatives of class (a) nouns keep intact the stress of their base – cf. Halle (1973) for Russian, Butska (2002) and below for Ukrainian. Then we expect pre-penultimate stress for *all* class (a)-based *-ov-yj* adjectives:[9] e.g. *labradór, labradór-ov-yj; káktus, káktus-ov-yj*. But this is not what (9) shows: a significant number of *-óv-yj* adjectives, most of which must be class (a)-based, have penult stress. Among them are *metal-év-yj* 'of metal', *lozung-óv-yj* 'of slogan', *fosfor-óv-yj* 'of phosphor' from the class (a) nouns *metál, lózung, fósfor*. Pre-antepenultimate main stress is rare, even though most bases – like *káktus, lózung, fósfor* – are penult stressed and expected to produce pre-antepenult stressed *-ov-yj* forms. Antepenult stress is well attested but less frequent than the proportion of class (a) bases leads one to expect.

It appears then that in a significant number of derivatives accentual markedness overrides base faithfulness, shifting main stress to the penult. We assume that final main stress is disfavored by NONFINALITYMAIN: this rules out unfaithful alternatives like **làbradòr-ov-ýj, *fósfor-ov-ýj,* limiting the choices to just two, faithful but marked (e.g. *làbradór-ov-yj, fósfor-òv-yj*) and unfaithful, unmarked (**labràdor-óv-yj, fósfor-óv-yj*).

A final observation confirms the preference for penult stress. 94 *-ov-yj* adjectives are listed in ISUM as having two variants. Most are written with two accents, e.g. <náftóvyj> 'of oil', or <káktusóvyj> 'of a cactus', to abbreviate two accentual options: e.g. *káktusovyj* and *kaktusóvyj*. There is a striking fact about all these doublets. The majority (81/94) limit variation between accent on a non-penult (final, antepenult or pre-antepenult) and the penult. Five apparent exceptions come from bases whose own accent varies: e.g. variable class (a) <fárfór> 'porcelain' gives rise to variable <fárfórovyj>. Setting those aside, there is no variation between stress on pre-penultimate positions: *káktusovyj,* from invariant *káktus,* never varies with **kaktúsovyj.* In eight forms, stress varies between the antepenult and the final: e.g. <stánovýj> 'of status', from class (a) *stán* 'social class'. In these cases, a lexicalized, inherited derivative with final stress, here *stanovýj* varies with a newer form that's accentually faithful to its base, *stán-ov-yj.*[10] Aside from these eight items, all ISUM doublets, 90% of all relevant forms, involve variation between *faithful non-penult stress and faithless penult stress*. Without a markedness preference for penult stress there is no reason why variation should be restricted in just this way.

We interpret this data by conjecturing that the variably accented derivatives reflect variation in the ranking between the markedness constraints that ensure penult stress (NonFinality (Main), MSR and *LapseR) and either (i) accentual faithfulness to the main stress of the base (Match Stem Stress (Main)), or (ii) faithfulness to a lexicalized, inherited derivative with final stress *-ov-ýj*.[11] Productive derivatives from the adjectival classes we study here generally don't have final-stressed variants: we infer from this that NonFinality (Main) isn't involved in the variation and can only be outranked by faithfulness to frozen derivatives like *stanovýj*. The major source of doublets then is just the relation between Match Stem Stress (Main) and, on the other hand, MSR and *LapseR. We analyze this type of variation next, as it will play a larger role in the analysis.

7.2.2 Analysis thus far: Lexicalized and free variation

If the stress variation in <náftóvyj>, <káktusóvyj> was general, we would propose to variably rank Match Stem Stress (Main) against *LapseR, MSR. The dictionary data suggests otherwise: variation is restricted to a subset of the recessive derivatives. Stress fluctuates in *kaktus-ov-yj*, but not in *gúmus-ov-yj* 'of humus' or in most other class (a) derivatives. Stress in unfaithful items like *metal-év-yj, fosfor-óv-yj* is fixed on the penult, with no reported variation.

To analyze all three options for derivatives of class (a), at least two constraints must be lexically indexed. We adopt Pater's (2010) analysis of lexical exceptions. A markedness or faithfulness constraint is cloned to produce a version that evaluates only L, a closed list of lexical items. We identify the constraints to be cloned in the present case as MSR and *LapseR and we refer to their lexically indexed clones as MSR$_{L1}$ and *LapseR$_{L2}$. We identify the lexical items contained in the L1 and L2 sets as the *bases* of the relevant *-ov-yj* derivatives. Thus the ranking MSR$_{L1}$ >> Match Stem (Main) >> MSR is a fragment of a grammar that shifts main stress only in derivatives of a closed L1-set that includes *káktus* and fósfor. Membership in the L1 set is invariant for *fósfor*, but it is variable for *káktus*. Similarly, membership in the L2 set is variable for *náfta* (cf. <náftóvyj>) but invariant for *metál* (cf. *metalévyj*).

On this view, no ranking fluctuates, but *membership* in the sets L1 and L2 may: it does fluctuate for items like *káktus*, *náfta*, with consequences for their derivatives. (10a) is the analysis of a derivative of *káktus,* understood as a member of L1: here lexically indexed MSR$_{L1}$ decides the outcome. (10b) is the analysis of a derivative of *káktus,* seen this time as a *non*-member of L1: with MSR$_{L1}$ moot, the ranking Match Stem Stress >> MSR is decisive. There is no variation for *gúmusovyj* because *gúmus* is never a member of L1. There is no variation for *fosforóvyj* because *fósfor* is always a member of L1. In (10c–d) we illustrate the same idea, applied this time to variation between antepenult and penult stress in cases like <náftóvyj>.

(10) Penult preference and accentual variants

a. Effect of MSR$_{L1}$ in unfaithful derivatives: *kaktusóvyj, fosforóvyj*

	Base: káktus$_{L1}$	Non Finality (Main)	MSR$_{L1}$	Match Stem (Main)
(a)	káktus -òv-yj		*!	
☞ (b)	kàktus -óv-yj			*
(c)	kaktùs -ov-ýj	*!		*

b. Effect of Match Stem (Main) in faithful derivatives: *káktusovyj, gúmusovyj*

	Base: káktus	MSR$_{L1}$	Match Stem (Main)	MSR
☞ (a)	káktus -òv-yj	moot		*
(b)	kàktus -óv-yj		*!	

c. Effects of *LapseR$_{L2}$ in unfaithful derivatives: *naftóvyj, metalévyj*

	Base: náfta$_{L2}$	*LapseR$_{L2}$	Match Stem (Main)
(a)	náft -ov-yj	*!	
☞ (b)	naft -óv-yj		*

d. Effect of Match Stem (Main) in faithful derivatives: *náftovyj, labradórovyj*

	Base: náfta	*LapseR$_{L2}$	Match Stem (Main)	*LapseR
☞ (a)	náft -ov-yj	moot		*
(b)	naft -óv-yj		*!	

Our claim is that penult-stressed unfaithful derivatives are due to the rise of penult main stress in Ukrainian. This is supported by diachronic observations in Veselovsjka (1970) and Vynnycjkyj (2002). Veselovsjka notes that the *-ov-yj* adjectives have been consistently moving towards penult stress from the late sixteenth century to the present. Vynnycjkyj discusses accentual variants of adjectives, underived and derived, where penultimate accent has become possible over the last two centuries, or has completely replaced an earlier accent on some other syllable.

Even if penultimate stress is on the rise now, final stress in some derivatives must have been a favored option at some recent point in the history of Ukrainian.[12] What matters here, however, is the current general preference for penult stress, supported both by the synchronic data discussed above, and by the historical evidence in Veselovsjka (1970) and Vynnycjkyj (2002). This markedness preference reveals the unusual faithfulness system of Ukrainian studied here.

7.2.3 Inflectional paradigms of derived adjectives

When we refer to an adjective, e.g. *velýk-yj* 'big', as having penultimate stress, we refer to a paradigm whose Nominatives and two-thirds of the oblique forms carry surface penultimate stress, but where forms with antepenult stress also exist. The latter contain disyllabic inflectional endings (e.g. *velýk-oju* 'big-fem.Instr.sg', *velýk-ymy* 'Instr.pl'). Stress in Ukrainian adjectives is invariant, so forms with the disyllabic endings keep stress on the same syllable as forms with monosyllabic endings (e.g. *velýk-a* 'fem. Nom.sg', *velýk-i* 'Nom.pl').

There are two related points here that require analysis: the very fact of accentual uniformity in adjectives, which differ in this respect from nouns, and the fact that what we call a 'penult-stressed' adjective has some inflected forms that aren't penult-stressed. We claim that the second of these facts – the deviations from penult stress – stems from the first: there is a base form in every adjectival gender/number subparadigm, the Nominative, and the accentual uniformity of adjectival paradigms is due to the fact that all other paradigm members must match the stress of that base. This point is not further reflected below: the reader will bear in mind that further Base-Derivative constraints on stress identity between the citation form and the rest of the derived adjective's paradigm must operate in the complete analysis.[13]

7.2.4 Ukrainian nominal accentual classes

We examine now the correlation between the stress assigned to the base noun in inflection and the accentual possibilities found in its recessive derivatives.

Ukrainian nouns fall into four main accentual classes, similar to Russian. These differ in the number of accentual allomorphs found in inflection: class (a) nouns have one stem allomorph, which is always accented; classes (b)–(d) have typically more than one, almost always including an unstressed allomorph. Within a class, gender differences create further accentual distinctions, triggered by differences between gender-specific endings. Nouns may also be defective, having only plural or only singular forms. All these factors determine if and where the accent surfaces on the stem of the noun, and hence its full set of accentual allomorphs. Ultimately then, it is not just membership in one of the accent classes that affects how a noun's derivatives will be accented. It is that, plus all other circumstances about the inflection of the base.

7.2.5 The Ukrainian database

Our Ukrainian evidence comes from a database of adjectival derivatives in *-n-yj, -ov-yj*, and *-sjk-yj* whose base noun inflection is known to us. We have built this collection by looking up the adjectives derived from the core set of mobile nouns in Butska (2002), and later by adding derivatives of both mobile and immobile bases, through searches in Andrusyshen and Krett (1957), Pogribnyj (1984), ISUM (1985) and the http://lcorp.ulif.org.ua/dictua/ site. The database currently contains over 1,000 recessive adjectives. Variant forms are listed as distinct items. Where our sources disagree on the accent class of a base, we side with Pogribnyj (1984).

The purpose of this database is to check correlations between the accentual class of the base noun and the accent of its derivatives. In the early stages of assembling it we did not count derivatives with the monosyllabic suffixes *-n-yj* and *-sjk-yj* if they met two conditions: their base was a final-accented noun, e.g. *labradór*, and the adjective's stress was, as predicted, on the penult. Thus *labradór-sjk-yj* was initially excluded, while *labradór-ov-yj* wasn't. The reason was that the factor responsible for the penult stress *labradór-sjk-yj* is ambiguous between faithfulness to the base *labradór* and the markedness preference for penult stress. By contrast, the stress in *labradór-ov-yj* has a single explanation: faithfulness to the base.

In this way, numerous items like *labradór-sjk-yj* were initially omitted. We later decided that this omission was an error and attempted to remedy it when expanding the database. But the result is that, in its present form, the database underrecords penult-stressed derivatives that are faithful to their base.

A second exclusion emerged as advisable. We observed that a significant minority of the derivatives are unfaithful to their presumptive nominal bases, but perhaps faithful to a stem allomorph occurring in a lexically related form. Two examples in this class, *manevr-óv-yj* and *avstríj-sjk-yj*, are shown below. Both are penult-stressed, unlike the faithful derivatives we expected, **manévr-ov-yj* and **ávstrij-sjk-yj*.

(11) Base uncertainty

a. The stem allomorph used in the derivative does not occur in the inflection of the base, but occurs in a related verb:
   i. Presumptive base, class (a): *manévr* 'maneuver, stratagem'
   ii. Unfaithful penult-stressed derivative: *manevr-óv-yj* 'shunting'
   iii. Related verb: *manevr-uvá-ty* 'to shunt, to maneuver'

b. The stem allomorph used in the derivative does not occur in the inflection of the base, but occurs in a co-derivative:
   i. Presumptive base, class (a): *Ávstrij-a* 'Austria'
   ii. Unfaithful penult-stressed derivative: *avstríj-sjk-yj* 'from Austria'
   iii. Related lexical item with identical stress: *avstríj-etsj* 'Austrian (person)'

These cases are of interest to us because they suggest, in the spirit of our proposal, that the forms consulted to check satisfaction of MATCH STEM STRESS are not limited to the underlying form of the base noun. They may include co-derivatives of that noun, if this allows satisfaction of markedness constraints that would otherwise be out of reach.[14] Adjectives like those in (11) appear to satisfy markedness by referencing such co-derivatives. A subset of these revealing forms is ambiguous: the syntactic base of *manevr-óv-yj* could be the verb *manevr-uvá-ty*, not the noun *manévr*. When unable to decide the syntactic filiation of items like *manevr-óv-yj*, we have excluded them from our count. Derivatives like *avstríj-sjk-yj* whose stress matches the stress of a non-verbal derivative were kept on the list on the grounds that, had they been derived from co-derivatives like *avstríj-etsj,* the derivational suffix of that derived noun would have surfaced in the result, **avstríjetsjkyj*. We suspect then that a subset of the adjectives studied here, including *avstríj-sjk-yj*, licence their penultimate stress by reference to forms that are only indirectly related to their base noun.

7.2.6 Derivatives of type (a) nouns

Class (a) nouns have fixed accent on the same stem syllable throughout their inflectional paradigm. Like our predecessors, we attribute this to the fact that they contain an underlyingly accented syllable. The lack of alternations in their inflection is explained by Butska (2002): any underlying stress on inflectional affixes is protected by inactive faithfulness constraints. Accentual faithfulness to stems competes only with markedness, and normally outranks it.

Our database contains 581 recessive denominal adjectives from type (a) bases. A breakdown of this set according to stress position and faithfulness is given below. The category 'Faithful-Base' contains derivatives that preserve the main stress of the base noun, like *káktus-ov-yj*. The category 'Faithful-Related' refers to derivatives that preserve the stress of a form related, but not identical, to their base noun, as discussed in connection to *avstríj-sjk-yj*. 'Not Faithful' are adjectives whose main stress does not match any related form we could find: *kaktus-óv-yj* fits in here. Many such 'Not Faithful' forms have faithful variants, like *káktus-ov-yj*. The majority of class (a) derivatives belong only to the 'Faithful-Base' class: e.g. *gúmus-ov-yj* 'of humus'. For each of these categories we indicate in (12) the lexical frequencies of attested main stress positions. For example, in 10% of the 'Faithful-Base' derivatives from type (a) nouns have main stress on a pre-antepenult syllable, as *gúmus-ov-yj*.

(12) Derivatives from type (a) bases. $N = 581$; 380 *-ov-yj*; 201 *-n-yj* and *-sjk-yj* forms.

	Faithful-Base: 78%	Faithful-Related: 8%	Not Faithful: 14%
Pre-antepenult (9%)	10%	0	0
Antepenult (58%)	75%	0	0
Penult (27%)	14%	64%	74%
Final (5%)	0	36%	26%

The revealing fact in (12) is that forms faithful to their base have predominantly (85%) pre-penultimate accent, while the 'Faithful-Related' and 'Not-Faithful' categories have predominantly penultimate accent (64% and 74% respectively). This asymmetry is explained in the same way as the variation in <káktus-óvyj>, (10). That is, the derivatives that don't preserve the stress of their base, the 'Faithful-Related' and 'Not Faithful' categories, rank constraints inducing penult main stress above MATCH STEM STRESS. It is then expected that penult stress predominates in this unfaithful class.

The majority of Ukrainian recessive derivatives place MATCH STEM STRESS above all accentual markedness constraints. The low frequency of penult stress in the faithful majority of class (a) derivatives is related to this.

The fact that most base-faithful adjectives are stressed on a *pre*-penultimate syllable stems from three facts. First, a majority of class (a) derivatives in our database (65%) are suffixed with disyllabic *-ov-yj*, so faithful stress in the derivative must be prepenultimate, e.g. *labradór-ov-yj*. Second, as noted above, we delayed recording ambiguous adjectives like *labradór-sjk-yj*, where faithfulness and markedness converge to produce penult stress. Had we recorded these from the start, the proportion of penult stress in class (a) derivatives may have been higher. Finally, most bases have non-final stress, as seen in (8).

There are 37 derivatives of class (a) nouns that carry final stress, e.g. *birž-ev-ýj* from *bírž-a* 'exchange'. These are neither faithful to their base nor acentually optimal. We think they are lexicalized survivors of earlier stages in East Slavic, where a large number of *-ov-yj* adjectives had final stress in accordance with Hartmann's Law (Hartmann 1936).[15] We present some evidence on this in section 7.2.10. As this predicts, recent loanwords (*káktus, gúmus, labradór, fósfor, metál, manévr*) normally produce non-final stressed derivatives.

7.2.7 Interim summary: Derivatives of constant-stress nouns

Up to this point, we have shown that a form of accentual correspondence, in competition with markedness, explains the predominant accent pattern of derivatives from class (a) nouns, the deviations from these patterns, and the limits on attested variation. We have not yet presented evidence that favors MATCH STEM STRESS over alternatives like IDENT STRESS IO or IDENT STRESS BD, the latter conceived as faithfulness to the stress of *one* base item. Indeed, the derivatives of fixed-stress class (a) nouns cannot provide such evidence. The argument must come from derivatives discussed next: when bases provide several allomorphs of the inflected stem, we can distinguish the effects of MATCH STEM STRESS from the other forms of faithfulness.

7.2.8 Derivatives of type (b) nouns

Class (b) nouns stress their inflectional endings whenever these contain an overt vowel:

(13) Ukrainian type (b) nouns

(a) Stressed stem allomorph in Nom.sg. *garbúz* 'watermelon'			(b) Stressed stem allomorph in Gen. pl. *knjažná* 'princess'		
Sg		Pl	Sg		Pl
N,A	garbúz □■	garbuz-ý □□-●	N	knjažn-á □-●	knjažn-ý □-●
G	garbuz-á □□-●	garbuz-ív □□-●	G	knjažn-ý □-●	knjažón □■
D	garbuz-ú □□-●	garbuz-ám □□-●	D	knjažn-í □-●	knjažn-ám □-●
I	garbuz-óm □□-●	garbuz-ámy □□-●○	A	knjažn-ú □-●	knjažón □■
L	garbuz-é □□-●	garbuz-áx □□-●	I	knjažn-óju □-●○	knjažn-ámy □-●○
			L	knjažn-í □-●	knjažn-áx □-●

We follow Butska (2002) in assuming that the root of these nouns is underlyingly unaccented. If the inflectional suffix is unaccented as well, some surface stress must be assigned. In that case, faithfulness to the unstressed root makes it preferable to locate this default stress on the suffix. In addition to the default suffix stress, we must also derive the invariant stem-final stress in zero-suffixed forms of this class, e.g. Nom. Sg. forms like *garbúz*. Butska (2002) proposes to index to class (b) nouns a constraint COINCIDE-RIGHT, favoring adjacency between main stress and the right stem edge. Stress on the ending, e.g. *garbuz-ý*, satisfies that constraint while keeping the stem unstressed. When no ending surfaces, in *garbúz*, only stem-final stress satisfies COINCIDE-RIGHT. Another possibility is to assume an opaque scenario in which the ending is a jer bearing stress, yielding intermediate *garbuz-ь́*. When the jer deletes, its stress is transferred to the preceding syllable: *garbuz- ь́* => *garbúz*. (Cf. Zaliznjak 1967 for Russian.) Evidence discussed below perhaps favors this option, as does Russian data discussed in section 3. We leave the choice between these scenarios open: they are not strictly relevant to what follows, and the evidence favoring one or another remains unclear.

What is important here is that most type (b) nouns – 90% of those in our database – will have acquired *two* stem allomorphs in inflection: the unstressed and the final-stressed one. The MATCH STEM STRESS hypothesis predicts that both of these allomorphs can be deployed to facilitate satisfaction of markedness constraints (*LAPSER, MSR, NONFINALITY (MAIN)) in both types of derived adjectives: those followed by two affixal syllables (*-ov-yj*) and those followed by one (*-sjk-yj*, *-n-yj*). Derivatives of *obrúč* 'hoop' illustrate this below. The final-stressed stem is used in *obrúč-n-yj*. The stressless stem originating in the other inflected forms (*obruč-í*, *obruč-ú*, *obruč-ý*, etc.) appears in *obruč -óv-yj*.

(14) Class (b) derivatives can satisfy both markedness and MATCH STEM STRESS (MAIN)

a. Derivatives with a disyllabic suffix

	Base: obrúč-, obruč-	MATCH STEM STRESS (MAIN)	MARKEDNESS
☞ (a)	òbruč -óv-yj		
(b)	obrúč -ov-yj		*! (*LAPSER)
(c)	obrúč -ov-ỳj		*! (MSR)
(d)	obrùč -ov- ýj		*! (NONFINAL(MAIN))

b. Derivatives with a monosyllabic suffix

	Base: obrúč-, obruč-	MATCH STEM STRESS (MAIN)	MARKEDNESS
(a)	òbruč-n-ýj		*!(NONFINAL(MAIN))
☞ (b)	obrúč -n-yj		

Pairs like *obruč-óv-yj*, *obrúč-n-yj* are common, as predicted. From class (b) we cite: *lemíš-n-yj, lemeš-év-yj* from *lemíš* 'plowshares'; *jazýč-nyj, jazyk-óv-yj* from *jazýk* 'language';[16] *tabún-nyj*, *tabun-óv-yj* from *tabún* 'herd'; and *čavún-ny-j*, *čavun-óv-yj* from *čavún* 'cast iron'.

On our analysis, both *-ov-yj* and *-n-yj, sjk-yj* derivatives from class (b) nouns can satisfy markedness without violating MATCH STEM STRESS. The analysis is confirmed if such derivatives are both penult-stressed and belong to the Faithful-Base category defined earlier. This is essentially what we find: all class (b) derivatives but one match the stress an attested stem allomorph, and the majority is penult-stressed.

(15) Derivatives of class (b) bases. $N = 221$; 61 derived with *-sjk-yj, -n-yj*, 160 with *-ov-yj*

	Faithful-Base: 220	NotFaithful: 1
Pre-penultimate	2 %	
Penult	74%	1
Final	24%	

Further details on the stress of class (b) derivatives support the analysis. The nouns of class (b) differ on whether a suffixless form exists in their paradigm and, if one does, which case/number combination it expresses: in masculines like *obrúč,* it will be the Nominative singular, but in feminines it will be the Genitive plural. Thus *jaryn-á* 'grain (fem.)' has a suffixless Gen. pl. *jarýn*, the only inflected form providing a stem-stressed allomorph. This form licenses the penult stress in *jarýn-nyj* 'of grain'. We will encounter similar Gen. pl.-based items in other mobile classes: they bear out our claim that any member of the inflectional paradigm of the base noun can provide the stem allomorph needed for a faithful, penult-stressed derivative.

(16) Class (b) bases of feminine nouns

	Base: jaryn-, jarýn (G.pl.)	MATCH STEM STRESS	MARKEDNESS
(a)	jàryn-n-ýj		*! (NON FINAL(MAIN))
☞ (b)	jarýn-n-yj		

What happens if a class (b) noun lacks any stem-final stressed allomorph? That question arises if all its forms have an overt ending, as in pluralless feminines like *tajg-á* 'taiga' or *taft-á* 'taffeta', or in *pluralia tantum* items like *xarč-í* 'food, provisions'. There are 17 derivatives of such nouns in our database.[17] Six other derivatives are based on class (b) pluralless feminine mass nouns whose only stem-stressed allomorph would be a Vocative: e.g. *xalv-á* 'halvah' with a potential Vocative *xálv-o*. We doubt that the Ukrainians address themselves to the halvah in this or any other fashion and count these in the set of defective class (b) nouns lacking any stressed stem. We expect all these nouns to lack penult-stressed *-n-yj* and *-sjk-yj* derivatives, such as **táft-n-yj* etc. Such forms, from such defective bases, would violate MATCH STEM STRESS. But at the same time we expect all these defective nouns to use their *stressless* stem in *-ov-yj* forms. Both expectations are met. Of the 23 derivatives from these defective class (b) bases all but one, the sole unfaithful derivative of class (b) nouns,[18] are *-ov-yj* forms using the stressless stem of their base: e.g. *xalv-óv-yj*, *tajg-óv-yj*, *taft-óv-yj*, *xarč-óv-yj*.[19]

As with class (a), we find a minority of final stressed items – e.g. *dnipr-ov-ýj* from *Dnipr-ó* 'Dniepr' – which we identify again as lexicalized archaisms. This final-stressed minority is larger for class (b) derivatives than for class (a): 25% vs. 5%. The likely reason is that class (a) has a larger share of new words: recent loanwords and productively derived nouns. Their derivatives, e.g. *káktus-ov-yj,* exclude older lexicalized adjectives. It is the latter that provide the main source of final stress. Class (b) derivatives, with fewer loan-based items among them, include a larger proportion of such older forms. If this is the reason, even higher rates of final-stress will be found in classes (c)–(d): class (b) contains some productive derivatives, the agentives in *-ár* and *-ák*, while classes (c) and (d) lack these. This prediction will be supported.[20]

7.2.9 Type (c) nouns and their derivatives

The next two sections are dedicated to M.M. Zoščenko's (1895–1958) portrayal of the painful dilemmas posed by accentually mobile Genitive plurals: for *kočerg-á* 'poker' should that form be *kočérg, kóčerg, kočeróg*, nothing?

Type (c) nouns have stem stress in the singular, and shift it to the ending in the plural: e.g. *jármarok, jarmark-ý* 'fair'. The position of stress inside the stem is unpredictable, as seen in pairs like *učýtelj* 'teacher' *vs. pérepel* 'quail'; *profésor* vs. *jármarok*. All polysyllabic nouns whose Nom.sg. carries word-final stress, e.g. *sekretár*, are excluded from this class and go instead to classes (a) or (b);[21] nonetheless, no property of class (c) stems positively predicts their stress. Accordingly, we posit underlying stress in class (c). Sample class (c) inflectional alternations are seen below.

(17) Ukrainian type (c) nouns with two and three stem allomorphs; selected case forms.

(a) Three allomorphs: *nébo* 'heaven'			(b) Two allomorphs: *profésor* 'professor'		
Sg		Pl	Sg		Pl
N	néb-o ■-○	nebes-á □□-●	N	profésor □■□	profesor-ý □□□-●
G	néb-a ■-○	nebés □■	G	profésor-a □■□-○	profesor-ív □□□-●
D	néb-u ■-○	nebes-ám □□-●	D	profésor-u □■□-○	profesor-ám □□□-●
L	néb-i ■-○	nebes-áx □□-●	L	profésor-i □■□-○	profesor-áx □□□-●

The mechanisms generating accentual alternations in class (c) are briefly discussed next.

7.2.9.1 Accentual contrast between singular and plural in class (c)

Both classes (a) and (c) contain underlyingly stressed stems. What differentiates them? In Yanovich and Steriade (2010), we claim it is class (c)'s preference to keep the singular and plural stems accentually distinct. The analysis can be summarized as follows. A group of Ukrainian nouns are subject to a lexically indexed constraint demanding an accentual contrast between the singular and the plural stems: the two stems must differ in the position of main stress.[22] Without this constraint, stress in each singular and plural form would have been individually optimized relative to the ranked Markedness and Faithfulness constraints. The contrast condition forces one number subparadigm to differentiate its stem from that of the other. The study cited shows that, in all Ukrainian noun types that enforce the singular-plural contrast, it is the singular forms that better satisfy Markedness and

Faithfulness. This is explained if the singular is generated on its own, while the plural, generated in the next step, adjusts its stress to keep it distinct from the already fixed singular. The adjusted stress of the plural necessarily contains additional violations of Markedness and/or Faithfulness.

In the subset of nouns subject to the contrast condition, some stems have underlying stress. These surface faithfully with stem stress in the singular. They are the type (c) nouns. Underlyingly unstressed nouns subject to the contrast constraint surface with ending stress in the singular, and shift stress to the stem in the plural. These are the type (d) nouns. A small third class, the *kóleso* nouns, satisfy paradigm contrast through stem-internal accent shifts.

For present purposes, three properties of class (c) bases matter, and they remain independent of how we derive accent mobility. First, class (c) stems have underlying stress. Their stress can, but need not, be stem-final: it is in *pidóšv-a*, it isn't in *jármarok* or *profésor*. Second, accent mobility creates in *all* class (c) nouns multiple accentual allomorphs: normally two, as in *profésor*; three in nouns like *nébo* or *pidóšva* (cf. (17)). Finally, some class (c) nouns alternate segmentally: Nom. sg. *néb-o,* Nom. pl. *nebes-á*, Gen. pl. *nebés*; Nom. sg. *pidóšv-a,* Nom. pl. *pidošv-ý*, Gen. pl. *pidošóv*. In the next section we use the first two base properties to explain the derivatives' stress. The segmental alternations become relevant later.

7.2.9.2 The derivatives of class (c) nouns

Stress distributions among adjectives derived from class (c) are summarized below.

(18) Class (c) derivatives $N = 164$; 75 with *-n-yj, sjk-yj*, 89 with *-ov-yj*

	Faithful-Base: 93%	Faithful-Related: 6%
Pre-penult	23%	
Penult	39%	100%
Final	38%	

Like class (b), the vast majority of class (c) nouns have accentually faithful derivatives: the Faithful-Base rates are 99% and 93% in classes (b) and (c) vs. 78% in class (a). This difference is expected, since we define faithfulness as matching the stress pattern of any stem allomorph of the base: classes (b)–(c) offer more allomorphs and thus more faithfulness options.

With respect to markedness, class (c) derivatives differ systematically from those of class (b) *and* of class (a). We see this in the rates of penult (unmarked) vs. pre-penult (marked) stress:

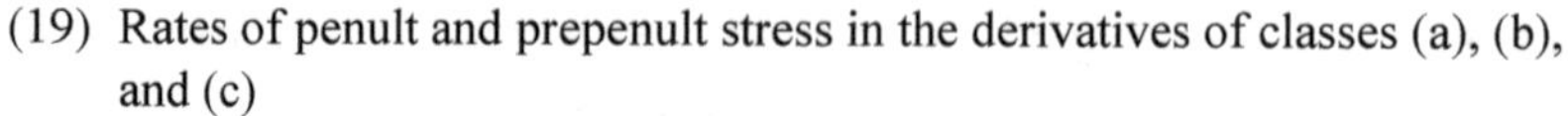
(19) Rates of penult and prepenult stress in the derivatives of classes (a), (b), and (c)

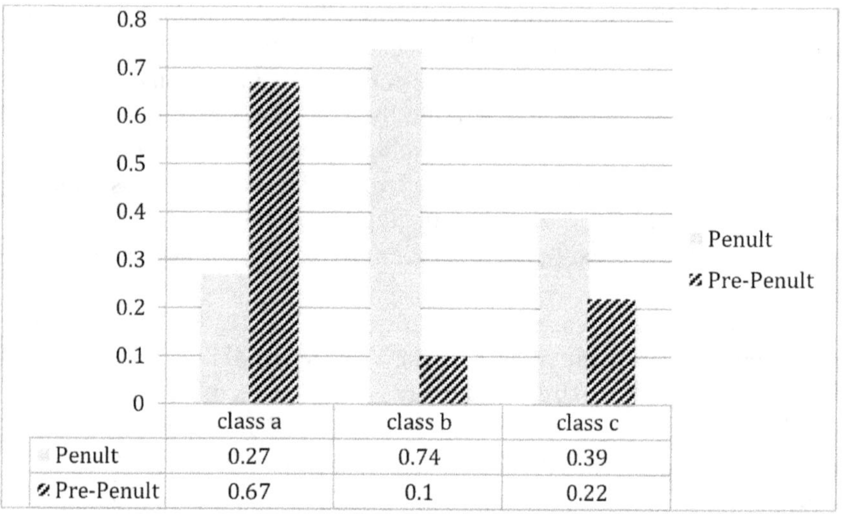

	class a	class b	class c
Penult	0.27	0.74	0.39
Pre-Penult	0.67	0.1	0.22

(19) shows that class (c) derivatives have increased rates of pre-penult stress compared to class (b). What explains this? It's the large number of class (c) bases with pre-final stress, a pattern necessarily absent in class (b). Of the 144 class (c) bases, 90 have pre-final stress, as *jármarok* and *profésor* do. Their derivatives can satisfy both markedness and faithfulness in only one form: the combination of stressless stem + penult-stressed *-óv-yj*, as in *jarmark-óv-yj*. In faithful derivatives suffixed with *-n-yj* or *-sjk-yj*, on the other hand, some markedness constraint must be violated: penult stressed **jarmárk-n-yj, *profesór-sjk-yj* aren't faithful, on any interpretation of faithfulness. We see below that the lesser violation of markedness is to stress the antepenult, e.g. *profésor-sjk-yj*. How does class (b) differ? Most class (b) bases can generate *two* faithful-unmarked combinations: final-stressed stem + *C-yj*, as in *obrúč-n-yj*; and stressless stem + *-óv-yj*, as in *obruč-óv-yj*. It is for this reason that prepenult rates are lower in class (b).

(19) also shows that increased rates of penult stress in class (c) derivatives compared to class (a). What explains that? In faithful derivatives suffixed with *-ov-yj*, class (c) bases provide a stressless stem: e.g. *jarmark-óv-yj*, using the stem of plural *jarmark-ý*. Class (a) nouns lack this variant: a class (a) faithful *-ov-yj* form must have prepenult main stress: e.g. *gúmus-òv-yj*.

Our analysis predicts a further difference between class (a) and class (c) derivatives: pre-antepenult stress is possible among the former, as seen in *gúmus-òv-yj*, but not the latter: **jármark-òv-yj* or **jármark-ov-yj* should be impossible, as seen below.

(20) Class (c) bases can't be stressed before the antepenult

	Base: jármarok, jarmark-	MATCH STEM STRESS	MARKEDNESS
(a)	jármarok-òv-yj		*! (MSR)
(b)	jármarok-ov-yj		*!**(*LAPSER)
☞ (c)	jàrmark-óv-yj		

Indeed, all 35 derivatives with pre-penult stresses from class (c) bases are *antepenult*-stressed (e.g. *profésorsjkyj*). A related prediction is that all such proparoxytone forms should contain *n-yj* and *sjk-yj* suffixes: as seen in (20), the *-ov-yj* derivatives not only have the option of penult stress but must exercise it. This is largely correct: of the 35 items with pre-penult stress, 31 are suffixed with *-sjk-yj* or *-n-yj*. Two of the remaining four have bases that are variously listed as class (a) or (c) in our sources, and a third has the expected variant with penult stress.

Several class (c) nouns have a final-stressed stem allomorph in the zero-suffixed Genitive plural: e.g. *nébo* 'heaven', *nebés,* cf. (17a). We expect this stem to be usable before *-n-yj* and *-sjk-yj,* where it ensures penult stress: e.g. *nebés-n-yj* 'heavenly'. Derivatives from at least four other bases have this third stem. All bear out the expectation:

(21) Class (c) derivatives from the third (Gen.pl.) stem

Base	Base Gen. pl.	Derivative	Gloss
čud-o, čudes-á	čudés	čudés-n-yj	'miracle' 'wonderful'
molýtv-a, molytv-ý	molytóv	molytóv-n-yj	'prayer'
pidóšv-a, pidošv-ý	pidošóv	pidošóv-n-yj	'sole (of a foot)'
tíl-o, tiles-á	tilés	tilés-n-yj	'body', 'corporeal'

A large proportion of class (c) derivatives have final stress, e.g. *step-ov-ýj* 'of a steppe', *porox-ov-ýj* 'of powder'. Many have penult-stressed variants, e.g. *vijsjk-ov-ýj* and *vijsjk-óv-yj* 'military' from *víjsjk-o* 'troups, army', but not all do. It has been our contention throughout that final-stressed recessive derivatives represent lexicalized archaisms. For class (c), this claim is supported by derivatives of recent loans, which are more likely to reflect the currently productive system. The corpus contains 10 such forms from class (c) loans. They behave uniformly. Those suffixed with *-ov-yj* carry penultimate stress and use the stressless plural stem: *tenor-óv-yj* 'of a tenor' based on *ténor*, *tenor-ý*. Those suffixed by *-n-yj, -sjk-yj* carry antepenult stress, as in *kórpus-n-yj*.[24] The absence of final stress in this set shows that NONFINALITY (MAIN) outranks *LAPSER, a point anticipated in (10).

(22) Class (c) productive derivatives: MSR, NONFINALITY (MAIN) >> *LAPSER

	Base: kórpus-, korpus-	MATCH STEM STRESS	NONFINALITY (MAIN)	*LAPSER
(a)	korpus-n-ýj		*!	
(b)	korpús-n-yj	*!		
☞ (c)	kórpus-n-yj			*

We consider now an analysis in which source of antepenult stress in class (c) derivatives is not MSR, NONFINALITY (MAIN) >> *LAPSER but faithfulness to the citation form, the Nominative singular. We name this constraint MATCH CITATION STRESS (defined in the Appendix) and observe that it would have to outrank *LAPSER to select *kórpus-n-yj*.

(23) Class (c) productive derivatives: MATCHCITATIONSTRESS >> *LAPSER

	Base: kórpus, korpus-	MATCHSTEMSTRESS	MATCHCITATION	*LAPSER
(a)	korpus-n-ýj		*!	
(b)	korpús-n-yj	*!	*	
☞ (c)	kórpus-n-yj			*

However, the ranking MATCH CITATION STRESS >> *LAPSER does not generalize to other classes. It predicts antepenult stress as the productive option for all class (b) *-ov-yj* derivatives. This is a first wrong result: of the *-ov-yj* forms from class (b), there are 113 penult-stressed items, like *obruč-óv-yj,* to only three with pre-penult stress (e.g. *targán-ov-yj* from *targán* 'cockroach'). Class (d) will pose comparable difficulties.

(24) Class (c) productive derivatives: MATCHCITATIONSTRESS >> *LAPSER

	Base: obrúč-, obruč-	MATCH STEMSTRESS	MATCHCITATION	*LAPSER
(a)	obruč -óv-yj		*!	
☞ ✖ (b)	obrúč -ov-yj			*

The overall analysis must predict both penult main stress in class (b) *-ov-yj* forms like *obruc-óv-yj* and pre-penult stress in class (c) *-n-yj* and *-sjk-yj* derivatives like *kórpus-n-yj*. The only ranking that achieves both results is MATCH STEM STRESS, NONFINALITY (MAIN) >> *LAPSER, as in (22). Still only an appeal to MATCH CITATION STRESS helps derive the few antepenult-stressed class (b) derivatives like *targán-ov-yj*. As MATCH CITATION STRESS will play a significant role later, we outline the analysis: the constraint is indexed to a lexical class L3 that includes *targán*.

(25) Class (b) antepenult-stressed *-ov-yj* derivatives: MATCHCITATIONSTRESS$_{L3}$ >> *LAPSER

	Base: Nom.sg. targán$_{L3}$, targan-	MATCH STEMSTRESS	MATCH CITATION$_{L3}$	*LAPSER	MATCH CITATION
(a)	targan-óv-yj		*!		*
☞ (b)	targán-ov-yj			*	*

Returning now to class (c) bases like *kórpus, profésor, jármarok* we must ask what MATCH CITATION STRESS$_{L3}$ might predict for them. It predicts that, if any of these items belongs to the L3 set, *its -ov-yj* derivative will carry stress on a pre-antepenult syllable. This, however, we have seen is impossible in class (c). We resolve the difficulty without abandoning the basic idea. MATCH CITATION STRESS$_{L3}$ can induce violations of *LAPSER, but not of MSR or *EXTENDED LAPSER. To illustrate the necessary ranking we assume now that class (c) *jármarok* belongs to the same lexical class L_3 as *targán*.

(26) Class (c) pre-antepenult stresses are impossible, even in items belonging to the L3 class. *EXTLAPSER, MSR >> MATCH CITATION$_{L3}$

	Base: Nom.sg. jármarok$_{L3}$, jarmark-	*EXTLAPSER	MSR	MATCH CITATION$_{L3}$
(a)	jármarok-ov-yj	*!*		
(b)	jármarok-òv-yj		*!	
☞ (c)	jàrmark-óv-yj			*

7.2.10 Derivatives of type (d) nouns

Our corpus contains 101 derivatives from class (d). In this class, as in (c), a contrast between the singular and the plural stems is enforced. Class (d) stems are unaccented in all singular forms. In the plural, some stem syllable carries the accent. We attribute this to the fact that (d)-roots are underlyingly unstressed: singular forms stress the endings because the singular is faithful to the stressless quality of the root. The stressed stems of the plural result from contrast-driven stress retraction.

Most class (d) nouns retract stress in the plural to the last stem syllable, as in (27). A few retract to the initial, but keep final stress in one plural form, the Genitive, (27b). Class (d) stems are further differentiated by epenthesis: many end in consonant clusters that require epenthesis in the zero-suffixed Genitive plural, (27c): /jadr/→ [jáder].

(27) Class (d) accentual alternations in inflection: selected case-number forms

a. Two stem allomorphs: *kovbas-á* sausage'			b. Three allomorphs: *syrot-á* 'orphan'		
Sg		Pl	Sg		Pl
N	kovbas-á □□-●	kovbás-y □■-○	N	syrot-á □□-●	sýrot-y ■□-○
G	kovbas-ý □□-●	kovbás □■	G	syrot-ý □□-●	syrít □■

c. Stems with epenthesis: *jadr-ó* 'grain'		
Sg		Pl
N, A	jadr-ó □-●	jádr-a ■-○
G	jadr-á □□-●	jáder ■□

Our analysis predicts that derivatives of *kovbasá* and *syrotá* type-nouns behave like those of class (b) *obrúč*: that's because all three types have an unstressed stem allomorph, plus a final-stressed one. For derivatives of nouns like *jadr-ó*, predictions are more complex: before a suffixal consonant, stems like *jadr-* must undergo epenthesis to avoid sonority-dipping CrC, e.g. **jadr-nyj*. To satisfy MATCH STEM STRESS, the epenthetic stem should have initial stress, i.e. *jáder-n-yj,* as its base counterpart does. These predictions are partly borne out, as seen below. First, an overview of stress in class (d) derivatives:

(28) Derivatives from class *d* bases. *N* = 101; 45 in *-ov-yj*, 56 in *-sjk-yj, -n-yj.*

	Faithful-to-Base : 94%	Faithful-Related: 3%	Not Faithful: 3%
Pre-penult	2%	0	0
Penult	61%	100%	100%
Final	35%	0	0

All faithful adjectives in *-n-yj, -sjk-yj* from (d)-bases like *kovbas-á, syrot-á* use the stem of the Genitive plural, e.g. *kovbás, syrít,* and thus achieve penult stress: e.g. *kovbás-n-yj, syrít-sjk-yj.* These are parallel to class (c) items like *čudés-n-yj, molytóv-n-yj* and, like them, they confirm the use of oblique allomorphs of the stem in the formation of derivatives. As anticipated, the Gen. pl. stem of class (d) nouns functions in the same way as the Nom. sg. of class (b) items.

Epenthetic bases like *jadr-ó, jáder* yield both penult and antepenult-stressed derivatives: *jáder-n-yj* but also *jadér-n-yj.* The variation between these is parallel to the variation between faithful *káktus-ov-yj* and unmarked *kaktus-óv-yj* from class (a) bases. Penult stressed *jadér-n-yj* and similar forms[25] represent the small minority of class (d) derivatives that do not belong to the 'Faithful-to-Base' class. Given the structure of stem allomorphs from class (d), the only source of penult stress in a not-'Faithful-to-Base' derivative is stress on such epenthetic vowels.

The high rate of final accented derivatives from class (d) is the only deviation from predicted patterns. Examples include *golov-n-ýj* (*golov-á,* pl. *gólov-y* 'head'), *stin-n-ýj* (*stin-á,* pl. *stín-y* 'wall'), *groz-ov-ýj* (*groz-á,* pl. *gróz-y* 'threat'). These satisfy MATCH STEM STRESS, but alternative forms like *stin-n-ýj* and *groz-ov-ýj* could have been both faithful and unmarked **stínnyj, *grozóvyj*. The constraint MATCH CITATION$_{L3}$ explored in (25) could be at work in favouring the final stress of *golov-n-ýj, stin-n-ýj*. There is variation: similar bases – e.g. *stin-á* 'wall' vs. *strun-á* 'cord, string' – have different derivatives, *stin-n-ýj* vs. *strún-n-yj*. This is expected: MATCH CITATION$_{L3}$ is lexically indexed.

Appeal to MATCH CITATION does not however explain why two-thirds of the class (d) derivatives in *-ov-yj* (30/45) have final stress. Having by now surveyed derivatives from all major classes, we can address this problem more generally. We compare in (29) final stress rates in *-ov-yj* vs. *-n-yj*, *-sjk-yj* forms across all accent classes: in each class, we calculate the percentage of *-ov-yj* and of *-n/sjk-yj* derivatives with final stress. We observe a steady increase in the relative frequency of final stress going from class (a) to the less productive classes (b), then (c), then (d). The increase affects mostly the *-ov-yj* forms. The comparison suggests that final stress is concentrated in the *-ov-yj* adjectives and, among these, that it resides mostly in the less productive classes, especially (d), the class with the smallest membership.

(29) Rates of final stress in *-n-yj* and *-sjk-yj* vs. *-ov-yj* forms across accent classes 's, n' = forms suffixed with *-n-yj and -sjk-yj*; 'v' = forms suffixed with *-ov-yj*.

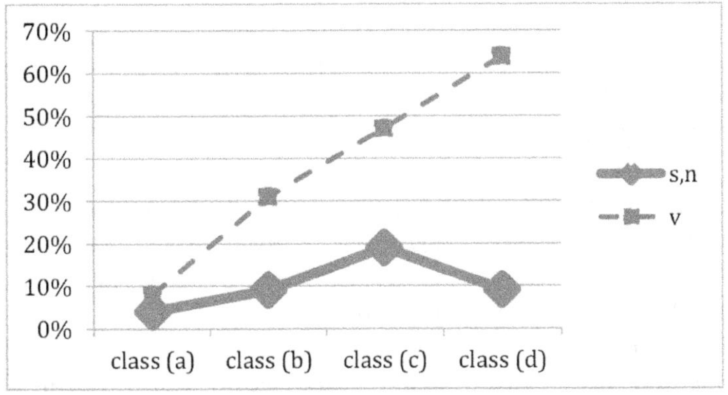

The trends in (29) suggest that the historical source of final stressed adjectives is to be found among *-ov-yj* forms, where it is still to some extent preserved. This is consistent with our claim that most final-stressed adjectives are archaisms.

7.2.11 Derivatives of *kóleso*-type nouns

A fifth accentual class involves stem-internal accent shifts: in every singular form, stress falls on a non-final stem syllable (e.g. *kóles-o* 'wheel', *kóles-a, kóles-u,* etc.), while the plural has stress on a later syllable, still inside the stem (e.g. *kolés-a* 'wheels', *kolís, kolés-am*). The corpus contains nine derivatives from such nouns, eight of which satisfy MATCH STEM STRESS. The remaining one (*pered-ov-ýj* 'foremost', from *péred, peréd-y* 'front') belongs to the final-stressed category, common among older *-ov-yj* forms. All but one faithful derivative of the *koleso* class are stressed on the penult. This one deviation, a lawful one, is *postél-ev-yj* (30b): no other stress pattern in a faithful class (d) *ov-yj*-derivative could be both faithful and less marked.

(30) Faithful derivatives of *kóleso* nouns
  a. Penult stressed
     tsygán-sjk-yj 'of a Gypsy' (from *tsýgan, tsygán-y* 'Gypsy')
     kolés-n-yj 'of a wheel' (from *kóles-o, kolés-a* 'wheel')
  b. Stressed on a pre-penult
     postél-ev-yj 'of bed' (*póstilj, postél-i* 'bed')

These adjectives are consistent with our overall picture of Ukrainian recessive derivatives: they carry penult stress, but only if a stem allomorph is available to license it. The stem allomorph they use is never identical to the one contained in the citation form: markedness precludes that.

7.2.12 Matching segmental and prosodic properties in stem allomorphs

In some Ukrainian nouns, stems that differ accentually differ also segmentally. One example is *kóleso, kolís* (Gen. pl.). Another is 'evening', *véčir* (Nom.sg.) *večor-ý* (Nom.pl.), from class (c). A no-longer productive process changes *o* to *i* before the former jers appearing in some Nom. sg. and Gen. pl. forms: e.g. *véčor-ъ → véčir, kolés-ъ → kolís* (cf. Zhovtobrjux *et al.* 1979: § 75 for a description of the change).

The question for us is how the derivatives of such nouns combine the accentual and segmental information provided by their bases in forming their own stems.

Imagine a faithful *-ov-yj* derivative of *véčir.* If optimally stressed on the penult, it could be *večir-óv-yj* or *večor-óv-yj*. MATCH STEM STRESS is satisfied either way. Its formulation in (4), and the revised Appendix formulation, demand only that each syllable, independently of others, find an identically stressed counterpart in some allomorph of the base. That matching process is represented in (31), where candidate stems appear, separated into syllables, in the second row. Stem allomorphs appear in the leftmost column. A perfect match between syllables is a cell marked by '+'. When syllables match accentually but not segmentally, the cell is marked by a (+). Even if we consider only perfect matches, it can be seen that both candidates, *večir-óv-yj* and *večor-óv-yj*, pass MATCH STEM STRESS in its present formulation: each syllable, in each stem, *večir-* or *večor-,* is marked by a + in this table.

(31) Matching syllables of the derivative's stem in the base stem

	večor-óv-yj		*večir-óv-yj*	
	ve -	*čor*	*ve -*	*čir*
véčir		(+)		+
véčor-a		+		(+)
večor-ý	+	+	+	(+)

In fact however only *večor-óv-yj* is attested.[26] To constrain the selection, we consider a more restrictive matching system that requires the entire stem of the candidate to find *one* correspondent among the allomorphs of the inflected base stem. We replace MATCH STEM STRESS with two constraints, both undominated. One of them, call it MATCH STEM, requires each derivative's stem to find a correspondent stem in one of the base forms. The other, IDENT MAINSTRESS BD (abbreviated IDMSTRESS) requires identity of main stress between each pair of correspondent syllables in each pair of correspondent stems. Further identity constraints, including MAX, DEP, IDENT F, promote segmental identity between correspondent stems. This system favours candidate derivatives whose stem corresponds, in the case in (31), to *véčir*, or to *véčor-*, or to *večor-,* but not to composites created, Frankenstein-style, from bits and pieces of each:[27] unattested *večir-óv-yj* is excluded because its stem is just such a composite. Below superscripts identify correspondent stem pairs.

(32) MATCH STEM + IDENT MAINSTRESS BD instead of MATCH STEM STRESS

	Base: véčir¹, večor²-	MATCH STEM	IDMSTRESS	MARKEDNESS
(a)	véčir¹-òv-yj			*! (MSR)
(b)	vèčir¹-óv-yj		*!	
☞ (c)	vèčor² -óv-yj			

Candidates based on the third stem *véčor-* don't contribute to the argument and are ignored.

The point thus far is that the combination Match Stem + IdentMStress succeeds in selecting the one attested candidate, *vèčor-óv-yj*, while Match Stem Stress (either (4) or the version in the Appendix) can't decide between *vèčor-óv-yj* and *vèčir-óv-yj*: both satisfy markedness and both pass Match Stem Stress.

The more restrictive mechanism Match Stem + IdentMStress is representative of the entire Ukrainian system. Nouns comparable to *véčir* have *-ov-yj* derivatives parallel to *vèčor-óv-yj*, not **vèčir-óv-yj*. As predicted, the same kinds of bases opt for a stem-stressed allomorph like *véčir* before *-n-yj*, *-sjk-yj*. Bases generating both derivative types are in (33a), others in (33b-c). Indices are used as in (32); stems superscripted as ^{1} appear in the Nom.sg.

(33) Distribution of stems in derivatives of *véčir*-type bases

	Base stems	Class	*-ov-yj* forms	*-n-yj, -sjk-yj*	Gloss
a.	jávir^1, jávor^2-, javor^3-	(c)	javor^3-óv-yj	jávir^1-sjk-yj	'maple sp.'
	kólir^1, kólor^2-, kolor^3-	(c)	kolor^3-óv-yj	kólir^1-n-yj	'colour'
	tábir^1, tábor^2-, tabor^3-	(c)	tabor^3-óv-yj	tábir^1-n-yj	'camp'
	bolót^1-, bolot^2-, bolít^3	(c)	bolot^2-óv-yj	bolót^1-n-yj	'swamp, bog'
b.	óvid^1, óvod^2-, ovod^3-	(c)	ovod^3-óv-yj		'cleg'
	óbid^1, óbod^2-, obod^3-	(c)	obod^3-óv-yj		'rim'
	txír^1, txor^2-	(b)	txor^2-év-yj		'ferret'
	čol^1-, čól^2-, číl^3	(d)	čol^1-óv-yj		'forehead'
c.	lemíš^1, lemeš^2-	(b)		lemíš^1-n-yj	'ploughshare'
	jákir^1, jákor^2-, jakor^3-	(c)		jákir^1-n-yj	'anchor'
	syrot^1-, sýrot^2-, syrít^3-	(d)		syrít^3-sjk-yj	'orphan'

This table illustrates the following. When a final CiC syllable appears only in a stressed allomorph of the base (as with *jávir, lemíš, syrít*), the CiC syllable appears only in derivatives whose stem is stressed (e.g. *jávirsjkyj, lemíšnyj, syrítsjkyj*). Conversely, when the stem of the derivative must be stressless, the CiC syllable belonging to the stressed stem allomorph is absent: e.g. *javoróvyj, txorévyj, čolóvyj*, not **javiróvyj*, **txirévyj*, **čilóvyj*. This is exactly as predicted by the new mode of evaluation in (32).

The same table reveals a new detail. Under the analysis on (32), some derivatives retain a choice between CVCiC and CVCoC if the two allomorphs have identical accentual properties. Thus (32) allows both *jávir^1-sjk-yj* and hypothetical **jávor^2-sjk-yj*, both *bolót^1-nyj* and hypothetical **bolít^3-nyj*. In fact, when the CVCiC stem is the Nom. sg. only derivatives using the

CVCiC stem are found: e.g. *jávir¹-sjk-yj, kólir¹-n-yj, tábir¹-n-yj, lemíš¹-n-yj, jákir¹-n-yj*. On the other hand, forms like *bolót¹-nyj* show that when this jer-induced [i] appears at the end of the Gen.pl. (*bolít*), and markedness is equally satisfied by using the Nom.sg. stem (*bolót-o*), the [i] is being kept out of the derivative. Finally, items like *syrít³-sjk-yj* reconfirm a point made earlier: the Gen.pl. stem (*syrít*) can be used if it alone satisfies accentual markedness.

What we observe here is a *general* MATCH CITATION effect: the lexically unindexed MATCH CITATION constraint breaks a tie between otherwise equivalent candidates. The general MATCH CITATION constraint must be lower ranked than markedness, to avoid *LAPSER or MSR violating forms like **jávir-ov-yj, *jávir-òv-yj*.

(34) MATCH CITATION can break a tie, but can only to do that.

	Base: jávir¹, jávor²-, javor³-	MARKEDNESS		MATCH CITATION
(a)	jàvor³-sjk-ýj	*!(NFIN)		
☞ (b)	jávir¹-sjk-yj		* (*LAPSER)	
(c)	jávor²-sjk-yj		* (*LAPSER)	*!

	Base: jávir¹, jávor²-, javor³-	MARKEDNESS	MATCH CITATION
(a)	jávir¹-òv-yj	*!(MSR)	
☞ (b)	jàvor³-óv-yj		*

Several items deviate from the pattern in (33), but do so in a systematic way: all are unfaithful derivatives whose stems are segmentally identical to a citation form but which mismatch its stress.

(35) Accentually unfaithful derivatives whose stem is segmentally identical to the Nom.sg.

Base stems	Class	*-n-yj, -sjk-yj* forms	Gloss
próstir¹, próstor²-, prostor³-	(c)	prostír¹-n-yj	'space'
storon¹-, stóron²-, storín³	(d)	storón¹-n-ij	'side'

These are further instances of lexically indexed MARKEDNESS outranking faithfulness, an option formalized earlier as MARKEDNESS$_L$ >> MATCH STEM STRESS. In the analysis below, we follow the decision to substitute MATCH STEM + IDENT STRESS BD for the earlier MATCH STEM STRESS: MATCH STEM is kept undominated and lexically indexed Markedness (here *LAPSER$_{L2}$) is allowed to outrank only IDENT STRESS BD. Among the resulting unfaithfully stressed stems, MATCH CITATION again chooses the citation form, this time in accentually modified form.

(36) Match Citation breaks a tie among unfaithfully stressed options

	Base: próstir^{1}, próstor^{2}-, prostor^{3} (L2)	*LapseR$_{L2}$	IdMStress BD	Match Citation
(a)	próstir^{1}-n-yj	*!		
☞ (b)	prostír^{1}-n-yj		*	
(c)	prostór^{2}-n-yj, prostór^{3}-n-yj		*	*!

Forms like *targán-ov-yj* (from class (b) *targán*) and *golov-n-ýj* (from class (d) *golov-á*) had earlier suggested that lexically indexed Match Citation$_{L3}$ outranks at least some accentual markedness constraints. This too is expressible in the revised analysis:

(37) Match Citation$_{L3}$ >> Markedness

	Base: golov^{1}-, gólov^{2}-, golív^{3} (L3)	IdMStress BD	Match Citation$_{L3}$	Markedness
☞ (a)	golov^{1}-n-ýj			*(NonFinal)
(b)	golív^{3}-n-yj	*!	*!	
(c)	golóv^{1}-n-ýj	*!		

	Base: targán^{1}, targan^{2}- (L3)	IdMStress BD	Match Citation$_{L3}$	Markedness
☞ (a)	targán^{1}-ov-yj			*(LapseR)
(b)	targan^{2}-óv-yj		*!	

The partial rankings established above are integrated below into a single hierarchy.

(38)

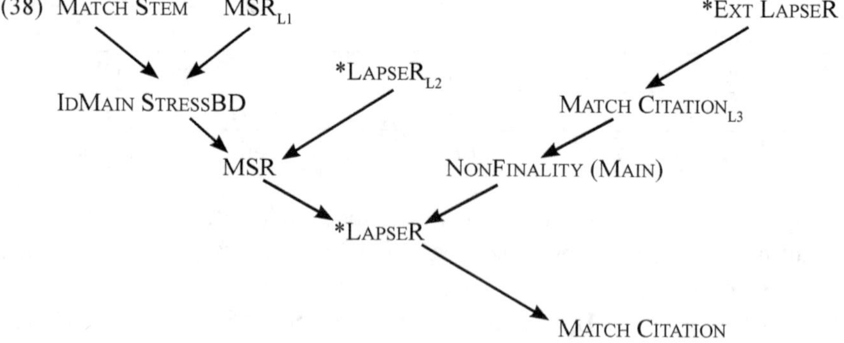

Ranking arguments summarized:

MATCHSTEM, MSR_{L1} >> IDMAINSTRESS BD	*fòsfor-óv-yj* ≻ **fósfor-òv-yj* (L_1)
MATCHSTEM, IDMAINSTRESS BD >> MSR	*gúmus-òv-yj* ≻ **gùmus-óv-yj* ($\neg L_1$)
MATCHSTEM, $*LAPSER_{L2}$ >> IDMAINSTRESS BD	*mètal-év-yj* ≻ **métal-èv-yj* (L_2)
*EXTLAPSER >> $MATCHCITATION_{L3}$	*jàrmark-óv-yj* ≻ **jármark-ov-yj* (*if* the base is in L_3)
$MATCHCITATION_{L3}$ >> NONFINALITY(MAIN)	*golov-n-ýj* ≻ **golóv-n-yj* (L_3, cit. *golov-á*)
$MATCHCITATION_{L3}$ >> *LAPSER	*targán-ov-yj* ≻ **targan-óv-yj* (L_3, cit. *targán*)
NONFINALITY(MAIN) >> *LAPSER	*profésor-sjk-yj* ≻ **profesor-sjk-ýj*
*LAPSER >> MATCHCITATION	*obruč-óv-yj* ≻ **obrúč-ov-yj*
MSR >> MATCHCITATION	*tènor-óv-yj* ≻ **ténor-òv-yj*

Having earlier acknowledged variation, we should also highlight the existence of a predicted invariant aspect in the accent of Ukrainian derivatives. There are only two circumstances under which pre-penultimate main stress occurs in these derivatives: (a) when the base offers no stem whose use can license a penult stress (*gúmusòvyj, profésorsjkyj, postélevyj)* and (b) when the derivative's stem is evaluated by $MATCHCITATION_{L3}$ (*targánovyj)*. Among the 1091 forms of the database, there are 430 pre-penultimate stressed derivatives and all but two fit this description.[28] Our analysis predicts exactly this.

We close this section with a summary of how our analysis derives each position where main stress is attested in the Ukrainian recessive derivatives.

(39) Main stress positions of Ukrainian derivatives and their grammatical sources

Final stress:

- Lexically listed
- Ranking: IDENTSTRESS BD, MATCH $CITATION_{L3}$ >> MARKEDNESS (NONFINALITY(MAIN))
  - *-n-yj, sjk-yj* forms like *golov-n-ýj,* whose base citation form is ending-stressed.

Penult stress:

- Ranking: IDENTSTRESS BD >> MARKEDNESS
  - *-n-yj, sjk-yj* forms like *obrúč-n-yj*, whose bases have a final-stressed allomorph;
  - *-ov-yj* forms like *obruč-óv-yj* whose bases have a stressless stem allomorph
- Ranking: MSR_{L1} or $LAPSER_{L2}$ >> IDENT STRESS BD (any base+suffix combination)
  - *-ov-yj* forms like *fòsfor-óv-yj*
  - *-n-yj, sjk-yj* forms like *jadér-n-yj*

Pre-penult stress:

- Ranking: IDMSTRESS BD >> MARKEDNESS (*LAPSER or MSR)
  - *-n-yj, sjk-yj* forms like *profésor-sjk-yj*, whose base lacks a final-stressed allomorph
  - *-ov-yj* e.g. *gúmus-òv-yj*, *làbradór-ov-yj,* whose bases lack a stressless allomorph.
- Ranking: IDMSTRESS BD, NONFINALITY(MAIN) >> *LAPSER
  - *-n-yj, sjk-yj* forms like *profésor-sjk-yj*, *jávir-sjk-yj*
- Ranking: IDMSTRESS BD, MATCH CITATION$_{L3}$ >> MARKEDNESS (*LAPSER)
  - *-ov-yj* forms like *targán-ov-yj*, whose base citation stem is final-stressed

7.2.12 Summary: Evidence for MATCH STEM STRESS in Ukrainian adjectives

Recall the expectations derived in section 7.1.4 from current theories of what may count as a base. Consider first the idea that each derivative type has exactly one base. Had the stress of adjectival derivatives been derived by reference to just one form – the underlying form or some surface form, such as the base citation form – the stress system of Ukrainian derivatives would be quite different. If the base was the citation form, no noun with a *stressed* citation stem, e.g. *obrúč,* could generate a derivative like *obruč-év-yj*. If the base was the underlying form, no noun with an underlyingly stressless root, e.g. */obruč/*, could generate a faithful stressed-stem derivative like *obrúč-n-yj.* Both types are in fact used in adjectival derivatives. We conclude that accentual faithfulness is not evaluated relative to a unique reference term.

Having shown that a unique-base model is inadequate for this system, we now review the argument that Faithfulness plays *some* role in it. Suppose that the Ukrainian derivatives' stress was entirely free to deviate from their bases: then penult-stressed pairs like *obruč-év-yj*, *obrúč-n-yj* would be predicted, but it would be hard to explain the basic difference between class (a) derivatives and those from other classes. This difference is that class (a) derivatives are, as a rule, pre-penult stressed (*gúmus-ov-yj, labradór-ov-yj*), while most other derivatives are penult stressed. MATCH STEM explains this fact in a general way. If faithfulness is satisfied by reference to any surface allomorph of the base, the attested distribution is the expected one: bases with *no* allomorph useable to promote penult stress (class (a) *gúmus*) get pre-penult stress in all their faithful derivatives; bases with just *one* useful allomorph provide a chance at penult stress for one of their faithful derivatives and force Markedness violations in others (*jávir, javor-*), while bases with two useful allomorphs (*obrúč, obruč-*) can have two distinct types of unmarked and faithful derivatives.

7.3 Russian evidence for Match Stem Stress

We analyse next an inflection dependence effect involving MATCH STEM in the derivational morphology of Russian. The accent in Russian inflected nouns is broadly similar to that of Ukrainian. The two languages also have accentually similar derivational suffixes.

There are differences too. First, Russian has additional accentual types, variants of classes (b) and (c), where the Nom. pl. bears stem stress. These were illustrated by *volk* and *gvozdj* in (2). Nouns from these classes are so frequent that Zaliznjak (1985) sets them up as the distinct accentual classes (e) and (f). Second, Russian adjectival inflection distinguishes 'short' and 'long' forms, the former mostly used as predicates. In the long forms, Russian adjectives have columnar stress like most Ukrainian adjectives. But in the short forms, Russian has many different accentual types, exemplified below. As there is almost no accentual mobility in Ukrainian adjectives, we did not consider any deadjectival derivatives in that language. In Russian, we will.

Turning to the derivational morphology, both Ukrainian and Russian derivational suffixes are divided into dominant and recessive. In recessive derivatives, stress is determined jointly by properties of the base stem and of the affix. It is such suffixes that provide the Russian evidence for an analysis in terms of MATCH STEM + IDENT STRESS BD. In this section, we discuss three recessive suffixes whose stress behavior is expected if these constraints are undominated. The Russian suffixes we consider have distinct accentual preferences reflecting, we argue, their underlying accentual status: one is stressed, the others are stressless.

(40) Russian recessive suffixes:

a. Stressed: *-išš-* (denominal, forming augmentative nouns)
okn-íšš-e 'huge window' <= *okn-ó* 'window'

b. Stressless: *-ov-* (denominal, forming possessive adjectives):
vín-ov 'of wine' <= *vin-ó*, Nom.pl *vín-a* 'wine'

c. Stressless: *-ostj-* (de-adjectival, forming creates nouns denoting qualities):
grámotn-ostj 'literacy' <= *grámotn-yj* 'literate'

We show that the accentual properties of these affixes are preserved only when an appropriate stem allomorph is found among the inflected forms of the base noun, allowing an underlyingly stressed suffix to surface with stress, and a stressless one to surface without it. When the base offers no allomorph allowing the affix to maintain its underlying stress value, the derivative is faithful to its unique base, or else a paradigm gap arises. None of these suffixes is allowed to generate an accentual allomorph of the stem that is not already present in the inflectional paradigm of the base: all are lexically conservative.

The idea of lexical conservatism is, to our knowledge, new in the literature on Russian stress. In particular, it distinguishes our take on the data from that of Zaliznjak (1985), to whom we are indebted for finding affixes relevant for our argument and for descriptive generalizations. In addition to Zaliznjak's high-level descriptions, we use primary data from the accentual dictionary Zaliznjak (1977), and from work with native speakers of Russian.

7.3.1 *-išš-* keeps its underlying accent, subject to MATCH STEM STRESS

Ivlieva (2009) shows that the augmentative *-išš-* surfaces as stressed when attached to a base that independently possesses a stressless stem allomorph (41b-f). Below, we amplify her evidence. When no such allomorph is generated in the inflection of the base, the suffix surfaces stressless, (41a). The stressless stem allomorph that *-išš-* prefers is underlined below. It may come from any case/number combination: in type (b) masculines, a stressless stem is found in any form other than the Nom.sg., (41b); in type (c), it is the plural forms that offer it, (41c); in type (d), it is the singular that has stressless stems, (41d); bases of types (e), (f) behave like (c), (b), except that the Nom. Pl. stem is stressed and thus unusable with *-išš-*.

(41) Russian derivatives with *-išš-* from bases of major accentual paradigms

a. type *a* noun → no stress on *-išš-* (35 examples in Zaliznjak 1977)
Base: NomSg. *jám-a*, GenSg. *jám-y* 'pothole'
=>Derivative: *jám-išš-a*, **jam-íšš-*a

b. type *b* noun → stressed *-íšš-* (25 examples in Zaliznjak 1977)
Base: NomSg. *xvóst*, GenSg. *xvost-á* 'tail'
=>Derivative: *xvost-íšš-e*,* *xvóst-išš-e*

c. type *c* noun → stressed *-išš-* (11 examples in Zaliznjak 1977)
Base: NomSg. *dóm*, GenSg. *dóm-a*, NomPl *dom-á*, GenPl. *dom-óv* 'house'
=>Derivative: *dom-íšš-e*, **dóm-išš-e*

d. type *d* noun → stressed *-íšš-* (11 examples in Zaliznjak 1977)
Base: NomSg *okn-ó*, GenSg *okn-á*, NomPl *ókn-a*, GenPl *ókon* 'window'
=>Derivative: *okn-íšš-e*, **ókn-išš-*e

e. type *e* noun → stressed *-íšš-* (8 examples in Zaliznjak 1977)
Base: NomSg *vólk*, GenSg *vólk-a*, NomPl *vólk-i*, GenPl *volk-óv* 'wolf'
=>Derivative: *volč-íšš-e*, **vólč-išš-e*

f. type *f* noun → stressed *-íšš-* (7 examples in Zaliznjak 1977)
Base: NomSg *pleč-ó*, GenSg *pleč-á* NomPl *pléč-i*, GenPl *pleč-éj* 'shoulder'
=>Derivative: *pleč-íšš-e*, **pléč-išš-e*

In sum, whenever the base provides a stressless stem allomorph – everywhere except in class (a) – the suffix *-íšš-* preserves its stress. We analyse this by ranking IDENT STRESS$_{išš}$, a lexically indexed IO faithfulness constraint, above root-faithfulness, IDENT STRESS ROOT IO. In turn, IDENT STRESS$_{išš}$ is outranked by MATCH STEM and IDENT STRESS BD: we abbreviate the pair as MATCH + IDSTRESS. The ranking MATCH STEM + IDSTRESS >> IDENT STRESS$_{affix}$ prevents the suffixal properties from being preserved at the expense of stem faithfulness. This ranking is a hallmark of recessive affixes in modern Russian.

(42) Analysis of *-íšš-* derivatives.

a. The base has no stressless stem allomorph: type (a) base.

	Base: škól- Suffix: -íšš	MATCH+IDSTRESS	IDENT STRESS$_{išš}$ IO	IDSTRESS ROOT IO
☞ (a)	škól-išš-e		*	
(b)	škol-íšš-e	*!		*

b. The base has a stressless stem allomorph: type (c) base.

	Base: dóm¹-, dom²- Suffix: -íšš	MATCH+IDSTRESS	IDENT STRESS$_{išš}$ IO	IDSTRESS ROOT IO
(a)	dóm¹-išš -e		*!	
☞ (b)	dom²-íšš-e			*

This analysis is confirmed by the *-išš*-derivatives of two less common accentual types. The first of these is the Russian counterpart of the Ukrainian *kóleso* type, a set of nouns where stress shifts stem-internally in the plural: e.g. Russian *ózer-o* 'lake', pl. *ozjór-a*. Accordingly, these nouns lack a stressless stem allomorph. As predicted, the *ózero*-nouns of Russian give rise to stem-stressed *-išš*-derivatives, differing in this respect from all other Russian mobile stress types.

(43) Russian *-išš-* derivatives from *ózer-o*-nouns
Base: NomSg *ózer-o*, GenSg *ózer-a*, NomPl *ozjór-a* 'lake'
=>Derivative: *ózer-išš-e*, **ozer-íšš-e*[29]

A last class of *-išš-* derivatives is based on class (a) nouns that have an exceptionally stressed Locative singular ending. These class (a) nouns thus possess a stressless stem allomorph in their inflectional paradigm, e.g. *grjaz-í* 'dirt-2nd Loc.sg'. The *-išš-* derivatives based on this type are listed by Zaliznjak (1977) as having suffixal stress, unlike all other type (a) derivatives.

(44) Type (a) nouns with exceptional LocSg → stressed *-išš-* (3 examples in Zaliznjak 1977)
Base: NomSg *grjázj*, GenSg *grjázj-i*, 2nd LocSg *(v) grjazj-í* 'dirt'
=>Derivative: *grjazj-íšš-a*, **grjázj-išš-a*

Our analysis explains all but two of the 104 augmentative *-išš-* derivatives in Zaliznjak (1977). These exceptions – *skuč-íšš-a* 'great boredom' and *von-íšš-a* 'great stink' – are based on class (a) nouns: they are unexpected in that the base nouns lack a stressless stem allomorph.[30]

Additional relevant data is presented by Melvold (1989: chapter 1) in her discussion of derivatives labelled as [-dominant] and either [+accented], like *-išš-* or [-accented], like *-nyk-*. A preliminary check of Melvold's evidence suggests that it is consistent with our analysis: all [-dominant] affixes are lexically conservative, like *-išš-*.

7.3.2 Unstressed possessive *-ov-*

The suffix *-ov-* forms possessive adjectives and family names. Data on its accentual behaviour can be found in V. Kiparsky (1962: 264ff). In the terms of the current analysis, *-ov-* is the stressless counterpart of *-išš-*: it seeks a stressed stem. We infer from this that the suffix is underlyingly unstressed.[31] As most noun paradigms provide at least one stressed allomorph of the stem, this requirement is usually satisfied. The only bases that force *-ov-* to be stressed are from class (b): all (b) nouns create *-ov-* derivatives with suffix stress.[32]

(45) Russian derivatives with the possessive *-ov-*:
a. type (a) base (constant stem stress):
Base *arbúz* 'watermelon'
=> Derivative *arbúz-ov*
b. type (b) base (ending stress):
Base: *most*, GenSg *most-á* 'bridge'
=> Derivative *most-óv*
Base: *staríк*, GenSg *starik-á* 'old man'
=> Derivative *starik-óv*
c. type (c) base (stem stress in the Sg, ending stress in the Pl):
Base: *glaz*, GenSg *gláz-a*, NomPl *glaz-á*, DatPl *glaz-ámi* 'eye'
=> Derivative *gláz-ov*

d. type (d) base (ending stress in the Sg, stem stress in the Pl):
Base: *vin-ó*, GenSg *vin-á,* NomPl *vín-a*, DatPl *vín-ami* 'wine'
=> Derivative *vín-ov*
e. type (e) base (stem stress in the Sg and NomPl, end. stress in the rest of the Pl):
Base: *volk*, GenSg *vólk-a,* NomPl *vólk-i*, GenPl *volk-óv*, DatPl *volk-ámi*, 'wolf'
=> Derivative *vólk-ov*
f. type (f) base (ending stress everywhere except NomPl, stem stress in NomPl):
Base: *ruk-á*, GenSg *ruk-í,* NomPl *rúk-i*, DatPl *ruk-ámi* 'hand'
=> Derivative: *rúk-ov*
Base: *golov-á*, GenSg *golov-ý,* NomPl *gólov-y*, DatPl *golov-ámi* 'head'
=> Derivative: *gólov-ov*

(46) Summary of the stress of possessive *-ov-* derivatives:
a. base is of accentual type *a, c, d, e, f* => *-ov-* derivative
b. base is of accentual type *b* => *-óv-* derivative

If *-ov-* is underlyingly stressless, a parallel ranking to that used for *-išš-* (MATCH STEM STRESS >> IDENT STRESS$_{OV}$ >> IDENT STRESS ROOT IO) derives most of the data in (45). The *ov*-derivatives of class (b) nouns pose a problem, and this is addressed below.

(47) Analyses of *-ov-* derivatives from nouns of types (a) and (c-f).
a. The base is a type (c) noun:

	Base: gólos[1]-, golos[2]- Suffix: -ov	MATCH+IDSTRESS	IDENT STRESS$_{OV}$
☞ (a)	gólos[1]-ov		
(b)	golos[2]-óv		*!

b. The base is type (f) noun:

	Base: ruk[1]-, rúk[2]- Suffix: -ov	MATCH+IDSTRESS	IDENT STRESS$_{OV}$
☞ (a)	rúk[2]-ov		
(b)	ruk[1]-óv		*!

(48) lays out the difficulty posed by the type (b) derivatives. Most of these should behave like those of types (a, c-f) – since most type (b) bases possess a stressed allomorph – but they don't.

(48) Analyses of *-ov-* derivatives from type (b) nouns

	Base: móst^1, most^2- Suffix: -ov	MATCH+IDSTRESS	IDENT STRESS$_{OV}$
☞ (✗) (a)	móst^1-ov		
(b)	most^2-óv		*!

An analysis of Russian phonology that acknowledges the underlying presence of *jers* – the high vowels that lower before another *jer* and otherwise delete (Lightner 1972, Halle 1973) – can detect an independent difference between the type (b) nouns and all other nouns. The difference is that, prior to *jer*-deletion, *no form of a type (b) noun has stem stress*. The only form with surface stem stress in type (b) has, prior to jer-deletion, stress on the desinential jer: at that stage *móst* is *most-ъ́*. All other noun classes differ from type (b) in this respect: each possesses a paradigm cell in which stress falls on the stem itself independently of *jer* deletion. Type (f) nouns, type (b)'s closest counterpart, have stem stress in the Nom. Pl., e.g. *rúk-i*: at the pre-*jer*-deletion stage, stress is already on the stem.

The behaviour of type (b) *ov*-derivatives is exactly what our analysis predicts, *if intermediate representations like most-ъ́ are the only ones being accessed by the faithfulness constraints*. Some aspect of our analysis seems to be on the right track: there is a level of representation at which this analysis, and only it, draws the right distinction between accent classes. In classes (a) and (c–f) there exists a stressed stem allomorph both befeore and after the fall of jers, in class (b), before jers fall, there is no stressed stem: this is why *-ov* is forced to take on stress when attached to class (b). However the assumption that faithfulness evaluates intermediate representations is problematic in the context of any surface-oriented approach to East Slavic stress. The reader will recall that the Ukrainian 'jer-final' forms – e.g. the class (b) Nominative singular *obrúč* or the class (d) Genitive plural *syrít* – must be evaluated in their surface forms, as if they are stem-stressed: this is what explains forms like *obrúč-n-yj* and *syrít-sjk-yj*. Why should Ukrainian differ in this way from Russian? Thus, while appeal to the stressed *jer* in intermediate *most-ъ́* sheds light on why the class (b) derivatives are being singled out by Russian *-ov*, it seems unlikely that the actual mechanism consults a stressed *jer*.

A possibility whose verification we leave for future work is that there is a residual *surface* distinction in Russian between class (b) Nominative sg. like *móst,* where stress lands on the stem only as a consequence of *jer*-loss, and class (c) Nominative sg. like *gláz*, where stress is on the stem independently of the fate of jers. Specifically, we speculate that the realization of *móst* is distinct from that of other stressed syllables of Russian, perhaps because stress is *transferred* to the stem from the lost *jer*. (A phonetic distinction between an original stressed syllable and a syllable onto which stress retracts is also documented in Latvian: cf. Endzelin 1922, and Derksen 1991: 52.) If so, this difference causes forms like *móst* to count as distinct from fully stressed stems. The Ukrainian counterparts of such forms may, but need not, be identical to other stressed syllables. We have no further evidence to bear on these speculations at present, and we note that they are consistent with all aspects of our analysis of East Slavic.

There are considerably more recessive derived adjectives in Russian than possessive *-ov*. Their accent patterns are sketched by V. Kiparsky (1962: 258ff). We have not as yet obtained the full data allowing us to propose an analysis for these.

7.3.3 Unstressable *-ostj-*

The suffix *-ostj-* creates deadjectival nouns denoting qualities. Its accentual behaviour is similar to that of *-ov-*, suggesting that *-ostj-* too is underlyingly stressless. The difference between them is that *-ov-* can be stressed if necessary, while *-ostj-* is never stressed. Derivatives where *-ostj-* would have to be stressed are missing from the language.[33]

In the simple case when the base adjective has constant stem stress, MATCH STEM STRESS has no effect: stressing the stem satisfies all forms of faithfulness to the stem and to the suffix.

(49) *-ostj-* derivatives of invariant, stem-stressed adjectives:
Base: *grámotn-yj*, GenSgMasc *grámotn-ogo* => Derivative: *grámotn-ostj* 'literacy'

When the base adjective has both stressless and stressed stem allomorphs in its inflection (50a–b), the *-ostj-* derivative selects a stressed allomorph. When the base has only stressless allomorphs, (51), no *-ostj-* derivative is formed.

(50) *-ostj-* derivatives of adjectives with multiple stem allomorphs
a. derivatives of mobile-stress Adjectives with one stem-stressed form:
Base: *molod-ój*, PredNeut *mólod-o* 'young'
=> Derivative: *mólod-ostj* 'youth'
Base: *udal-ój*, PredNeut *udál-o,* 'able'
=> Derivative: *udál-ostj* 'high ability'
b. derivatives of mobile-stress Adjectives with two stem-stressed forms:
Base: *xolódn-yj*, PredNeut *xólodn-o*, PredFem *xolodn-á* 'cold'
=> Derivative: *xólodn-ostj* 'coldness (towards a person)', also ?*xolódn-ostj*

Base: *zeljón-yj*, PredNeut *zélen-o*, PredFem *zelen-á* 'green'
=> Derivative: *zeljón-ostj* 'greenness', also ?*zélen-ostj*
Base: *vesjól-yj*, PredNeut *vésel-o*, PredFem *vesel-á* 'cheerful'
=> Derivative: *vesjól-ostj* 'cheerfulness', no alternative **vésel-ostj.*

(51) *-ostj-* derivative of adjectives lacking a stem-stressed allomorph:
Base: *golub-ój*, PredFem *golub-á*, but no **gólub, *golúb*; 'blue'
=> Derivative: None. **golub-óstj, *gólub-ostj, *golúb-ostj* are all impossible.

With more than one stressed stem allomorph, as in (50), at least some adjectives allow two *-ostj-* forms: e.g. *xólodn-ostj* and non-standard but acceptable *xolódn-ostj*; *zeljón-ostj* and non-standard *zélen-ostj.* These variants support the simplest version of our analysis, where only MATCH STEM, IDENT STRESS BD and affixal faithfulness control the selection of stem allomorphs. In still other cases only one *-ostj-* derivative seems possible, for reasons that remain unclear: e.g. only *vesjólostj* 'cheerfulness', from *vesjól-yj, vésel, vesel-á* 'cheerful'. Summing up the key findings, *-ostj-* derivatives select a stressed stem allomorph, and when there is a choice of more than one, further preferences apply.

The ranking MATCH STEM STRESS >> IDENT STRESS$_{OSTJ}$ >> IDENT STRESS ROOT IO, parallel to those used for *-išš-* and *-ov-*, is helpful here too.

(52) Analyses of *-ostj-* stress:
a. Bases with one stressed stem allomorph yield one *-ostj* form:

	Base: molod[1], mólod[2]- Suffix: -ostj	MATCH+IDSTRESS	IDENT STRESS$_{OSTJ}$
☞ (a)	mólod[2]-ostj		
(b)	molód-ostj	*!	
(c)	molod[1]-óstj		*!

b. Bases with two stressed stem allomorphs yield two *-ostj* variants:

	Base:		
	xolodn[1]-, xólodn[2]-, xolódn[3]-	MATCH+IDSTRESS	IDENT STRESS$_{OSTJ}$
☞ (a)	xólodn[2]-ostj		
☞ (b)	xolódn[3]-ostj		
(c)	xolodn[1]-óstj		*!

The *-ostj-* derivatives differ from *-išš-* and *-ov-* forms when the base adjective does not provide any stressed stem allomorph, (51). In such cases, faithfulness to the affix is overridden in *-išš-* and *-ov-* forms. But for *-ostj-*, among thousands of such forms in Zaliznjak (1977), there is just one with stress on the suffix: *zl-ostj* 'anger', from *zl-ój* 'angry', with a non-syllabic stem. This suffix is then subject to a stricter faithfulness requirement than the others: the combination of suffix and stem faithfulness yields a paradigm gap in its case.[34]

The form of this stricter requirement is not immediately relevant here, but we offer, for illustrative purposes, a ranking of the constraint M-PARSE (Prince and Smolensky 1993)[35] below MATCH + IDSTRESS and IDENT STRESS$_{OSTJ}$ and above IDENT STRESS$_{ISS}$, IDENT STRESS$_{OV}$: this allows the analysis of other Russian suffixes to stand unchanged, while correctly blocking any *-ostj-* derivative that violates either MATCH + IDENT STRESS or IDENT STRESS$_{OSTJ}$.

(53) Analyses of *-ostj-* stress: Bases without a stressed stem allomorph yield paradigm gaps

	Base: golub- Suffix: -ostj	MATCH+IDSTRESS	IDENT STRESS$_{OSTJ}$	M-PARSE
(a)	gólub-ostj	*!		
(b)	golúb-ostj	*!		
(c)	golub-óstj		*!	
☞ (d)	⊙			*

The total ranking for the phenomena discussed here is then MATCH STEM, IDENT STRESS BD, IDENT STRESS$_{OSTJ}$ >> M-PARSE >> IDENT STRESS$_{ISS,}$ IDENT STRESS$_{OV}$ >> IDENT STRESS ROOT.

A comparison between impossible **golub-ostj* (with any stress) and parallel forms like *cvétn-ostj* suggests an extension to the set of forms accessed by MATCH STEM. The adjectives *golub-ój* 'blue' and *cvetn-ój* 'coloured' have fixed stress on the ending, the same pattern as in nouns of type (b). In the only form of the adjectival paradigm that has a null ending, the "short" masculine singular, stress is expected to surface on the last syllable, as in comparable type (b) nouns. But both adjectives lack that form. For *golub-ój*, other short forms do exist, e.g. the feminine singular *golub-á*, but any version of the short masculine – **gólub*, **golúb* – is impossible. For *cvetn-ój* no short form – **cvétn-a, *cvétn-o, *cvéten* – is attested at all (Zaliznjak 1977). *Cvetn-ój*, however, differs from *golub-ój* in possessing a related form with stem stress: the Adjective's own base, the noun *cvét* 'color'.This noun is of the type (c), with stem stress in the singular. Apparently the *-ostj-* derivative *cvétn-ostj* – and a number of other forms – is formed by accessing the stressed form of the root *cvét*, its base's base. This is enough to satisfy MATCH STEM. This case is thus akin to the use of stem allomorphs from co-derivatives we recorded in Ukrainian as 'Faithful-Related'.[36]

(54) Using the base's base to form an *-ostj-* derivative:

a. <u>Base$_1$</u>: *cvét*, GenSg *cvét-a*, NomPl *cvet-á*, GenPl *cvet-óv* 'color'
=> <u>Base$_2$</u> *cvet-n-ój* (no predicative forms) 'colored'
=> <u>Derivative</u> *cvétn-ostj* 'property of being colored'

b. <u>Base$_1$</u>: *krúžev-o*, GenSg *krúžev-a* NomPl *kružev-á*, GenPl *kružev-óv* 'lace'
=> <u>Base$_2$</u> *kružev-n-ój* no predicative forms 'lacy'
=> <u>Derivative</u> *krúžev-n-ostj* 'property of being lacy'

(55) Analysis of *-ostj-* stress: A base's base is accessed to provide a stressed stem allomorph

	Base$_1$: cvét- Base$_2$: cvet-	MATCH +IDSTRESS	IDENT STRESS$_{OSTJ}$	M-PARSE
☞ (a)	cvét-n-ostj	(Base$_1$)		
(b)	cvet-n-óstj	(Base$_2$)	*!	
(c)	⊙			*!

7.3.4 Summary: Russian recessive suffixes provide evidence for MATCH STEM

The Russian recessive derivatives illustrate the interaction between faithfulness to the accentual properties of the suffix and the higher-ranked stem faithfulness conditions MATCH STEM, IDENT STRESS BD. These Russian recessive derivatives preserve the underlyingly [±stress] status of their outer suffix, but only if this is compatible with using an allomorph of the base that is independently available in its inflectional paradigm. Russian recessive derivatives are lexically conservative too.

The accentual class of the base does not directly affect the derivative's stress in the case of *-ostj* and *-išš-* nouns: what does matter is the existence of a stem allomorph with accentual properties that allow the derivational suffix to surface with its underlying accentual value.

In the case of the possessive/family-name suffix *-ov-*, the accentual class of the base appears to determine the stress of the derivative, in the sense that only type (b) nouns yield *-óv* derivatives. We have tentatively proposed to explain this by noting that at an intermediate stage of the mapping to the surface form such type (b) nouns lack any stem-stressed accentual allomorph. On this interpretation, we can maintain that the recessive derivatives of Russian – or at least all the ones analysed here – determine their stress independently of the accentual type of the base noun.

Though the accentual facts of Ukrainian and Russian differ, as do the properties of cognate affixes, the combination MATCH STEM and IDENT

STRESS is a force in the phonology of both, creating the landscape of options for stressing recessive derivatives.

The patterns characterized by MATCH STEM appear to be an innovation in East Slavic. Proto-Slavic accent placement followed the same transparent rules in inflection and in derivation (Dybo 1981). Later, this earlier transparent system gave way to the modern East Slavic split between inflectional and derivational accent. In inflection, accent is now determined by the underlying representation of the stem and the set of paradigm contrast and uniformity constraints indexed to a particular stem. This creates the vast accentual diversity found in the East Slavic inflection especially for nouns, which feature half a dozen major accentual types, with over a dozen subtypes. This complexity, however, is largely irrelevant for accent placement in derivatives: there are virtually no cases in which the specific accentual type of the base directly affects the placement of stress in the derivative.

The derivational system of East Slavic features two essential innovations. First, many affixes of East Slavic have become accentually dominant, overriding all accentual properties of the base lexeme. This allows the language to avoid introducing complexity into the derivation, by collapsing all bases into one class. Second, for derivatives using recessive affixes, accent placement in the base still matters, but in a limited way: the stress of the derivative may depend on the range of surface stem allomorphs found in the base's inflection, but not on any of its other accentual properties. In this way, most accentual types of bases are again collapsed into supertypes as far as the derivational morphology goes. These two East Slavic innovations result in a simpler system of accent placement in derivatives.

7.4 MATCH STEM outside East Slavic

Analyses parallel to the one offered here are needed outside Slavic. The closest counterpart is found in the phonology of Romanian, where consonantal processes are allowed to apply in derived forms only if *some* stem allomorph matching the output of the relevant process exists in an inflected form of the base (Steriade 2007). One process is velar palatalization: k → ʧ, g → ʤ before front vowels. Palatalization applies automatically before eligible inflectional endings. Any velar-final noun whose inflectional paradigm contains an ending beginning with *e* or *i*, e.g. plural *-i*, is thus guaranteed to have a stem allomorph ending in ʧ or ʤ (56a). Any velar final noun lacking such an ending lacks the palatalized stem allomorph (56b).

(56) Velar palatalization in Romanian inflected nouns (Steriade 2007)

a. Palatalization applies before front vowels
kolák, pl. *koláʧ-i* 'bagel' *stíŋg-ə,* pl. *stínʤ-i* 'left side'

b. No palatalization before back vowels
fok, pl. *fók-uri* 'fire', *lok,* pl. *lók-uri* 'place' tɨrg, pl. *tɨ́rg-uri* 'market'

Derivational suffixes are potential triggers of velar palatalization. But the version of this process triggered in derivation applies only if there is a palatalized stem allomorph in the inflectional paradigm of the base. This restriction takes two forms. In one case, the same derivational suffix triggers the process in forms whose bases undergo palatalization in inflection (57a), and is blocked in other bases (57b):

(57) Velar palatalization in Romanian derivatives

a. Palatalization applies in derivation:
Base: *stíŋg-ə,* pl. *stínʤ-i* 'left' => Derivative: *stinʤ-íst,* **stiŋg-íst* 'leftist'

b. Palatalization is blocked in derivation
Base: *fok,* pl. *fók-uri* 'fire' => Derivative: *fok-íst, *foʧ-íst* 'locomotive engineer'

Second, when there is a choice of suffixes for a given derivative, bases that undergo palatalization in inflection can choose *i-* or *e-*initial derivational suffixes, because they can allow palatalization to proceed (58a); velar-final bases that have not undergone palatalization in inflection, for lack of a trigger ending, avoid the palatalizing derivational suffixes (58b).

(58) Base allomorphs dictate the choice among derivational suffixes: *-i* vs *-ui*

a. Palatalization has applied in inflection and can apply in derivation:
Base: *kolák,* pl. *koláʧ-i* 'bagel'
=> Derivative: *iŋ-koləʧ-í* 'to roll up'

b. Palatalization could not apply in inflection, and is blocked in derivation
Base: *lok,* pl. *lók-uri* 'place'
=> Derivative: *ɨn-lok-uí, *ɨn-lok-í, *ɨn-loʧ-í* 'to replace'

Selecting the suffix *-ui* over *-i* is a means to satisfy both markedness (the trigger of palatalization, *KI below, violated in **ɨn-lok-í*) and faithfulness to the pool of allomorphs found in the inflectional paradigm (violated in **ɨn-loʧ-í*).

All major consonantal alternations of Romanian display this effect. The equivalent of Slavic MATCH STEM is needed here. The stem of a candidate derivative must find *some* correspondent among stems already generated in inflection, containing identical counterparts to the root consonants to be used in the derivative. (59) is a simplified illustration. To highlight the similarity to the East Slavic pattern, no distinction is made below between the constraint establishing global correspondence between stems (MATCH STEM), and the constraint enforcing segmental identity between corresponding consonants, *stɨndʒ-íst*, **stɨŋg-íst*.

(59) MATCH STEM effects in Romanian derivatives:
b.i.1.a a base with palatalization in inflection: *stɨndʒ-íst.*

	Base: stɨ́ŋg-, stɨ́ndʒ- Suffix: -ist	MATCH STEM	*KI
☞ (a)	stɨndʒ-íst		
(b)	stɨŋg -íst		*!

b.i.1.b a base without palatalization in inflection: *fok-íst*

	Base: fok- Suffix: -ist	MATCH STEM	*KI
☞ (a)	fok-íst		*
(b)	fotʃ-íst	*!	

In this way, palatalization in the derivative – or any other consonantal process caused by the derivational suffix – is conditioned by its applicability in the plural of the base. This is parallel to the East Slavic fact that stem destressing (as in *obruč-óvyj*) or the stressing of the last stem syllable (as in *obrúč-nyj*) is much more likely to happen in derivatives whose bases, like *obrúč,* have acquired the appropriate stems in inflection. As in East Slavic, the MATCH STEM constraint needed in Romanian is concerned with productively generated stems allomorphs, and it is non-selective: if a base offers a choice of stems, any one, regardless of the morphological features expressed by the form it surfaces in, will do as long as it improves markedness.

7.5 Models of correspondence

OT models the phonological influences between pairs of morphologically related forms through constraints on Base-Derivative Correspondence (Benua 1997), and Input-Output Correspondence in Stratal OT (Kiparsky 2000; Bermúdez-Otero 2011). In the domain of inflectional paradigms, Uniform Exponence (Kenstowicz 1996) and Optimal Paradigms (McCarthy 2005) constraints are employed. All the works just cited take a restricted view of the conditions under which related forms may correspond. The pairs that qualify must be either derivatives and their bases, provided that the latter are contained as immediate constituents in the former; or they must coexist as members of the inflectional paradigm of the same lexeme.

In this study we have documented phenomena that favour extending the range of correspondent pairs, a point anticipated by Burzio (1998) and Steriade (1999a,b). The patterns reported here involve the asymmetric correspondence for which Base-Derivative constraints are best suited: one form has been independently generated, while the second must be generated in a way that maintains similarity to the first. The bases of our study differ in multiple ways from those studied in Benua (1997) and later work, making certain components of the theory advocated by Benua unworkable for the East Slavic data.

They differ, first, in that East Slavic bases need not be morphologically contained in their derivatives. Benua (1997:30), adapting to OT generalizations inherited from rule-based phonology, claimed that morphological containment is a necessary restriction on Base-Derivative correspondence. The East Slavic data shows it isn't. The Russian derivative *dom-íšš-e* 'house-Augm.' takes its accent from the plural of *dóm* (Nom.pl. *dom-á*, Gen.pl. *dom-óv*) but does not contain a plural ending. Nor does the Ukrainian class (c) derivative *tenor-óv-yj* contain any of the plural endings justifying its stressless stem *tenor-*. Ukrainian *syrít-sjk-yj* 'of an orphan' may be said to contain the Genitive plural *syrít* of *syrot-á* 'orphan', but surely not in a syntactic sense. If a syntactic reason existed for Genitive plurals inside *-sjk-yj* adjectives, *all* such derivatives would contain Genitive plurals, independent of the calculus of stress.

Relatedly, the East Slavic base-derivative relations studied here are unusual in being *unselective*: the derivative can use any one of its inflected base's stems. This property of correspondence derives from the first, the absence of a containment restriction. If the base must be the exponent of an immediate constituent of the derivative, there is a unique base for each derivative. If this containment condition is abandoned, as it seems it must be, then multiple bases may in principle become available for any one derivative. The East Slavic data support this second point as well. We have observed, for instance, that the Ukrainian adjectives *obrúč-n-yj* and *obruč-év-yj* or *jávir-sjk-yj*, *javor-óv-yj,* use different stems from their base noun, a Nominative sg. in the first cases, and an oblique or plural form in the second ones. That means that both stems are available as bases, again regardless of the morphosyntactic features expressed in the relevant case-number form. Which one is chosen depends solely on the phonological markedness of the result.

To analyse the East Slavic pattern we have proposed MATCH STEM, a modified Base-Derivative correspondence constraint. The modifications it incorporates bear on the two distinctive aspects of correspondence outlined above. MATCH STEM requires only that a stem of the base correspond to the stem of the candidate derivative, allowing the endings of the base form to lack corresponding material in the derivative. This constraint can be satisfied by any pair like {B *dom-á*, D *dom-íšš-e*}, whether the former is contained or not in the latter.

Second, MATCH STEM allows unselective correspondence between a candidate derivative stem and any one in a pool of base stems. It does this by requiring only that *some inflected form* of the base, with non-specific *some*, contain a stem that accentually matches the derivative stem.

While MATCH STEM itself favours no stem, a preference exists in Ukrainian for using in derivatives the stem of the Nominative singular, the form used in East Slavic and elsewhere as the citation form of the noun. Recall the derivatives of class (c) nouns like *jávir*. MATCH STEM is equally satisfied by *jávir-sjk-yj* and **jávor-sjk-yj*, but only the form using the citation stem is a productive option. The constraint MATCH CITATION expresses this.

Because it is a weak preference, MATCH CITATION plays a minor role in our analysis of East Slavic. But it is a significant component of the analysis because it helps place the data analysed here in broader perspective. It provides the missing link between our conception of a collective base consisting of many stems, any of which is available to derivatives, and the restrictive hypothesis of a unique base upon which earlier work on the cycle was founded. To analyse standard 'one-base' cyclic phenomena, like the relation between *oríginal* and *orìginálity* or that between Palestinian Arabic *fíhim* and *fihím-na*, one need not appeal to a fundamentally different model of grammar from the one we used in East Slavic: one must only rank above MARKEDNESS a Base-Derivative constraint, the counterpart to our MATCH CITATION, which favours *a particular base* over others that are in principle available.[37]

It would be surprising if the only change needed in the grammar of Base-Derivative relations was limited to MATCH STEM constraints. Recent work in Correspondence Theory has uncovered evidence for changes that go beyond this. In particular, the use of morpheme variants originating in one syntactic context but deployed in others to improve markedness, is discussed in Bonet and Torres Tamarít (2009), Lloret (2009), Rebrus and Törkenczy (2005), Steriade (1999a,b). Most of these works document the extended distribution of affixes to contexts that mismatch their basic exponence functions. The overall picture emerging from all these studies is one in which markedness constraints interact freely with exponence conditions, as well as a variety of correspondence constraints.

We conclude by summarizing the main result. Accent in East Slavic recessive derivatives is computed by selecting, among all the stems of the inflected base, one that optimizes satisfaction of Markedness, in Ukrainian, and of affixal Faithfulness, in Russian. This generalization can be analysed in a modified theory of Base Derivative correspondence where markedness competes with both unselective and targeted faithfulness constraints, represented here, respectively, by MATCH STEM and MATCH CITATION.

Notes

* We are indebted to the editors, to two anonymous reviewers, and to Jonathan Borowsky, Edward Flemming, Bruce Hayes, Paul Kiparsky, Mikhail Oslon, Kie Zuraw, as well as audiences at FASL 20 and UCLA for comments on this work. We also thank the native speakers who filled in our questionnaires on stress in Russian possessive *-ov* derivatives.

1. Recent developments in Slavic historical accentology suggest that the Proto-Slavic inflectional accent was more complex. See Shrager (2007, Ch. 1) for a recent overview.
2. In (2) we write both reconstructed acute and circumflex accents with the acute mark '´'.
3. See Kiparsky (2009) for recent discussion.
4. In **mǫž-ьsk-á*, accent is on the ending because the ending itself is underlyingly stressed, while the derivational suffix *-ьsk-* is underlyingly stressless. In **vorž-ьj-ь́*, the suffix *-ьj-* is underlyingly stressed but, because it has a short vowel, stress is realized on the following syllable, according to the regular post-accentuation pattern.
5. Squares stand for stem syllables, circles for desinential syllables; black shapes denote stressed positions. The words in (3) are of the same declension class: endings *-y*/*-i* (Nom Pl) and *-ov*/*-ej* (Gen Pl) are allomorphs whose selection is conditioned by the palatalization of the stem-final consonant; all other endings are strictly identical. We use Zaliznjak's (1977) labels for accentual types. Russian accent is discussed in section 3. We use standard transliteration for Russian and Ukrainian rather than IPA notation.
6. The alternation between *-ev-yj* and *-ov-yj* is controlled by the palatality of the preceding consonant.
7. Modern Ukrainian type (c) nouns must be analysed as having underlyingly stressed stems. See section 7.2.8.
8. It's unclear if Proto-Slavic had dominant derivational suffixes. Dybo (1981: 258–259) discusses the most likely candidates and argues that there are reflexes of recessivity for all of them.
9. We did not conduct a count of how many of the 3385 *-ov-yj* derivatives have bases that are not of class (a). However, Butska (2002) found only 722 nouns of types other than (a), so the proportion of type (a) bases in our sample must be significantly higher than the 46% of forms with stem stress in the *-ov-yj* derivative.

10. By 'inherited', we mean inherited from the Ukrainian of the eighteenth–nineteenth centuries at the earliest, not inherited from Proto-Slavic. The accentuation of East Slavic adjectives underwent a period of high instability in the sixteenth–seventeenth centuries, see Zaliznjak (1989) among others, so one cannot assume without argument continuity between modern accentuation and the earlier stages.
11. The historical source of final accented *-ov-ýj* forms is discussed by Hartmann (1936), Reiter (1969), Lehfeldt (2001). For derivatives of final-stressed bases, like *budják* 'thisle' we don't exclude the possibility that an older final-stressed form, *budjak-ov-ýj,* could vary with base-faithful, antepenult stressed *budják-ov-yj.* Such variation is indeed found among the other derived adjectives and its infrequent status for *-ov-yj* should be considered accidental. It is only for derivatives of non-final stressed bases like *káktus* plus disyllabic *-ov-yj* that the remarks in the text hold. A further remark on the subject of final accented derivatives is that these either do not come from recent loanwords or they have close counterparts in Russian suggesting that they could be borrowed fully formed from Russian: e.g. *grup-ov-ýj* 'of a group' *stilj-ov-ýj* 'of a style'.
12. Stress shifts from the penult to the final have also happened in the very recent history of Ukrainian. For example, Vynnycjkyj (2002) discusses *pux-ov-ýj* 'down (Adj)', where in the late nineteenth century the penult-stress form *pux-óv-yj* was common (Vynnycjkyj 2002: 309), or *vognj-an-ýj* 'fire (Adj)', with *vognj-án-yj* dominant in the first half of the nineteenth century, but then becoming marginal (2002: 301). The factors generating these shifts remain unclear to us. A related fact are loanwords that occasionally yield final stressed derivatives: e.g. *šljuz-ov-ýj* 'of a (water) lock' from *šljúz* '(water) lock', from Dutch *sluis*, German *Schleusse*, or Polish *śluza*.
13. Other instances of paradigms levelled in favour of the citation form (Nom.sg.) of one of the genders in multiple-gender paradigms are documented by Kraska-Szlenk (1995), Booij (1986), Kenstowicz (2005).
14. A case of this sort is found in English (Steriade 1999a); a related Russian case is documented in section 7.3.
15. As before, by 'earlier stages' we mean the 18th–19th centuries at the earliest.
16. Velars regularly palatalize (k → č) before *-nyj*.
17. Relevant bases are the feminines *mišur-á, tertj-á, vzuttj-á, žyttj-á, šeljug-á, taft-á, tajg-á, česuč-á, alyč-á, birjuz-á, lobod-á, parč-á*; the neuters *tepl-ó, pysjm-ó-* and the pluralia tantum nouns *xarč-í, svjatk-ý, partf-í.*
18. This exceptional word is *mišúr-n-yj*, from *singulare tantum mišur-á* 'tinsel, trumpery'.
19. Final-stressed derivatives like **tajg-n-ýj,* from defective class (b) bases like *tajgá*, would be faithful to their stressless stems. They are nonetheless unattested. Perhaps **tajg-n-ýj* is eliminated by competition with forms like *tajg-óv-yj,* which are both faithful and accentually unmarked. Competition is possible between *-n-yj* and *-ov-yj* because they seem to be syntactically and semantically equivalent (unlike *-sjk-yj*, which is restricted to human

referents). We have not tested the hypothesis of a grammatically regulated competition between *-ov-yj* and *-n-yj*.

20. Another possibility is to appeal to a fact that singles out just class (b). Historically, and perhaps underlyingly, class (b) zero-suffixed forms like *garbúz* end in a stressed jer. If the derivation *garbuz-ъ́* => *garbúz* is justified, then nouns like *garbúz*, the majority of our class (b) bases, lack any stressed allomorphs at the intermediate level of representation that precedes the loss of jers in a stepwise derivation (cf. Pesetsky 1979). We discuss in section 7.3 how this might play a role in the stress of Russian derivatives. We find the Russian evidence for this idea more persuasive and incline, for Ukrainian, in favour of the explanation given in the text.
21. The one apparent exception to this generalization that we're aware of, *nebíž* 'nephew', has a common initial-stressed variant *nébiž*. Some dictionaries list the latter only.
22. See Kenstowicz (2005) for a survey of paradigm-internal contrast effects.
23. An example of the 'Faithful-Related' category is *lymár-n-yj* 'of a saddler', based on *lýmar*, *lymar-í* 'saddler', and related to *lymár-nj-a* 'saddlery'. All *-ar-nj-a* nouns denoting the site of a trade are stressed on the penult.
24. The others are: *buxgálter-sjk-yj* 'of an accountant (< *Buchhalter*)', *káter-n-yj* 'of a small boat' (English *cutter*), *dóktor-skj-yj* 'of a doctor', *ávtor-sjk-yj* 'of an author', *dyréktor-sjk-yj, redáktor-sjk-yy, profésor-sjk-yj*, *asésor-sjk-yj*.
25. They are: *stegén-n-yj, jarém-n-yj, vidér-n-yj, tjurém-n-yj, rebér-n-yj* from, respectively, *stegn-ó, jarm-ó, vidr-ó, tjurm-á, rebr-ó*. All have epenthetic genitive plurals stressed on the first stem syllable.
26. Historically, the choice between segmental allomorphs like *večor/večir* was conditioned by the following syllable: a syllable with a full vowel selected *večor*, e.g. *večor-ov-yj*, while a syllable with a reduced yer, later lost, selected *večir*, e.g. *večir-n-yj*. Later processes of levelling extended each of these allomorphs. The result is that the modern system no longer represents the original distribution of the CoC/CiC allomorphs.
27. We thank Bruce Hayes for reminding us to address the Frankenstein option. Cf. Steriade (1999b) for relevant evidence.
28. The two exceptions are *nóvyn-sjk-yj*, listed alongside expected *novýn-sjk-yj*, on *novyn-á* 'novelty' (class (b) or (d); plural stem *novýn-*) and *kamfór-ov-yj* on *kamforá* ('camphor', (d), *singulare tantum*). *Kamfór-ov-yj* is possibly modelled on attested *kamfór-n-yj,* an unfaithful derivative that follows the ranking in (35b).
29. Why do we observe *ózer-išš-e*, rather than **ozjór-išš-e* with the plural stem allomorph? This could be an effect of MATCH CITATION, but we have not systematically explored this for Russian.
30. Both *skuka* 'boredom' and *vonj* 'stink' have related verbs providing a stressless stem allomorph: *skuč-átj* 'to be bored' and *vonj-átj* 'to stink'. Whether the verbs are the bases of the nouns or their co-derivatives, we expect such forms to be available to the formation of *-íšš-* forms, as belonging to the 'Faithful-Related' category. On this point, see also the discussion of Section 7.3.3.

31. There are too few *-ov-* derivatives in Zaliznjak (1977) to show the behaviour of all accentual types of bases: aside from derivatives of proper names, Zaliznjak provides only 16 *-ov-* derivatives from class (a), five from class (b), five from class (c), and one from class (e). To supplement his data, we asked eight native speakers to fill a questionnaire that asked them to choose which of the accentual variants for an *-ov-* derivative sounds better, for two words from each accentual type of base from (a) to (f). In (45), we report a somewhat simplified picture of the results. For types (a), (b), (c) and (e), there was virtually no variation among our subjects. For types (d) and (f), some speakers reported suffixal rather than stem stress: these responses are not reflected in (45) because such preferences were not consistent across speakers or across items. However, they did correlate with the speakers' interpretation of the base word as a family name rather than a common noun. This suggests, contra Zaliznjak, that the family-name forming suffix *-ov-*, unlike the possessive *-ov-*, prefers or tolerates suffixal stress.
32. The data in (45) includes stress patterns of *potential* family names. *Common* family names may have different stress, perhaps because they're archaisms. The differences mostly affect type (b) nouns: fossilized family names from such nouns often have stem stress, e.g. *Kótov, Sómov* (from V. Kiparsky 1962), *Stárikov* (Mikhail Oslon, p.c.).
33. There are between 2,500 and 3,000 *-ostj-* derivatives in Zaliznjak (1977). To our knowledge all but one stress the stem. We did not conduct an exhaustive check of this class and only provide illustrative examples, without counts.
34. The suffix *-ostj* enjoys the kind of unrestricted productivity that allows the creation of novel forms from any adjectival base: e.g. English *cool*, borrowed as *kúlj-n-yj,* yields nonce *kúlj-n-ostj*. For this reason, the impossibility of *golubostj* (side by side with attested, otherwise parallel forms like *zelenostj*) seems to be non-accidental.
35. For similar analyses of different ineffability phenomena see Pertsova (2005), Albright (2009).
36. Many comparable forms are found: *vétrov-ostj* 'windiness' (<= *vetrov-ój* <= *véter, vetr-á* 'wind'), among others. In other cases, the use of stressed root allomorphs in *-ostj* forms is impossible, perhaps for reasons of segmental correspondence: *sméx* 'laughter' → *smeʃ-n-ój, *sméʃ-n-ostj*.
37. This point is developed in Steriade (2007).

References

Albright, Adam (2002) *The Identification of Bases in Morphological Paradigms*. Doctoral dissertation, University of California, Los Angeles.

Albright, Adam (2005) The morphological basis of paradigm leveling. In Laura Downing, Tracy Alan Hall and Renate Raffelsiefen (eds) *Paradigms in Phonological Theory*, 17–43. Oxford: Oxford University Press.

Albright, Adam (2009) Lexical and morphological conditioning of paradigm gaps. In Curt Rice (ed.) *When Nothing Wins: Modeling Ungrammaticality in OT*. London: Equinox Publishing.

Albright, Adam (2010) Base-driven leveling in Yiddish verb paradigms. *Natural Language & Linguistic Theory* 28 (3): 475–525.

Andrusyshen, C. H. and Krett J. N. (1957) *Ukrainian-English Dictionary*. Toronto: University of Toronto Press.

Benua, Laura (1997) *Transderivational Identity: Phonological Relations Between Words*. Doctoral dissertation, University of Massachusetts Amherst. [available on http://roa.rutgers.edu/files/259-0498/roa-259-benua-2.pdf]

Baerman, Matthew (1999) *The Evolution of Fixed Stress in Slavic*. Munich: LINCOM EUROPA.

Bermúdez-Otero, Ricardo (2011) Cyclicity. In Marc van Oostendorp, Colin Ewen, Elizabeth Hume and Keren Rice (eds) *The Blackwell Companion to Phonology*, vol. 4, 2019–2048. Malden, MA: Wiley-Blackwell.

Bonet, Eulàlia, Lloret, Maria-Rosa and Mascaró, Joan (2007) Allomorph selection and lexical preferences: Two case studies. *Lingua* 117 (6): 903–927.

Bonet, Eulàlia and Torres-Tamarit, Francesc (2009) *Allomorph selection in Catalan encliticized imperatives*. Paper presented at the Linguistic Symposium on Romance Languages. University of Arizona, 26–29 March 2009. [Published as: Allomorphy in pre-clitic imperatives in Formenteran Catalan. An output-based analysis. In Sonia Colina, Antxon Olarrea, Ana María Carvalho (eds) *Romance Linguistics 2009. Selected Papers from the 39th Linguistic Symposium on Romance Languages*, 337–351. Amsterdam: John Benjamins, 2010.]

Booij, Gert (1986) Form and meaning in morphology: The case of Dutch 'agent' nouns. *Linguistics* 24 (3): 503–518.

Bulaxovsjkyj, L. A. (1927) Naholos ukrajinsjkyx prykmetnykiv. *Zapiski istoryčno-filolohičnogo viddilu Ukrajinsjkoji Akademiji nauk*, 13–14: 294–303.

Burzio, Luigi (1998) Multiple Correspondence. *Lingua* 104: 79–109.

Burzio, Luigi (2005) Sources of paradigm uniformity. In Laura J. Downing, T. Alan Hall and Renate Raffelsiefen (eds) *Paradigms in Phonological Theory*, 65–106. Oxford: Oxford University Press.

Butska, Luba (2002) *Faithful Stress in Paradigms: Nominal Inflection in Ukrainian and Russian*, Doctoral Dissertation, Rutgers University.

Chomsky, Noam, Halle, Morris and Lukoff, Fred (1956) On accent and juncture in English. In Morris Halle, Horace Lunt, Hugh McLean and Cornelius van Schooneveld (eds) *For Roman Jakobson: Essays on the Occasion of his Sixtieth Birthday*, 65–80. The Hague: Mouton.

Chomsky, Noam, and Morris Halle (1968) *The Sound Pattern of English*. New York: Harper and Row. Birthday. The Hague: Mouton, pp. 65-80.

Derksen, Rick (1991) An introduction to the history of Lithuanian accentuation. *Studies in Slavic and General Linguistics* 16: 45–84.

Drachman, Gaberell, Kager, René and Malikouti-Drachman, Angeliki (1996) Greek allomorphy: An Optimality Theory account. *OTS Working Papers* 10: 1–12.

Dybo, Vladimir Antonovich (1981) *Slavjanskaja akcentologija. Opyt rekonstrukcii sistemy akcentnyx paradigm v praslavjanskom*. Moscow: Nauka.

Feldstein, Ronald F. (1984) Stress restrictions in Russian nominal derivation. *Slavic and East-European Journal* 28 (4): 502–510.

Feldstein, Ronald F. (2006) Accentual base forms of Russian nouns and their relation to nominative and genitive endings. In Robert Allen Rothstein, Ernest A. Scatton and Charles Edward Townsend (eds) *Studia Caroliensia: Papers in Linguistics and Folklore in Honor of Charles E. Gribble*, 105–115. Bloomington, IN: Slavica.

Garde, Paul (1976) *Histoire de l'accentuation slave*. Paris: Institut d'Études Slaves

Halle, Morris (1973) The accentuation of Russian words. *Language* 49 (2): 312–348.

Halle, Morris and Kiparsky, Paul (1981) Review of Garde (1976). *Language* 57: 150–181.

Hartmann, Hans (1936) *Studien über die Betonung der Adjektiva im Russischen*. Leipzig: Otto Harrassowitz.

Illich-Svitych, Vladislav (1963) *Imennaja akcentuacija v baltijskom i slavjanskom*. Moskow: Nauka.

Ivlieva, Natalia (2009) Nominal stress in Russian. Unpublished ms. Massachusetts Institute of Technology.

ISUM (1985) – *Inversijnyj Slovnyk Ukraïnsjkoï Movy*. Kyiv: Naukova Dumka

Kager, René (1996) On affix allomorphy and syllable counting. In Ursula Kleinhenz (ed.) *Interfaces in Phonology*, 155–71. Berlin: Akademie Verlag.

Kager, René (1999) *Optimality Theory*. Cambridge: Cambridge University Press.

Kenstowicz, Michael (1996) Base identity and uniform exponence: Alternatives to cyclicity. In Jacques Durand and Bernard Laks (eds) *Current Trends in Phonology: Models and Methods*, 363–394. Manchester: European Studies Research Institute, University of Salford.

Kenstowicz, Michael (2005) Paradigmatic uniformity and contrast. In Laura J. Downing, T. Alan Hall, and Renate Raffelsiefen (eds) *Paradigms in Phonological Theory*, 145–169. Oxford: Oxford University Press.

Kiparsky, Paul (2000) Opacity and cyclicity. *The Linguistic Review* 17 (2–4): 351–367.

Kiparsky, Paul (2009) *Compositional vs. paradigmatic approaches to ccent and ablaut*. [Available at http://www.stanford.edu/~kiparsky/Papers/ucla_IE_09.submitted.new.pdf.]

Kiparsky, Valentin (1962) *Der Wortakzent der russischen Schriftsprache*. Heidelberg: Carl Winter.

Kraska-Szlenk, Iwona (1995) *The Phonology of Stress in Polish*. Doctoral dissertation, University of Illinois, Urbana-Champaign.

Lehfeldt, Werner (2001) *Einführung in die morphologische Konzeption der slavischen Akzentologie*. München: Verlag Otto Sagner.

Lightner, Theodore M. (1972) *Problems in the Theory of Phonology, Vol. I: Russian Phonology and Turkish Phonology*. Edmonton: Linguistic Research, Inc.

Lloret, Maria-Rosa (2009) Changes in inflectional class as a means to repair phonology. In Fabio Montermini (ed.) *Selected Proceedings of the 6th Décembrettes: Morphology in Bordeaux,* 22–34. Somerville, MA: Cascadilla Press.

McCarthy, John (2005) Optimal paradigms. In Laura J. Downing, T. Alan Hall and Renate Raffelsiefen (eds) *Paradigms in Phonological Theory,* 170–210. Oxford: Oxford University Press.

McCarthy, John J., and Prince, Alan (1994) The emergence of the unmarked: Optimality in prosodic morphology. In Mercè González (ed.) *Proceedings of the North East Linguistic Society 24,* 333–379. Amherst, MA: GLSA.

Melvold, Janis L. (1989) *Structure and stress in the phonology of Russian*. Doctoral dissertation, Massachusetts Institute of Technology.

Paster, Mary (2005) Subcategorization vs. output optimization in syllable-counting allomorphy. In John Alderete, Chung-hye Han and Alexei Kochetov (eds) *Proceedings of the 24th West Coast Conference on Formal Linguistics,* 326–333. Somerville MA: Cascadilla Press.

Pater, Joe (2010) Morpheme-specific phonology, Constraint-indexation and inconsistency resolution. In Steve Parker (ed.) *Phonological Argumentation: Essays on Evidence and Motivation,* 123–154. London: Equinox.

Pertsova, Katya (2005) How lexical conservatism can lead to paradigm gaps. In Jeff Heinz and Katya Pertsova (eds) *UCLA Working Papers in Linguistics: Papers in Phonology*, vol. 6, 13–38. Los Angeles, CA: University of California at Los Angeles.

Pesetsky, David (1979) Russian morphology and lexical theory. Unpublished ms. Massachusetts Institute of Technology.

Pogribnyj, Mykola Ivanovych (1984) *Orfoepičnyj Slovnyk*. Kyiv: Radjanska Škola.

Prince, Alan and Smolensky, Paul (1993 [2004]) *Optimality Theory: Constraint Interaction in Generative Grammar*. Technical Report, Rutgers University Center for Cognitive Science and Computer Science Department, University of Colorado at Boulder. Malden, MA and Oxford: Blackwell. [Available at http://roa.rutgers.edu/files/537-0802/537-0802-PRINCE-0-0.PDF.]

Pugh, Stefan M. and Press, Jan (1999) *Ukrainian: A Comprehensive Grammar*. London: Routledge.

Rebrus, Peter and Törkenczy, Miklos (2005) Uniformity and contrast in the Hungarian verbal paradigm. In Laura J. Downing, T. Alan Hall and Renate Raffelsiefen (eds) *Paradigms in Phonological Theory,* 263–295. Oxford: Oxford University Press.

Reiter, Norbert (1969) Über einige Ausnahmen vom Hartmannschen Gesetz. *Scando-Slavica* 15: 129–137.

Shrager, Miriam (2007) *The accentual system of Masculine nouns in the 'Krivichi' dialects*. Doctoral Dissertation, Indiana University.

Stang, Christian S. (1957) *Slavonic accentuation*. Oslo: Universitetsforlaget.

Steriade, Donca (1999a) Lexical Conservatism. In *Linguistics in the Morning Calm, Selected Papers from SICOL 1997,* 157–179. Seoul: Hanshin.

Steriade, Donca (1999b) Lexical conservatism in French adjectival liason. In Jean-Marc Authier, Barbara E. Bullock and Lisa A. Reed (eds) *Formal Perspectives on Romance Linguistics,* 246–270. Amsterdam: John Benjamins.

Steriade, Donca (2007) A pseudo-cyclic effect in the Romanian declension. In Asaf Bachrach and Andrew Nevins (eds) *Inflectional Identity,* 313–361. Oxford: Oxford University Press.

Tranel, Bernard (1996) French liaison and elision revisited: A unified account within OT. In Claudia Parodi (ed.) *Aspects of Romance Linguistics: Selected Papers from the Linguistic Symposium on Romance Languages XXIV,* 433–455. Washington, DC: Georgetown University Press.

Truckenbrodt, Hubert and Luba Butska (2003) *Ukrainian Nominal Inflection and Conditions on asymmetric faithfulness.* Unpublished ms. University of Tubingen and Ryerson University, Toronto.

Veseljovjsjka, Z.M (1970) *Nagolos u sxidno-slovjansjkyx movax počatkovoji doby formuvannja rosijskoji, ukrajinsjkoji ta bilorusjkoji nacij (kinecj XVI – počatok XVIII stolitj).* Kharkiv: Vydavnyctvo Xarkivsjkogo universytetu.

Vynnycjkyj, Vasylj (2002) *Ukrajinsjka akcentna systema: stanovlennja, rozvytok.* Lviv: Biblios.

Yanovich, Igor and Donca Steriade (2010) Uniformity, Subparadigm Precedence and Contrast derive stress patterns in Ukrainian nominal paradigms. Paper presented at OCP 6, Berlin.

Zaliznjak, Andrej Anatolyevich (1967) *Russkoe imennoe slovoizmenenie.* Moscow: Nauka.

Zaliznjak, Andrej Anatolyevich (1977) *Grammaticheskij slovarj russkogo jazyka.* Moscow: Russkij jazyk.

Zaliznjak, Andrej Anatolyevich (1985) *Ot praslavjanskoj akcentuacii k russkoj.* Moscow: Nauka.

Zaliznjak, Andrej Anatolyevich (1989) O nekotoryx svjazjax mezhdu znacheniem i udareniem u russkix prilagateljnyx. In *Slavjanskoe i balkanskoe jazykoznanie: Prosodija,* 148–164. Moscow: Nauka.

Zhovtobrjux, Mikhail Andreevich, Vitalij Makarovich Rusanovskij and Vitalij Grigorjevich Skljarenko (1979) *Istorija ukrajinskoji movy. Fonetyka.* Kyiv: Naukova Dumka.

Zilynskyj, Ivan (1979) *A Phonetic Description if tbe Ukrainian Language.* Cambridge, MA: Harvard University Ukrainian Research Institute, Harvard University Press.

Zoshchenko, Mikhail (1961) Kocherga (The Poker). In *Scenes from the Bathhouse,* translated by Sidney Monas. Ann Arbor, MI: University of Michigan Press.

Appendix: Constraints used in the text

Markedness

*CLASH: No adjacent stressed syllables.
*LAPSE: No adjacent stressless syllables
MAINSTRESSRIGHT (MSR): The main stress is not followed by another stress.
MAINSTRESSRIGHT$_{LEX}$ (MSR$_{lex}$): like MAINSTRESSRIGHT (MSR) but lexically indexed.
NONFINALITY (MAIN): No main stress on the final.

Faithfulness

IDENTSTRESS BD: corresponding syllables in base and derivative have identical stress values.
IDENT STRESS IO: corresponding syllables in the UR and SR have identical stress values.
MATCHCITATION: the derivative's stem corresponds to the stem of the Nom.Sg. of the base noun.
MATCHCITATION$_{LEX}$: same, lexically indexed.
MATCHSTEMSTRESS (MAIN): for each syllable s_d of the derivative's stem, there is a corresponding syllable s_b in a stem of some inflected form of the base noun such that s_d carries main stress if and only if s_b carries main stress.
MATCHSTEM: the derivative's stem corresponds to a stem of the inflected form of the base noun.

8 Syllable-counting allomorphy by prosodic templates

Jochen Trommer (Leipzig University)

8.1 Introduction

In syllable-counting suppletive allomorphy (SCA), different allomorphs of an affix are used according to the syllable number of the base. Thus in Estonian, the genitive plural is expressed by the suffix *-te* after bisyllabic and quadrisyllabic noun stems, but by the allomorph *-tte* after trisyllabic stems. Since Estonian doesn't have a productive phonological process of (de-)gemination triggered by the syllable count of the word, this is obviously an instance of phonologically triggered suppletive allomorphy (in the following shortly 'phonological suppletion'), which in contrast to better-known cases such as the morphologically/lexically triggered allomorphy of plural affixes in *ox-en* vs. *fox-es* is sensitive to phonological, not to morphological properties of the bases selected by the allomorphs (see Carstairs-McCarthy 1987 for the first detailed theoretical discussion of this phenomenon). The same distribution is found with the partitive plural allomorphs *-sit* and *-it*:

(1) *Syllable-counting phonological suppletion in Estonian* (Kager 1996: 157)

	Nom.sg.	Gen.sg.	Gen.pl.	Part.pl.	
2 σ	visa	visa	visa-te	visa-sit	'block'
3 σ	paras	paraja	paraja-tte	paraja-it	'suitable'
4 σ	atmiral	atmirali	atmirali-te	atmirali-sit	'admiral'

The classical optimality-theoretic analysis of the Estonian data, and of syllable-counting allomorphy more generally, is due to Kager (1996) (see Perlmutter 1998; Rubach and Booij 2001; Mascaró 1996, 2007 for analyses of the same type) who assumes that phonologically determined allomorphs

Affiliation: (Heisenberg fellow) Universität Leipzig, Leipzig, Germany enter the OT-evaluation as unordered input sets undergoing selection by the phonological optimization of corresponding outputs, using standard constraints on prosody such as the ones in (2):

(2) *Constraints governing SCA in Estonian* (Kager 1996)
  a. ONSET: Syllables should start with an onset.
  b. ALIGNSTR: The right edge of a stem should coincide with the right edge of a foot.
  c. STRESS2WEIGHT: Stressed syllables should be heavy.

For the Estonian Partitive Plural, OT-evaluation now considers all candidates produced by GEN for the inputs *visa-it* and *visa-sit*, as shown in (the highly simplified version of) Kager's analysis in (3) (additional high-ranked constraints ensure that all feet are binary trochees, and that each word starts with the head foot of the prosodic word).[1] All outputs using input *-it* either violate Onset (3c) or ALIGNSTR (3b), whereas the input *-sit* allows to satisfy both constraints by erecting a bisyllabic foot over the first two syllables (3a):

(3) *Estonian allomorph selection for a bisyllabic stem* (Kager 1996)

Input: visa+{-sit,-it}	ONSET	ALIGNSTR	STR2WT
☞ a. [(ví.sa)sit]			*
b. [(ví.sái̯)t]		*!	*
c. [(ví.sa)it]	*!		*

For stems consisting of three light syllables, there is no well-formed footing for either allomorph which would allow to satisfy ALIGNSTR. At this point, STR2WT gets relevant, which favours heavy stressed syllables and thus *-it* (4a) over *-sit* (4b):

(4) *Estonian allomorph selection for a trisyllabic stem* (Kager 1996)

Input: paraja+{-sit,-it}	ONSET	ALIGNSTR	STR2WT
☞ a. [(pá.ra)(jái̯)t]		*	*
b. [(pá.ra)(já.si)t]		*	*!
c. [(pá.ra)(já.i)t]	*!	*	*

Kager's approach to phonological suppletion is conceptually attractive since it captures the phenomenon with minimal theoretical means: the disjunctive listing of the attested allomorphs, and the evaluation of independently motivated phonological constraints. Moreover, it makes the non-trivial falsifiable prediction that phonological suppletion should always be phonologically optimizing, i.e., transparently motivated by the general phonological constraint ranking of the language where it occurs.

In fact, Paster (2005) claims that this prediction is wrong, and argues, based on a broad typological survey of the phenomenon that SCA is not in general phonologically optimizing (see also Paster 2006; Bye 2008 on the same claim for phonological suppletion in general). As illustrative examples she cites cases from Tzeltal and Dyirbal. In Tzeltal, the perfective aspect of verbs is marked by *-oh* with monosyllabic (5a), but by *-ɛh* with polysyllabic bases (5b).

(5) *Syllable-counting allomorphy in Tzeltal* (Walsh Dickey 1999: 32–329)

a. *Monosyllabic bases*		b. *Polysyllabic bases*	
s-ku'͡tʃ-óh	'she carried it'	s-ku͡tʃ-laj-ɛ́h	'she carried it repeatedly'
s-nuts-óh	'he chased something'	h-pak'-anta'j-ɛ́h	'I patched it'

As Paster (2005:328) points out, in Tzeltal '[o] and [ɛ] do not alternate elsewhere …, so the allomorphy is probably truly suppletive … Stress in Tzeltal is word-final …, so the allomorphy is not stress-conditioned and … A constraint banning [ɛ] in the second syllable has not been proposed for UG … so this appears to be a case where we would not want to describe the distribution of allomorphs as phonologically optimizing in any way.'

In contrast to SCA in Estonian, the choice of allomorphs in these cases does not lead to straightforward phonological optimization and cannot be derived by submitting candidates with different allomorphs to standard OT-evaluation. Instead Paster proposes to capture SCA by subcategorization frames associated with the affix entries of single allomorphs that select bases of specific phonological shapes. Thus Tzeltal *-oh* would select monosyllabic stems (6a), whereas *-ɛh* is the default allomorph (without a subcategorization frame) applying to all other perfective forms of different shapes (6b):

(6) *SCA in Tzeltal as morphological subcategorization* (Paster 2006: 105)
   a. -oh ↔ perf / [#σ#] ___
   b. -ɛh ↔ perf

Similarly, under Paster's analysis, Estonian *-sit* selects input stems with a final foot (such as [(ví.sa)], but not [(pá.ra)já]) (7a) in contrast to the default allomorph *-it* (7b):

(7) *SCA in Estonian as morphological subcategorization*
   a. -sit ↔ [+part +pl] / [Foot#] ___
   b. -it ↔ [+part +pl]

In this chapter, I will show that the data presented by Paster do not require the adoption of prosodic subcategorization, but can be captured by a conservative extension of Kager's approach, namely the association of specific allomorphs with prosodic templates. The simplest implementation of this idea employs 'indexing' of prosodic constraints for single suppletive allomorphs, i.e. restricting them to phonological material that overlaps with the phonological exponence of a specific allomorph, an approach implicit in much OT-based work on prosodic morphology, and advocated most explicitly for morphologically sensitive phonology by Pater (2007, 2009), see also Flack (2007). Under this approach, perfective suppletion in Tzeltal can be derived from the standard requirement that prosodic words consist of binary syllabic feet relativized to the allomorph *-oh* (PWD=BINFT$_{oh}$), which in turn is the allomorph preferred by the relevant morphological constraint on affixal spellout (PERF=oh).[2] For monosyllabic stems, this leads to straightforward selection of *-oh* since both allomorphs result in a binary foot and -oh is effectively the default allomorph:

(8) *Evaluation for Tzeltal with monosyllabic input*

Input: skutʃ+{-ɛh,-oh}	PWD=BINFT$_{oh}$	PERF=oh
☞ a. (sku.tʃoh)		
b. (sku.tʃɛh)		*!

With longer stems (9), neither affixation of *-oh* nor of *-ɛh* leads to a bisyllabic word (and both would violate the general constraint PWD=BINFT). However, the relevant undominated constraint PWD=BINFT$_{oh}$ is only violated by the candidate (9a) since only here the imperfect prosodic word overlaps phonologically with the allomorph *-oh*. In effect, *-ɛh* is chosen (9b) because it allows to avoid the offensive violation of prosodic well-formedness tied to *-oh*.

(9) *Evaluation for Tzeltal with polysyllabic input*

Input: skutʃlaj+{-ɛh,-oh}	PWD=BINFT$_{oh}$	PERF=oh
a. sku.tʃ(la-j.oh)	*!	
☞ b. sku.tʃ(la.jɛh)		*

The resulting approach is empirically more restrictive than the one by Paster because SCA and phonological suppletion in general is still restricted to cases where it allows to avoid a phonologically marked output configuration, but more liberal than the original model of Kager because the winning output candidate is not necessarily less marked than the candidate employing the losing allomorph – it might simply be exempt from the well-formedness requirements excluding the losing allomorph.

The chapter is structured as follows: in section 8.2, I introduce in detail my theoretical assumptions on the morphology-phonology interface, and show how these allow the capture of a simple instance of syllable-counting morphophonology – morphologically triggered truncation. In section 8.3, I present my extension of this analysis to the SCA data of Paster (2005). Section 8.4 shows that this analysis extends to cases of opaque SCA under the assumption that affixation is stratal. Section 8.5 compares empirical predictions of both approaches, and shows that the template-optimization account is more restrictive than the subcategorization approach. In section 8.6, I discuss further alternatives to phonological subcategorization and argue that assuming affixation of defective prosodic structure is a serious theoretical competitor for the indexed-constraint approach.

8.2 Theoretical assumptions

I make two crucial theoretical assumptions. First, I assume that morpheme-specific phonology derives from constraints indexed for specific (classes of) morphemes (Pater 2007). Second, I adopt the standard architecture of Stratal Optimality Theory, where optimization applies at two ordered levels: the Stem and the Word Level (Bermúdez-Otero 2007, 2013, in preparation). Constraint indexing can be conveniently illustrated with velar deletion in Turkish which deletes velar stops intervocalically in word forms involving the dative suffix *-e* (10a), but not in other morphological contexts such as aorist forms (10b):

(10) *Velar deletion in Turkish* (Inkelas and Zoll 2005)

	a. *Dative suffix:*	*Velar deletion*		b. *Aorist suffix:*	*No deletion*	
	Nominative	*Dative*		*Past*	*Aorist*	
	bebek	bebe-e	'baby'	gerek-ti	gerek-ir	'be necessary'
	inek	ine-e	'cow'	bırak-tı	bırak-ır	'leave'

Intervocalic velar deletion is a crosslinguistically frequent phonological process (see e.g. Pycha 2008: 20) phonetically grounded in the preference for intervocalically voiced obstruents and the concurrent aero-dynamic difficulty to produce voiced back obstruents in this context (cf. Ohala 1997). Thus it is natural to derive it from the optimality-theoretic constraint in (11a). However, *VkV by itself would also incorrectly predict velar deletion in non-dative forms (/gerek-ir/ => [*gereir]) a problem avoided by the indexed version of *VkV in (11b):

(11) *Constraint indexing*

a. *VkV: Avoid the sequence Vowel-[k]-Vowel.

b. *VkV_e: Avoid the sequence Vowel-[k]-Vowel (indexed by dative *-e*).

The evaluation of indexed markedness constraint is governed by the general interpretation convention in (12), which I will call the 'Overlap Condition':

(12) *The Overlap Condition*: (Pater 2007:275)

*X_L: Assign a violation mark to any instance of X
that contains a phonological exponent.
of a *morpheme* specified as L.

Under (12), the distribution of Turkish Velar Deletion can be captured by the ranking *VkV_e >> MAX-C, as shown in (13). In (13aii), the constraint locus (McCarthy 2003a,b) – here a sequence of a vowel followed by [k] and a further vowel instantiated by [eke], overlaps with the exponent of the dative suffix *-e* (in fact contains it), and leads hence to a violation of *VkV_e resulting in selection of the deletion candidate (13ai). On the other hand the sequence [eki] in (13bii) doesn't overlap with dative *-e*, and is hence not violated such that lower-ranked MAX-C selects the non-deleting output (13bii):

(13) *Turkish velar deletion by indexed constraints*

a. *Dative*

Input: inek-e	*VkV_e	MAX-C
☞ i. ine-e		*
ii. inek-e	*!	

b. *Aorist*

Input:gerek-ir	*VkV_e	MAX-C
i. gere-ir		*!
☞ ii. gerek-ir		

The only departure from Pater's approach I will assume here is a minimal modification of the Overlap Condition, which is formulated with respect to allomorphs and not morphemes:

(14) *The Overlap Condition: (revised version)*

*X_L: Assign a violation mark to any instance of X
that contains a phonological exponent
of an *allomorph* specified as L.

This reformulation doesn't make any difference for morphemes with a single allomorph such as the Turkish dative and aorist, but will become crucial for the derivation of syllable-counting allomorphy below.

The second important theoretical tool for the derivation of syllable counting allomorphy is Stratal OT. Thus, in line with Bermúdez-Otero (2013), I assume that word phonology comprises two strata of constraint evaluation, a first cycle at the Stem Level followed by a second one at the Word Level. In the following subsection, I will show how the combination of assumptions adopted here allows for deriving basic patterns of morphologically triggered truncation. In section 8.3, we will see that syllable counting allomorphy exhibits close structural parallels to truncation. In the following section, I will show that SCA exhibits basically the same patterns as truncation.

Morphologically triggered truncation shares an important property with SCA: it is typically syllable- (or mora-) counting. Thus the pattern of hypocoristic truncation in German discussed below maps an input of arbitrary length to an output of two-syllable length. Descriptively, templatic truncation of this type can be classified into the three groups in (15).[3]

(15) *Types of morphological truncation*

a.	Truncation with internal affixation:	An overt affix is part of the template.
b.	Truncation with external affixation:	A morphological category is expressed by templatic truncation and subsequent overt affixation.
c.	Truncation without overt affixation:	Truncation doesn't involve any affixation.

In truncation with internal affixation, a base word is truncated to a specific prosodic shape, incorporating at the same time an additional affix such that the affix becomes part of the templatic structure created by the morphological construction. A typical case is German hypocoristic formation which adds the suffix *-i* to base nouns and adjectives and shortens this combination to bisyllabic size, as shown in (16).[4]

(16) *Truncation with internal affixation (German hypocoristics)* (Féry 1997)

Base		*Hypocoristic*	
Stu(dent)	→	(Studi)	'student'
spon(tan)	→	(sponti)	'spontaneous'
(Hausauf)(gabe)	→	(Hausi)	'homework'
(Kinder)(garten)	→	(Kindi)	'kindergarten'

On the other hand, in truncation with external affixation, the prosodic template targeted by truncation does not include the affix introduced by the morphological construction. A case in point are hypocoristics with the suffix *-čan* in Japanese, which are formed by truncating the base to bimoraic size, and adding *-čan* to the resulting constituent (Poser 1990; Mester 1990; Benua 1995):

(17) *Truncation with external affixation (Japanese hypocoristics)* (Benua 1995: 119)
Midori → (Mido)-čan, (Mii)-čan
Yooko → (Yo.ko)-čan, (Yoo)-čan
Akira → (A.ki)-čan

Under the standard assumption that the targets of truncation coincide with the inventory of possible prosodic constituents (McCarthy and Prince 1993, 1996 [1986]; Alber and Arndt-Lappe 2012), the only consistent interpretation of this pattern is truncation to a bimoraic foot (i.e. a single bimoraic syllable, or two monosyllabic syllables) and affixation of *-čan* to the resulting foot (the complex of truncated base + *-čan* has no consistent syllable count, and no known prosodic constituent has a typical 4-μ size). The third descriptive type of truncation is truncation without overt affixation. This is found in hypocoristic formation in Spanish as shown by the examples in (18):

(18) *Truncation without overt affixation (Spanish hypocoristics)* (Roca and Felíu 2003: 188)
Isabél → (Í.sa)
Federíco → (Fé.de)
Gertrúdis → (Gér.tru)

All three types of truncation receive a natural formal interpretation under the theoretical framework introduced above: internal-affix truncation is a direct effect of affixing and concomitant constraint indexing. Thus for German hypocoristic formation (16), we can simply assume that a version of the constraint PWD=BINFT indexed for the affix *-i* is ranked above the faithfulness constraint MAX that penalizes segment deletion. For words that do not contain *-i* such as the underived noun *Student*, the constraint is vacuously satisfied, and hence ineffective (19a), but in forms which contain *-i*, it requires the prosodic word erected over the word form to coincide with a syllabic binary foot, which can only be achieved by deleting part of the underlying segmental material (19b):[5]

(19) *Internal-affix truncation by indexing*
a. *Evaluation of the base*

Input: Student	PWD=BINFT$_i$	MAX	WEIGHT2STRESS
☞ i. Stu(dént)			
ii. (Stú.dent)			*!

b. *Evaluation of hypocoristic*

Input: Student-i	PWD=BINFT$_i$	MAX	WEIGHT2STRESS
i. Stu(dén.ti)	*!		
☞ ii. (Stú.di)		***	

Of course, the analysis in (19) contains a slight simplification in that the unmarked coincidence of prosodic words with a binary foot is captured as a specific constraint – whereas there is a substantial body of evidence from the literature on prosodic morphology (cf. Kager 1999, and references cited there) that it can be decomposed into more general constraints. Thus we may assume that PWD=BINFT$_i$ is actually an abbreviation for the two constraints ALLFTLFT$_i$ ('The left edge of every foot should coincide with the left edge of a prosodic word') and PARSE σ_i ('Every syllable should be parsed by a prosodic word'). PARSE σ_i has the effect that the syllable containing *-i* must be part of a foot (excluding (20b)), and ALLFTLFT$_i$ requires that this foot appears at the left edge of the word (excluding (20a)). Only candidates such as (19bii) that consist exhaustively of a single foot fulfil both constraints.

(20) *Internal-affix truncation by indexing: PWD=BINFT$_i$ decomposed*

Input: Student-i	ALLFTLFT$_i$	PARSE σ_i
a. Stu(dén.ti)	*!	
b. (Stú.den)ti		*!

Truncation without overt affixation seems at first glance to be at odds with an approach that derives truncation as an effect of constraint indexing for affixes, i.e. phonologically overt affixal material. I assume that as in the classical approach to Prosodic Morphology (McCarthy and Prince 1996 [1986]) this pattern derives from the affixation of prosodic material, in this case suffixation of a foot node. I will call this analysis in the following 'covert-affix truncation'. Under this assumption, the derivation of affix-less hypocoristic truncation in Spanish is completely parallel to the internal-affixation case in German, as shown in (21) (where the subscript 'F' indicates the templatic foot suffix):[6]

(21) *Covert-affix truncation by indexing*

a. *Evaluation of the base*

Input: Isabel	PWD=BINFT$_F$	MAX
☞ i. I.sa(bel)		
ii. (I.sa)		*!**

b. *Evaluation of hypocoristic*

Input: Isabel-F	PWD=BINFT$_F$	MAX
i. I.sa(bel)$_F$	*!	
☞ ii. (I.sa)$_F$		***

Truncation with external affixation results if a morphological construction involves two affixes, a templatic foot affix at the Stem

Level, and an 'external' affix at the Word Level. Thus truncation with external affixation is a transparent combination of covert-affix truncation and straightforward segmental affixation at the subsequent phonological stratum. (22) illustrates this approach for Japanese hypocoristics, where the input of Word-Level optimization is the output of the Stem-Level optimization plus the suffix *-čan*:

(22) *External-affix truncation*

a. *Stem-Level evaluation*

Input: Midori-F	PWD=BINFT$_F$	MAX
i. Mi.do(ri)$_F$	*!	
☞ ii. (Mi.do)$_F$		**

b. *Word-Level evaluation*

Input: Mido-čan	PWD=BINFT$_F$	MAX
☞ i. Mi.do-čan		
ii. Mi.do		*!**

The Japanese data also illustrate a further important point. Just as there are prosodic systems with strictly syllabic feet and other systems (languages) with moraic feet, prosodic templates may employ either foot type. Whatever the concrete constraint-based implementation of this parameter in foot formation is, it can be exported via constraint indexing to specific morphological templates in truncation, and, as we will see below, to prosodically conditioned suppletive allomorphy. These cases are not strictly syllable-counting, but rather 'mora-counting', but for ease of reference I will continue to use the simple term 'syllable-counting allomorphy' for both types of suppletion.

8.3 Reanalysis: Simple cases of syllable-counting allomorphy

It should be obvious by now that SCA in Tzeltal is structurally closely analogous to cases of truncation with internal affixation as in German hypocoristics. Just as hypocoristic *-i*, Tzeltal *-oh* only occurs in words which form a perfect binary foot, and in both cases the restriction of prosodic words to binary feet is affix-specific, i.e., not a general property of the relevant languages (cf. Tzeltal *s-kut͡ʃ-laj-éh* 'she carried it repeatedly' in (5), and German *Student-en* 'students'). The crucial difference between both cases is that the only strategy available to *-i* to ensure the bisyllabic template is deletion, whereas Tzeltal *-oh* has an escape hatch in the form of an allomorph which is free from the burden of prosodic perfection. The logic of this relationship is shown schematically in (23):

(23) *Structural relation of truncation and syllable-counting allormorphy*

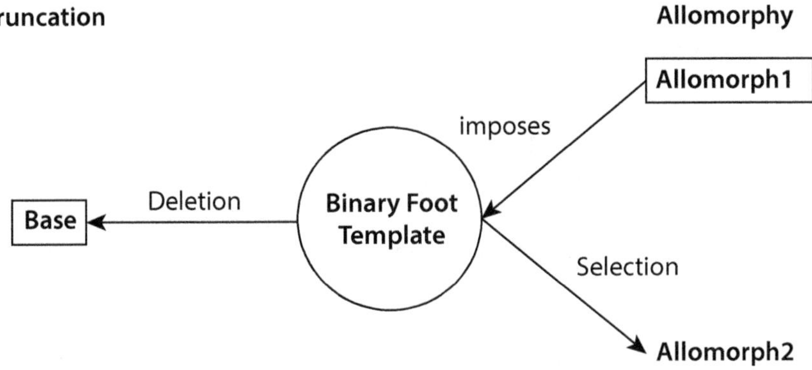

The full analysis for Tzeltal is shown in (24) and (25) extending tableaux (8) and (9) to show the interaction with faithfulness, and highlighting the close relation to the truncation analysis for German. With a monosyllabic base, all three constraints, PWD=BINFT$_{oh}$, MAX, and PERF=oh can be satisfied by affixing the allomorph *-oh*:

(24) *Tzeltal perfective allomorphy: Monosyllabic base*

Input: skutʃ+{-ɛh,-oh}	PWD=BINFT$_{oh}$	MAX	PERF=oh
☞ a. (sku.tʃoh)			
b. (sku.tʃɛh)			*!

For bases with more than one syllable the ranking of MAX above PERF=oh is crucial: the allomorph *-ɛh* is chosen (25c) although PERF=oh prefers *-oh* to satisfy PWD=BINFT$_{oh}$ (violated by (25a)) and to avoid also violation of MAX by truncation (25b):

(25) *Tzeltal perfective allomorphy: Polysyllabic base*

Input: skutʃlaj+{-ɛh,-oh}	PWD=BINFT$_{oh}$	MAX	PERF=oh
a. sku.tʃ (la.joh)	*!		
b. (sku.tʃ-oh)		*!**	
☞ c. sku.tʃ (la.jɛh)			*

Interestingly, under the indexed-constraint analysis, most cases of SCA collected by Paster are structurally completely parallel to Tzeltal. Consider for instance, Paster's examples from Zuni and Kaititj. In Zuni, singular nouns are marked by the suffix *-ʔleʔ* if they are monosyllabic (26a), and by *-nne* if they have more than one syllable (26b):

(26) *SCA in Zuni (language isolate, New Mexico)* (Newman 1965:24,56)

a. *Monosyllabic bases*		b. *Polysyllabic bases*	
ɬí-ʔleʔ	'sinew'	hóma-nne	'juniper leaf'
ʃí-ʔleʔ	'piece of meat'	téna-nne	'song'

Obviously, this is exactly the same pattern as in Tzeltal, both under Paster's approach and the one proposed here. Under Paster's account, *-ʔleʔ* would subcategorize for monosyllabic bases, whereas *-nne* is the corresponding default affix. Under the templatic approach proposed here, the preferred and indexed allomorph *-ʔleʔ* is chosen if it results in a word constituting a perfect bisyllabic output foot, hence with monosyllabic bases. The dispreferred (and not indexed) allomorph (*-nne*) appears when this would not be possible without truncation, i.e., with longer bases. A virtually identical pattern as in Zuni is found in Kashaya (Oswalt 1960; Buckley 1994), where according to Paster (2006: 169) (citing Buckley 1994) 'monosyllabic stems take *-cin*', while polysyllabic stems take *-men*"'. Hence the uniform output of the preferred allomorph *-cin*' is again a bisyllabic foot.

The allomorphy for ergative/instrumental/locative marking in Kaititj (Pama-Nyungan) provides an interesting twist. As shown in (27), *-ŋ* appears with bisyllabic nouns (27a) and *-l* with longer nouns (27b) (apparently there are no monosyllabic nouns in the language):

(27) *Ergative allomorphy in Kaititj* (Koch 1980:264–266)

a. *Bisyllabic nouns*		b. *Polysyllabic nouns*	
akí-ŋ	'head'	alíki-l	'dog'
iltyí-ŋ	'hand'	aʈúyi-l	'man'
aNmí-ŋ	'red ochre'	aɣírki-l	'sun'

Crucially, in Paster's theory, the subcategorization frame of Kaititj *-ŋ* has a different specification (it selects bisyllabic bases) from the one assumed for Tzeltal *-oh* and Zuni *-ʔleʔ* (selecting monosyllabic bases). On the other hand, the analysis of Kaititj in the template-based account is virtually identical to the ones for Tzeltal and Zuni. Kaititj *-ŋ* consists of a single consonant, it is subsyllabic, hence all outputs where it is affixed to a bisyllabic noun result in a bisyllabic foot as in *akí-ŋ* 'head'. This points to an important difference between subcategorization- and template-based approach. The template approach predicts that the preferred output variants in SCA should be prosodically well-formed templates such as binary feet.

Hence we would not expect a syllabic affix such as Tzeltal *-oh* to select bisyllabic bases because this would not result in an unmarked binary foot. On the other hand there would be nothing strange about such a pattern in the subcategorization approach. Thus the template/coindexing account makes clearly the more restrictive predictions. In fact, most of the data collected by Paster follow the bisyllabic output pattern we have seen in Tzeltal, Zuni, and Kaititj. Since bisyllabic feet are also one of the few standard templates observed in other areas of morphological exponence, such as truncation (Alber and Arndt-Lappe 2012) and reduplication (Inkelas to appear), this lends crucial support to the approach proposed here.

The only example of non-optimizing SCA cited by Paster, which is not roughly isomorphic to Estonian (one allomorph cooccurs with even-syllable-numbered bases, the other one with odd-syllable-numbered stems), or to Tzeltal and Kaititj (one allomorph results in bisyllabic outputs, the other one in longer polysyllabic outputs) is Dyirbal where one allomorph of the ergative suffix (*-ŋku*) selects bisyllabic bases, and the other one (*-ku*) longer noun stems:

(28) *SCA in the Dyirbal ergative* (Dixon 1972: 42,224)

a. *Bisyllabic nouns*		b. *Polysyllabic nouns*	
ˈyara-ŋku	‘man’	ˈya.maˈni-ku	‘rainbow’
ˈyugu-ŋku	‘stick’	ˈdu.ɲaˈŋunu-ku	‘from leaves in water’

Crucially, the outputs of *ŋku*-forms are consistently trisyllabic, a size which does correspond to a well-formed prosodic constituent, nor to a standard template in other areas of Prosodic Morphology such as reduplication (Downing 2006) or truncation (Alber and Arndt-Lappe 2012; see also Hayes 1995, Elenbas and Kager 1999 for critical discussion on alleged cases of trisyllabic feet in metrical theory).

However, from a morphological perspective, the analysis of the *-ŋku/-ku* alternation as suppletive allomorphy between two unrelated alternants is problematic. Under the standard assumption that the cognitive representation and segmentation of affixes is to a high degree governed by ‘islands of reliability’ (Albright 2002; Albright and Hayes 2003), i.e. highly regular syncretism patterns in the morphosyntactic distribution of potential affixes, Dyirbal has only a single ergative affix *-ku*, since this string of segments is used in ergative forms of all nouns throughout the language (Dixon 1972). On the other hand, *-ŋ* does not only occur in ergative, but also in locative forms giving rise to exactly the same SCA pattern: *-ŋka* appears with bisyllabic, and *-ka* with longer nouns (Dixon 1972; Wolf 2008, this volume).

(29) *SCA in the Dyirbal locative* (Dixon 1972)
a. jaɽa-ŋka 'man'
b. jamani-ka 'rainbow'

As shown by Wolf (2008, this volume), ergative and locative form a natural class in Dyirbal, they correspond to the case feature [–free] proposed by Halle and Vaux (1998).[7] Taken together, the much more plausible analysis of the data in (28) (and (29)) is that *-ku* is the unique ergative affix of the language, whereas *-ŋ* is a stem extension expressing the feature [–free] with a suppletive Ø-allomorph. Under the natural assumption that stem extensions are Stem-Level (see Bermúdez-Otero 2007, 2010, and Trommer 2013 for similar cases in Spanish and Albanian), and the ergative suffix a Word-Level affix, as shown in (30):

(30) *Alternative morphological segmentation of Dyirbal ergative suffixation*

a. *Bisyllabic Nouns*
['yara-ŋ]-ku 'man'
['yugu-ŋ]-ku 'stick'

b. *Polysyllabic Nouns*
['ya.ma'ni-Ø]-ku 'rainbow'
['du.ɲa'ŋunu-Ø]-ku 'from leaves in water'

Under this morphological interpretation, the analysis of Stem-Level allomorphy in Dyirbal is completely analogous to the cases in Tzeltal, and Kaititj: *-ŋ* appears in bisyllabic (31a), -Ø in polysyllabic outputs (31b) at the Stem Level, and Word-Level affixation of *-ku* doesn't involve any allomorphy.

(31) *Dyirbal by indexed-constraint stem optimization*

a. *Bisyllabic input at the Stem Level*

Input: yara+{-ŋ,-Ø}	PWD=BINFT$_{ŋ}$	[–free]=ŋ
☞ i. (ya.ra-ŋ)		
ii. (ya.ra-Ø)		*!

b. *Polysyllabic input at the Stem Level*

Input: yamani+{-ŋ,-Ø}	PWD=BINFT$_{ŋ}$	[–free]=ŋ
i. ya(ma.ni-ŋ)	*!	
☞ ii. ya(ma.ni-Ø)		*

Thus the pattern in Dyirbal is a close counterpart to external affixation cases in truncation: in a form such as *(yara-ŋ)-ku*, the suffix *-ku* is external to the bisyllabic template in exactly the same way as *-čan* in the Japanese hypocoristic form (*Mido*)-*čan*. A case of allomorphy which is structurally virtually identical to Dyirbal is the diminutive formation in a number of Spanish dialects for which Paster (2006: 148) following Harris (1979) argues that the allomorph *-cito/-cita* appears after bisyllabic (32a), but *-ito/-ita* after longer stems (32b) (orthographic <u> and <i> in <saurie> correspond phonologically phonologically to the glides [w] and [j], hence <saurie> is bisyllabic).

(32) *Diminutive SCA in Spanish dialects* (Harris 1979:291)

a.	i.	madre-cita	*madr-ita	b. i.	comadr-ita	*comadre-cita
	ii.	saurie-cito	*saur-ito	ii.	dinosaur-ito	*dinosaurie-cito

As in Dyirbal the 'allomorph' surfacing with bisyllabic stems consists of the default allomorph extended by an initial consonant. Thus exactly the same analysis applies: *-c* is a Stem-Level diminutive marker that is by constraint indexing restricted to bisyllabic bases, and otherwise supplanted by a zero allomorph; in addition there is a general Word-Level diminutive *-ito/-ita* that applies to all diminutives. Interestingly, under this analysis, the case of redundant diminutive affixation in Spanish follows exactly a pattern identified by Inkelas and Caballero (2013) as typical for multiple affixal exponence: an innermost phonologically 'weak' affix of low salience is supplemented by a phonologically 'strong' outermost affix of high salience.[8]

An interesting variant to the Dyirbal (and Spanish) pattern is found in a closely related language, Warlpiri, where ergative is marked by *-ŋku* or *-rlu*, and the locative by *-ŋka* or *-rla* (Paster (2006: 180, page numbers in brackets) refer to Nash (1986); unlike for Dyirbal, in Warlpiri orthography, <rC> indicates a retroflex C):

(33) *Mora-counting allomorphy in the Warlpiri ergative* (Nash 1986)

a. i.	ŋurrpa-ŋku	'unknowing-ERG'	(34)	b. i.	nyanuŋu-rlu	'he-ERG'	(235)
ii.	ŋapa-ŋku	'water-ERG'	(41)	ii.	ŋuurrpa-rlu	'throat-ERG'	(34)
iii.	kurdu-ŋku	'child-ERG'	(227)	iii.	Jakamarra-rlu	(name)-ERG	(217)

(34) *Mora-counting allomorphy in the Warlpiri locative* (Nash 1986)

a. i.	karru-ŋka	'creek-LOC'	(203)	b. i.	turaki-rla	'vehicle-LOC'	(145)
ii.	karti-ŋka	'cards-LOC'	(203)	ii.	yaali-rla	'that-LOC'	(176)
iii.	pirli-ŋka	'rock-ERG'	(176)	iii.	Yalikaraŋu-rla	(place name)-ERG	(132)

In close parallel to Dyirbal, Warlpiri, marks [–free] (ergative and locative) by *-ŋk* for 'shorter' (prosodically lighter) nouns, *-u* expones ergative, and *-a* locative. In contrast to Dyirbal, the suppletive [–free] allomorph for longer nouns is non-zero *-rl,* and the weight/length parameter that triggers suppletion is slightly different. Bimoraic stems take *-ŋk*, and longer stems *-rl*, as is obvious from word forms such as *yaali-rl-a* (3bii), which is bisyllabic but trimoraic due to the long vowel in its first syllable (only vowels are moraic in Warlpiri, coda consonants are irrelevant for the mora count), and takes the same alternants as trisyllabic *turaki* (34bi). Thus the Warlpiri analysis is virtually identical to the one for Dyirbal apart from the fact that the prosodic constraints indexed for *-ŋk* enforce bimoraic, not bisyllabic feet.

Again, the same structural pattern is also found outside of Australia. In Axininca Campa (Payne 1981) according to Paster (2006: 172) 'there is a genitive suffix that takes one of two forms, *-ni* or *-ti*, depending on whether the stem (not including the person marking prefix) has two vocalic moras or more than two, respectively':

(35) *Mora-counting allomorphy in Axininca Campa* (Payne 1981: 244--246)

a. i.	no-sari-ni	'my macaw'	b. i.	a-toniro-ti	'our palm (aquaje)'
ii.	p-ana-ni	'your black dye'	ii.	pi-wiiri-ti	'your bat'
iii.	o-çaa-ni	'her anteater'	iii.	o-itairiki-ti	'her wild pig'
iv.	i-yimi-ni	'his squash'	iv.	n-aawana-ti	'my mahogany'

Again the suffix can be straightforwardly subsegmented into a unique Word-Level affix *-i* and two Stem-Level allomorphs *-n* and *-t* (as in Paster's account, prefixes must be added derivationally later, hence also at the Word Level). Thus under the natural assumption that Axininca has moraic binary feet, PWD=BINFT$_n$ >> GEN=n derives the correct distribution of *-n* and *-t*.

Note finally an important point about the morphological side of the reanalysis for the Spanish diminutive, Axininca, and similar cases: whereas the subanalysis of *-cito* into *-c* and *-ito* is new for the case at hand, it doesn't require any novel theoretical devices apart from the possibility of multiple exponence, i.e., of realizing the same set of morphosyntactic features by more than one affix. As things stand, virtually all major approaches to morphological spellout acknowledge that multiple exponence is a pervasive feature of natural language, and allow to derive it by principled means, either by not restricting the cooccurrence of affixes expressing the same features, as long as these are part of different rule blocks (Anderson 1992; Stump 2001), or by capturing it through postsyntactic copying operations as in Distributed Morphology (Halle and Marantz 1993; Müller 2007). The analyses proposed here simply combine multiple exponence with allomorphy, constraint indexing, and the assignment of affixes to morphophonological strata. Whereas many cases of multiple exponence discussed in the literature are more obvious than the case of *-c-ito* either because the two cooccurring affixes occur both independently in some contexts (cf. Paster 2007 on nominal plural in Jubba Maay, and also the Dyirbal and Warlpiri cases discussed above) or because they may be separated by other affixes (cf. Inkelas and Caballero 2013 on the applicative in Choguita Rarámuri), all the subanalyses assumed here are rather traditional in executing the classical structuralist principle that 'a sequence of phonemes which has meaning, and which is not composed of smaller sequences having meaning, is a morpheme' (Harris 1942: 169).

8.4 Opaque SCA and morphological stratification

Apart from instances of non-optimizing allomorphy, Paster adduces a further strong argument against capturing SCA by phonological optimization: cases where SCA could in principle be captured by output optimization, but where for a subset of inputs/stems the motivation for the selection of the correct allomorph is opaquely obscured by later phonological or morphological processes. The first such case Paster cites is SCA in the verbal inflection of Saami (Dolbey 1997), which is structurally closely parallel to the Estonian case discussed above. Many affixes such as the 2du suffix have two allomorphs, where one appears with nominal bases of even-numbered syllable count (e.g. 2du *-be͜ahtti*) and the other one with odd-numbered bases (e.g. 2du *-hppi*).

(36) *Simple SCA in Saami* (Dolbey 1997:103,105)

	jearra- 'to ask'	veahkehea- 'to help'	even	odd
1du	je:r.re.-Ø	ve͜ah.ke.he:-t.ne	-Ø	-tne
2du	je͜ar.ra.-be͜aht.ti	ve͜ah.ke.he͜a-hp.pi	-be͜ahtti	-hppi
2pl	je͜ar.ra.-beh.tet	ve͜ah.ke.he:-h.pet	-behtet	-hpet
passive	je:r.ro.-juv.vo	ve͜ah.ke.hu-v.vo	-juvvo	-vvo

Once again this pattern can also be straightforwardly understood in terms of optimizing phonological outputs. Thus the choice of allomorphs systematically ensures that the resulting output forms have an even-numbered syllable count. Assuming that Saami allows only bisyllabic trochaic feet, this may be captured as a straightforward effect of high-ranked PARSE σ, as shown in (37):

(37) *Saami SCA by pure output optimization*

a. *Even-numbered-σ input*

Input: je:r.re+{-Ø,-tne}	PARSE σ
☞ i. (je:r.re-Ø)	
ii. (je:r.re)-tne	*!

b. *Odd-numbered-σ input*

Input: veah.ke.he+{-Ø,-tne}	PARSE σ
i. (veah.ke).he-Ø	*!
☞ ii. (veah.ke).(he-t.ne)	

Opacity arises in cases of recursive affixation of the SCA-affixes in (36), such as in the example in (38), where 2du affixation applies to a form that already bears a passive suffix.

(38) *Recursive SCA in Saami* (Dolbey 1997)
je:r.ro-juv.vo-beaht.ti 'you (two) ask'
ask-passive-2du
*je:r.ru-v.vo-hp.pi

Both suffixes show the (bisyllabic) allomorph used for even-numbered bases. This follows directly from a subcategorization analysis in Paster's approach if the affix entries for Saami are adapted from the correspondingly behaving Estonian affixes in (7) as in (39) and affixation is taken to be cyclically interleaved with phonology.

(39) *SCA in Saami as morphological subcategorization*

a. -juvvo ↔ [+pass] / [Foot#] __
b. -vvo ↔ [+pass]
c. -beaht.ti ↔ [+2 –pl –sg] / [Foot#] __
d. -hppi ↔ [+2 –pl –sg]

Thus in the first phonological cycle of (38), the root gets a bisyllabic foot structure by phonological optimization: je:rro ⇒ (je:r.ro), consequently it satisfies the subcategorization requirement of *-juvvo*, which is therefore preferred over *-vvo*: (je:r.ro) ⇒ (je:r.ro)-juvvo. In the second phonological cycle, the affix also receives a binary foot, which in turn gives rise to affixation of *-beaht.ti* since the resulting stem ends in a foot: (je:r.ro)-juvvo ⇒ (je:r.ro)-(juv.vo) ⇒ (je:r.ro)-(juv.vo)-beaht.ti.

On the other hand, in the framework assumed by Kager – fully parallel OT– recursive SCA in Saami turns out to be problematic, as shown in the tableau in (40). Whereas the correct 2du passive form with two bisyllabic allomorphs (40a) satisfies PARSE σ, so does (40b) with the two monosyllabic variants, since the output also results in perfect binary foot formation.

(40) *Parallel evaluation of recursive SCA*

Input: je:r.ro+{-juvvo,-vvo}+{-beahtti,-hppi}	PARSE σ
☞ a. (je:r.ro)-(juv.vo)-(beaht.ti)	
☛ b. (je:r.ru-v)(vo-hp.pi)	
c. (je:r.ru-v)(vo-beaht)ti	*!
d. (je:r.ro)-(juv.vo-hp)pi	*!

However, the subcategorization model is not more successful because it is fully morphological, where Kager relies on phonological optimization, but because it is cyclic.[9] Once cyclicity is imported into OT-evaluation, Saami is perfectly amenable to an analysis in terms of phonological optimization. Thus under the assumption that passive is a Stem-Level affix, whereas 2du is Word-Level, Stem-Level evaluation will correctly select *-juvvo* (41ai) for a bisyllabic stem since (je:r.ru-v)vo cannot be completely footified:

(41) *Stratal optimization of recursive SCA*

a. *Stem Level*

Input: je:r.ro+{-juvvo,-vvo}	PARSE σ
☞ i. (je:r.ro)-(juv.vo)	
ii. (je:r.ru-v)vo	*!

b. *Word Level*

Input: je:r.ro.juv.vo+{-beahtti,-hppi}	PARSE σ
☞ i. (je:r.ro)-(juv.vo)-(beaht.ti)	
ii. (je:r.ro)-(juv.vo-hp)pi	*!

Paster (2006:160) adduces a further case for opaque SCA from in Spanish, where there are two competing almost identical suffixes which derive nouns from adjectives. *-eza* is used with mono- and bisyllabic input stems, and *-eza* with longer adjectives (orthographic <c> and <qu> in Spanish denote phonological [k]):

(42) *Opaque SCA in Spanish (σ-number of input stems)*

1 σ	2 σ (final V)	2 σ (final C)	3 σ	4 σ
vil	franco	gentil	maduro	hediondo
vil-eza	franqu-eza	gentil-eza	madur-ez	hediond-ez
'vile'	'truthful'	'gentle'	'mature'	'smelly'

As pointed out by Aranovich and Orgun (1998), this pattern is opaque in the sense that the σ-number of the input adjective, not its eventual output seems to be decisive for the selection of the correct allomorph. Thus the exponents of both *gentil* and *maduro* are bisyllabic in the resulting nominalizations due to a general morphophonological process in Spanish that deletes stem-final theme vowels before vowel-initial suffixes such as *-ez(a)* (Bermúdez-Otero 2007, 2013), but only *gentil* nominalizes with *-eza*.

(43) *Opaque SCA in Spanish (σ-number of output stems)*

1 σ	2 σ	3 σ
vil	gentil	hediondo
vil-eza	gentil-eza	hediond-ez
franc	maduro	
franqu-eza	madur-ez	

Thus apparently vowel deletion is counterbleeding allomorph selection. This is a natural consequence in the cyclic architecture of Paster's subcategorization approach where morphological selection by an affix precedes phonological optimization of the affix-stem combination, but is problematic for approaches deriving SCA from output optimization since phonological outputs as in (43) do not deterministically predict allomorphy.

However, as in the case of Dyirbal ergative allomorphy, it is highly unlikely that the different realizations of Spanish nominalization result from a simple choice between two atomic allomorphs in the first place. Virtually all current analyses of Spanish nominal inflection agree that the final vowels of Spanish nouns represent a segmentable formative, the 'theme vowel' which maintains at least some independence from roots and affixes to which it attaches (cf. Harris 1991, 1996; Oltra-Massuet and Arregi 2005; Bermúdez-Otero 2007, 2013, and Wunderlich 1996 for a minority position).[10]

Now, if *-a* is an independent formative, the allomorphy analysis of the Spanish data proposed by Paster would amount to the claim that Spanish has two homophonous affixes *-ez* forming deadjectival nouns, one that selects mono- or bisyllabic bases, and triggers a vocalic theme marker, and a second one that selects longer bases, and selects the zero theme marker (or no theme marker at all). But under these premises, it is much more likely that there is only one affix *-ez*, and the interdependence of syllable number and theme marker selection is due to independent factors.

Since there are a substantial number of exceptions to the distribution claimed by Aranovich and Orgun (Mascaró p.c., see also the discussion below), it is possible that the distribution of theme markers is actually the result of the full-form storage for deadjectival nouns including theme vowels. This would be a natural assumption in the approach to Spanish theme vowels by Bermúdez-Otero (2007, 2013), who argues that all occurrences of theme vowels in Spanish are the result of lexical listing for complex stems (i.e., stems with internal structures) including theme vowels. Thus *franqueza* would be stored as [[[*franqu*$_A$]-*ez*$_N$]]-*a*$_{Th}$], and *madur-ez* would simply instantiate the regular pattern of deadjectival adjective formation.[11]

But even if the SCA pattern identified by Aranovich and Orgun is taken to be the productive one, and theme vowels are interpreted as independent exponents of inflectional class, the Spanish data are compatible with an analysis based on phonological optimization. For concreteness, I will sketch a Distributed Morphology analysis for the morphological facts. I adopt the approach to Spanish nominal inflection developed in Halle and Marantz (1994), where theme vowels spell out inflectional class features that are introduced by vocabulary items and postsyntactic morphological rules, and [I] is the class feature whose default realization is *-a* (as in *gentil-ez-a*). I assume that deadjectival nominalization in Spanish is bimorphemic, consisting of a Stem-Level affix (little a), and a Word-Level affix (little n) (+ the inflectional class marker/theme vowel in *-ez-a*), whereas little n is consistently *-ez*, little a has two allomorphs, the templatic affix -F (a foot), and Ø, where -F carries the class feature [I]. -F is subject to the same kind of indexing as Tzeltal *-oh* and all structurally parallel allomorphs in other languages discussed so far. Crucially, at the Stem Level, vowel deletion has not applied yet, and thus -F is selected for all monosyllabic and bisyllabic adjectival stems whether they are vowel-final or consonant-final (*vil, franco*, and *gentil*) (44a) and Ø for all longer stems (*maduro, hediondo*) since these do not give rise to the complete coincidence of the prosodic word with a foot.[12]

(44) *Stem-Level optimization of Spanish nominalization*

a. *Bisyllabic stem*

Input: gentil+{-F,-Ø}	PWD=BINFT$_F$	a=F
☞ i. (gen.til)$_F$		
ii. (gen.til)-Ø		*!

b. *Polysyllabic stem*

Input: maduro+{-F,-Ø}	PWD=BINFT$_F$	a=F
i. ma(du.ro)$_F$	*!	
☞ ii. ma(du.ro)-Ø		*

In effect, nominalizations based on mono- or bisyllabic adjectives carry the class feature [I], which is later spelled out by *-a*, whereas nominalizations built on longer stems do not. Independent evidence for the close link of the *-ez/-ez-a* alternations to inflectional class features comes from other uses of these formatives. As pointed out by Aranovich and Orgun (1998), *-ez* (without thematic *-a*) also occurs regularly with denominal nominalizations as in (45):

(45) *Denominal nominalizations with* -ez (Aranovich and Orgun 1998: 120)
  a. niño 'child' niñ-ez
  b. viudo 'widow' viud-ez

This is expected under the analysis here: In both cases, deadjectival and denominal nominalizations there is the same category head with an abstract reading spelled out by *-ez*, but denominal forms do not involve little a which might lead to the introduction of the class feature [I], thus do not trigger insertion of a thematic vowel. In addition, there are exceptional deadjectival nouns which carry the theme vowel, as shown in (46):

(46) *Deadjectival nominalizations with polysyllabic inputs* (Aranovich and Orgun 1998: 120)
  a. ligero 'light' ligereza
  b. agudo 'sharp' agudeza
  c. delicado 'delicate' delicadeza

Again, this type of exception is expected if the distribution of thematic *-a* is governed by lexical class features. It can be captured straightforwardly by assuming that little a has a third, lexically conditioned allomorph which is phonologically Ø, but introduces the class feature [I]. Thus the morphological approach sketched allows one to capture all patterns of *-ez/-eza*-nominalizations by assuming only one affix *-ez*, and the regular class suffix *-a*, where Aranovich and Orgun (and Paster) must stipulate a wide set of isofunctional homophonous and semi-homophonous word formation affixes.

There is one final advantage of the approach developed here. If the different shapes of deadjectival formation are derived by phonological selection of *-eza*, it requires a subcategorization frame that specifies a minimally trisyllabic base, as in the analysis proposed by Paster:

(47) *Subcategorization analysis of Spanish* (Paster 2006:160)
  -ez ↔ N / [...σσσ#] ___
  -eza ↔ N

This runs counter to the standard assumption in theoretical phonology that the upper bound for counting in OT-constraints is 2 (see McCarthy 2003b and references cited there for discussion), a hypothesis which is impressively supported by Paster's SCA data, once they are captured by indexed constraints and phonological optimization. Conversely, the subcategorization approach does not provide a principled tackle on the typological generalization that virtually all cases of SCA involve affixed targets that are bisyllabic.

Paster (2006:167) discusses a further case that shows a similar type of opacity as Spanish nominalization, instrumental allomorphy in Nancowry, where the infix *-an-* (48a) is used for monosyllabic input verbs, and *-in-* for bisyllabic ones (48b):

(48) *Infixing SCA in Nancowry* (Radhakrishnan 1981:61–63)

a.	i.	káp	'to bite'	k-an-áp	'tooth'
	ii.	tián	'to file'	t-an-ián	'a file'
	iii.	léʔ l-an-léʔ	'to catch'	l-an-éʔ	'an object to catch with'
	iv.	rɯ́k	'to arrive'	r-an-ɯ́k	'a vehicle'
b.	i.	kaʔap	'to close'	k-in-ʔáp	'a trap'
	ii.	tikóʔ	'to prick'	t-in-kóʔ	'pin, needle'
	iii.	sahuáŋ	'cool'	s-in-huáŋ	'something that cools'
	iv.	ha-kiõk	'to inflate'	h-in-kiõk	'a pump'

Although *-an-* and *-in-* are both infixes that surface after the first consonant of the base verb they differ in their morphophonological effects: whereas *-an-* precedes the first stem vowel *-in-* triggers its deletion. In effect, the output forms for both are bisyllabic, again the kind of opacity which provides prima facie evidence against an output optimization approach, whereas a subcategorization approach might simply capture the distribution of the infix allomorphs by subcategorization requirements on *-an-* for monosyllabic, and on *-in-* for bisyllabic stems. Since phonological subcategorization in Paster's approach applies to the phonological structure of bases before they are concatenated with the subcategorizing affix, the ultimate levelling to bisyllabic outputs across the board is irrelevant.

However, the output optimization system proposed here which makes use of indexed constraints and strata offers a number of straightforward options to capture Nancowry instrumental allomorphy, depending of course on the analysis of infixation and vowel deletion.

For example we might assume that *-an-* is infixed after the first base consonant (and before the first stem vowel), whereas *-in-* is inserted after the first vowel of the base (standard targets for infixation in the systems of Yu 2007 and Fitzpatrick 2004), and that stem-vowel deletion in hiatus contexts is strictly a Word-Level process in Nancowry. *-an-* is indexed in the standard way to a bisyllabic foot template. Thus at the Stem Level, a monosyllabic base would form an optimal output for *-an-* because both allomorphs lead to bisyllabic results and *-an-* is favoured by lexical preference (49a). On the other hand, the combination of a bisyllabic base with any allomorph would result in trisyllabic outputs, which leads to selection of *-in-* which is not restricted to bisyllabicity by indexed markedness constraints:

(49) *Stem-Level optimization in Nancowry SCA*

a. *Monosyllabic input at the Stem Level*

Input: rúk+{-an-,-in-}	PWD=BINFT$_{an}$	INS=an
☞ i. (ra.núk)		
ii. (rú.ink)		*!

b. *Biysyllabic input at the Stem Level*

Input: kaʔap+{-an-,-in-}	PWD=BINFT$_{an}$	INS=an
i. ka(na.ap)	*!	
☞ ii. ka(in.ʔap)		*

The Stem-Level output ka(in.ʔap) is then shortened to bisyllabic (kin.ʔap) at the Word Level to avoid hiatus (or to satisfy a more general bisyllabicity requirement), whereas (ra.núk) is faithfully conserved.

In fact, neither the recourse to different constraint rankings at Stem and Word Level, nor to different linearization requirements for *-an-* and *-in-* is strictly necessary to account for the Nancowry case if we abandon the idea that the distribution is strictly driven by syllable counting, i.e., by foot-level prosody. An alternative option is to employ the insight that none of the *-an*-forms, but all *-in*-forms in (48) have complex codas which we may implement by the undominated indexed constraint NOCODA$_{an}$, and extending the bisyllabic foot requirement to both allomorphs as in (50), where both allomorphs might surface after the first consonant or after the first vowel (with concomitant deletion of the stem vowel).[13] For monosyllabic stems, INS=an again ensures preference for *-an-*, and PWD=BINFT$_{\{an,in\}}$ selects a bisyllabic output (50a). For a bisyllabic input there is no output that would be both bisyllabic (and meet PWD=BINFT$_{\{an,in\}}$) and without a coda. Since the effect of NOCODA is limited to *-an-* by lexical indexing, this leads to preference for *-in-* (50b):

(50) *Alternative analysis of Nancowry SCA (Stem Level)*

a. *Monosyllabic input at the Stem Level*

Input: rúk{-an-,-in-}	NOCODA$_{an}$	PWD=BINFT$_{\{an,in\}}$	INS=an
☞ i. (ra.núk)			
ii. (ri.núk)			*!
iii. (r.ink)			*!
iv. (rank)	*!	*	*

b. *Biysyllabic input at the Stem Level*

Input: kaʔap+{-an-,-in-}	NoCoda$_{an}$	PWd=BinFt$_{\{an,in\}}$	Ins=an
i. ka(na.ʔap)		*!	
ii. ki(na.ʔap)		*!	
iii. (kan.ʔap)	*!		
☞ iv. (kin.ʔap)			*

8.5 Empirical predictions of subcategorization and template optimization

Whereas the indexed-constraint approach to non-optimizing SCA can capture all attested data uncovered by Paster, it is inherently more restrictive, imposing narrow limits on the possible phonological shapes of affixes for specific types of SCA. Thus consider again Kaititj, where the first of two subsyllabic affix allomorphs combines with bisyllabic bases (e.g. *akí-ŋ* 'head') while the second allomorph appears longer bases (e.g. *alíki-l* 'dog'). This is shown schematically in (51a). As argued above, this distribution can be captured both by Paster's subcategorization approach and the indexed-constraint approach developed here. However, in the subcategorization approach, where phonological selection is an arbitrary feature of allomorphs, we also expect to find systems as in hypothetical Kaititj' (51b), where both allomorphs are monosyllabic (say *-ŋa* and *-lo*), resulting in trisyllabic outputs for the preferred allomorph (e.g. *akí-ŋa*) and quadrisyllabic (*alíki-lo*) or correspondingly longer forms for the default allomorph, and Kaititj'' (51c), where a monosyllabic allomorph selects bisyllabic, and a subsyllabic allomorph longer bases.

(51) *Attested and unattested SCA patterns predicted by prosodic subcategorization*

a. *Kaititj (two subsyllabic allomorphs)*

		Allomorph$_1$	Allomorph$_2$
Base	2 σ	akí-ŋ	*
	n σ	*	alíki-l

b. **Kaititj' (two monosyllabic allomorphs)*

		Allomorph$_1$	Allomorph$_2$
Base	2σ	akí-ŋa	*
	nσ	*	alíki-lo

c. **Kaititj" (one mono-/one sub-syllabic allomorph)*

		$Allomorph_1$	$Allomorph_2$
Base	2σ	akí-ŋa	*
	nσ	*	alíki-l

On the other hand, there is no analysis of the distributions in (51b,c) in the approach to SCA based on prosodic optimization since this would require an (indexed) constraint ranking that selects trisyllabic words as optimal, which is impossible under standard assumptions on foot structure and prosodic markedness.[14]

Similar points could be made for potential cases of SCA involving bisyllabic allomorphs. These can be captured straightforwardly in Paster's subcategorization approach, but not in a phonological-optimization account, which would presuppose unmarked trisyllabic or quadrisyllabic templates, not available in standard approaches to prosodic phonology. Since all known cases of SCA show exactly the correlation of affix size and base shape predicted by a template optimization approach, this provides striking evidence for the systematic correlation of phonological affix and stem shape, and for a template optimization approach.

Let us now consider further possible systems predicted by the templatic-optimization approach. Recall from section 2 (see the discussion of tableau (20)) that PWD=BINFT is actually a shorthand for the independently motivated constraints PARSE σ and ALLFTLFT. This opens up the possibility that only one of these constraints might be indexed for a primary allomorph (the one sanctioned by a lexical preference constraint). Here, I will show for SCA systems with monosyllabic allomorphs that this results in output distributions also predicted by the subcategorization approach. Consider first a putative language Tzeltal', where PARSE σ, but not ALLFTLFT is indexed for *-oh* and prosodic parsing generates left-aligned syllabic feet, with final unfootified syllables for word forms with odd syllable number.[15] Hence, for a monosyllabic base, PARSE σ_{oh} is satisfied (52a), but not for a bisyllabic base (52b) which occurs hence with *-ɛh* (52b):

(52) *Tzeltal': Short bases*

a. *Monosyllabic base*

Input: σ+{-ɛh,-oh}	PARSE σ_{oh}	PERF=oh
☞ a. (σ.oh)		
b. (σ.ɛh)		*!

b. *Bisyllabic base*

Input: σσ+{-εh,-oh}	PARSE $σ_{oh}$	PERF=oh
a. (σ.σ)oh	*!	
☞ b. (σ.σ)εh		*

The same distributional pattern would be found with longer bases: bases with odd syllable number surface with *-oh* (53a), bases with even syllable number surface with *-εh* (53b):

(53) *Tzeltal': Long bases*

a. *Trisyllabic base*

Input: σσσ+{-εh,-oh}	PARSE $σ_{oh}$	PERF=oh
☞ a. (σ.σ)(σ.oh)		
b. (σ.σ)(σ.εh)		*!

b. *Quadrisyllabic base*

Input: σσσσ+{-εh,-oh}	PARSE $σ_{oh}$	PERF=oh
a. (σ.σ)(σ.σ)oh	*!	
☞ b. (σ.σ)(σ.σ)εh		*

Thus effectively Tzeltal' results in a system similar to Estonian and Saami where one allomorph appears with even numbers and one with odd numbers of base syllables, which can be captured in Paster's system by subcategorization of one allomorph (here: *-εh*) for bases with final bisyllabic feet. (Paster 2005: 331). If PARSE σ is not indexed for *-oh*, but only ALLFTLFT, we get a minimally different pattern where *-oh* appears with monosyllabic (54a) and even-numbered bases (54b), (55b), and *-εh* with longer odd-numbered bases (55a) (if *-oh* is not part of a foot, ALLFTLFT_{oh} is vacuously satisfied since there is no foot overlapping with *-oh*):

(54) *Tzeltal'':* *Short bases*

a. *Monosyllabic base*

Input: σ+{-εh,-oh}	ALLFTLFT_{oh}	PERF=oh
☞ a. (σ.oh)		
b. (σ.εh)		*!

b. *Bisyllabic base*

Input: σσ+{-εh,-oh}	ALLFTLFT_{oh}	PERF=oh
☞ a. (σ.σ)oh		
b. (σ.σ)εh		*!

(55) *Tzeltal'':* *Long bases*

a. *Trisyllabic base*

Input: σσσ+{-ɛh,-oh}	ALLFTLFT$_{oh}$	PERF=oh
a. (σ.σ)(σ.oh)	*!	
☞ b. (σ.σ)(σ.ɛh)		*

b. *Quadrisyllabic base*

Input: σσσσ+{-ɛh,-oh}	ALLFTLFT$_{oh}$	PERF=oh
☞ a. (σ.σ)(σ.σ)oh		
b. (σ.σ)(σ.σ)ɛh		*!

Also Tzeltal'' follows naturally in Paster's approach if *-oh* subcategorizes for a base with a final foot (the single unary foot of a monosyllabic base or the final binary foot of even-numbered bases; by assumption, odd-numbered bases end with an unfootified syllable). Note finally that the distribution of allomorphs for monosyllabic bases in Estonian is actually more complex than in Tzeltal' and Tzeltal'', where some (heavier) monosyllabic bases take even-syllable allomorphs and other (lighter) bases odd-syllable allomorphs. These complications are not discussed in Paster (2006), see Kager (1996) for discussion.

A further combinatorial possibility is that one of the two competing allomorphs is indexed for by ALLFTLFT, and the other one by PARSE σ. If the primary allomorph (*-oh*) is indexed for PARSE σ, and the secondary allomorph (*-ɛh*) for ALLFTLFT, this results in a pattern where one affix appears with odd-numbered bases (56a), (57a), and the other one with even-numbered bases (56b), (57b):[16]

(56) *Tzeltal''': Short bases*

a. *Monosyllabic base*

Input: σ+{-ɛh,-oh}	ALLFTLFT$_{ɛh}$	PARSE σ$_{oh}$	PERF=oh
☞ a. (σ.oh)			
b. (σ.ɛh)			*!

b. *Bisyllabic base*

Input: σσ+{-ɛh,-oh}	ALLFTLFT$_{ɛh}$	PARSE σ$_{oh}$	PERF=oh
a. (σ.σ)oh		*!	
☞ b. (σ.σ)ɛh			*

(57) *Tzeltal''': Long bases*

a. *Trisyllabic base*

Input: σσσ+{-εh,-oh}	ALLFTLFT$_{εh}$	PARSE σ$_{oh}$	PERF=oh
☞ a. (σ.σ)(σ.oh)			
b. (σ.σ)(σ.εh)	*!		*

b. *Quadrisyllabic base*

Input: σσσσ+{-εh,-oh}	ALLFTLFT$_{εh}$	PARSE σ$_{oh}$	PERF=oh
a. (σ.σ)(σ.σ)oh		*!	
☞ b. (σ.σ)(σ.σ)εh			*

This is once again the Estonian-type pattern of SCA, and can be derived in Paster's approach as well as with other constraint rankings in the template-optimization account. Of course, the 'cross-indexing' of allomorphs could be reversed, which results in a pattern where one affix (here: *-oh*) appears with monosyllabic (58a) and all even-numbered bases (59b), and the other one (here: *-εh*) with longer even-numbered bases (59a):

(58) *Tzeltal'''': Short bases*

a. *Monosyllabic base*

Input: σ+{-εh,-oh}	ALLFTLFT$_{oh}$	PARSE σ$_{εh}$	PERF=oh
☞ a. (σ.oh)			
b. (σ.εh)			*!

b. *Bisyllabic base*

Input: σσ+{-εh,-oh}	ALLFTLFT$_{oh}$	PARSE σ$_{εh}$	PERF=oh
☞ a. (σ.σ)oh			
b. (σ.σ)εh		*!	*

(59) *Tzeltal'''': Long bases*

a. *Trisyllabic base*

Input: σσσ+{-εh,-oh}	ALLFTLFT$_{oh}$	PARSE σ$_{εh}$	PERF=oh
a. (σ. σ)(σ.oh)	*!		
☞ b. (σ.σ)(σ.εh)			*

b. *Quadrisyllabic base*

Input: σσσσ+{-εh,-oh}	ALLFTLFT$_{oh}$	PARSE σ$_{εh}$	PERF=oh
☞ a. (σ.σ)(σ.σ)oh			
b. (σ.σ)(σ.σ)εh		*!	*

Hence the constraint ranking of Tzeltal'''' generates the same output distribution as the one of Tzeltal''. Thus overall, the empirical patterns that can be captured by templatic optimization are a proper subset of the ones predicted by the subcategorization account.

8.6 Further alternatives to phonological subcategorization

In the preceding sections, I have shown that apparently non-optimizing types of SCA cited by Paster (2005) in favour of a subcategorization-based and against a phonological-optimization account can be captured through minimally upgrading Kager's (1996) original analysis by a Stratal organization of grammar and indexed constraints relativized to single morphs, two theoretical devices that have been widely argued for in the recent literature. In this section, I discuss other alternatives to prosodic subcategorization which might partially or entirely derive the same result. (60) shows Paster's complete sample for cases of SCA, where (60b) contains the cases she regards as problematic for a pure-optimization approach. Crucially, I have provided above reanalyses for all these cases apart from the genitive and durative in Jivaro for which Paster (2006: 82–85) convincingly argues that the apparent syllable counting in allomorphy assumed by de María (1918) are an accidental side effect of suppletion sensitive to conditions on vowel harmony and the identity of base-final segments (vowels vs. consonants).

(60) *Paster's SCA sample* (Paster 2005:332)

a. *Phonologically predictable*

Estonian		
Finnish		illative
Kimatuumbi	(Bantu, Tanzania)	perfective
Nakanai	(Austronesian, New Britain)	nominalizer
Nancowry	(Mon-Khmer, Nicobar Islands)	causative
Saami	(Lappic, Norway)	person markers, passive
Shipibo	(Panoan, Peru)	ergative, repetitive
Turkana	(Nilotic, Kenya)	abstract noun suffix

b. *Phonologically unpredictable*

Dyirbal	(Pama-Nyungan, Australia)	ergative*
Jivaro	(Jivaroan Ecuador)	genitive*negative*
Kaititj	(Pama-Nyungan/Australia)	ergative/instrumental/ locative*
Kashaya	(Pomoan, California)	durative*
Nancowry	(Mon-Khmer, Nicobar Islands)	instrumental*
Spanish		diminutive*
Tzeltal	(Mayan, Mexico)	perfective*
Warlpiri	(Pama-Nyungan, Australia):	ergative*
Zuni	(isolate, New Mexico)	singular*

Other semiderivational versions of OT: note first that the stratal architecture assumed here might be supplanted by other semi-derivational implementations of OT, such as Optimality Theory with Candidate Chains (OTCC, McCarthy 2007). Thus Wolf (this volume) develops based on an earlier unpublished version of this chapter a version of the Dyirbal analysis above which is couched in Harmonic Serialism (McCarthy 2008, 2010; McCarthy *et al.* 2012).[17] In Wolf's approach, the insertion of an exponent (allomorph) is achieved by the same OT-grammars also carrying out phonological optimization and counts as a single optimization step, i.e., one cycle of OT-evaluation might either lead to the insertion of an exponent or to a standard phonological operation such as deleting a single segment, but not to the simultaneous execution of more than one step; thus a single cycle could neither delete two segments, nor insert two exponents, nor delete a segment and simultaneously insert an exponent. Thus, as above, the first cycle of optimization chooses *-ŋ* over -Ø for bisyllabic stems, and the second cycle inserts *-ku.*[18]

All the cases of derivationality above that crucially invoke strata can be reanalysed by a version of Harmonic Serialism or OT-CC, that achieves allomorph insertion along the lines developed by Wolf since they only require that specific innermost affixes are inserted derivationally prior to specific outermost affixes. Since in Wolf's approach all inner affixes are inserted derivationally before all outer affixes, this possibility follows a fortiori.[19] There is a second crucial difference between HS/OT-CC and Stratal OT. In Stratal OT, the constraint ranking in the Word-Level and the Stem-Level phonology of a given language might be different, whereas HS/OT-CC assumes a single consistent constraint ranking for a given language. Again, this difference is unproblematic for a reconstruction of the Stratal-OT analyses developed here since they are all consistent with a fixed constraint ranking for Stem Level and Word Level.

Cophonology Theory: Given that different combinations of derivational OT-implementations and morpheme- (or allomorph-) specific phonology allow to reconstruct the templatic approach to SCA proposed here, Cophonology Theory (Inkelas and Zoll 2005) is another framework promising to convey the same effect. Cophonology embraces the assumption that every morphological construction *C* (and a fortiori every distinct affixation pattern involving the affix *A*) confers a distinct type of phonological optimization employing a constraint ranking specific to *C*, and – in the case of affixation – to *A*. On the one hand, this allows for analyses which seem to be close to notational variants of analyses in terms of indexed constraints. Thus the account of intervocalic velar deletion provided by Inkelas and Zoll (2005) is almost isomorphic to the indexed-constraint approach sketched in (10), where the ranking for the indexed versions of *VkV constraints with respect to MAX-C corresponds one-by-one to the different rankings of *VkV for the corresponding cophonologies.

(61) *Cophonology analysis for Turkish velar deletion* (Inkelas and Zoll 2005)

a. *Dative Cophonology*

Input: inek-e	*VkV	MAX-C
☞ i. ine-e		*
ii. inek-e	*!	

b. *Aorist Cophonology*

Input: gerek-ir	MAX-C	*VkV
i. gere-ir	*!	
☞ ii. gerek-e		*

Since, as shown by Orgun (1996), the declarative formulation of conditions on the complex feature structures employed in the theory allows a complete reconstruction for the effects of cyclic phonology (i.e. of a phonological optimization cycle applying after every affixation step, or more generally after every morphological operation), we would expect that Cophonology Theory allows a simple way to emulate the templatic approach to SCA developed here. Interestingly enough, it turns out that SCA is one of the areas where morphological indexing of constraints and employing cophonologies is not equivalent (see Pater 2007, 2009; Inkelas and Zoll 2007; Jurgec 2010; Trommer 2011b for more general discussion).

Consider first the possibility that the templatic effects in SCA fall out from cophonologies that are relativized to morphemes in the sense that the same ranking applies to all allomorphs of an affix *A*. For Tzeltal, this would mean that both allomorphs of the perfective suffix are subject to the same (un-indexed) constraint PWD=BINFT, ranked at the same position of the constraint ranking. Since the resulting outputs (e.g. (sku.tʃɛh) vs. (sku.tʃoh), and skutʃ(la.jɛh) vs. skutʃ(la-j.oh)) are prosodically completely isomorphic, they will incur exactly the same violations for this constraint weighted in the same way. Thus relativizing Cophonologies to morphemes doesn't allow to capture a differential templatic effects for different allomorphs. It might seem that there is a more promising Cophonology approach to SCA which employs different Cophonologies for different allomorphs of an affix, but there is no effective way to integrate this intuition into the basic architecture of Cophonology Theory. The essence of the Cophonology approach is that there is a 1:1 correspondence between rankings specific to a morphological construction *C* and the phonological material introduced by *C* (i.e. in the case of affixation, the segments of the affix). This perfect correspondence is the essence of Cophonology's tackle on affix-specific constraints without the need to index constraints for specific affixes. But this implies that the different rankings for the Tzeltal perfective allomorphs (PWD=BINFT >> PERF=oh for *-oh*, and PERF=oh >> PWD=BINFT for *-ɛh*) involve different evaluation processes, e.g. for a disyllabic stem, the optimization procedures in (62), but OT doesn't provide any effective way to compute a single output from parallel distinct evaluations.

(62) *Evaluation for Tzeltal by allomorph-specific cophonologies*

a. *Input based on* -oh

Input: skutʃ+*oh*	PWD=BINFT	PERF=oh
☞ i. (sku.tʃoh)		
ii. sku.(tʃoh)		*!

b. *Input based on* -ɛh

Input: skutʃ+*ɛh*	PERF=oh	PWD=BINFT
☞ i. (sku.tʃɛh)	*	
ii. sku.(tʃɛh)	*	*!

On the other hand, merging (62a) and (62b) would either require to commit the analysis to one of the rankings for the involved constraints – thus losing the allomorph-specific effect of PWD=BINFT, or to index PWD=BINFT, hence obviating Cophonologies by reintroducing the indexed-constraint-based approach to SCA developed above.

Note also that the indexed-constraint analysis of SCA requires to abandon a standard condition on constraint indexing, implicitly underlying most optimality-theoretic research on Prosodic Morphology (e.g. McCarthy and Prince 1994 and morphophonology (Alderete 1999, 2001; McCarthy and Prince 1995), and explicitly advocated in the literature on lexical stratification (Fukazawa, Kitahara and Ota 1998, Ito and Mester 1999) that indexing is restricted to faithfulness constraints (Inkelas and Zoll 2007 call this assumption 'Faith-based Variation'). Under the general approach adopted here, indexing of faithfulness constraints seems to be systematically irrelevant for prosodically governed allomorphy since the involved constraints either encode arbitrary lexical preference for affix variants, or well-formedness constraints on prosody.

Allomorphic Templates by Underlying Prosody: there is one final alternative to both, to the subcategorization approach and to morpheme-specific constraints, an analysis based on the assumption that templatic effects follow from floating prosodic structure which is part of the underlying phonological representation of affixes (i.e., affix allomorphs) much as in Classical pre-OT Prosodic Morphology (McCarthy and Prince 1996 [1986]; see Kirchner 2010, 2013, Bermúdez-Otero 2012, Bye and Svenonius 2012 for recent reconstructions of prosodic affixation in OT). Thus the first allomorph of the Tzeltal perfective would consist of the string of segments *ɛh*, whereas the second allomorph is represented as a prosodic word dominating two syllables (via an intermediate foot node not shown here), where the second syllable in turn dominates the segments *o* and *h*, $[(\sigma\sigma_{oh})]_{\omega}$, as shown in (63) (the morphological 'color', i.e., affiliation of the phonological affix material is indicated here and in the following by grey background boxes). Hence the second, templatic allomorph is a partially incomplete prosodic tree (a 'treelet' in the terms of Bermúdez-Otero (2012)). A complex of different constraints abbreviated here as TEMPLATESATISF requires that the output corresponds in shape to the prosody of the templatic affix. Again, a monosyllabic base as in (63a) allows the establishment of the bisyllabic prosodic word without MAX violations; Candidates resulting from *-ɛh* fulfil TEMPLATESATISF vacuously since they don't involve an underlying template. Thus both outputs in (63a) are phonologically perfectly equivalent, and the variant $[(\text{sku.tʃoh})]_{\omega}$ is selected due to the low-ranked constraint PERF=oh encoding morphological preference for *-oh*. In contrast, a bisyllabic base as in (63b) results in too much segmental material to fit into the bisyllabic Procrustes bed, the simultaneous fulfilment of TEMPLATESATISF and PERF=oh, and would involve deletion (63bii). Since MAX is ranked above PERF=oh the form with the dispreferred suffix variant and without deletion is chosen instead (63biii):

(63) *Tzeltal by underlying prosodic templates*

a. *Monosyllabic base*

Input: skutʃ + {ɛh, $[(\sigma\sigma_{oh})]_{\omega}$}	TEMPLATESATISF	MAX	PERF=oh
☞ i. $[(\text{sku.tʃoh})]_{\omega}$			
ii. $[(\text{sku.tʃɛh})]_{\omega}$			*!

b. *Bisyllabic base*

Input: skutʃlaj+ {ɛh, $[(\sigma\sigma oh)]_{\omega}$}	TEMPLATESATISF	MAX	PERF=oh
i. $[\text{skutʃ(la.joh)}]_{\omega}$	*!		
ii. $[(\text{sku.tʃoh})]_{\omega}$		*!**	
☞ iii. $[(\text{skutʃ.la.jɛh})]_{\omega}$			*

The explanatory success of a templatic prosodic-affixation analysis depends crucially on the details of TEMPLATESATISF. The proposal I will make here is to require that underlyingly floating syllables must be headed by segmental material, with prosodic faithfulness ensuring that the affix syllable surfaces in the prosodic environment specified in its affix entry. This is implemented in the following in the autosegmental approach to floating morphology developed in Trommer (2011a), where the Containment Assumption (i.e., the unviolable ban on literal deletion of phonological input material; cf. Prince and Smolensky 1993, McCarthy and Prince 1993, van Oostendorp 2006, Revithiadou 2007, Finley 2008) allows generalized versions of markedness constraints on association to refer indiscriminately to underlying ('morphological') and surface ('phonetic') phonology. Thus σ → • (64b) is satisfied by a surface syllable that dominates surface segments, but also by underlying syllables dominating underlying segments.[20]

(64) *TEMPLATESATISF decomposed*
  a. PW≈GW: Assign * to every phonetic prosodic word which doesn't coincide with a phonetic grammatical word.
  b. σ → •: Assign * to every σ-node which is not headed by segmental material morphologically or phonetically.
  c. MAX π–π: Assign * to every phonetic prosodic node π which is associated morphologically to a prosodic node π' but is not phonetically associated to π'.
  d. DEP π–π: Assign * to every phonetic prosodic node π which is associated phonetically to a prosodic node π' but is not morphologically associated to π'.

The tableau in (65) shows how the constraints in (64) effectively derive TEMPLATESATISF (grey and white background boxes in candidates indicate the morphological affiliation to base and suffix respectively, epenthetic material is notated without background box). By PW≈GW the output is restricted to a single prosodic word (65f). σ → • has the effect that the first syllable of the affix prosody must be retained in the output to grant it domination of segmental material, whereas it freely allows deletion of stem-syllables and the syllable dominating *-oh* because these already dominate segments morphologically (in the input) (65e).[21] By the faithfulness constraints MAX π–π and DEP π–π, the presence of σ in the output sets in motion an implicational chain reaction. By MAX π–π, σ cannot be associated to another foot (i.e., an epenthetic foot or a foot node provided by the base), thus the affix foot must be retained (cf. (65e) vs. (65f)). By the same logic, the affix foot requires presence of the affix PWord, and the affix PWord consequently implies retaining the second σ-node of the affix (cf. (65b) vs. (65c)). Given these premises, DEP π–π enforces the affix template on the entire form: Since the obligatory (and unique) affix PWord is not allowed to dominate any heteromorphemic or epenthetic syllable the output is limited to the original bisyllabic PWord of the affix. Thus the constraints in (64) can only be entirely fulfilled for a polysyllabic base under deletion of segmental material (or with monosyllabic inputs).

(65) *TEMPLATESATISF decomposed*

Input: $(\sigma_{skut\int}\ \sigma_{laj})\ [(\sigma\ \sigma_{oh})]$	PW≈GW	σ → •	MAX π–π	DEP π–π
a. $[(\sigma_{sku}\ \sigma_{t\int oh})]$				
b. $[\sigma_{skut\int}\ (\sigma_{la}\ \sigma_{joh})]$				PW-σ!
c. $[\sigma_{skut\int}\ (\sigma_{la}\ \sigma_{joh})]$			PW-F!	
d. $[(\sigma_{skut\int}\ \sigma_{la})\ \sigma_{joh}]$			F-σ!	
e. $[(\sigma_{skut\int}\ \sigma_{la})\ \sigma_{joh}]$		*!		
f. $(\sigma_{skut\int}\ \sigma_{laj})\ [(\sigma\sigma_{joh})]$	*!			

Obviously the template-affixation analysis is compatible with the stratal architecture assumed in the preceding sections to account for opaque SCA, and the derivational-OT alternatives sketched in this section. Moreover, the template-affixation analysis also extends straightforwardly to templatic truncation as shown for the case of German hypocoristics in (66):[22]

(66) *Truncation by templatic affixation*

Input: $(\sigma_{Stu}\ \sigma_{dent})\ [(\sigma\sigma_{i})]$	PW≈GW	σ → •	MAX π–π	DEP π–π	MAX
☞ a. $[(\sigma_{Stu}\ \sigma_{di})]$					***
b. $[\sigma_{Stu}\ (\sigma_{den}\ \sigma_{ti})]$				PW-σ!	
c. $[\sigma_{Stu}\ (\sigma_{den}\ \sigma_{ti})]$			PW-F!		
d. $[(\sigma_{Stu}\ \sigma_{den})\ \sigma_{ti}]$			F-σ!		
e. $[(\sigma_{Stu}\ \sigma_{den})\ \sigma_{ti}]$		*!			
f. $(\sigma_{Stu}\ \sigma_{den})\ [(\sigma\sigma_{ti})]$	*!				

Thus neither the SCA nor the truncation data discussed in this paper (and by Paster 2005, 2006) provide by themselves evidence for an indexed-constraint approach over a template-affixation approach or vice versa. Conceptually, both types of analysis tightly integrate SCA with general prosodic constraints, which make them in principle preferable to accounts in terms of phonological subcategorization. However, as argued in detail by Bermúdez-Otero (2012), prosodic-affixation approaches to templatic effects are inherently more restrictive than indexed-constraint accounts since they require consistency of the constraint ranking enforcing affix prosody with the overall phonology of the respective language. Thus the evaluation of this approach to SCA would require a thorough study of the effects discussed here in the context of the language-specific phonologies of the respective languages, a challenge far beyond the scope of the present paper.[23] Still the discussion here shows that the argument for the necessity of morphological subcategorization to account for SCA is surprisingly weak since there are not too few, but rather too many purely phonological alternatives.

Notes

1. The bracket notation employed in (4) effectively encodes a set of specific inputs resulting from computing the expansions of all brackets in the overall input as in the bracket extension employed by Chomsky and Halle (1968). Thus an overall input containing one bracket with two allomorphs and a second bracket with three allomorphs would generate six specific inputs. See also (41) for a concrete example of an OT-evaluation employing allomorphs of multiple allomorphs.
2. Following Kager (1996), Wolf (this volume), I encode arbitrary lexical preference for specific allomorphs by preference constraints for single allomorphs, which is natural in a system where all phonological constraints may be relativized specific to allomorphs. Equivalently, preference for allomorphs could be encoded by specifying morphological allomorph hierarchies and a general PRIORITY constraint which sanctions insertion of allomorphs higher in this hierarchy during phonological evaluation, as proposed by Bonet, Lloret and Mascaró (2007) and Mascaró (2007).
3. See Alber and Arndt-Lappe (2012) for a thorough typological and theoretical survey of truncation and related phenomena, especially for a discussion of non-templatic truncation, and for detailed references to the literature.
4. Féry (1997) treats the occurrence of *i* here not as affixation but as a phonological Emergence-of-the-Unmarked (TETU) effect (McCarthy and Prince 1994), but this move is not unproblematic since usually [ə], not [i] is taken to be the unmarked unstressed vowel in German (Wiese 1996). Note also that the string of base segments preceding *i* in truncated structures is not necessarily a well-formed syllable of German as in *depressiv* ⇒ (de.pri), 'depressive' – the sequence *pr* is not licit syllable-finally (or word-finally). This sets the German internal-affixation case crucially apart from external-affixation truncation as in Japanese, discussed below.
5. An alternative candidate for (19b) not shown here would delete the affix and leave the base intact (*Student*). I assume that this is excluded by the undominated constraint REALIZE MORPHEME (van Oostendorp 2005, Trommer 2012), which is violated once for any input morpheme for which a candidate doesn't contain at least one piece of output phonology. The fact that deletion targets a contiguous portion of segments at the right edge, and not elsewhere in the base, is probably an effect of high-ranked ANCHOR-LEFT, a standard (but not universal) condition on truncation patterns (cf. Alber and Arndt-Lappe 2012: 298–299, 306).

6. I leave it open here whether the suffixal status of the affix foot is enforced by an Alignment constraint, such as ALIGN(F_{hyp},R,PWORD,R) (cf. Prince and Smolensky 1993), or follows by right-peripheral concatenation of the foot to the prosody of the base noun in underlying representations, which is then conserved by faithfulness constraints against metathesis operations (Horwood 2002). What is crucial is that either kind of undominated constraint ensures that the right edge of the templatic affix foot coincides with the rightmost surviving segment of the base. Note also that PWD=BINFT$_F$ here amounts simply to ALLFTLFT$_F$. PARSE σ_F applies only to syllables which overlap with, hence are dominated by -F, and is thus vacuously satisfied by any syllable.
7. '… Halle and Vaux (1998) have proposed that Ergative and Locative share a feature [–free], which designates "nominals with a consistent role in argument structure". The other two cases which have this feature in the Halle/Vaux feature system are the Instrumental (whose phonological realization is identical to that of Ergative in Dyirbal) and Accusative, which Dyirbal doesn't have' (Wolf 2008: 91).
8. See Inkelas and Caballero (2013) for an intriguing theoretical derivation of this generalization in a Harmonic-Serialism-based approach to morphological exponence. However, the empirical generalization Inkelas and Caballero describe is also consistent with the general tackle on Stem-Level affixes (which undergo synthetic listing as parts of stems, and hence tend to 'fuse' with stems) vs. Word-Level affixes (which might only be stored analytically) taken by recent work in Stratal OT (Bermúdez-Otero 2012).
9. Without cyclic morphology-phonology interleaving, Paster could not ensure that bases have the required prosody to trigger the correct allomorphs. Thus if all morphology/subcategorization would apply before all phonological optimization, it could not be ensured that *-juvvo* bears a binary foot and triggers selection of *-beaht.ti* (cf. the explicit discussion of the necessary ordering of phonological and morphological operations for Saami in Paster's approach below (39)).
10. In contrast to the earlier literature, Bermúdez-Otero assumes that the theme vowel is not the spell-out of inflectional-class features (as assumed below), but stored as part of a complex tree together with respective nouns. See immediately below for more discussion.
11. Presupposing the lexicalist framework of Bermúdez-Otero, the regular derivational history of *madur-ez* would of course not prohibit that it also undergoes full-form listing.
12. To be sure, final vowels in adjectives are theme vowels of the same type as nominal theme vowels, hence Word-Level affixes. Thus the derivation here involves a Stem-Level affix and a Stem-Level cycle of phonological evaluation outside of a Word-Level affix (and Word-Level evaluation). See Bermúdez-Otero (in preparation) and references there for detailed arguments that Word-Level affixes may occur inside of Stem-Level affixes, i.e. that the Affix Ordering Generalization of Siegel (1974) assumed in Lexical Phonology and Morphology is wrong. On the background of recent research

which links the effects of lexical affix stratification with morphosyntactic phases tied to category-defining heads such as little n and little a (Marvin 2003, Scheer 2010, Embick 2010), category changing word formation process is a highly plausible context for this configuration.

13. Thus (50) implicitly presupposes undominated status for MAX-V$_{\{an,in\}}$, MAX-C, and for a constraint penalizing hiatus.

14. A potential loophole to derive Kaititj' and Kaititj'' in the templatic approach is to generalize the Distributed-Morphology analysis of the Spanish *-ez/-eza* nominalization sketched above. This would require one to assume double allomorphy: a pair of Stem-Level allomorphs (-Ø and -F) inducing the templatic distinction between bisyllabic and polysyllabic bases, and a second pair of Word-Level allomorphs corresponding to *-ŋa* and *-lo* which are triggered by the corresponding Stem-Level morphs. Whether such an analysis would be tenable depends essentially on the adopted theory of morphologically triggered allomorphy. Thus under the natural assumption that morphologically triggered allomorphy may only be sensitive to morpho-syntactic features of other morphs, the Word-Level affixes would have no means to distinguish -Ø and -F (which would both mark ergative). Hence the crucial difference between Kaititj' and the Spanish nominalization case would be that at the Word Level Spanish doesn't involve allomorphy, but simply the spellout of class features. However, in morphological approaches where class features are rejected for independent theoretical reasons (cf. Wunderlich 1996), even the Spanish data would have to be captured in a different way, which might be the correct result given the fact that the phonological nature of the *-ez/-eza-* allomorphy is highly questionable (cf. the discussion in section 8.4). Note also that no other case of allomorphy discussed here involves any selection between Stem-Level and Word-Level exponents. Thus in the Spanish diminutive analysis above, Stem Level *-c/-Ø* and Word-Level *-ito* cooccur, but the choice of the Stem-Level allomorph doesn't have any effect on the Word-Level morpheme, which is consistently *-ito*.

15. In a system with right-aligned feet, PARSE σ_{oh} would be always satisfied, and would hence not have any relevant effect.

16. Note that the relative ranking of the indexed markedness constraints for Tzeltal''' (and for Tzeltal'''' below) is irrelevant for the outcome. If the morpheme preference constraint PERF=oh is ranked highest, we get consistent realization of the underlying morpheme as *-oh* (thus this ranking would be equivalent to a grammar where *-oh* is the only allomorph). If one of the indexed constraints is ranked above, and the other one below PERF=oh, we get the same allomorph distributions as in Tzeltal' and Tzeltal''. Thus the rankings in (56)–(59) are effectively all cross-indexing rankings that have potentially different outputs from the ones discussed above.

17. Roughly speaking, OT with Candidate Chains is an enriched version of Harmonic serialism that allows one to impose an arbitrary language-specific order on optimization cycles by so-called PREC constraints. Thus, as pointed

out by Wolf (this volume), his Harmonic-Serialism analysis could be straightforwardly taken over to the richer system (simply by assuming that there are no high-ranked PREC constraints that would intervene).The Dyirbal analysis developed in Wolf's (2008) extension of OT-CC to morphological exponence and allomorphy shares the assumption that *-ŋ-ku* is bimorphic, but is actually implemented in a parallel version of OT since it is developed in an early expositional chapter of his thesis.

18. Wolf also adopts constraint coindexing for *-ŋ*, but applies this to the markedness constraint COINCIDE(AFFIX, HEAD FOOT), which requires that *-ŋ* coincides (is part of the head foot) of the word, not to PWD=BINFT (or the constraints that constitute it) as I have assumed above. Since Dyirbal has binary syllabic trochees, this constraint also enforces a bisyllabic foot template. A virtue of Wolf's proposal is that it builds slightly more directly on the general prosodic system of Dyirbal such that only one atomic constraint must be indexed for *-ŋ*. A drawback is that the stipulation of an indexed version for COINCIDE(AFFIX, HEAD FOOT) predicts the existence of its generalized version, i.e. of languages where all affixed words are restricted to a foot template whereas monosyllabic words may have any prosodic size. Since such systems are probably non-existent, COINCIDE is empirically problematic.
19. In fact, the stratal approach that I follow here makes the interesting (and potentially incorrect) empirical prediction that the type of SCA-opacity occurring in Dyirbal is restricted to combinations of a Stem-Level and a Word-Level affix.
20. The effects derived here by Autosegmental Containment and generalized constraints could also be achieved by high-ranked constraints which require the output realization of underlyingly floating material (e.g. MAX FLOAT in Wolf 2005, 2007 or MAX SUBSEGMENT in Zoll 1996). The advantage of the Containment-based approach adopted here is that it actually *derives* (predicts) the structural priority of floating material under appropriate constraint ranking.
21. $\sigma \rightarrow \bullet$ has also the effect that the output doesn't contain floating epenthetic syllables, since these would not dominate any segments at any level of representation.
22. This is of course not surprising given the fact that the classical prosodic-affixation approach (cf. McCarthy and Prince 1996 [1986]) was i.a. developed to capture truncation. An interesting complication for the prosodic-affixation approach is how to represent a bimoraic foot template. Under the assumption that templatic affixes (and maybe affixes in general) must form structurally contiguous phonological objects such a template should either be $[\sigma_\mu\ \sigma_\mu]$ or $[\sigma_{\mu\mu}]$, none of which would encode the full range of outputs generated by Japanese hypocoristic formations as in (Mido)-č an/(Mii)-č an (cf. (17)). On the other hand, the phonological part of a templatic affix such as $[\mu\mu]_F$, as assumed by Mester (1990), is not a contiguous phonological object if feet are not allowed to directly dominate moras. However, Japanese hypocoristics

might simply follow from the affix $[\ ]_F$ – a bare foot template without internal prosodic structure since feet in Japanese are generally bimoraic, which would require a slightly different implementation of TEMPLATESATISF as the one sketched here. An interesting prediction of the resulting system would be that strictly bisyllabic and monosyllabic templates are possible in languages with moraic feet (in fact, Japanese also has monosyllabic truncation, cf. Mester 1990), but languages with strictly syllabic feet should not exhibit bimoraic templates of the type exemplified by Japanese hypocoristics since bimoraicity could neither be stipulated as a template nor derived from the general prosodic constraints of the language.

23. See e.g. Flack (2007) for a detailed argument that underlying prosody is not sufficient to account for templatic effects, and Trommer (2011a) for critical discussion.

References

Alber, Birgit and Arndt-Lappe, Sabine (2012) Templatic and subtractive truncation. In Jochen Trommer (ed.) *The Morphology and Phonology of Exponence,* 289–325. Oxford: Oxford University Press.

Albright, Adam (2002) Islands of Reliability for regular morphology: Evidence from Italian. *Language* 78: 684–709.

Albright, Adam and Hayes, Bruce (2003) Rules vs. analogy in English past tenses: A computational/experimental study. *Cognition* 90: 119–161.

Alderete, John (1999) *Morphologically governed accent in Optimality Theory.* Doctoral dissertation, University of Massachusetts at Amherst.

Alderete, John (2001) Dominance effects as Transderivational Anti-Faithfulness. *Phonology* 18: 201–253.

Anderson, Stephen R. (1992) *A-Morphous Morphology*. Cambridge: Cambridge University Press.

Aranovich, Raúl and Orgun, Orhan (1998) Opacity in *-ez/-eza* suffixation. In Timothy L. Face and Carol A. Klee (eds) *Selected Proceedings of the 8th Hispanic Linguistics Symposium,* 116–122. Somerville, MA: Cascadilla Proceedings Project.

Benua, Laura (1995) Identity effects in morphological truncation. In Jill Beckman, Suzanne Urbanczyk and Laura Walsh-Dickey (eds) *Papers in Optimality Theory,* 78–136. Vol. 18 of *University of Massachusetts Occasional Papers in Linguistics*. Amherst, MA: GLSA.

Bermúdez-Otero, Ricardo (2007) Morphological structure and phonological domains in Spanish denominal derivation. In Fernando Martínez-Gil and Sonia Colina (eds) *Optimality-theoretic Studies in Spanish Phonology,* 278–311. Amsterdam: John Benjamins.

Bermúdez-Otero, Ricardo (2010) Cyclicity. In Marc van Oostendorp, Colin J. Ewen, Elizabeth Hume and Keren Rice (eds) *The Blackwell Companion to Phonology*. Vol. 4: *Phonological Interfaces*, chapter 85, 2019–2048. Malden, MA: Wiley-Blackwell.

Bermúdez-Otero, Ricardo (2012) The architecture of grammar and the division of labour in exponence. In Jochen Trommer (ed.) *The Morphology and Phonology of Exponence,* 8–83. Oxford: Oxford University Press.

Bermúdez-Otero, Ricardo (2013) The Spanish lexicon stores stems with theme vowels, not roots with inflectional class features. *Probus* 25 (1): 1–101.

Bermúdez-Otero, Ricardo (in preparation) *Stratal Optimality Theory*. Oxford: Oxford University Press.

Bonet, Eulàlia, Lloret, Maria-Rosa and Mascaró, Joan (2007) Allomorph selection and lexical preferences: Two case studies. *Lingua* 117 (6): 903–927.

Buckley, Eugene (1994) *Theoretical Aspects of Kashaya Phonology and Morphology*. Stanford, CA: CSLI Publications.

Bye, Patrick (2008) Allomorphy: Selection, not optimization. In Sylvia Blaho, Patrik Bye and Martin Krämer (eds) *Freedom of Analysis?,* 63–92. Berlin: Mouton de Gruyter.

Bye, Patrik and Svenonius, Peter (2012) Exponence, phonology, and non-concatenative morphology. In Jochen Trommer (ed.) *The Morphology and Phonology of Exponence,* 427–495. Oxford: Oxford University Press.

Carstairs-McCarthy, Andrew (1987) *Allomorphy in Inflexion*. London: Croom Helm.

Chomsky, Noam and Morris Halle (1968) *The Sound Pattern of English*. New York: Harper and Row.

de María, José (1918) *Gramática y vocabulario jíbaros*. Quito: Impr. de la Universidad Central.

Dixon, R. M. W. (1972) *The Dyirbal Language of North Queensland*. Cambridge: Cambridge University Press.

Dolbey, Andrew (1997) Output optimization and cyclic allomorph selection. In *Proceedings of WCCFL 15:* 97–112, Stanford, CA: CSLI Publications.

Downing, Laura J. (2006) *Canonical Forms in Prosodic Morphology*. Oxford: Oxford University Press.

Elenbaas, Nine and Kager, René (1999) Ternary rhythm and the *LAPSE constraint. *Phonology* 16 (3): 273–330.

Embick, David (2010) *Localism versus Globalism in Morphology and Phonology*. Cambridge, MA: MIT Press.

Féry, Caroline (1997) *Uni* und *Studis*: die besten Wörter des Deutschen. *Linguistische Berichte* 172: 461–490.

Finley, Sara (2008) *Formal and cognitive restrictions on vowel harmony*. Doctoral Dissertation, Johns Hopkins University.

Fitzpatrick, Justin (2004) A concatenative theory of possible affix types. In I. Andrés Pablo Salanova (ed.) *Papers from EVELIN I*. MIT Working Papers in Linguistics.

Flack, Kathryn (2007) Templatic Morphology and indexed markedness constraints. *Linguistic Inquiry* 38 (4): 749–758.

Fukazawa, Haruka, Kitahara, Mafuyu and Ota, Mitsuhiko (1998) Lexical stratification and ranking invariance in constraint-based grammars. In M. Catherine Gruber, Derrick Higgins, Kenneth Olson and Tamra M. Wysocki (eds) *Proceedings of CLS 32, Part 2: The Panels,* 47–62. Chicago IL: Chicago Linguistic Society.

Halle, Morris and Marantz, Alec (1993) Distributed Morphology and the pieces of inflection. In Ken Hale and Samuel J. Keyser (eds) *The View from Building 20,* 111–176. Cambridge, MA: MIT Press.

Halle, Morris and Marantz, Alec (1994) Some key features of Distributed Morphology. In Andrew Carnie and Heidi Harley (eds) *Papers on Phonology and Morphology,* 275–288. Vol. 21 of *MIT Working Papers in Linguistics*. Cambridge, MA: MITWPL.

Halle, Morris and Vaux, Bert (1998) Theoretical aspects of Indo-European nominal morphology: The nominal declensions of Latin and Armenian. In Jay Jasanoff, H. Craig Melchert and Lisi Olivier (eds) *Mi'r Curad: Studies in Honor of Clavert Watkins*, 223–240. Innsbruck: Innsbrucker Beitraege zur Sprachwissenschaft.

Harris, James W. (1979) Some observations on 'substantive principles in Natural Generative Phonology'. In Daniel A. Dinnsen (ed.) *Current Approaches to Phonological Theory,* 281–293. Bloomington, IN: Indiana University Press.

Harris, James W. (1991) The exponence of gender in Spanish. *Linguistic Inquiry* 22: 27–62.

Harris, James W. (1996) The syntax and morphology of class marker suppression in Spanish. In Karen Zagona (ed.) *Grammatical Theory and Romance Languages,* 99–122. Amsterdam: John Benjamins.

Harris, Zellig Sabbatai (1942) Morpheme alternants in linguistic theory. *Language* 18: 169–180.

Hayes, Bruce (1995) *Metrical Stress Theory: Principles and Case Studies*. Chicago, IL: University of Chicago Press.

Horwood, Graham (2002) Precedence faithfulness governs morpheme position. [Available on http://roa.rutgers.edu/article/view/527]

Inkelas, Sharon (to appear) The Morphology-phonology connection. In Proceedings of the Berkeley Linguistics Society.

Inkelas, Sharon and Caballero, Gabriela (2013) Word construction: tracing an optimal path through the lexicon. In Jochen Trommer (ed.) *New Tools in the Modelling of Morphological Exponence.* Issue 23(2) of *Morphology*.

Inkelas, Sharon and Zoll, Cheryl (2005) *Reduplication: Doubling in Morphology*. Cambridge: Cambridge University Press.

Inkelas, Sharon and Zoll, Cheryl (2007) Is grammar dependence real? A comparison between cophonological and indexed constraint approaches to morphologically conditioned phonology. *Linguistics* 45 (1): 133–171.

Ito, Junko and Mester, Armin (1999) The phonological lexicon. In Natsuko Tsujimura (ed.) *The Handbook of Japanese Linguistics,* 62–100. Oxford: Blackwell.

Jurgec, Peter (2010) Disjunctive lexical stratification. *Linguistic Inquiry* 41 (1): 149–161.

Kager, René (1996) On affix allomorphy and syllable counting. In Ursula Kleinhenz (ed.) *Interfaces in Phonology* 155–171. Berlin: Akademie-Verlag.

Kager, René (1999) *Optimality Theory*. Cambridge: Cambridge University Press.

Kirchner, Jesse Saba (2010) *Minimal Reduplication.* Doctoral Dissertation, University of California at Santa Cruz.

Kirchner, Jesse Saba (2013) Minimal Reduplication and reduplicative exponence. In Jochen Trommer (ed.) *New theoretical tools in the Modeling of Exponence. Morphology* 23 (2): 227–244.

Koch, Harold J. (1980) Kaititj nominal inflection: Some comparative notes. In B. Rigsby and P. Sutton (eds) *Papers in Australian Linguistics* 13: *Contributions to Australian Linguistics,* 259–274. Number 59 in 'Pacific Linguistics Series A', Australian National University.

Marvin, Tatjana (2003) *Topics in the stress and syntax of words*. Doctoral Dissertation, MIT.

Mascaró, Joan (1996) External allomorphy as emergence of the unmarked. In Jacques Durand and Bernard Laks (eds) *Current Trends in Phonology: Models and Methods,* 473–483. Salford, Manchester: European Studies Research Institute, University of Salford.

Mascaró, Joan (2007) External allomorphy and lexical representation. *Linguistic Inquiry* 38: 715–735.

McCarthy, John J. (2003a) Comparative Markedness. *Theoretical Linguistics* 29: 1–51.

McCarthy, John J. (2003b) OT constraints are categorical. *Phonology* 20: 75–138.

McCarthy, John (2007) *Hidden Generalizations: Phonological Opacity in Optimality Theory*. London: Equinox.

McCarthy, John (2008) The gradual path to cluster simplification. *Phonology* 25: 271–319.

McCarthy, John (2010) An introduction to Harmonic Serialism. *Language and Linguistics Compass* 4: 1001–1018.

McCarthy, John, Kimper, Wendell and Mullin, Kevin (2012) Reduplication in Harmonic Serialism. *Morphology* 22: 173–232.

McCarthy, John and Prince, Alan (1993) Prosodic Morphology. Constraint interaction and satisfaction. [Available on http://roa.rutgers.edu/article/view/485.]

McCarthy, John and Alan Prince (1994) The emergence of the unmarked: Optimality in Prosodic Morphology. In Mercè Gonzàlez (ed.) *Proceedings of NELS 24,* 333–379. Amherst, MA: GLSA Publications.

McCarthy, John and Prince, Alan (1995) Faithfulness and reduplicative identity. In Jill N. Beckman, Laura Walsh Dickey and Susanne Urbanczyk *University of Massachusetts Occasional Papers in Linguistics* 18: 249–384.

McCarthy, John J. and Prince, Alan (1996) Prosodic Morphology 1986, Technical Report 32, Rutgers University Center for Cognitive Science.

Mester, Armin (1990) Patterns of truncation *Linguistic Inquiry* 21 (3): 478–485.

Müller, Gereon (2007) Extended exponence by enrichment: Argument encoding in German, Archi, and Timucua. In Tatjana Scheffler, Joshua Tauberer, Aviad Eilam and Laia Mayol (eds) *Proceedings of the 30th Annual Penn Linguistics Colloquium* 253–266. Vol. 13 of *Penn Working Papers in Linguistics*.

Nash, David (1986) *Topics in Warlpiri grammar*. New York: Garland Publishing, Inc.

Newman, Stanley S. (1965) *Zuni Grammar*. Vol. 14 of *University of New Mexico Publications in Anthropology*. Albuquerque: University of New Mexico Press.

Ohala, J. J. (1997) Aerodynamics of phonology. In Proceedings of the 4th Seoul International Conference on Linguistics [SICOL]: 92–97.

Oltra-Massuet, Maria Isabel and Arregi, Karlos (2005) Stress-by-structure in Spanish. *Linguistic Inquiry* 36 (1): 43–84.

Orgun, Cemil Orhan (1996) *Sign-based morphology and phonology with special attention to Optimality Theory*. Doctoral dissertation, University of California at Berkeley.

Oswalt, Robert L. (1960) *A Kashaya grammar (Southern Pomo)*. Doctoral Dissertation, University of California at Berkeley.

Paster, Mary (2005) Subcategorization vs. output optimization in syllable-counting allomorphy. In John Alderete, Chung-hye Han, and Alexei Kochetov (eds) *Proceedings of WCCFL 24*, 326–333. Somerville, MA: Cascadilla Proceedings Project.

Paster, Mary (2006) *Phonological conditions on affixation*. Doctoral Dissertation, University of California at Berkeley.

Paster, Mary (2007) Aspects of Maay phonology and morphology. *Studies in African Linguistics* 35 (1): 73–120.

Pater, Joe (2007) The locus of exceptionality: Morpheme-specific phonology as constraint indexation. In Leah Bateman, Michael O'Keefe, Ehren Reilly and Adam Werle (eds) *Papers in Optimality Theory* III, 259–296. Amherst, MA: GLSA.

Pater, Joe (2009) Weighted constraints in generative linguistics. *Cognitive Science* 33: 999–1035.

Payne, David L. (1981) *The Phonology and Morphology of Axininca Campa*. Dallas, TX: The Summer Institute of Linguistics and the University of Texas at Arlington.

Perlmutter, David M. (1998) Interfaces: Explanation of allomorphy and the architecture of grammars. In Steven G. Lapointe, Diane K. Brentari and Patrick M. Farrell (eds) *Morphology and its Relation to Phonology and Syntax*, 307–338. Stanford, CA: CSLI.

Poser, William J. (1990) Evidence for foot structure in Japanese. *Language* 66: 78–105.

Prince, Alan and Smolensky, Paul (1993 [2004]) *Optimality Theory: Constraint Interaction in Generative Grammar*. Technical Report, Rutgers University Center of Cognitive Science Department, University of Colorado at Boulder. Malden, MA and Oxford: Blackwell.

Pycha, Anne (2008) *Morphological sources of phonological length*. Doctoral Dissertation, University of California at Berkeley.

Radhakrishnan, Ramaswami (1981) *The Nancowry Word: Phonology, Affixal Morphology, and Roots of a Nicobarese Language*. Edmonton, Alberta: Linguistic Research, Inc.

Revithiadou, Anthi (2007) Colored turbid accents and containment: a case study from lexical stress. In Sylvia Blaho, Patrik Bye and Martin Krämer (eds) *Freedom of Analysis?*, 149–174. Berlin and New York: Mouton De Gruyter.

Roca, Iggy and Felíu, Elena (2003) Morphology in truncation: the role of the Spanish desinence. *Yearbook of Morphology* 2002: 187–243.

Rubach, Jerzy and Booij, Gert (2001) Allomorphy in Optimality Theory. *Language* 77: 26–60.

Scheer, Tobias (2010) Intermodular argumentation: Morpheme-specific phonologies are out of business in a phase-based architecture. In Nomi Shir and Lisa Rochman (eds) *The Sound Patterns of Syntax* 333–351. Oxford: Oxford University Press.

Siegel, Dorothy (1974) *Topics in English morphology*. Doctoral Dissertation, MIT.

Stump, Gregory T. (2001) *Inflectional Morphology*. Cambridge: Cambridge University Press.

Trommer, Jochen (2011a) Phonological Aspects of Western Nilotic Mutation Morphology. Habilitation thesis, University of Leipzig.

Trommer, Jochen (2011b) Phonological sensitivity to morphological structure. In Marc van Oostendorp, Colin J. Ewen and Keren D. Rice (eds) *The Blackwell Companion to Phonology*, chapter 103, 2464–2489. London: Wiley Blackwell.

Trommer, Jochen (2012) Constraints on multiple-feature mutation, *Lingua* 122: 1182–1192.

Trommer, Jochen (2013) Stress uniformity in Albanian: morphological arguments for cyclicity. *Linguistic Inquiry* 44: 109–143.

van Oostendorp, Marc (2005) Expressing inflection tonally. *Catalan Journal of Linguistics* 4(1): 107–127.

van Oostendorp, Marc (2006) A Theory of Morphosyntactic Colours. Ms., Meertens Institute, Amsterdam. [Available under: http://egg.auf.net/06/docs/Hdt%20 Oostendorp%20coulours.pdf.]

Walsh Dickey, Laura (1999) Syllable count and Tzeltal segmental allomorphy. In John R. Rennison and Klaus Kühnhammer (eds) *Phonologica 1996: Syllables!?* 323–334. The Hague: Thesus.

Wiese, Richard (1996) *The Phonology of German*. Oxford: Clarendon Press.

Wolf, Matthew (2005) An Autosegmental Theory of quirky mutations. In John Alderete, Chung-Hye Han and Alexei Kochetov (eds) *Proceedings of the 24th West Coast Conference on Formal Linguistics,* 370–378. Somerville, MA: Cascadilla Proceedings Project.

Wolf, Matthew (2007) For an autosegmental theory of mutation. In Leah Bateman, Michael O'Keefe, Ehren Reilly and Adam Werle (eds) *University of Massachusetts Occasional Papers in Linguistics* 32: *Papers in Optimality Theory* III, 315–404. Amherst, MA: GLSA.

Wolf, Matthew (2008) *Optimal Interleaving: Serial phonology-morphology interaction in a Constraint-based Model*. Doctoral dissertation, University of Massachusetts at Amherst.

Wolf, Matthew (this volume) Lexical insertion occurs in the phonological component.

Wunderlich, Dieter (1996) Minimalist Morphology: The role of paradigms. *Yearbook of Morphology* 1995: 93–114.

Yu, Alan C. L. (2007) *A Natural History of Infixation*. Oxford: Oxford University Press.

Zoll, Cheryl (1996) *Parsing below the segment in a constraint-based framework*. Doctoral dissertation, University of California at Berkeley.

9 Lexical insertion occurs in the phonological component

Matthew Wolf

9.1 Introduction

A morpheme (or a collection of morphological features) may be pronounced in different ways when it appears in different contexts. The term 'allomorphy' in the broadest sense refers to any instance where this occurs. Some cases of allomorphy involve purely morphosyntactic suppletion, a parade example being the English irregular verb which is pronounced [gow] in the present tense and [wɛnt] in the past tense. While the grammar must choose between these pronunciations, the choice is not made on the basis of any phonological information; knowing the morphosyntactic tense of the verb is sufficient to make the right choice. At another extreme lie cases of allomorphy which arise solely from phonological alternations. In such cases, the morphology consistently selects a single underlying pronunciation for some morphological object, and this undergoes different phonological changes in different phonological contexts where it may be found.

This chapter is concerned with systems of allomorphy which fall in the territory between these two extremes. Since the work of Carstairs (-McCarthy) (1987, 1988, 1990), it has been widely familiar that there are systems of allomorphy where the allomorphs are distributed according to a phonological generalization, but where we could not derive the different surface allomorphs from a single underlying form via plausible phonological processes. What these cases demand is that there be a selection between multiple different listed pronunciations (like the first type), but that this selection make reference to information about the phonological context in which the chosen pronunciation will appear (like the second type). A fairly well-known example is that of the third-person masculine singular

Affiliation: None.

possessive/direct object enclitic in Moroccan Arabic (Heath 1987: 34, 238; Mascaró 1996b), which is /-u/ after a consonant-final base, but /-h/ after a vowel-final one:

(1) a. [ktab-u] 'his book'
 b. [xtˤa-h] 'his error'

Following Paster (2005, 2006, 2009, this volume), I will refer to this phenomenon as 'phonologically conditioned suppletive allomorphy', or PCSA for short.

A longstanding question in phonological and morphological theory is that of how these different kinds of allomorphy are distributed in the grammar. A relatively traditional response would go something like this. There is a module of grammar, which we may call the morphological component, in which non-phonologically-conditioned suppletion like that involving *go* ~ *went* is handled. This component takes abstract morphological structure and consults the list of arbitrary sound-meaning pairs stored in the language's lexicon to decide which collection of sounds is appropriate for expressing which bit of morphological structure. When this is finished, the output of the morphology – a collection of phonological underlying representations – becomes the input to the phonological component. The phonology takes this string of underlying forms and maps it onto the phonological surface form. The second type of allomorphy thus arises in the phonological component.

So far all this is relatively straightforward, perhaps even banal. The trickier (and thus more interesting) matter, under the standard assumptions just laid out, is that of where in the grammar PCSA arises. It is with this question that the present chapter is concerned. In the existing literature, three general responses to this question can be identified.

The first answer is that PCSA arises in the phonological component. This view has become widespread since the appearance of Optimality Theory (Prince and Smolensky 2004 [1993]). In parallel Optimality-Theoretic models of phonology, the selection of the surface pronunciation of some form results from considering various candidate pronunciations and determining which best satisfies a set of ranked and violable constraints. It is easy to see the intuitive appeal of treating PCSA in such a framework, since PCSA seems by definition to involve using phonological criteria to choose between competing alternative pronunciations. It is thus not surprising that in the first few years of OT, a number of different researchers (Mester 1994; Hargus 1995; Tranel 1995, 1996, 1998; Drachman *et al.* 1996; Kager 1996a; Mascaró 1996a,b) proposed OT analyses of PCSA effects in a variety of languages. Many works since these (far too numerous to list) have pursued this same line of analysis.

The second response is that some cases of PCSA happen in the phonology component and others in the morphology component. Lapointe and Sells (1996), Dolbey (1997), and Lapointe (1999) note that there are at least some attested PCSA systems in which typologically-plausible and strictly *phonological* OT constraints are not available which will produce the correct distribution of allomorphs. If PCSA is to be kept in the phonology component, these cases seem to require that the phonological constraints be augmented with additional constraints which impose preferences which are, from a phonological standpoint, arbitrary (Kager 1996a; Bonet 2004; Mascaró 2007; Bonet *et al.* 2007; Trommer 2008). An alternative suggestion, put forth by the authors cited at the beginning of this paragraph, is that the cases of PCSA which are not clearly phonologically optimizing are not really part of the phonology at all, but are instead like English *go/went*: they involve arbitrary subcategorization for features of the environment in which each allomorph appears, and it simply happens that some of the features subcategorized for are phonological.

The third response goes further. If some cases of PCSA need to be attributed to arbitrary preferences imposed by nonphonological constraints, then this seems to vitiate the argument for PCSA ever representing optimization according to phonological criteria. If arbitrary morphological subcategorization frames are needed in order to cope with some cases of PCSA (as well as with nonphonological suppletion like *go~went*), then, the argument goes, it is most economical to assign all suppletion to the morphology component. Versions of this position are staked out, notably, by Paster (2005, 2006, 2009, this volume), Bye (2008) and Embick (2010).

This chapter suggests that a different response is in order. Perhaps, if there are systems of suppletive allomorphy which seem to show the mixed influence of phonological criteria and morpho-lexical, non-phonological ones, this is because the two kinds of criteria are enforced by constraints which belong to a single component of the grammar, meaning that it is unsurprising that they should interact. That is, perhaps there is no crisp dividing line between cases of allomorphy which seem to belong to the morphological module and cases which seem to belong to the phonological module because *these are not in fact separate modules*. Instead, I would like to suggest, there is a single module of grammar in which all lexical insertion occurs, along with all phonological operations.

The argument is developed as follows. In section 9.2 I present the structure of the standard approach to PCSA in OT, taking as a central illustration Mascaró's (1996b) analysis of the Moroccan Arabic example mentioned above. Having seen how this mode of analysis works, we will then consider a well-known case in which arbitrary preferences seem to be required, namely that of the Ergative suffix in the Pama-Nyungan language Dyirbal. Section 9.3 lays out an analysis of the Dyirbal facts cast within a theoretical framework which assumes that phonology and lexical insertion occupy a single module of grammar, namely Optimal Interleaving (OI: Wolf 2008). This section also compares the OI analysis to an alternative approach to arbitrary preference based on the constraint PRIORITY (Bonet 2004; Bonet *et al.* 2007). Comparison with approaches which remove PCSA from the phonology entirely is made in section 9.4. Section 9.5 discusses some additional types of interactions between phonological and morphological constraints which are expected if the two types of constraints belong to the same component and are freely re-rankable with respect to one another. Section 9.6 gives a concluding summary.

9.2 PCSA as phonological optimization: The standard treatment, and its limits

The idea that PCSA occurs in the phonological component has been implemented in a variety of different ways, but to the extent that a standard implementation of this idea exists, it is probably the one presented by Mascaró (1996a,b). The analysis of the Moroccan Arabic third-person masculine singular possessive/direct object enclitic in Mascaró (1996b) assumes that this morpheme has two underlying forms, /-u/ and /-h/,[1] and that the following convention (originally stated in explicit form in Mascaró 1996a) is applicable in such cases:

(2) For a lexical item L such that $\Phi = a, b$:
Eval(Gen (a, b)) = Eval(Gen(a) $\cup$ Gen(b))

That is: when a morph L's phonological representation Φ consists of two underlying forms *a* and *b*, the candidate set evaluated when L is in the input is defined as the union of two candidate sets: Gen(a), the candidate set produced with just *a* in the input, and Gen(b), the candidate set produced with just *b* in the input.[2] When some morphs in the input have multiple underlying forms, candidates thus differ not only in what surface form they contain, but also in which underlying form they select for those morphemes which have multiple disjunctive URs.

When the Moroccan Arabic third person masculine singular enclitic is added to a vowel-final base, a candidate using the /-h/ allomorph will win, provided that having an onsetless syllable, as using /-u/ would give rise to, is a more serious problem than having a coda in the word-final syllable, as using /-h/ would give rise to. Mascaró's (1996b) analysis expresses this idea via the OT constraint ranking ONSET >> NOCODA:[3]

(3)

/xtˤa – {h, u}/ Inputs:	Outputs:	ONSET	NOCODA
/xtˤa-h/	a. ☞ [xtˤah]		1
/xtˤa-u/	b. [xtˤa.u]	W1	L

For consonant-final bases, the same ranking will result in the selection of a candidate that uses /-u/:

(4)

/ktab – {h, u}/ Inputs:	Outputs:	ONSET	NOCODA
/ktab-u/	a. ☞ [kta.bu]		
/ktab-h/	b. [ktabh]		W1

Let us now consider the general requirements that must hold for an instance of PCSA to be analysable under these assumptions. Suppose that a morpheme is realized, depending on its context, by one of two listed allomorphs X and Y, which appear respectively in the phonological contexts A_B and C_D. If the choice between X and Y is made by an OT grammar in the manner illustrated for Moroccan Arabic, then two things must be the case:

(5) a. Some (markedness) constraint M_1 that exerts the preference AXB ≻ AYB must dominate all constraints that exert the preference AYB ≻ AXB.
  b. Some other (markedness) constraint M_2 that exerts the preference CYD ≻ CXD must dominate all constraints that exert the preference CXD ≻ CYD.

These requirements result directly from the basic logic of constraint ranking in OT. For a pair of competing options like AXB and AYB, the highest-ranked constraint which prefers one over the other must prefer AXB, since otherwise unattested *AYB would be chosen instead.[4] In some allmorphy systems, like /-h/ ~ /-u/ in Moroccan Arabic, it is easy to find the required M_1 and M_2 among markedness constraints which are well motivated by phonological typology. In Mascaró's (1996b) analysis of Moroccan Arabic depicted in (3)–(4), for instance, we can call on standard, widely-used, not-especially-controversial constraints like ONSET and NOCODA.

For other allomorphy systems, it is not apparent that the required M_1 and M_2 can be found. The system that arises most frequently in discussions of this issue (McCarthy and Prince 1990, 1993: ch. 7; Bonet 2004; McCarthy and Wolf 2005; Paster 2005, 2006, this volume; Bye 2008; Trommer 2008) involves the marking of Ergative Case on vowel-final stems in the Pama-Nyungan language Dyirbal (Dixon 1972):[5]

(6) jaɽa-ŋku 'man-ERG'
jamani-ku 'rainbow-ERG'
palakara-ku 'they-ERG'

As the data illustrate, disyllabic vowel-final stems are suffixed with /ŋku/ in the Ergative, while longer stems are suffixed with /ku/.[6] (Stems ending in a nasal or [j] mark the Ergative with [Tu], where [T] is a stop homorganic with the stem-final consonant; with stems ending in a liquid, the final liquid is deleted, and the Ergative is marked with [-ɽu].) It is reasonably clear that there will be constraints that prefer /ku/ over /ŋku/, regardless of context, since nasals, velars, and consonant clusters are all marked. However, given that /ku/ and /ŋku/ resemble each other so much, it is not so obvious that we would be able to find a typologically-plausible universal constraint which could prefer /ŋku/ over /ku/ just in case the stem were disyllabic.

If we can't, then it seems that in addition to substantively phonological preferences among allomorphs like those imposed by constraints like ONSET and NOCODA, at least some cases of PCSA require a role for *arbitrary* preferences among allomorphs, in the Dyirbal case in favour of /-ŋku/. Some authors have retained the same sort of OT framework illustrated for Moroccan Arabic while adding constraints that impose arbitrary, lexically-specified preferences (Kager 1996a; Kenstowicz 2005; Mascaró 2007; Bonet *et al.* 2007; Trommer 2008). Others have drawn a different lesson, concluding that if PCSA cannot be adequately treated without recourse to arbitrary preferences, there is nothing conceptually gained by treating PCSA as involving phonological optimization at all (Paster 2005, 2006, 2009, this volume; Bye 2008; Embick 2010). That is, the preference-relations among allomorphs which have been understood as being exercised by substantively phonological constraints could be replaced by arbitrary statements expressing the same preferences. In this way, non-phonological selection criteria would do all the work, and there would be no need to have both phonological and morpholexical constraints on allomorph selection.

As mentioned, this chapter will argue for a quite different conclusion: that allomorph selection is governed by both phonological and morphological constraints, and that these constraints occupy one and the same OT grammar and are freely re-rankable with respect to one another. The next section presents the assumptions of the framework being argued for here.

9.3 Optimal Interleaving theory and its treatment of arbitrary preference in allomorph selection

The framework in which I will present my analysis of Dyirbal is called Optimal Interleaving (OI: Wolf 2008, 2009, 2010, 2013, to appear; Kimper 2009; Staubs 2011; McCarthy 2012; McQuaid 2012). OI, in brief, assumes (a) a realizational view of morphology, and (b) that morphological realization occurs together with phonology in a single OT grammar, specifically one with the serial architecture of OT-CC (McCarthy 2007) or Harmonic Serialism (Prince and Smolensky 2004 [1993]: §5.2.3.3). As it happens, serialism is not logically necessary to the analysis of Dyirbal I will present, but I will couch the analysis in HS terms for ease of comparison with existing discussions of OI. First let us briefly explicate these two basic assumptions of OI.

9.3.1 Realizational morphology

Stump (2001) presents a taxonomy of morphological theories which distinguishes between *incremental* theories and *realizational* ones. In an incremental theory, morphemes are regarded as meaningful collections of phonological material, which are assembled together to make words. That is, the construction of the abstract semantico-syntactic structure of words and the construction of the words' (underlying) phonological form proceed hand-in-hand. On the other hand, *realizational* theories assume that a purely abstract morphological structure is built first, and then at a later step, this structure is 'realized' or 'spelled out' by associating units of the abstract structure with collections of phonological material (and possibly also by applying phonological process like truncation, feature changes, etc.). Rules or constraints of one sort or another are responsible for dictating which abstract morphological features can be paired with which collections of phonological structure.

On a realizational view, the derivation of the English word *cats* will proceed something like this: first an abstract structure which we may represent as CAT+PLURAL is built. The process of spell-out then associates the abstract unit CAT with the underlying phonological string /kæt/ and PLURAL with the underlying string /z/. The collection of underlying forms /kætz/ then undergoes voicing assimilation to yield the surface form [kæts]. Within this general picture, there is substantial room for disagreement, for instance with regard to the extent to which words do or do not contain internal syntax-like structure organizing their abstract features; Distributed Morphology (Halle and Marantz 1993) and A-Morphous Morphology (Anderson 1992) are prominent realizational theories which take markedly different positions on this issue. In this chapter, I will attempt to remain agnostic about such issues to the extent possible. I will use the term 'morpheme' to refer to structures at the abstract level of morphological structure and the term 'morph' to refer to the bundles of phonological material which are used to spell out morphemes (i.e., what is known in Distributed Morphology as a 'vocabulary item'). My use of the term 'morpheme' in this way should not be taken as indicating disagreement with frameworks like A-Morphous Morphology which reject the classical morpheme; rather, it should be taken as referring to any structural positions or layers within the abstract representation of a word which are smaller than the whole word but (potentially) larger than an individual morphosyntactic feature.

At least two general theoretical arguments can be given for a realizational view.[7] First, it is generally assumed that it is only the abstract morphological structures, and not their spell-out, which are built in or interact with syntax; spell-out, in derivational terms, occurs after syntax is done. This predicts that the syntax will be insensitive to the phonological composition of words, which seems to be right; this prediction is dubbed 'Feature Disjointness' in Distributed Morphology (Marantz 1995), and similar empirical conclusions are argued for (though from a standpoint quite different from DM's) under the rubric of the Principle of Phonology-Free Syntax (Zwicky 1969; Zwicky and Pullum 1986a,b; Pullum and Zwicky 1988; Miller *et al.* 1992, 1997).

The other argument in favour of a realizational view is that it permits us to analyse at least some morphological syncretisms without having to resort to accidental homophony. A straightforward illustration involves adjective inflection in Dutch (Sauerland 1995). Neuter singular strong adjectives have no overt inflectional ending; strong adjectives of other number-gender combinations carry an ending /-ə/:

(7) *Number/gender endings in Dutch strong adjectives*

	[+neuter]	[−neuter]
[+plural]	-ə	-ə
[−plural]	Ø	-ə

On an incremental view of morphology, this would require us to posit three accidentally-homophonous /-ə/ suffixes, with the meanings 'neuter plural', 'non-neuter plural', and 'non-neuter singular'. This is because in an incremental theory, morphological features inhere in and are introduced by the formatives which represent them, and so the observed formatives must carry all of the features which are possessed by the word which they appear in. Realizational theories are different, because while all the required dimensions of morphosyntactic feature contrast exist at the level of abstract morphological structure, it is possible that some of these contrasts may be neutralized in the mapping from morphemes to morphs – that is, a single morph of the language may be used to express multiple distinct morphemes.

Following Sauerland (1995)'s Distributed Morphology analysis, in a rule-based realizational framework we might set up the following two rules for Dutch:

(8) a. Spell out the inflectional ending as /Ø/ if it contains the features [−plural, +neuter].
b. Spell out the inflectional ending as /-ə/.

Since rule (8a) is applicable in a proper subset of the places where rule (8b) is, the rules will effectively apply in the order shown if they are disjunctively ordered in accordance with the Elsewhere Condition (Pāṇini, by way of Anderson 1969, Kiparsky 1973, and others). In other words, the null form of the inflectional ending is the default, but when the feature-combination required for the use of this form is absent, the elsewhere form /-ə/ is used instead. In Distributed Morphology, such default/elsewhere relationships between morphs (or 'vocabulary items' in DM parlance) is generally taken to be expressed via the Subset Principle (Halle 1997):

(9) *Subset Principle*
The phonological exponent of a Vocabulary item is inserted into a morpheme in the terminal string if the item matches all or a subset of the grammatical features specified in the terminal morpheme. Insertion does not take place if the vocabulary item contains features not present in the morpheme. Where several Vocabulary items meet the conditions for insertion, the item matching the greatest number of features specified in the terminal morpheme must be chosen.

On this view, morphs (vocabulary items) can be thought of as ordered pairs consisting of a bundle of morphological features and a bundle of phonological material. When determining which morph to pair up with a particular morpheme, the grammar compares the features of the morpheme with the features of each morph in the language's lexicon. The morph which is chosen is the one which matches the greatest number of the features present in the abstract morpheme, provided that the morph does not contain any features which the morpheme lacks. Expressed in these terms, we can set up the following two morphs for Dutch (Sauerland 1995):

(10) a. <[−plural, +neuter], Ø>
b. <Ø, /ə/>

Couched in these theoretical terms, the default status of the phonologically-null morph is a consequence of the fact that its bundle of morphological features contains a proper superset of the morphological features of the /-ə/ morph. In a short while, we will see that a similar mode of analysis can be called on in order to implement the required arbitrary preference among the competing allomorphs of the Dyirbal Ergative. The main architectural innovation this will require, naturally, is that constraints on the goodness of feature-matching in morphological spell-out must be able to interact with phonological constraints. Before addressing either the Dyirbal Ergative or these broader theoretical questions, though, we need to consider how a Subset-Principle-like mechanism of morph selection could be set up using OT constraints.

9.3.2 Constraints on morpheme-morph correspondence

Let us suppose that the input to the phonology consists of an abstract morphological structure.[8] Let us assume that the abstract representation consists of a set of nodes called *morphemes*, and that individual morphosyntactic features are autosegmental dependents of these nodes. (In principle the features might not be direct dependents of morphemes, but instead arranged in a more elaborate multi-layered feature geometry, as in Harley and Ritter 1998.) To the extent possible, I will try to be neutral about what kind of superordinate structure the morphemes themselves may be organized into (e.g. whether the morphemes are terminal nodes of a syntactic tree, or slots in a morphological template, or something else.) Following Trommer (2001), I will refer to a morpheme together with its dependent morphological features as a *feature structure*, or FS.

As before, let us suppose that a language's lexicon contains a list of *morphs*, and that morphs are ordered pairs consisting of an FS and an underlying phonological representation. Under these assumptions, a candidate in the phonology will consist of:

- A set of morphs;
- A surface phonological representation;
- An input-output Correspondence relation (McCarthy and Prince 1995) between the surface phonological representation and the underlying phonological representations contained in the morphs;
- A Correspondence relation between the FSes of the morphs and the FSes of the morphemes in the input. (Call this the MM Correspondence relation.)

For the English word *cats*, the winning candidate will then look something like this (coindexation indicates that two elements stand in Correspondence with one another; to emphasize the existence of distinct Correspondence relations, Greek letters indicate MM Correspondence, and Arabic numerals indicate IO Correspondence):

(11)

input	*morphs*	*surface form*
CAT$_{\alpha}$-PLURAL$_{\beta}$	<CAT$_{\alpha}$, /k$_1$æ$_2$t$_3$/>, <PLURAL$_{\beta}$, /-z$_4$/>	[k$_1$æ$_2$t$_3$s$_4$]

Similar assumptions about the nature of candidates can be found in Zuraw (2000) and Walker and Feng (2004), as well as in much recent work in the Bidrectional Phonology and Phonetics programme making use of 'lexical' or 'M-Phon' constraints, including Boersma (2001, 2011), Escudero (2005), Apoussidou (2007), Eisenstat (2009), Hamann *et al.* (2009), Jesney (2009), Jesney *et al.* (2010), Pater *et al.* (2010, 2012), Pater and Smith (2011), Smith (2012), and Staubs and Pater (to appear).[9]

As in standard OT, phonological markedness constraints will evaluate the surface phonological representation, and phonological IO-faithfulness constraints will evaluate the Correspondence relation between the underlying and surface phonological structures. One thing which will be new is that there will be faithfulness constraints on the morpheme-morph dimension of Correspondence which assess the 'goodness of fit' between the input FSes and the FSes of the morphs employed in a given candidate.

Let us now return DM's Subset Principle. Given the assumptions and terminology just laid out, we can rephrase the Subset Principle as follows:

(12) a. If F is a feature-structure of a morpheme and *F′* is a feature structure of a morph that it corresponds to, *F′* must not contain any features which are not present in F.

b. If F is a feature-structure of a morpheme and *F′* is a feature-structure of a morph that it corresponds to, *F′* must contain as many of F's features as possible.

c. In case of conflict between them, satisfying requirement (a) takes priority over satisfying requirement (b). However, requirement (b) must still be satisfied to the fullest extent possible, without violating requirement (a).

Once it's rephrased in this way, it becomes clearer that the Subset Principle contains an implicit OT-type constraint ranking: constraint (12a) dominates (12b). That ranking means that (12a) will be obeyed in case of conflict, but even then (12b) is satisfied to the fullest extent that it can be. The minimal violation of disobeyed constraints forms the core argument for OT's assumption that constraints are ranked, rather than being parameterized as on or off (Prince and Smolensky 2004 [1993]; see also McCarthy and Prince's 1994 discussion of The Emergence of the Unmarked, which is a case of this minimal-violation effect). Therefore, it seems fruitful to reformulate (12a-b) as OT constraints.

Requirement (12a) can be stated as a constraint of the Dep family, which on the IO dimension of Correspondence serve to militate against epenthesis:[10] the introduction of items in the output representation which lack correspondents in the input representation. Specifically, let us assume that for every morphosyntactic feature *F*, there is a constraint of the following form:[11]

(13) Dep-M(F)
Let φ′ be an instance of the feature F at the morph level. Assign one violation-mark if there does not exist some φ at the morpheme level, such that φ and φ′ stand in MM-Correspondence.

In addition to the Dep-M constraints for features, there will also presumably be Dep-M(FS) constraints, requiring that every feature structure at the morph level have a corresponding FS at the morpheme level.

Similarly, requirement (12b) can be stated as a constraint of the Max family, which in IO Correspondence militate against deletion: the presence of items in the input which lack correspondents in the output. On the MM dimension of Correspondence there will exist constraints of the following form for every feature F (as well as for FSes):[12]

(14) Max-M(F)
Let φ be an instance of the feature F at the morpheme level. Assign one violation-mark if there does not exist some φ′ at the morph level, such that φ and φ′ stand in MM-Correspondence.

To show these constraints put to analytic use, let's return for one last time to the Dutch example. Recall that the two morphs we posited were:

(15) a. <[−plural, +neuter], Ø>
b. <Ø, /ə/>

When the morpheme containing an adjective's inflectional features has any person/number feature combination besides [-plural, +neuter], it will be the <Ø, /ə/> allomorph which is used. This creates a conflict between Dep-M and Max-M constraints for feature-combinations like [+plural, +neuter] and [−plural, −neuter]. For the latter of these, the question is, is it more important to give a correspondent to the morpheme's [−plural] feature or to avoid using a morph containing a token of [+neuter] which isn't present at the morpheme level? The attested result follows if Dep-M(+neuter) outranks Max-M(-plural) (in (16), MM-Correspondence is indicated by Greek-letter co-indices):

(16)

FS_α / \\ $[-plural]_\beta$ $[-neuter]_\gamma$	Dep-M(+neuter)	Max-M(−plural)
a. ☞ $\|FS_\alpha\|$ $/ə_1/$ $[ə_1]$		1
b. $\|FS_\alpha\|$ / \\ $[-plural]_\beta$ $[+neuter]_\delta$ *(no phonological material)*	W1	L

By an exactly analogous argument, Dep-M(−plural) must outrank Max-M(+neuter) in order to get the /ə/ morph to win with adjectives which are [+plural, +neuter].[13]

9.3.3 Harmonic Serialism

The original OI proposal in Wolf (2008) is cast within an OT architecture called OT with Candidate Chains (McCarthy 2007). In OT-CC, each candidate is (approximately) a chain of successively more harmonic forms, each differing from the last by only one of some hypothesized set of minimal changes. OT-CC is an elaboration on Harmonic Serialism (Prince and Smolensky 2004 [1993]: §5.2.3.3) designed to cope with counter-feeding and counterbleeding opacity. As mentioned, serialism is not actually required to cope with the Dyirbal facts in the analysis which will follow, but I will present the analysis in HS terms both in order to facilitate comparison with other literature in and about OI; in addition, the one-step-at-a-time character of the derivational HS presentation will make it easier to isolate and explain the individual pieces of the analysis.[14]

In HS, the candidate-generating function Gen is taken to consist of some particular set of basic operations. At the beginning of a derivation, the input is presented to Gen, and the candidate set consists of every form which can be produced from the input by performing one of these operations, as well as the fully-faithful candidate identical to the input. If the winner from this candidate set is anything other than the fully-faithful candidate, the output of the current round of optimization is returned to GEN as an input, with the process continuing until a fully-faithful candidate is chosen (*convergence*).

The overall HS framework is compatible with any number of different hypotheses about what exactly the set of basic operations in GEN consists of. The goal of this paper is to advance one such hypothesis: that 'insert one morph' is amongst the operations of the GEN of the phonological component.

9.3.4 Analysis of the Dyirbal Ergative

In Dyirbal, the competing Ergative morphs /-ŋku/ and /-ku/ stand in a special-general relationship: /ŋku/ appears in one specific context (after a disyllabic stem), and /ku/ appears elsewhere. In this case, the context of the special morph is phonologically defined. As we have already seen, special-general relations of the same sort also exist in systems of suppletive allomorphy in which there is no evidence of phonological conditioning. The inflection of Dutch strong adjectives discussed earlier in this chapter is just such an example: null inflection is used with neuter singular adjectives (the special case) and /-ə/ is used otherwise (the general case).

In order for the general case to emerge, the preference for the special case has to be overruled in certain contexts. In OT terms, this means that in the contexts where the general case appears, the relevant MAX-M(F) constraints are dominated by a constraint which, in just those contexts, prefers the use of the general case over the use of the special case. As we saw in (16), in the case of Dutch, the relevant constraints are DEP-M(+neuter) and MAX-M(-plural), and DEP-M(-plural) and MAX-M(+neuter).

For Dyirbal, the analytic strategy will be the same. The arbitrary preference for /ŋku/ over /ku/ can be derived from the assumption that /ŋku/ spells out more features than /ku/ does. The main difference between Dutch and Dyirbal will be in the nature of the constraint that dominates MAX-M(F) and which triggers use of the general case. For Dutch, these were morpheme/morph faithfulness constraints, but for Dyirbal, the constraint will have to involve phonology, since a phonological generalization is at work.

In order to justify the particular assumptions that I'll make about the morphosyntax of /ŋku/ and /ku/, we need to consider one further fact about the Dyirbal Case system. This is that the Locative Case shows a pattern of allomorphy which is identical to that of that of the Ergative, except that the Locative has [a] where the Ergative has [u]. So, among V-final stems, disyllabic stems take [ŋka] in the Locative, whereas longer stems take [ka] (Dixon 1972):

(17) jaɽa-ŋka 'man-LOC'
jamani-ka 'rainbow-LOC'

That there should be this kind of partial syncretism between the Ergative and Locative is unsurprising in light of proposals about Case features. Specifically, Halle and Vaux (1998) have proposed that Ergative and Locative share a feature [−free], which designates 'nominals with a consistent role in argument structure.' The other two Cases which have this feature under Halle and Vaux's proposal are Instrumental (whose phonological realization is identical to that of Ergative in Dyirbal) and Accusative, which Dyirbal doesn't have.[15,16]

We can therefore make the following generalization about Dyirbal:

(18) a. The feature [−free] is marked by /ŋ/ on disyllabic roots, but receives no overt phonological realization with longer roots.
b. In the [−free] Cases, the other case features besides [−free] may be spelled out by other morphs, i.e. /ku/ in the Ergative and Instrumental or /ka/ in the Locative.

Before showing the analysis, one bit of preview on the phonological constraints to be employed. As in most previous analyses of the Dyirbal Ergative (and indeed as with most phonological analyses of syllable-counting PCSA), the constraint lying behind the non-use of /-ŋ/ with longer-than-disyllabic stems will be one involving foot structure. Dyirbal has left-to-right trochaic stress (Dixon 1972: §7.2.2; McCarthy and Prince 1990): the initial syllable and all non-final odd-numbered syllables get stress. Dixon (1972: 275) reports that there are no phonetic differences between stressed syllables that would permit us to identify one particular stress as the primary stress. However, he says so after mentioning that one could conceivably posit that the initial syllable bore primary stress. (Dixon himself rejects this as 'a mere analytic ploy', due to the just-mentioned lack of phonetic distinctions between degrees of stress.) The basis for this possibility is that there are a number of morphemes in Dyirbal (not just the Ergative) which show one allomorph with two-syllable bases and a different allomorph with longer bases. Transitive verbalizations of nouns (Dixon 1972: 86) are formed by adding /-mal/ to a two-syllable stem, and /-(m)bal/ to a longer stem. Second, reflexive forms of [j]-final verbs are formed by adding /-ˈmarij/ to disyllabic stems, and /-(m)ˈbarij/ to longer stems.[17] There are other allomorphic processes which refer to proximity to *any* stress (e.g. the reflexives of [l]-final roots: Dixon 1972: 89), but there are no allomorphic alternations which are conditioned by proximity to any *particular* non-initial stress (to the exclusion of other stresses). This might be seen as evidence that all word-initial stresses in Dyirbal have a property which no medial stresses have. If that's right, the obvious candidate for this property is that initial stresses are primary stresses, while medial stresses are all secondary.

Assuming that primary stress in Dyirbal is indeed word-initial, we may attribute the blocking of /-ŋ/-affixation on greater-than-disyllabic stems to the following constraint:

(19) COINCIDE(ŋ, head ft)$_{ŋ}$
Assign one violation-mark for every instance of the segment /-ŋ/ which is not in the head foot. (Due to indexed nature of constraint, only evaluate instances of /-ŋ/ which belong to the morph that spells out the feature [-free].[18])

This constraint is a member of the COINCIDE family of positional markedness constraints introduced by Zoll (1998). These constraints impose requirements to the effect that marked structures are allowed only when affiliated with certain prominent positions. In the present case, this constraint will discourage introducing an [-ŋ] if that segment would not fall in the head foot, which by hypothesis is coextensive in Dyirbal with the first two syllables of a word. This requirement, it can be noted, is quite similar to the restriction in Guugu Yimidhirr (Haviland 1979; Kager 1996b) that long vowels are permitted only in the first two syllables of a word; it is this pattern which is one of the empirical bases upon which Zoll (1998) argues for the existence of licensing constraints like (19).

Now, to see how the analysis of Dyirbal works, let us begin by considering the derivation of [jaɽaŋku], 'man-ERGATIVE'. I will assume that the input to the phonology for this word contains two abstract morphemes: a root morpheme MAN, and a Case morpheme having as its dependants the features [−free, −oblique, +structural, +superior] (i.e., the full composition of Ergative Case in the theory of Case features in Halle and Vaux 1998). I will assume that the insertion of any one morph from the language's lexicon can occur as a single step in the Harmonic-Serialist derivation. Additionally, I will assume that the construction of prosodic structure – syllables and feet, for present purposes – can occur simultaneously with any operation that occurs on a single step. (This is assumed strictly for purposes of expositional simplicity, and should not be taken as a rejection of proposals that construction of syllables, Pater (2012), and/or feet, Pruitt (2010), are derivational steps of their own.)

Supposing that MAX-M(root) is undominated in Dyirbal, the first thing to occur will be the insertion of the root morph /jaɽa/. (For visual simplicity in the tableaux illustrating the analysis of Dyirbal, I will depict direct co-indexation between phonological surface forms and the FSes of the input; it should be understood that the link between these two representations is mediated by MM-Correspondence between the morpheme and morph levels, and by IO-Correspondence between the phonological portion of those morphs, and the phonological surface form):

(20)

MAN$_1$- {−fr$_2$, −obl$_3$, +str$_4$, sup$_5$}	MAX-M (root)	COINCIDE (ŋ, head ft)$_n$	MAX-M (−free)	MAX-M (−obl)	MAX-M (+struc)	MAX-M (+sup)
a. ☞ MAN$_1$- {−fr$_2$, −obl$_3$, +str$_4$, +sup$_5$} [(jaṛa$_1$)$_{Ft}$]$_{PWd}$			1	1	1	1
b. MAN$_1$- {−fr$_2$, −obl$_3$, +str$_4$, +sup$_5$} ŋ$_2$	W1	W1	L	1	1	1
c. MAN$_1$- {−fr$_2$, −obl$_3$, +str$_4$, +sup$_5$} ku$_{3,4,5}$	W1		1	L	L	L
d. MAN$_1$- {−fr$_2$, −obl$_3$, +str$_4$, +sup$_5$}	W1		1	1	1	1

On the second pass, our choices are either to insert /-ŋ/, whose feature structure contains the feature [−free], or to insert /-ku/, whose feature structure contains [−oblique, +structural, +superior]. Assuming that MAX-M(-free) is higher ranked than the MAX-M constraints for the other three features, the candidate which inserts /-ŋ/ will beat the one that inserts /-ku/:

(21)

MAN$_1$- {−fr$_2$, −obl$_3$, +str$_4$, +sup$_5$} [(jaɽa$_1$)$_{Ft}$]$_{PWd}$	MAX-M (root)	COINCIDE (ŋ, head ft)$_ŋ$	MAX-M (−free)	MAX-M (−obl)	MAX-M (+struc)	MAX-M (+sup)
a. ☞ MAN$_1$- {−fr$_2$, −obl$_3$, +str$_4$, +sup$_5$} [(jaɽa$_1$ŋ$_2$)$_{Ft}$]$_{PWd}$				1	1	1
b. MAN$_1$- {−fr$_2$, −obl$_3$, +str$_4$, +sup$_5$} [(jaɽa$_1$)$_{Ft}$ ku$_{3,4,5}$]$_{PWd}$			W1	L	L	L
c. MAN$_1$- {−fr$_2$, −obl$_3$, +str$_4$, +sup$_5$} [(jaɽa$_1$)$_{Ft}$]$_{PWd}$			W1	1	1	1

As can be seen, I'm assuming here that upon being inserted, the suffix /-ŋ/ is immediately incorporated into a foot. Because the root is disyllabic, the foot which /-ŋ/ becomes part of is the head foot of the word, and so the indexed constraint COINCIDE(ŋ, head ft)$_ŋ$ is not violated.

On the next and, for our purposes, final pass, /-ku/ is inserted:

(22)

MAN$_1$- {−fr$_2$, −obl$_3$, +str$_4$, +sup$_5$} [(jaɽa$_1$ŋ$_2$)$_{Ft}$]$_{PWd}$	MAX-M (root)	COINCIDE (ŋ, head ft)$_ŋ$	MAX-M (−free)	MAX-M (−obl)	MAX-M (+struc)	MAX-M (+sup)
a. ☞ MAN$_1$- {−fr$_2$, −obl$_3$, +str$_4$, +sup$_5$} [(jaɽa$_1$ŋ$_2$)$_{Ft}$ ku$_{3,4,5}$]$_{PWd}$						
b. MAN$_1$- {−fr$_2$, −obl$_3$, +str$_4$, +sup$_5$} [(jaɽa$_1$ŋ$_2$)$_{Ft}$]$_{PWd}$				W1	W1	W1

Now let us consider longer bases, with which /ŋ/ will not appear. On the assumptions that Dyirbal foot structure is left-to-right trochaic, and that the [ŋ] of an intervocalic [ŋk] cluster is parsed as a coda (the justification for which will be discussed shortly), we may propose that the spell-out of [−free] by the /ŋ/ morph is blocked because MAX-M(−free) is outranked by the indexed positional licensing constraint which requires instances of the segment /-ŋ/ to coincide with the head foot:

(23)

THEY$_1$- {−fr$_2$, −obl$_3$, +str$_4$, +sup$_5$} [('pa.la)$_{Ft}$(ˌka.ra$_1$)$_{Ft}$]$_{PWd}$	MAX-M (root)	COINCIDE (ŋ, head ft)$_ŋ$	MAX-M (−free)	MAX-M (−obl)	MAX-M (+struc)	MAX-M (+sup)
a. ☞ THEY$_1$- {−fr$_2$, −obl$_3$, +str$_4$, +sup$_5$} [('pa.la)$_{Ft}$(ˌka.ra$_1$)$_{Ft}$ ku$_{3,4,5}$]$_{PWd}$			1			
b. THEY$_1$- {−fr$_2$, −obl$_3$, +str$_4$, +sup$_5$} [('pala)$_{Ft}$(ˌkara$_1$ŋ$_2$)$_{Ft}$]$_{PWd}$		W1	L	W1	W1	W1
c. THEY$_1$- {−fr$_2$, −obl$_3$, +str$_4$, +sup$_5$} [('pa.la)$_{Ft}$(ˌka.ra$_1$)$_{Ft}$]$_{PWd}$			1	W1	W1	W1

At this point we can see why assumptions about the syllabification of [VŋkV] sequences as [Vŋ.kV] is essential to the success of the analysis of the disyllabic stems. We assumed that /-ŋ/ is inserted before /-ku/, which requires that MAX-M(-free) outrank the MAX-M constraints for the other three features making up the Ergative Case. If COINCIDE(ŋ, head ft)$_ŋ$ dominates MAX-M(−free), the former constraint will by transitivity also dominate the MAX-M constraints for the three features spelled out by /-ku/. If adding /-ku/ would cause /-ŋ/ to resyllabify as an onset, then it follows that adding /-ku/ will create a new violation of COINCIDE(ŋ, head ft)$_ŋ$. Given the constraint rankings just adduced, insertion of /-ku/ would then be blocked, which obviously is not what we want:[19]

(24)

MAN$_1$- {−fr$_2$, −obl$_3$, +str$_4$, +sup$_5$} [(jaɽa$_1$ŋ$_2$)$_{Ft}$]$_{PWd}$	MAX-M (root)	COINCIDE (ŋ, head ft)$_ŋ$	MAX-M (−free)	MAX-M (−obl)	MAX-M (+struc)	MAX-M (+sup)
a. ☞ MAN$_1$- {−fr$_2$, −obl$_3$, +str$_4$, +sup$_5$} [(ja.ɽa$_1$)$_{Ft}$ ŋ$_2$ku$_{3,4,5}$]$_{PWd}$		W1		L	L	L
b. 💣 MAN$_1$- {−fr$_2$, −obl$_3$, +str$_4$, +sup$_5$} [(jaɽa$_1$ŋ$_2$)$_{Ft}$]$_{PWd}$				1	1	1

The same assumption about syllabification will be necessary if we alternatively assumed that /-ku/ were inserted earlier in the derivation than /-ŋ/ (meaning that /-ŋ/ would be a kind of infix). This is because /-ŋ/ would end up in onset position to begin with, again resulting in a new violation of COINCIDE(ŋ, head ft)$_ŋ$:

(25)

MAN$_1$- {−fr$_2$, −obl$_3$, +str$_4$, +sup$_5$} [(jaɽa$_1$)$_{Ft}$ ku$_{3,4,5}$]$_{PWd}$	MAX-M (root)	COINCIDE (ŋ, head ft)$_ŋ$	MAX-M (−free)	MAX-M (−obl)	MAX-M (+struc)	MAX-M (+sup)
a. ☞ MAN$_1$- {−fr$_2$, −obl$_3$, +str$_4$, +sup$_5$} [(ja.ɽa$_1$)$_{Ft}$ ŋ$_2$ku$_{3,4,5}$]$_{PWd}$		W1	L			
b. 💣 MAN$_1$- {−fr$_2$, −obl$_3$, +str$_4$, +sup$_5$} [(jaɽa$_1$ŋ$_2$)$_{Ft}$ku$_{3,4,5}$]$_{PWd}$			1			

Is this assumption about syllabification justified? Dixon (1972: 274) states that '[i]t is not easy to formulate a criterion for dividing up Dyirbal words into syllables', but there are a couple of pieces of evidence hinting that [Vŋ.kV] is the right syllabification for intervocalic nasal-stop clusters. First, these clusters occur only word-medially in Dyirbal, never as word-initial onsets or word-final codas (Dixon 1972: 272–273). Second, there is at least one other case in the language where the choice of [VŋkV] versus [VkV] is sensitive to the degree of prosodic prominence of the material *preceding* the intervocalic consonants. This involves the Dative marker, which is generally [-ku], but which appears as [-ŋku] when it immediately follows a stressed syllable (Dixon 1972: 284).[20] In any case, there does not appear to be any evidence which would argue in favour of [V.ŋkV] being the correct syllabification.

9.3.5 Comparison with the PRIORITY approach to arbitrary preference

The line of analysis pursued here is that arbitrary preference amongst phonologically-conditioned allomorphs arises because: (a) realization of abstract morphosyntactic structure occurs in the same component as the phonology; and (b) allomorphs may differ in how fully they express the features of the abstract structure. A different strategy – probably the most prominent one in the OT literature – is proposed by Bonet and Mascaró (2006), Bonet *et al.* (2007), Mascaró (2007), and Bonet (2004), the last of whom presents an analysis of the Dyirbal ergative in terms of this approach. It involves the following constraint:

(26) PRIORITY: Respect lexical priority (ordering) of allomorphs.
Given an input containing allomorphs m_1, m_2, …, m_n, and a candidate m_i', where m_i' is in correspondence with m_i, PRIORITY assigns as many violation marks as the depth of ordering between m_i and the highest dominating morph(s).
(Definition from Mascaró 2007)

PRIORITY-based analyses are architecturally identical in form to multiple-underlying-form analyses like the one presented earlier for Moroccan Arabic: there is only one pass of constraint evaluation, and all of the competing allomorphs are in the input at once. The following tableaux, adapted from Bonet (2004), illustrate how the PRIORITY approach handles the Dyirbal facts:

(27) Dyirbal 'man.ERG' with PRIORITY

/jaɽa -{ŋku > ku}/	RESPECT	PRIORITY
a. ☞ [(ˈja.ɽa)$_{HeadFt}$ ŋku]$_{PWd}$		
b. [(ˈja.ɽa)$_{HeadFt}$ ku$_{Ft}$]$_{PWd}$		W1

Ranked above PRIORITY is a constraint RESPECT, which is violated if a candidate uses a certain allomorph but does not comply with the allomorph's lexically-specified subcategorization requirements, in this case [-ŋku]'s requirement to be suffixed to the head foot. (RESPECT thus does the same work as COINCIDE(ŋ, head ft)$_{ŋ}$ did in the OI analysis, and in principle the PRIORITY analysis could use that licensing constraint in place of RESPECT.) With a disyllabic stem, as in (27), /-ŋku/ and /-ku/ can both be suffixed to the head foot. Candidate (27a) thus satisfies RESPECT and (27b) satisfies the same constraint, vacuously because /-ku/ has no subcategorization requirements. Since RESPECT is indifferent as to the choice of allomorphs, the choice is made by the lower-ranked constraint PRIORITY. The winning candidate chooses the first-listed underlying form /-ŋku/ and thus gets no marks from PRIORITY. By contrast, candidate (27b) chooses the second-listed underlying form /-ku/. It therefore gets one mark from PRIORITY, and thus loses.

Now consider what happens with a greater-than-disyllabic stem:

(28) Dyirbal 'rainbow.ERG' with PRIORITY

/jamani-{ŋku > ku}/	RESPECT	PRIORITY
a. ☞ [(ˈja.ma)$_{HdFt}$(ˌni.ku)$_{Ft}$]$_{PWd}$		1
b. [(ˈja.ma)$_{HdFt}$(ˌni.ŋku)$_{Ft}$]$_{PWd}$	W1	L

Because, when the stem is more than two syllables long, the head foot is no longer at the right edge of the Prosodic Word, neither allomorph of the Ergative suffix can be suffixed to the head foot. As a result, the candidate that chooses the first-listed underlying form /-ŋku/ incurs a violation from RESPECT. The candidate that chooses /-ku/ gets no such violation (again vacuously because /-ku/ has no subcategorization requirements), and so the /-ku/-selecting candidate now emerges as the winner, because RESPECT is higher-ranked than PRIORITY.

The PRIORITY model is conceptually extremely similar to the OI-based one in how it handles this or any other specific example. The difference between them, and the likeliest basis for preferring one over the other, lies in exactly *how* arbitrary preference relations are encoded in the lexicon. In the OI approach, arbitrary preference relations have an epiphenomenal status; they arise from the way that the grammar seeks to pair the feature-structures of abstract morphemes with those of morphs, and are necessarily encoded in the morphosyntactic feature specifications of the competing morphs.

For the OI framework, this means that the analyst's ability to posit arbitrary preferences in any given case is constrained by the need to be consistent with overall patterns of morphological exponence in the language as a whole. As we saw in the proposed analysis of Dyirbal, separating out /-ŋ/ as an independent affix expressing one of the features making up Ergative creates the possibility that /-ŋ/ could also be used in expressing other cases involving that same feature. Indeed, /-ŋ/ does surface under the same phonological conditions with the Locative, permitting us to identify the feature it expresses as [−free].

By contrast, in a PRIORITY account, no particular predictions of this sort will arise, since this approach does not attribute arbitrary-preference effects to the competition of *separate* morphs to realize morphosyntactic structure: the alternative allomorphs are simply packaged together as part of a single lexical entry, possibly with priority relations specified amongst them. Setting up, for instance, {-ŋku > -ku} as the lexical entry for Ergative in Dyirbal commits us to no particular expectations about what the realization of Locative or any other Case should look like. The OI approach is different because it relies on the mechanics of a DM-type realizational system in which, in principle, every morph of the language competes for insertion onto every morpheme. Claims about arbitrary preference among certain morphs, and hence about their FSes' content, thus potentially give rise to consequences which reverberate throughout the language as a whole. The PRIORITY approach is more permissive in that it takes the pairing of morphological functions to lexical entries (such as [Ergative] to {-ŋku > -ku}) as given, and treats arbitrary preference as wholly internal to each such entry.

The greater flexibility allowed by PRIORITY might arguably be necessary in a case where the morphosyntactic features involved did not give us 'room' to make the higher-priority allomorph spell out more features than the lower-priority one. For example, Bonet and Mascaró (2006; see also Mascaró 2007, Bonet and Harbour 2012) discuss the Spanish conjunction meaning 'and', which is *y* [i] everywhere except when followed by [i], where it is [e]; they analyse this using PRIORITY with a lexical representation of {i > e} for the conjunction. Assuming that this case must be attributed to listed allomorphy rather than a phonological alternation caused by indexed constraints, the worry for an OI-type analysis like the one presented for Dyribal is: just how do the feature specifications of the /i/ and /e/ differ? How much they *could* differ depends on how many morphosyntactic features the 'and' morpheme consists of. If it's just one feature [AND], the simplest analysis would be that the allomorphs have the representations <AND, i> and <Ø, e>. (This would resemble the analysis of Dutch earlier, where the lower-priority 'elsewhere' form has an empty FS.) What we would need to ensure in such an analysis is that the empty FS of the <Ø, e> allomorph does not allow it to be used for morphemes other than the conjunction.

This may well be achievable, say if high-ranked MAX-M constraints compel the use of more-specified morphs everywhere that <Ø, e> might otherwise show up. But difficulties might arise in cases where we need some *other* morph with an empty FS to be used rather than <Ø, e>. For instance, the conjunction meaning 'or' is [o] everywhere except before [o], where it is [u]; for this case Bonet and Mascaró (2006) propose a lexical representation {o > u}. If, in an OI analysis, the Spanish lexicon contained both <Ø, e> and <Ø, u>, what would ensure that the former is used for 'and' but the latter for 'or'? Any worries about these specific examples might well be moot if we were to have a reason to think that the morphemes meaning 'and' and 'or' consist of multiple morphosyntactic features – in that case we could assume that /e/ and /u/ realize smaller, but still non-empty, subsets of those features than /i/ and /o/ do – but this discussion hopefully serves to illustrate the kind of situation in which PRIORITY would arguably have an advantage.

To whatever extent empirical considerations do not resolve the choice, it could be argued that the OI type of approach is preferable to PRIORITY on grounds of parsimony. To the extent that the DM-style feature-based system of realizational morphology is independently motivated (see discussion in section 9.3.1 earlier), Occam's Razor would seem to recommend that we call upon this same machinery to handle arbitrary-preference PCSA, rather than invoking the additional innovations in the structure of lexical entries assumed by the PRIORITY model. Similarly, OI is also arguably at an advantage in that its account of how phonological constraints can compel the use of non-default allomorphs relies on the same machinery used to account for other types of phonologically-induced mismatches in morphological spell-out (which we will consider in section 9.5); PRIORITY, by contrast, is a single-purpose device which deals only with the phenomenon of arbitrary preference.

9.4 Comparison with subcategorization-only approaches

All cases of 'arbitrary preference' PCSA are recognizable as such, and are theoretically challenging, because the distribution of allomorphs involves preferences which could not be exerted by any plausible constraint we'd expect to be part of the phonology on strictly phonological grounds (e.g. as a motivator of processes like deletion or epenthesis). Both OI and the PRIORITY approach deal with this problem by adding to the phonology additional constraint types which will exert the necessary preferences, but only in relation to allomorph choice. Essentially the opposite response is to remove PCSA from the purview of the phonology, placing it in a separate morphology component where arbitrary subcategorization frames enforce all selectional restrictions of affixes, including selection for phonological properties. Versions of this general stance can be found in Paster (2005, 2006, 2009, this volume), Bye (2008) and Embick (2010), amongst others.

The strongest argument for adopting the first rather than the second type of solution (Mester 1994; Tranel 1996; González 2005; Itô and Mester 2006; Wolf 2008: 101–108; Alber 2011) is based on cases where there is a conspiracy (Kisseberth 1970) between a PCSA system and phonological processes or restrictions in the same language. In these cases, the suppletive allomorphs are distributed in such a way as to avoid some phonological configuration X, and the phonology of the language (segmental alternations, static phonotactic restrictions, syllabification, stress placement, etc.) independently prohibits, avoids, or eliminates other instances of the same configuration X. If PCSA is not part of the phonology, then the dispreference for X would have to be enforced at two separate places in the grammar: in the morphological component and the phonological one. This would exactly parallel the Duplication Problem (Clayton 1976; Kenstowicz and Kisseberth 1977; Prince and Smolensky 2004 [1993]) faced by theories of phonology which make use of morpheme structure constraints: restrictions defining the phonological form of inputs to the phonology often duplicate restrictions which are active in the phonology itself (see also Cook 1971; Kiparsky 1972: 216; and Ross 1973 for early suggestions that syntactic or morphological rules, or MSCs, could participate in a conspiracy alongside phonological rules).

Examples of conspiracies in PCSA are numerous. For instance, in the analysis of Moroccan Arabic /-u/~/-h/ suppletion which we adopted from Mascaró (1996b), the use of /-h/ rather than /-u/ after a vowel-final stem was attributed to the constraint ONSET. This constraint makes itself felt in numerous other places in the language. Heath's (1987) study of colloquial Moroccan Arabic phonology reports all of the following strategies for avoiding onsetless syllables. First, stems cannot begin with a short vowel; this is rectified through epenthesis of a glottal stop (p. 19). Second, vowel-initial loan verbs from French and Spanish undergo either initial glottal-stop epenthesis or deletion of the initial vowel. Third, borrowed vowel-initial nouns can also undergo glottal-stop epenthesis, though 'there are indications that speakers find the glottal-initial form awkward' (p. 19), and as an alternative they will use the noun with the definite prefix /l-/, even in morphosyntactically non-definite contexts (pp. 19, 38):

(29) /ʃi l-anˤanˤasˤ/ 'some pineapples'
some DEFINITE-pineapples

For some nouns this has progressed to full re-analysis of definite /l-/ as part of the stem, as indicated by the presence of a double lateral in the definite form: /l-lasˤ/ 'the ace [playing card]'.[21] Finally, there are also alternations involving devocalization of suffixal high vowels following a vowel-final stem (pp. 199, 237)[22] and deletion of suffixal short vowels following a vowel-final stem, and indeed short vowels never appear on the surface adjacent to another vowel (p. 252).

A comparable argument involving constraints on segmental features is made by Alber (2011) for the realization of the past participle prefix in Mòcheno, which alternates between a prefix [ga-] and a floating-feature bundle [-cont, -voice]. The latter is used on verbs beginning with a fricative, which consequently changes to a voiceless affricate; voiceless stops, however, take the [ga-] allomorph:

(30) a. [zuaxən] 'to look for' ~ [tsuaxt] 'look for-P.PPL.'
b. [drukʰən] 'to press' ~ [gadrukʰt] 'press- P.PPL.' (*[trukʰt])

Alber connects this asymmetry with the fact that voicing in this language is contrastive in stops but not in fricatives. (In words like (30a), fricatives are normally voiced word-initially before a vowel or sonorant.) High-ranked faithfulness to voicing in stops both accounts for their supporting a voicing contrast as well as their resistance to realizing the participle through a devoicing mutation. For a subcategorization-based approach, however, there is no connection between these facts.

9.5 Other predicted forms of phonological interference with morphology

Our analysis of the Dyirbal ergative posits that satisfaction of a phonological constraint COINCIDE(ŋ, head ft)$_{ŋ}$ results in violation of a lower-ranked morphological constraint of the MAX-M(feature) family.[23] If phonological constraints are freely re-rankable with constraints on morpheme/morph Correspondence, then we expect that there should also be effects where satisfaction of a phonological constraint forces violation of a conflicting DEP-M constraint. In the case of DEP-M(feature) constraints, this would mean that the phonology forced insertion of a morph which bore grammatical features that were not present in the morpheme to which it corresponded. In the case of DEP-M(FS) constraints, this would mean that the phonology was forcing insertion of an entire morph which didn't correspond to any morpheme – a kind of 'dummy affix' which was there for solely phonological reasons, but which did not express any of the grammatical features of the word it appeared in.

One of the best-known phenomena which has been analysed as morphological feature mismatch induced by a phonological requirement occurs in French. A number of adjectives and determiners have a masculine form ending in a vowel and a feminine form ending in a consonant, with the C-final feminine form (or at least an allomorph homophonous with it) also being used pre-vocalically in *liaison* environments, even when the word is morphosyntactically masculine:

(31) *Masculine* liaison *form homophonous with feminine form*:

	Citation masc.	Citation fem.	Masc. liaison form	
'new'	[nuvo]	[nuvɛl]	[nuvelɑ̃]	
	nouveau	*nouvelle*	*nouvel an*	'new year'
'beautiful'	[bo]	[bɛl]	[bɛ.lɔm]	
	beau	*belle*	*bel homme*	'handsome man'
'this'	[sœ]	[sɛt]	[sɛ.ta.mi]	
	ce	*cette*	*cet ami*	'this friend'

A number of different analyses of these facts have been given. Some have proposed that this in fact involves the use of feminine morphs in morphosyntactically masculine contexts (Tranel 1995; Perlmutter 1998; Steriade 1999), which in OI terms would mean violation of DEP-M(feminine) as well as MAX-M(masculine).

(32)

{THIS$_1$ [masc]$_2$} {FRIEND$_3$, [masc]$_4$}	ONSET	DEP-M (fem)	MAX-M (masc)
a. ☞ *morphs*: <{THIS$_1$ [fem]$_5$}, /sɛt/> <{FRIEND$_3$, [masc]$_4$}, /ami/> *surface phonology*: [sɛ.ta.mi]		1	1
b. *morphs*: <{THIS$_1$, [masc]$_2$} /sœ/> <{FRIEND$_3$, [masc]$_4$}, /ami/> *surface phonology*: [sœ.a.mi]	W1	L	L

Other analyses have argued that the apparent feminine allomorphs in these examples are not really morphologically specified as feminine; however, even under these analyses, the phonology can be seen to be forcing morphological defectiveness of one sort or another. For example, Lapointe and Sells (1996) and Tranel (1998) propose that in a pair like *ce/cet(te)*, [sœ] is indeed [masculine], but [sɛt], which can appear in both masculine and feminine contexts, is unspecified for gender. In OI terms, this means that forms like *cet ami* do not violate DEP-M(feminine), but they would still involve violation of MAX-M(masculine). An analysis conceptually similar to this one is found in Lamarche (1996), who proposes that lexical items like *ce/cet(te)* have two listed allomorphs, neither of which is specified for gender, and which are ordered, [sœ] being the default form and [sɛt] the elsewhere form; use of the default form is proposed to be blocked before a vowel and in morphosyntactically feminine contexts. On a view of this kind, forms like *cet ami* would involve phonologically-motivated violation of arbitrary preferences among allomorphs, just like the one in Dyirbal which was discussed earlier.

Another example of gender mismatch which appears to be phonologically motivated occurs with the plural suffix in Modern Hebrew. This language has two plural suffixes: [-im], which for the most part is used with masculine nouns, and [-ot], which for the most part is used with feminines. There are exceptions with both suffixes, though: there are masculine nouns which take [-ot] and feminines which take [-im]. A phonological tendency underlies the use of [-ot] with masculines: Bolozky and Becker (2006) found that of 230 native masculine nouns which take [-ot], 146 have [o] as the rightmost stem vowel. The tendency of such masculine nouns to be more likely to take [-ot] has been found to manifest in experimental tasks with nonce forms (Berent *et al.* 1999, 2002; Becker 2009).

An OT analysis of this pattern is given by Becker (2009: ch. 3). His proposal begins with the fact that with most native nouns in Hebrew, as well as all deverbal nouns, suffixes attract stress off of the stem (Bat-El 1993; Becker 2003). This means that using [-im] when the stem's rightmost vowel is [o] results in the configuration [...C_0oC_0ím], as opposed to [...C_0oC_0ót] which would result from using [-ot]. Becker proposes that the first structure is dispreferred relative to the second by a constraint which requires that the mid-vowel features of [o] must be licensed by being linked to a stressed nucleus. In [...C_0oC_0ím] the [o] is unstressed, but in [...C_0oC_0ót], assuming that the two [o]s share place features, these features will be linked to the second, stressed [o], licensing them and avoiding violation of the constraint. Assuming that this constraint is variably ranked above MAX-M(masculine) and DEP-M(feminine), we get the observed pattern of a tendency towards the use of gender-mismatched [-ot] with masculine nouns having [o] as their rightmost vowel. For further details and discussion of this phenomenon, see Becker (2009: ch. 3) and Wolf (2008: §2.4.2).

A third and final possible example of a phonologically-driven feature mismatch, again involving gender, is the Spanish 'feminine *el*'; see Wolf (2008: §2.4.1) for an OI analysis, and Bonet, Lloret and Mascaró's paper in this volume for another perspective.

Now let us turn to violation of DEP-M(FS): cases in which phonological constraints force insertion of an entire 'dummy' affix. Perhaps the best-known case of this comes from the Western Desert language Pitjantjatjara. Hale (1973) argues that Pitjantjatjara has the following word-final augmentation rule:

(33) Ø → pa / C_#

The process is clearly conditioned by the presence of what would otherwise be a word-final consonant. When the stem is followed by a V-final suffix, the augmentative /pa/ doesn't show up:

(34)

uninflected	*Ergative*	*Dative*	
man'kurpa	man'kur-tu	man'kur-ku	'three'
punpunpa	punpun-tu	punpun-ku	'fly'

The /pa/ also appears after certain verbal suffixes: /-n, -n'in, -ŋin, -nin/ ~ /-npa, -n'inpa, -ŋinpa, -ninpa/.

This augmentation process is theoretically challenging because the marked status of [labial] place means that epenthesis of [labial] consonants should be impossible. The tableau below illustrates the analysis that I propose for Pitjantjatjara, and the markedness problem that would arise for the assumption that the augmentative [-pa] were epenthetic. For the sake of brevity and to avoid enmeshing the argument in potentially distracting HS-specific considerations, the tableau shows a parallel analysis, with insertion of one or more morphs and epenthesis of one or more segments possible in a single direct mapping. Subscripts on root and affix substrings indicate morpheme-morph Correspondence; the lack of an index on a word-final substring therefore indicates that it is phonologically epenthetic (as such strings do not belong to morphs and cannot bear an MM-correspondence relation). For visual emphasis, epenthetic segments are also italicized.

(35)

$\vert$THREE$_1\vert$	DEP-IO	*C]$_{PWd}$	DEP-M(FS)	*[labial]
a. ☞ mankur$_1$-pa$_2$			1	2
b. mankur$_1$		W1	L	1
c. mankur$_1$-*ta*	W2		L	1
d. mankur$_1$-*pa*	W2		L	2

The markedness constraint responsible for /pa/-insertion is what we can call $*C]_{PWd}$, which bans Prosodic Words from ending in a consonant (see Flack [2007, 2009] for extensive typological justification of this constraint). For the input |THREE$_1$|, i.e. the root meaning 'three' alone, with no inflection, the winning candidate is [mankurpa]. This candidate has inserted the root morpheme /mankur/, as well as the semantically-empty affix /pa/. The presence of /pa/ means that the winning candidate satisfies $*C]_{PWd}$, but it also means that the candidate incurs an extra violation of *[labial], by virtue of containing the segment /p/.

One competitor of the observed winner is (35b), which inserts only the root morpheme /mankur/. This candidate does better than the winner on *[labial], due to the absence of [-pa], but it loses by virtue of violating the higher-ranked constraint $*C]_{PWd}$. Of greater interest are the competitors (35c-d), with epenthesis. Both of these candidates violate the anti-epenthesis constraint DEP-IO, by virtue of epenthesizing the sequences [ta] or [pa]. By contrast, the winner does not violate DEP-IO, because all of its surface segments – including the [pa] – stand in IO-Correspondence with the segments in the underlying form of some morph.

Crucially for my argument, (35d), which is surface-homophonous with the winner, is harmonically bounded by (35c), which epenthesizes [ta] rather than [pa]. The two perform identically on DEP-IO and $*C]_{PWd}$, but (35b) is more harmonic than (35c) because the coronal [t] is less marked than the labial [p]. This means that if morph insertion were not available as a 'repair' in the phonological component of the grammar – that is, if the depicted winner in tableau (35) were not a possible candidate – there would be no way for $*C]_{PWd}$ – violation to be avoided by insertion of [pa], since [pa]-epenthesis should always be harmonically bounded by [ta]-epenthesis (except in specific contexts that might favour the presence of a labial, e.g. adjacent to another labial).

The prediction of markedness theory that marked segment types like labials can never be epenthetic is largely supported by typological surveys (e.g. de Lacy 2002). The analysis that I offer thus somewhat complicates the status of epenthetic quality as evidence about markedness, since any segment, no matter how marked, could in principle belong to the UR of a morph inserted for phonological reasons. This does not seem tremendously worrisome, though, as there are various diagnostics that will often be available to distinguish epenthetic segments from affix segments. In some cases, it might be possible to identify the inserted string as an affix based purely on its length. Epenthetic alternations typically involve only one segment, which in OT we can understand as an effect of DEP-IO: even when outranked by a markedness constraint, DEP-IO still favours inserting as few segments as possible. As such, when the inserted string is longer than necessary to resolve the markedness violation(s) that are plausibly at issue (say, inserting /-ʔaʔaʔa/ rather than simply /-ʔa/ at the end of C-final words), it would be easier to say with confidence we are looking at a dummy affix and not at true epenthesis.[24]

Another possible diagnositic is that dummy affixes may be subject to morphotactic restrictions limiting where they can appear. De Lacy (2002) notes that apparent epenthetic round vowels in Seri, Hungarian and Icelandic are restricted to particular morphological contexts, and suggests that these segments are therefore likely to be affixes of some kind rather than true epenthetic segments. Hale (1973) identifies similar conditions on the distribution of augmentative /-pa/ in Pitjantjatjara —it does not appear with vocatives or after the 2nd person singular clitic /-n/— and argues on this basis that /-pa/ is an affix. Similar arguments for the morph(eme)-hood of apparent epenthetic segments have been put forth by Cardinaletti and Repetti (2007) regarding vowel epenthesis in standard and dialectal varieties of Italian (see also Tranel and Del Gobbo 2001: 198) and by Kager (1999: 130) in relation to vowel epenthesis in Mohawk.[25] Looking beyond surface evidence, there are also likely to be experimental means for disentangling the epenthetic vs. affixal status of segments. For example, lexical and epenthetic segments may be acoustically different, i.e. epenthesis is at least sometimes incompletely neutralizing (Gouskova and Hall 2010); we might also ask whether speakers display 'perceptual epenthesis' of the inserted material (Dupoux *et al.* 1999).

Now let's consider the MAX-M family. We've already dealt with cases like the Dyirbal ergative which arguably involve MAX-M(feature) violation. What about violation of MAX-M(FS)? This would involve entire morphemes failing to be spelled out by any morph at all.

A familiar and typologically common way in which consecutive identical or near-identical morphs are avoided is via haplology – i.e., omitting one of them (Stemberger 1981; Menn and MacWhinney 1984; de Lacy 2000). A simple example from English is discussed by Jaeger (to appear) and Walter and Jaeger (2005). In English, use of the overt complementizer *that* is normally optional:

a. She said you left.
b. She said that you left.

In the studies just cited, it was found that omission of complementizer *that* was significantly more likely when the complementizer would have appeared adjacent to demonstrative *that*, as in *She said (that) that inspector visited yesterday*. Cases like this can be analysed by assuming that a phonological OCP constraint (perhaps variably) dominates the MAX-M constraints that favour spelling out one of the two relevant morphemes (see Golston 1995, Yip 1998 for proposals in this direction):[26]

(37)

COMP$_1$ DEMONST$_2$	OCP	MAX-M(complementizer)
a. ☞ ðæt$_2$		1
b. ðæt$_1$ ðæt$_2$	W1	L

Evidence has also been reported of *that*-omission being sensitive to rhythmic factors. Jaeger (to appear: §5) and Lee and Gibbons (2007) found that the complementizer was less likely to be omitted before stressed than before unstressed syllables. Since the complementizer itself is generally unstressed, this makes sense in terms of pressure to avoid stress clashes and lapses.

Another well-known case of phonologically-motivated morph omission occurs in the pausal phonology of Classical Arabic, of which McCarthy (2012) gives an OI analysis. Bonet, Lloret and Mascaró (this volume) (see also Bonet 2012 [2013] and Wolf 2008: 110–115 for OI-specific discussion) present an example from Northeastern Central Catalan in which the plural suffix /-s/ is omitted in inter-consonantal position in the pre-nominal portion of a DP. Selkirk (2002) discusses an example from Hausa, where general constraints on the size and layering of prosodic constituents compel the non-realization of the focus particle /fa/ in certain environments. Another proposed example comes from Tohono O'odham (Fitzgerald 1994) where the presence or absence of the *g*-determiner is attributable to a requirement that utterances begin with a trochaic foot.

All in all, it seems reasonable to conclude that both DEP-M and MAX-M constraints can be violated for phonological reasons. This suggests that we are on the right track in assuming that phonological constraints and constraints on spell-out reside in a single module of the grammar, and can be freely re-ranked with respect to one another.

9.6 Conclusion

Some types of suppletive allomorphy make reference to phonological properties of the environments in which the allomorphs appear, but at the same time seem to show the influence of arbitrary and non-phonological preferences. These cases have been the subject of much debate regarding whether they should be treated as arising in the phonology or in the morphology. Here I have argued that the answer to that question is, effectively, 'both' – that phonology and morphological spell-out occur in one and the same grammar. This permits an analysis of cases like the Dyirbal Ergative which avoids difficulties for various proposals about how to incorporate arbitrary-preference constraints into the phonology, as well as letting us deal with the wide range of attested cases in which satisfaction of morphological constraints on spell-out is sacrificed in order to ensure satisfaction of phonological constraints.

The same theoretical conclusion is pointed to by facts, beyond the scope of this chapter, which bear on the *interleaving* part of Optimal Interleaving. The implementation of phonology and spell-out in a single OT-CC grammar lets us use OT-CC's opacity-handling machinery to model serial interactions between phonological and morphological processes. Elsewhere I have argued that with respect to several such types of interaction, the OT-CC approach gives rise to desirable results. These include cyclic effects (Wolf 2008: ch. 5), non-derived environment blocking (Wolf 2008: ch. 4), underapplication in derived environments (Wolf 2008: ch. 5, 2010), 'local ordering' interactions (Anderson 1969, 1972, 1974) between phonological and morphological processes (Wolf 2009, to appear), and the conditions under which PCSA can be phonologically transparent and 'outwards looking' as opposed to opaque and 'inwards looking' (Wolf 2013). To the extent that OT-CC gives us the results we want regarding phonology/morphology derivational interactions, this is a strong hint that phonology and morphology belong in one and the same OT-CC grammar, consistent with the conclusion argued for in the present chapter, namely that lexical insertion occurs in the phonological component of the grammar.

Acknowledgements

I have received many valuable comments, suggestions, and other assistance in relation to the various forms in which portions of this chapter's content have been presented since 2006. I would particularly like to thank my dissertation committee members, John McCarthy, Joe Pater, Lisa Selkirk, and Mark Feinstein; Bernard Tranel; and the editors of this volume, Eulàlia Bonet, Maria-Rosa Lloret, and Joan Mascaró. I also received valuable thoughts and feedback on this material from Stephen R. Anderson, Diana Apoussidou, Michael Becker, Kathryn Flack-Potts, Gaja Jarosz, Karen Jesney, Dasha Kavitskaya, Shigeto Kawahara, John Kingston, Kathryn Pruitt, Erich Round, Anne-Michelle Tessier, and members of audiences at

HUMDRUM 2006 (especially Luigi Burzio, Paul de Lacy, Alan Prince, and Bruce Tesar), Reed College (especially Matt Pearson), the 15th Manchester Phonology Meeting (especially Patrik Bye, Bruce Morén-Duolljá, Mary Paster, Ricardo Bermúdez-Otero, Jochen Trommer, and Christian Uffman), the Workshop on the Division of Labor Between Phonology and Morphology in Amsterdam (especially Geert Booij, Diane Lesley-Neuman, Andrew Nevins, Marc van Oostendorp, and Dieter Wunderlich), and the University of Pennsylvania (especially David Embick and Rolf Noyer). The standard disclaimers apply.

Notes

1. The idea of a morpheme as having more than one UR – or, somewhat differently put, of the UR as a set of allomorphic alternants – has its roots in work by Hudson (1974) and Hooper (1976).
2. An essentially identical formulation is also put forth by Perlmutter (1998: 319).
3. Combination violation/comparative tableaux (Prince 2002, 2003) are used throughout this chapter. Numerals indicate the number of violation marks incurred from each constraint. In rows for losing candidates, W indicates that the constraint prefers the winner over that loser, and L that the constraint prefers that loser over the winner.
4. See Prince (2002, 2003) for formal discussion in relation to this. The formulation that the highest-ranked constraint which distinguishes between a winning and a losing candidate must prefer the winner is originally due to Jane Grimshaw.
5. Dyirbal has a single (voiceless unaspirated) stop series; to represent these I use IPA [p t k …] rather than [b d g …] as used by Dixon (1972) and others. Similarly, I use [j] rather than [y] to represent the glide used in Dyirbal.
6. In their study of Dyirbal song, Dixon and Koch (1996:44) report finding one instance of the /-ŋku/ allomorph being used with a trisyllabic base. They suggest that this may be an archaism, reflecting an earlier stage (retained in other Australian languages) where the /–ŋku/ form was used with all vowel-final stems.
7. These are in addition to several lines of psycholinguistic evidence suggesting a separation in the mental lexicon between the morphosyntactic and phonological features of words; see Wolf (2008: 16–18) for some references and discussion.
8. Zuraw (2000) makes the same assumption; she refers to the abstract semantic/morphosyntactic structure that forms the input to the phonology as the *intent*. That the input to the phonology may contain some not-yet-spelled-out morphosyntactic features is also proposed by Yip (1998).
9. See also the works cited in Notes 11 and 12 for Correspondence-theoretic approaches to morphological selection (though which do not necessarily

take the view that spell-out and phonology are in the same module of the grammar).

10. See also Gouskova (2007) for discussion of other roles played by DEP constraints on various dimensions of Correspondence.
11. A non-exhaustive list of similar constraints in OT treatments of morphology includes Curnow's (1999) IDENT constraints, Ackema and Neeleman's (2004, 2005) FAITHFULNESS, Wunderlich's (2001) IDENT constraints, Xu's (2007) DEP constraints, and Aronoff and Xu's (2011) IDENT constraints.
12. A non-exhaustive list of similar constraints includes Noyer's (1993) PARSE-PROPERTY, Bonet's (1994) ELSEWHERE, Kiparsky's (2005) EXPRESSIVENESS, Donohue's (1998) PARSE constraints, Curnow's (1999) MAX and IDENT constraints, Selkirk's (2002) REALIZE constraints, Trommer's (2001) PARSE constraints, Wunderlich's (2000, 2001, 2003) MAX constraints, Ackema and Neeleman's (2004, 2005) PARSE, Teeple's (2008a,b) FAITH-SM and EXPRESSIVENESS, Strigin's (2007) MAX-STRUCT, Xu's (2007) MAX constraints, and Aronoff and Xu's (2011) IDENT constraints.
13. As an alternative (or perhaps in addition) to using faithfulness constraints to regulate morpheme/morph correspondents, it would be possible to propose constraints which directly stated 'morphosyntactic feature *F* should be realized by underlying form *U*'. The 'lexical' constraints of Bidirectional Phonology and Phonetics (see references below (11)) and the realization constraints of Realization OT (Xu 2007, Aronoff and Xu 2010, 2011) work this way. Constraints of the same form appear in several works in the OT literature on PCSA systems requiring arbitrary preference, for instance Kager (1996a).
14. OT-CC is in certain respects more powerful than HS because in the former, rather than constructing just a single serial derivation, the grammar produces multiple derivations (chains), which then compete as candidates, thereby combining features of serialism and parallelism. Ultimately, adopting an OT-CC rather than HS version of OI is arguably necessary in order to deal with cases of allomorphy and cyclic process application which involve outwards-sensitivity, which can arise under special conditions due to OT-CC's partly global character: for more details see Wolf (to appear) on cyclicity, and Wolf (2008: 174–186, 2013) on allomorph selection. For two interacting examples in Catalan which are problematic for HS-OI, see Bonet (2012 [2013]), and see Wolf (2008: 110–115, to appear: 159) for discussion of these in an OI context.
15. Superficially, Dyirbal has a Nominative-Ergative system in nouns but a Nominative-Accusative system in pronouns. However, Dixon (1972: §5.2) argues that the pronouns too underlyingly pattern as Nominative-Ergative. In any case, if Accusative Case does exist in Dyirbal, it and its morphosyntactic exponence is limited to a closed class of forms (the pronouns) and can probably be safely ignored when advancing a proposal about the phonological exponence of the Case feature [−free].

16. For an account of the gradual collapsing together of the various allomorphs of the Ergative and Locative by younger Dyirbal speakers as the language dies out, see Schmidt (1985: ch. 4). She finds that 'reduction in the range of locative allomorphs operates on the same principles as ergative allomorph reduction' (p. 52).
17. It might be taken as worrisome that the behaviour of these two suffixes is the reverse of the Ergative: they *avoid* nasal-stop clusters after disyllabic bases, and allow them otherwise. (This also runs counter to the phonological tendency I mention below in Note 20.) To the extent that the operative markedness constraints have to be morphologically indexed (as I will assume for the Ergative in a moment), there is probably no danger of analytic inconsistency.
18. I assume here that morphologically-indexed constraints operate as proposed in Pater (2010).
19. An analysis of Dyirbal conceptually quite similar to the one in this chapter is independently developed by Trommer (2008). In his analysis, the indexed constraint which bars using /-ŋ/ with long stems is PWD=BINFT$_{ŋ}$, which forbids the Prosodic Word to be longer than a binary foot. Cast within Stratal OT (Kiparsky 2000, amongst many others), adding /-ŋ/ to a greater-than-disyllabic base at the stem level is barred because it would create a violation of this constraint (the PWd to which /-ŋ/ would belong would be bigger than a foot). Crucially, this constraint (like COINCIDE(ŋ, head ft)$_{ŋ}$ under the syllabification assumed in (24)), *will* be violated after adding /-ku/ to an intermediate form like [(jaɽaŋ)$_{Ft}$]$_{PWd}$, since doing so adds a third syllable. The choice of PWD=BINFT$_{ŋ}$ as the constraint enforcing the base size requirement would therefore dictate against the use of HS and in favour of Stratal OT. I am not aware of any Dyirbal-specific empirical argument for using one constraint versus the other.
20. Dixon discusses this (197: 283–286) as one reflex of a process of nasal insertion, whereby 'the sooner a medial consonant cluster, C_2, comes after a stressed vowel the more tendency there is for it to include a nasal ... [this process] involves the insertion of *-n-* at certain grammatical boundaries' (283). The fact that proximity to *preceding* stress is what makes conditions favorable for the insertion of the nasal seems to be consistent with the assumption being made here that nasals are syllabified as codas. Now, if there is such a general process, the reader may naturally wonder whether the [-ŋku] ~ [-ku] alternation is actually the result of a phonological rule, not a matter of listed allomorphy at all. The best response to this objection seems to be that insertion of nasals at morpheme boundaries occurs at different degrees of proximity to stress for different suffixes: following the head foot for the Ergative and Locative, but immediately following stress for the Dative.
21. The fact that in French the definite article is *l'* [l] before a vowel, and that in Spanish the masculine definite article is *el*, doubtless helps in causing V-initial nouns of these languages to be borrowed with an initial [l].

22. This fact creates an apparent problem for the analysis shown in (3) wherein ONSET crucially prefers [xtˤah] over *[xtˤa.u]: what about a competitor [xtˤaw] which uses the /-u/ allomorph, devocalizes, and has no onsetless syllables? It is here that serial evaluation plays a critical role. In general, PCSA choices always interact opaquely with phonological processes (other than prosodification) that any of the allomorphs would trigger or undergo (Paster 2006, 2009: §5.2; Wolf 2008: §3.6), which is predicted in a derivational model like OI where allomorph choice, and phonological changes, occur as separate, successive steps (Wolf 2008: §3.4.2). If this is right, then the competition indeed is between [xtˤah] and *[xtˤa.u]; *[xtˤaw] is not even part of the candidate set at the point where allomorph choice is made. Thus, PCSA of the clitic bleeds devocalization of high vowels in hiatus, but both are driven by ONSET. (For a few possible examples of crucially-transparent PCSA, and a proposal about what special conditions are needed for this to happen, see Wolf 2013).
23. For another example of this, see McQuaid's (2012: ch. 5) OI analysis of Appalachian English *a*-prefixing.
24. I am grateful to the editors for pointing this out.
25. See Wolf (2008: 4) for references to additional proposed cases of 'dummy' affixes inserted for phonological reasons.
26. The OCP effect on adjacent instances of *that* also seems to control allomorph choice in restrictive relative clauses. Normally there is optional variation between *that* and *which* to introduce a relative clause: *The book {which/that} I ordered arrived today*, though use of *which* is generally frowned upon by prescriptivists. Pullum (2010) points out that *which* becomes the only acceptable option when another *that* precedes: *That which/*that doesn't kill you might give you stomach trouble.* (The version of the example sentence with *which* is a caption from a cartoon in the 5 July 2010 issue of *The New Yorker*.) My intuitions are that *that* is not entirely ill-formed in this context, though it is clearly degraded relative to *which*. (The option of using *which* to avoid the OCP violation is also mentioned in passing by Walter and Jaeger [2005].)

References

Ackema, Peter and Neeleman, Ad (2004) *Beyond Morphology: Interface Conditions on Word Formation*. Oxford: Oxford University Press.

Ackema, Peter and Neeleman, Ad (2005) Word-formation in Optimality Theory. In Pavol Šteckauer and Rochelle Lieber (eds) *Handbook of Word-Formation* 285–313. Dordrecht: Springer.

Alber, Birgit (2011) Past participles in Mòcheno: Allomorphy, alignment, and the distribution of obstruents. In Michael Putnam (ed.) *Studies on German-Language Islands*, 33–64. Amsterdam: John Benjamins.

Anderson, Stephen R. (1969) *West Scandinavian vowel systems and the ordering of phonological rules*. Doctoral dissertation, Massachusetts Institute of Technology.

Anderson, Stephen R. (1972) On nasalization in Sundanese. *Linguistic Inquiry* 3: 253–268.

Anderson, Stephen R. (1974) *The Organization of Phonology*. San Diego, CA: Academic Press.

Anderson, Stephen R. (1992) *A-Morphous Morphology*. Cambridge: Cambridge University Press.

Apoussidou, Diana (2007) *The learnability of metrical phonology*. Doctoral dissertation, University of Amsterdam.

Aronoff, Mark and Xu, Zheng (2010) A realization Optimality-Theoretic approach to affix order. *Morphology* 20: 381–411.

Aronoff, Mark and Xu, Zheng (2011) A Realization Optimality-Theoretic approach to full and partial identity of forms. In Martin Maiden, John Charles Smith, Maria Goldbach and Marc-Olivier Hinzelin (eds) *Morphological Autonomy: Perspectives from Romance Inflectional Morphology,* 257–286. Oxford: Oxford University Press.

Bat-El, Outi (1993) Parasitic metrification in the Modern Hebrew stress system. *The Linguistic Review* 10: 189–210.

Becker, Michael (2003) Hebrew stress: Can't you hear those trochees? In Elsi Kaiser and Sudha Arunachalam (eds) *University of Pennsylvania Working Papers in Linguistics* 9.1: *Proceedings of the 26th Annual Penn Linguistics Colloquium,* 45–57. Philadelphia, PA: Penn Linguistics Club.

Becker, Michael (2009) *Phonological trends in the lexicon: The role of constraints*. Doctoral dissertation, University of Massachusetts Amherst.

Berent, Iris, Pinker, Steven and Shimron, Joseph (1999) Default nominal inflection in Hebrew: Evidence for mental variables. *Cognition* 72: 1–44.

Berent, Iris, Pinker, Steven and Shimron, Joseph (2002). The nature of regularity and irregularity: Evidence from Hebrew nominal inflection. *Journal of Psycholinguistic Research* 31: 459–502.

Boersma, Paul (2001) Phonology-semantics interaction in OT, and its acquisition. In Robert Kirchner, Joe Pater and Wolf Wilkey (eds) *Papers in Experimental and Theoretical Linguistics* 6: *Workshop on the Lexicon in Phonetics and Phonology,* 24–35. Edmonton: Department of Linguistics, University of Alberta.

Boersma, Paul (2011) A programme for biderectional phonology and phonetics and their acquisition and evolution. In Anton Benz and Jason Mattausch (eds) *Bidirectional Optimality Theory,* 33–72. Amsterdam: John Benjamins.

Bolozky, Shmuel and Becker, Michael (2006) Living lexicon of Hebrew nouns. [Available on http://becker.phonologist.org/LLHN/.]

Bonet, Eulàlia (1994) The person-case constraint: A morphological approach. In Heidi Harley and Colin Phillips (eds) *MIT Working Papers in Linguistics* 22: *The Morphology-Syntax Connection,* 33–52. Cambridge, MA: MIT Working Papers in Linguistics.

Bonet, Eulàlia (2004) Morph insertion and allomorphy in Optimality Theory. *International Journal of English Studies* 4 (2): 73–104.

Bonet, Eulàlia (2012 [2013]) A challenge for Harmonic Serialism with Optimal Interleaving. *Phonology* 30: 399–421. [Available on http://filcat.uab.cat/clt/membres/professors/bonet/A%20challenge%20for%20HS-OI-Bonet.pdf.]

Bonet, Eulàlia and Harbour, Daniel (2012) Contextual allomorphy. In Jochen Trommer (ed.) *The Morphology and Phonology of Exponence,* 195–235. Oxford: Oxford University Press.

Bonet, Eulàlia, Lloret, Maria-Rosa and Mascaró, Joan (2007) Allomorph selection and lexical preferences: Two case studies. *Lingua* 117: 903–927.

Bonet, Eulàlia, Lloret, Maria-Rosa and Mascaró, Joan (this volume) The prenominal allomorphy syndrome.

Bonet, Eulàlia and Mascaró, Joan (2006) *U* u *o* e *y* o *e*. In Antonio Fábregas, Natalia Curto and José Maria Lahoz (eds) *Cuadernos de Lingüística XIII,* 1–9. Madrid: Instituto Universitario de Investigación Ortega y Gasset.

Bye, Patrik (2008) Allomorphy – selection, not optimization. In Sylvia Blaho, Patrik Bye, and Martin Krämer (eds) *Freedom of Analysis?* 63–92. Berlin: Mouton de Gruyter.

Cardinaletti, Anna and Repetti, Lori (2007) Vocali epentetiche nella morfologia dell'italiano e dei dialetti italiani. In Roberta Maschi, Nicoletta Penello and Piera Rizzolatti (eds) *Miscellanea di studi linguistici offerti a Laura Vanelli da amici e allievi padovani,* 115–126. Udine: Forum.

Carstairs, Andrew (1987) *Allomorphy in Inflexion*. London: Croon Helm.

Carstairs, Andrew (1988) Some implications of phonologically-conditioned suppletion. In Geert Booij and Jaap van Marle (eds) *Yearbook of Morphology 1988,* 67–94. Dordrecht: Foris.

Carstairs, Andrew (1990) Phonologically conditioned suppletion. In Wolfgang U. Dressler, Hans C. Luschützky, Oskar E. Pfeiffer and John R. Rennison (eds) *Contemporary Morphology,* 17–23. Berlin: Mouton de Gruyter.

Clayton, Mary L. (1976) The redundancy of underlying morpheme structure conditions. *Language* 52: 295–313.

Cook, Eung-Do (1971) Phonological constraint and syntactic rule. *Linguistic Inquiry* 2: 465–478.

Curnow, Timothy Jowan (1999) Maung verbal agreement revisited: A response to Donohue (1998). *Australian Journal of Linguistics* 19: 141–159.

de Lacy, Paul (2000) Haplology and correspondence. In Paul de Lacy and Anita Nowak (eds) *University of Massachusetts Occasional Papers in Linguistics* 24: *Papers from the 25th Anniversary,* 51–88. Amherst: GLSA.

de Lacy, Paul (2002) *The Formal Expression of Markedness*. Doctoral dissertation, University of Massachusetts at Amherst.

Dixon, R.M.W. (1972) *The Dyirbal Language of North Queensland.* Cambridge: Cambridge University Press.

Dixon, R.M.W. and Koch, Grace (1996) *Dyirbal Song Poetry: The Oral Literature of an Australian Rainforest People*. St. Lucia, QLD: University of Queensland Press.

Dolbey, Andrew (1997) Output optimization and cyclic allomorph selection. In Brian Agbayani and Sze-wing Tang (eds) *Proceedings of the 15th West Coast Conference on Formal Linguistics,* 97–112. Stanford, CA: CSLI.

Donohue, Mark (1998) A note on verbal agreement in Maung. *Australian Journal of Linguistics* 19: 73–89.

Drachman, Gaberell, Kager, René and Malikouti-Drachman, Angeliki (1996) Greek allomorphy: An Optimality Theory account. *OTS Working Papers* 10: 1–12.

Dupoux, Emmanuel, Kakehi, Kazukhiko, Hirose, Yuki, Pallier, Cristophe and Mehler, Jacques (1999) Epenthetic vowels in Japanese: A perceptual illusion? *Journal of Experimental Psychology: Human Perception and Performance* 25: 1568–1578.

Eisenstat, Sarah (2009) *Learning underlying forms with MaxEnt*. Master's thesis, Brown University.

Embick, David (2010) *Localism versus Globalism in Morphology and Phonology*. Cambridge, MA: MIT Press.

Escudero, Paola (2005) *The attainment of optimal perception in second-language acquisition*. Doctoral dissertation, University of Utrecht.

Fitzgerald, Colleen (1994) Prosody drives the syntax: O'odham rhythm. In Susanne Gahl, Andrew Dolbey, and Christopher Johnson (eds), *Proceedings of the Twentieth Annual Meeting of the Berkeley Linguistics Society,* 173–183. Berkeley: BLS.

Flack, Kathryn (2007) *The sources of phonological markedness*. Doctoral dissertation, University of Massachusetts Amherst.

Flack, Kathryn (2009) Constraints on onsets and codas of words and phrases. *Phonology* 26: 269–302.

Golston, Chris (1995) Syntax outranks phonology. *Phonology* 12: 343–368.

González, Carolina (2005) Phonologically conditioned allomorphy in Panoan: Towards an analysis. In Jeffrey Heinz, Andrew Martin and Katya Pertsova (eds) *UCLA Working Papers in Linguistics* 11: *Papers in Phonology 6,* 39–56. Los Angeles, CA: UCLA Working Papers in Linguistics.

Gouskova, Maria (2007) DEP: Beyond epenthesis. *Linguistic Inquiry* 38: 759–770.

Gouskova, Maria and Hall, Nancy (2010) Acoustics of epenthetic vowels in Lebanese Arabic. In Steve Parker (ed.) *Phonological Argumentation: Essays on Evidence and Motivation,* 203–225. London: Equinox.

Hale, Kenneth (1973) Deep-surface canonical disparities in relation to analysis and change: An Australian example. In Thomas Sebeok (ed.) *Current Trends in Linguistics*, vol. 11, 401–458. The Hague: Mouton.

Halle, Morris (1997) Distributed Morphology: Impoverishment and fission. In Benjamin Bruening, Yoonjung Kang and Martha McGinnis (eds) *MIT Working Papers in Linguistics* 30: *PF: Papers at the Interface,* 425–449. Cambridge, MA: MIT Working Papers in Linguistics.

Halle, Morris and Marantz, Alec (1993) Distributed Morphology and the pieces of inflection. In Kenneth Hale and Samuel Jay Keyser (eds) *The View from Building 20: Essays in Linguistics in Honor of Sylvain Bromberger,* 111–176. Cambridge, MA: MIT Press.

Halle, Morris and Vaux, Bert (1998) Theoretical aspects of Indo-European nominal morphology: The nominal inflections of Latin and Armenian. In Jay Jasanoff, H. Craig Melchert and Lisi Olivier (eds) *Mír Curad: Sudies in Honor of Calvert Watkins,* 223–240. Innsbruck: Institut für Sprachwissenshaft der Universität Innsbruck.

Hamann, Silke, Apoussidou, Diana and Boersma, Paul (2009) Modeling the formation of phonotactic restrictions across the mental lexicon. In Ryan Bochnak, Nassira Nicola, Peet Klecha, Jasmin Urban, Alice Lemieux and Christina Weaver (eds) *Proceedings from the Annual Meeting of the Chicago Linguistic Society* 45, vol. 1: *The Main Session,* 193–206. Chicago, IL: CLS.

Hargus, Sharon (1995) The first person plural subject prefix in Babine/Witsuwit'en. [Available on http://roa.rutgers.edu/article/view/119.]

Harley, Heidi and Ritter, Elizabeth (1998) Person and number in pronouns: A feature-geometric analysis. *Language* 78: 482–526.

Haviland, John B. (1979) Guugu Yimidhirr. In R.M.W. Dixon and Barry Blake (eds) *Handbook of Australian Languages*, vol. 1, 27–180. Canberra: Australian National University Press.

Heath, Jeffrey (1987) *Ablaut and Ambiguity: Phonology of a Moroccan Arabic Dialect*. Albany, NY: State University of New York Press.

Hooper, Joan (1976) *An Introduction to Natural Generative Phonology*. New York: Academic Press.

Hudson, Grover (1974) The representation of non-productive alternation. In John M. Anderson and Charles C. Jones (eds) *Historical Linguistics II: Theory and Description in Phonology,* 203–229. Amsterdam: North-Holland.

Itô, Junko, and Mester, Armin (2006) Indulgentia parentum filiōrum perniciēs: Lexical allomorphy in Latin and Japanese. In Eric Baković, Junko Itô and John J. McCarthy (eds) *Wondering at the Natural Fecundity of Things: Essays in Honor of Alan Prince,* 185–194. Santa Cruz: Linguistics Research Center, University of California, Santa Cruz.

Jaeger, T. Florian (to appear) Phonological optimization and syntactic variation: The case of optional *that*. *Proceedings of the 32nd Annual Meeting of the Berkeley Linguistics Society*. [Available on http://www.bcs.rochester.edu/people/fjaeger/papers/E_Jaeger_2006_bls.pdf.]

Jesney, Karen (2009) Uniformity effects as a consequence of learning with lexical constraints. Poster presented at the KNAW Colloquium on Language Acquisition and Optimality Theory, Amsterdam, July 2–3. [Handout available on http://www-bcf.usc.edu/%7Ejesney/Jesney2009KNAW.pdf.]

Jesney, Karen, Pater, Joe and Staubs, Robert (2010) Restrictive learning with distributions over underlying representations. Paper presented at the Workshop on Computational Modeling of Sound Pattern Acquisition, University of Alberta, Edmonton, February 13–14. [Handout available on http://people.umass.edu/rstaubs/slides/Edmonton%20presentation%20full.pdf.]

Kager, René (1996a) On affix allomorphy and syllable counting. In Ursula Kleinhenz (ed) *Interfaces in Phonology* 155–171. Berlin: Akademie Verlag.

Kager, René (1996b) Stem disyllabicity in Guugu Yimidhirr. In Marina Nespor and Norval Smith (eds) *Dam Phonology: HIL Phonology Papers II,* 59–101. The Hague: Holland Institute of Generative Linguistics.

Kager, René (1999) *Optimality Theory*. Cambridge: Cambridge University Press.

Kenstowicz, Michael (2005) Paradigmatic uniformity and contrast. In Laura J. Downing, T. A. Hall and Renate Raffelsiefen (eds) *Paradigms in Phonological Theory,* 145–169. Oxford: Oxford University Press.

Kenstowicz, Michael and Kisseberth, Charles W. (1977) *Topics in Phonological Theory*. New York: Academic Press.

Kimper, Wendell (2009) Constraints on what's not there: The role of serial derivations in subtractive truncation. Paper presented at HUMDRUM 2009, University of Massachusetts Amherst, April 18. [Available on http://personal-pages.manchester.ac.uk/staff/wendell.kimper/humdrum_09.pdf.]

Kiparsky, Paul (1972) Explanation in phonology. In Stanley Peters (ed) *Goals of Linguistic Theory,* 189–227. Englewood Cliffs, NJ: Prentice-Hall.

Kiparsky, Paul (1973) 'Elsewhere' in phonology. In Stephen R. Anderson and Paul Kiparsky (eds) *A Festschrift for Morris Halle,* 93–106. New York: Holt, Rinehart and Winston.

Kiparsky, Paul (2000) Opacity and cyclicity. *The Linguistic Review* 17: 351–367.

Kiparsky, Paul (2005) Blocking and periphrasis in inflectional paradigms. In Geert Booij and Jaap van Marle (eds) *Yearbook of Morphology 2004,* 113–136. Dordrecht: Springer.

Kisseberth, Charles (1970) On the functional unity of phonological rules. *Linguistic Inquiry* 1: 291–306.

Lamarche, Jacques (1996) Gender agreement and suppletion in French. In Karen Zagona (ed.) *Grammatical Theory and Romance Languages,* 145–157. Amsterdam: John Benjamins.

Lapointe, Steven G. (1999). Stem selection and OT. In Geert Booij and Jaap van Marle (eds) *Yearbook of Morphology 1999,* 263–297. Dordrecht: Kluwer.

Lapointe, Steven G. and Sells, Peter (1996) Separating syntax and phonology in Optimality Theory: The case of suppletive segment/Ø allomorphy. Unpublished manuscript, University of California, Davis, and Stanford University.

Lee, Ming-Wei and Gibbons, Julie (2007) Rhythmic alternation and the optional complementizer in English: New evidence of phonological influence on grammatical encoding. *Cognition* 105: 446–456.

Marantz, Alec (1995) 'Cat' as a phrasal idiom: Consequences of late insertion in Distributed Morphology. Unpublished manuscript, Massachusetts Institute of Technology.

Mascaró, Joan (1996a) External allomorphy and contractions in Romance. *Probus* 8: 181–205.

Mascaró, Joan (1996b) External allomorphy as emergence of the unmarked. In Jacques Durand and Bernard Laks (eds) *Current Trends in Phonology: Models and Methods,* 473–483. Salford: European Studies Research Institute, University of Salford.

Mascaró, Joan (2007) External allomorphy and lexical representation. *Linguistic Inquiry* 38: 715–735.

McCarthy, John J. (2007) *Hidden Generalizations: Phonological Opacity in Optimality Theory*. London: Equinox.

McCarthy, John J. (2012) Pausal phonology and morpheme realization. In Toni Borowsky, Shigeto Kawahara, Takahito Shinya and Mariko Sugahara (eds) *Prosody Matters: Essays in Honor of Elisabeth Selkirk,* 341–373. London: Equinox.

McCarthy, John J. and Prince, Alan S. (1990) Foot and word in Prosodic Morphology: The Arabic broken plurals. *Natural Language and Linguistic Theory* 8: 209–282.

McCarthy, John J. and Prince, Alan (1993) *Prosodic Morphology: Constraint Interaction and Satisfaction*. Technical report #3, Rutgers University Center for Cognitive Science.

McCarthy, John J. and Prince, Alan (1994) The Emergence of the Unmarked: Optimality in Prosodic Morphology. In Mercè Gonzàlez (ed.) *Proceedings of the North East Linguistic Society 24,* 333–379. Amherst, MA: GLSA.

McCarthy, John J. and Prince, Alan (1995) Faithfulness and reduplicative identity. In Jill N. Beckman, Laura Walsh Dickey and Suzanne Urbanczyk (eds) *University of Massachusetts Occasional Papers in Linguistics* 18: *Papers in Optimality Theory* 249–384. Amherst, MA: GLSA.

McCarthy, John J. and Wolf, Matthew (2005) Less than zero: Correspondence and the null output. [Available on http://roa.rutgers.edu/article/view/732; revised version published as Wolf and McCarthy (2009).]

McQuaid, Goldie Ann (2012) *Variation at the morphology-phonology interface in Appalachian English*. Doctoral dissertation, Georgetown University.

Menn, Lise and MacWhinney, Brian (1984) The repeated morph constraint: Toward an explanation. *Language* 60: 519–541.

Mester, Armin (1994) The quantitative trochee in Latin. *Natural Language and Linguistic Theory* 12: 1–61.

Miller, Philip, Pullum, Geoffrey K. and Zwicky, Arnold M. (1992) Le principe d'inaccessibilité de la phonologie par la synatxe: trois contre-exemples apparents en français. *Lingvisticæ Investigationes* 16: 317–343.

Miller, Philip, Pullum, Geoffrey K. and Zwicky, Arnold, M. (1997) The principle of Phonology-Free Syntax: Four apparent counter-examples in French. *Journal of Linguistics* 33: 67–90.

Noyer, Rolf (1993) Optimal Words: Towards a declarative theory of word-formation. Paper presented at Rutgers Optimality Workshop-1, Rutgers University, New Brunswick, NJ, October 22–24. [Available on ftp://babel.ling.upenn.edu/facpapers/rolf_noyer/optimal_words.ps.]

Paster, Mary (2005) Subcategorization vs. output optimization in syllable-counting allomorphy. In John Alderete, Chung-hye Han and Alexei Kochetov (eds) *Proceedings of the 24th West Coast Conference on Formal Linguistics,* 326–333. Somerville, MA: Cascadilla Proceedings Project.

Paster, Mary (2006) *Phonological conditions on affixation*. Doctoral dissertation, University of California at Berkeley.

Paster, Mary (2009) Explaining phonological conditions on affixation: Evidence from suppletive allomorphy and affix ordering. *Word Structure* 2: 18–37.

Paster, Mary (this volume). Phonologically conditioned suppletive allomorphy: cross-linguistic results and theoretical consequences.

Pater, Joe (2010) Morpheme-specific phonology: Constraint indexation and inconsistency resolution. In Steve Parker (ed) *Phonological Argumentation: Essays on Evidence and Motivation* 123–154. London: Equinox.

Pater, Joe (2012) Serial Harmonic Grammar and Berber syllabification. In Toni Borowsky, Shigeto Kawahara, Takahito Shinya and Mariko Sugahara (eds)

Prosody Matters: Essays in Honor of Elisabeth Selkirk, 43–72. London: Equinox.

Pater, Joe and Smith, Brian W. (2011) Le 'e' en français: élision, épenthèse, les deux, ni l'un ni l'autre? Paper presented at Phonologie du français contemporain, Paris, 11–13 December. [Slides available on http://people.umass.edu/pater/pater-smith-pfc.pdf.]

Pater, Joe, Smith, David, Staubs, Rober, Jesney, Karen and Mettu, Ramgopal (2010) Learning hidden structure with a log-linear model of grammar. Paper presented at the 84th Linguistic Society of America Annual Meeting, Baltimore, 7–10 January. [Available on http://people.umass.edu/rstaubs/slides/pater-smith-staubs-jesney-mettu.lsa.2010.pdf.]

Pater, Joe, Staubs, Robert, Jesney, Karen and Smith, Brian (2012) Learning probabilities over underlying representations. In *Proceedings of the Twelfth Meeting of the ACL-SIGMORPHON: Computational Research in Phonetics, Phonology, and Morphology,* 62–71.

Perlmutter, David M. (1998) Interfaces: Explanation of allomorphy and the architecture of grammars. In Steven G. Lapointe, Diane K. Brentari and Patrick M. Farrell (eds) *Morphology and its Relation to Phonology and Syntax,* 307–338. Stanford, CA: CSLI Publications.

Prince, Alan (2002) Entailed ranking arguments. [Available on http://roa.rutgers.edu/article/view/510.]

Prince, Alan (2003) Arguing optimality. In Angela C. Carpenter, Paul de Lacy and Andries W. Coetzee (eds) *University of Massachusetts Occasional Papers in Linguistics* 26: *Papers in Optimality Theory II,* 269–304. Amherst, MA: GLSA.

Prince, Alan and Smolensky, Paul (2004 [1993]) *Optimality Theory: Constraint Interaction in Generative Grammar*. Malden, MA and Oxford: Blackwell. Technical Report, Rutgers University Center for Cognitive Science and Computer Science Department, University of Colorado at Boulder.

Pruitt, Kathryn (2010) Serialism and locality in constraint-based metrical parsing. *Phonology* 27: 481–256.

Pullum, Geoffrey (2010) That which doesn't apply to English. [Available on http://languagelog.ldc.upenn.edu/nll/?p=2425.]

Pullum, Geoffrey K. and Zwicky, Arnold M. (1988). The syntax-phonology interface. In Frederick J. Newmeyer (ed.) *Linguistics: The Cambridge Survey,* Volume I*: Linguistic Theory: Foundations* 255–280. Cambridge: Cambridge University Press.

Ross, John Robert (1973) Leftward, ho! In Stephen R. Anderson and Paul Kiparsky (eds) *A Festschrift for Morris Halle,* 166–173. New York: Holt, Rinehart and Winston.

Sauerland, Uli (1996) The late insertion of Germanic inflection. [Available on http://www2.sfs.nphil.uni-tuebingen.de/~uli/morph.pdf.]

Schmidt, Annette (1985) *Young People's Dyirbal: An Example of Language Death from Australia*. Cambridge: Cambridge University Press.

Selkirk, Elisabeth (2002) On the phonologically driven non-realization of function words. In Charles Chang, Michael J. Houser, Yuni Kim, David Mortensen, Mischa Park-Doob and Maziar Toosarvandani (eds) *Proceedings of the*

Twenty-Seventh Annual Meeting of the Berkeley Linguistics Society, 257–270. Berkeley, CA: BLS.

Smith, Brian W. (2012) Ineffability and UR constraints in Optimality Theory. Poster presented at 20th Manchester Phonology Meeting, University of Manchester, May 24–26. [Available on http://people.umass.edu/bwsmith/papers/bws_mfm20.pdf.]

Staubs, Robert (2011) Operational exponence: Process morphology in Harmonic Serialism. Paper presented at Challenges of Complex Morphology to Morphological Theory, Linguistic Society of America Summer Institute, Boulder, CO, 27 July. [Available on http://people.umass.edu/rstaubs/slides/staubs.operationalexponence.workshop.pdf.]

Staubs, Robert and Pater, Joe (to appear) Learning serial constraint-based grammars. In John McCarthy and Joe Pater (eds) *Harmonic Grammar and Harmonic Serialism*. Sheffield: Equinox.

Stemberger, Joseph Paul (1981) Morphological haplology. *Language* 57: 791–817.

Steriade, Donca (1999) Lexical conservatism in French adjectival liaison. In J.-Marc Authier, Barbara Bullock and Lisa Reed (eds) *Formal Perspectives on Romance Linguistics,* 243–270. Amsterdam: John Benjamins.

Strigin, Anatoli (2007) Paradigmatic scale building in OT: The case of strong verbs in German. [Available on http://roa.rutgers.edu/article/view/966.]

Stump, Gregory T. (2001) *Inflectional Morphology: A Theory of Paradigm Structure*. Cambridge: Cambridge University Press.

Teeple, David (2008a) Prosody can outrank syntax. In Charles B. Chang and Hannah J. Haynie (eds) *Proceedings of the 26th West Coast Conference on Formal Linguistics,* 454–462. Somerville, MA: Cascadilla Proceedings Project.

Teeple, David (2008b) Lexical selection and strong parallelism. [Available on http://roa.rutgers.edu/article/view/1022.]

Tranel, Bernard (1995) Exceptionality in Optimality Theory and final consonants in French. In Karen Zagona (ed.) *Grammatical Theory and Romance Languages,* 275–291. Amsterdam: John Benjamins.

Tranel, Bernard (1996) French liaison and elision revisited: A unified account within Optimality Theory. In Claudia Parodi, Carlos Quicoli, Mario Saltarelli and Maria Luisa Zubizareta (eds) *Aspects of Romance Linguistics,* 433–455. Washington, DC: Georgetown University Press.

Tranel, Bernard (1998) Suppletion and OT: On the issue of the syntax/phonology interaction. In Emily Curtis, James Lyle and Gabriel Webster (eds) *The Proceedings of the Sixteenth West Coast Conference on Formal Linguistics,* 415–429. Stanford, CA: Stanford Linguistics Association/CSLI Publications.

Tranel, Bernard and Del Gobbo, Francesca (2001) Local Conjunction in Italian and French phonology. In Caroline R. Wiltshire and Joaquim Camps (eds) *Romance Phonology and Variation: Selected Papers from the 30th Linguistic Symposium on Romance Languages, Gainsville, Florida, February 2000,* 191–218. Philadelphia, PA: John Benjamins.

Trommer, Jochen (2001) *Distributed Optimality*. Doctoral dissertation, University of Potsdam.

Trommer, Jochen (2008) Syllable-counting allomorphy by indexed constraints. Paper presented at Old Word Conference on Phonology 5, Toulouse, 23–26

January. [Slides available on http://www.uni-leipzig.de/~jtrommer/papers/ocp5.pdf.]

Walker, Rachel and Feng, Bella (2004) A ternary model of phonology-morphology correspondence. In Vineeta Chand, Ann Kelleher, Angelo J. Rodríguez and Benjamin Schmeiser (eds) *WCCFL 23: Proceedings of the 23rd West Coast Conference on Formal Linguistics,* 773–786. Somerville, MA: Cascadilla Press.

Walter, Mary Ann and Jaeger, T. Florian (2005) Constraints on optional *that*: A strong word form OCP effect. In Rodney L. Edwards, Patrick J. Midtlyng, Colin L. Sprague and Kjersti G. Stensrud (eds) *Proceedings from the Annual Meeting of the Chicago Linguistic Society* 41, vol. 1: *The Main Session,* 505–519. Chicago, IL: CLS.

Wolf, Matthew (2008) *Optimal Interleaving: Serial phonology-morphology interaction in a constraint-based model*. Doctoral dissertation, University of Massachusetts Amherst.

Wolf, Matthew (2009) Local ordering in phonology/morphology interleaving: Evidence for OT-CC. Talk presented at 83rd Linguistic Society of America Annual Meeting, San Francisco, 8–11 January. [Available on http://wolf.phonologist.org/LSA%202009%20handout.pdf.]

Wolf, Matthew (2010) Implications of affix-protecting junctural underapplication. In Jon Scott Stevens (ed.), *Penn Working Papers in Linguistics* 16.1: *Proceedings of the 33rd Annual Penn Linguistics Colloquium,* 235–234. Philadelphia, PA: Penn Linguistics Club.

Wolf, Matthew (2013) Candidate chains, unfaithful spell-out, and outwards-looking phonologically-conditioned allomorphy. *Morphology* 23: 145–178.

Wolf, Matthew (to appear) Cyclicity and non-cyclicity in Maltese: Local ordering of phonology and morphology in OT-CC. In John J. McCarthy and Joe Pater (eds) *Harmonic Serialism and Harmonic Grammar*. Sheffield: Equinox.

Wolf, Matthew and McCarthy, John J. (2009) Less than zero: Correspondence and the null output. In Sylvia Blaho and Curt Rice (eds) *Modeling Ungrammaticality in Optimality Theory,* 17–66. London: Equinox.

Wunderlich, Dieter (2000) A correspondence-theoretic analysis of Dalabon transitive paradigms. In Geert Booij and Jaap van Marle (eds) *Yearbook of Morphology 2000,* 233–252. Dordrecht: Kluwer.

Wunderlich, Dieter (2001) How gaps and substitutions can become optimal: The pronominal affix paradigms of Yimas. *Transactions of the Philological Society* 99: 315–366.

Wunderlich, Dieter (2003) On generating and constraining morphological objects: A reply to Harbour. *Transactions of the Philological Society* 101: 137–147.

Xu, Zheng (2007) *Inflectional morphology in Optimality Theory*. Doctoral dissertation, Stony Brook University.

Yip, Moira (1998) Identity avoidance in phonology and morphology. In Steven G. Lapointe, Diane K. Brentari and Patrick M. Farrell (eds) *Morphology and its Relation to Phonology and Syntax,* 216–246. Stanford, CA: CSLI Publications.

Zoll, Cheryl (1998) Positional asymmetries and licensing. [Available on http://roa.rutgers.edu/article/view/292.]

Zuraw, Kie (2000) *Patterned exceptions in phonology*. Doctoral dissertation, University of California, Los Angeles.

Zwicky, Arnold M. (1969) Phonological constraints in syntactic descriptions. *Papers in Linguistics* 1: 411–463.

Zwicky, Arnold M. and Pullum, Geoffrey K. (1986a) The Principle of Phonology-Free Syntax: Introductory remarks. *Ohio State University Working Papers in Linguistics* 32: 63–91.

Zwicky, Arnold M. and Pullum, Geoffrey K. (1986b) Two spurious counterexamples to the Principle of Phonology-Free Syntax. *Ohio State University Working Papers in Linguistics* 32: 92–99.

Index

Languages

Terms